Getting Away

Getting Away

75 EVERYDAY PRACTICES FOR FINDING BALANCE IN OUR ALWAYS-ON WORLD

Jon Staff

A TARCHERPERIGEE BOOK

tarcherperigee

An imprint of Penguin Random House LLC
penguinrandomhouse.com

Illustrations by Amelia Detwiler

Grateful acknowledgment is made to reprint from the following:

Arthur Aron et al., "The Experimental Generation of Interpersonal Closeness: A Procedure and Some Preliminary Findings," *Personality & Social Psychology Bulletin* 23 (4): 374–75. Copyright © 1997. Reprinted by permission of SAGE Publications, Inc.

"In my medicine cabinet" from *The Book of Haiku* by Jack Kerouac, edited by Regina Weinreich. Copyright © 2003 by The Estate of Stella Kerouac, John Sampas, Literary Representative. Used by permission of Penguin Books, an imprint of Penguin Publishing Group, a division of Penguin Random House LLC. All rights reserved.

Most TarcherPerigee books are available at special quantity discounts for bulk purchase for sales promotions, premiums, fund-raising, and educational needs. Special books or book excerpts also can be created to fit specific needs. For details, write: SpecialMarkets@penguinrandomhouse.com.

ISBN 9780593189399

Printed in the United States of America
10 9 8 7 6 5 4 3 2 1

Book design by Katy Riegel

Contents

PART 2
Balance Your Relationships

PART 3
Balance Your Home

PART 4
Balance Your Work

PART 5
Balance Your Downtime

x | Contents

Introduction

THE DIGITAL AGE has left us unbalanced. We're not just connected; we're suffering from social and technological overload. We rarely experience the joy of solitude or the respite of nature. We're always on; we never turn off.

In 2015, my friend Pete Davis and I started our company, Getaway, to help counterbalance these digital-age excesses. Seeking balance isn't a new (or even New Age) idea: we can trace it all the way back to Aristotle, who taught that virtue could be found in the balance—he called it the "golden mean"—between extremes. For years, Pete and I had been talking about how we could build something to provide disconnection to our fellow tech addicts, nature to our fellow city dwellers, and leisure to our fellow workaholics. To our surprise and delight, we've been able to weave these goals together into a single project, Getaway, which designs tiny cabins, places them in the woods, and invites folks to rent them out by the night. While on a Getaway, guests disconnect from their devices and work to reconnect with the world beyond the daily grind.

It's exactly the kind of respite we were looking for ourselves. After college—where we met and became friends—we got wrapped up in the hustle of city living and stressful, time-consuming jobs. While Pete worked on political causes in Washington, I worked for startups in Boston. It seemed like we could never work hard enough, or long enough, as our time on the clock spilled over into nights and weekends. When we weren't working, we were thinking about work, worrying about work, refreshing our email, updating our calendars. We were cranky and tired and often joked to each other about wishing we could just run away to the woods.

In the midst of this, in desperate need of a break, Pete booked a night's stay at an RV on a farm a few hours away from his home outside of DC. He went out alone, with just a book and a change of clothes. The RV was dilapidated and full of bugs, but it still felt like a haven to him: a simple, solitary, distraction-free space, physically and psychologically removed from the anxieties and responsibilities of his day-to-day life, where he could give himself permission to unwind and do nothing at all.

I had a similarly eye-opening experience when friends and I booked a stay at a farm in Connecticut where guests were invited to sleep in a geodesic dome. It was a freezing-cold week in January, and our group arrived to find that the wind was blowing snow under the sides of the unheated dome. I grew up in rural northern Minnesota, but my city friends did not share my enthusiasm for this particular kind of adventure, especially when we realized we might wind up sleeping in snowdrifts. Luckily, the farmer who owned the property took pity on us and offered to let us stay in his nearby toolshed instead. It wasn't the Ritz, but with four sturdy walls, floorboards under our feet, and a roof over our heads, it offered basic protection from the elements. That was enough. We bundled inside with a pile of blankets, then stayed up all night talking and playing cards by the light and heat of a single bulb.

These trips have stayed with us as some of our favorite memories: pockets of space and time that allowed us to escape the stresses of our daily lives both physically and mentally, enabling us to reconnect with versions of ourselves that feel truer to who we really are—or, at least, who we aspire to be. You'd be surprised by the places your mind can go when you spend a day alone in an RV with nothing but farmland for miles around, or the kinds of conversations you end up having with friends when you're bundled into an old shed with a snowstorm raging outside.

A few years after that, I was working remotely for a friend while living and traveling in an Airstream trailer. The Airstream was my introduction to tiny homes: I had all the basics I needed to get by, but none of the distractions. A lightbulb went off in my head, and I thought that maybe I could buy one of these and stick it in the woods outside of Boston, where I was based at the time. I love the city, and people, and technology, but I also need to escape all of those things fairly frequently. I wanted to be able to leave it all behind without traveling too far, and spend some time unplugging in solitude, surrounded by trees.

These were the seeds that would grow into Getaway: a desire to carve out the space and time to slow down, take stock, connect with nature, and return to a more analog way of living. In 2015, after some late-night brainstorming, a few months of sketching with Harvard Graduate School of Design students, a few weeks of carpentry (with the help of my very handy dad), and a harrowing drive north on Interstate 93 with a tiny cabin in tow, the first Getaway house arrived in southern New Hampshire. We named it Ovida, after our then-intern's grandmother. When that house filled up, we added a second, Lorraine (after my grandmother), and then a third, Clara (after Pete's).

Three Getaway cabins became ten, then thirty, and then three hundred. It's been a great adventure, one that has taken us and our tiny cabins from the mountains of New Hampshire to Virginia's Shenandoah Valley, California's San

Bernardino Mountains, the forests of East Texas and northern Georgia, and even to the set of *Shark Tank*. As we grow, we do our best to remember that if Getaway is successful, that has less to do with us than with the simple idea at the center of the business: helping people restore balance to their lives.

It's why we have a cell phone lockbox in each of our cabins—to help guests experience the joy of disconnection. It's why our cabins are in the woods and come with constellation maps—to help folks get closer to nature. And it's why we have no Wi-Fi—to help guests break away from their work. Internally, we're also working hard to build a company culture that provides balance to everyone who works at Getaway, one we hope will become a model for other workplaces.

Pete has moved on to other projects since starting Getaway with me, but the ideas and values we developed together remain at the core of the business, which extends far beyond tiny cabins in the woods. Finding balance isn't just about reconnecting with nature and ourselves every now and then—it's about the choices we make every day, even when we can't literally get away. In this book, I'll share tips, tricks, and ideas for practices that help make everyday life more balanced and sustainable. I'm not advocating radical lifestyle overhauls here, or to abandon city life, technology, and work. I've come to love living in New York City; I use my smartphone and computer every day; and I still work too much and care deeply about my job. But in this age of constant anxieties and overload, there are plenty of small, actionable steps we can take to lessen stress and restore balance—at work, at home, in our communities, and in ourselves.

About the Book

Getting Away is divided into five sections dedicated to bringing balance to the following areas of your life:

- **Balance Yourself** includes tips for self-care, stress reduction, and maintaining healthy relationships to technology.
- **Balance Your Relationships** offers practices for improved communication and bonding with friends, family, colleagues, and romantic partners.
- **Balance Your Home** details convenient and affordable tips for organizing and outfitting your living space for relaxing and entertaining while limiting reliance on digital devices.
- **Balance Your Work** includes practices for maintaining focus and productivity while avoiding burnout, and for creating better boundaries to prevent work from spilling over into leisure time.
- **Balance Your Downtime** takes these ideas further, offering tips for committing dedicated stretches of time to new adventures as well as rest, relaxation, and even boredom.

There's no right or wrong way to read this book. Start at the beginning, skip around to different sections, or flip through the pages to see what catches your eye.

In the opening lines of his iconic book *Walden,* Henry David Thoreau writes, "I went to the woods because I wished to live deliberately." If you're looking for woods, we've got tiny cabins for you at ten Outposts and counting. In the meantime, *Getting Away* aims to help you live a little more deliberately, wherever you are.

PART 1

Balance Yourself

"SELF-CARE" is an expression that's been overused to the point of meaninglessness. As product marketers have attached the phrase to luxury goods and services— scented candles, cashmere socks, skincare creams, detoxifying drinks, spa treatments—it's gotten a bad rap as nothing more than an excuse for conspicuous consumption and a hashtag for Instagram influencers. But genuine self-care isn't about indulgent purchases or aspirational slogans; it's about making space for your physical, mental, and emotional health. Taking good care of yourself and caring about others aren't mutually exclusive, and you don't need huge amounts of free time or disposable income to make a habit of prioritizing your well-being. Real self-care isn't luxury bath oils, though it might be unwinding with a bath at the end of the day. It might also be making a point to spend less time on your phone and more time outside, seeing a therapist, or getting lost in an unputdownable novel.

Keep a Gratitude Journal

GROWING UP, like a lot of kids, I loved Bobby McFerrin's "Don't Worry, Be Happy." As catchy as the song is, I bet most of us would agree that living a worry-free, joy-filled existence is a lot easier said (or sung) than done. We may not be able to sing away our troubles, but research reveals that there *is* a fairly easy, cost-free way to improve our overall health and well-being: the simple act of gratitude.

In study after study, scientists have found that when people feel and express gratitude, they become more patient and forgiving, their relationships improve, they take better care of their bodies through diet and exercise, and they sleep better, feel less depressed, and even report lower levels of physical pain.

How does this work? Dr. Robert Emmons, a leader in the field of positive psychology, explains that our brains have a natural tendency to pay more attention to bad input than good, a phenomenon known as "negativity bias." This trait was likely an evolutionary adaptation designed to make our primitive brains more attuned to danger so that we could avoid it; in the twenty-first century, it means we tend to remember insults and criticism more

clearly than compliments, and we dwell on those times our loved ones have let us down rather than the times when they've been there for us. In his research, Dr. Emmons has found that when we express gratitude—making a conscious effort to find and affirm the good in our lives—we can override our brain's tendency to fixate on the negative. "Gratitude allows us to celebrate the present," he says. "It magnifies positive emotions."

If thinking grateful thoughts is good for us, writing them down is even better. "Writing helps to organize thoughts, facilitate integration, and helps you accept your own experiences and put them in context," Dr. Emmons explains. "In essence, it allows you to see the meaning of events going on around you and create meaning in your own life."

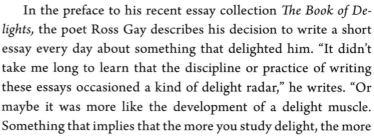

In the preface to his recent essay collection *The Book of Delights,* the poet Ross Gay describes his decision to write a short essay every day about something that delighted him. "It didn't take me long to learn that the discipline or practice of writing these essays occasioned a kind of delight radar," he writes. "Or maybe it was more like the development of a delight muscle. Something that implies that the more you study delight, the more delight there is to study."

The same could be said of gratitude. The more you seek it out, the more you'll find.

When I started counting my blessings,
my whole life turned around.
—Willie Nelson

Try It Out

Put in real effort. Researchers have found that you'll get much more out of keeping a gratitude journal if you're genuinely motivated to feel happier, so don't just go through the motions. Before putting pen to paper, spend a few minutes really thinking about what makes you grateful. Only write once you've tapped into that feeling.

Quality over quantity. Don't worry about trying to list *everything* you're grateful for; instead, work on describing a few subjects in depth, making sure to consider not just what or who inspires your gratitude but *how* and *why.* The more detail you include, the more you'll be able to connect with the sentiment, and the more benefits you'll reap.

Prioritize people over things. "Gratitude is a social emotion," says Dr. Emmons. "It requires us to see how we've been supported and affirmed by other people." While there's nothing wrong with journaling about beloved objects, studies show that focusing on your gratitude for the people in your life can help alleviate loneliness and boost self-esteem.

Find the time and place that works for you. Some lifestyle gurus recommend working on your gratitude list first thing in the morning in order to start your day with feelings of goodwill. Others suggest journaling as a way to wind down before bed, when you can reflect on the events of the day. But according to Dr. Emmons, "There is no one right way to do

it." The important thing is establishing a regular habit.

It's okay to skip days. Concentrating on gratitude regularly can make us more grateful overall, but we may diminish its positive effects if we overdo it. Psychologist Sonja Lyubomirsky and her colleagues found that people who wrote in gratitude journals only once a week reported greater happiness after six weeks than those who wrote three times a week. If you're starting to feel burned out, feel free to scale down—but try to maintain the practice at least once a week.

Feeling stuck? Tim Ferriss, the bestselling author of *The 4-Hour Workweek,* relies on four categories to jump-start his inspiration.

1. Relationships
Do you have a childhood friend you feel grateful for? Who makes you laugh? What qualities do you admire most in a friend, family member, or partner?

2. Opportunities
What is one thing you can do this week that will make you feel good? What element of your life can you appreciate that isn't necessarily accessible to other people? What obstacles have you overcome?

3. Great events

What is one thing that surprised you in a good way this month? What future date are you looking forward to, and why? Describe the memory of a past event that you cherish.

4. Simple things

Reflect on a favorite book, movie, album, or meal, and why you love it. Describe something ordinary in your line of sight that becomes beautiful when you look at it closely.

Meditate for Five Minutes Daily

FEELING STRESSED OUT lately? You're not alone. A recent Gallup poll found that Americans are among the most stressed people in the world. Eight in ten US adults report feeling stressed at some point every day, and 55 percent of us admit we're stressed "a lot of the day" (compared with 35 percent worldwide). We also outpace other countries when it comes to worry and anger.

Stress isn't just a bad feeling: it prompts our bodies to release cortisol, the hormone linked to our "fight-or-flight" response. While this was useful for keeping early humans safe from threats like wild animals, most of our current problems can't be solved by fighting or fleeing. Without a mechanism for release, cortisol builds up in our bloodstream and can lead to serious health problems, from lower bone density and decreased immune function to weight gain, elevated blood pressure and cholesterol, and an increased risk of heart disease and diabetes. It can even impair our learning and memory.

While there's no quick fix for resolving the underlying issues that cause us anxiety, studies find that meditating for even five minutes a day can reduce stress and its symptoms. Just taking a few deep breaths is enough to send signals to our nervous system to lower our blood pressure and slow our heart rate. A regular meditation practice can also improve focus, attention, and mood. Meditation and mindfulness can make us more compassionate toward others, more resilient when confronted with stressful situations, and less likely to ruminate.

And here's the best part: you can do it *right now,* wherever you are. You might be on the subway, in your living room, or on a flight to a family reunion; all you need is your own mind and body to give mindfulness a try. In fact, some airlines have started offering in-flight meditation options through the entertainment console in front of your seat. So if you *are* on a red-eye to Toledo, now would be a great time to try it out before diving into that *New York Times* bestseller or latest Hollywood hit.

One of the simplest forms of meditation begins with, as the renowned meditation teacher and bestselling author Sharon Salzberg puts it, "something you've known how to do all of your life: breathe." Deceptively simple—and incredibly powerful.

Try It Out

Begin with a short breathing meditation. An easy, common breathing meditation involves sitting in a comfortable position and noticing the inhalation and exhalation of your breath. You don't have to close your eyes, though closing them may help you to concentrate. Tune in to the flow of your breath. You don't need to do anything special— just turn your attention to it. Notice where you feel your breath in your body as it rises and falls. Do you feel it in your chest, your abdomen, or your throat? Let yourself feel each breath, one at a time. (And be gentle with yourself when your mind wanders. Every meditation expert basically tells you to *expect* your mind to wander—when it does, just gently guide it back to your breath.) Try setting a timer for a minimum of five minutes at first. You can always work your way up to longer meditations.

Harness the power of technology. Unsurprisingly, there are now a number of apps available for your phone (including Headspace, Breethe, and Simply Being) that can guide you through the process of meditation. While it might sound counterintuitive to turn to your phone for mindfulness and relaxation, these apps can help you get started with small meditation exercises, set reminders to get you meditating more consistently, and incrementally build your meditation practice.

Cultivate compassion—and a sense of humor. Alongside all its other benefits, the practice of meditation encourages you to be gentle and compassionate with others—*and* with yourself. If you become frustrated with yourself when your mind just won't settle

down, consider the advice of American Buddhist nun Pema Chödrön: "Every time we sit down to meditate, we can think of it as training to lighten up, to have a sense of humor, to relax."

Take It Further

There are lots of opportunities for exploring meditation further, and many are free or inexpensive. Sharon Salzberg occasionally runs on-line "meditation challenges" for a few weeks or a month, sending out daily guided audio meditations and reflective writings. You can find meditation centers and classes in many cities around the world. There are also many great books by authors who can help you deepen your practice, like Thich Nhat Hanh, Jon Kabat-Zinn, Pema Chödrön, and Jack Kornfield.

Turn off Push Notifications

IN THE BEGINNING, believe it or not, push notifications existed to keep us *off* our phones. BlackBerry first rolled out push email in 2003, with the theory that if users received notifications whenever a new email arrived, they could stop worrying about checking their inboxes all the time. Push notifications would tell them when something demanded their attention; otherwise, they were free to ignore their phones.

Mail

Times have changed, to put it mildly. As scores of apps compete for our attention, notifications aren't conveying important information so much as delivering bite-size advertisements for the apps themselves. Facebook wants you to know that someone you haven't spoken to since high school just uploaded a new photo. Twitter informs you that eight people you follow just liked a celebrity's tweet. Duolingo lays on a guilt trip by reminding you that you haven't practiced French in three weeks; you have a new podcast ready to download; Lyft has discounted rates for the next two hours; your meditation app thinks you could really use some mindfulness today (no kidding!). In 2013, Apple announced that 7.4 *trillion* push notifications had traveled across its servers. With all of that flashing, dinging, and buzzing, it's no surprise the average smartphone user checks their phone more than forty-seven times per day.

And for what? "Allowing an app to send you push notifications is like allowing a store clerk to grab you by the ear and drag you into their store," writes *Wired*'s David Pierce. "You're letting someone insert a commercial into your life anytime they want." Even when the notifications are actually relevant—a text from your mom, a calendar alert for an appointment, a notice from your bank letting you know a check has cleared—the constant onslaught is awful for our brains. It forces us into a state the tech writer Linda Stone calls "continuous partial attention," which she describes as "always-on, anywhere, anytime, any place behavior that involves an artificial sense of constant crisis."

Notifications disrupt our thinking whether we respond to them or not. Researchers at Florida State University found that merely receiving a push notification causes just as much distraction as answering a phone call or responding to a text, "even when participants did not directly interact with a mobile device during the task." The tech ethicist Tristan Harris refers to the intrusion of push notifications as a kind of mental hijacking, by "steering what people are paying attention to" and how we spend our time without our consent.

There's a straightforward solution: Turn off your notifications! That way, *you're* the one deciding when and how to use your phone.

Three Thanksgivings ago, I was pretty worn out from work. As a reward to myself and out of respect for my family, I turned off my push notifications. I thought it was just for the weekend, but I realized I felt a lot happier and didn't really miss anything. They've been off ever since.

Sleep

"SCIENTISTS HAVE DISCOVERED a revolutionary new treatment that makes you live longer," University of California, Berkeley, neuroscientist and psychologist Matthew Walker recently announced. "It enhances your memory, makes you more attractive. It keeps you slim and lowers food cravings. It protects you from cancer and dementia. It wards off colds and flu. It lowers your risk of heart attacks and stroke, not to mention diabetes. You'll even feel happier, less depressed, and less anxious. Are you interested?"

How could anyone not be? It turns out that this miraculous treatment is available to everyone on earth (at least in theory), and better yet, it's free. While it might seem too good to be true, the treatment Dr. Walker touts is good, old-fashioned sleep—about eight hours a night—and his internationally acclaimed book *Why We Sleep* presents evidence drawn from decades of research showing that sleep is the single most important factor in determining our mental and physical health and performance.

Sleep is vital to learning and memory. When we form new memories, they're stored in a region of the brain called the hippocampus. Our ability to absorb and retain new information diminishes the longer we stay awake, as the hippocampus fills to capacity. Sleep acts as a "file-transfer mechanism," moving those memories from short-term storage in the hippocampus to long-term storage in the cortex, restoring our brain's learning capabilities by clearing space for us to absorb new information.

Sleep is also essential for memory retention, which Dr. Walker likens to "click[ing] the 'save' button on those newly created files." Studies show that people who learn new facts and then sleep for eight hours are as much as 40 percent more likely to remember what they just learned than those who stay awake—so if you're planning to pull an all-nighter cramming for a test, you may want to reconsider.

Sleep is crucial for what we might call "muscle memory" (though it's actually *procedural* memory, which takes place in the brain)—enabling us to refine and perfect skills like riding a bike, swimming, or playing the piano. Even when you aren't actively practicing a motor skill, your sleeping brain continues working to improve your performance, which may be why record-breaking sprinter Usain Bolt takes naps before his races.

Sleep is also hugely beneficial when it comes to creativity and problem-solving. When we enter REM sleep and begin to dream, our brain begins testing out and making connections between distant, seemingly unrelated memories and information, which can lead to ingenious ideas and solutions that would never occur to our waking minds. When we're having trouble solving a problem, we say we need to "sleep on it." Dr. Walker points out that a version of this expression exists in most languages, from the French *dormir sur un problem* to the Swahili *kulala juu ya tatizo.*

In fact, some of the greatest innovations in science and art have emerged from sleep: the elegant design for the periodic table came to chemist Dmitri Mendeleev in a dream. Thomas Edison, who patented 1,093 different inventions over the course of his lifetime, including the lightbulb, the phonograph, the kinetoscope, and the alkaline battery, relied on daytime naps to jump-start his imagination. Paul McCartney awoke from a dream with the melody for "Yesterday" in his head. While staying at her friend Lord Byron's estate in the summer of 1816, young Mary Shelley had a frightening nightmare. The next morning, she turned her dream into a ghost story, which she later expanded into a novel called *Frankenstein* ("Wonderful work for a girl," declared Lord Byron).

I sleep a lot—at least eight hours a night, often nine. I go to bed around 11:30 p.m. every night and sleep until 7:30 or 8:00 a.m. I've never been the all-nighter type. If I don't get enough sleep, I make worse decisions, I find it harder to focus, and I'm snippier with people. It's not just me: anyone who's been sleep deprived knows that lack of sleep makes us cranky, destroys our focus, and impairs our decision-making abilities. It can also make us feel hungry no matter how much we eat, since sleep loss stimulates the hunger hormone ghrelin while suppressing leptin, the hormone that tells our brains we're full. As a result, studies find that sleep-deprived people eat up to three hundred calories more per day than those who sleep well, leading to a ten-to-fifteen-pound weight gain over the course of a single year.

Sleep loss increases our blood pressure and accelerates our heart rate, putting strain on the heart and elevating our risk of hypertension and heart attack.

It weakens the immune system, making us much more vulnerable to colds and flus. Multiple studies have found a correlation between insufficient sleep (six hours or less) and an increased risk of cancer. One of the functions of sleep is to clear away metabolic waste that develops between brain cells. With insufficient sleep, this waste builds up, impairing cognition and increasing the risk of Alzheimer's disease. And we're not just hurting ourselves when we don't get enough sleep: in the United States, sleepiness leads to 1.2 million car crashes every year, and those crashes tend to be more deadly than those caused by alcohol or drugs.

All of the global and historical research on sleep confirms that in order to function at our best and healthiest, we need between seven and nine hours of sleep per night. You're fooling yourself if you think you can function just as well with less, say sleep scientists. While a tiny percentage of the population carries a rare gene enabling them to thrive on fewer than six hours a night, "that number," says Dr. Thomas Roth of Henry Ford Hospital in Detroit, "expressed as a percent of the population, and rounded to a whole number, is zero."

In our hectic, high-speed lives, it's easy to fall into the trap of thinking about sleep as lost or wasted time. The science shows this couldn't be further from the truth. The activities of our sleeping brain—sorting and storing memories and information, constructing intricate webs of association, repairing cells, and maintaining the systems responsible for our mental and physical health—are the very functions necessary for getting the most out of our waking hours.

Even a soul submerged in sleep is hard at work
and helps make something of the world.
—Heraclitus

Try It Out

Maintain a sleep schedule. Make a point to go to bed and wake up at the same time every day. Sleeping in on weekends won't counteract sleep loss during the week (unfortunately, scientists say there's no such thing as "making up sleep"), and doing so may even make it harder to get up on Monday morning. If you need a reminder, consider setting an alarm for bedtime as well as when you wake up.

Exercise, but not before bed. Aim to get at least thirty minutes of exercise a day, but avoid working out two to three hours before you plan to go to bed, since that can make it harder to fall asleep.

Stay away from caffeine, nicotine, and alcohol before bed. The stimulating effects of caffeine can take up to eight hours to wear off, so avoid drinking caffeinated beverages in the afternoon or later. Nicotine is also a stimulant known to disrupt sleep. And while we may think of a "nightcap" as a sleep aid, drinking alcohol before bed can prevent sleepers from entering into the deeper stages of sleep that are necessary for meaningful rest.

Don't nap after 3:00 p.m. Naps can be wonderfully restorative, but taking a nap after 3:00 p.m. may interfere with your ability to fall asleep at bedtime. As for the ideal length of a nap, sleep scientists recommend ninety minutes— enough time to complete a full

cycle through the light and deep stages of sleep. If you can't spare ninety minutes, try a ten-to-twenty-minute "power nap" for a quick jolt of alertness, but avoid a thirty-minute nap, which will likely leave you groggy.

Optimize your bedroom for sleep. Dr. Walker offers this mantra: "Dark bedroom, cool bedroom, gadget-free bedroom." Experts say that the optimal temperature for sleeping well is around 65°F, while reducing artificial light will cue your body that it's time to sleep. See Practice No. 38 for tips on replacing your phone with a physical alarm clock to achieve a gadget-free sleep environment.

If you can't sleep, get out of bed. Feeling anxious about not falling asleep will make it even harder to fall asleep. If you find yourself tossing and turning after twenty minutes, sleep experts recommend getting out of bed and doing a relaxing activity like reading until you feel sleepy.

Audit Your Phone Usage

IT'S ONE THING to wonder whether you're on your phone too much; it's another to face up to the cold, hard evidence. According to data collected by RescueTime, an app that tracks screen time for iPhone and Android users, the average person uses their phone three hours and fifteen minutes every day. To put that number in starker terms: assuming we're not on our phones while we're asleep, we spend seventy-four full days a year—*two and a half straight months*—staring at our phone screens.

Don't blame yourself; blame the biological makeup of your brain, and the tech companies that are taking advantage of it. Human brains are hardwired to shift focus rapidly in response to aural and visual cues. This "orienting response" was an evolutionary advantage back in prehistoric times, when it helped us to evade wild animals and other dangers. But today, those cues aren't coming from panthers lurking in the bushes—they're coming from our flashing, buzzing, dinging phones.

And once our phones have captured our attention, app developers know how to hold on to it: social media platforms use the same strategies as casinos to get us

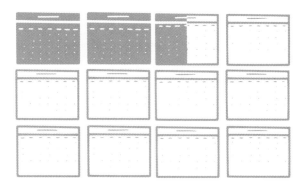

hooked. The pull-to-refresh and endless scroll features on Twitter, Facebook, Instagram, and Snapchat are a lot like the mechanics of a slot machine, says Tristan Harris: "You pull a lever and immediately receive either an enticing reward (a match, a prize!) or nothing." While you might try to curb a gambling addiction by swearing off casinos, it can be more complicated to scale back on phone use. Often, practicing moderation is harder than quitting—it requires both willpower and consistent mindfulness about when and how much you're consuming. Fortunately, there are a few easy steps you can take to ensure your phone usage stays in check and your time remains your own.

Try It Out

Track your total phone usage for one week. Go into your phone settings to enable Screen Time (for iOS) or Digital Wellbeing (for Android)—native software programs that provide daily and weekly reports of how much time you spend on your phone, including breakdowns of time spent on individual apps and the number of times you pick up your phone throughout the day. Decide how much time you want to spend on each app every day, and set limits accordingly. Once you hit your limit, Screen Time gives you the option to add another fifteen minutes—the app-use equivalent of hitting snooze—or disable the limit entirely. Digital Wellbeing is less permissive: after you've used up your allotted time, the program locks down the app for the remainder of the day.

Bury your most addictive apps in the back pages of your phone's home screen. This turns passive apps—apps you go to out of habit, just to zone out—into affirmative apps, which you consciously seek out for a purpose. You have much more control over affirmative browsing than you do over habitual, zoned-out scrolling.

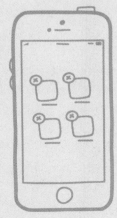

Download apps to keep your phone use in check. If you're willing to accept the irony of using tech to limit your tech use, there are dozens of additional apps that track and limit your screen time.

RescueTime will block distracting apps and websites for set periods of time, allowing you to work without interruption—and also includes a feature that reminds you to *stop* working during the hours you've designated for leisure time. **Siempo** (for Android) "de-brands" your apps by converting the logos into simple black icons on a white background, and continually moves the placement of apps on your home screen so you can't rely on muscle memory to open them unconsciously. **Freedom** allows you to create custom block lists for distracting apps and websites, which you can use across devices. With **Off the Grid**, your phone will lock down completely for the time you've selected: anyone who attempts to text you will receive a custom auto-reply (you can "whitelist" important contacts to allow their calls and texts), and if you want to use your phone during "off the grid" time, you'll have to pay a $1 fee.

Take It Further

Remove temptation altogether by switching to a dumbphone. Nokia offers a line of "classic phones" that take users back to the pre-smartphone days of keypads, small screens, week-long battery life, and the iconic game Snake. Other manufacturers are starting from scratch to build the perfect dumbphones for the digital age. The Light Phone, which can be used only for phone calls, is just a number pad with a single-line display. You keep your old number, use a normal SIM card, and get three weeks of use per battery charge. You can receive calls at your regular phone number, and if you don't pick up, the caller is informed you're in Light Phone mode and will call back later.

Spend Thirty Minutes Outside Every Day

IN THE NINETEENTH century, most American cities lacked public parks. City dwellers who wanted a breath of fresh air had to settle for taking walks and having picnics in cemeteries—and they did so in droves. In places like Denver, graveyards were so overrun with picnickers—"thousands strew the ground with sardine cans, beer bottles, and lunch boxes," according to one journalist—that officials considered police intervention.

This ghoulish pastime didn't last, mostly thanks to the work of Frederick Law Olmsted, a landscape designer who revolutionized urban park design across America beginning with New York City's famed Central Park. Olmsted believed that it was the government's responsibility to provide "great public grounds" where all people could freely enjoy "the choicest natural scenes in the country." Through his efforts, that vision became a reality.

We've come a long way from the era of graveside picnics. But today, despite an abundance of public parks nationwide, nature-based recreation has dropped by 35 percent. Americans spend 87 percent of our time indoors, and almost half of the remaining time in an enclosed vehicle. That means we're outside only 7 *percent* of the time.

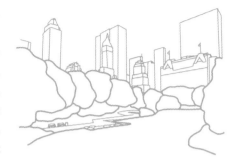

It's worth our while to get out more: spending time outdoors, especially in green spaces, makes us measurably healthier and happier. Researchers have found that regular exposure to nature offers a wide range of health benefits, from lower risk of type 2 diabetes and heart disease to better sleep, reduced stress, higher self-esteem, and improved memory. When we soak up sunlight, our body absorbs Vitamin D, which helps us process the calcium that strengthens our bones. Just *looking* at trees can reduce our blood pressure and stress hormones.

Studies show that people suffering from depression recover faster when they take regular nature walks, and being outside also improves concentration: researchers believe that "doses of nature" could be an effective tool for treating ADHD in children. In fact, the health benefits of spending time outside are so far-reaching that some doctors have started writing their patients prescriptions for visiting parks.

When I moved into my current apartment, I intentionally chose a place that's a twenty-five-minute walk to my office door-to-door: close enough that I don't need to rely on public transportation but far enough to feel like I'm getting a real walk. My commute ensures that I'm outside for almost an hour a day—in two and a half years, I've taken the subway to work only once—and when I'm there, I schedule walking meetings whenever I can. (See Practice No. 57 for tips on turning meetings into walking meetings.) When I head home in the evenings, my walk lets me unwind and release the stress of the workday. It allows me to be a better person and a better partner, since I arrive home refreshed and ready to ease into an evening of disconnection.

Spending at least thirty minutes outside every day will be good for your body and mind, and it will help you feel more connected to the world around you. Here are some ways to fit outdoor time into a busy schedule.

Try It Out

Commute to work on foot or by bike. Swapping the car or public transportation for a walk or bike ride will give you an opportunity to get outdoor exercise—and save you money at the same time.

Hit the streets (or trails) instead of the gym. Your jog will be a lot more interesting when you trade the treadmill for the real world, whether you're running on streets or in parks. And of course, there are no gym fees in the great outdoors.

Go on a picnic. Instead of meeting friends at a restaurant, suggest a picnic in your local park. In cooler weather, bring extra blankets and bundle up for a cozy alfresco meal. If you're stuck in an office all day for work, take a lunch break outside for a change of scenery and a chance to soak in some Vitamin D.

Walk a dog. Dogs are a great excuse for getting outside. If you don't have one of your own, offer to take a friend's dog for a walk. You'll be doing them a favor while reaping the benefits of fresh air.

Shop at a farmers' market. When you buy food from a farmers' market, you'll be supporting local vendors—an environmentally friendly practice that helps your community. You'll be able to stock up on farm-fresh seasonal produce, which tastes better and is often more affordable than supermarket options—all while getting to spend some time outside.

Observe a Digital Sabbath

THE IDEA OF the Sabbath originates in the book of Genesis, when God finishes creating the universe and chooses to rest on the seventh day. The third of the Ten Commandments mandates a day of rest for humans: "Six days you shall labor and do all your work, but the seventh day is a Sabbath to the Lord your God. On it you shall not do any work."

Like the Sabbath of the Bible, observing a digital sabbath means reserving one full day each week for taking a break: in this case, a break from digital technology. That means no phones, computers, television, video games, e-readers, or smartwatches. A digital sabbath is partly about getting away from work and partly about getting away from screens. But mostly, it's about changing your relationship to *time.*

When we're distracted, shifting our focus quickly from one thing to another to another, we're effectively breaking up our time into smaller and smaller pieces. As a result, time seems to fly by. (Think about opening a social media app "just for a minute" and then looking up to realize an hour has passed.) If we're not rushing, it often feels like time is rushing past us, so we've developed a million tips and tricks for maximizing our efficiency and productivity.

What if, instead of trying to beat time, we slowed it down? The scholar Rabbi Abraham Joshua Heschel has called the Sabbath a "palace in time." Just like a palace, the Sabbath is meant to be spacious and beautiful, a space where different rituals and rules apply. Inside the palace in time, Rabbi Heschel teaches that we should practice "divine rest"—rest that isn't just about recharging for more work later, but about reminding ourselves that work is not an end in itself and that our lives are about more than what we do. "The Sabbath was made for humankind," reads the Gospel of Mark 2:27. It's an opportunity to appreciate not only our own existence but time with family, friends, and community.

The food writer Mark Bittman began observing a weekly digital sabbath in 2008. As he reported for *The New York Times,* at first his tech-free day made him feel "jumpy, twitchy, and uneven." But over time, he became more comfortable, especially when he realized that "nothing bad has happened while I've been offline." He started taking pleasure from his long walks, naps, and uninterrupted stretches of reading. "I experienced what, if I wasn't such a skeptic, I would call a lightness of being," he writes. "I felt connected to myself rather than my computer. I had time to think, and distance from normal demands. I got to stop."

Try It Out

Find one day in the week when you can fully disconnect. If you struggle to imagine a day when you can go totally offline and

screen-free, consider rearranging your schedule. Do you have any digital obligations that absolutely *can't* wait twenty-four hours? If your answer is yes, ask yourself what makes them so essential and what would happen if you waited a day.

Find a community. A digital sabbath is easier to observe when you do it with others—especially when you're first trying it out. Enlist a friend, partner, or family member to go tech-free with you on your chosen day. You can also join the online community at www.digital sabbath.io, which challenges participants to "go without digital technology one day a week for three months" and sends weekly "gentle reminder" emails to help you commit to the practice.

Make a list of screen-free activities. Take a walk; cook a meal; work on a craft project; read a print newspaper or magazine; go to the beach; have a picnic; meet a friend for coffee; go to a concert; browse a flea market; read a book; clean your house; play tennis; go for a bike ride; take a nap; assemble furniture; write postcards—there are limitless possibilities for how to spend your offline time.

Carry a Book Wherever You Go

IT PROBABLY WON'T come as a huge surprise that reading is really good for us. It can make us smarter: studies find that kids who have a higher reading ability also have higher verbal and nonverbal cognitive skills than their peers, including their own siblings. Reading also improves our memory and can help ward off mental decline by up to 32 percent as we age, since it stimulates the brain to continue making new connections. Better yet, readers are also likely to live longer: a study at Yale found that people who spend at least thirty minutes a day reading may live up to twenty-three months longer than those who don't.

The Yale researchers found that those results were even stronger for readers of books, specifically. While reading newspapers, magazines, and blogs can expand our knowledge, books—and especially literary fiction—offer additional benefits. When we get swept up in a good book, we start caring about the characters and feel invested in their thoughts and lives, whether we love them, hate them, or love to hate them. This process helps to develop what cognitive scientists call our "theory of mind"—the ability to imagine how people outside ourselves think and feel.

That skill has real-world consequences, as the psychologist Keith Oatley found in his study of the relationship between reading, imagination, and social behavior. Reading stories about other people makes us more empathetic, better at appreciating thoughts and perspectives different from our own, and more cooperative with the people outside our books. "Because we're extremely social, we have to understand people," Oatley tells *The Washington Post*. "This is pretty much the center of what it means to be human."

So if you want to get smarter, improve your memory, live longer, and become an all-around better person, make sure to toss a book in your bag the next time you leave the house.

I love the writer Erik Larson, especially his book *The Devil in the White City*, which is a combination of architectural history and true crime. I'm so impressed by his ability to write nonfiction as if it's fiction, full of memorable characters and suspenseful plots. As a kid, and even into early adulthood, I struggled to read a lot because I felt pressure to read what I thought I should read (like *Robinson Crusoe* when I was way too young to tackle it, or presidential biographies when I thought I should be a politics/history nerd). I finally admitted to myself that I should just read what I enjoy— and that it's okay to ditch a book a couple chapters in without declaring failure. Now I read a lot more.

Never trust anyone who has not brought a book with them.
—Lemony Snicket

Try It Out

Reclaim your waiting time. We spend a lot of time waiting around: waiting for public transportation to carry us between work and home; waiting in line for groceries; waiting at the doctor's office; waiting for friends to show up to dinner or drinks. When you have a book with you, you can turn a tedious activity you can't control into a valuable opportunity for learning and entertainment. Reading a good book will make the time fly by.

Save money and battery life. Reading a book won't drain your phone battery, and a paper book doesn't require any equipment or software to keep you entertained for hours: all you need is enough light to see the words on the page. And if you have a library card, you'll be able to access a steady supply of new books without spending a cent.

Start a conversation . . . or gracefully avoid one. If you're feeling sociable, reading a book in public is a natural conversation starter. A friend of mine met his future wife at a café

when she complimented him on the story collection he was reading. When we read in public, books can signal our tastes and personalities to the people around us, which can be a quick way of finding common ground with a stranger. On the other hand, when you're *not* in a social mood, a book provides an easy and polite excuse to stop talking and return to minding your own business.

Take It Further

Inspire yourself to read more—and remember what you read—by keeping an annual list of books you've finished. Record the title, author's name, and the date you completed the book; then add a line or two summarizing its content or recording your opinion of it. Over time, this list can become a valuable reference guide, helping you keep track of what you like, what you don't, and how to find more books that align with your tastes.

Make a Physical Photo Album

WITH A SMARTPHONE in every hand, and a camera in every smartphone, there's a reason Gen Z folks have earned the title "Most Photographed Generation"—in 2018 alone, people around the world took 1.2 *trillion* photos. We might post some on social media and text others to our friends. But the vast majority of these images will be forgotten almost as soon as they're taken, buried in an ever-growing heap of digital data.

In theory, we could revisit our photos whenever we want, pulling them up onscreen from our clouds and flash drives. Most of us don't, though. Let's admit it: scrolling through digital photos isn't nearly as fun as flipping through an actual photo album. But when was the last time you printed your photos, much less pasted them into an album? If you're like the majority of us, the answer is probably *never*. By some estimates, only one photo is printed for every one hundred thousand shots.

While printing photos today can feel as retro as sending a fax, it's never been easier or more affordable. Unlike in the old days of film photography, when

you'd develop a roll to find half your shots blurry, overexposed, or ruined by a thumb in the frame—or was that just me?— digital technology allows us an unprecedented degree of quality control. Online photo printing services such as Snapfish, Shutterfly, and Mpix offer fast and affordable delivery in a range of sizes, paper options, and finishes. If you're skeptical about your album-making skills, many of these companies can also print your photos in book form.

Making physical copies of your photos won't just inspire you to look at them more often; it's also the most reliable way to ensure you'll still have them in the future. JPEGs can degrade in quality through compression, while photos printed on archival paper can last over a hundred years. And given the speed at which our digital storage systems evolve, state-of-the-art methods for file saving are rapidly becoming obsolete. Case in point: in the early days of digital photography, DVDs were the best way to store images; today, it's hard to find a computer with a disc drive. Even flash drives from a few years ago are incompatible with new computers, as USB ports give way to Thunderbolt ports. Cloud storage works well now, but who knows where we'll be in another fifteen years?

For all the logical and logistical reasons to print your photos, the best reason is emotional. We take photos to capture moments that are meaningful to us, whether that meaning comes from who we're with, where we are, or what we're doing. Creating photo albums we can hold and share is the best way to honor and preserve those memories.

Try It Out

Gather materials. If you plan to make your own album or scrapbook, you'll need some basic supplies: the album, labels or pens, and adhesive for attaching photos (double-stick tape, photo-safe glue sticks, and self-adhesive mounting corners all work well). You can buy scrapbook-making materials at craft and art supply stores like Michaels, Blick, and Paper Source.

Build your printed photo collection. "To collect photographs is to collect the world," wrote the critic Susan Sontag. If you're not sure where to begin, start by making a commitment to print your ten favorite photos each month—images that showcase *your* world, whether they're selfies, candid shots of friends and family, memorable meals, or random beautiful/funny sights that have caught your eye. You may want to send small batches to different online printing services to figure out which you prefer. Once you've found a service you like, print larger batches or order a custom photo book.

Stay organized. Before assembling an album, keep your photos (and any other scrapbook memorabilia) in order with inexpensive photo storage boxes or old shoeboxes. Use index cards as dividers to organize photos and other materials by date or theme. Once you're ready to create your album, use an acid-free pen or labels to caption photos so you'll be able to remember the who-what-where-when details for years to come.

Control your digital camera roll with regular purges. The more limited your options, the easier it will be for you to choose your favorite images for printing. How many pictures do you currently have stored on your smartphone—and when was the last time you looked at any of them? Keep your phone memory manageable by deleting unwanted photos from your digital roll at regular intervals. Depending on how many photos you take, you may want to schedule twenty-to-thirty-minute sessions for photo cleanup on a weekly or monthly basis. Do the same if you have a huge backlog of photos stored on your computer, external hard drive, or cloud.

Take It Further

Print extra copies of your favorite photos to gift to friends. Stick them in frames or use them to personalize birthday and holiday cards. If you're feeling extra ambitious, make a mini album for someone you love to commemorate a special occasion.

Volunteer

AS A NATION, we like volunteering—at least in theory. Ninety percent of Americans say they'd like to volunteer, but according to the Corporation for National and Community Service, only about 30 percent actually do. How come? Some people say they aren't sure how to get involved or that no one has asked for their help. Others say they don't have enough free time—the most common excuse by far among would-be volunteers. But Amy Yotopoulos, a director at the Stanford Center on Longevity, notes that people between the ages of thirty-five and forty-four, who often have young kids and full-time jobs, volunteer at similar or higher rates than retirees. Yotopoulos suggests that people who don't volunteer may be experiencing "volunteering inertia"—in other words, unless you've made a habit of volunteering, it can be a challenge coming up with the motivation to get started.

Here's something to motivate you: volunteering isn't just good for the communities or organizations you serve; it's one of the best things you can do for yourself. Doing good deeds for others can reduce stress and anxiety, alleviate loneliness and depression, and improve your mood. Researchers have found that charitable acts stimulate our brain's reward center, leading to the "warm glow" we feel when we know we've helped someone out. (Yes, "warm glow" is the actual scientific term.) And regular volunteer work with an organization can create an opportunity to forge meaningful relationships and build an enduring support network.

As a hands-on learning environment, volunteering is also a great way to acquire new skills. Want to learn about art history? Volunteer as a docent at a museum. If you like building things, consider donating some of your time to an organization like Habitat for Humanity. Many nonprofit organizations and corporations provide leadership-training opportunities for volunteers—the *Stanford Social Innovation Review* even calls service-based learning "the new executive training ground."

Along those lines, volunteering is a great way to gain experience in new fields and try out possible careers without needing to make any long-term commitments. It can also be helpful in demonstrating your skills, experience, and commitment to prospective employers. According to *The Wall Street Journal,* "Skilled volunteer work—such as helping a nonprofit with its finances—makes job applicants look more appealing to hiring managers." And the personal connections you make doing volunteer work can become valuable assets in your professional life.

One last point for the folks who claim they don't have time to volunteer: a study by Wharton professor Cassie Mogilner found that people who give their time away to help others feel they have *more* time to spare afterward than those who don't. How to explain this seeming paradox? "People who give time feel more capable, confident, and useful," Mogilner tells *Harvard Business Review*. "They feel they've accomplished something and, therefore, that they can accomplish more in the future." That sense of accomplishment makes people more productive, so even if they objectively have less time than the people who haven't volunteered, they're able to accomplish more.

> Service to others is the rent you pay
> for your room here on earth.
> —Muhammad Ali

Try It Out

Think about what you'd like to do. Do you want to help out your local community? Learn a new skill? Share a skill you already have? Travel and experience a different culture? Test out a possible career path? Work with a specific population (children, the elderly, animals)? "The best way to volunteer is to find a match with your personality and interests," recommends *HelpGuide,* a mental health and wellness website.

Look for opportunities. Organizations that regularly provide volunteer opportunities include museums, libraries, theaters, youth organizations, historic sites and state parks, animal shelters, senior centers,

food banks, and places of worship. You can find a list of online resources below.

Find the right fit. Volunteer opportunities are practically limitless, so you may want to explore a few different options to find out what works best for you. You might love an organization's mission but not quite click with its staff. Or you may adore the team but struggle to make the hours fit with your work schedule. As you sort through options, it's important to learn what a given organization's needs are and whether they align with your interests and availability. Don't be shy about asking questions before you commit your time.

VolunteerMatch (volunteermatch.org) matches volunteers with nonprofit organizations based on interests including location and type of work.

The Corporation for National & Community Service (nationalservice .gov) is the federal organization that oversees AmeriCorps and Senior Corps, and offers volunteer positions nationwide.

Idealist (idealist.org) is a database of service-oriented jobs, internships, organizations, graduate programs, volunteer opportunities, and more. The organization also hosts "Idealist Days," monthly days of action that bring people together for local gatherings worldwide.

Volunteer.gov (volunteer.gov) is a portal for environmental service opportunities.

Catchafire (catchafire.org) helps professionals donate their skills to the mission-driven organizations that need them, allowing prospective volunteers to filter for options based on skill set and time commitment.

For longer-term and international opportunities, check out the **US Peace Corps** (peacecorps.gov), the **American Red Cross** (redcross.org), and **MovingWorlds** (movingworlds.org).

Take a Bath

IN THE RUSH to feel productive, fine-tune our efficiency with life hacks, and stay endlessly connected, our most basic restorative routines and rituals can get squeezed out. Take getting clean, for instance. The majority of Americans shower about once a day. While there's no doubt a shower can be refreshing, for many of us, it's a hurried, mechanical part of our routine—a means to an end—rather than a valuable experience in its own right. Soaking in a tub is an easy, low-cost way to relax, reconnect with the senses, and find peaceful sanctuary—but only around 13 percent of Americans take baths on a regular basis.

We could take a tip from the Japanese, for whom *ofuro*—the nightly ritual of soaking in a warm bath—is a national tradition that goes back centuries. "Here bathing isn't about getting clean, it's about doing nothing," explains Japanese-American author Hanya Yanagihara in an essay for *Town & Country*. "It is a time and place reserved for pleasing the senses, for enjoying the luxury of

feeling, for the wonder of experiencing the simplest, most satisfying sensations: heat, water, scent."

Not only does a bath give you the opportunity to slow down and return to your body, there's plenty of evidence that baths are good for your physical and mental health. The British psychologist Neil Morris found that people who took daily baths for two weeks experienced "a significant drop in feelings of pessimism about the future," while researchers at Yale found that taking a hot bath can make people feel less lonely. Dr. John Harcup, who chairs the Medical Advisory Committee for the British Spa Foundation, suggests that we experience a primal form of comfort when we're submerged in warm water: it "gives us connotations of being in the womb, and it is very comforting," he told *The Telegraph.*

The immersive heat we get from baths also improves our circulation, lowering blood pressure, increasing blood flow, and helping sore muscles to relax. A bath can help you fight off colds and flus, since elevated body temperature helps with our immune response. If you need help falling asleep at night, a bath can be invaluable: relaxing in hot water raises your body's core temperature, so that when you get out, it drops to a cooler one—a key signal to your system that it's bedtime.

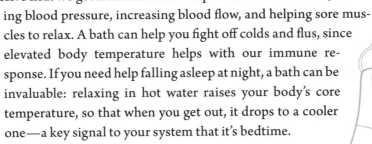

Most importantly, a bath can be a great way to put space between you and the day's activities—evaporating stress, creating a space for reflection, and preparing you for deep rest.

Try It Out

YLANG YLANG

BERGAMOT

Put some space between yourself and the world. Take an evening bath as a relaxing transition from the daily grind to reclaiming your own time and space—your own personal "going off the grid" ritual. Power down your laptop, phone, or any other screens as you're filling the tub. Let a hot bath be your gateway to a quiet, peaceful night—and easier sleep.

Take joy in the senses. While hot water can feel wonderful on its own, the addition of essential oils or Epsom salts can enhance your experience with restorative effects. Lavender or coconut oil can help hydrate and heal your skin, while bergamot orange, ylang-ylang, and clary sage have been found to reduce anxiety through aromatherapy. Dissolving Epsom salts in bathwater is an effective way to reduce inflammation in joints and soothe sore muscles.

SAGE

Wind down. Listen to some soothing music or read a book for pleasure. To make the ambience even more relaxing, use low lighting or light some candles. Once you've created a soothing atmosphere, give yourself license to do nothing at all.

LAVENDER

Take It Further

Many cultures around the world have a rich tradition of public bathing, from the Japanese *onsen* to the Turkish *hamam,* the Russian *banya,* and the Korean *jjimjilbang.* I've enjoyed public baths in Seoul, South Korea, and under Mount Fuji in Japan. But you don't need to fly across the globe to experience these international bathing traditions firsthand: you can find a variety of public bathhouses and spas in many American cities. In Brooklyn, there are a number of Russian *banya*s, and I really like visiting them for friend reunions. It's a great opportunity to relax and catch up while doing something a little out of the ordinary. At public bathhouses, in addition to hot and cold pools, you'll often encounter saunas, steam rooms, spa treatment options, and even designated areas for taking naps. Depending on your level of comfort, you may find bathing with strangers unnerving at first. (I know I did!) But if you allow yourself to embrace the experience, you'll likely adapt quickly. As Hanya Yanagihara writes of her first time visiting a Japanese *onsen:* "The self-consciousness I, like so many of us, carry with me everywhere feels like scaffolding squeezing my heart. But then, unfailingly, one or five minutes in, I feel it: that letting go, that falling away, that lightness. When I get out, everything is softer—my skin, of course, but something unseeable as well." I agree.

PRACTICE NO. 12

Treat Yourself to a Massage

FOR THE PAST few years, I've been making an effort to get a massage about once a month. I used to go to a spa with a hundred different aromatherapies, but lately I've been going to a no-frills place in the basement of an unassuming building a few blocks from my apartment. I don't need my massage to be fancy. I think of it like getting a haircut: an hour of self-care that creates a space for total disconnection from the outside world.

While luxury spas have lent the practice an aura of upscale self-indulgence, massage therapy is a clinically approved technique for addressing a wide range of physical and mental health issues. In other words, it's for everyone. Therapeutic massage dates back five thousand years and has roots in cultures around the world. We get acupuncture from China, reflexology from Egypt, shiatsu from Japan, aromatherapy from Greece, and Swedish massage from . . . you guessed it.

Massage is great for athletes, since it can improve flexibility and range of motion while easing muscle tension and reducing the risk of injury. It's also great for office workers, since it helps to correct posture problems caused by sitting for extended periods of time. Massage therapy can help diabetics to process insulin more effectively and improve immune function in cancer patients. Massage also increases levels of the mood-boosters dopamine and serotonin while decreasing the stress hormone cortisol, which makes it helpful in treating anxiety, depression, and insomnia.

For me, massages are an opportunity to relax. In addition to working out my knots, I love that I can't go anywhere, look at anything, or do anything besides lie still and allow myself to get lost in thought. Whether you're treating a specific issue or just looking for a chance to step outside your life for an hour of dedicated relaxation, think of a massage as an investment in your overall health and well-being. You deserve it.

A Global History of Massage

3000 BCE: Indians practice massage as part of a holistic system known as Ayurvedic healing, which focuses on creating a harmonic balance between the body and the surrounding environment.

2600 BCE: The first written reference to massage appears in the Chinese text *The Yellow Emperor's Classic of Medicine*. This influential work, based in Taoist philosophy, describes acupuncture methods that form the basis of contemporary acupressure therapy.

2500 BCE: Tomb paintings show ancient Egyptians practicing reflexology, the method of applying pressure to specific points in the hands and feet for full-body healing.

1000 BCE: Buddhist monks bring massage therapy from China to Japan, where the Japanese develop a technique called *anma*—later known as shiatsu—pressure-point massage with a focus on balancing energy levels throughout the body.

800–700 BCE: Greek athletes use massage as sports medicine, applying pressure to loosen tight muscles before and after competition. Physicians add fragrant herbs and oils to their massages, giving rise to aromatherapy.

500 BCE: "Father of Medicine" Hippocrates—who created the ethical standards for medicine still observed today with the Hippocratic oath ("do no harm")—prescribes friction to heal injuries and strengthen muscles, writing, "The physician must be experienced in many things, but most assuredly in rubbing."

100 BCE: Roman physician Galen practices massage on emperors, and ordinary Romans seek massage treatments at public bathhouses to loosen their joints and improve circulation.

1800s: Swedish gymnastics teacher Per Henrik Ling pioneers a treatment for his own chronic pain that combines gymnastics, stretching, and massage. Thirty years after Ling's death, Swedish gymnast and doctor Johann Georg Mezger outlines five therapeutic techniques—stroking, kneading, rubbing, tapping, and shaking of muscles—that serve as the basis for Swedish massage, the most common form of massage practiced today.

1950s: The American Massage Therapy Association is established. By the 1970s, massage therapy is a common treatment for pain management and is recognized as an important component in general health and well-being.

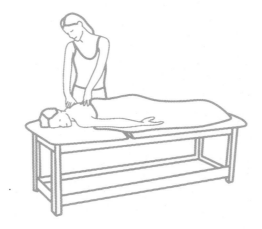

Try It Out

Give yourself time. While you don't need to do anything special to prep for a massage, you should give yourself plenty of time for getting to your appointment, since rushing will make it harder to relax once you arrive. Show up well hydrated, but avoid eating a meal right before your massage, so that your body isn't actively working to digest food during the session.

Communicate with your massage therapist. Before your session begins, your massage therapist should ask you about your medical history, any symptoms you're experiencing, and your reasons and

expectations for the massage. The therapist should also explain the techniques they'll be using for your massage so you know what to expect. Let them know if you're allergic to any oils, lotions, or powders, since these may be used to reduce friction during the massage—your therapist can find a substitute. And if you have any questions or concerns, don't hesitate to voice them.

Make your comfort a priority. Your massage therapist may ask you to undress and cover yourself with a sheet. They'll leave the room to give you privacy while you undress, and during the massage, they'll uncover only the areas of your body that they're actively working on. If you'd prefer not to remove your clothes, wear loose-fitting clothing so that the therapist can reach and move different parts of your body with ease. Some styles of massage can cause mild discomfort or soreness the next day, but a massage shouldn't cause you pain or make you uncomfortable. Speak up if you're uncomfortable in any way.

Give feedback. During your massage, let your therapist know whether you'd like them to adjust their pressure or speed, or to focus on specific areas of your body. If you're

bothered or distracted by anything in the environment—the temperature of the room, lighting, music, aromatherapy, conversation if you'd prefer silence—make sure to communicate this as well. Everyone has different preferences. The massage therapist's job is to ensure that you're getting the experience you want.

Relax and breathe. Deep breathing circulates oxygen to your blood supply and lowers your heart rate, which will help your muscles and mind to relax. If your therapist is working on a painful knot, try not to tense up. Keep breathing, and each time you exhale, imagine pushing the discomfort out of your body. Try to let thoughts pass freely in and out of your mind. If you find yourself ruminating on something, refocus by concentrating on the feeling of your therapist's hands on your body.

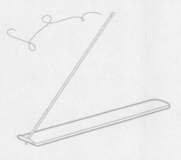

Allow yourself time after your massage. To extend the relaxation benefits of your massage, take your time getting up, dressing, and returning to your regular life. Massage can be dehydrating, so make sure to drink lots of water after your session.

Schedule multiple sessions. The health benefits of massage therapy are cumulative: like exercise, you'll get the most out of it when you make it a regular practice. Massage therapy is available at a range of price points, so look around for a place that fits your budget.

Try Therapy

FOR YEARS, my friend and I kept having the same argument about therapy. He didn't see the point. Sure, he'd say, it's helpful to talk through the things we're struggling with, but isn't that what our friends and family are for?

I'd argue back that it is great to have supportive friends and family, but they're not a good substitute for therapy. Unlike talking to friends and family, when we see a therapist, we never have to worry that we're taking up too much of their time or being too needy. We don't have to worry about whether they'll maintain confidentiality, judge us, or get offended by something we say. Family and friends have a personal stake in our lives, which can color their opinions and advice. Therapists are trained professionals—their job is to offer us neutral, unbiased feedback and help us to develop long-term skills and strategies for navigating the challenges we face.

I suspect that whether he was aware of it or not, my friend had absorbed some of the stigma surrounding mental healthcare. A lot of people see going to therapy as a sign of weakness or self-absorption, while others believe it's only for those suffering from serious mental illness. But as

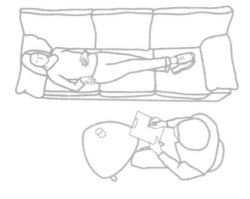

the psychologist Ryan Howes points out in *Psychology Today,* most of us don't think twice when it comes to taking care of our physical health: if we're feeling sick, we go to the doctor; if we want to improve our strength and fitness, we go to the gym or work out with a trainer. Why shouldn't we treat our mental health with the same level of care? Therapy can be a great resource if you're feeling depressed or facing a crisis. But you don't need to be struggling with a problem to reap its benefits: "Therapy is just as useful in the wellness model of getting healthy, achieving potential, and making a good life better," says Dr. Howes.

Therapy is a mechanism that enables me to think more deeply about whatever is going on in my life and how I relate to the world. Therapy has helped me to better manage my stress, communicate more clearly in my personal life, and be a more effective leader at work. And after years of debate, I've finally won over my friend: he started seeing a therapist recently, and now he says it's changed his life!

Here are some reasons to try therapy:

- If you're feeling down, depressed, or isolated
- If you've experienced trauma or loss
- If you want resources to manage stress and anxiety
- If you're engaging in behaviors you think may be unhealthy
- If you're going through a big life change
- To improve your self-esteem
- To make a good relationship even stronger
- To create healthier habits in your personal and professional lives
- To strategize about how to get the most out of your career
- To set actionable goals and priorities for your life
- To develop leadership skills
- To become more organized and motivated
- To improve your communication skills at home or at work
- To become more assertive

Try It Out

Check with your insurance provider to learn about your mental health coverage. The Affordable Care Act requires most individual and group health plans to offer coverage for mental health services. Call your insurer for the specifics of your coverage, including your own financial responsibility and a database of local providers. If you don't have insurance or your coverage is limited, don't panic! Many therapists offer a sliding scale for clients who can't afford to pay their full rate. Other options, like group therapy or online counseling, may be more affordable.

Get a referral. There are a lot of therapists out there, and finding the right one for you can involve some trial and error. You might start by asking your primary care doctor for a referral or soliciting recommendations from friends. (If you don't want to see the same therapist as your friend, see if they can refer you to someone else in the practice.)

Do some research. Many therapists have profiles on the website PsychologyToday.com, where they list their qualifications, specializations, and general philosophy. Once you have a few names, spend some time on the site to learn whether their interests and approaches align with your own needs.

Arrive prepared. Before your first session, spend some time thinking about your goals for therapy. What do you think you'd like to work on? It's okay if you don't have all of this figured out. Remember that your goals and concerns may change over time. When you arrive, make sure you bring your insurance information and any relevant medical history.

Listen to your instincts. While it's not an exact science, after a few sessions you may have a gut feeling about whether or not your therapist is a good fit for you. If you have doubts, it's okay to speak directly to your therapist about your concerns and ask for their perspective on your treatment. Your therapist isn't there to be your friend, but you should feel comfortable and safe with them.

Don't expect easy answers. Good therapists won't tell you what to do; their job is to help you develop the resources to understand your thoughts, feelings, and behaviors—and then find your own solutions.

Implement a "No Screens While Moving" Policy

I SHOULD GIVE credit to Getaway friend Jess Davis for this next practice. The award-winning brand consultant and digital strategist (or, as she might put it, *recovering* digital strategist) had built a successful career in tech, but even as her professional life flourished, she admits, "My brain was struggling. Memory, attention, and creativity were all lacking." She sought medical advice, but doctors couldn't figure out what was going on. Then, while on vacation in Hawaii, she took a "family-imposed digital detox"—in other words, her husband locked up her cell phone and laptop for the full ten days of the trip. At first, like any addict, she felt anxious and frustrated. But on the eighth day, she had an epiphany: "I was well again and the only difference was my presence, lack of technology, and slower pace."

The revelation was life-changing. As soon as she got back from vacation, Jess quit her job. Soon after, she launched Folk Rebellion, a media brand and advocacy organization on a mission to foster digital well-being. "We aren't anti-tech," she clarifies, but she believes having a healthier relationship with digital technology requires setting firm boundaries around screen time. "Mindful tech is a practice. It's you controlling your technology, not it controlling you. It's making conscious choices about how, when, and where you use it."

One of the easiest ways to fall into mind*less* tech use is while commuting. I can't count the number of times I've gotten onto the subway, pulled out my phone . . . and then looked up to realize forty-five minutes have gone by while I've been scrolling aimlessly through social media. To break the habit, I've adopted one of Jess's ideas: her "no screens while moving" policy.

"No screens while moving" means that whenever you're in transit, you're not on your phone or tablet: you don't text while walking; you don't check email in a cab; you don't use Instagram on the subway. (It should go without saying that if you're driving, or riding a bike, you should definitely not be on your phone.) By making it a rule, you create a clear boundary for your-self, which eliminates the temptation for indecision, waffling, and bargaining. You don't have to spend time wondering, *Should I really be on my phone right now?* The answer is no, and you're way less likely to do it if you've got a "no screens while moving" policy in place.

Try It Out

Don't be afraid to start small. If the idea of getting rid of *all* screens across *all* modes of transit feels like too drastic a change, break it down into more manageable goals. You could start by making a commitment to stop using your phone while walking. This isn't just for the sake of mindfulness: researchers have found that in the past decade, over eleven thousand people have sustained injuries walking while texting. (And those, we may assume, are just the ones who admit it.)

Bring analog entertainment for your commute. Newspapers, magazines, and books are great company for commuters, as are crossword and Sudoku puzzles. (See Practice No. 59.) If you're craft-inclined, the daily commute is a great time to make headway on that scarf you've been meaning to knit for the past three winters.

Be present in your surroundings. You might be amazed by how much you notice when you move around without your face buried in a screen: seasonal changes, new houses or shops popping up in your neighborhood, street art and buskers, the mini-dramas of your fellow commuters.

Let yourself daydream. Studies show that allowing your mind to wander is actually good for your brain; it exercises your working memory, the system that allows you to juggle multiple thoughts at once. Daydreaming can also cause the mind to connect unrelated ideas, which spurs creative thinking and imagination.

Take It Further

Once you've mastered the habit of screen-free transit, expand the practice to other parts of your routine, like meals or before bed. (See Practice No. 32 for tips on establishing no-phone zones.)

Give up Headphones for a Week

I HAVE NOTHING against headphones in principle. Like billions of people around the world, I like listening to music. I also like having the ability to take my music and podcasts on the go. Still, I've realized that on busy days, if I have my headphones in as I rush from home to office to meetings and back, I end up filling every single minute of my day with content. My brain doesn't get a break, and I don't get any time to spend with my own thoughts. By the time I get home in the evening, I feel burned out and even a little dizzy.

It's not just that I'm not listening to myself think. It's amazing how quickly you can tune out the world by turning on a podcast. I live in New York City, a place full of strange and fascinating people, but if I'm immersed in whatever is streaming through my AirPods, I'm way less likely to notice what's going on around me. That lack of attention can pose real risks: a 2012 study conducted by researchers at the University of Maryland found that the rate of pedestrians who were killed or critically injured while wearing headphones had more than tripled over the previous six years (not coincidentally, the same years that saw the meteoric rise of iPods and smartphones). "I'm not suggesting that pedestrians wearing headphones be pulled over," the study's lead author, Dr. Richard Lichenstein, told *The New York Times*. "But wearing them at the gym is different from using them wherever you're walking around. You're distracted, and you can't hear the surrounding environment."

Speaking of hearing, audiologists warn that continual exposure to headphones can lead to long-term hearing loss, especially if you're turning up the volume in an effort to drown out other noises around you.

Of course, the desire to drown out other noises is exactly why lots of people wear headphones. "Our ear shields are barriers against barbaric city attacks like catcalls, construction or unwanted conversation," writes journalist Lindsay Mannering in *The New York Times*. They don't just give us something else to listen to: Mannering reports that headphones are so effective as Do Not Disturb signs that people have started wearing them even when they're not listening to anything at all.

This is exactly what former Assistant Surgeon General Douglas Kamerow dislikes about headphones: "It is profoundly isolating," he writes in *HuffPost*. "We are floating past each other in our individual cocoons, walled off from everyone else." If you live in a crowded city, the ability to retreat into an "individual cocoon" may feel like a blessing. But it's also limiting: when we put up barriers between ourselves and our immediate surroundings, we experience less of the world, including opportunities for connecting with the people around us.

Going headphones-free doesn't mean you have to chat up every stranger on the street, but fleeting daily exchanges with the folks you encounter can be entertaining and rewarding. As writer Sage Anderson observes in *Mashable* of her headphones-free week visiting Cuba: "Being plugged in would've made me miss the wholesome, weird, and wacky moments. I formed a light rapport with our doorman once he found out I was Cuban. . . . Taxi rides felt much shorter after I started some interesting chats with the drivers. Waiting (and complaining) in line was now a communal experience."

I'm not suggesting you renounce headphones forever—I wouldn't want to, myself. But taking a weeklong headphones break can be a useful experiment in observing where your thoughts go, and what you notice, when you unplug.

Healthy Headphones: How Loud Is Too Loud?

If you . . .

- have trouble hearing someone speaking from a few feet away
- hear sound coming from your headphones when you hold them at arm's length
- hear ringing or buzzing in your ears after listening

. . . your headphones are too loud. Audiologists recommend the 60–60 rule: you should only listen to music at 60 percent volume for a maximum of 60 minutes.

Write a Letter to Your Future Self

WHEN I WAS growing up, my teachers occasionally gave my classmates and me the assignment of writing letters to our future selves. When I opened these letters a year or two later, I always felt slightly embarrassed—sometimes more than slightly. But as much as the letters made me cringe—so naïve!—with a little bit of reflection I could also see that I'd grown up. Even if I didn't feel as though my life had changed in major ways, when I read my old letters, I could clearly see that I was no longer the person who'd written them. I'd become at least a *little* bit wiser; I knew a little bit more about myself and the world.

It's easy to look back and see how far we've come. But most people find it difficult to imagine that we'll continue changing in the future, a phenomenon social psychologists call the "end of history illusion." In a study of more than nineteen thousand people between the ages of eighteen and sixty-eight, researchers found that most people believe that the present versions of themselves are "who they really are" and that their interests, values, preferences, and priorities will stay the same in the future. "Middle-aged people—like me—often look back on our teenage selves with some mixture of amusement and chagrin," one of the study's authors, Harvard psychologist Daniel T. Gilbert, told *The New York Times*. "What we never seem to realize is that our future selves will look back and think the very same thing about us. At every age we think we're having the last laugh, and at every age we're wrong."

In this light, writing letters to our future selves can be a worthwhile practice for keeping ourselves honest, benchmarking who we are and what matters to us now as a reminder (and data point) for our future selves. "We are well advised to keep on nodding terms with the people we used to be, whether we find them attractive company or not," Joan Didion suggests in her classic 1966 essay "On Keeping a Notebook."

David G. Allan, CNN's editorial director of Features, believes we can also use these letters to set ourselves on a course for achieving the future we want, using a technique called backcasting. Unlike forecasting, which uses patterns from the past and present to predict the future, backcasting starts by asking us to imagine the future in detail. What do we want it to look like? And even if we can't control all possible outcomes (spoiler alert: we can't), what can we start doing right now to make that vision of the future more likely? "Consider the present as the past of your own future," he writes. "At any given time, our actions have a personal butterfly effect on what happens later. The more we ruminate on this seemingly obvious fact and then start to plan accordingly, the greater influence we will have on our future."

Allan has been writing letters to his future self for nearly twenty years. In the letters, he describes his current life and lists milestones he hopes to hit in the future. He notes that after Frederick Law Olmsted designed New York City's Central Park, the park took decades to grow into his intended vision for it. "Our lives are like designing Central Park," Allan writes. "We can't totally predict what will sprout and how exactly it will look, but we are largely in charge of what we plant and how often we tend to those saplings."

Real generosity towards the future lies
in giving all to the present.
—Albert Camus

Try It Out

Start by describing your current life. How do you spend your time, and who do you spend it with? List your recent accomplishments, new skills you've acquired, and your current interests.

Write down your fears and preoccupations. What thoughts keep you up at night? What challenges are you facing? If you struggle with self-doubt, consider when and why this feeling shows up. You may find that the things that worry you most now are no big deal to your future self, which could help your future self to gain perspective on his or her own worries.

Identify your values and lessons learned. What matters most to you on a day-to-day basis? What are your guiding principles? What have you learned about yourself and your surroundings (your work, your relationships, etc.), and how does that knowledge impact the decisions you currently make?

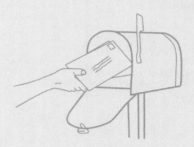

Lay out your goals and dreams. What does your ideal future look like? Think about career, family, where you want to live, skills you hope to develop, and experiences you'd like to have. Then jot down some notes about what you plan to do now and over the next few years to begin—or continue—laying the groundwork for that future.

Prep your letter for future delivery. You can always seal your letter in an envelope and leave it in a drawer for future you to find, but it might be easier to outsource: a number of online and analog services have stepped up to fill the role of our former grade school teachers and camp counselors. FutureMe (futureme.org) is a free online service that invites users to submit letters on the site, to be delivered via email anytime between one month and fifty years in the future. Dear Future Me (dearfutureme.org) allows writers to send and receive their letters through the mail: the company charges users a small monthly fee to store the letters in a "locked, fireproof safe at a secure location" for up to five years, sending them out on the user's chosen date. Letter to Future Self (lettertofutureself.com) allows users to submit their letters on the website and will print and mail them at a future date of the user's choice for $9.99.

PART 2

Balance Your Relationships

THOUGH SOME OF US are more introverted and others more extroverted, humans are fundamentally social creatures. Maintaining strong relationships with others is essential for our health and well-being. Relationships improve the quality of our lives and can help us live longer. But even as technology makes it easier to connect with friends near and far, people are reporting higher levels of loneliness and isolation than ever. While our smartphones can bridge long distances, they can also create barriers by distracting us from the people right in front of us. Some social scientists warn that as we move deeper into the digital age, overreliance on screen-mediated communication and social media is threatening our ability to communicate comfortably face-to-face. In her book *Reclaiming Conversation*, MIT professor Sherry Turkle writes, "When digital media encourage us to edit ourselves until we have said the 'right thing,' we can lose sight of the important thing: Relationships deepen not because we necessarily say anything in particular but because we are invested enough to show up for another conversation." Showing up can take lots of forms: sending a handwritten letter; asking meaningful questions and really listening to the answers; bonding over board games; or bringing people together to share a home-cooked meal.

Schedule a "Day of Jubilation"

WHEN I WAS in college, I took a class called Introduction to Science and Technology in Society. One class assignment required students to give up all electronic communication (laptops, cell phones, and even debit and subway cards) for twenty-four hours as a demonstration of how ubiquitous electronic communication is. At the time, I thought it would be a real inconvenience. After all, I had term papers to write, exams to study for, and pre-newsfeed Facebook pages to browse through endlessly.

In reality, it ended up being the best day of my college years. Several classmates and I had arranged to meet up in the morning, and I left my dorm room without checking my phone or email for the first time I could remember. Once we got outside, our group began walking around with nothing in our pockets besides keys and some cash. It was thrilling to realize how vibrant and strange the world around us was when we didn't have anything to distract us from it. We came across a string quartet rehearsal and a group of women playing rugby in prom dresses. We stopped on the banks of Boston's Charles River and had deep, meandering talks about life. We ran into friends, who joined our group when

they saw how happy we were. Ten years later, we still refer to it as the Day of Jubilation and hold reunions regularly.

What is jubilation? It's a feeling of joy, delight, and triumph. Our electronics-
free day reminded my classmates and me that for however much our day-to-day
lives are mediated by texts, emails, social media, podcasts, and Netflix, we don't
actually *need* any of it to be entertained, connected, and happy. All we need is an
uninterrupted stretch of time to pay attention to the people we care about and
the world around us.

Try It Out

Recruit friends and choose a date. Find a time when you can all disconnect together for a full twenty-four hours. (Don't worry: you don't
need to spend all twenty-four hours together.) While weather can be
tricky to predict, you may want to aim for a time of year when it's
likely to be nice outside, so you have more options to explore.

**Power off your phone and set an email auto-
reply.** Give advance warning to folks who might
otherwise worry if they can't get in touch with
you immediately. For everyone else, calls that go
straight to voicemail and auto-response emails
should make it clear that you're not ignoring
anyone; you're just not available.

Prearrange a meet-up spot. Just like we did in the days before cell phones, set up a specific time and place to meet your friends in advance. And get there on time! You won't be able to send any "running late" or "on my way!" texts.

Be adventurous. You might have some ideas for how you plan to spend your day, but keep yourself open to whimsy and spontaneity. Follow your instincts and curiosities; allow yourself to be guided by happenstance and unexpected encounters. Let the day take you where it will, even if that means going off the map and out of your comfort zone.

Take It Further

A Day of Jubilation is a great way to refresh your relationship to familiar surroundings. It can also be an exciting and unconventional way to discover a new place. The next time you travel somewhere new, try an electronics-free day to wander around and see what you discover without the aid of recommendation websites and GPS. (See Practice No. 64 for more tips on exploring new places without the help of digital technology.)

Write Thank You Notes

WHEN'S THE LAST TIME you sent a thank you note? Not just a text or an email, but a real ink-on-paper, signed-sealed-and-delivered letter through the mail? Unless you've recently had a wedding or baby shower, you might have to go back to that time in grade school when your parents made you write to Grandma Lorraine to thank her for that encyclopedia set.

We've been exchanging letters of appreciation for thousands of years. The ancient Chinese and Egyptians wrote each other well wishes on papyrus. Fourteenth-century Europeans delivered notes to friends and family by hand. In the late 1880s, the card-sending tradition took off in the United States when Polish-born printer Louis Prang introduced a technique called chromolithography to reproduce colorful motifs on card stock. And America's original etiquette guru, Emily Post, included entire chapters on card and letter writing in her ground-breaking 1922 guidebook, *Etiquette in Society, in Business, in Politics, and at Home.* "In writing notes or letters, as in all other forms of social observance," Post instructed readers, "the highest achievement is in giving the appearance of simplicity, naturalness and force." Her detailed dos and don'ts extended to paper type ("should never be ruled, or highly scented, or odd in shape"), the style of an envelope's flap ("should be plain and the point not unduly long"), how to fold a note ("*neatly*"), and closing lines ("No lady should ever sign a letter 'respectfully,' not even were she writing to a queen").

While the regular exchange of thank you notes may have been the *mode du jour* in Emily Post's day, today these expressions of gratitude have become a rarity. Have we gotten ruder? Maybe. But a recent study conducted at the University of Texas, Austin, found that people often hesitate to send thank you letters because they worry their notes might come across as insincere or poorly written, and that they might make recipients feel awkward or uncomfortable. At the same time, they doubt how much recipients will appreciate such notes. But the research team discovered that getting a thank you note—even an email that took its author less than five minutes to write—*was* a big deal to the people who received them. Most reported feeling "ecstatic" and perceived the letters as warmer and better written than their nervous authors had imagined.

Meanwhile, as Practice No. 1 (Keep a Gratitude Journal) discusses, tapping into gratitude is good for our health: feeling grateful can make us more patient, improve our relationships, ease depression, and even help us to sleep. "Saying thanks can improve somebody's own happiness, and it can improve the well-being of another person as well," says Dr. Amit Kumar, an author of the UT study. So why not make a regular habit of this low-cost, high-reward activity? Emily Post would approve.

Try It Out

Sometimes sending a thank you note is a must-do. While letters of appreciation are a nice gesture at any time, in certain circumstances they're pretty much mandatory. *Always* send a thank you note after a job interview (whether or not you get the job), after receiving a gift, after someone writes you a letter of recommendation or does you a favor, after someone hosts an event in your honor, and after staying over at someone's house.

Personalize your note. If you're expressing gratitude for a gift, let the person know how much you enjoy it or how you plan to use it. If you're thanking someone for a letter of recommendation, you might mention how much you value their opinion.

Make a practice of sending thank you notes after dinners, parties, and other social events. It's not necessary to send a formal note of thanks to the host after a party (as long as it's not a party *for* you), but that doesn't mean it won't be appreciated. I send a lot of handwritten notes around the holidays, and lately I've gotten in the habit of sending them after dinner parties, too. It's the easiest thing in the world, and it makes me feel good to sit down and say a proper thank you—sometimes I even spot my note on a friend's fridge the next time I visit them.

Take It Further

Challenge yourself to send at least one spontaneous appreciation text every day. You don't need to wait for a special occasion to send a quick text thanking someone for being a good friend, or giving you advice that's served you well, or sharing a joke that makes you laugh whenever you think of it. Sending a thank you text might take you only a few seconds, but it's likely to brighten the recipient's mood for much longer.

Go the Distance

Step up your thank you game by investing in blank cards, a few good pens, and a book of Forever stamps. "It is so important, in a digital world, to have the dignity to sit down and write something in your own hand," the fashion publicist Cristiano Magni told *The New York Times.* "It not only strengthens the bonds between people, in your personal life and in business, it also rings an emotional chord." If you're feeling nervous about what to write, remember that the gesture itself is what the recipient will remember.

Tell Ghost Stories

SOMETIME AROUND 100 CE, the ancient Roman lawyer Pliny the Younger wrote a letter to the senator Licinius Sura. "I am extremely desirous to know whether you believe in the existence of ghosts," Pliny wrote. "What particularly inclines me to believe in their existence is a story which I heard . . ." He went on to describe a woman of "unusual size and beauty more than human" who appeared before a young man and accurately predicted his future; an old house in Athens where "in the dead of the night," frightened guests awaken to "the form of an old man, with a long beard and disheveled hair, rattling the chains on his feet and hands"; and a mysterious figure who visits Pliny's servant in the night, cuts off his hair, and scatters it around the room. Could these hauntings be real? "The subject deserves your examination," Pliny wrote to Sura, concluding the world's first known ghost story on a spookily ambiguous note.

Ghosts and ghost stories exist in cultures throughout the world. Nearly half of all Americans believe in ghosts, and we love telling ghost stories, from whispered tales at sleepovers, to creepy yarns spun around a campfire, to the perennial popularity of horror movies. The fantasy and horror writer Neil Gaiman believes that we're attracted to ghost stories because "fear is a wonderful thing, in small doses."

What's so wonderful about fear? It turns out that when we're frightened, we get a rush of adrenaline, even if the threat is imaginary. Adrenaline heightens our senses and speeds up our metabolism, making us feel excited and alive. "You ride the ghost train into the darkness, knowing that eventually the doors will open and you will step out into the daylight once again," Gaiman says. "It's always reassuring to know that you're still here, still safe."

There's a lot that's objectively scary in the real world: war, famine, and climate change, to name a few. On a more personal level, we might dread losing our jobs or homes, facing a serious illness, or getting our hearts broken. Ghost stories offer us a version of fear we can control. They can give us a way to explore things we don't understand or offer us a connection to the past. And telling them brings us together to share a collective act of imagination, whether we're huddling around the campfire or in the living room lit with flashlights on a dark and stormy night.

Try It Out

Craft an original story based on your own experience. According to Colin Dickey, the author of *Ghostland: An American History in Haunted Places,* everyone has a potential ghost story inside them. "For so many people, they have, somewhere in their history, something they can't quite explain, but yet don't want to dismiss out of hand," Dickey told *The Washington Post.* While you might not count yourself among the 18 percent of Americans who claim to have seen a ghost, you've probably had at least one strange or mysterious experience you can develop into an original ghost story. The more verifiable truth there is in your story, the creepier it will be for your listeners.

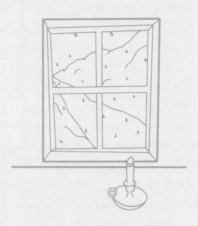

Set a familiar scene. If you're telling ghost stories in the woods, have your story take place in the woods. If you're in a house, set the story in a similar house. Scan your surroundings for details you can work into your story in order to blur the line between fantasy and reality.

Take your time. For building up dread, suspense is more effective than gore: you'll probably frighten your audience more by describing the sound of mysterious footsteps getting closer than you will with the nitty-gritty details of a bloody ax murder.

End with a surprise twist or cliffhanger. Keep your listeners on the edge of their seats to the very end . . . or longer. Open-ended stories extend the mystery and the creepy feeling that comes with it, so don't shy away from endings like ". . . and as far as we know, she's still out there."

Take It Further

Try your own spin on a classic ghost story. For resources, check out *Grimm's Fairy Tales*—the Bible of folktales—or more recent takes on old favorites, such as Angela Carter's *The Bloody Chamber* and Carmen Maria Machado's *Her Body and Other Parties*.

Make a Habit of "Phone Stacking" When out with Friends

WE'RE PROBABLY ALL familiar with the frustration of trying to enjoy a meal with companions who are so glued to their phones that they barely notice the food in front of them, much less the company around them. (From time to time, we might even be guilty of doing this ourselves.) But it can be awkward asking our friends to put away their phones and pay attention—no one wants to be *that* person. According to Internet lore, in early 2012, a blogger came up with a solution that turned dining and phone etiquette into a game. Originally called "Don't Be a Dick During Meals with Friends" (quickly rebranded as "The Phone Stack"), the rules are as follows: At the start of a restaurant meal, players take out their cell phones and stack them facedown in the center of the table. For the duration of the meal, participants are forbidden from checking their phones, no matter how much they buzz, beep, or chime. The first person who gives in to temptation

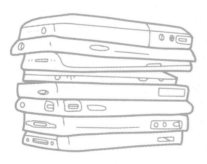

and reaches for their phone loses the game, which can come at a high price, depending on the restaurant—the loser has to pick up the check for everyone else. (If there are no losers, participants split the bill.)

The blog post struck a chord, and soon other media outlets were hyping the game. "I like to think of it as a free market exercise," writes Anthony Ha of *TechCrunch*. "After all, people love to say, 'Sorry, but I have to take this.' Do you *have* to answer it? Really? Is it that important to you? Great, then you can pay."

The challenge at the heart of the game comes from resisting not just the temptation of social media but also more personal alerts. What if your mom is trying to get in touch? Your partner? Your boss? The game encourages participants to move away from the expectation that having a mobile phone means we should be perpetually reachable and available. It can also be fun to discover what you can learn when everyone commits (or *attempts* to commit) to going phone-free. In addition to helping the group stay focused and engaged, the game forces you to exercise your memory, since you won't be able to look things up online.

If the Phone Stack game feels too gimmicky for you, make a commitment to keep your phone in your bag or pocket for the entirety of the meal and ask your friends to do the same. Important: sneaking a peek during a restroom break is cheating! To guarantee a screen-free meal, consider asking the restaurant whether you can leave your group's phones at the host station or bar until you're ready to leave.

My friend and Getaway cofounder Pete Davis takes a different approach. If he's at dinner with friends and gets the urge to look something up on his phone, he makes sure to ask the whole group for permission before he takes it out. At first, his friends used to laugh whenever Pete said, "May I bring a cell phone into this conversation?" But now, some of them have started doing it, too. This kind of affirmative consent turns phone use into an intentional, collective decision rather than a reflexive, self-motivated action. And in the time it takes to ask our friends' permission, we just might realize we don't really need to check our phones after all.

Strike up a Conversation with a Stranger

IT'S POSSIBLE THAT *Humans of New York* creator Brandon Stanton has had more conversations with strangers than anyone else on earth. In 2010, the aspiring photographer moved to New York and started taking pictures of ordinary people he met on the street. With the ambitious goal of taking ten thousand portraits of his fellow New Yorkers, Stanton began posting the photos—along with quotes from his subjects—on a Facebook page he called "Humans of New York." As his following grew, Stanton's interactions with his subjects deepened: he started asking serious, intimate questions like "What's the thing you struggle with the most?" and "What was the saddest moment of your life?" More often than not, his subjects answered honestly, telling Stanton—a man they'd met only moments before—about extremely personal moments in their lives, along with their hopes, frustrations, and fears. Today, Stanton's project has evolved into two bestselling books, and the "Humans of New York" Facebook page boasts nearly eighteen million followers. While Stanton admits he's not the world's greatest photographer, his unique talent is getting strangers to

open up to him, creating authentic moments of intimacy. "People like to feel like they have a story worth telling," he says.

To those of us who grew up hearing about "stranger danger," striking up a conversation with a stranger can feel awkward at best, scary at worst. But we should do it anyway, says Kio Stark, the author of *When Strangers Meet: How People You Don't Know Can Transform You.* When we make eye contact, smile, and say hello to strangers, we're acknowledging them as fellow human beings. Whether we're wishing them good morning or commenting on the weather, our specific words don't really matter, says Stark. "What we mean when we say those things is: I see you there."

In fact, once we get started, we might discover it's easier to talk to a stranger than to a close friend. "We often avoid using people who are close to us as confidants," says Harvard sociologist Mario Luis Small, "exactly *because* they are important to us." Unlike friends and family, who know us well and have a personal stake in our lives, a stranger is a blank slate—and a temporary one. No matter what we might share with each other in the moment, we'll soon be returning to our separate lives, unlikely to meet again.

In the most basic sense, meeting strangers outside of your social circle expands your world. It can help us to overcome bias and make us more open-minded: Stark explains that when we engage with strangers, we stop seeing them as abstractions and start seeing them as individuals. "The more we can have contact with people who aren't like us, the more we are challenged, invited, required to see them as humans, as specific individuals with a context," she says.

It can also be a great way to learn more about your neighborhood or larger community. I try to make conversation with bartenders when I can—they're some of the easiest strangers to talk to. Over time, I've become real friends with

Natasa, a bartender at my favorite Brooklyn bar (the sadly now closed Hank's Saloon). She's older than me and moved to New York fifteen years before I did—she and her partner live in a very different version of New York than I do. But I get to learn about it through her, and when she invites me to places I've never heard of before, where my other friends don't go, I even get to experience it for myself.

Kio Stark's Tips for Breaking the Ice with Strangers

Make eye contact. Catching the eye of a stranger is the best way to make initial contact. If someone avoids your eyes, they're probably not interested in chatting.

Comment on something you both might notice. "There's you, there's a stranger, there's some third thing that you both might see," says Stark. The third thing could be something in the environment, like a street musician, or something you're both experiencing, like a long line or an unexpected change in the weather. It's a quick way to find common ground.

Offer a compliment. Perhaps it goes without saying, but complimenting a stranger is not the same as catcalling! While you might compliment a specific article of clothing that a stranger is wearing ("That's a beautiful scarf!" "I love your shoes!"),

avoid commenting on the person's body or hair, which could be invasive.

Use dogs and babies as a gateway. If you're feeling awkward about launching into conversation with a stranger, start by directing your attention to their dog or baby—assuming they have one, of course. Many dog owners and new parents are used to being approached by curious strangers, and you'll be able to gauge their interest in further conversation based on how they respond.

Try It Out

If you've been chatting with a stranger for a little while and feel comfortable, challenge yourself to be vulnerable: move beyond pleasantries to share something meaningful and true. Often, opening up to a stranger will inspire them to open up to you as well. Kio Stark calls these moments "beautiful interruptions into the expected narrative of your daily life and theirs." It might give you something to smile about in the moment—or become a memory you cherish for the rest of your life.

Organize a Game Night

BOARD GAMES HAVE made a major comeback recently, and not just for kids. Game sales are booming in the US and around the world; in 2016, board games were the top-funded category on Kickstarter, the crowd-funding website. Retailers and enthusiasts credit this renaissance to the popularity of so-called Euro games like the German-made Settlers of Catan, which rely on strategy and cooperation more than luck.

Games are good for the brain: studies show that playing strategic board games can boost creativity, problem-solving, and critical-thinking skills. Maybe more importantly, games bring us together. Nearly half of all Americans report feeling lonely on a regular basis, and 27 percent of millennials say they have "no close friends," according to a 2019 YouGov poll. Meanwhile, MIT professor Sherry Turkle notes that as we've gotten used to digital age communication—the texts, DMs, and emails that she refers to as "little 'sips' of online connection"—we're losing our ability to have

face-to-face conversations. It makes sense, then, that we'd start gravitating toward activities that bring us into the same room to work together toward shared goals—like bartering sheep to build a settlement, for instance.

As the neuroscientist Jon Freeman told *The Atlantic*, "Adults who spend all day sitting in front of a computer want to spend time with people." Several years ago, Freeman left his post directing a clinical research facility in order to open the Brooklyn Strategist, a board-game café near

my apartment. "It's really about people having like-minded, shared experiences," says Freeman. "We'd lost access to that, and places like board-game cafés have opened up access." At the Strategist, which has a library of over five hundred board games, customers can pay $10 for up to four hours of play. Today, you can find board-game cafés and bars around the world.

When my boyfriend, Michael, and I are looking for a low-key evening or weekend activity, we'll go head-to-head over Scrabble, or invite friends to join us at the Brooklyn Strategist for Catan or Ticket to Ride. But you don't need a nearby board-game café—or even a board—to organize a game night with friends. You can play games like Charades, Pictionary, and Bowl of Nouns with nothing more than friends, imagination, and common household items like paper and pens.

Try It Out

Give some thought to your group and goals. When planning a game night, it's useful to start by thinking about who you'll be inviting and whether there's a specific purpose to your evening (beyond fun). Is this an opportunity to get to know new colleagues or neighbors? A chance to reconnect with old friends or bring separate friend groups together? Different occasions may call for different types of games, to make sure everyone is comfortable and has a good time. You'll also want to think about how many people are needed for each of the games, and whether any games involve pairing up (in which case you should avoid inviting an odd number of guests).

Provide refreshments. Game-playing and grazing go hand in hand, so make sure to have plenty of snacks for keeping your players' spirits and energy up. If you're playing a game that involves handling cards or other pieces, you may want to avoid greasy or powdery foods and stick to low-mess classics like tortilla chips, pretzels, and cut-up veggies.

Take game suggestions in advance. One of the best things about getting a group together is the chance for everyone to learn new games from one another. Ask your guests to bring game suggestions—or to bring along their favorite board games—for a night of variety.

Make it a tradition. Get friends together on a regular basis to play favorite games and learn new ones. Take turns hosting and introducing games, or find a local board-game café and go as a group.

Send Postcards to Your Friends

I'M ALWAYS DELIGHTED when I go to pick up my mail and discover a handwritten letter or postcard tucked in with all the catalogs, bills, and flyers. (Usually, they're addressed to my boyfriend, since his friend group has made a better habit of this than mine.) In an age of instant communication through email and texts, snail mail has taken a hit: mail sent through the US Postal Service has dropped by 50 percent in the past decade, and the average household gets only one piece of personal mail every seven weeks.

For as little as we're sending mail, most of us enjoy being on the receiving end: 75 percent of millennials report that getting personal mail "makes them feel special," according to a recent survey by the USPS Office of the Inspector General. While Practice No. 18 focused on the value of sending thank you notes, you don't need any specific reason to send snail mail to the people you care about. Although a postcard may take its sender only a few minutes to write, the gesture of thought and care extends far beyond the actual written message. In the words of Nancy Pope, former head curator at the

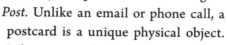

National Postal Museum, "When you're able to actually hold something in your hand, that trumps reading something electronically any day."

Sending a postcard is all about making a personal connection, using "this piece of cardboard—to emphasize, create, or establish a memory," Pope told *The Washington Post*. Unlike an email or phone call, a postcard is a unique physical object. When we send our friends postcards

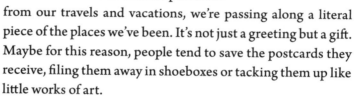

from our travels and vacations, we're passing along a literal piece of the places we've been. It's not just a greeting but a gift. Maybe for this reason, people tend to save the postcards they receive, filing them away in shoeboxes or tacking them up like little works of art.

Of course, you don't need to travel anywhere to send postcards. In the early 1900s, people who lived along the same mail delivery routes would use postcards to invite their neighbors over for tea later that day. You can send cards to say thanks, offer condolences, wish someone a happy birthday, or just to let the recipient know you're thinking of them. The car salesman Joe Girard made a habit of writing personalized thank you notes to every customer who bought a car from him, but he didn't stop there: each month, he sent handwritten notes to his clients that simply read "I like you." The humor writer David Sedaris sends

cards to fellow writers to let them know what he appreciates about their work: "I loved it on Page 38 when you did this."

"It makes me feel good, and it's not that hard," Sedaris told *The New York Times*. In fact, studies find that people who write positive letters to others report higher levels of happiness and satisfaction with their own lives. Less than five minutes to write, and 35 cents to send—it's hard to find happiness at a better bargain.

Did you know? A postcard collector is called a deltiologist. Deltiology is one of the most popular collector hobbies in the world, along with stamp and coin collecting.

Try It Out

Stockpile postcards and stamps. Keep a supply of postcards and stamps so that you can send them anytime. Pick up a book of postcard stamps at your local post office, or order them online from usps. com or Stamps.com. (A current postcard stamp costs 35 cents, and Forever stamps remain valid regardless of future price increases.) You don't need to be on vacation to buy postcards: you can find them at tourist shops in your own town, gas stations and rest stops, airports, museum gift shops, flea markets, and antique stores.

Don't worry too much about the wording. You don't have to write like Shakespeare to send a good postcard. Assuming your message is positive, your recipient will be happy no matter what you write. If you're worried, keep it short and simple.

Write one postcard every day for a week. Jump-start your new habit by writing a postcard to a different friend each day for a week. Mail them as you write them, or save them to mail in a batch at the end of the week. You might even inspire the recipients to respond by sending postcards of their own, launching a new tradition among your friends.

Take It Further

Stretch your creativity by making your own postcards. Use sturdy paper as a base, like card stock or an index card, then embellish the non-address side by drawing, painting, making a collage, or using a photograph. Alternatively, design a card online using a service like Vistaprint or Adobe Spark.

To qualify for postcard pricing, USPS advises that your postcard must be:

- Rectangular
- At least 3½ inches high by 5 inches long by 0.007 inch thick (about the thickness of an index card)
- No more than 4¼ inches high by 6 inches long by 0.016 inch thick

Ask Your Loved Ones Deep Questions

IN HER VIRAL 2015 essay for *The New York Times,* "To Fall in Love with Anyone, Do This," Mandy Len Catron wrote about a study the psychologist Arthur Aron had conducted at Stony Brook University more than twenty years earlier. Dr. Aron wanted to explore whether it was possible to create feelings of closeness between people who didn't know each other. To do so, he asked pairs of strangers to sit down in his lab and talk to each other for

forty-five minutes. Some of the pairs were instructed to make casual small talk, while others were given a set of thirty-six questions to ask each other—questions that grew more and more personal as the list went on. By the end of the session, two of the strangers who'd asked each other deep questions had fallen in love. Six months later, they got married and invited everyone from the lab to the wedding.

Catron decided to try Dr. Aron's experiment on a first date with a casual acquaintance. While sitting at a bar with her date, she pulled up the study's thirty-six questions on her phone. Then she and her date took turns asking and answering. "The questions reminded me of the infamous boiling frog experiment in which the frog doesn't feel the water getting hotter until it's too late," Catron writes. "Because the level of vulnerability increased gradually, I didn't notice we had entered intimate territory until we were already there, a process that can typically take weeks or months."

WOULD YOU LIKE TO BE FAMOUS? IN WHAT WAY?

The questions did more than fast-track the conversation between Catron and her date: they forced the two near-strangers to reveal their true selves. "We all have a narrative of ourselves that we offer up to strangers and acquaintances, but Dr. Aron's questions make it impossible to rely on that narrative," Catron notes.

If you're wondering whether Catron's experiment worked, it did. She and her date fell in love. But this isn't just a story about romance, she cautions: "It's about what it means to bother to know someone, which is really a story about what it means to be known."

GIVEN THE CHOICE OF ANYONE IN THE WORLD, WHOM WOULD YOU LIKE AS A DINNER GUEST?

I'm somewhat infamous among my friends for disrupting a perfectly pleasant conversation by asking questions like *Why are you doing that? Do you really believe that?* We tend to say what we think people want to hear—we're almost always in pitch mode. I find that asking challenging questions always leads to a much more interesting conversation. *Now* we're having a conversation that's new to both sides.

And I have to receive what I put out, even when it makes me uncomfortable. Sometimes I pause and say out loud, "Let me take a moment to make sure I'm telling you the truth." The deeper answers usually aren't immediately on hand, and it can take real thought to say, "Wait a minute, is this true, or is it just what I *want* to be true?" But it's important to do that work if we are going to deepen our relationships.

When we ask deep questions of the people in our lives, we're saying, *I want to know who you really are and what you really think.* When we answer those questions honestly, we're saying, *I trust you not to judge me for who I really am.* Though these exchanges don't have to be limited to romantic partners, we can still think of them as an act of love.

Try It Out

Try Dr. Aron's questions with a friend or partner. See page 114 for the thirty-six questions. Take turns asking and answering questions, spending about fifteen minutes with each of the three sets, and alternate who answers first each time. Make eye contact as you ask and answer. Remember to be honest, even if it makes you feel nervous or vulnerable.

Replace small talk with meaningful questions. You don't need to replicate a landmark psychological study to get into the habit of asking deep questions. Next time you find yourself chatting about work or weather with friends, switch gears and ask your companions something more meaningful.

Be an active listener, and ask follow-up questions. There's no point in asking deep questions if you zone out during the answers. See Practice No. 30 for tips on deep listening. Push your conversations further by asking follow-up questions and challenging basic assumptions. Possible follow-ups include: *Why do you think that? Have you always felt this way? What caused you (or could cause you) to change your mind?*

Ask yourself questions. One of the best ways to develop, improve, and expand your own thinking is to ask yourself questions that challenge your assumptions and beliefs. You'll keep your mind flexible while getting to know yourself better as you continue to grow and change.

The Experimental Generation of Interpersonal Closeness: *Arthur Aron's Thirty-Six Questions*

Set 1

1. Given the choice of anyone in the world, whom would you want as a dinner guest?
2. Would you like to be famous? In what way?
3. Before making a telephone call, do you ever rehearse what you are going to say? Why?
4. What would constitute a "perfect" day for you?
5. When did you last sing to yourself? To someone else?
6. If you were able to live to the age of ninety and retain either the mind or body of a thirty-year-old for the last sixty years of your life, which would you want?
7. Do you have a secret hunch about how you will die?
8. Name three things you and your partner appear to have in common.
9. For what in your life do you feel most grateful?

10. If you could change anything about the way you were raised, what would it be?

11. Take four minutes and tell your partner your life story in as much detail as possible.

12. If you could wake up tomorrow having gained any one quality or ability, what would it be?

SET 2

13. If a crystal ball could tell you the truth about yourself, your life, the future, or anything else, what would you want to know?

14. Is there something that you've dreamed of doing for a long time? Why haven't you done it?

15. What is the greatest accomplishment of your life?

16. What do you value most in a friendship?

17. What is your most treasured memory?

18. What is your most terrible memory?

19. If you knew that in one year you would die suddenly, would you change anything about the way you are now living? Why?

20. What does friendship mean to you?

21. What roles do love and affection play in your life?

22. Alternate sharing something you consider a positive characteristic of your partner. Share a total of five items.

23. How close and warm is your family? Do you feel your childhood was happier than most other people's?

24. How do you feel about your relationship with your mother?

SET 3

25. Make three true "we" statements each. For instance, "We are both in this room feeling . . ."
26. Complete this sentence: "I wish I had someone with whom I could share . . ."
27. If you were going to become a close friend with your partner, please share what would be important for him or her to know.
28. Tell your partner what you like about them; be very honest this time saying things that you might not say to someone you've just met.
29. Share with your partner an embarrassing moment in your life.
30. When did you last cry in front of another person? By yourself?
31. Tell your partner something that you like about them already.
32. What, if anything, is too serious to be joked about?
33. If you were to die this evening with no opportunity to communicate with anyone, what would you most regret not having told someone? Why haven't you told them yet?
34. Your house, containing everything you own, catches fire. After saving your loved ones and pets, you have time to safely make a final dash to save any one item. What would it be? Why?
35. Of all the people in your family, whose death would you find most disturbing? Why?
36. Share a personal problem and ask your partner's advice on how he or she might handle it. Also, ask your partner to reflect back to you how you seem to be feeling about the problem you have chosen.

Find Your Local Place

WHEN I WAS a kid, my parents owned a bar called the Backwoods Bar. In our one-street town of fifty-four people, you didn't need to use the term "local bar"—there was only one, so that's where everyone went. At the Backwoods Bar, the bartenders knew all the customers, and the customers knew one another. Sadly, the bar burned down when I was three and my parents found other work, but everywhere I've lived as an adult, I've sought out a local bar to make "mine"—less because I love bars, and more because it's important for me to be able to go to a place where the people there know who I am and I can get to know them.

Recent studies reveal that loneliness is reaching "epidemic levels" worldwide. According to a 2018 Cigna survey, nearly half of all Americans report feeling alone or left out "sometimes or always." A third of the UK's residents feel lonely often or very often. And in Japan, over half a million people between the ages of fifteen and thirty-nine report that they haven't left their houses or had social interactions in at least *six months*. There's even a new term for these "modern day hermits": *hikikomori,* which translates to "pulling inward" or "being confined."

Loneliness isn't just making us depressed and anxious; it's literally killing us.

Researchers at UCLA found that social isolation makes people more susceptible to heart disease, stroke, cancer, and Alzheimer's disease. A 2015 analysis by researchers at Brigham Young University found that lonely people have a 26 percent higher risk of dying early; if they live alone, that figure jumps to 32 percent.

What's the antidote? *Belonging.* We humans are social beings: we thrive when we feel connected to our communities. Numerous studies show that people who have active social lives and are involved with their communities tend to live longer, get sick less often, feel happier, and run a lower risk of developing dementia than those who are more socially isolated. And one way to foster a sense of belonging is to achieve "regular" status at your local bar or coffee shop. In the words of the iconic eighties TV show *Cheers:* "Sometimes you want to go / Where everybody knows your name / And they're always glad you came."

Thanks to a recent study by researchers at Oxford, we now have scientific evidence that becoming a regular at your local watering hole is good for your health. The team of anthropologists and psychologists found that people who frequent their local bars tend to have more close friends, be more trusting of community members, and report higher levels of satisfaction than those who don't. "Friendship and community are probably the two most important factors influencing our health and well-being," explains lead researcher Robin Dunbar. "Given the increasing tendency for our social life to be online rather than face-to-face, having relaxed accessible venues where people can meet old friends and make new ones becomes ever more necessary."

Local bars and coffee shops aren't just good for their patrons. They often form the beating heart of a neighborhood by hosting musicians' gigs, game and trivia nights, and clubs and meetings. They can be a hub for on-the-ground intel about issues affecting the community, from construction projects to rent hikes to new ordinances. They provide jobs for local workers and funnel money back into the community through tax revenue.

Whether you're new to the neighborhood or a longtime resident, there's no better time to adopt a nearby bar, café, or coffee shop as "yours." Consider it your civic duty. As a bonus, it might help you live longer.

Try It Out

Find a comfortable place. That hip new bar that always has a line around the block is probably not the best candidate for becoming your "local." While you don't need to devote yourself to an abandoned hole-in-the-wall, you'll have better luck becoming a regular at a place where the atmosphere is relaxed and you don't have to start a brawl to get a seat.

Learn your bartender/barista/server's name. Once you've started coming around regularly, you can begin to forge a more meaningful connection by exchanging names and basic life details with the people who serve you. Remembering someone's name goes a long way.

Make conversation, but pick your moment wisely. If you'd like to strike up conversation with your bartender or barista but aren't sure how, an easy opener is to ask them a work-related question, like their recommendation for beer or coffee. Once you're talking, it'll be easier to segue into other subjects. Many bartenders and baristas are naturally conversational—they're in the hospitality industry, after all, so it comes with the territory. But be aware of your surroundings. Don't try starting a conversation if you can see your server is backed up with work. And no matter how friendly you get, remember: your bartender isn't your therapist. If you'd find it helpful to talk through complicated issues in your life, consider enlisting a professional. (See Practice No. 13 for tips on trying therapy.)

Tip generously! Being a good tipper is one of the most effective ways to win over the staff at your local spot. What's a good tip? Most bartenders today agree that the old "dollar per drink" tip standard is outdated, especially in an era of complex craft cocktails that require skill and time to create. "If you order one beer, a shot, or something very simple, then a $1 tip for pouring a draft is acceptable," Jeremy Barrett of Billy Sunday bar in Chicago told *Thrillist.* Otherwise, a 20 percent tip is industry standard if you're happy with your service.

Unlike bartenders and servers, baristas don't rely on tips for the majority of their income, but that's no reason to skip the tip. Most baristas are paid minimum wage, which doesn't go very far these days no matter where you live. While many baristas say that any tip will be appreciated, Blue Bottle Coffee founder James Freeman takes a stronger stance: "I don't think you should ever tip less than a dollar," he told *Business Insider.*

Surprise Someone with a Gift

MY FRIEND JONATHAN Finn-Gamiño is always giving gifts. Sometimes it's a special occasion; often it's not. Usually it's some small thing he came across that made him think of me, like a lapel pin of a marshmallow being roasted over a campfire flame. I always find it so thoughtful when he thinks of me, and I know he does the same for others.

Gift-giving is embedded in our cultural DNA. Though the particulars of the ritual vary from one country to the next, humans practice this tradition everywhere on earth. We give gifts to express friendship and love, to say thank you, to apologize, to facilitate business deals, to commemorate life events like birthdays, weddings, anniversaries, and retirements.

As good as it feels to be on the receiving end of a gift, psychologists say that the giver may reap even greater benefits. "When you give a gift, it makes you feel generous, it makes you feel in control, it's good for your self-esteem, and it's good for the relationship," says Harvard psychologist Ellen Langer. Studies have found that people feel happier when they give money away than when they spend it on themselves, and subjects who were asked to perform five acts of kindness a week reported greater satisfaction with their lives. That warm fuzzy feeling we get from doing good deeds for others has a biological basis: behaving generously releases endorphins and activates regions of the brain associated with rewards and pleasure, leading to what scientists call a "helper's high." Additional studies show that providing social support to others can reduce stress, lower blood pressure, and even increase our longevity.

Giving also strengthens social bonds. When you give someone a gift, you're letting the recipient know that you're thinking about them, that you care about them, and that their happiness matters to you. Those sentiments matter at least as much as the gift itself—and probably more. Generosity tends to be contagious, spreading outward in a ripple effect that benefits the larger community: your act of giving is likely to inspire others to give, whether they're returning the favor or paying it forward.

You don't need a special occasion to give someone a gift—in fact, an impromptu "just because" gift is likely to be even more meaningful to your recipient. And the more you do it, the more you'll get out of it: generosity truly is the gift that keeps on giving.

> The gift is to the giver,
> and comes back most to him—
> it cannot fail.
> —Walt Whitman

Try It Out

Make it personal. Gifts mean more when you give them with specificity and intention. Before choosing a gift, spend some time thinking about your recipient. What sort of person are they? What do you  know about their tastes and preferences? What is the nature of your relationship with them? Dr. Langer notes that gift-giving "provokes mindfulness in us" as we pause to reflect on our connection to another person. That act of reflection then helps to deepen and enrich our connection.

Practical or sentimental gifts matter more than expensive ones. You don't need to spend a ton of money to be a great gifter. If your recipient is sitting in the dark, a lightbulb makes a better gift than jewelry or a deluxe box of chocolates. One of my friends—a champion gift-giver—sends groceries as a housewarming gift, knowing that people who've just moved into a new home probably haven't had time to go food shopping. Whether your gift evokes a shared memory, reflects how well you know someone, or makes their life easier in some way (even a small way), its value will go far beyond its cost in dollars.

Give something you love. Do you have a favorite book, record, brand of tea or coffee, kitchen implement, tote bag, cooking spice, or travel mug? If you're not sure what the other person will like, your best bet is to gift a copy of something *you* love. Even if you don't have the exact same tastes, you'll be sharing a part of yourself with the other person, which is meaningful in its own right.

Get crafty. Handmade gifts are extra special, since they take time and effort to create, and each handmade item is one-of-a-kind. You don't have to be an expert artisan to make a gift your recipient will cherish. Here are some ideas to get you started:

- Bake cookies or muffins
- Grow sourdough starter and reserve some to give away
- Pour candles
- Carve a wooden spoon
- Tie-dye a T-shirt
- Make a bookmark by pressing flowers or leaves and gluing them onto card stock. (See Practice No. 70 for tips on identifying and preserving flowers.)
- Use markers or crayons to create a colorful card
- Turn old wine corks into coasters or a trivet

PRACTICE NO. 27

Start a Book Club

PRACTICE NO. 8 ("Carry a Book Wherever You Go") discussed the many benefits of reading: digging into a book can lower your stress, teach you new things, improve your memory, make you more empathetic, and even help you to live longer. Every year, I try to read mostly books that don't have anything to do with my work. I've found that one of the best ways to commit to reading is with a book club, which adds a social aspect to a solitary activity and gives me a roomful of accountability partners. I'm much more likely to finish a book when I know I'll be discussing it in a group. And yes: sometimes I don't finish the book and just go for the coffee and conversation.

My book club meets around once a month. We take turns choosing what the group will read, and because we all have different tastes, our selections vary a lot from month to month. Some months we're reading a literary novel; other months we're reading a how-do-we-fix-the-world type book. This is another thing book clubs are good for: you don't just read more; you tend to read more widely, which helps expand your perspective across a range of new subjects and ideas.

Beyond the books themselves, group discussion creates a space for friendly debate and exchange among people with different ideas and responses. "Companionship and intellectual stimulation—and thinking quickly during book club discussions—all of these things are very healthy," says Dr. Michael Roizen, chief wellness officer at the Cleveland Clinic. Warby Parker cofounder Neil Blumenthal, who started a series of employee book clubs at his popular eyewear company, notes that book clubs can be valuable for team-building: "It helps build trust when you create what is a safe environment to share ideas, or to debate ideas."

It doesn't always have to be books, either. In grad school, my friends and I took turns hosting what we called "Enlightenment Dinners": the host would choose a long magazine feature about some issue in the world, everyone would read it, and then we'd all come to the dinner prepared to discuss it.

Whether you're choosing books or articles, a reading-based club is a great excuse for meeting new people or getting together with friends on a regular basis. Since book clubs often take place in homes, they tend to be more affordable than meeting up for dinner or drinks, and they offer a natural way to deepen and expand conversation beyond the typical (and tedious) "how's work, how's the family" topics. And of course, they give you a reason to make reading a regular part of your life.

Try It Out

Figure out who (and how many) to invite. When thinking of your invite list, figure out whether you're looking for an opportunity to spend more time with close friends, get to know your neighbors (Practice No. 42), expand your social circle, bond with coworkers over non-work subjects (Practice No. 52), or some combination of the above. If you're planning to hold meetings at home, make sure you limit the group to a size you can comfortably accommodate. If you don't have bookish friends or colleagues, check in with your local bookstore or library branch to see if they offer book clubs for patrons/members. Or start an online book club through Facebook, Goodreads, or another social media platform, and host your meetings over Skype.

Decide on the frequency of meetings. Scheduling a time that works for everyone can be tricky, especially if you have a lot of members. Set dates far in advance, and stick to a regular schedule if possible, like the first Tuesday of the month. Once-a-month meetings should give everyone a chance to get and read the book, but if your members have very busy schedules, consider aiming for every other month.

Decide how to nominate books. Your club will probably be happiest if you have a democratic process for choosing books, whether you take turns selecting the next month's book or nominate titles and vote as a group. You may want to set some ground rules, like page limits and availability. Is your selection available in paperback or as an ebook? Is it easy to get from the library? (You might want to avoid brand-new bestsellers, which often have long waitlists for library check-out.)

Be open-minded. One of the pleasures—and occasional frustrations—of a book club is that you're likely to end up reading some books you wouldn't have thought (or thought you wanted) to read on your own. You probably won't love every book your club chooses to read, but you may also discover unexpected favorites this way. If you'd asked me last year if I wanted to read a book about China's Cultural Revolution, I would've said no. I didn't know anything about the subject, and I wasn't especially interested in it. But when my book club chose *Do Not Say We Have Nothing* by Madeleine Thien, a multigenerational novel that takes place partly during Mao Zedong's reign, I read the book, loved it, and learned a lot about a period in history that had been unfamiliar to me.

Give your meetings some structure. For a lot of book clubs, getting together is more about wine and snacks than the book itself. If you want to make sure you actually discuss the book, come prepared with a few questions to talk about. Many publishers print discussion questions in a book's back pages or make questions available online. You can take turns leading discussion or ask book club members to come prepared with a question for the group.

Start an Email Listserv for Your Friends

WHEN MY FRIENDS and I finished grad school, we worried about falling out of touch as we went our separate ways. One of my friends suggested starting an email listserv for our group, and we still keep it up four years later. Every two weeks, my friend kicks off a new round of emails, and we all reply. The emails aren't formal—in fact, our rule is that whatever we write has to be formatted into no more than five bullet points. We can include anything in the bullet points, such as personal news, updates about work or family, a link to a song we love or an interesting article we just read, a funny GIF. I suspect the bullet-point format is the secret to our success, because it takes away the pressure of thinking about what and how to write.

By circulating our listserv every two weeks, my friends and I have been able to keep up with the important details of one another's lives—and some of the random minutia, too. It's not the same as being in the same place, but it still feels like a community. We make jokes that can feel lighthearted, but it's also a space where we can be vulnerable with one another and talk honestly about the real stuff going on in our lives. We've seen one another through leaving jobs and starting new adventures, weddings and breakups, deaths in the family, new babies, and major moves.

Maintaining these relationships is important, and not just for my friends and me. A long-running Harvard study that tracked subjects over the course of their lives found that people who maintain close relationships tend to stay healthier and live longer than those who don't. "Staying connected and involved is actually a form of taking care of yourself, just like exercise or eating right," says Dr. Robert Waldinger, the director of the Harvard Study of Adult Development. "This is an important prescription for health." (Read more about the health benefits of a strong social network in Practice No. 25, "Find Your Local Place.")

Some people feel comfortable sharing the intimate details of their lives with anyone who follows them on social media, and more power to them. As a somewhat private person, I'm grateful for our listserv, which allows my friends and me to keep up with one another's lives and is only for us.

Try It Out

Get a group together. Solicit friends to participate in your listserv, especially those who live far away or whom you don't see on a regular basis. You may want to poll prospective participants on how often they'd like to send and receive updates.

Create a circulation schedule. Once you've determined the frequency of your group emails, set dates to launch each new round and add them to your calendar with alerts. If you're willing to take the lead each time, set reminders for yourself to make sure you don't skip a round. If you're taking turns, make sure each person knows when it's their date to start a new round of emails. The more organized you are, the more likely you'll be to keep it up.

Decide on a format for your updates. Bullet points work well for my group, but you may want to choose another organizing principle—or go freeform. You could organize your dispatches by theme (for example: a great meal you recently enjoyed, something that made you want to scream, a funny phrase you overheard on the street); have everyone respond to a standard set of questions; or anything you like—just remember that the quicker and easier it is for folks to respond, the higher the likelihood they will.

Keep it up. This is the hardest part, but it's not actually that hard. If you're too busy to write more than a sentence when the next round of emails appears, just write a sentence. If you're too busy for *that*—perhaps it is time to reevaluate your life!

Take It Further

If you're interested in writing regular dispatches for a wider audience, consider starting a personal newsletter using a service like TinyLetter (tinyletter.com) or Substack (substack.com). Readers can subscribe to receive your newsletter direct to their inbox when you release it, and Substack offers users the option to monetize their newsletters with a paid subscriber option.

Host a Potluck

EVERYONE LOVES a home-cooked meal, but hosting a dinner party can be stressful, especially if your cooking skills are dubious (no judgment!) or your kitchen is tiny. Even for a seasoned chef in a state-of-the-art kitchen, cooking for a group is a labor-intensive—and often expensive—endeavor. By hosting a potluck and asking each guest to bring a dish, you can gather your loved ones together to enjoy home cooking without the stress of handling all the prep yourself.

According to some sources, the term "potluck" dates back to the Middle Ages, when guests who showed up unexpectedly would be served "the luck of the pot" by their hosts—whatever leftover food happened to be around or still simmering on the stove. Today's potlucks are closer in concept to the folktale "Stone Soup," where a clever traveler persuades the villagers to help "season" a soup allegedly made from a magical stone by pitching in their vegetables, meats, and herbs. The

delicious result, of course, comes not from the stone but from the food that the villagers have collectively contributed.

I grew up in Minnesota, where people have potlucks all the time—my mom's famous potluck dish is called calico beans. A potluck wedding is not uncommon, with the family making the main dishes and the guests bringing sides. My own sister had a taco potluck at her wedding reception. (Weddings when I was growing up were a lot more casual than they seem to be now.)

While potlucks have been a staple of American gatherings since the nineteenth century, they've gotten a bad rap among younger folks due to their association with church basements, flavorless casseroles, soggy potato salads, and bean dip. But it doesn't have to be that way: here are some tips for hosting a potluck that's contemporary, well-organized, low-stress, and delicious.

Try It Out

A little organization goes a long way. Make sure you've got all your courses covered by assigning your guests categories like "side dish," "main course," "salad/veggies," or "dessert" when you invite them. To avoid repeat dishes, you may want to create a shareable sign-up sheet where guests can add their planned contributions and note any dietary restrictions. (Google Docs works well for this, and SignUpGenius (www.signupgenius.com) even has a tab specifically for potlucks.) Beyond that, *Modern Potluck* author Kristin Donnelly advises to "control your inner control freak." You never know quite what you'll get with a potluck, but that's part of the fun.

Make it a theme party. If you want to ensure that guests will bring dishes with complementary rather than competing flavors, consider hosting an "international dinner": the host picks the country, and the guests research and prepare different dishes representing that country's cuisine. Or make it a seasonal dinner by asking guests to bring dishes based on whatever foods are local and currently in season.

Here are some other themes to consider:

- Old family recipes: Each guest brings a dish that's a classic in their own family. Extra credit for bringing copies of the recipe to share.
- Book club: like a regular book club, but members bring dishes inspired by the book. (A spin on this is cookbook club, where the host chooses a cookbook and participants each make a different recipe from it.)
- Swap party: In addition to a dish, guests bring gently used household items, clothing, and books to trade with other guests.

Theme parties can add fun and structure to a potluck. Donnelly advises that they work best for smaller groups where most people already know one another.

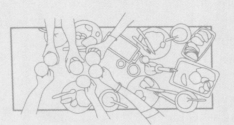

Label your dishes. If you're hosting a larger potluck and can't fit all the dishes on the dinner table, set them out buffet-style and offer your guests blank index cards and markers for labeling their dishes. Labels might also note ingredients for those with allergies and other dietary restrictions ("Gluten-free!" "Includes dairy"). As a shortcut, pick up a pack of color dot stickers for color-coding dishes (for example: green = vegetarian, yellow = nuts, red = spicy) and post a key nearby for guests.

Check your meal service supplies. Before the event, make sure you have enough plates, glasses, utensils, and serving dishes for all your guests and their contributions. You may want to buy disposable plates, cups, and utensils if you're hosting a larger group. (For an environmentally friendly approach, look for compostable options or invest in reusable bamboo or melamine dinnerware.) Don't expect your guests to bring their dishes on serving plates unless you specifically ask them to. Make sure trash, recycling, and composting containers are labeled and visible to help with cleanup.

Clean your kitchen in advance. It's likely that your guests will ask to pop their dishes into the oven for a warm-up or require counter space for prepping last touches. Put away anything you don't need before your guests arrive, making sure your sink, stovetop, and counters are clean and clear.

My Mom's Famous Calico Beans

Yield: 10–14 servings

INGREDIENTS

1 lb. bacon (Mom recommends bacon ends and pieces), diced

1½ lbs. lean ground beef

1 large onion, chopped

1 teaspoon salt

½ teaspoon pepper

3 (16.5-oz.) cans Bush's Beans (original)

2 (16-oz.) cans dark red kidney beans, rinsed and drained

1 (16-oz.) can butter beans, rinsed and drained

1 cup packed brown sugar

1 cup ketchup

½ cup dark molasses

1 teaspoon prepared mustard

DIRECTIONS

1. In a large skillet, cook bacon over medium heat until crisp. Remove to paper towels to drain. Discard drippings.

2. In the same skillet, cook beef and onion, seasoned with the salt and pepper, over medium heat until the meat is no longer pink; drain. Combine the beef mixture, bacon, beans, brown sugar, ketchup, molasses, and mustard.

3. Bake, covered, at 325°F for 45–60 minutes, or until the beans are hot. This can also be cooked in a Crock-Pot, and the recipe can be easily doubled for a larger group.

Practice Deep Listening

IN 1957, Ralph G. Nichols and Leonard A. Stevens wrote in the *Harvard Business Review:* "It can be stated, with practically no qualification, that people in general do not know how to listen." If we were bad at listening back then—decades before the Internet, social media, smartphones, and smartwatches arrived to distract us—we've only gotten worse. A recent study by Microsoft found that the average adult attention span is only *eight seconds.* Eight!

It's not just our conversations that are suffering—digital distraction affects our capacity to connect as a whole. MIT professor Sherry Turkle explains that empathy grows from attention: "In conversations where you look somebody in the eye and you sense their body, you sense their pauses, their stops, their starts." The Center for Contemplative Mind in Society defines deep listening as "a way of hearing in which we are fully present with what is happening in the moment without trying to control it or judge it. We let go of our inner clamoring and our usual assumptions and listen with respect for precisely what is being said." As we replace face time with FaceTime and other screen-mediated exchanges, we lose that experience—what Turkle calls "a complex dance that we know how to do to each other" in the same physical space.

The philosopher William James wrote that "voluntarily bringing back a wandering attention over and over again is the very root of judgment, character, and will." By that standard, practicing the art of deep listening won't just help us build and sustain meaningful relationships with our family, friends, and colleagues; it can also help us to become better people.

When I want to have a meaningful conversation with someone, I'll often suggest meeting in person and going for a walk. Why? When we're sitting inside, it can be hard to resist the temptation to sneak glances at our phones. When we're walking and talking outside, I don't even think about checking my texts or emails. It also avoids the risk of being interrupted by others.

Try It Out

Have conversations in person. Next time you're texting with a local friend, suggest meeting up to continue the conversation face-to-face.

Put away your phone. Researchers have found that even when subjects aren't actively using their cell phones, just having them within  reach is enough to reduce their listening comprehension by up to 20 percent. To be a better listener, keep your cell phone stowed away with notifications turned off—or even better, leave it behind entirely.

Make eye contact. Conversations aren't staring contests—that would be creepy and distracting in its own right—but looking at the person you're speaking with can help you stay focused and more closely attuned to the nonverbal cues that get communicated through facial expressions and gestures. Sometimes you can't get together in person. If you need to have a conversation over the phone, suggest a video chat like FaceTime, Skype, or Google Hangouts so that you and the person you're speaking with can see each other. Turn off notifications so they won't interrupt you during the call. I always try to do job interviews by video call if we can't be together in person—the truth is that I listen better when I can look into someone's eyes.

Be curious and ask questions. When you think about your conversation as an opportunity to learn something new, you're less likely to tune out. Asking questions is a good way to enlarge a conversation while demonstrating your interest in the speaker and the subject at hand. It can take courage: at times I've been tempted to avoid asking a question for fear it will sound dumb or be potentially off-putting. But I've found that if asked the right way, these are the questions that tend to make

conversations much more interesting. It can be helpful to frame a difficult question by saying, "I have a question that might be ignorant," or "Can I ask you something that I am hesitant to ask for fear of offending you?" This way, you set up the listener to engage with you.

Repeat back what you hear. Sometimes our own preconceived ideas and expectations can interfere with our ability to really hear what another person is saying to us. This active-listening technique is useful for refocusing your attention on the other person, clarifying intentions, and ensuring that everyone is on the same page.

Create a Perpetual Birthday Book

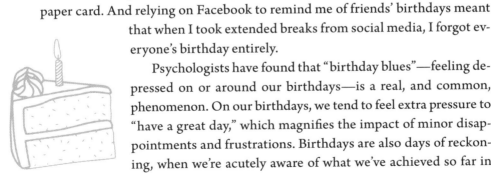

FOR A WHILE, I was great at remembering everyone's birthday: all I had to do was log on to Facebook and there they were, listed right at the top of the screen. With a single click, a few words, and an exclamation point, I could wish anyone with a Facebook account a happy birthday in a matter of seconds. Of course, because it was so easy, it was a relatively meaningless, automatic gesture. Posting "HBD!" on someone's Facebook wall is nicer than nothing (I guess), but it lacks the personal touch of a text, phone call, or the gold standard of birthday greetings: an actual paper card. And relying on Facebook to remind me of friends' birthdays meant that when I took extended breaks from social media, I forgot everyone's birthday entirely.

Psychologists have found that "birthday blues"—feeling depressed on or around our birthdays—is a real, and common, phenomenon. On our birthdays, we tend to feel extra pressure to "have a great day," which magnifies the impact of minor disappointments and frustrations. Birthdays are also days of reckoning, when we're acutely aware of what we've achieved so far in

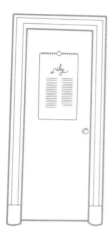

our lives—and also where we've fallen short. And then there's the social element. "One has expectations that others are going to congratulate them, remember the birthday, give a gift," the epidemiologist Myrna Weissman told *Vice*. "If that doesn't happen, it's very disappointing."

Luckily, there are lots of ways to keep track of birthdays, whether you're "very online" or have sworn off the Internet entirely. You can take a tip from the Dutch, who are so committed to their *verjaardagskalenders* (perpetual birthday calendars) that they hang them on the backs of their bathroom doors, where they can be seen on a daily basis. If that's not your ideal bathroom décor, there are plenty of other options, from wall hangings to portable paper planners to cell phone apps and other software.

Try It Out

Update your smartphone contacts' birthdays. The easiest way to transfer birthdays from Facebook is to sync your contacts to your smartphone. If you'd prefer not to sync across platforms, or you don't have a Facebook account, solicit your friends and family for their birthdays to start making a record. Android and iOS users can add a "Birthday" field to contact information in their smartphones, which will then automatically populate on a Google calendar or iCal account.

Make a perpetual wall calendar. A perpetual calendar lists months (and sometimes dates) without designating days of the week or years, so it will never go out of date. Creating a DIY perpetual wall calendar is as easy as drawing a grid of twelve squares on a large piece of paper, one for each month. Label each square with the name of a month. Include enough space inside the individual squares to record significant birthdays and other annual occasions. More artful versions, including multipiece wooden wall hangings, are available at paper goods stores like Paper Source and craft-based websites like Etsy.

Fill out a desk calendar or planner. If you'd rather not mount birthdays on the wall, you can achieve the same effect with a perpetual desk calendar or planner. All you need is paper, a ruler, and markers to make your own. Alternatively, you can download PDFs online, or order from a retail store or website. If you're recording birthdays in a planner, make sure to keep it somewhere visible so that you remember to look at it on a regular basis.

Use an app-based or online service. There are numerous birthday reminder apps available to Android and iOS users (including HIP, Birthday Cards, and Birthday Reminder & Countdown), which will send alerts in advance of birthdays to give you a head start on gifts, cards, or party planning. You can also sign up for a variety of web-based services (like Birthday Lab, moMinder, and BirthdayAlarm) that will send reminders to your email and allow you to select and send birthday e-cards.

Take It Further

Once you've learned and recorded your loved ones' birthdays, schedule reminder alerts for two weeks in advance. This will give you time to pick up a small gift, or get/make a birthday card to send through the mail—a small gesture that will go a long way toward making someone's special day.

PART 3
Balance Your Home

IN 2014, JAPANESE decluttering guru Marie Kondo took the world by storm with her bestselling book *The Life-Changing Magic of Tidying Up*, which urged readers to inventory every item they owned, asking of each one: "Does this spark joy?" Kondo advised, "Keep only those things that speak to your heart. Then take the plunge and discard all the rest." Kondo and her "KonMari method" became an international sensation as millions of people worldwide rushed to purge unwanted items from their homes. Some were intimidated by the KonMari process, which requires substantial time, as well as physical and emotional energy. Others felt that Kondo's clean, minimalist aesthetic simply didn't appeal to them. They liked having lots of things around. Whether you're a Kondo convert or not, your home should be a place where you can relax, unwind, and be yourself. Decluttering is one way to create a well-balanced home; you can also cultivate low-maintenance houseplants, construct a cozy reading nook, or develop a morning routine that makes you feel calm and energized for the day ahead.

Establish No-Phone Zones

ENTERING THE NATIONAL Radio Quiet Zone, which stretches thirteen thousand square miles across eastern West Virginia, you might feel like you've traveled back in time. There's no cell service, no Wi-Fi, and the radio picks up only the lowest-frequency stations. There's a good reason for this: the zone surrounds and protects the National Radio Astronomy Observatory, where the massive Robert C. Byrd Green Bank Telescope tracks and reads energy waves from stars in galaxies thousands of light-years away. The signals that the telescope picks up are so faint that even a

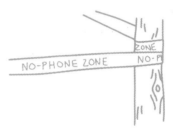

tiny amount of interference can throw off its readings, so federal and state laws prohibit cell service, Wi-Fi, and other signal-generating devices in the area. "If you want to hear quiet noises, you need to keep the noise down," explains the telescope's principal scientist, Jay Lockman. The community is so serious about disconnection that it even has "RFI policemen"—roving disconnection cops who come after anyone who produces any radio frequency interference.

The townspeople of Green Bank, West Virginia, who rely on landlines, ham radios, and walkie-talkies, love their disconnected lives. And the town has even attracted former city dwellers seeking a peaceful reprieve from the clamor of the digital age. But you don't have to move to Green Bank to find time and space for disconnection. Tech-free spaces have flourished in recent years. Some are one-off gimmicks, like a Kit Kat campaign where the company built a public bench with a device nearby to block Wi-Fi signals. They called it a "Free No-Wi-Fi Zone" and invited passersby to "take a break," in line with their classic slogan. Others are more immersive, like the London restaurant the Bunyadi, which banned phones, turned off the electricity, illuminated tables by candlelight, cooked food over an open fire, and even banned clothes. (Perhaps too far for some of us!)

In our daily lives, we can achieve a similar effect by instituting no-phone zones in our homes. The best place to start is the bedroom. Michael and I also try to keep our phones tucked away inside when we are having our end-of-the-day beer on our patio.

Try It Out
CREATE A NO-PHONE ZONE . . .

At the dinner table. For millennia, humans have connected with one another over shared meals. Having phones out at the table—even if we're not actively engaging with them—diminishes the quality of our interactions by suggesting that our attention could be drawn away at any time. Researchers at the University of British Columbia found that diners who bring their phones to the table take less pleasure from their meals. Banish phones to restore the dinner table as a site of emotional, intellectual, and physical nourishment.

In the car. We already know we shouldn't be texting, browsing, or dialing while at the wheel. Here's the next step: even if you're just along for the ride, try locking your phone away. How many friendships have been forged in the idle time on road trips? How many family challenges have surfaced on rides home from school? How many new ideas pop up while staring out the window at passing scenery?

While watching TV. If you're in the habit of scrolling through your phone while streaming Netflix, you're not alone: According to a 2018 study, over 178 million Americans report using another device while in front of the TV. This is known as media multitasking, and neuroscientists warn that it's bad for our brains. In tests of attention and working memory, heavy media multitaskers perform notably worse than those who stick to a single screen. So savor leisure—and save your memory—by watching one thing at a time.

In the bedroom. There are lots of good reasons to keep our phones far away from our beds: the screen's blue light that disrupts our body's melatonin production; the addictive allure of social media that keeps us scrolling mindlessly past our bedtimes; the way phones distract us from downtime with our partners; the non-ionizing electromagnetic radiation they emit that our body tissue absorbs. If you use your phone alarm to wake up in the morning, see Practice No. 38 on trying out a physical alarm clock.

Take It Further

As the old saying goes, "Out of sight, out of mind." Maintain your no-phone zones more easily by stowing your cell in a lockbox. See Practice No. 44 for details.

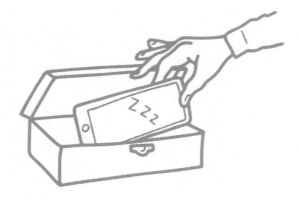

Get a Houseplant

IF YOU DON'T live near a forest or park, you can still reap the benefits of nature with the help of houseplants. Not only do plants make for stylish and affordable home décor, there's plenty of evidence that indoor plants benefit our health. They help purify the air: NASA researchers have found that by absorbing carbon dioxide and particulates, some houseplants can remove up to 87 percent of airborne toxins in just twenty-four hours. Other studies show that being around green leafy plants can improve our concentration and productivity, help us to feel more satisfied at work, reduce stress and anxiety, boost creativity, and even help us get along better with others.

Plants can also help us heal. In 1981, the researcher Roger Ulrich observed that patients recovered faster from surgery and reported less pain when their rooms faced a tree-filled courtyard, compared to those patients whose windows looked out on other buildings. Another study found that patients recovering in rooms filled with potted plants had lower blood pressure, heart rate, and pain levels than those in plant-free rooms.

Michael and I recently went to a nursery and bought

six plants for our apartment. We did manage to kill one right away, but we've replaced it with two more from the Sill (thesill.com), an online plant shop that helps you choose the right plants for your space and offers a variety of helpful care tips. I'm happy to report that there have been no additional plant murders—our new plants are thriving.

Plant and Chill

Snake Plants

These do best with indirect sunlight and a sandy soil mix that allows plenty of drainage to avoid root rot. Allow the soil to dry out between waterings. Water every two weeks or so, depending on the humidity of your home.

Bonus: snake plants release oxygen at night, so keep one in your bedroom for better sleep!

Succulents

These dry-climate plants like a lot of sunlight, so put them near a south-facing window if you have one. They store water in their leaves, so it's best to plant them with a soil or gravel mix that allows for lots of drainage, and water only when the soil gets dry.

Pothos

These adaptable plants grow heart- or spade-shaped leaves from vines, and they do well in indirect or low-light settings like bathrooms and offices. They can be grown in pots or hanging baskets, and they need to be watered only when their soil is dry.

Try It Out

Choose the right plant for your space and lifestyle. Do you have lots of windows or none at all? Some plants love full sunlight; others thrive in the shade. And if you're habitually forgetful or travel a lot, you'll do best with a super-low-maintenance plant like a succulent, pothos, or snake plant. Keep in mind that some plants (including beginner-friendly aloe vera and jade) can be toxic to pets.

Go easy on watering. The easiest way to kill a plant is by overwatering, so adopt a philosophy of benign neglect. Before you reach for your watering can, test the moisture of the soil: it should feel dry to the touch an inch or two below the surface. When you do water your plant, use lukewarm water (which plants can absorb faster), and aim for the roots rather than the leaves.

Give your plant room to grow. Most plants will benefit from repotting. You can buy inexpensive terra-cotta pots from garden stores, craft and hardware stores, and online. Choose a planter that's only a few inches larger than your current container and has a drainage hole at its base. Otherwise, the soil may retain more water than your plant needs, leading to root rot.

Take It Further

Turn one plant into many by propagating new plants from cuttings. For certain species, growing a new plant is as easy as clipping off a four-to-six-inch stem and dropping the cut end into a glass of water, where it will grow roots. Once it roots, you can transfer it to a pot with soil. Expand your collection, or gift it to a friend!

Subscribe to the Print Edition

OF ALL THE WAYS the Internet has changed our lives, its impact on the way we consume news might be starkest. In 1990, more than 62 million Americans subscribed to daily print newspapers. By 2018, though the country's population had grown by over 77 million people, the number of print newspapers in circulation had dropped by more than half, to 28.5 million. It's easy to see why: digital subscriptions are cheaper and more convenient than print editions; the articles are easier to save and share; they don't create piles of clutter in your home; and they're updated in real time. Besides, all  the content-sharing and commentary on social media platforms means that it's fairly easy to get news without subscribing to anything at all.

Conceding all that, I still maintain it's worthwhile to subscribe to a print edition of your preferred newspaper or magazine, and a lot of journalists—including ones who write exclusively for the web!—agree. Although *Politico* writer Jack Shafer has been an online journalist for over twenty years, he calls his commitment to newsprint "almost cultistic." When he's reading online, he says, "I often forget why I clicked a page in the first place and start clicking on outside links until I'm tumbling through cyberspace like a marooned astronaut." A physical newspaper or magazine presents articles without the distraction of flashing ads, pop-ups, and links. Schafer finds he reads and finishes more articles in print. He also remembers them better: "It has the power to focus me," he says.

The print edition also offers more opportunities for discovery and surprise. Online, algorithms calculate the kind of stories that interest us in order to serve us more of the same, according to the "If you liked *this,* then you'll probably like *that*" model. By contrast, turning the pages of a print newspaper and letting your eyes skim across its pages (which, Schafer notes, have been designed and refined "for more than two centuries . . . over hundreds of millions of editions" to give you the best reading experience possible), you're able to "explore for the news like a hunter in a forest, making discoveries all the way."

Farhad Manjoo, a *New York Times* reporter, describes his return to print subscriptions as "life-changing." He writes, "Turning off the buzzing breaking-news machine I carry in my pocket was like unshackling myself from a monster who had me on speed dial, always ready to break into my day with half-baked bulletins." A lot of the "news" we read online isn't really news, Manjoo realized. After all, it takes time to report stories with depth and accuracy. To appease readers accustomed to the twenty-four-hour news cycle, media outlets churn out commentary and hot takes as the real work of information-gathering slowly unfolds behind the scenes. This turns readers into amateur investigators, trying to figure out "what really happened"—and often propagating inaccuracies and conspiracy theories on social media—before most of the facts are in. By waiting for the story until the next morning's paper, Manjoo avoids the whiplash of commentators' competing theories, and the headache of trying to sift real information from speculation. "Hundreds of experienced professionals had done the hard work for me," he writes.

And then there's the physical pleasure of reading in print. After getting his news digitally for more than a decade, Andrew Ferguson, a staff writer for *The Atlantic,* waxes poetic about switching back to print: "There is the steaming cup of coffee . . . and then the plumping of the reading chair—the quick scan of the front page to get your bearings and then the plunge inside. . . . I unfold the paper, and the world opens up to me as through a parting cloud," he writes.

Taking a tip from the food writer Michael Pollan, who famously summed up his nutrition advice as, "Eat food. Not too much. Mostly plants," Farhad Manjoo suggests, "Get news. Not too quickly. Avoid social."

A couple years ago, Michael and I decided to subscribe to the weekend edition of *The New York Times.* I didn't expect to be hooked. Initially I thought, This will be more clutter in the house, and I hate clutter! And it does create more clutter in the house, so we have a rule that when each week's newspaper arrives, we have to throw out any remainders of the previous week's edition.

I didn't anticipate how much it would become part of our cozy weekend routine. Someone has to get up and make coffee, go get the paper, and come back to bed. We spread it out and read it and talk to each other about what we read. I go for the Real Estate section first, then Metropolitan, then Arts and Style. Michael goes straight for the hard news (which makes it easy to share). I'll read The Ethicist column aloud and ask Michael what he would do, without telling him what the Ethicist says. And we both get excited about doing the crossword puzzle in the *Times* magazine.

Try It Out

Find out which newspapers deliver to your area. Think about where you most like to read your news online, and check that outlet's subscription page to find out whether home delivery is available for your zip code.

Look into limited subscription deals. Many newspapers offer steep, limited-time discounts to new subscribers, along with cancel-anytime exit options. This will give you an opportunity to try out a print subscription for a few weeks or months, without leaving you on the hook for longer than you want to be. Most newspapers also offer substantial discounts for teachers and students.

Opt for a weekend-only or Sunday subscription. For those who don't have the time, space, or resources for newspaper delivery on a daily basis, consider signing up for a lower-commitment weekend edition. Most major newspapers offer subscriptions for weekend or Sunday-only print editions, which come with 24/7 digital access.

Try a newsmagazine instead. If you're in the market for concise summary and analysis of the major news in a given week, consider subscribing to a newsmagazine like *The Economist.* If you love reading long reported features, you may prefer a magazine like *The New Yorker, The Atlantic, The New Republic,* or *Harper's,* which focus on delivering not only news but detailed, compelling storytelling. These magazines all offer budget subscription deals for new subscribers.

Audit Your Belongings

HOW MANY THINGS do you own? According to professional organizer Regina Lark, the average American owns three hundred thousand items, so much stuff that it's spilling out of our homes entirely: offsite storage is the fastest

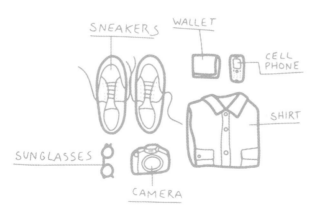

growing area of the American real estate market, with more than fifty thousand facilities and counting. Then there's author and podcaster Joshua Fields Millburn of the Minimalists, who owns a mere 288 belongings. Whether you have a lot or a little, most organizers agree that there's no "right" number of items to own. "We all have different standards for what is too much," writes interior designer and life coach Tisha Morris in her book *Clutter Intervention.* "What may seem cluttered to me may feel like a cozy haven to you. What may seem cold and stark to one person may feel liberating to another." The important thing is to make sure your belongings meet your needs and make you happy—and that you're not saving space for those that don't.

There are lots of reasons people hold on to things they don't need (and sometimes even things they don't like). We save clothes we've outgrown, hoping that with a new diet and exercise regime, we'll fit into them again. We save books and magazines we've been meaning to read but haven't gotten to yet. We save odds and ends buried at the back of closets or deep in drawers because we don't even remember that we own them. We keep things because they're sentimental, because they were expensive to buy, or because we "might need them later."

But organizers say that these aren't good excuses to hold on to things. An object is sentimental because of the memory associated with it: while there's nothing wrong with holding on to a few items for purely sentimental reasons, if you don't love or have space for something, you can keep the memory while discarding the object. You won't lose money by getting rid of an expensive object you don't use—you've already spent it!—but you *can* save yourself some space. And if you haven't read or used that thing in the last year, odds are you never will.

Letting clutter pile up doesn't just cost you surface space. According to a recent survey by the location app Pixie, the average American spends two and a half full days per year looking for misplaced items like car and house keys, remote controls, cell phones, eyeglasses, and wallets. Sixty percent of respondents admitted that lost items had made them late to work or school, while nearly half had missed meetings or appointments. Losing things around the house is an expensive habit, too: collectively, Americans spend around $2.7 *billion* a year replacing things we already own, either because we can't find them or because we've forgotten we own them.

Beyond our time and wallets, clutter can impact our health: research has shown that people with cluttered, messy bedrooms have a harder time falling and staying asleep, and people with "chaotic kitchens" tend to eat more junk food than those with well-organized kitchens.

It can be helpful to think of our things as "a physical extension of ourselves," says Tisha Morris. Our identities shift and change with time, but objects are static. Not only do they not change, they can hold us back. International organizing superstar Marie Kondo advises us to hold on to only those things that "spark joy." Tisha Morris takes a slightly different approach. As you look over all of the belongings you've acquired over time, she suggests asking yourself the following questions: *What from your past do you want to take forward? Which items are still relevant to you now and to where you want to go?*

Instead of making a big occasion of spring or fall cleaning, I try to throw things away on a regular basis. The other day while waiting for the water to boil to make pasta, I went into our linen closet, which has gotten overrun. I took everything off one shelf—it happened to be the one with all of our random medicines—and set it all on the counter to sort through. It turned out that practically everything was expired, so I threw it away—all before the pasta water boiled. I resisted the temptation to feel as though I should clean out the whole closet, which would've taken more time and might've discouraged me from doing any cleaning at all.

Try It Out

Enter your home like a new visitor. We can get so accustomed to our homes and belongings that we stop truly seeing them. Next time you return home, scan your space as if you're seeing it for the first time. What do you notice? Are certain areas more crowded or cluttered than others? Are there things you could put away or remove entirely?

Designate a place for everything. You wouldn't put a hairbrush in your utensil drawer or stow your spatula in the bathroom. Apply the same philosophy to shoes, clothes, mail, loose change, and anything else that tends to pile up where it doesn't belong. If you can't find a space in your home for something you own, it might be a sign that it's time to let it go.

Follow the "thirty-second" rule. According to Sandra Felton, the founder of Messies Anonymous, "If it takes thirty seconds or less to do a job, do it immediately." This means hanging up clothes and putting away shoes after wearing them, loading dirty dishes into the dishwasher after finishing a meal (or at least soaking them in the sink), returning tools to their homes after using them, and sorting/recycling junk mail as soon as you bring it into your home. Making a habit of putting things away immediately after use will save you lots of time in the long run.

Store items temporarily to see what you actually use. This technique works especially well for decluttering kitchens and closets. To

figure out what you actually use, stow kitchen supplies and closet items in a closed cardboard box. Remove each item from the box when you need it and return it to its original home (a shelf, drawer, etc.) after use. After a few months, see what's still in the box. These are the items you don't use or need, so get rid of them.

Work on decluttering with a partner. The psychologist Joseph Ferrari suggests that one reason we find it hard to get rid of personal items is because we have an "over-attachment" to them. "Once you touch the item, you are less likely to get rid of it," he told *The New York Times*. "If you're going to declutter, don't touch the item. Don't pick it up. Have somebody else hold the pair of black pants and say, 'Do you need this?'"

Practice one-in, one-out. For each new item you bring into your home, select one item you already own to give away or recycle. If the thought of getting rid of something gives you pause, consider whether you really need that new thing after all.

Plant a Garden

WE'RE ASKED TO pay attention to a lot in our day-to-day lives: emails, texts, and phone calls; meetings and appointments; communication with colleagues, friends, and family; when those bills and library books are due; where we left our house keys; whether it's safe to cross the street; when our subway stop is coming up; how to get from Point A to Point B; where we parked; what time it is; whether we're running late. With so much to focus on, it's easy to get worn out, a phenomenon psychologists call directed attention fatigue (DAF). You might recognize the symptoms, which include distractibility, forgetfulness, impatience, and irritability. I feel this way frequently.

DAF isn't a permanent condition. It turns out that the most effective way to rest and restore our directed attention is to shift our attention over to something that engages us without requiring sustained focus. The natural world offers an ideal fix, stimulating our senses—rustling leaves, birds in flight, clouds drifting overhead—without demanding heavy concentration. If you're looking for something more active than simply

soaking in the great outdoors, try gardening. "When you sit at a desk all day, there's something about literally putting your hands in the dirt, digging and actually creating something that's really beautiful," magazine editor and gardener Gillian Aldrich told CNN.

We already know that exposure to nature is good for us: being in green spaces reduces our stress, lowers our risk of heart disease and type 2 diabetes, and improves our self-esteem, memory, sleep, and concentration. Gardening takes these benefits and multiplies them. A recent study found that gardening helps people relax even more than leisure activities like curling up with a book, and it can ease a variety of mental and physical health issues, from depression to chronic pain. It burns calories, improves cardiovascular health, and can increase bone density among people who perform weight-bearing activities like digging and raking. The pulling, twisting, and bending involved in basic gardening tasks help to improve balance, coordination, and strength. Just being exposed to soil makes us less likely to suffer from asthma and allergies. Maybe most striking of all, gardening is so effective at stimulating brain nerve growth that older

people who garden regularly are up to 36 percent less likely to develop dementia than their non-gardening peers.

Gardens aren't just for folks with big yards or acres of land. In recent years, community gardens have sprung up in cities across the country as a way to build community, liven up neighborhoods, promote healthy living, and provide "backyards" for apartment dwellers. Today we can find community gardens in vacant lots and city parks, elementary schools and state

prisons, and even on the South Lawn of the White House, thanks to Michelle Obama's "Let's Move!" program.

Let's not forget the (literal!) fruits of this labor. The produce you grow in a garden will be fresher—and probably taste better—than any you can buy from a store. It will almost certainly be more affordable. You'll have the pride of eating something you grew yourself. And you'll be doing something good for the earth, too: not only do plants absorb the greenhouse gas carbon dioxide, growing your own food reduces the packaging waste and fuel needed to transport crops from commercial farms to grocery stores.

Try It Out

Start small. If you don't have much gardening experience, experts recommend beginning with just five to seven plants, so choose a few you're excited about and focus on those. You can always add more next season.

Choose a spot that gets sunlight and access to water. Kathleen Frith, president of the sustainable agriculture organization Glynwood (and former managing director of Harvard's Center for Health and the Global Environment), recommends selecting a plot that gets at least six hours of sunlight per day. Frith also suggests building

or using a raised garden bed, which gives you control over your ratio of soil and nutrients.

Weed before you plant. If you take time to clear your plot of pesky 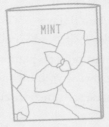 weeds before you start planting, you'll save yourself the headache later in the season.

Label your plants. It's easy to forget which plants are which, or where exactly you buried those seeds. As you're planting, set labels in the soil to keep track of your plot. You can use the ones that come with store-bought plants or make your own with markers and popsicle sticks.

Water your crop. After planting, add water around the roots to help them expand and grow. Keep your plants well-watered by testing the soil on a regular basis: stick your finger about two inches into the soil near the base of the plant. If the soil feels dry, it's time to grab the watering can. If the soil is still moist, check back in a few days.

Join a community garden in your neighborhood. The American Community Gardening Association (communitygarden.org) offers a database of community gardens nationwide (and additional sites around the world) as well as resources ranging from "Super Foods" to "Garden Politics." Many local food co-ops and natural food stores can also provide resources and information for aspiring urban gardeners.

Create an Offline Morning Routine

HOW WE START the day matters. You probably already know from experience that having a good morning can boost your mood, energy, and productivity throughout the day, whereas spending your first waking hours stressed or rushing can ruin your mood and keep you on edge for hours—but in case you need further evidence, this is also backed up by research. "Start-of-the-day mood can last longer than you might think—and have an important effect on job performance," writes Wharton professor Nancy P. Rothbard for *Harvard Business Review.*

The best way to ensure that you're consistently starting your day on the right foot is to establish a healthy morning routine. Think of your morning—the stretch between waking and beginning your responsibilities for the day—as sacred time for yourself. If you tend to check email or scroll through social media first thing, you're giving your time away to other people. So stay off your screens and focus on you. (I promise, you'll still have plenty of time throughout the day to get bogged down in email, feel jealous of other people's vacations on Instagram, and worry about the state of the world on Twitter.)

You don't want to rush through your morning routine, so you may need to get up a little earlier than you're used to. But that doesn't mean skimping on rest. The sleep specialist Stephanie Silberman recommends adapting your schedule incrementally: start by going to bed and waking up fifteen minutes earlier, take a few days to let your body get used to the new times, then adjust by another fifteen minutes until you reach your desired wake-up time.

My morning routine isn't especially interesting, but it does help me to start my day feeling balanced. The most important part is my coffee-making ritual: grind whole beans, boil water, use the French press. I shower in our Nebia Spa Shower (which is genuinely spa-like and uses 65 percent less water than regular showerheads). Then I walk to work, which takes me about twenty-five minutes. I've always tried to live within walking distance of work if possible, since walking connects me to the neighborhood and gives me head-clearing time. Sometimes I listen to the news. Sometimes I call friends or family to check in. Otherwise, I just take in the sights and sounds around me before arriving at the office.

On the following pages, you'll find a list of practices for a morning routine that will make you feel calm, grounded, and energized as you head into the rest of your day. Feel free to pick and choose among the practices to find the ones that work for you. For best results, start by "habit stacking"—attaching a new practice to an action you already do regularly. (For example, reserve a few minutes for meditation immediately after brushing your teeth.) Once the new practice becomes a habit, add another. Repetition is the key to routine.

> We are what we repeatedly do. Excellence,
> then, is not an act, but a habit.
> —Will Durant, paraphrasing Aristotle

Try It Out

Stretch. According to the science writer Luis Villazon, there's a reason we have the impulse to stretch out and wiggle our limbs when we  first wake up: "When you sleep, your muscles lose tone and fluid tends to pool along your back. Stretching helps to massage fluid gently back into the normal position." You don't even need to get out of bed for this one!

Open your blinds to let in the sun. Our circadian rhythm is an internal clock that regulates our sleep, waking, metabolic function, and hormone levels on a roughly twenty-four-hour cycle. Getting morning sunlight helps to keep our light-sensitive circadian rhythm in sync

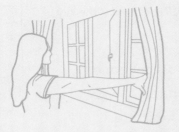

with the natural world, the same way that winding a watch helps it to keep perfect time. Exposure to sunlight also stimulates the body to produce Vitamin D, which is good for bone growth and triggers the brain to release serotonin, a hormone associated with improved mood and focus.

Rehydrate. Drinking a glass of water when you first wake up can make you more alert, flush toxins from the body, jump-start your metabolism, and keep your immune system running well. (Squeeze fresh lemon juice into your water for flavor and additional health benefits like Vitamin C, improved digestion, and healthier skin.)

Journal. The creativity guru Julia Cameron advocates writing "morning pages"—three handwritten pages capturing your stream-of-consciousness thoughts—when you first wake up in the morning. This exercise is designed to draw our goals and desires to the surface of our minds, while training ourselves to tune out our inner critic. "Morning pages may hold insights and intuitions that startle you. Typically, they puncture denial," Cameron writes in her landmark book on creativity, *The Artist's Way.* If you don't consider yourself a writer, don't worry: morning pages "are not even 'writing,'" Cameron assures readers. "They are about anything and everything that crosses your mind—and they are for your eyes only. Morning pages provoke, clarify, comfort, cajole, prioritize and synchronize the day at hand."

Meditate. Meditation can calm your nerves, improve your concentration, reduce depression and anxiety, make you more compassionate, and enable you to clarify your intentions. A mere five or ten minutes of morning meditation can help you to greet the day's challenges with a calm and focused mind-set. (See Practice No. 2 for more information.)

Exercise. You already know you should get regular exercise to stay healthy. There are also specific advantages to incorporating exercise into your morning routine. Researchers at Brigham Young University found that people who exercise first thing in the morning tend to stay more active throughout the day compared to those who don't. Exercising in the morning can also help to curb appetites in dieters and lower blood pressure for folks at risk of heart attacks (which often occur in the morning). Morning exercise works wonders for improving the length and quality of your sleep, says the National Sleep Foundation. And you'll likely feel good about yourself and carry a sense of accomplishment into your day.

End your shower with thirty seconds of cold water. Sure, it sounds like torture. But studies show that cold showers can improve circulation, boost immunity, reduce your risk of infection, and stimulate alertness—there's nothing like icy water to shock you awake. Maybe unsurprisingly, subjecting yourself to regular cold showers can also help you build resilience and become better at tolerating stress.

Write down your goals for the day. Committing your goals to paper will make them more tangible. It will also help you to keep them in mind, increasing your focus and motivation. Researchers at Dominican University found that the simple act of recording your goals and dreams makes you 42 percent more likely to achieve them.

Eat breakfast. Eating a healthy breakfast will kick your metabolism into gear, give you energy, and improve your focus as you start your day. Steer clear of sweet cereals and fruit juice, which are high in sugar and can cause you to crash after a few hours. Instead, opt for oatmeal, berries and other fruits, multigrain toast with nut butter, or lean proteins like Greek yogurt, cottage cheese, and eggs.

Wake up with a Physical Alarm Clock

OF THE MANY tools and gadgets that the all-in-one smartphone has replaced (camera, notepad, calculator, address book, road map, dictionary, etc.), the alarm clock might be the most obsolete. While lots of people still use cameras and paper notebooks, these days it's hard to find anyone who depends on a reliable old clock radio to wake up in the morning. But we should.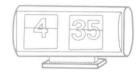

If it strikes you as unnecessary to buy another device when the alarm on your phone does its job perfectly well, here's some incentive: waking up with a physical alarm clock is one of the easiest and most impactful steps you can take to achieve a healthier and more balanced life.

Using your smartphone as an alarm clock is bad for sleep hygiene. When your phone is on hand, you're much more likely to scroll through social media feeds, refresh your email, or check the news before turning in. In addition to the blue light your phone emits—which can interfere with your circadian rhythm and make it harder to fall asleep—flipping through your apps will rev up your mind (and quite possibly your anxiety) at the exact time when it should be winding down.

It's also bad for relationships: If you share your bed with a partner, the minutes between crawling into bed and dozing off are invaluable time for building intimacy, whether you're decompressing about your day, sharing thoughts and concerns, cuddling, or whatever else you like to do (which is none of my business!). If you're both on your phones, your thoughts and attention will be far away from each other, even if you're sharing the sheets.

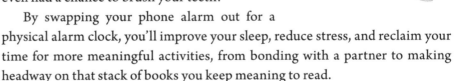

Smartphones are bad for managing insomnia: if you wake up in the night and can't fall back to sleep, the *last* thing you need is a glowing screen containing all the information in the world.

And it's bad for your morning routine, as discussed in Practice No. 37. When your smartphone is the first thing you see after waking up, you're likely to start checking email and social media before you even lift your head off the pillow. Why invite the day's stress into your mind before you've even had a chance to brush your teeth?

By swapping your phone alarm out for a physical alarm clock, you'll improve your sleep, reduce stress, and reclaim your time for more meaningful activities, from bonding with a partner to making headway on that stack of books you keep meaning to read.

Another reason to keep phones away from bed: a ten-year study by the US government's National Toxicology Program found that prolonged exposure to the radio frequency radiation (RFR) emitted by cell phones "can produce adverse biological effects," according to senior scientist John Butcher of the

National Institute of Environmental Health Sciences. The study found "clear evidence" that rats exposed to RFR developed tumors in their hearts, as well as "some evidence" that RFR resulted in tumors in the rats' brains and adrenal glands. While it's not clear whether this radiation poses a similar threat to humans, Butcher notes that the risk level goes up with "prolonged and persistent use." One easy way to limit exposure is to stop relying on your phone as your alarm clock, so that you can keep it farther from your body while you sleep.

Try It Out

Pick up a physical alarm clock. As a kid, I had a truly horrible alarm clock—instead of beeping, it told bad jokes. There were only about seven jokes in all, and they'd rotate. *Maybe* they were funny the first time, but hearing the same joke a hundred times—when I already didn't want to wake up and go to school—was, dare I say, no longer funny. Luckily, options for alarm clocks abound. From no-frills, battery-operated devices to vintage mid-century beauties, you can find the right alarm clock to suit your needs, aesthetics, and budget. Big-box and home goods stores offer a wide array of clocks with different features and price points. For a vintage model, check out yard sales, antique shops, Etsy, and eBay.

Keep a stack of books beside your bed. Trading late-night Instagramming for a novel won't just help you get through your aspirational reading list; it'll also help you fall asleep. "Losing yourself in a book is the ultimate relaxation," the cognitive neuropsychologist David Lewis told *The Telegraph.* In a study he conducted at the University of Sussex, Dr. Lewis found that reading is better at reducing stress and lowering your heart rate than listening to music, taking a walk, or even drinking a cup of tea. Reading also stimulates creativity, imagination, and empathy.

Develop a screen-free unwinding routine before sleep. Whether you're settling in with a good book, chatting with your partner, filling in a crossword or Sudoku puzzle, journaling, or doing some gentle stretches, creating a regular pre-sleep routine will cue your mind and body to relax and get ready to drift off.

Silence your phone. When you don't need to rely on your phone to wake you up, you can silence it, set it on airplane mode, or turn it off entirely. If you want to be available in case of emergency, enable Emergency Bypass in your iOS (or equivalent Android) settings to allow calls and texts from specific contacts.

Ease into morning. Once your alarm clock wakes you up, turn it off (or hit Snooze—no judgment!) and spend a few minutes taking stock of your body and mind. Open your curtains to get some natural light.

Consider jotting down your dreams, if you remember them, or doing a few stretches to get your blood flowing. (See Practice No. 37 for more suggestions.)

Take It Further

Turn your bedroom into a no-phone zone (see Practice No. 32) and leave your phone to charge in another room overnight. If you live in a studio, charge your phone somewhere you can't easily reach from bed.

Make Your Home Cozier

DENMARK IS A COUNTRY of long, cold winters: Danes spend as many as seventeen hours a day in darkness in the winter, often at freezing temperatures. As gloomy as that sounds, Danish citizens consistently rate among the world's happiest people. What's their secret? Maybe it's the government-subsidized higher education, universal healthcare, and fifty-two weeks of paid parental leave—but we could also credit the role of *hygge*, the centuries-old Danish concept of coziness, sharing, and joy in simple things.

hy·gge
[hue-gah] *noun*

In recent years, *hygge* has caught on as a lifestyle trend around the world. In the United States and elsewhere, the rise of *hygge* #goals has coincided with ads, magazine features, and books encouraging us to invest in rustic furniture, throw pillows, soft blankets, fluffy socks, Edison bulbs, and sheepskin rugs in order to bring Danish-style coziness into our homes.

But true coziness isn't about *stuff;* it's about *feeling.* "Hygge is about an atmosphere and an experience," writes Meik Wiking in *The Little Book of Hygge: Danish Secrets to Happy Living.* "It's about being with the people we love. A feeling of home. A feeling that we are safe." In addition to happiness, Denmark ranks among the top countries in the world when it comes to leisure time, self-care, and trust in others. Stockpiling candles and blankets is definitely one way to make your home more *hyggeligt* (*hygge*-like), but so is inviting friends and family over to share a meal, curling up with a good book, or savoring a hot cup of coffee in your favorite mug.

Try It Out

Simplify your space. To create a space that feels welcoming and comfortable, clear out junk mail, clothes you don't wear, and obsolete electronics. After all, clutter isn't very cozy. But neither is ultra-minimalism: hold on to things that are meaningful, whether it's furniture you inherited from your family, or art and other objects that hold special associations for you.

Light your home with candles and lamps. The warm, flickering glow of candles can instantly make a space feel cozier and more intimate; Danes consider candlelight a key factor in creating a *hygge* home. In fact, Danes are the world's top candle consumers, burning through an average of thirteen pounds of candle wax per person per year. (The Danish word for spoilsport, *lyseslukker,* literally means "one who puts out the candles.") Add additional cozy accents by swapping out overhead lights for lamps, which create warm pools of light and shadow.

Create a cozy nook. The impulse to create safe and cozy spaces is hardwired in us. Remember building forts out of couch cushions and blankets as a kid? In Denmark, the adult version of this is called a *hyggekrog,* which Wiking describes as "the place in the room where you love to snuggle up in a blanket with a book and a cup of tea." You can create your own *hyggekrog* by placing a comfy chair in a corner

or near a window. Add a lamp, a blanket for chilly days, and a small table where you can set a hot drink and a stack of books or crossword puzzles. **Invite friends over for a home-cooked meal.** Capturing that cozy feeling isn't just about *what* you have but *whom* you have in your space. If you're worried your kitchen space or cooking skills aren't up to par, consider investing in a slow cooker: all you have to do is dump in the raw ingredients, plug it into an outlet, and give it four to eight hours to slow-cook your meal for you. You'll delight your guests and fill your home with delicious cooking smells in the meantime.

Take pleasure in the little things. Even if you're not yet living in the home of your dreams, home should still be a space where you feel safe and comfortable. Think of ways to appreciate and cultivate what you do have, whether it's the warmth of sunlight through your window, a cup of hot tea with lemon and honey, the feeling of crawling into bed with freshly laundered sheets, or a leisurely bath.

Take a Break from Streaming Services

ACCORDING TO CRITICS and consumers alike, we're living in a new golden age of television. Beginning around the new millennium, shows like *The Sopranos, The Wire, Breaking Bad,* and *Mad Men* introduced a new standard for TV entertainment, with high production value and complex antiheroes portrayed by A-list actors. Now we're not just watching TV to relax and veg out; we're watching to participate in Important Cultural Moments. Binge-watching has become a badge of honor—according to a recent survey by YouGov, 58 percent of Americans say they binge-watch shows, and nearly three-quarters of binge-watchers say it's their preferred way of consuming TV.

The clinical psychologist Renée Carr explains that when we binge our favorite shows, our brains produce dopamine, which causes us to feel a rush of pleasure and satisfaction. "It is the brain's signal that communicates to the body, 'This feels good. You should keep doing this!'" Dr. Carr told NBC News. "Your body experiences a drug-like high. You experience a pseudo-addiction to the show because you develop cravings for dopamine."

This has been made possible, of course, by streaming services, which deliver us an endless supply of content anytime we want it. And we want it a *lot:* according to Netflix, its subscribers cumulatively spend around 140 million hours a day streaming content. In 2018, Netflix users spent 52 billion minutes streaming episodes of *The Office.* If that number is too big to mean anything to you,

 here's another way of looking at it: those minutes add up to 99,103 years. As the *Hollywood Reporter*'s Rick Porter puts it, this is "an amount of time that would stretch back to the Pleistocene epoch, around when, scientists hypothesize, pre-modern *Homo sapiens* began to use language." And that's just for a single show!

If our brains' chemical reward system prompts us to stay glued to our screens, streaming services' autoplay feature makes it even easier, serving up the next episode of a show while the credits are still rolling on the episode we just watched. With 150 million Netflix subscribers, 100 million Amazon Prime subscribers, 28 million Hulu subscribers, and over a hundred other streaming services to choose from, it's no surprise that the US Bureau of Labor Statistics found that we spend more time streaming shows than exercising, reading, and socializing with friends combined—and nearly twice as much time watching TV as we do bonding with family.

All that streaming takes a toll, not just on our social lives but also on our health. When asked about his biggest competitor, Netflix CEO Reed Hastings replied, "We actually compete with sleep. And we're winning!" In addition to cutting into our sleep time (and making it harder to fall asleep when we finally turn in), experts warn that extended periods of sitting can lead to a higher risk of heart disease, stroke, type 2 diabetes, and obesity. Heavy TV consumption can also impact our mood and worldview: a 2015 Boston University study found that the more hours viewers spend watching shows that portray violence, the more likely they are to see the world as "a mean and scary place."

I love *Narcos* as much as the next person, but it's good to take a break every once in a while—for our mental and physical health, for our relationships, and in order to remind ourselves of all the other things we could be doing with our time. The great thing about streaming services is that, unlike live TV, you probably won't miss anything by taking some time off. Your shows will still be waiting for you when you sign back on.

Try It Out

Commit to a duration for your no-streaming break. You'll be more likely to succeed if you set a clear goal for yourself. Can you manage a full week streaming-free? Ten days? What about a month? Mark your chosen end-date on a calendar, and let others know about your intentions to help hold yourself accountable. Even better, ask a friend, partner, or family member to go streaming-free with you, so that you can motivate each other to stick to your goal.

Sign out of your services. It will be easier to resist the temptation of your streaming services if you can't access them with a single click. As an extra precaution, consider asking someone you trust to change your passwords for the duration of your break. If you're planning to quit for a month or longer, you can even temporarily unsubscribe from your streaming services, which offers the added incentive of saving you money.

Make a list of activities to do in your new free time. According to the Bureau of Labor Statistics, the average American spends nearly twenty hours a week watching TV. That's time that could be spent learning to play a musical instrument, picking up a new language, cooking gourmet meals every night of the week, taking care of all the household chores, training for a marathon, reading books cover to cover, writing your own books, bonding with friends and family . . . the list is literally endless. Is there an activity you've always wanted to try, if only you had the time? Put it on your list. The more streaming substitutes you identify and pursue, the less you'll miss your shows.

Record your progress. Every time you feel tempted to watch TV but opt for another activity instead, write it down. At the end of your break, you may be so impressed with all of your recent accomplishments that you won't even want to pick up your remote again. (Okay, we can dream. . . .)

Once your break ends, implement systems to keep bingeing under control. Start by disabling autoplay on your streaming services. While this won't prevent you from bingeing, it will at least require you to make a conscious choice about whether you want to load a new episode. If you're itching to watch multiple episodes in a row, turn each one into a reward for accomplishing a specific task, like washing the dishes or sorting laundry. And if you do decide to settle in for a marathon streaming session, make a point to get up regularly to stretch and move around.

Get a Comfy Bathrobe and Slippers

COGNITIVE SCIENTISTS USE the term "embodied cognition" to describe the idea that while the brain might be the control center for the body, the body also has influence over the mind—that our experiences in the physical world influence the way we think and feel. In 1979, researchers George Lakoff and Mark Johnson published a study exploring the ways we use physical descriptions as metaphors to express our thoughts and feelings: When we're optimistic, we say things are looking *up;* when we're sad, we say we're feeling *down.* We describe a friendly person as *warm* and an unfriendly one as *cold.* Something serious or important is *heavy,* while something fun or frivolous is *light.*

More recently, Northwestern University psychologists Hajo Adam and Adam Galinsky coined the term "enclothed cognition" to describe the ways in which our mood and behavior are influenced by the clothes we wear. In a series of sustained attention tests, the researchers found that subjects who were asked to put on white lab coats performed better than those who stayed in their street clothes. The doctor's coat wearers also performed better than subjects who were asked to wear painter's coats, even though the "doctor's coats" and "painter's coats" were identical. The study demonstrated that the clothes we wear have an influence on our psychological state, not just because of how they feel on our body but also because of the symbolic meaning we project onto them.

Let's bring this theory from the lab into our homes. Ideally, our homes are spaces where we can rest, relax, and be ourselves. And there may be no better way to ease into a state of relaxation than by putting on a bathrobe and slippers. These loungewear classics are symbols of warmth, comfort, and coziness. We may also associate them with the luxury of hotels and spas, where slipping on a robe means a temporary escape from the pressures of everyday life. According to the writer and ethnographer Leah Reich, a bathrobe is "your gateway to glamour, to leisure, to comfort, to relaxation, to a singular and very personal joy." Over the years, Reich has collected a full wardrobe of robes, from the plush, oversize Nautica bathrobe she stole from her dad that "doubles as a comforting hug when I'm sick," to the vintage silk 1920s flapper robe she bought for when she's "in the mood to play dress-up and transport myself" but doesn't feel like leaving home. "My bathrobes, more than any other garment I own, are both comfort and fantasy, home and away," Reich writes.

Just as Reich collects robes, the journalist Margarita Gokun Silver "hoards" slippers. To Silver, slippers "symbolize the domestic space, the feeling of leaving the worries of the world at the door, and the safety and comfort that only one's abode can offer," she writes in *The Atlantic*. "When I slip them on my feet are freer, my floors stay cleaner, and I always feel as if I've truly come home."

Whether you put them on just before bed or spend whole weekends in them, a good robe and slippers can be grounding or transporting. Either way, they'll make you feel as though you're exactly where you need to be.

Pair Your Loungewear with a Hot Beverage

Cognitive psychologists have found that people who hold a hot drink in their hands are more likely to consider others around them warm and trustworthy. If you're relaxing at home with company, serve tea, coffee, or hot toddies to bring out the best in your companions.

PRACTICE NO. 42

Get to Know Your Neighbors

IN HIS ICONIC 1835 book *Democracy in America,* the French sociologist Alexis de Tocqueville declared, "Americans of all ages, all conditions, all minds constantly unite." Today, between our bitterly divided politics, our hectic lives, and the sheer volume of entertainment we can access without needing to leave our homes, it feels as though we've drifted a long way from Tocqueville's America. For instance, when was the last time you talked to a neighbor? Do you and your neighbors even know one another's names? If not, you're not alone: according to the Pew Research Center, more than half of Americans know only a few of their neighbors' names, and one-third say they never have any interactions with their neighbors at all.

Given that the average American moves more than eleven times in a lifetime, spending time and energy getting to know neighbors might seem like a pointless exercise. But studies show that people who trust their neighbors and feel connected to their local community—whether or not they're planning to stay long-term—are happier and healthier than those who don't. There's a reason that *Mr. Rogers' Neighborhood,* a show about sharing with and caring for your neighbors, was beloved by children (including me!) and adults alike during its thirty-three years on the air.

In addition to lending that proverbial cup of sugar, neighbors can serve as an important safety net, helping you shovel in a snowstorm, carrying groceries when your arms are full, looking after your plants and pets when you go on vacation, and coming to your aid in an emergency. If you and your friends tend to share similar tastes and opinions, getting to know your neighbors can be an opportunity to expose yourself to new and different perspectives. Even if you and your neighbors don't become close friends, the simple act of exchanging greetings when you see one another will deepen your sense of belonging. Home isn't only about what's inside your house or apartment—it's also about the community just outside your door.

> As man draws nearer to the stars, why should he
> not also draw nearer to his neighbor?
> —Lyndon B. Johnson

Try It Out

Spend time outside. It's pretty hard to meet new people when you don't leave your house. Whether you're hanging out on a porch or stoop, reading on a balcony, doing yard work, or taking a walk around the block, spending time outside gives you the opportunity to see and interact with the people around you. The more often you see new faces, the more quickly they'll become familiar.

Smile and say hi. Getting to know your neighbors doesn't require that you show up at every doorstep on your block with a plate of freshly baked cookies (though I bet no one would object). If you're not sure how to break the ice, start by simply saying hello and smiling when you see a neighbor.

Ask questions. Neighbors can be an invaluable resource for getting to know your neighborhood, whether they're recommending a delicious restaurant, a trustworthy mechanic, a block that's best to avoid after dark, or guidance about a local custom. Asking for tips about the area is an easy way to start up a conversation—people are usually flattered to have their opinions solicited.

Join a local group. Become a member of a food co-op, join a community garden, volunteer at a local shelter or food pantry, or find out where your neighborhood association meets and attend the next meeting. Getting involved with your community is a great way to meet new people while supporting the place where you live.

Take It Further

HOST A NEIGHBORHOOD POTLUCK OR BLOCK PARTY

Years ago, I lived in an apartment in Somerville, Massachusetts, with my roommate, Karen. We wanted to get to know our neighbors and other new people, so we decided to host a potluck every Thursday. (See Practice No. 29 for tips.) Having casual dinner parties with lots of new faces was a great, low-pressure way to get to know people better. We kept it up every week for over a year, sometimes with as many as twenty-five people, sometimes as few as five. We had regulars, new people, and one guy whose contribution to the potluck was a microwave he'd found on the street. (We were pretty skeptical, but it still worked . . . so we cleaned it out and used it for the rest of the time we lived in that apartment.) If your home isn't big enough for a dinner crowd, consider throwing a block party. You'll probably need to coordinate with neighbors to make sure the date doesn't interfere with another event. Visit your local police precinct for advice about closing your street off to traffic during the party.

Explore Your Local Library

WHEN I MOVED to the neighborhood where I live now, I was delighted to discover that my new apartment was just a few blocks away from a branch of the Brooklyn Public Library. Whenever I walk in, I'm reminded of my hometown library, where I spent time as a kid flipping through books, playing with toys and games in the children's section, and hiding from my dad in the stacks. Even though my new library in Brooklyn is different, so much is immediately familiar: the sound of papers rustling and people whispering; the librarian leaning over the circulation desk to answer a question; the slightly musty, comforting smell of books. It's easy to feel at home in a library, which is the point. At a public library, everyone's welcome, and anyone can belong.

At the risk of sounding curmudgeonly, things have changed since I was young! The library used to be the first and most obvious place to go for information on practically any subject—now we have the Internet for that. My friends and I used to borrow CDs from the library when we didn't want to buy them— now we can stream albums on Spotify. In the digital age, with unlimited information and entertainment available on our smartphones and laptops, some critics have questioned whether we even need public libraries anymore.

The answer is an emphatic *yes*—and not just when you ask librarians. Recent surveys by the Pew Research Center find that over 90 percent of Americans believe libraries are important, and 66 percent say that if their local library branch were to close, it would have a "major impact" on their community. From a strictly economic sense, that's true: proximity to libraries causes property values to go up. But a library's value to its community can't really be quantified.

> The America I love still exists at the front desks
> of our public libraries.
> —Kurt Vonnegut

While it's true that the main function of a library is to loan books, today's libraries do much, much more. With more than 16,500 branches around the country, libraries are more widespread in the US than Starbucks or McDonald's. Librarians across the country answer an average of 6.6 *million* questions a week. Eight in ten Americans say they consider public libraries and librarians trustworthy resources for information, while only one-third have similar faith in the news media.

Libraries adapt their collections to serve the specific needs of their local communities. In Richmond, California, home gardeners can "borrow" seeds from the public library to grow tomatoes, lettuce, beans, and peas. (The library asks that borrowers let some of their new plants go to seed, then bring those second-generation seeds back to the library for others to borrow. "Don't worry,"

the library's website adds. "We don't have fines if you don't return seeds.") In Iowa City, Iowa, the public library's Art to Go! collection allows patrons to check out framed art prints and original works by local artists to hang in their homes for up to two months at a time. The Dallas Public Library's "Fairy Tale Closet" opens up during prom season for teens to browse and borrow donated gowns. The public library in Ann Arbor, Michigan, lends out musical instruments and equipment; the Chicago Public Library lends fishing poles and tackle boxes; and the Maine Tool Library in Portland, Maine, as you might expect, lends out tools and appliances ranging from blowtorches to cake pans.

Beyond what you can borrow, libraries host cultural events like readings, concerts, lectures, and film screenings that are free and open to the public. Sometimes called "the people's university," many libraries offer a wide range of educational programming: classes in history, art, and music appreciation; creative writing workshops; knitting and painting classes; job and interview training; and more.

Libraries are a quiet workspace for remote workers and freelancers. They're a welcoming sanctuary for folks without stable housing. They offer support to patrons trying to navigate complex tax forms, immigration documents, and health insurance policies. And they offer a community to those who are lonely or just looking for other people who live nearby and share their interests. In the words of Harvard political science professor Robert

Putnam: "People may go to the library looking mainly for information, but they find each other there."

If you want to feel more at home in your neighborhood, there's no better place to begin than your local library.

The publicness of the public library is an increasingly rare commodity. It becomes harder all the time to think of places that welcome everyone and don't charge any money for that warm embrace.
—Susan Orlean, *The Library Book*

Make a Cell Phone Lockbox for Your Home

STEP INTO ANY of Getaway's tiny cabins, and one of the first things you'll see is our signature cell phone lockbox. Getaway cofounder Pete Davis's sister, Rebecca, came up with the idea for the lockbox, but our early guests were the inspiration for it. When we started out, we knew we wanted to create a space that felt separated from everyday concerns. As a part of that, we didn't think the cabins should have Wi-Fi. (To be totally honest, we didn't know how to provide it, anyway.) But we were worried that our guests would hate not having Wi-Fi access. Then, to our surprise, a number of guests started writing in to thank us for the forced disconnection. Not only did they not hate it; they *liked* it. We wanted to build on that in some way, and after some brainstorming, the cell phone lockbox was born. Guests are encouraged to stow their phones in the

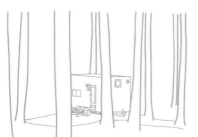

lockbox when they check in and keep them there until checkout.

We're not the first to come up with an idea like this. Digital Detox cofounder Levi Felix championed unplugging by establishing Camp Grounded, a summer camp for adults where campers' phones are sealed in bags labeled "biohazard" while they're on-site. And California entrepreneur Graham Dugoni's company Yondr supplies event spaces with portable, autolocking neoprene pouches for cell phones. After silencing their phones and sealing them into the pouches, guests can hold on to them, but if they want to use them, they need to visit unlocking stations outside the phone-free zone. Dugoni compares Yondr to old-time smoking and nonsmoking sections. "If you're waiting for a call from the babysitter, for instance, you'll still feel your phone vibrate in your pocket, and then you can step out into the phone-use area and unlock it," he says.

Our lockboxes aren't fancy or high-tech—they're just cigar boxes with "Cellphone Lockbox" engraved on the lid and a little metal clasp to keep them closed. People ask us how we make sure that people use the lockbox. Do we have a cell phone police force on-site? Not at all—it's completely up to guests if they follow the rules. But based on the feedback we've received, it seems like almost everyone is using the lockbox voluntarily during their stay.

The power of the lockbox is that by creating a physical barrier between you and your phone—even one that can easily be breached—you also create a psychological barrier. When you need to take a few extra seconds and a few extra steps to access your phone, you may find yourself asking, *Do I really need my phone right now?* More often than not, the answer is no.

Try It Out

Get the supplies to build your own cell phone lockbox. Getaway's lockboxes are made of wood, but yours doesn't need to be. You can buy a simple box at any craft store, or even repurpose an empty shoebox. If you share your home with multiple people, you'll want to

make sure your box is big enough to hold everyone's phones at once. Next, decorate it, label it, or keep it simple— it's up to you.

Install your lockbox at home. The best place to keep your lockbox is near your front door, so you can deposit your phone as soon as you enter your home.

Silence your phone before stowing it in the lockbox. The lockbox won't do much good if you can still hear your phone buzzing or chiming. Silence it, or set it on Do Not Disturb mode before you put it away.

Give yourself time to adjust. The first few times you use your cell phone lockbox, you may find yourself itching to take it right back out. You can build up phone-free endurance by setting rules around when you're allowed to check it. At first, you might ask yourself to wait an hour. The next day, try to increase the time you leave your phone in the box, and build up incrementally.

Invite guests to use your lockbox. Next time you have friends over, ask them to leave their phones in the lockbox, and see how your dynamic changes when no one is glued to their screens.

Listen to an AM/FM Radio

AT GETAWAY, EVERY cabin is stocked with an AM/FM radio. I tune in whenever I'm in one of our cabins, switching on the receiver and scrolling through static until I land on a local station. You can learn a lot about a place from its radio stations—from hyperlocal news reports to the personalities of talk show hosts and DJs and the kind of music they choose to play.

Back at home in Brooklyn, I tend to keep my radio tuned to NPR. I love the way both radio and podcasts offer long-form content to listeners, going in-depth on different stories and subjects. But I find that radio provides an added level of discovery. When I listen to podcasts, I tend to click on programs and topics I'm already interested in. When I stream music, I choose albums I already know I like. With the radio, your choices are more limited— you can switch stations, but you can't control what plays. You're a lot more likely to hear something brand new, whether it's a news story on an unfamiliar topic or a song you've never heard before.

"Perhaps no invention of modern times has

delivered so much while initially promising so little," the science reporter Guy Gugliotta wrote of the humble radio in *Discover Magazine*. In a little over a century, the radio has gone from a transmitter of brief electrical pulses to an essential tool for education, entertainment, emergency management, and democracy around the world. For poor rural populations worldwide, where cell phones and Internet access are scarce, community radio stations give locals a platform for sharing important concerns and information. In emergencies and disaster zones, radios are often able to continue transmitting life-saving information when other signals go down. On a daily basis, across every age group, income bracket, and region of the world, people tune into radios for breaking news, weather and traffic reports, storytelling, new and long-beloved music, and more. It's free, universal, and ever-changing. Next time you go to turn on a playlist or podcast, consider switching on the radio instead.

Try It Out

Wake up to the radio. Practice No. 38 discussed why it's better to use a real alarm clock rather than your cell phone for waking up in the morning. If you use a clock radio, you can ease out of sleep to the sound of music or a news program instead of a beeping alarm. "Human beings are conditioned to hear voices; they're not conditioned to hear beeps," the forensic scientist Niamh Nic Daéid told *The Guardian*. Listening to the radio may help you wake up faster and in a less jarring way than a conventional alarm—and make you less likely to hit the snooze button.

Get the news while you get ready for your day. If your morning routine includes time spent scanning Twitter or news headlines on your phone or computer, consider listening to a morning news program on the radio instead. There are lots of things you can do while listening to the radio—showering, getting dressed, making coffee—that you can't do with your eyes glued to a screen (or a newspaper).

Get a battery-operated radio for power outages. When the power goes out, so do your lights, TV, and Internet. If you keep an inexpensive, battery-powered radio on hand, you'll be able to stay informed—and entertained—during a power outage.

Strip down to basics with the Public Radio. A pair of Brooklyn-based engineers have designed a radio so simple it's literally just a mason jar with a volume/power knob and an antenna. Called the Public Radio, it plays only one station, which buyers can preselect. The radio hardware is built onto the metal lid, while the glass jar amplifies the sound. If you're dedicated to a single station, this is the radio for you.

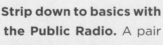

PART 4

Balance Your Work

THROUGHOUT HISTORY, WORKERS have taken to the streets and picket lines and sometimes even sacrificed their lives fighting for rights like the eight-hour workday and the forty-hour workweek. We could think of these as the original struggles for "work-life balance." Fast-forward to today: thanks largely to the Internet and digital technology, the line between work and life has become so blurred that we're answering emails during family dinner and watching cat videos during meetings. I call this phenomenon "The Great Spillover." We might think we're squeezing more out of our days: more emails, more entertainment, more connection, more progress on our projects. But in reality, we are struggling with everything. We rarely have sustained, uninterrupted time for deep thought and deep work. We fail to give colleagues and collaborators our full attention. And we never have a chance to truly escape and rejuvenate. Productivity can't be our only metric for career success; we also need to place real value on our mental and physical well-being and our sense of fulfillment. That might mean going for walking meetings to get fresh air while discussing a project with a colleague, or taking breaks to recharge throughout the workday. It means creating firm boundaries around when and how we work, and making sure that our time off is truly off.

Set Out-of-Office Messages

IF YOU WRITE to anyone at Getaway while we're on vacation, you'll get an auto-reply message a lot like this one:

Subject: Disconnecting and recharging

Hi,
At Getaway, we believe it is important that everyone have the opportunity to take real time off.

It's my turn—I'll be offline through Tuesday, October 8.

In the meantime, Henry can point you in the right direction if you need anything.
Be well,
Jon

That's because every Getaway employee is required to set an out-of-office message when they take vacation, including myself (and taking vacation is a requirement). Some employees are reluctant to advertise that they're taking a break, fearing it will seem as though they're not taking their work seriously if an important contact tries to get in touch. I relate to this anxiety, especially when it comes to our investors. If they find out I'm going on vacation, will they think I'm not working as hard as I could be?

Then I remind myself that taking time off to relax and recharge isn't just important in theory—it's the core philosophy of our company. We *should* advertise that we're going on vacation, not just so people trying to get in touch will know where we are and how long we'll be away (though that's helpful, too) but because vacations are good for our general health and well-being. And taking a real vacation means disconnecting from work, email and all. (See Practice No. 54 to learn more about the benefits of taking vacations.)

Of course, setting an out-of-office message won't prevent you from checking and replying to email if you really want to. But it will take the pressure off, allowing you to do so on your own terms and schedule—or to stay offline entirely. If nothing else, it's good to get periodic reminders that the world doesn't end when you take some time away from your inbox.

What Makes a Good Out-of-Office Message?

Keep it simple. While it can be fun to add personal touches to an auto-reply, such as where you'll be and what you'll be doing, it's best to be clear and concise about the most important information: that you're away from your desk, when you'll be back, whether you're reachable, and who to contact if you're not.

Proofread carefully. A typo or incorrect date in an email is bad enough when it goes to one person. Your out-of-office message will get sent to everyone who tries to contact you while you're away, so double- and triple-check to make sure all the information is accurate, or ask a colleague to proofread your message before enabling it.

Be careful with humor. Remember that your message will go out indiscriminately, and not all recipients respond to humor in the same way. What's funny to one person may seem unprofessional (or just plain confusing) to another.

Be clear about how reachable you are. Clarify whether you'll be checking in periodically or disconnecting completely. Avoid promising a concrete date for responses: rather than writing, "I'll reply to all emails on January 5," consider something like: "I'll respond once I'm back in the office" or "I'll respond as soon as I'm able."

Try It Out

Let colleagues and important contacts know about your time off in advance. Your out-of-office message shouldn't come as a surprise to anyone you're working closely with, especially if you have deadlines coming up. Being transparent about an upcoming vacation isn't just good for ensuring that work runs smoothly in your absence, it'll also help you to relax once you're finally away.

Designate a point person for time-sensitive queries. If you don't have an assistant or team member who will do this anyway, ask a colleague if you can redirect important questions or concerns to them while you're away. Make sure to get permission before listing their contact information in your auto-reply. And let them know how to contact you directly if you'd like to be reachable for higher-level work issues or in case of emergency.

Remember to turn off your auto-reply once you're back at work. Most email programs allow you to enter an expiration date when you set your out-of-office message, but you may want to leave a note for yourself just in case. If you anticipate having a lot of unread email to sort through upon your return, you may want to leave your out-of-office message up until the day *after* you return, so you have uninterrupted time to catch up.

Take It Further

You don't need to be on vacation to take advantage of an out-of-office message. Consider configuring your email to send auto-replies outside of work hours, so you don't feel pressured to respond immediately to emails that come in later in the evening or early in the morning. Learning that you aren't available outside of regular work hours may encourage your contacts to reconsider their own email habits.

Declutter Your Desktop

IN 2017, twenty-one-year-old marketing intern Aida Said tweeted out screenshots of her friend Carley's desktop, which showed thousands of files and images stacked on top of one another, filling the screen with digital chaos. The tweet quickly went viral, as Twitter users reacted with collective horror: "I'm calling the police on Carley," wrote one responder. "This is like looking through a portal to hell," wrote another. Then there were the people who identified with Carley, tweeting out screenshots of their own wildly cluttered desktops. Websites picked up the story with headlines like "Woman's Cluttered Desktop Is the Worst Thing on the Web," and "Messy Desktops Are Your Worst Nightmare or Your Shameful Reality."

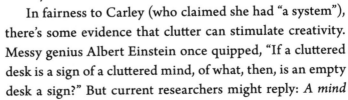

In fairness to Carley (who claimed she had "a system"), there's some evidence that clutter can stimulate creativity. Messy genius Albert Einstein once quipped, "If a cluttered desk is a sign of a cluttered mind, of what, then, is an empty desk a sign?" But current researchers might reply: *A mind*

better able to focus. The brain can absorb only about 1 percent of the visual information it receives at any time, so the more objects there are in the surrounding environment, the harder the brain has to work to tune out these distractions. "The clutter competes for your attention in the same way a toddler might stand next to you annoyingly repeating, 'Candy, candy, candy, candy, I want candy, candy, candy, candy, candy, candy,'" writes the decluttering guru Erin Doland on her blog *Unclutterer.* "Even though you might be able to focus a little, you're still aware that a screaming toddler is also vying for your attention."

Studies at Princeton and UCLA have found that in addition to making it harder to maintain focus, clutter can reduce productivity, increase stress and anxiety, and cause mental fatigue. Clutter is closely linked to procrastination, because when you can't find what you're looking for, it's tempting to put it off until later. We could even think of clutter as the physical evidence of procrastination, itself. As the author of *The Clutter Diet,* Lorie Marrero, told *Fast Company,* "Think about everything you have sitting around on your counter or on your desk, that's an action you haven't taken or a decision you haven't made."

I don't have a desk. I suspect if I did, it would quickly pile up with papers and clutter, so my trick for maintaining an organized workspace is not to have one at all. When I'm at the office, I move around with my laptop. I hate screens, so I print out the documents I need (on recycled paper!). At the end of the day, I digitize everything by taking photos of anything I need to keep, then recycle the hard copies.

Whether you work on the go or return to the same desk every day, decluttering your digital and physical desktop will help you stay organized and focused, improve your productivity, and reduce your stress. Even Carley might approve: A few days after her original tweet, Aida Said tweeted an updated screenshot of her friend's desktop. In the midst of the chaos, Carley had created a new folder titled "aida i wanna clean my desktop."

Try It Out

PHYSICAL DESKTOP

Identify the necessities, and donate or discard the rest. Before you can get organized, you'll probably need to do some purging. Remove everything from your desktop, drawers, and anywhere else you keep office supplies. Sort into three piles: keep, give away, and trash. You might need a couple of pens, but you probably don't need a dozen, and you definitely don't need old, dried-up highlighters, stretched-out rubber bands, and your name tag from last year's conference. As you go through each item, ask yourself what purpose it serves, whether it's redundant, and how likely you are to use it in the next month. Save only the items you actually use on a regular basis, and discard or give away the remainder.

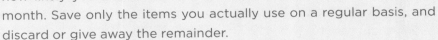

Organize your paper. Paper clutter tends to pile up faster than anything else, so finding an efficient way to deal with it is a key step in maintaining a tidy workspace. Jennifer Lifford, the author of *The Home Decluttering Diet,* suggests following the "one-touch" rule: "Once you touch a piece of paper, either act upon it immediately, file it in the appropriate place, or throw it away/shred it," she writes.

Leave your desk to eat lunch. Even if you're a tidy eater, having meals at your desk makes it more likely that you'll accumulate clutter like dirty dishes, takeout containers, utensils, and napkins in your workspace. Besides, getting up is good for your mental health and productivity—research shows that workers who take breaks away from their desks return with greater energy and focus.

Organize your cords. Create a DIY charging station to keep your cords organized and your devices charged. Make a dock from an old shoebox, letter organizer, or utensil tray. Drill holes to run the cords through the dock, then connect to a power strip. Whether you use a dock or not, you can keep excess cords neat by coiling and securing them with twist-ties.

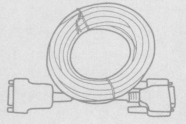

DIGITAL DESKTOP

Start with a blank slate by moving your entire desktop into a temporary folder. While it might feel like cheating, you need clear space to get organized. Create a new folder called "old desktop" and drag everything into it. Now the only thing you should be able to see on your desktop is that one folder.

Create three additional folders. One for whatever you're currently working on; one for anything you've finished that can be archived; and one for incoming media—screenshots, photos, music, etc. Now you have a system for keeping your files in order. It's up to you to maintain it!

Download a read-it-later program. Programs like Evernote, Instapaper, and Pocket allow you to download, save, and organize articles for future reading across devices—without needing to clutter up your desktop.

Say No to Multitasking

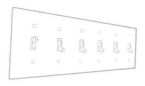

HERE'S A WAKE-UP CALL: no matter what you wrote on your résumé or promised your boss, *you are not a good multitasker.* I'm not trying to insult you. I can't multitask, either. In fact, none of us can; our brains are wired to focus on only one thing at a time. Neuroscientists explain that what we refer to as multitasking is actually task-*switching:* transferring our attention from one thing to another and then back in rapid succession. When we answer emails during a meeting, we're not doing two things at once; we're just answering emails and then engaging in the meeting and then answering emails and then engaging in the meeting.

While multitasking has long been touted as a productivity tool, experts say it actually *decreases* our productivity—by as much as 40 percent. "Your brain has to reorient its attention every time you switch from one task to another," explains Gloria Mark, a professor of informatics at the University of California, Irvine, in an interview with *BuzzFeed.* When our focus on one task is interrupted by the need to attend to another task at the same time, blood rushes to an entirely different part of the brain to make a decision about what task to perform next, before rushing back to perform the task—a task that, of course, will be interrupted again shortly. "That loss of mental resources wastes time, causes stress, and means that the quality of the things you're working on decreases," says Dr. Mark.

Multitasking doesn't just slow us down, stress us out, and decrease the quality of our work. It degrades our ability to pay attention over extended periods of time, which can make it difficult to engage in the deep processing required to learn new things. It makes us less creative and can damage personal relationships—think of how you feel when you're trying to talk to someone who keeps looking at their phone. It can even lower our IQ. Researchers at the University of London's Institute of Psychiatry found that their test subjects' IQ points dropped twice as much when subjects were distracted by email and phones as when subjects smoked pot right before work. Maybe most alarming of all, multitasking might actually alter our brain structure for the worse: after taking MRI scans of their subjects, researchers at the University of Sussex found that heavy multitaskers had less brain density in their anterior cingulate cortex, the region associated with decision-making, impulse control, and empathy.

There are plenty of ways to improve our focus, work quality, and productivity, but none of them includes trying to do it all at the same time. As a first step, let's dispel the myth of multitasking once and for all.

Try It Out

Create designated times for checking your email. Otherwise, keep your email closed and turn off alerts to avoid the temptation of

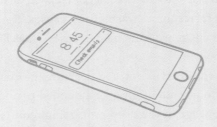

getting pulled away from your work every time a new message comes in. **Keep your phone out of sight when you're not actively using it.** Studies have found that people are more distracted when their phones are nearby, even if they're not engaging with them. If you can't see or hear your phone, you're less likely to be tempted by it.

Make a to-do list. The process of mentally sifting through your tasks, naming and listing them, can make you feel more organized and less stressed about forgetting anything important. In fact, the mere act of writing them down will help you remember them. And breaking down abstract or long-term goals into smaller, concrete steps helps reduce the sense of being overwhelmed while giving you better control over planning.

Work in timed intervals with breaks. In the late 1980s, the entrepreneur and author Francesco Cirillo came up with a deceptively simple productivity technique he called the Pomodoro Method, named after the bright red plastic tomato timer found in many kitchens. The guiding principle of Cirillo's method—which has since been adapted by dozens of different focus apps and programs—is to work in relatively short, timed bursts that allow you to concentrate deeply on a single task at a time, followed by a short break. I like to use a program called SelfControl (which locks me out of tempting apps and websites) and set a timer whenever I really need to focus. I usually do fifty minutes on, ten minutes off. (Cirillo's Pomodoro Method calls for twenty-five minutes on, five minutes off.) I've found that working this way turns a daunting project into one I can make a lot of progress on, and the combination of focused work and forced break time makes my work much more enjoyable.

Take care of your top-priority work first. One reason many of us feel compelled to multitask is the anxiety that we haven't accomplished everything we set out to do. If you start your day with the most important tasks on your list, you'll feel more relaxed and maintain better focus as the day goes on.

Get others on board. Dave Crenshaw, the author of *The Myth of Multitasking,* suggests having a direct conversation with your boss and colleagues about your desire to check email (and other work-related communication like Slack) less often in order to be more focused on your work. Approaching the issue collaboratively will create a better work environment for everyone.

Take Swedish-Style *Fika* Breaks

WHEN IT COMES to balancing our work lives, we could all take a lesson from the Swedes. Only around 1 percent of Swedish employees report working very long hours, and a 2010 study found that Swedes are the least stressed work-

ers in the world. What's their secret? It may be the twice-daily breaks Swedish workers take to enjoy a leisurely coffee and snack, a national tradition known as *fika* (pronounced "*fee*-kah"). *Fika* is an inversion of the Swedish word for coffee, *kaffi*, but thinking of *fika* as a mere coffee break leaves out the essence of the tradition. Sure, coffee's a part of it—Sweden is one of the top three consumers of coffee worldwide—but more important, *fika* is about slowing down and taking time to appreciate the simple, good things in life.

"You can do it alone, you can do it with friends," explains Anna Brones, co-author (with Johanna Kindvall) of *Fika: The Art of the Swedish Coffee Break*. "You can do it at home, in a park or at work. But the essential thing is that you do it, that you make time to take a break."

In Sweden, workers generally break for *fika* once in midmorning and again in midafternoon. While the ritual often includes coffee and a treat known as *fikabröd* (cinnamon buns, apple tarts, and almond cake are popular), what you choose to eat and drink doesn't really matter. As Brones puts it, "There's no *fika* police." Having a cup of coffee and a pastry at your desk while you check email? That's not *fika*. Savoring time and companionship with the people around you? Classic *fika*.

In the workplace, *fika* is an opportunity for colleagues to exchange knowledge and opinions in an informal setting. "The hierarchy breaks down during the *fika*; we're all in it together regardless of power and position," says Swedish communications professor Viveka Adelswärd. It can also facilitate interpersonal bonding: "We sound each other out and let a little of our private lives come out, which can create sympathy for colleagues who are having a tough time."

While taking multiple breaks throughout the workday for bonding, relaxing, and snacking with coworkers might sound bad for productivity, studies show that the opposite is true. Researchers have found that breaks restore our energy and attention while improving our decision-making abilities. They can also spur "goal reactivation"—if we're getting lost in the minutia of a task, stepping away and shifting focus for a while can clear our minds, allowing us to see the bigger picture when we return. And breaks can boost our creativity. As Adelswärd puts it, "We get a chance to blow the dust off our brains, fill them with inspiration from others, and have an opportunity to test our thoughts and ideas." Given all the benefits, it's no surprise that some Swedish companies have made *fika* mandatory.

If you want to enjoy *fika* in true Swedish style, consider bringing a homemade treat to share. For *fika*-focused recipes, check out the Swedish Institute's cookbook *The Swedish Kitchen: From Fika to Cosy Friday*.

My boyfriend Michael's parents live in an old mill in Devon, England, that dates back to at least the year 1100. (There are mentions of a mill on that site in the Domesday Books.) Michael's eighty-nine-year-old grandfather Alan lived in the house for decades, and he still comes every morning to work on the house and yard. I suspect some of his amazing energy comes from the fact that he has his own version of *fika*: regular tea and biscuit breaks he calls "pre-sies" (before work), "one-sies" (mid-work), and "two-sies" (at the end of work). Don't ask me about the logic behind the names!

Announce the End of Your Workday

IF YOU WANT to create a clear separation between your work and leisure time, make a point to *say* that you're ending your workday. According to the executive coach and author Deborah Bright, creating end-of-day rituals or routines is key to building a "psychological barrier" between work and home life. Bright suggests choosing a particular action—what she refers to as an "anchor quick charge"—that signals to yourself and others that you're ready to stop thinking about work for the day. Maybe it's powering down your computer, switching off the lights in your office, or sending a text to someone at home to let them know you're on your way. "Consistent use of this designated anchor will enable you to take control of your emotions and shift your mental state, just as if you were clocking out on a timesheet," Bright explains.

You could simply say out loud, "I'm done with work!"—even if you're the only one around to hear it. While it may feel silly, research shows that talking to yourself out loud can motivate you to follow through on your intentions.

When you say something aloud, you force your brain to focus closely on what's being said, bringing it to the forefront of your attention and making it easier to remember. If you hear yourself say that you're finishing work for the day, you'll be more likely to act accordingly. If your colleagues hear you say it, they can hold you accountable—for example, by dropping by your desk to ask why you're still there when you told them you were leaving fifteen minutes ago. And if you've made your announcement to someone who's expecting you after work—whether it's family waiting at home, or a friend you're meeting for dinner or drinks—then you'll need to follow through in order to uphold your social commitment. On multiple occasions, Michael and I have moved from work mode into personal mode while still on our computers (for instance, switching from Slack to reading the news), patiently waiting for each other to "finish the workday" without realizing that we're both already done. Now we make a point to let each other know when we're wrapping up.

"How you end the day is critical," national workplace expert Lynn Taylor told *Forbes*. While we tend to be more focused on "getting off on the right foot" to ensure a productive and successful workday, Taylor notes that closing the day with intention also matters: "The end of your day sets the stage for tomorrow."

Try It Out

Announce you're wrapping up in advance. Give yourself and/or your colleagues a fifteen- or thirty-minute warning as you approach the end of your workday, in order to make sure you have a chance to address anything major before you leave.

Make a to-do list for the next day. List the tasks you need to accomplish in order of priority. This will help you feel prepared for the following day, reducing stress and creating an easier transition upon your return to work.

Complete one small, final task. Sign a document, mail off a letter, or return a brief email or call—a way to end your day on a note of closure and accomplishment.

Clean up your workspace. Taking a few minutes to straighten your desk or work area can help you ease into an end-of-day mind-set by giving you a task that engages a different part of your brain—the pile-making and where-does-this-thing-go? part—without causing additional mental strain. You can also think of it as a gift to your future self, since studies show that workers who return to cluttered, messy desks in the morning feel more stressed than those who arrive to well-organized workspaces.

Announce you're signing off. Say out loud that your workday is over, even if you're alone. If you're with colleagues, say goodbye to them. "We tend to think about the importance of checking in and saying good morning to kick off the day, but we forget that it can

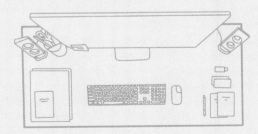

be just as important, and make us feel good as well, to say a friendly and proper goodbye to everyone," international business speaker Michael Kerr told *Forbes*.

Actually leave. The quality of your work matters more than the quantity of time you spend at your desk. Instead of striving to be the last one in the office, make it your priority to leave work at work. You'll be more innovative and productive if you give yourself meaningful time off to rest and recharge.

Alternate Between Sitting, Standing, and Walking Throughout the Day

STANDING DESKS have been around for a long time: Charles Dickens, Ernest Hemingway, and *Spider-Man* creator Stan Lee all worked standing up. But the current craze for standing desks took off around 2010, after a series of high-profile studies warned that sitting all day wasn't just bad for the back—it might even be life-threatening. The studies found that sitting for long periods of time was linked to higher rates of obesity, heart disease, diabetes, and certain forms of cancer, prompting health reporters to declare that sitting was "the new smoking." In response, many employers and home office workers rushed to install standing desks.

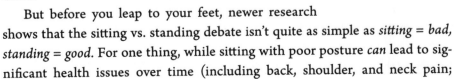

But before you leap to your feet, newer research shows that the sitting vs. standing debate isn't quite as simple as *sitting = bad, standing = good*. For one thing, while sitting with poor posture *can* lead to significant health issues over time (including back, shoulder, and neck pain;

headaches; and fatigue), doing your work from a chair isn't necessarily as deadly as researchers once believed. Those earlier reports hadn't differentiated between people who are sitting for *work* and those who are, say, watching TV on a couch twelve hours a day, or sedentary because of preexisting health problems. Studies that focused exclusively on people in workplaces found little evidence to link "occupational sitting" to poor health outcomes.

And standing for long periods of time presents its own set of problems, including foot pain, joint compression, varicose veins, and heart disease. "You

shouldn't be doing anything inactive for six to eight hours a day—whether that's sitting at a computer or standing at a computer," says Dr. Michael Fredericson, who directs the sports medicine program at the Stanford University Medical Center. "Our bodies are meant to move," he told *Men's Health*.

What's the solution? Alternate between sitting, standing, and walking over the course of your workday. Studies show that desk workers who are active throughout the day are more focused and productive—and experience less physical discomfort—than those who are stationary. According to experts, the optimal ratio is about twenty minutes of sitting, followed by eight minutes standing and two minutes moving (such as a short walk or gentle stretching). And you don't need to invest in an expensive adjustable-height desk to follow this regime: I made my own standing desk by stacking a milk crate on a tabletop.

Try It Out

Shift position periodically. Whether you're sitting or standing, shifting position will engage different muscle groups and improve circulation, helping to minimize stiffness and fatigue. If you're standing, you can use a footstool to shift your weight from foot to foot.

Set a timer to remind you to move. If you're looking for more than a simple countdown clock, a variety of mobile and desktop apps for Windows and iOS (including Stretchly, Stand Up!, Workrave, and Awareness) will prompt you to take micro-breaks for standing, stretching, drinking water, and readjusting your gaze to reduce eye fatigue.

Stretch at your desk. Regular stretching can improve flexibility, reduce pain, and ease physical and mental stress. There are lots of different stretch routines you can do without leaving your desk: upper body stretches like overhead reaches, shoulder shrugs, and torso rotations; as well as hip, knee, and hamstring stretches you can do from your chair.

Ease into standing. If you want to try out a standing desk for longer periods, give your body time to adjust. Start by standing for just fifteen minutes at a time. Listen to your body: if you feel tired or uncomfortable, it's a sign that you should change your position.

Get exercise throughout the day. Dr. Fredericson recommends "bracketing your workday with exercise"—walking or biking to and from work, finding excuses to get up and walk around throughout the workday, taking a longer walk at lunch, and doing exercises and stretches to improve flexibility before bed. "It really has to be a lifestyle," he says. "Not 'Okay, I'll sit all day (even though it's really bad) and then I'll try and make up for it at another time.' Think about your lifestyle and how you can work around inactive periods."

Start an Office Kickball Team

IF YOU WORK full-time, there's a good chance you spend more waking hours with your coworkers than you do with your family and friends. So it probably won't come as a surprise that the relationships you form with your colleagues—not just as collaborators, but as people—can have a significant impact on your well-being, both on and off the clock.

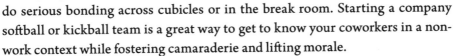

People who like one another tend to work better together. "When we get to know our coworkers and strengthen our bonds with them, it becomes a little easier to meet challenges as a team," the career performance coach Jacqueline Dolly told *Bustle*. But it can be tough to do serious bonding across cubicles or in the break room. Starting a company softball or kickball team is a great way to get to know your coworkers in a non-work context while fostering camaraderie and lifting morale.

Spending time outside and getting exercise are tried-and-true methods for reducing stress and increasing happiness. Participating in an organized sport with colleagues is also a natural way to escape office hierarchies and departmental divisions—at least temporarily. Regardless of your titles at work, you're all on an even playing field (literally!) when you play sports together. It's a fresh way to see and be seen: if you're athletic, you'll be able to show off skills that you probably don't get to use at work; if you're not, you can still impress your colleagues (and quite possibly your managers) with good sportsmanship and enthusiasm. Likewise, it's a great opportunity to discover your colleagues' hidden talents and to create new memories and inside jokes that will strengthen your bonds and add new dimensions to your relationships.

Playing sports with coworkers can give you a chance to team up with folks you don't often cross paths with, helping you feel more connected to your organization as a whole. Meanwhile, the shared goal of winning a match (and cheering for teammates) can create a powerful sense of solidarity that lasts after you're back in the office.

When employees feel as though they're part of a supportive work community, they tend to experience higher levels of satisfaction in their careers and are less likely to suffer burnout. Recent research by Gallup finds that employees who report having close friends at work are more than twice as engaged with their jobs as those who don't. When morale is high, performance improves across the board. And it's not just our work that benefits. A 2016 study published in the journal *Personality and Social Psychology Review* found that having friends at work makes us happier and healthier. It makes sense: feeling good about the people we work with makes us feel better about our work. And when we feel good about work, we're far more likely to feel good about our lives overall.

It's important to note that while these coworker-bonding activities are meant to be fun, they'll be a lot less fun if they begin to feel like just another work-related obligation. If you find that you don't really enjoy hanging out with your coworkers outside of work, whether through organized sports or otherwise, don't feel bad about skipping out and reserving your free time for the people and activities you prefer. (See Practice No. 56 for tips on separating your work life from your social life.)

Not a sports person? Here are some other ways to bond with coworkers outside of work:

- Launch an office book club (see Practice No. 27).
- Start a band with colleagues.
- Invite coworkers to your home for a game night (see Practice No. 22).
- Sign up for an evening art/language/exercise class with colleagues.
- Suggest an office-wide outing to a park or museum.

Schedule a No-Contact Production Day

ANYONE WHO WORKS in a busy office—especially one with an open floor plan—knows that some days, it can feel practically impossible to get any real work done. Walking into the office, you get caught

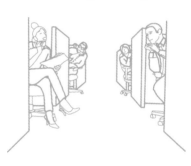

up in conversation with a colleague who wants to tell you about their weekend. As you settle in to check your email, you get a phone call; when you hang up the phone, your boss drops by to ask if you've finished the latest report. You have to race to a meeting, then back to your desk for a conference call, but there's a problem with your log-in information and you have to talk to someone in tech.

Meanwhile emails are piling up, your friend at the next desk wants to show you a meme, your coworkers are pinging you with questions on Slack, and you haven't even looked at that big project you meant to finish today.

Sound familiar? It's not just you. Researchers at the University of California, Irvine, found that the typical office worker gets interrupted every *three minutes and five seconds.* This would be challenging enough if we had the ability to snap straight back into focused work following an interruption—but we generally don't. The Irvine researchers found that after we're interrupted, it can take us over twenty-three minutes to return to the task at hand.

And that's not even counting meetings! Studies find that mid-level office workers spend up to 35 percent of their work time in meetings; for executives it can be closer to 50 percent. Not only are meetings notorious for running long while accomplishing little, by pulling us away from our desks, they break up time we might otherwise be using to engage in focused work. It's not just the meetings themselves that hurt our productivity: a recent study from Ohio State University found that we tend to waste the time immediately *before* our meetings, too. People with upcoming commitments perceive their free time before-hand as more limited than it objectively is. "We seem to take a mental tax out of our time right before an appointment," explains one of the study's authors, Selin Malkoc. "As a result, we do less with the available time."

The workplace efficiency expert Edward G. Brown refers to all these inter-ruptions as "Time Bandits"—the people and obligations that steal our time and hurt our productivity, however well-intentioned they may be. While coordina-tion and collaboration are important, we also need to set aside blocks of quiet time for ourselves, when we can focus on the work in front of us.

Whenever I'm working on a big project that requires my full attention, I schedule a No-Contact Production Day. On that day, I set an out-of-office message for my email, and I don't take any meetings or phone calls. My col-leagues know how to reach me in an emergency; otherwise, I'm offline for the day. Knowing I'll be able to go the whole workday without interruptions allows me to clear mental space and sharpen my focus. I can fully immerse in my work, getting into a state of deep concentration that often eludes me on busier days.

No-Contact Production Days create a rhythm and flow for my work by separating the responsibilities of my job into individual tasks I can focus on one at a time. When I know I can carve out interruption-free time for focused work, I don't worry as much about interruptions or meetings on other days. This doesn't just make me a better worker—it also makes me a better colleague and boss.

Try It Out

Communicate with your supervisor and team. Be open about your needs. Say that you believe you'll be more productive and produce better work if you're able to reserve time to work without any interruptions. "Every Time Bandit has a Time Bandit," says Brown; in other words, everyone knows what it's like trying to get work done in the face of constant interruptions. By starting this dialogue, you may find that your colleagues are eager to get on board, too. If a full No-Contact Production Day feels daunting, start by requesting a two-hour block.

Try working remotely. Despite stereotypes of the lazy worker who loafs around at home when they don't have to come into the office, studies show that people who work from home are actually *more* productive than their colleagues in the office. There are a number of reasons for this: working from home saves transportation time, allows for fewer distractions from colleagues, and incentivizes workers to prove they're putting their time to good use. Working from home is ideal for No-Contact Production Days— that is, assuming you don't have anyone distracting you at home.

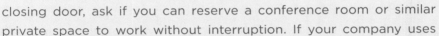

Reserve space for solo work. If your company doesn't have a telecommuting policy, and you don't have your own office with a closing door, ask if you can reserve a conference room or similar private space to work without interruption. If your company uses shared calendars, block out the time on your calendar to let your colleagues know that you're unavailable—and also where to find you in an emergency.

Avoid being your own Time Bandit. We're often our own worst interrupters, given how easy it is for us to get distracted by social media, email, texts, chatting with coworkers, and more. Maintain focus by committing to work on only one thing at a time, and take regular breaks to keep your mind fresh. (See Practice No. 48 to learn more about the multitasking myth.) You'll save time—and the mental energy of switching tasks—if you batch your work so that you move from one task to a similar one, and schedule your meetings to follow one another rather than spreading them out.

Take Vacations

IN 1910, President Taft announced that every working American ought to be granted two to three months' vacation per year, arguing that such lengthy respite was "necessary in order to enable one to continue his work the next year with that energy and effectiveness which it ought to have." If only! To this day, the United States remains the only advanced economy in the world that doesn't mandate *any* paid vacation for its workers. According to a recent report by the Center for Economic and Policy Research, while most full-time American workers receive some paid holidays and vacation days from their employers, only 40 percent of part-time workers get these benefits, and nearly a quarter of the country's workers have no paid time off at all. (By contrast, laws in the European Union, Australia, and New Zealand require a minimum of four weeks' paid vacation for all workers; Canada and Japan guarantee ten paid vacation days.)

Even when Americans *do* get vacation

time, we don't take it: more than half of Americans fail to use all of their vacation days each year. And it turns out that our days off aren't really so "off" after all:

many of us admit to carving out a few hours of each vacation day to do work, or taking work calls on holidays. It's no wonder one in five Americans say they "never fully relax" on vacation.

We can't blame it all on our bosses. Over the past few decades, millions of American workers have bought into the "cult of busy"—so much so that 59 percent of millennials report feeling "shame" for taking a vacation. A recent study by researchers from Columbia University, Harvard, and Georgetown found that when subjects were told a person was busy, they immediately perceived that person as more competent, ambitious, and successful. Whereas leisure and luxury goods were once aspirational status symbols, the new status symbol is having no time for leisure at all. "Like a rare gemstone, a busy individual is seen as in high demand and scarce," the researchers wrote in the *Journal of Consumer Research*.

The study describes a recent sea change in advertising campaigns: in the late eighties and nineties, Cadillac's "Only Way to Travel" commercials featured shots of polo matches, scenic road trips, and families playing together in parks and swimming pools and on tennis courts. By contrast, Cadillac's 2014 Super Bowl commercial opens with an actor turning away from a pristine, unused swimming pool and scoffing: "Other countries—they work, they stroll home, they stop by the café, they take August off—off! Why aren't you like that? Why aren't we like that? Because we are crazy, driven, hard-working believers, that's why!"

In fact, we should really take a tip from those "other countries," because we need to start taking our time off as seriously as we take our work. Studies show that vacations are crucial for our physical and mental health. They substantially decrease our risk of heart attacks and depression, lower our blood pressure, and improve our sleep. They also help with family cohesion: according to William Doherty, a University of Minnesota professor of family social science, "Vacations tend to create memories more than any other family activity." And vacations even improve our *work:* A study conducted by Ernst & Young found that an employee's performance rating improved 8 percent for every additional ten hours of vacation time she took. When the *Harvard Business Review* studied twelve thousand employees to find out what made people feel more engaged at work, one of the most popular responses was "opportunities to regularly renew and recharge."

When I started Getaway, I was committed to building a company that held work-life balance as one of its core values. So I was surprised by how hard it was to get folks who worked for the company to stop texting about work on weekends, sending emails late at night, and working too many hours in general. I quickly learned I had to set a clearer example, both by limiting my own bad behavior (like not checking email after hours) and by actively discouraging it in employees (like resisting the impulse to praise someone who clearly gave up their Sunday to work). Now I send a lot of emails to staff on vacation that read "Get offline!"

Cultivate honorable relationships, resist absentminded busyness, tell the world how to treat you, embrace enoughness, and more.
—Bertrand Russell

Try It Out

BEFORE YOU GO . . .

Schedule vacations in advance. If you keep waiting until "later" to re-quest time off, you may never get the chance. Flip through your calen-dar to find a time to get out of town—or at least to get away from work.

Get organized before you leave. For a guilt-free break, strive to complete important tasks and delegate ongoing work before your vacation begins.

Set your out-of-office auto-reply. Make sure to include another col-league's contact information for notifications that can't wait until your return. You may also want to ask a trusted coworker to monitor your inbox while you're away, just to make sure nothing crucial slips through the cracks.

WHILE YOU'RE AWAY . . .

Turn off notifications on your phone. Try to resist checking your work email entirely, but if you find yourself feeling *more* anxious that way, limit yourself to a quick scan of your inbox no more than once a day. Leave your phone behind whenever you can.

Don't overschedule your days. If you're traveling somewhere new, you might be tempted to pack your trip with sightseeing excursions and tours. Try to resist the impulse to schedule more than one

244 | BALANCE YOUR WORK

organized activity per day—remember how fleeting time off really is, and make sure you actually enjoy it.

Practice slowing down. Give yourself permission to sleep in. Linger over meals. Read a few chapters of a book in a single sitting. Go for a long walk. Let the hours of the day unfold slowly around you without worrying too much about what, or how much, you're accomplishing.

WHEN YOU GET BACK . . .

Block time for catching up. Keep your out-of-office auto-reply on for your first day back at work so that you can get up to speed with as few interruptions as possible.

Stick to your normal work hours. If you exhaust your-self trying to make up all the work you missed while you were away, you'll squander the benefits of your time off. There will always be more work to do no matter what, so go home at the usual time.

Keep up your best vacation de-stress routines. If you adopted relaxation rituals on vacation— long swims, meandering strolls, card games after dinner—try to maintain these activities once you're back.

Set Specific and Limited Goals for Every Workday

WHEN IT COMES to getting things done, making a list of daily goals is one of our oldest and most reliable productivity tools. In spite of this, we often fall short of our own best intentions. A 2012 LinkedIn survey found that only 11 percent of respondents manage to get through all the tasks on their list each day, and a review by the progress-tracking software I Done This revealed that 41 percent of the tasks on its users' lists are *never* completed.

It's hard to beat the feeling of pride and accomplishment that comes from checking off everything on your list. To improve your odds, experts recommend making sure your goals are specific, realistic, and *limited.* If you make an epic to-do list, you'll only end up overwhelmed. Researchers have found that most people have about three to six hours of truly productive time in any day, and our concentration tends to wane around the fifty-minute mark. We need to take regular breaks to stay sharp, and no matter how carefully we plan, unexpected distractions will inevitably pop up to interrupt us. (As an old Yiddish proverb goes, *Der Mentsch Tracht, un Gott Lacht*—"Man plans, and God laughs.")

CALL PETE!

It may take some trial and error to figure out how much you can reasonably accomplish over the course of the average workday. If you narrow your focus to just a few significant goals per day (and allow yourself a margin of error for unexpected interruptions), you'll likely be more focused, more productive, and more satisfied at the end of each day.

In a 1981 article, the business consultant George T. Doran introduced the concept of SMART goals. Doran wrote that goals should be:

SPECIFIC
What do you want to accomplish? Why does it matter? Who is involved?

MEASURABLE
What are the component parts? How will you know when the goal is reached?

ACHIEVABLE
Is the goal realistic given your available time and resources?

RELEVANT
Is this the best use of your time and energy right now? Does it help to move your project or related goals forward in a concrete way?

TIME-BOUND
What is your deadline? What do you need to accomplish today? What do you need to accomplish over the next week, month, or six months?

In the decades since, some business leaders have come to feel that SMART goals are outdated for today's fast-paced, fluid work environments. Entrepreneur and Olympic gold medalist Adam Kreek has proposed an updated system of CLEAR goals:

COLLABORATIVE
Who are you working with? What support do you need? Who are you serving?

LIMITED
When does your goal begin and end? What constraints may limit your ability to achieve it? Are you being realistic?

EMOTIONAL
Does the goal serve your purpose? Will it feel fulfilling? Are you dedicated to achieving it?

APPRECIABLE
Is your goal actionable? Can you break it down into smaller component parts? What is the first step? What significant milestones can you track along the way?

REFINABLE
What factors might change as you work toward your goal? Can you adapt and revise your goal to accommodate new information or issues beyond your control?

Try It Out

Lay out your daily goals the night before. "If you're waiting until the morning to organize your day, it's too late; the day is already crashing down upon you," warns Julie Morgenstern, the author of *Never Check E-Mail in the Morning*. Making your list the previous night will save you time and mental energy in the morning.

Apply the 1-3-5 Rule to your to-do list. "On any given day, assume that you can only accomplish one big thing, three medium things, and five small things," writes Alex Cavoulacos, a cofounder of *The Muse* and coauthor (with Kathryn Minshew) of *The New Rules of Work*. If you tend to field a lot of unexpected or last-minute requests over the course of your workday, Cavoulacos suggests leaving a few tasks on your list blank to give yourself a buffer.

Break large tasks into smaller actions. Doing so reduces your risk of procrastinating because you're overwhelmed or don't know where to begin. The narrower and more descriptive your tasks are, the easier it will be for you to dive into them. Avoid vague catchall words like "plan" and "develop" in favor of concrete action items like "enter new contacts into database."

Take care of your worst tasks first. Mark Twain famously said, "Eat a live frog first thing in the morning and nothing worse will happen to you the rest of the day." Kick off your day by tackling the task you're dreading most. (It probably can't be worse than eating a live frog.) Putting it behind you will be a relief and boost your morale moving forward.

Synchronize your list with your calendar. Writing out your goals in a list won't do you any good if you haven't scheduled time for them. Designate blocks of time in your calendar for making progress on the specific items on your to-do list. Check in with yourself routinely to make sure you're being realistic about how much time you allocate to each task, and adjust as needed.

Take breaks. No matter how busy you are, you need to take regular breaks in order to keep your mind sharp and focused. When you feel your concentration beginning to flag, get up from your desk and do a few stretches, take a short walk, or get a drink or snack. Working in intervals fol-

September 20
Friday

10 AM — clean out inbox
11 AM — meet with James
12 AM — Lunch Break
1 PM
2 PM — Design event materials
3 PM
4 PM — afternoon break
5 PM — meeting with marketing team
6 PM

lowed by breaks can improve your focus and productivity. (See Practice No. 49 for more information.)

Create a fresh list every day. Even if you don't check off everything on your list by the end of the day, don't recycle or add to the old list—start a brand-new one for the next day. Your priorities change from day to day, and your list should reflect that.

Separate Your Work Life from Your Social Life

IN THE EARLY DAYS of Getaway, in an effort to be close to what we were building and learn as much as possible, we moved our team to a cobwebby old house in the Catskill Mountains of New York, near our tiny cabins. The house was both our office and our home; our co-workers were also our roommates. So, of course, our lives and work were indistinguishable. We talked about the broken refrigerator during meetings. We talked about the latest website launch during dinner. I tried instituting a "No Work Talk After 7:00 p.m." rule to create some semblance of work-life balance, but it was an ongoing challenge. When your work, social life, and leisure are in the same place with the same people, it's impossible to draw hard lines between them.

It didn't take us long to put an end to that experiment, though we still make an effort to maintain our "No Email, Calls, or Texts After Hours" policy. But for many companies, the culture of mixing leisure with work has become the norm. Google was a pioneer in the field of workplace perks, and lots of other companies have followed the tech giant's lead, offering employees free meals, coffee bars, foosball and Ping-Pong tables in common areas, on-site gyms, dry-cleaning services, and more.

These amenities are designed not only to make us like a workplace but to make us stay at work longer. Why leave work to go to the gym when there's a state-of-the-art gym at work? Explaining why she'd spent her day off in the office, one Google employee told *The New York Times,* "I live in a studio apartment. And I don't have free food."

While workplace perks may distract us for a little while, they can end up feeling coercive. According to Dr. Barbara Plester of Auckland University, only one in five people have a good time at "fun" events their employers organize. And activities designed to stimulate employee bonding aren't very effective. As Columbia professors Paul Ingram and Michael W. Morris discovered in a study called "Do People Mix at Mixers?"—they don't. After outfitting participants with electronic name tags and tracking their movements at a party, the researchers found that the partygoers generally stuck close to people they already knew, "even though they overwhelmingly stated before the event that their goal was to meet new people."

Work can be a lot of things—fulfilling, productive, meaningful—but it shouldn't have to be fun. When we feel good about our work, that feeling should come from our motivation and sense of pride for the work itself. Let's reserve our fun for when we're *not* working.

Try It Out

Don't mistake "perks" for "benefits." An easy way to tell the difference between perks and benefits is that perks make it easier or more appealing to spend longer hours at work, whereas benefits are designed to make your life *outside* work more sustainable. These include things such as health insurance, paid vacation and sick time, contributions to your retirement account, and paid parental leave. Think of it this way: perks ultimately serve your employer; benefits serve *you.*

Leave the office for happy hour. Maintaining a healthy balance between your work and social life doesn't mean you can't hang out with your coworkers when you're off the clock—but it shouldn't feel like an extension of your workday. The company Kegerator.com suggests that employers install kegerators in their offices in order to "bring the bar to the meeting." I disagree: your office doesn't need a kegerator any more than a bar needs a Xerox machine. If you want to share a beer with coworkers at the end of the day, leave your office and head to a bar.

At happy hour, leave work-talk at the office. When we're socializing with our colleagues after hours, we're probably still talking about work, thanks to a phenomenon called the "common information effect"—the tendency to gravitate toward, and prioritize, subjects we have in common. The next time you and your coworkers go for drinks, suggest making work-talk off-limits. Talking about subjects beyond work will give you an

opportunity to get to know your colleagues as *people*. If you find that you don't have much in common beyond work, you may want to reevaluate how much of your leisure time you're spending with them.

Set your schedule around your personal time. Make personal or family time a priority rather than something you squeeze in between work commitments. If you feel anxious or guilty about setting work aside, remember that the restorative benefits of leisure time will actually improve your creativity and productivity.

Add downtime to your calendar. It may not feel natural to input something so basic into your calendar. But it probably doesn't feel natural to answer work calls during your evening walk

> Downtime ⬤

through the park, either! Downtime should help you decompress from work and relax. Resist the urge to get distracted, or skip downtime altogether, by giving yourself rules: Reading a book or the newspaper might be okay; scrolling Instagram might not be. Do your best to hold yourself accountable.

Turn Meetings into Walking Meetings

GETAWAY'S HEADQUARTERS IS A ten-minute walk from Fort Greene Park in Brooklyn. The park is named for a Revolutionary War general, Nathanael Greene, who oversaw a military fort on the site. Today, the park—designed by Central Park's landscape architects Frederick Law Olmsted and Calvert Vaux—features rolling hills, trees, walking paths, tennis courts, and the towering column of the Prison Ship Martyrs Monument, a tribute to the men and women who died in captivity on British ships during the war.

> All truly great thoughts are conceived while walking.
> —Friedrich Nietzsche

I tend to get stir-crazy if I have too many meetings in our conference room, so for one-on-ones, I like to ask if we can go for a walk in the park. Since we print out everything we need for meetings to avoid relying on our screens, it's easy to grab the relevant pages and head for the door.

I'm not just looking for an excuse to go outside. (Okay, that, too.) Researchers have found that we think better when we're walking. Moving our bodies elevates our heart rate, circulating additional blood and oxygen through the body and brain. When we do it regularly, walking can stimulate neuron growth and connections between brain cells. And a recent study at Stanford University found a clear connection between walking and creativity: subjects who were asked to perform creative tasks and problem-solving tests did much better when they were out walking than when they were sitting still. The researchers believe that this is because walking doesn't require much conscious effort, which leaves our minds open to wander, activating the neural network responsible for associative thinking and flashes of insight.

Other studies have found that spending time in green spaces like parks and forests can lower our stress and anxiety levels while improving our concentration, energy, and mood. I've found that going on walking meetings makes the dynamic between my colleagues and me feel more comfortable and casual—it's way easier to open up when you're walking side by side through the trees, rather than squaring off across a conference table. When conversation flows freely, we tend to be more productive. Besides, a change of scenery is a great way to inspire fresh ideas. And yes, I admit it—it's nice to leave the office and get outside.

Methinks that the moment my legs begin to move,
my thoughts begin to flow.
—Henry David Thoreau

Try It Out

Be mindful of your surroundings. Your walking meeting won't be as effective if you have to shout to be heard. Try to avoid areas with traffic, construction, and heavy pedestrian congestion—head for parks or quiet side streets instead.

Bring portable materials. Print out any documents you'll need for your meeting, so you won't need to rely on your smartphone. Bring a pocket notebook and pen for jotting down notes on the go. If you don't have a chance to take notes during your walk, reserve five to ten minutes for notetaking after you return to the office, when ideas are still fresh.

Keep it small. Walking meetings work best with two people, or three at the most; otherwise it will turn into a parade.

Have fun! Studies show that workers who take walking meetings are more satisfied with their jobs than those who don't, so enjoy this opportunity to get fresh air and exercise while taking care of business!

PRACTICE NO. 58

End Your Workday with a Workout Class

THANKS TO MY colleague Rachel for this tip. It can be tough getting out of the office at the end of the workday. There are always more emails to respond to, calendars to update, coworkers with "quick questions," reports to finish, and items to cross off your to-do list. If you're one of those people who consistently finds yourself stuck at your desk long after you meant to leave, try signing up for an after-work exercise class.

Adding planned exercise sessions to your end-of-day schedule allows you to accomplish multiple goals at once. First, it gives you an excuse—not just an excuse, an *obligation*—to leave work on time. If you're expected somewhere else, you'll be less likely to linger over your inbox or entertain last-minute questions from colleagues. Exercise classes start at a set time: you can't exactly text to ask your spin instructor to wait twenty minutes for you to wrap up a project, the way you might when meeting friends for happy hour.

Second, it creates a transitional space for you to move out of your work-mind and into your downtime. You're in a different place, surrounded by different people, with a different purpose: to take care of your body. While work worries might not disappear entirely, going to an exercise class forces you to shift focus and concentrate on something else, at least for the duration of the session.

Speaking of work worries, what's better than converting that anxious energy into sweat, muscle strengthening, and burned calories? Exercise circulates oxygen and nutrients throughout your body, which is especially useful if you've been sitting all day. The endorphin rush of a workout will improve your mood while lowering your stress, allowing you to decompress before heading home for the evening. The benefits of exercise are cumulative: over time, consistent workouts will give you an energy boost by day and help you sleep more soundly at night.

Finally, signing up for a workout class will make you more likely to commit to a regular fitness routine, which is important for your overall health and well-being. Researchers have found that working out in groups creates "positive peer pressure" that encourages exercisers to show up and push themselves harder, increasing their workout time and intensity by as much as 200 percent. "For most people, it's difficult to stay consistent with workout routines, but having a certain group there waiting for you provides you with the motivation and accountability everyone needs to be successful," trainer Michael Yabut told NBC News. Numerous studies also show that people who exercise with others feel more inspired and enjoy their workouts more.

So next time you're tempted to stay late at work, work *out* instead—it's good for you, and it will make you feel good, too.

Try It Out

Join a gym near your workplace. You'll be more likely to commit to after-work exercise if you don't need to travel a long way to get there. Most gyms have class offerings throughout the day; look at the class schedule before joining to ensure that you'll be able to get the most out of a membership. You may want to check with your employer before beginning your search, since some companies offer discounted gym memberships (as well as other wellness-related benefits) to their employees.

Choose a class that feels right for you. If you tend to have a lot of energy at the end of the day, you may want to sign up for a cardio-centric class. If you worry that a high-intensity evening workout will make it hard for you to sleep, look into yoga, Pilates, or strength-training classes.

Try a gym alternative. If joining a gym sounds like your personal nightmare, there are lots of other ways to get exercise after work, including dance classes, rock climbing and bouldering, swimming, kayaking, and boxing. You could also join a running, biking, or hiking club that offers evening activities. The most important thing is to choose an activity that makes you feel good and that you'll want to commit to.

Socialize while you sweat. Joining an exercise class is a great way to expand your social circle and meet new friends. "There's a bond that is created when a group struggles, sweats, fights, and grinds their way through a tough workout," says Yabut. Nothing creates camaraderie like a shared challenge. You'll have an opportunity to meet people with careers and passions beyond your usual social circle, which can lead to enduring friendships.

PART 5

Balance Your Downtime

IN HIS 1948 philosophy treatise *Leisure: The Basis of Culture*, the German theologian Josef Pieper observed that we treat work as the center of our culture. We tend to overvalue activity for its own sake—the idea that we must always be doing something—and what he called "the social function of work," the notion that our worth comes from how useful we are to one another. Pieper wondered: What if we valued leisure in the same way? When we experience deep leisure, we escape our inner frenzy and enter into a more open and receptive relationship with the world around us. For Pieper, leisure is not simply spare time, a weekend, a vacation, or a stretch of non-activity. It is an "attitude of the mind and a condition of the soul." And it's more than just a break from work, designed to reenergize us for more work. "The essence of leisure," Pieper writes, "is not to assure that we may function smoothly but rather to assure that we, embedded in our social function, are enabled to remain fully human." Even if you love what you do for work, you are more than your labor. When you make space for leisure and the experiences that bring you pleasure—whether that means going hiking, making art, stargazing, or sleeping in—you honor the qualities that make you who you are and create the conditions to thrive in all aspects of your life.

Complete a Word or Number Puzzle

YOU MAY HAVE heard that "brain games" like crossword puzzles and Sudoku can improve cognition and even prevent Alzheimer's disease. Sounds great, but is it true? "Yes and no," says the cognitive neurologist Sandra Bond Chapman. "Brain games improve the specific function that is being trained," Dr. Chapman explains, so making a regular habit of filling in crossword and Sudoku squares will almost certainly improve your crossword and Sudoku skills. But there isn't much evidence to suggest these brain games significantly improve cognitive function or ward off dementia. If you're interested in boosting brain health long-term, researchers say, it's better to pursue activities that offer continuous new challenges, like learning a new language, photography, or even gardening.

But that's no reason to give *up* these classic puzzles. While they may not prevent us from growing forgetful in old age, they offer plenty of benefits to us now. For starters, they're fun, readily available, and transportable, making them popular with commuters who use them to wake up or wind down at the end of the workday. (They're also popular with celebrities: the cellist Yo-Yo Ma, the quarterback Brett Favre, the actor Natalie Portman, and the former president Bill Clinton are all committed crossword fans, to name just a few.) By giving us a single low-stakes task to focus on, these puzzles temporarily take our minds off other worries and preoccupations—which can in turn lower our stress levels and help us relax. Crosswords can improve our vocabulary and verbal fluency, and the feeling of accomplishment we get from completing a puzzle can boost our self-esteem.

```
D O W E C R N F R S
M S Z B E A J I T E
P N V H X F B L U K
Y T N E O U A I L R
S B R A I N O C N T
W S O L Z I T T B H
T N V T X U S L T K
M S A H Y L E I T E
P O Q E T R N A R S
```

We may get even more out of these puzzles when we work to complete them in groups. "Although the crossword seems engineered for solo consumption, it's just as important in its social function," writes Adrienne Raphel in her new exploration of crosswords and culture, *Thinking Inside the Box*. (Raphel is also the creator of this book's original crossword puzzle, "Off the Grid, On the Grid," which you can find on pages 268–69. The answer key is on page 272.)

Researchers have found that collaborating on puzzles can improve participants'

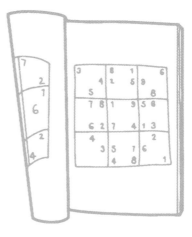

problem-solving and strategic-thinking skills, encourage creativity, and strengthen social bonds. "The crossword draws already close people still closer together, letting their brains sync as they solve," writes Raphel. "It gives people a way to interact who otherwise might have nothing in common."

Three years ago, when Michael and I were living in Catskill, New York, getting the second Getaway Outpost off the ground, we bought a book of *New York Times* crosswords for $9.99 at Inquiring Mind Bookstore in the nearby town of Saugerties. It was the best ten bucks we've ever spent. We've since gotten a second book, and we subscribe to the *Times* weekend edition, so every Sunday we do the crossword, usually at the end of the day as we're winding down and getting ready to fall asleep. I used to be intimidated by crosswords—I'd get stuck on clues and think, *There's no way I'm going to figure out who the King of Prussia was.* But I've learned to trust that some of the answers will work themselves out. And it's nice quality time to spend together: relaxing, sort of mindless, and productively distracting from life's many worries.

cruciverbalist (n.) cru·ci·ver·bal·ist | \ ˌkrüsəˈvərbələst\ :
a person skillful in creating or solving crossword puzzles
(Merriam-Webster)

Off the Grid, On the Grid

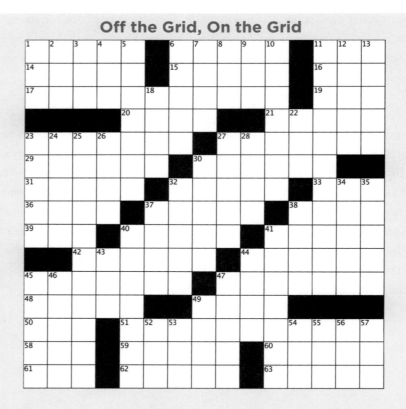

ACROSS

1. Plant _____ (suggest; or, literally, plant something!)
6. Dark weather
11. Philosophy
14. Guy
15. Author Lois (The Giver)
16. Austin to Dallas dir.
17. Autumn color seekers
19. Indian lentil dish
20. What you might use to solve crosswords, if you're bold
21. _____ up (prepare)
23. Splash pools

27. How a black diamond trail might rise
29. Parenthetical comments
30. What Richard III offered "my kingdom" for
31. Oxidizes
32. Like a slug's trail
33. Tarheel state, in multiple
36. Egg containers
37. Spoke like a sailor
38. Eve's man
39. "Mr. Blue Sky" band
40. Time on the job
41. Tableau
42. Not at all
44. Carbolic acid
45. Delights
47. Seasons, for one
48. A dandelion, for example
49. Catch a wave
50. Business end?
51. Moments in your Getaway cabin after long hikes
58. Rent out
59. Holy one
60. Wipe out
61. Graduating grp.
62. Uber-cozy
63. Pitted fruits

DOWN
1. CIO's partner
2. Intuit
3. She, in Portuguese
4. Woodland sprite
5. Speckles, as on a horse
6. Narrow valleys
7. Cuts off
8. Be in debt to
9. Bruin Bobby
10. Cozy thing to curl up with on a dark and stormy night . . . if you dare
11. How you'll feel at a Getaway, instead of needing all your screens
12. Mobile home resident?
13. Like marshmallows on hot cocoa
18. Huge shoe sizes
22. Certain plural ending
23. Analyze grammatically
24. Same old, same old
25. What one does vis-a-vis one's smartphone at a Getaway cabin
26. Banned insecticides
27. Button-down or polo

28. The Complete Works of Shakespeare, e. g.
30. Not together
32. Roll or Miss
34. Summer camp craft
35. Small silvery fish
37. Mix in
38. One who crushes tests, say
40. Type of fish, maybe
41. Given the short end of the stick
43. Words of praise
44. Cat's sound of contentment
45. Cries of agony
46. Titleholder
47. "And I _____"
49. Bird call
52. Aye's opposite
53. Archaeological site
54. Lyricist Gershwin
55. Downward-facing dog site
56. Portland, OR, to Atlanta, GA, dir.
57. French possessive

Try It Out

Keep it classic with paper and pencil. While you can download a plethora of puzzle apps to your phone, you'll reap more stress-relieving benefits—and probably more satisfaction—the old-fashioned way, using a pencil to fill in a puzzle on paper. Most major newspapers feature daily crossword and Sudoku puzzles, but if you don't subscribe to a print newspaper, you can invest in a puzzle book (available in bookstores and at supermarket checkout counters) to keep you well stocked for weeks or months to come. Use a pencil rather than a pen so you can risk guesses and mistakes.

Use puzzles as a mental refresher during the workday. There's plenty of evidence that taking breaks throughout the day can keep our minds fresh, help renew focus, and improve productivity. If you're feeling stuck on a project, take a few minutes off to fill in a puzzle. Concentrating on something different, even briefly, can give you the critical distance you need to return to your project with fresh ideas.

Collaborate or compete. Turn this solo activity social by pulling in friends and family to help you finish a puzzle. Sharing strategies can help individuals become more effective and creative problem solvers, and when it comes to crosswords, it can be fun to learn which obscure information is lodged in your companions' memories. Alternatively, add stakes to your game by making copies of a single puzzle and seeing who can solve it first.

Take It Further

If you're an expert crossword or Sudoku solver, challenge yourself to create an original puzzle. You can even download software for constructing your grid: www.beekeeperlabs.com/crossfire and www.crossword-compiler.com are popular options for novices as well as pros. Not sure how to get started? Raphel suggests choosing a theme and thinking of three to five long "anchor" words or phrases that fit the theme. Wordplay is the key to a crossword's fun, so get creative. (For instance, a 2005 *New York Times* crossword included five answers that ended in parts of a tree: "squareroot," "tableleaf," "wardrobetrunk," "brainstem," and "bankbranch.") Once you have your anchors in place on the grid, start filling in around them. When coming up with answer words, "Think of common Scrabble letters," Raphel recommends. "A, S, E, and T are going to help. If you have words with J and Z, that's going to be hard." Crossword creation involves a lot of trial and error, even for seasoned cruciverbalists. To save time and frustration, get all of your words set on the grid before you start writing clues.

Go the Distance

Create an original crossword as a unique and memorable birthday or special-occasion card by including answers that have personal meaning for your recipient. Or take a tip from former *Daily Show* host Jon Stewart, who enlisted the help of *New York Times* crossword editor Will Shortz to create a marriage proposal crossword for his now-wife, Tracey.

Go Forest Bathing

IF YOU WANT to really immerse yourself in nature—while reaping benefits like reduced stress, lower blood pressure, and improved focus, memory, and immune function—consider taking a forest bath.

The term comes from Japan, where the phrase *shinrin-yoku* was coined in the 1980s to describe the practice of "taking in the forest atmosphere," or "forest bathing" for short. Originally, *shinrin-yoku* was aimed at encouraging

Japanese citizens to make use of the country's expansive network of forest trails. Then, in 1990, Chiba University researcher Yoshifumi Miyazaki decided to investigate whether the activity led to any measurable health benefits. Dr. Miyazaki sent one group of volunteers to walk for forty minutes in a laboratory and another group to walk for the same amount of time on a forest trail. When he tested each group's stress hormone levels after their walks, he found that the forest walkers had much lower levels of stress than their laboratory

counterparts. Forest bathing became a beloved national pastime in Japan, and in recent years, the practice has gone global.

So what exactly *is* forest bathing? It's not hiking, but walking doesn't really capture it, either. To take a forest bath is to stroll through the woods while paying close attention to your senses. Your goal is to slow down, quiet your mind, and take in the sights, sounds, scents, textures (and occasionally tastes) of the forest. Dr. Qing Li, president of Japan's Society of Forest Medicine, says that *shinrin-yoku* "bridges the gap between us and the natural world."

When researchers tested whether a forest or a hospital was the best place to recover from depression, they found that the forest group's improvement rate was almost three times higher than the hospital group's. Better still, trees and plants release chemicals called phytoncides, which boost our immune function by increasing the activity of the white blood cells our body uses to fight tumors and infections.

You don't need a guide to try forest bathing—and in truth, you don't even need a *forest*. According to Dr. Li, "Once you have learned how to do it, you can do *shinrin-yoku* anywhere—in a nearby park or in your garden. Look for a place where there are trees, and off you go!"

Between every two pine trees there is a door
leading to a new way of life.
—John Muir

Wildness reminds us what it means to be human, what we are connected to rather than what we are separate from.
—Terry Tempest Williams

Try It Out

Find an outdoor space that makes you feel peaceful and relaxed. While you don't need to be in total isolation, you'll want to avoid crowded places. If you love the sound of running water, see if you can start your forest bath near a river or stream. If the smell of damp soil makes you happy, seek out a shady grove.

Leave your cell phone behind. Even better, leave behind as much as you can. The fewer possessions you're carrying, the more you'll be able to focus on the feeling of your body moving through the landscape. Don't worry about where you're going; let your senses and curiosity be your guide.

Open your senses. Listen for birds and the rustling of leaves. Look at the different colors of foliage and the pattern of shadows from sunlight through the branches. Inhale to smell and taste the aroma of the soil, moss, and trees. Press your hands against tree trunks to feel the texture of the bark; sit or lie on the ground to get a fresh perspective. **Take your time.** Unlike a hike or even a walk, you're not trying to get from Point A to Point B. You might not wander more than a few dozen yards in any direction. The goal is to open yourself up to the landscape and let it work its gentle magic to relax and restore you.

Take It Further

If you want to brush up on basics before heading out on your own, consider signing up for a guided forest bathing session. Certified Forest Therapy guides offer private and group sessions throughout the United States and worldwide. Think of it like an in-motion meditation session—the guide will provide you with information and strategies to get the most out of your experience.

Make Art

ART-MAKING IS A regular part of our lives when many of us are growing up. We make sculptures out of Play-Doh and clay, string beads into necklaces, finger-paint and use watercolors, sing in the school chorus, learn to play simple songs on the recorder. But as we get older, folks who pursue careers in the arts often specialize in one form or another, and those of us who don't consider ourselves "real artists" often fall out of the habit of making any art at all. As Pablo Picasso once observed, "Every child is an artist. The problem is how to remain an artist once he grows up."

It's a problem worth trying to solve, because art (both making it and consuming it) can enrich our lives in lots of ways. Art has the power to change how we see and experience the world around us. Making art allows us to explore other sides of ourselves and even surprise ourselves. It can also be an important mode of self-expression: a way of translating our thoughts, experiences, and emotions into new forms, then using those forms to connect with others.

You don't have to possess any special talent or formal education to make art. You just have to be willing to try it out. A former boyfriend and I used to make regular trips to Michaels to buy canvases, paint, and brushes. Then we'd experiment with what we could make. No one would've called our paintings masterpieces (except possibly our moms), but we had fun and ended up with work that was decent enough to hang on our walls. "There's no diploma in the world that declares you as an artist—it's not like becoming a doctor," says the artist Kara Walker. "You can declare yourself an artist and then figure out how to be an artist." Even if you're never able to paint like Michelangelo or compose like Bach or dance like Martha Graham, everyone has creative potential. Once you tap into it, it can benefit you in surprising ways.

Researchers have found that making art can reduce anxiety and stress. It can improve focus and memory: a study in the journal *Applied Cognitive Psychology* found that people who doodle when bored tend to remember the boring information better than those who don't. Making art can also strengthen connections in the brain known as the default mode network, the system engaged with thinking about the past and planning for the future. It can make us more resilient and help us to cope with grief by giving us a way to explore and process feelings that are hard to articulate. And according to the psychologist Mihaly Csikszentmihalyi, getting immersed in an art project allows us to enter a "flow state," which he describes as the "optimal state of consciousness where we feel our best and perform our best."

Of course, we don't need to make art just because it's *good* for us. "I make art primarily because I enjoy the process," Academy Award–winning Pixar animator and director Pete Docter told *Greater Good Magazine*. "It's fun making things."

Artists on Art

Edward Hopper, painter: "If I could say it in words, there would be no reason to paint."

Kwame Dawes, poet: "I want to somehow communicate my sense of the world—that way of understanding, engaging, experiencing the world—to somebody else. I want them to be transported into the world that I have created with language. The ultimate aim of my writing is to create an environment of empathy."

Miles Davis, musician: "I'm always thinking about creating. My future starts when I wake up in the morning and see the light."

Agnes Martin, painter: "Art is the concrete representation of our most subtle feelings."

James Baldwin, writer: "All art is a kind of confession, more or less oblique. All artists, if they are to survive, are forced, at last, to tell the whole story; to vomit the anguish up."

Louise Bourgeois, sculptor: "Every day you have to abandon your past or accept it, and then, if you cannot accept it, you become a sculptor."

Try It Out

Carry a blank notebook for inspiration. Make a conscious effort to notice and record the things that interest and inspire you. Use your notebook as a pressure-free space to jot down rough ideas and

sketches. Or take pictures on your smartphone or a camera to create a visual diary.

Carve out time. Developing an artistic practice is like developing any other skill: it requires dedicated time. "Stay firmly in your path and dare; be wild two hours a day!" advised the Postimpressionist painter Paul Gauguin. If you can't find two hours in your daily schedule for artistic wildness, start by reserving at least one hour a week.

Be creative anywhere. When it comes to making art, the sky's the limit: you don't need to be sitting in front of an easel, a potter's wheel, or a grand piano. The British landscape artist Andy Goldsworthy creates temporary installations using materials he finds in the natural world—leaves, branches, rocks, ice, moss. The experimental composer John Cage's famous "4'33"" instructs performers *not* to play their instruments for the duration of the piece, forcing the audience to become aware of the ambient noises in the surrounding environment. In the Chinese practice of *dishu,* calligraphers use brushes and water to paint evaporating forms on sidewalks. You can make art from anything you can imagine—gum wrappers, tire tracks, or the movement of your own body.

Take a class. Signing up for an art class will force you to commit to a regular artistic practice, at least for the duration of the course. Take the opportunity to improve on a skill you've practiced before, or try something brand new.

Give yourself permission to make bad art. Julia Cameron, the author of the bestselling creativity guide *The Artist's Way,* keeps a sign in her workspace that reads: I AM WILLING TO MAKE BAD ART. That doesn't mean she's *planning* to make bad art, Cameron explains to visitors who are taken aback by the sign. But, she says, "we must not deny ourselves the dignity of growth. . . . By being willing to make bad art, I am free to make any art—and often, art that is very good. Willing to make 'bad' art, what we actually are is *willing to make progress.*"

Make art social. Instead of throwing a dinner party or meeting at the bar, invite friends over for a craft night. Get some basic supplies (like drawing and construction paper, colored pencils and pens, watercolors, glue, etc.) and encourage people to contribute their own craft materials.

Getaway runs an Artist Fellowship program, providing a free overnight stay in one of our tiny cabins to artists looking to harness their talents in a focused environment surrounded by nature. We use the term "artist" loosely: anyone involved in creative work is considered a good candidate for the fellowship. Writers, illustrators, chefs, game makers, poets, sculptors, composers, urban planners, musicians, and more are all welcome to apply. Visit www.getaway.house/artist to fill out an application.

Visit a State or National Park

IF YOU LIVE in or near a city, it can be easy to forget that our sprawling country encompasses a wealth of diverse landscapes: dense forests and snow-capped mountain ranges, arid deserts and canyons, volcanoes and glaciers, vast rivers and lakes, thousands of miles of coastline. Much of this beautiful wilderness can be explored through our na-

tional park system, which comprises nearly eighty-five million acres of protected land. The writer and historian Wallace Stegner called our national parks "the best idea we ever had. Absolutely American, absolutely democratic, they reflect us at our best rather than our worst."

Thank Teddy Roosevelt. The twenty-sixth president might be best known for his foreign policy motto, "Speak softly and carry a big stick," but Roosevelt was also a passionate conservationist who used his time in office to create the US Forest Service and protect over 230 million acres of public land. Drawing inspiration from the naturalist John Muir, who persuaded Roosevelt to preserve

Those who contemplate the beauty of the earth find reserves of strength that will endure as long as life lasts. There is something infinitely healing in the repeated refrains of nature—the assurance that dawn comes after night, and spring after winter.

—Rachel Carson

the Yosemite wilderness during a three-day camping trip, Roosevelt's administration established 150 national forests, fifty-one federal bird reserves, four national game preserves, five national parks, and eighteen national monuments—more than all of his predecessors combined. In 1916, President Woodrow Wilson expanded on this legacy by creating the National Park Service (NPS), and today the United States boasts over four hundred park sites, including nearly 2,500 historic landmarks and sixty-one formally designated National Parks.

From the Florida Everglades to Denali in Alaska, the United States park system offers something for everyone. Rock climbers make pilgrimages to scale the sheer granite face of Half Dome in Yosemite, while cave enthusiasts get their spelunking fix in the passageways and chambers of Mammoth Cave National Park in Kentucky. Park visitors can try out whitewater rafting at the Grand Canyon or sandboarding at Great Sand Dune National Park in Colorado. If you aren't an adrenaline junkie, parks nationwide offer bike and

hiking trails, campsites and cabins, archaeological sites, educational programming, and plenty of spots to sit back and enjoy a pristine view of the wilderness. Best of all, visiting them won't break the bank. While day rates vary from park to park, an annual US Park Pass costs just $80, admits a full family (including up to four adults), and can be shared among friends.

Try It Out

Explore your local landscape. With 418 park sites across fifty states and territories, including Puerto Rico, American Samoa, and the US Virgin Islands, you won't have to venture far from home to find a  park. Visit the NPS's website (www.nps.gov) for a state-by-state listing of parks, monuments, preserves, and heritage areas.

Time your trip. If you have a flexible schedule, you may want to avoid visiting parks in the summer, which is peak tourist season. If summer is your only free time, try scoping out less popular trails and attractions to avoid crowds, or plan your visit during off-hours, like early morning or dusk.

Do your homework. Before venturing off into the wilderness, do some research into the various offerings of the park you plan to visit. You can usually learn the difficulty of different hikes, the relative comfort of campsites, and the best places to swim or watch the

sunset before you arrive, which will help you to make the most of your time.

Travel light. When visiting a park, you want to focus your attention on the landscape around you, not your stuff. Avoid packing anything that you'd be devastated to damage or lose. *Do* make sure to bring layers, bug spray, sunscreen, a water bottle or two, and a flashlight or head-lamp, even if you're not planning to be out after dark.

Check in with park rangers. When you enter a park, stop by the visitors' center and speak to a ranger. They can provide valuable information about road and trail closures, weather and animal warnings, and more.

Practice LNT (Leave No Trace). Leave No Trace means striving to leave trails, campsites, and other outdoor spaces better than you found them in or-der to protect the landscape's biodiversity and en-sure its continued existence for future generations. The Center for Outdoor Ethics lists seven principles for minimizing impact on the natural world: 1) Plan ahead and prepare; 2) Travel and camp on du-rable surfaces; 3) Dispose of waste properly; 4) Leave what you find; 5) Minimize campfire impacts; 6) Respect wildlife; and 7) Be consid-erate of other visitors.

Take It Further

Dig into History with a Shared Heritage Itinerary. The NPS has teamed up with the National Conference of State Historic Preservation Officers, along with state and local organizations, to create travel itineraries based on historic and cultural legacies of the United States. The itineraries—which include "Where Women Made History," "Asian American and Pacific Islander Heritage," "Sites of Aviation," "The Amistad Story," "Florida Shipwrecks," and more—combine travel tips and site-specific history lessons.

The environment, after all, is where we all meet, where we all have a mutual interest. It is one thing that all of us share. It is not only a mirror of ourselves, but a focusing lens on what we can become.

—Lady Bird Johnson

Complete a Jigsaw Puzzle

I RECENTLY WENT on vacation, and when I got back to work, I discovered that my Getaway colleagues had special-ordered a large jigsaw puzzle featuring a goofy photo of me. (Mildly embarrassing, to say the least!) They set it out on a table in the middle of our office, thinking puzzles would be a nice diversion for anyone in need of a break during the workday. Sometimes I'll see a few of my coworkers hovering over it, fitting pieces together while having a sidebar conversation. It's been coming together pretty slowly—most of it is still in pieces—though unsurprisingly, my colleagues managed to assemble the "Jon section" of the puzzle right away.

You might not know it from the puzzle in our office, but the first jigsaw puzzles were prized as educational tools. In 1766, the English mapmaker and engraver John Spilsbury glued a map of Europe onto a wooden board, then cut out the shape of each country. Teachers used Spilsbury's multipiece map for geography lessons, with their students learning the location of each country by fitting the pieces back together.

By the early twentieth century, jigsaw puzzles had

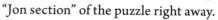
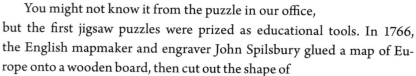

become a popular pastime for adults as well as children. During the Great Depression, many turned to puzzles as an inexpensive source of entertainment, a way to feel a degree of escapism and accomplishment during hard times. By 1933, people were buying puzzles at the incredible rate of ten million per week.

While we don't exactly have the same level of puzzle fever a century later, the jigsaw remains a timeless source of entertainment: a low-cost investment that can keep individuals and groups occupied for hours, days, and even weeks. Teaming up to put a puzzle together is an easy way to build camaraderie among friends, family, or colleagues. It's also great for our brains, since it gives both hemispheres a workout at the same time. The analytical left hemisphere uses sequencing and logic to sort through the different shapes and colors, while the creative right hemisphere uses intuition to see the "big picture." When both sides of the brain are engaged, our neural network builds new connections across hemispheres, which helps to improve our memory and cognition. And each time we fit a correct piece into the puzzle, we activate our brain's reward network, which can in turn increase our concentration, confidence, and motor skills.

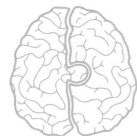

Whether you're piecing together a map of the world or a goofy photo of a colleague, working on a jigsaw puzzle is a great way to give your mind a break from its everyday concerns while strengthening your brainpower at the same time.

Explore New Places Without the Help of Digital Technology

IN 2016, an American named Noel Santillan became briefly famous in Iceland when the GPS in his rental car led him very far astray. Instead of directing Santillan to his hotel in Reykjavik, about forty minutes' drive from the airport, the device led the twenty-eight-year-old tourist on a six-hour, 250-mile journey to the opposite end of the country. The error stemmed from a minor typo: instead of entering his destination as "Laugavegur," the name of a popular shopping street in downtown Reykjavik, Santillan had typed "Laugarvegur," which turned out to be a road in the remote northern fishing village of Siglufjörður.

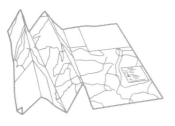

Santillan didn't seem too bothered by his very long detour. "I did enjoy the scenery on the way," he told a local reporter. "I've never seen anything quite like it. And the horses!" For their part, the villagers of Siglufjörður were delighted to host the lost American, taking him to their award-winning Herring Era Museum and introducing him to a local delicacy, putrefied shark.

While Santillan's GPS misadventure made him a local celebrity, the author George Michelsen Foy worries about how digital navigation systems (and our dogged reliance on them) impact our intuition and even our long-term brain function. In his book *Finding North: How Navigation Makes Us Human,* Foy argues that putting our faith in GPS devices and smartphones causes us to disregard our own instincts. For hundreds of years, humans have practiced a navigation technique called "dead reckoning," relying on guesswork and reasoning to determine where we are based on information like our last known location, direction, speed, and duration of travel. When we switch on the GPS, we become passive followers and stop paying attention to the surrounding environment. We may even disregard obvious warning signs—news reports document alarming cases of drivers who've driven off roads and bridges, or gotten caught on railroad tracks, while following GPS navigation. (Santillan admits he saw road signs for Reykjavik pointing in the opposite direction but chose to trust his GPS over his eyes.)

These perils aren't just limited to drivers. Our brains have an internal navigation system made up of complex neural networks that encode information about our movement through space. "Place cells" in the hippocampus light up when we move from one location to another, creating a mental map of our surroundings that enables us to, for example, find our way back after taking a walk through an unfamiliar neighborhood. If we aren't actively engaging these networks, they can atrophy, increasing our risk of developing Alzheimer's disease and memory loss. On the other hand, figuring out where to go the old-fashioned way—by identifying landmarks in relation to one another—can actually cause our brains to expand. When researchers used MRI scans to look at the brains of London taxi drivers (who need to memorize over twenty-three thousand different roads to qualify for a license), they found the taxi drivers had larger hippocampi and more neuron-dense gray matter than the average person.

"Humans evolved and progressed by seeking to explore and understand the unknown," Foy writes. "Exploring the unknown as our ancestors did means, very exactly, not knowing where we are to start with, physically, intellectually or both. It means getting lost." Foy describes that act of getting lost—and then using our curiosity, memories, insight, and intuition to find our way again—as "the most deeply human process of all."

Sometimes on weekends, Michael and I like to leave our phones behind and go explore a new neighborhood. We'll find real estate listings for open houses and use them to walk us from place to place. (We're not in the market for a new place, but getting a chance to peek inside other people's apartments is an evergreen NYC pastime.) Wandering from one place to the next, we'll discover coffee shops, parks, specialty stores, street art, interesting architecture—all things we might not notice if we were just trying to get from Point A to Point B. Without our phones, we can't rely on Google or Yelp ratings to let us know where the four- and five-star restaurants are when we get hungry, which is just as well. We've outsourced so much of our decision-making to maps and apps that we've forgotten we're our own best judges of what want we when we use our eyes and instincts.

As for Noel Santillan, the "Lost Tourist" of Iceland, he eventually found his way to Reykjavik. But a few days later, his GPS got him lost *again,* when he followed it to a deserted building while trying to find the Blue Lagoon, Iceland's famous geothermal spa. This time, he decided to forgo the GPS and ask a real human being for directions. Then he drove on, looking out for landmarks along the way. Before long, he'd arrived exactly where he wanted to be. "I'm not afraid to get lost. I love getting lost," he later told reporters. "That's how you find interesting things. If you don't lose yourself, you're never going to find yourself."

Listen to an Album from Start to Finish

WE LIVE IN an era of singles. While it was once standard for artists to release a single song or two as teasers for an upcoming album, these days it's common for musicians to put out four, five, or even six singles—with or without a full album to promote. "It's all about throwing out content," the songwriter Savan Kotecha (who's written hits for One Direction, Ariana Grande, and the Weeknd) told *Rolling Stone*. And between streaming services, satellite radio, and YouTube, it's never been easier to listen to the songs we want, when we want them.

Despite the temptation to skip ahead to our favorite tracks, or stream individual songs without bothering with the album itself, it's worth taking the time to listen to a full album from start to finish. It's not even that time-consuming—as the music writer Sarah Eldred points out, most full albums are shorter than a single episode of a TV drama. "You wouldn't read every other chapter in a book, would you?" Eldred asks. Like novelists, musicians think about the big picture as they assemble their albums, paying careful attention to elements like pacing, storytelling, how to begin, and where to end. When we cherry-pick individual songs, we miss an opportunity to understand the artist's project on a deeper level.

Listening to a full album can pay off in other ways, too. It's often the only way to discover "deep cuts"—the songs that might not make it on to the radio as singles but are still great in their own right. You can gain a better understanding of the songs you already love when you hear them in the context of the full album, and you can hone your critical listening skills by giving yourself a chance to really absorb the work and its impact on you.

"Good art often takes time to make, and it often takes time to understand, too," writes *The New Yorker*'s music critic Amanda Petrusich. "Who hasn't lived with a record for weeks, only to wake up one morning and find that it has suddenly unlocked a whole new suite of rooms deep in one's subconscious?" The more time and attention you give to an album, the greater your reward.

Try It Out

Go retro with a record. With the rise of digital music, CD sales are down . . . but vinyl has made a major comeback: *Rolling Stone* recently reported that vinyl records are on pace to outsell CDs for the first time since 1986. These days, a number of companies are producing lightweight and affordable turntables, and most current records come with a digital download code so that collectors can also take their music on the go. Why is everyone going crazy for vinyl again? "There's something wonderfully interactive about putting on a record, listening to a side, and then flipping it over to hear the other side," writes *Gizmodo*'s Mario Aguilar. "It makes the listening experience something in which you are constantly physically and emotionally involved."

Consider sound quality. If you'd rather stick to digital files, think about downloading your album rather than streaming it, since Internet speed and connection can impact or interrupt the streaming process. And if you're playing music off your computer, it's worthwhile to connect to external speakers, which will give you better sound quality than what's built into your laptop.

Host a listening party. Celebrate a new album release—or show love for an old favorite—by inviting friends over to listen to an album out loud in its entirety. Learning what your friends love about an album can help you to hear and appreciate the music in a whole new way.

Put on headphones and take a long walk. Studies show that walking outside can help us concentrate, so for a more focused listening experience, consider putting on headphones and taking your album out for a stroll. Be careful if you're walking on busy streets or bike trails, especially if you have noise-cancelling headphones—concentrating on your music doesn't mean you should disregard your surroundings. For safety, you may want to wait until you've reached a good resting place—a shady spot under a tree or a park bench—before pressing play.

Write a Six-Word Story

ACCORDING TO LEGEND, Ernest Hemingway once bragged to a friend that he could write a complete novel in just six words. When the friend offered him $10 to make good on the boast, Hemingway scrawled the following story on a bar napkin: *For sale: baby shoes, never worn.*

Even for a writer with a reputation for terse, matter-of-fact prose, these six words are a masterpiece of bare-bones storytelling. The single brief sentence contains a full emotional arc: expectation ("baby shoes"), followed by heartbreak ("never worn"), and an attempt at moving on ("for sale").

Unfortunately, the legend has been debunked—whoever wrote the story, it wasn't Hemingway (and it probably wasn't on a napkin, either). But it's still an impressive feat. Anyone can string together a six-word sentence. But how do you get those words to tell a *story*? According to *Narrative Magazine*, which features an entire section dedicated to these tiny works of literature, "a six-word story should provide a movement of conflict, action, and resolution

Not that the story need be long, but it will take
a long while to make it short.
—Henry David Thoreau

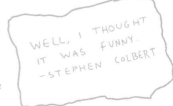

that gives the sense of a complete story transpiring in a moment's reading."

Easier said than done! Crafting a six-word story is a brain-stretching challenge, even for professional writers. In the anthology *Not Quite What I Was Planning: Six-Word Memoirs by Writers Famous & Obscure,* many give it their best shot, from the novelist Dave Eggers ("Fifteen years since last professional haircut") to the journalist and filmmaker Nora Ephron ("Secret to life: marry an Italian") to *Late Show* host Stephen Colbert ("Well, I thought it was funny").

When it comes to crafting your own tiny tale, consider drawing from experiences in your own life: a memory, a fear, a dream, a funny or challenging moment. Or you could invent something brand-new. If you're feeling stuck, start by writing a list of words you like, images that interest you, or an outline of events you'd like to include. You probably won't write the perfect story on your first try, but as the French Enlightenment philosopher Voltaire famously said (in six words!), *"Le mieux est l'ennemi du bien"*—*Best is the enemy of good.* Give yourself the freedom to experiment and even to write sentences that are just plain bad.

Writing a six-word story is a great way to give your brain a workout and expand your creativity. Best of all, you can do it anywhere: commuting to work or waiting in line at the grocery store, on the beach or at the bar, alone or with friends.

Writing is 1 percent inspiration,

99 percent elimination.

—Louise Brooks

Go on a Hike

THE APPALACHIAN TRAIL begins at Springer Mountain in Georgia, then moves north, crossing fourteen states, eight national forests, and six national parks before ending at the peak of Mount Katahdin in Maine. There, hikers who've walked the full length of the trail line up to have their photo taken next to a weather-beaten wood sign. By the time these backpackers (known as "thru-hikers") arrive at Mount Katahdin, they've spent at least five straight months trekking along the 2,178-mile trail—the longest marked path in the United States.

The trail got its start a hundred years ago, in 1921, when a Massachusetts forester and conservationist named Benton MacKaye published an article laying out his idea for a walking path across the Appalachian Mountains. Over the next fifteen years, volunteer hiking clubs turned his dream into a reality, clearing brush and painting blazes to mark the route.

MacKaye, who believed that the stress and speed of urban life were bad for people's health, envisioned the trail as a destination for worn-out city dwellers in need of recreation and refreshment in nature. When journalists asked him what the trail's purpose was, MacKaye's reply was Zenlike in its simplicity: "To walk, to see, and to see what you see."

In the century since, the pace of city life has only sped up, and we're spending less and less time outside. MacKaye's concern for our health, and his proposed solution of getting out into nature for a reset, are as relevant as ever. Researchers have found ample evidence that hiking is good for your body, your mind, and even your relationships. Hiking is a great workout: Biomechanics professor Daniel Ferris explains to *Time* that while walking on a level surface doesn't require much energy: "When you walk on uneven terrain"—like trails through the woods—"your heart rate and metabolic rate go up, and you burn more calories." Hiking with a backpack can burn up to five hundred calories an hour, and the cardiovascular benefits include lower blood pressure and cholesterol, as well as reduced risk of heart disease, type 2 diabetes, and stroke. And it's easier on the joints than running—trails tend to be softer underfoot than sidewalks and streets, reducing strain on the knees and hips.

Look deep into nature, and then you will
understand everything better.
—Albert Einstein

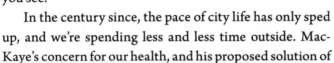

It had nothing to do with gear or footwear or the backpacking fads or philosophies of any particular era or even with getting from point A to point B. It had to do with how it felt to be in the wild. With what it was like to walk for miles with no reason other than to witness the accumulation of trees and meadows, mountains and deserts, streams and rocks, rivers and grasses, sunrises and sunsets.

—Cheryl Strayed, *Wild: From Lost to Found on the Pacific Crest Trail*

Hiking is also therapeutic: studies find that people who spend time walking in nature are less likely to ruminate on negative thoughts, and they report lower levels of stress, anxiety, and depression. As REI Outdoor Programs manager Leigh Jackson-Magennis told *HuffPost,* "Being out in nature, away from the business of our daily lives and technology, can allow people to connect with themselves and nature in a way that brings about peace and a sense of well-being." In addition to heightening mindfulness, studies show that hiking can enhance our creative problem-solving abilities by up to 50 percent—so if you're stumped by a work problem, you might be better off leaving the office and heading for the hills to find a solution.

Hiking is a great way to bond with friends and family, creating the opportunity for shared experiences and enduring memories. There's a low barrier to entry, since for the most part, anyone who can walk can hike (at least on easier trails), making it an activity that folks of all ages and levels of fitness can enjoy together. And it's inexpensive, since it only really requires a sturdy pair of shoes. Whether you're embarking on a multiday camping trip or just heading out for an hour or two, it's worth your while to hit the trails and—as Benton MacKaye would suggest—see what you can see.

Try It Out

Locate a nearby trail. You don't need to live in the middle of the wilderness to find good places to hike. Many cities and towns have parks and other greenspaces with walking paths, and you can find good hiking trails just an hour away from major cities like New York, Los Angeles, Washington DC, Chicago, Milwaukee, and Miami. (See "Useful Websites for Hikers" on page 306 for a list of online trail-finding resources.)

Warm up with simple exercises. One of the most common hiking injuries is a sprained ankle, but you can reduce your risk with exercises to expand your range of motion and build core strength, which will help to stabilize you on an uneven trail. Crunches, squats, and lunges will strengthen your core, while a resistance band can help to improve muscle strength and extension.

Break in new footwear in advance. Blisters are a buzzkill. If you plan to wear new or rarely used shoes or boots on your hike, spend some time walking around in them in advance. While lightweight hiking shoes might feel comfortable right away, heavier leather boots may

take up to a few weeks to soften to the shape of your feet. Start by wearing new shoes/boots inside, then take walks around your neighborhood, extending your wear-time as you feel more comfortable.

Prepare before you go. Check the weather a few hours before you plan to set out. Even if you plan to hike for only a few hours, bring a backpack with water, sunscreen, bug spray, snacks, extra layers, and a basic first aid kit. You may also want to bring a flashlight if you think there's a chance you'll be out after dark, and a compass if you have one— relying on smartphones in the wilderness is never a great idea. While it's safer to hike with a partner, if you're planning to go out alone, make sure to tell someone where you're going and when you expect to be back. (See Practice No. 62 for tips on hiking in a state or na-tional park.)

Budget extra time. Hiking is usually slower than walking, since rug-ged terrain and changes in elevation will slow your pace. Depending on the landscape and your level of fitness, assume you'll cover one to two miles of trail per hour. Add an extra hour for every one thousand feet of elevation gain. If you're new to hiking, start with a shorter, easier trail, and err on the safe side by budgeting in a few extra hours. **Walk, see, and see what you see.** You knew that was coming, right?

In every walk with nature, one receives

far more than he seeks.

—John Muir

Useful Websites for Hikers

AllTrails (www.alltrails.com) is a database (and app) with listings for over one hundred thousand trails. Enter the name of your city, park, or local trail for detailed maps, reviews, and information about length, condition, and difficulty of each route. You can save a list of your favorite trails, create and share custom maps, and get driving directions that take you straight to the trailhead.

Hiking Project (www.hikingproject.com) features an international trail directory with listings by state and country. Listings include key information like trail length and conditions, as well as flora and fauna to look out for on your hike. And there's an app!

Outdoor Project (www.outdoorproject.com) offers a wealth of resources for all kinds of outside adventures, including tips, tricks, guides, and itineraries—all searchable by region and activity.

TrailLink (www.traillink.com) is a website and app hosted by the Rails-to-Trails Conservancy, a nonprofit that turns old railroad lines into hiking paths nationwide. After registering for free, you can enter your zip code to access maps, itineraries, and the history behind nearby trails.

Listen to Live Music

I LOVE SEEING live music; it's one of the things that makes me most happy. Sometimes people ask me whether it's worthwhile to spend money on tickets to live shows. After all, it's usually less expensive to buy an album, which I could listen to whenever I wanted, and even cheaper—free, in fact!—to listen to the music over streaming services. But while I like listening to albums, for me, there isn't a comparison. When you hear music live, you get to experience something being created right in front of you. I've always found it amazing that just by moving their hands or vocal cords, musicians are creating something that literally didn't exist one second earlier—and if they stopped moving, it would disappear again. To be right there, witnessing that moment of creation, feels like magic to me. At a live performance, you also get the stories, the jokes, all the little ad-libbed moments that don't show up on a studio album. And if you go to see music at smaller venues, which I prefer, there's a sense of intimacy, a give-and-take between the performer and the audience that creates a special energy and makes each show unique.

No matter how you choose to consume it, listening to music is good for you. Researchers have found that people who listen to music are better at managing

and recovering from stressful situations. Music also works as a mood booster by stimulating the brain to release the feel-good hormone dopamine. Even when your music is on in the background and you're barely paying attention to it, it's still impacting you in positive ways: studies show that upbeat background music can improve processing speeds on cognitive tasks, and both upbeat and downbeat music are correlated with improved memory.

A few recent studies suggest that listening to live music is even more advantageous. For one thing, it might just be objectively better: researchers at Doshisha University in Japan found that musicians tend to play better in front of live audiences than they do in studios. Then there's the social component. Whether you're in a small room with a dozen other people or standing in a crowd of thousands at a festival, that communal experience has a powerful, positive impact on emotional health and well-being. In surveys, two-thirds of respondents say they feel happier, healthier, and more engaged when listening to music with others compared to listening on their own.

For all the reasons listening to live music is good for you, it's also vital for

the musicians. While a report by Citigroup found that the music industry raked in a whopping $43 billion in 2017, the artists themselves received only around 12 percent of the proceeds. With the exception of megastars, musicians don't make money from record sales or streaming—they earn their incomes touring. (Even megastars make most of their money from live shows.) So if you want to support the musicians you love, make a point to see them live. You'll be investing in their success and your own health and happiness, all at the same time.

Try It Out

Read local listings to find shows near you. Local newspapers, alt-weeklies, and magazines like *Time Out* offer weekly listings for concerts happening in your area. Most venues post event calendars on their websites so that you can see who will be playing there in the coming month. And apps like Songkick and Bandsintown make it even easier by curating lists of upcoming concerts in your area based on your music preferences and alerting you when your favorite artists go on tour.

Try out different kinds of live music experiences. Go to a show at your local bar or coffee shop. Check out a sit-down performance at a concert hall. Get a festival pass to discover new artists playing alongside your favorites. Or spend some time with a musician who's performing for spare change on a subway platform or street corner, and you might get a sneak preview of a future star—pop dynamos Ed Sheeran, Sheryl Crow, and Tracy Chapman all started out as buskers.

Take It Further

Host a concert in your home. If you love hearing music in intimate settings, nothing beats a house show. Last summer, my favorite singer-songwriter, Joe Pug, launched his new album by announcing that he'd play a few house shows. My friend and Getaway cofounder, Pete, and I decided to sponsor one at my apartment. It was amazing to have this hero of ours in my home. He was as kind, smart, and charming in person as he'd seemed onstage. He brought his dad, and we squeezed around fifty people into the space. The whole night was incredible.

Revisit a Book or Movie You Loved When You Were Young

I'M A SUCKER for coming-of-age films. As long as they keep making them, I'll keep watching (and rewatching) them. I've seen *Stand by Me* more times than I can count. And I've watched *Love Actually* at least five times, since it's Michael's favorite movie and he rewatches it every Thanksgiving. Are these the greatest movies ever made? I will admit they probably are not. Could we have spent our time watching any of the hundreds of other movies we haven't yet seen instead? Of course. But there's a special feeling that comes from watching a movie you've

seen enough times to know all the dialogue and plot twists by heart—it's comforting and familiar, like hanging out with an old friend.

In 2011, researchers Cristel Antonia Russell and Sidney Levy set out to discover why people take so much pleasure from "reconsuming" experiences they've already had: rewatching movies and TV shows, reading the same books multiple times, repeatedly listening to songs and albums, and revisiting places they've gone before. Given that there are more movies, TV shows, books, records, and tourist destinations than any person could possibly experience in a lifetime, what keeps us coming back to what we already know?

For one thing, while it might seem that we'd get bored watching, reading, or listening to the same things over and over, the opposite is true—repetition tends to make us like those things even more. Studies find that we feel greater affection toward people and things that are familiar to us, even if that affection is subconscious, a phenomenon psychologists call the "mere exposure effect."

Then there's the nostalgia factor. According to the psychologist Clay Routledge, there are two different types of nostalgia: historical (nostalgia for an earlier time in history) and autobiographical (nostalgia for an earlier time in our own personal lives). We could credit historical nostalgia for the popularity of TV shows like *Mad Men* and *Stranger Things,* with their pitch-perfect renderings of the fashion, hairstyles, technology, and cultural mores of decades past. But it's autobiographical nostalgia that keeps me coming back to *Stand by Me.* Whenever I see it, I remember watching the movie for the first time as a kid. As *The Atlantic's* Derek Thompson puts it, "It's using entertainment as a time machine to revisit a lost memory." It makes me feel more connected to the version of my-

self I used to be, even though I'm glad to be the person I am today. There's a distinct pleasure in remembering the way we were, with all the perspective we've gained since then.

Returning to old favorites can even be therapeutic. Studies show that feeling nostalgic gives us a heightened sense of physical warmth, which may explain why we tend to seek out nostalgic experiences in colder temperatures. (Think about the classic movie marathons that run on TV during the winter holidays, for example.) Revisiting familiar experiences can also help us regulate our emotions: when we already know what will happen in a book or movie, we can't be surprised or disappointed. With repetition, we can also gain a deeper understanding and appreciation by noticing things we didn't catch the first time.

Revisiting old favorites is also a great opportunity for bonding with other people. In their study, Russell and Levy found that sharing these experiences with friends, family, and partners often increased their subjects' enjoyment and made them feel closer to the people they were with. As wonderful as new experiences can be, there are times when nothing compares to a walk down memory lane—especially in the company of someone you love.

Stop and Smell the Flowers

WHEN WE TELL someone to "stop and smell the roses," we don't mean it literally: the expression speaks to the importance of slowing down to appreciate moments of beauty in our everyday lives. But a recent study suggests that we could use more actual roses in our lives—and other types of flowers, too.

Researchers at Rutgers University's Human Emotions Lab presented subjects with one of three gifts—a fruit basket, a decorative candle, or a bouquet of flowers—in order to monitor subjects' facial expressions upon receiving the gift. While responses to the candle and fruit basket varied, every single person who received a floral bouquet responded with a heartfelt smile. "I was shocked," lead researcher Jeannette Haviland-Jones told *Rutgers Magazine.* "In the Emotions Lab, you never get a 100 percent response unless you're dropping a snake on people, which gives you a nice 100 percent fear response. But happy? No." Days later, the flower recipients reported higher levels of happiness and lower stress than the other subjects, suggesting that flowers can have a long-lasting positive impact on mood.

ROSE

NEW YORK

Additional studies by the team found that flowers make us more so-cial, reduce anxiety and depression, and can even improve memory among elderly subjects.

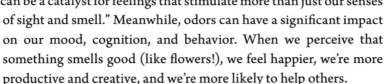

Why do flowers make us so happy? Experts say we're likely re-sponding to their color and fragrance. According to the color special-ist Leatrice Eiseman, "Our response to color is intensely emotional, and flowers can be a catalyst for feelings that stimulate more than just our senses of sight and smell." Meanwhile, odors can have a significant impact on our mood, cognition, and behavior. When we perceive that something smells good (like flowers!), we feel happier, we're more productive and creative, and we're more likely to help others.

Some studies have found that the more appreciation we feel, the greater our overall satisfaction with life. When we look at flowers, whether growing wild or in a bouquet, we can appreci-ate their beauty and feel a stronger connection to the natural world. So if you're looking for a lasting mood-booster, pick up a farm-fresh bouquet from your local florist, take a stroll through a botanic gar-den, or simply observe the flowers growing around your own neighborhood.

Try It Out

Learn to identify different flowers in the wild. Look for talks and classes at your local botanic garden or park, or learn on your own by picking up a guide to area plants. Start small and local—what's

growing nearby your home? What are the native plants of your state? Next, look for the hallmark characteristics of the flower: What color is it? What size? How many petals? What shape and color are the leaves? Is it growing in the shade or in the sun? You may want to record notes or take a photo to help you remember. For a shortcut, download a plant identification app like PlantSnap, Pl@ntNet, or PictureThis to your smartphone. Simply take a picture of the flower, and the app's algorithm will identify it for you.

Buy a sustainably sourced bouquet to brighten up your home (or someone else's). Eighty percent of the cut flowers sold in the United States are imported from other countries, primarily Colombia. In addition to questionable labor practices at large-scale flower farms, the import of international flowers means that your blossoms have probably traveled thousands of miles in diesel-guzzling trucks before arriving at your local florist. To keep

your flower-buying as green as your stems, visit a farmers' market to pick up a local, sustainably grown bouquet, or check out the online directory Slow Flowers (www.slowflowers.com), which allows users to search for locally grown flower sources by city, state, and zip code.

Plant flowers in your vegetable garden. In addition to adding a pop of color to your plot, planting flowers beside your vegetables will attract pollinating bees and beneficial insects that discourage plant-eating pests, helping everything in your garden to grow. Flowers like marigolds, chamomile, daisies, and clover make great additions to a vegetable garden. (See Practice No. 36 for more gardening tips.)

Press your flowers for keepsakes. Cut flowers don't last very long. To preserve your blooms, press them and mount them in frames, or use them to decorate handmade bookmarks, cards, and scrapbooks. For best results, select freshly cut flowers that haven't started to wilt or brown. Flatter flowers like daisies and violets work best. Sandwich the flower between two clean sheets of paper, then set it in a flower press (two or more pieces of wood that tighten together with bolts) or between the pages of a book. Stack books or other heavy objects on top to add weight. Then wait two to three weeks for the flowers to dry completely, and remove them from the pages

AMERICAN BEAUTY ROSE

WASHINGTON D.C.

POPPY

CALIFORNIA

with care. If you want to speed up the process, you can use an iron instead. Set the flower between two pieces of paper, turn the iron on low, then press and hold it on top of the paper for fifteen seconds. Lift the iron and wait for the paper to cool, and repeat the process until the flower is dry.

Solve Riddles

YOU MAY HAVE heard this one before: *What's something that belongs to you, which others use more than you do?*

Humans have been puzzling over riddles for thousands of years. They exist in every language and culture around the world. There are riddles in the Bible, in folktales and songs, in *Alice in Wonderland* and *Harry Potter*. Today we can find them printed on cereal boxes, gum wrappers, and subway ads, but the earliest known riddles date all the way back to the ancient Sumerians in 2350 BCE, where they were recorded on clay tablets. (Q: *There is a house. One enters it blind and comes out seeing. What is it?* A: *A school.*) In Greek mythology, the Sphinx refuses to let travelers pass unless they solve her riddle: *What creature goes on four legs in the morning, two legs at noon, and three legs in the evening?* If they guess wrong, she devours them. According to the legend, Oedipus solves the riddle by announcing that the answer is *man,* who crawls on all fours as a baby, walks upright as an adult, and uses a cane in old age.

What explains the enduring popularity of these mental puzzles? Scholars say it's because riddles rely on flashes of insight—that "Aha!" moment—that is at the root of creativity and innovation. When we land on the right answer, we feel a rush of pleasure as the reward centers of our brain flood with dopamine. The brain-tickling challenge of solving a riddle can also serve as a much-needed escape from more serious issues in our daily lives. "It's all about you, using your own mind, without any method or schema, to restore order from chaos," the anthropologist and professor Marcel Danesi told *The New York Times*. "And once you have, you can sit back and say, 'Hey, the rest of my life may be a disaster, but at least I have a solution.'"

Recent studies suggest that if you want to improve your puzzle-solving skills, laughter might be the best medicine. "It really helps to be in a playful frame of mind," the science writer David Corcoran told NPR. Being in a good mood allows for looser, more flexible thinking, making you more likely to "spot connections or see things in the background that you might not otherwise pick up if you were feeling sober or serious," says Corcoran.

Much like a riddle, we want Getaway to feel like a happy escape from the stress and pressures of daily life. When you visit our tiny cabins, you'll find a guestbook that includes some of our favorite brainteasers.

Try It Out

1.
A precious stone, as clear as diamond.
Seek it out whilst the sun's near the horizon.
Though you can walk on water with its power,
Try to keep it, and it'll vanish within an hour.

2.

I am, in truth, a yellow fork
From tables in the sky
By inadvertent fingers dropped
The awful cutlery.
Of mansions never quite disclosed
And never quite concealed
The apparatus of the dark
To ignorance revealed.

3.

I come out of the earth,
I am sold in the market.
He who buys me cuts my tail,
takes off my suit of silk,
and weeps beside me when I am dead.

4.

I can run, but not walk.
Thought is not far behind me.
What am I?

5.

Dirty when white.
What am I?

6.
A natural state, I'm sought by all.
Go without me, and you shall fall.
You do me when you spend,
and use me when you eat to no end.
What am I?

7.
I have streets, but no pavement.
I have cities, but no buildings.
I have forests, yet no trees.
I have rivers, yet no water.
What am I?

8.
A prisoner is told: If you tell a lie we will hang you. If you tell the truth we will shoot you.
What can he say to save himself?

9.
What occurs once in every minute, twice in every moment, yet never in a thousand years?

10.
The more you take, the more you leave behind. What am I?

At Getaway we don't publish the answers because we believe that part of being balanced is accepting that you may not figure it out, but if you must . . .

Answers: Intro: Your name. 1. Ice. 2. Lightning. 3. Onion. 4. Nose. 5. Chalkboard. 6. Balance. 7. Map. 8. "You will hang me." 9. The letter M. 10. Footsteps.

Write a Haiku

HAIKU IS A FORM of poetry known for its brevity and simplicity. Originating over seven hundred years ago in Japan as the opening verses to longer poems, haiku were being written as stand-alone works by the sixteenth century. The legendary poet Matsuo Bashō mastered the form in the seventeenth century, using vivid images of the natural world to capture distinct moments in time:

> *An old silent pond—*
> *A frog jumps into the pond,*
> *splash! Silence again.*

A traditional haiku consists of three unrhymed lines of five, seven, and five syllables, in succession. It references nature by evoking the landscape, wildlife, or a season. And it relies on juxtaposition, a technique for creating contrast by setting two different images or ideas next to each other. (In Bashō's haiku, the poet contrasts the stillness of the old pond with the sound and movement of the jumping frog.)

Of course, when it comes to art, rules are made to be broken. "Above all, a haiku must be very simple and free of all poetic trickery and make a little picture," said the American writer Jack Kerouac, who enjoyed experimenting with the form but mostly ignored the 5-7-5 syllable rule:

In my medicine cabinet
the winter fly
has died of old age

Whether you choose to follow all the rules or bend them as you go, writing haiku isn't just about making poems. It's about slowing down to pay attention to the world around you. As you develop the practice of focusing closely on your surroundings, you'll begin noticing more and more. "Writing haiku takes you right into the heart of the moment," says the former Buddhist monk and author Clark Strand.

Try It Out

Find inspiration by walking in nature. Traditional haiku includes references to the natural world, so take a walk outside to find inspiration. If you live in the city and don't have parks nearby, you can still find elements of nature in

the sky and clouds overhead; the feeling of sunshine, rain, or wind on your skin; or even the sight of birds perching on wires.

Take notes. While haiku appear short and simple, they can be deceptively hard to write. Jot down notes about the things you notice, focusing on sensory details like sight, sound, scent, touch, and taste. Take your time. Record the time of day and the season. The more detail you include in your notes, the more material you'll have for shaping your haiku.

"Make a little picture," as Kerouac suggested. When you write, use language that will create a clear image in the reader's mind. Think of

your haiku like a photo that captures one moment in time. What's inside the frame?

Create contrast. A haiku should include a moment of change or surprise—think of the frog jumping into Bashō's pond, or the dead fly Kerouac finds in his medicine cabinet. For another example, consider this haiku from eighteenth-century Japanese poet Kobayashi Issa, which moves from affec-

tion to pain in the last two lines:

Everything I touch
with tenderness, alas,
pricks like a bramble.

Take It Further

Challenge yourself to write one haiku every day for a month. Notice how your attention evolves as you get into the habit of collecting images and other sensory details for your writing. If you're comfortable enough to share, consider gifting your original haiku to friends and family.

Dance Like No One's Watching

IN 1987, the songwriters Susanna Clark and Richard Leigh penned a country song called "Come from the Heart." While the song became a success—singer Kathy Mattea's 1989 version peaked at #1 on the Billboard Country Charts—a single phrase from the chorus, "dance like nobody's watching" took on a life of its own. Today the phrase adorns T-shirts, coffee mugs, inspirational posters, and even body parts (it's a popular tattoo request). As a metaphor, it evokes the idea of living life to the fullest, without worrying about what others think. Taken literally, it's solid advice for nudging wall-flowers out onto the dance floor.

Why dance? Anyone who's worked up a sweat on the dance floor knows that dancing is a fantastic workout. As with other cardio-focused exercise, dancing burns calories while increasing endurance, balance, flexibility, bone density, and muscle strength. It's low impact, making it easier on the joints than jogging, and involves movement in all directions, which gives smaller support muscles a workout while reducing the risk of repetitive stress injury.

A recent study published in the *Scandinavian Journal of Medicine & Science in Sports* found older women who dance regularly are 73 percent less likely than their non-dancing peers to develop disabilities that impact basic functions for daily living (like walking, eating, and getting dressed). And dancing doesn't just benefit the body: the lead researchers noted that "dancing requires not only balance, strength, and endurance ability, but also cognitive ability: adaptability and concentration to move according to the music and partner, artistry for graceful and fluid motion, and memory for choreography."

In other words, dancing is also a great workout for the brain. Studies find that dancing for 60 to 120 minutes per week can improve cognitive function and neuroplasticity—the ability to adapt to changing situations. While the brain's white matter degrades as we age, leading to cognitive decline, brain scans of elderly subjects showed that dancing actually increases the brain's white matter. Researchers at Yeshiva University's Albert Einstein College of Medicine found that dancing reduced their subjects' risk of dementia by a whopping 76 percent.

Dance is also hugely beneficial to our emotional health, boosting endorphins and the feel-good hormone serotonin. Dancing has been found to be so effective at reducing stress, anxiety, and depression that there's an entire therapeutic practice based around it, called dance/movement therapy. When we dance in groups, we benefit from the physical contact we make with each other, while also feeling more emotionally connected to the people around us. "Basically," says *Time* health reporter Markham Heid, "dancing with someone else is like exercise and a hug rolled together."

As a somewhat rhythmically challenged person, I don't just dance like nobody's watching—I only dance *if* nobody's watching. But given the wealth of evidence that dancing is one of the best things we can do for our mental, physical, and emotional well-being, I'm trying to take to heart the words of the great choreographer Martha Graham: "Nobody cares if you can't dance well. Just get up and dance. Great dancers are great because of their passion."

> And we should consider every day lost on which
> we have not danced at least once.
> —Friedrich Nietzsche

Try It Out

Dance on your own. One great thing about dancing is that you can do it basically anywhere. Put on some tunes and dance around your bedroom to wake up, or shimmy in the kitchen while you're preparing a meal or cleaning up—be careful with the knives, though! To turn casual at-home dancing into an exercise opportunity, stream a dance fitness class online.

Sign up for a dance class. Dance studios offer a variety of classes in different styles of dance for all levels of experience. Many gyms also offer dance-based workout classes like Zumba, which will allow you to test the waters of a group dance class without needing to commit to multi-week sessions.

Go out dancing with friends. Why stand around in a crowded bar when you could be dancing? You can find dance clubs—or at least bars with dance floors—in most cities. Alternatively, put together an upbeat playlist and host a dance party at home.

Start your day with a morning rave. Yes, this is a thing. The company Daybreaker hosts sober, early-morning dance parties in twenty-seven cities around the world for folks who want to "dance with reckless abandon for two hours before work," according to the website. With DJs, light shows, and bars that serve coconut water and coffee, these pop-up ticketed events offer early-morning workouts with a nightclub vibe.

Find the Constellations

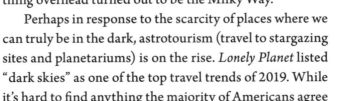

I'M NOT MUCH of an astronomer. When it comes to identifying stars, I can point out the Big and Little Dippers . . . and that's about it. Nonetheless, whenever I visit a Getaway Outpost, one of my favorite activities is to sit outside after dark, gazing up at the star-filled sky.

Based on the feedback we've received, a lot of our guests feel similarly. It makes sense that the chance to stargaze might seem like a special treat: an astonishing 99 percent of people in the United States and Europe can't see the Milky Way from where they live due to light pollution. Some of us wouldn't even know it if we saw it—in 1994, after an earthquake caused power outages across Los Angeles, numerous residents called 911 to report a mysterious gray, glowing cloud in the sky. That alarming thing overhead turned out to be the Milky Way.

Perhaps in response to the scarcity of places where we can truly be in the dark, astrotourism (travel to stargazing sites and planetariums) is on the rise. *Lonely Planet* listed "dark skies" as one of the top travel trends of 2019. While it's hard to find anything the majority of Americans agree on, in 2017, more than 215 million Americans—88 percent of the population—joined together for a very rare stargazing event: watching the solar eclipse on its path of totality. *The New York Times* reported that the eclipse "brought the United States together in greater numbers than most any national

event in recent memory"—the sky's audience that day was twice the size of the audience for the Super Bowl.

Few things make us feel awe—that sense of wonder mixed with a touch of both fear and reverence—like being immersed in nature. When we stare out across a vast ocean or canyon, take in the panoramic view from a mountaintop,

or gaze up at the stars, we recognize that we're a very small part of something much greater than ourselves. This can be an unnerving feeling—but as researchers at the University of California, Irvine, have found, it can also make us better people. In a series of experiments, the researchers found that participants

who had recently been awed by nature acted more generously toward others and were more inclined to make ethical decisions than those who hadn't. "By diminishing the emphasis on the individual self, awe may encourage people to forgo strict self-interest to improve the welfare of others," explains the lead researcher, Paul Piff. Further studies have found that in addition to inspiring awe (and the social benefits that go with it), stargazing can reduce stress and increase positivity.

The International Dark-Sky Association has designated over 120 dark-sky parks, reserves, and sanctuaries around the world. At these sites, light pollution is minimal or nearly nonexistent, making them ideal for stargazing. But the great thing about astrotourism is that you don't need to invest in pricey equipment or travel long distances to take part. You simply need to leave behind the bright lights of the city. Then, once it gets dark, look up.

WHEN I HEARD THE LEARN'D ASTRONOMER
by Walt Whitman

When I heard the learn'd astronomer,
When the proofs, the figures, were ranged in columns before me,
When I was shown the charts and diagrams, to add, divide, and measure them,
When I sitting heard the astronomer where he lectured with much applause in
  the lecture-room,
How soon unaccountable I became tired and sick,
Till rising and gliding out I wander'd off by myself,
In the mystical moist night-air, and from time to time,
Look'd up in perfect silence at the stars.

Try It Out

Invest in a red flashlight. The warm glow of a red flashlight will give you enough light to see without ruining your night vision, unlike the bright glare of a regular blue-white flashlight, which forces your eyes to readjust every time you switch it on and off. A red-light flashlight is essential equipment for professional and amateur starwatchers alike, and you can pick one up for less than $10—or make a DIY version by covering your flashlight with a piece of red cellophane.

Bring binoculars for a closer view. Especially if you're just getting started, astronomers advise holding off on investing in a costly, tricky-to-use telescope. Instead, pick up an inexpensive pair of binoculars, which will allow you to see the sky in far greater detail than with the naked eye.

Be strategic about timing. Crisp, cold nights are much better for stargazing than warm, muggy ones, when humidity creates haze in the air. And you'll see the stars more clearly if you choose a night when the moon is waxing or waning, since a full moon's brightness can wash out the pinpricks of starlight.

"Find your park after dark" with the National Park Service (NPS). The NPS's website (www.nps.gov) provides listings of park-sponsored evening events, activities, and educational programming nationwide, along with listings for observatories and stargazing tips.

Get help from apps. With a variety of apps for iOS and Android, users can simply point their phone cameras at the sky and instantly identify the stars, constellations, and planets overhead. SkyView Lite, SkySafari, Night Sky Lite, and Star Walk offer free versions for download. (Much like a flashlight, the blue light emitted by your phone can throw off your night vision, so proceed with caution.) Other apps, like Dark Sky Finder, can identify the levels of light pollution at different locations before you set out.

Take It Further

Do your part to reduce light pollution by pointing light sources downward and turning off outside lights once you're home for the night—or replacing them with motion sensor lights. You can also exchange your lightbulbs for ones with lower wattage and amber hues, which cause less light pollution overall.

Be Bored

THE IDEA FOR GETAWAY came to me during a five-month solo trip I took in an Airstream trailer. While the trip was amazing and active in some ways, there were other long stretches when I was just sitting inside a tiny trailer by myself with nothing to do. In other words, I was *bored.*

According to the psychologist John Eastwood, boredom is "the unfulfilled desire for satisfying activity"—when our minds and bodies are looking for, but failing to find, something that merits our meaningful attention. Anyone who's spent time waiting at an airport gate for a delayed flight knows this feeling well, but humans have been documenting their boredom for millennia:

graffiti on the subject was found in the ruins of Pompeii; the ancient Roman philosopher Seneca referred to boredom as a kind of nausea; Charles Dickens brought the word "boredom" itself into common usage with his (long, brilliant, and occasionally very boring) novel *Bleak House.* Suffice it to say that as long as humankind has taken interest in things, we've also had the capacity to be bored—and hated it. A recent study by social scientists at the

University of Virginia found that two-thirds of men and a quarter of women would rather *give themselves electric shocks* than sit alone in a room with their thoughts for fifteen minutes.

In spite of this, boredom isn't always a bad thing. Researchers have found that subjects who are asked to perform boring tasks later perform better than a control group at a creative activity. The scientists believe that when we're bored, we tend to start daydreaming, engaging in the kind of free and associative thinking that's fertile ground for creativity.

Boredom can also make us more productive. When we're uninspired by the task in front of us, it's easy to indulge in distractions like social media, online shopping, or texting. The productivity expert Josh Kaufman advises us to resist this impulse and embrace the boring task instead. He calls this "strategic boredom": when we don't allow ourselves anything else to focus on, we're more inspired to finish the boring task quickly.

The difficulty of always feeling that you ought to be doing something is that you tend to undervalue the times when you're apparently doing nothing, and those are very important times. It's the equivalent of the dream time, in your daily life, times when things get sorted out and reshuffled.

—Brian Eno

Try It Out

Don't dismiss boredom. Next time you find yourself in a potentially boring situation—waiting in line at the grocery store, sitting on a bus or train, stuck at your desk with an uninspiring assignment—resist the impulse to focus on something more entertaining. If you don't have pressing responsibilities, let your mind wander and see where it leads you. If you have to complete a dull assignment, immerse yourself in the tediousness of the work to get through it more quickly.

Approach boredom with curiosity. Researchers have identified multiple forms of boredom ranging from *indifferent* (calm but disengaged) to *reactant* (negative feelings, like a desperate wish to be doing something else). When you notice your boredom, ask yourself about the nature of that feeling. Which thoughts are passing through your mind? What feelings can you name? Can you locate a specific part of the body that seems to be responding or reacting to boredom? Once you're actively interrogating the feeling, boredom becomes . . . well, less boring.

Listen to your boredom. Your boredom may be sending you an important message. Being consistently bored at work is a good sign that your work isn't challenging you and it's time to pursue other goals. If you're bored around your friends or significant other, you may have gotten into a social pattern you no longer find stimulating or fulfilling. That doesn't mean you should ditch your friends or partner, but it could be worthwhile to introduce new dynamics: new conversation topics, different activities, fresher ways of relating.

Take It Further

Practice boredom on your daily commute, and avoid turning to your phone, book, music, or podcasts for a full week. See what you notice when you have nothing to distract you from your immediate surroundings. If you don't have a commute, practice boredom the next time you're waiting in line.

Conclusion

OUR LIVES WILL always be complicated, messy, and uncertain—the sum of many moving parts, some within our control, plenty of others beyond it. In today's high-speed, hyperconnected world, it can be easy to get caught up in the frenzy, but as Pulitzer Prize–winning writer Annie Dillard reminds us, "How we spend our days is, of course, how we spend our lives. What we do with this hour, and that one, is what we are doing."

There's no one-size-fits-all solution for finding and maintaining balance. Instead, we might think of the search for balance as a continuous process of trial and error. Every day presents innumerable opportunities to make choices—some big, some small—about how to invest our time, energy, and attention. This book offers seventy-five ideas. Feel free to pick and choose which ones work best for you, or discover new ones on your own. I wish you well.

Acknowledgments

I AM GRATEFUL to the neighbors, friends, and family who have supported (and endured) all things Getaway for years now, including the creation of this book. Thank you to Kirk Johnson and MJ Cantin for their caring and direct advice, and for introducing me to my collaborator (and so much more), Ariel Lown Lewiton, who was undaunted by high expectations and a tough timeline. I've always believed that design and details are essential to inspiring people, and so thanks are due to Abby Ciucias, Danielle Benincasa, and Amelia Detwiler for making this book come to life through illustration.

I've always felt that if we think what we are doing at Getaway matters, then we owe it to ourselves to bring Getaway and our values to as many people as possible. For this project, Katherine Latshaw and Folio Literary Management, as well as TarcherPerigee, Penguin Random House, and my editor, Joanna Ng, were the conduit to bringing this message to the masses. I am grateful for their collaboration and spirit of partnership.

I cared a lot about this book not being a brochure for the company, because I think these ideas are bigger and more important than one endeavor. Nonetheless, I'm deeply aware that I would not have the privilege of publishing this book without the platform that Getaway provides. I am deeply grateful to my colleagues at Getaway for being thoughtful co-creators on this adventure, and for the tremendous crowd of people on the sidelines cheering us on, supporting us, or inspiring us in all sorts of ways.

My family have been cheerleaders since day one, even though my mom was fully convinced the cabins would be "too tiny." Much love to Mom, Dad (builder of cabin #1), Cierra, Jerry, Andrea, and the kids.

Michael Thornton, my partner, is the most patient and even-keeled person I know—especially as I try and often fail to live a life of balance myself. He's smart, he's fun, and he's the best partner one could ask for in times of stress and times of leisure.

And finally: while he's moved on to other ways of changing the world, there'd be no Getaway without Pete Davis. I owe him especially for ensuring that our company was and is rooted in values ("no weasels!"), verve, and kindheartedness. I hope everyone has at least one friendship like the one Pete and I share.

Notes

Page 9. our brains have a natural tendency to pay more attention to bad input than good: Robert Emmons, "Why Gratitude Is Good," *Greater Good Magazine,* November 16, 2010, https://greater good.berkeley.edu/article/item/why_gratitude _is_good.

Page 10. "Writing helps to organize thoughts": Robert Emmons, *Thanks!: How Practicing Gratitude Can Make You Happier* (New York: Houghton Mifflin, 2008), 189.

Page 14. Stress isn't just a bad feeling: "Stress Symptoms: Effects on Your Body and Behavior," Mayo Clinic, April 5, 2019, https://www.mayoclinic.org /healthy-lifestyle/stress-management/in-depth /stress-symptoms/art-20050987.

Page 19. Researchers at Florida State University found: Cary Stothart, Ainsley Mitchum, and Courtney Yehnert, "The Attentional Cost of Receiving a Cell Phone Notification," *Journal of Experimental Psychology: Human Perception and Performance* 41, no. 4 (August 2015): 893–97.

Page 19. "steering what people are paying attention to": Nicholas Thompson, "Our Minds Have Been Hijacked by Our Phones. Tristan Harris Wants to Rescue Them," *Wired,* July 26, 2017, https://www.wired .com/story/our-minds-have-been-hijacked-by-our -phones-tristan-harris-wants-to-rescue-them.

Page 21. "Scientists have discovered a revolutionary new treatment": Matthew Walker, *Why We Sleep: Unlocking the Power of Sleep and Dreams* (New York: Scribner, 2018), 107.

Page 24. a correlation between insufficient sleep (six hours or less): Lara G. Sigurdardottir, Unnur A. Valdimarsdottir, Lorelei A. Mucci, Katja Fall, Jennifer R. Rider, Eva Schernhammer, Charles A. Czeisler, Lenore Launer, Tamara Harris, Meir J. Stampfer, Vilmundur Gudnason, and Steven W. Lockley, "Sleep Disruption Among Older Men and Risk of Prostate Cancer," *Cancer Epidemiology, Biomarkers & Prevention* 22, no. 5 (May 1, 2013): 872–79.

Page 24. sleepiness leads to 1.2 million car crashes every year: Jane E. Brody. "Personal Health; Dark Side of Holidays: Sleep Deprived Drivers," *The New York Times*, November 26, 2002, https://www.nytimes .com/2002/11/26/health/personal-health-dark-side-of -holidays-sleep-deprived-drivers.html.

Page 27. This "orienting response": Adrienne Matei, "Shock! Horror! Do You Know How Much Time You Spend on Your Phone?," *The Guardian*, August 21, 2019, https://www.theguardian.com/lifeandstyle/2019/aug/21/cellphone-screen-time-average-habits.

Page 30. The Light Phone: See *https://www.thelightphone.com*.

Page 32. "thousands strew the ground": Jonathan Kendall, "Remembering When Americans Picnicked in Cemeteries," *Atlas Obscura,* October 24, 2018, https://www.atlasobscura.com/articles/picnic-in-cemeteries-america.

Page 32. Olmsted believed that it was the government's responsibility: Frederick Law Olmsted, "Preliminary Report on the Yosemite and Big Tree Grove," 1865, in *The Papers of Frederick Law Olmsted,* ed. Victoria Post Ranney, vol. 5, *The California Frontier, 1863–1865* (Baltimore: Johns Hopkins University Press, 1990), 488–516.

Page 32. Americans spend 87 percent of our time indoors: N. E. Klepeis et al., The National Human Activity Pattern Survey (NHAPS): A Resource for Assessing Exposure to Environmental Pollutants," *Journal of Exposure Science and Environmental Epidemiology* 11, no. 3 (May–June 2001): 231–52, doi:10.1038/sj.jea.7500165.

Page 33. Researchers have found that regular exposure to nature: University of East Anglia, "It's Official—Spending Time Outside Is Good for You," ScienceDaily, July 6, 2018, www.sciencedaily.com/releases/2018/07/180706102842.htm.

Page 33. doctors have started writing their patients prescriptions: Perri Klass, "Writing Prescriptions to Play Outdoors," *The New York Times,* July 16, 2018, https://www.nytimes.com/2018/07/16/well/writing-prescriptions-to-play-outdoors.html.

Page 37. "palace in time": Abraham Joshua Heschel, *The Sabbath* (New York: FSG Classics, 2005).

Page 40. studies find that kids who have a higher reading ability: Stuart J. Ritchie, Timothy C. Bates, and Robert Plomin, "Does Learning to Read Improve Intelligence?: A Longitudinal Multivariate Analysis in Identical Twins from Age 7 to 16," *Society for Research in Child Development* 86, no. 1 (January–February 2015): 23–36.

Page 40. people who spend at least thirty minutes a day reading: S. S. Bassuk, D. Wypij, and L. F. Berkmann, "Cognitive Impairment and Mortality in the Community-Dwelling Elderly," *American Journal of Epidemiology* 151, no. 7 (April 2000): 676–88.

Page 46. JPEGs can degrade in quality through compression: Sue Chastain, "JPEG File Format Myths and Facts," *Lifewire,* May 17, 2019, https://www.lifewire.com/jpeg-myths-and-facts-1701548.

Page 47. "To collect photographs is to collect the world": Susan Sontag, *On Photography* (New York: Picador, 2001), 3.

Page 50. Researchers have found that charitable acts stimulate our brain's reward center: Jo Cutler and Daniel Campbell-Meiklejohn, "A Comparative fMRI Meta-Analysis of Altruistic and Strategic Decisions to Give," *NeuroImage* 184 (January 2019): 227–41, doi:10.1016/j.neuroimage.2018.09.009.

Page 54. 13 percent of Americans take baths on a regular basis: Kantar, "When the World Washes," December 2015, https://www.informationisbeautifulawards.com/showcase/1635-when-the-world-washes.

Page 55. The immersive heat we get from baths:
Leah Silverman, "8 Reasons Why Baths Are Great for
Your Health," *Town & Country,* November 6, 2019,
https://www.townandcountrymag.com/style
/beauty-products/a18673205/hot-baths-benefits.

**Page 56. Lavender or coconut oil can help
hydrate and heal your skin:** Rachel Nall, "Which
Essential Oils Can Relieve Anxiety?" *Medical News
Today,* February 18, 2019, https://www.medical
newstoday.com/articles/324478.php.

**Page 58. Therapeutic massage dates back five
thousand years:** Florida Academy, "The History of
Massage Therapy: 5,000 Years of Relaxation and Pain
Relief," May 17, 2019, https://florida-academy.edu
/history-of-massage-therapy.

Page 58. Massage is great for athletes: Katharine
Watts, "6 Surprising Benefits of Massage Therapy,"
Reader's Digest Best Health, https://www
.besthealthmag.ca/best-you/health/benefits-of
-massage-therapy.

**Page 59. help diabetics to process insulin more
effectively:** Jeanette Ezzo et al., "Is Massage Useful in
the Management of Diabetes?: A Systematic Review,"
Diabetes Spectrum 14, no. 4 (October 2001): 218–24;
doi:10.2337/diaspect.14.4.218.

**Page 59. improve immune function in cancer
patients:** S. M. Sagar, T. Dryden, and R. K. Wong,
"Massage Therapy for Cancer Patients: A Reciprocal
Relationship between Body and Mind," *Current
Oncology* 14, no. 2 (April 2007): 45–56.

**Page 60. "The physician must be experienced in
many things":** "Massage," *Journal of the American
Medical Association* 28 (January 1897).

**Page 76. Audiologists recommend the 60–60
rule:** Jeff Olsen, "Mayo Clinic Minute: The 60–60 Rule

for Safer Listening," *Mayo Clinic News Network,*
September 8, 2017, https://newsnetwork.mayoclinic
.org/discussion/mayo-clinic-minute-the-60-60-rule
-for-safer-listening.

**Page 89. a recent study conducted at the University
of Texas, Austin:** Amit Kumar and Nicholas Epley,
"Undervaluing Gratitude: Expressers Misunderstand the
Consequences of Showing Appreciation," *Psychological
Science* 29, no. 9 (2018): 1423–35.

Page 92. "I am extremely desirous to know":
Pliny the Younger, "LXXXIII. To Sura," in *The Harvard
Classics,* ed. Charles W. Elliot, vol. 9, *Letters* (New York:
P. F. Collier & Son Corporation, 1909). Accessed online
at https://www.bartleby.com/9/4/1083.html.

**Page 92. Nearly half of all Americans believe in
ghosts:** Jamie Ballard, "45 Percent of Americans Believe
that Ghosts and Demons Exist," YouGov, October 21,
2019, https://today.yougov.com/topics/lifestyle
/articles-reports/2019/10/21/paranormal-beliefs-ghosts
-demons-poll.

**Page 93. "fear is a wonderful thing, in small
doses":** Neil Gaiman, "Ghosts in the Machines," *The New
York Times,* October 31, 2006, https://www.nytimes
.com/2006/10/31/opinion/31gaiman.html.

**Page 93. 18 percent of Americans who claim to
have seen a ghost:** "Many Americans Mix Multiple
Faiths," Pew Research Center, December 9, 2009,
https://www.pewforum.org/2009/12/09/many
-americans-mix-multiple-faiths/#ghosts-fortunetellers
-and-communicating-with-the-dead.

**Page 99. "People like to feel like they have a
story worth telling":** Kathy Gurchiek, "'Humans of
New York' Blogger Shares Interviewing, Listening Tips
with D&I Conference," SHRM, October 24, 2018,
https://www.shrm.org/resourcesandtools/hr-topics

/behavioral-competencies/global-and-cultural
-effectiveness/pages/humans-of-new-york-blogger
-shares-interviewing-listening-tips-with-di-conference
-.aspx.

**Page 100. When we make eye contact, smile, and
say hello to strangers:** Kio Stark, "Why You Should
Talk to Strangers," TED2016, February 2016, https://
www.ted.com/talks/kio_stark_why_you_should
_talk_to_strangers.

**Page 100. "We often avoid using people who are
close to us as confidants":** Craig Lambert, "Choosing
Confidants," *Harvard Magazine,* January–February
2015, https://harvardmagazine.com/2015/01
/choosing-confidants.

**Page 100. "The more we can have contact with
people who aren't like us":** Kio Stark, "How to Talk to
Strangers: A Guide to Bridging What Divides Us," *The
Guardian,* November 12, 2016, https://www
.theguardian.com/lifeandstyle/2016/nov/12
/how-to-talk-to-strangers.

**Page 103. Game sales are booming in the US and
around the world:** Annaliese Griffin, "Playing Board
Games Can Make You a Nicer Person with Better
Relationships," *Quartz,* August 28, 2017, https://qz.com
/1063566/playing-board-games-like-magic-the
-gathering-can-make-you-a-nicer-person-with-better
-relationships.

**Page 103. Nearly half of all Americans
report feeling lonely:** Brian Resnick, "22 Percent
of Millennials Say They Have 'No Friends,'" *Vox,*
August 1, 2019, https://www.vox.com/science-and
-health/2019/8/1/20750047/millennials-poll
-loneliness.

Page 104. "little 'sips' of online connection":
Sherry Turkle, *Reclaiming Conversation: The Power
of Talk in a Digital Age* (New York: Penguin Books,
2016).

**Page 107. mail sent through the US Postal
Service has dropped:** Susan Shain, "We Could All Use a
Little Snail Mail Right Now," *The New York Times,*
October 18, 2018, https://www.nytimes.com/2018/10
/08/smarter-living/we-could-all-use-a-little-snail-mail
-right-now.html.

Page 111. Dr. Aron wanted to explore: Arthur
Aron et al., "The Experimental Generation of
Interpersonal Closeness: A Procedure and Some
Preliminary Findings," *Personality and Social
Psychology Bulletin* 24, no. 4 (April 1997): 363–77,
https://journals.sagepub.com/doi/pdf/10.1177
/0146167297234003.

Page 117. According to a 2018 Cigna survey: Ellie
Polack, "New Cigna Study Reveals Loneliness at
Epidemic Levels in America," Cigna, May 1, 2018,
https://www.cigna.com/newsroom/news-releases
/2018/new-cigna-study-reveals-loneliness-at-epidemic
-levels-in-america.

**Page 117. A third of the UK's residents feel lonely
often or very often:** Claudia Hammond, "Who Feels
Lonely? The Results of the World's Largest Loneliness
Study," BBC, *Anatomy of Loneliness,* October 2018,
https://www.bbc.co.uk/programmes/articles
/2yzhfv4DvqVp5nZyxBD8G23/who-feels-lonely
-the-results-of-the-world-s-largest-loneliness-study.

**Page 117. And in Japan, over half a million
people:** Lila MacLellan, "In Japan, Hundreds of
Thousands of Young People Are Refusing to Leave Their
Homes," *Quartz,* September 23, 2016, https://qz.com
/789082/the-hikikomori-problem-in-japan-hundreds
-of-thousands-of-young-people-are-refusing-to-leave
-their-homes.

Page 118. Researchers at UCLA found that social isolation: Veronique de Turenne, "The Pain of Chronic Loneliness Can Be Detrimental to Your Health," *UCLA Newsroom*, December 21, 2016, http://newsroom.ucla.edu/stories/stories-20161206.

Page 118. A 2015 analysis by researchers at Brigham Young University: Julianne Holt-Lunstad et al., "Loneliness and Social Isolation as Risk Factors for Mortality: A Meta-Analytic Review," *Perspectives on Psychological Science* 10, no. 2 (March 2015): 227–37, doi:10.1177/1745691614568352.

Page 118. becoming a regular at your local watering hole is good for your health: R. I. M. Dunbar, "Breaking Bread: The Functions of Social Eating," *Adaptive Human Behavior and Physiology* 3 (March 2017): 198–211, https://doi.org/10.1007/s40750-017-0061-4.

Page 122. "When you give a gift, it makes you feel generous": "The Psychological Benefits of Giving," *Day to Day*, NPR, December 23, 2008, https://www.npr.org/templates/story/story.php?storyId=98638778.

Page 122. Studies have found that people feel happier: Jill Suttie and Jason Marsh, "5 Ways Giving Is Good for You," *Greater Good Magazine*, December 13, 2010, https://greatergood.berkeley.edu/article/item/5_ways_giving_is_good_for_you.

Page 123. behaving generously releases endorphins and activates regions of the brain: James Baraz and Shoshana Alexander, "The Helper's High," *Greater Good Magazine*, February 1, 2010, https://greatergood.berkeley.edu/article/item/the_helpers_high.

Page 127. "Companionship and intellectual stimulation": Melanie Kindrachuk, "Why Book Clubs Are a Great Thing," *Stratford Writers Festival*, https://stratfordwritersfestival.com/six-reasons-to-join-a-book-club.

Page 127. Warby Parker cofounder Neil Blumenthal: Rebecca Greenfield, "The Warby Parker Book Club," *Fast Company*, May 9, 2014, https://www.fastcompany.com/3030178/the-warby-parker-book-club.

Page 131. A long-running Harvard study: "Can Relationships Boost Longevity and Well-Being?" *Harvard Health Publishing*, June 2017, https://www.health.harvard.edu/mental-health/can-relationships-boost-longevity-and-well-being.

Page 139. A recent study by Microsoft: Kevin McSpadden, "You Now Have a Shorter Attention Span Than a Goldfish," *Time*, May 14, 2015, https://time.com/3858309/attention-spans-goldfish.

Page 139. "In conversations where you look somebody in the eye": "Reclaiming Conversation," Podcast #155, *The Art of Manliness*, November 13, 2015, https://www.artofmanliness.com/articles/podcast-155-reclaiming-conversation.

Page 140. "voluntarily bringing back a wandering attention": William James, *The Principles of Psychology* (New York: Henry Holt, 1890).

Page 140. just having them within reach is enough to reduce their listening comprehension: Bob Sullivan and Hugh Thompson, "Now Hear This! Most People Stink at Listening," *Scientific American*, May 3, 2013, https://www.scientificamerican.com/article/plateau-effect-digital-gadget-distraction-attention.

Page 149. "If you want to hear quiet noises": Wayne Drash and Evelio Contreras, "America's Quietest Town: Where Cell Phones Are Banned," CNN, July 2015, https://www.cnn.com/interactive/2015/07/us/quiet-town-american-story.

Page 151. over 178 million Americans report using another device: André J. Szameitat, "A Neuroscientist Explains Why Multitasking Screens Is So Terrible for Your Brain," *ScienceAlert,* December 16, 2016, https://www.sciencealert.com/multitasking-is -not-a-good-way-to-train-your-brain-here-s-why.

Page 153. NASA researchers have found that by absorbing carbon dioxide and particulate: "Plants Clean Air and Water for Indoor Environments," *NASA Spinoff,* 2007, https://spinoff.nasa.gov/Spinoff2007/ps _3.html.

Page 153. the researcher Roger Ulrich observed that patients recovered faster from surgery: Roger S. Ulrich, "Health Benefits of Gardens in Hospitals," presented at *Plants for People* conference, 2002.

Page 153. patients recovering in rooms filled with potted plants: Seong-Hyun Park and Richard H. Mattson, "Ornamental Indoor Plants in Hospital Rooms Enhanced Health Outcomes of Patients Recovering from Surgery," *The Journal of Alternative and Complementary Medicine* 15, no. 9 (September 2009): 975–80, doi:10.1089/acm.2009.0075.

Page 157. By 2018, though the country's population had grown: "Newspapers Fact Sheet," Pew Research Center, July 9, 2019, https://www.journalism .org/fact-sheet/newspapers.

Page 157. Although *Politico* writer Jack Shafer has been an online journalist: Jack Shafer, "Why Print News Still Rules," *Politico,* September 10, 2016, https:// www.politico.com/magazine/story/2016/09/news papers-print-news-online-journalism-214238.

Page 158. Farhad Manjoo, a *New York Times* reporter: Farhad Manjoo, "For Two Months, I Got My News from Print Newspapers. Here's What I Learned," *The New York Times,* March 7, 2018, https://www .nytimes.com/2018/03/07/technology/two-months -news-newspapers.html.

Page 159. Andrew Ferguson, a staff writer for *The Atlantic,* waxes poetic: Andrew Ferguson, "There's No Substitute for Print," *The Atlantic,* April 10, 2019, https:// www.theatlantic.com/ideas/archive/2019/04 /andrew-ferguson-joys-reading-print-newspaper/586792.

Page 164. people with "chaotic kitchens" tend to eat more junk food: Lenny R. Vartanian, Kristin M. Kernan, and Brian Wansink, "Clutter, Chaos, and Overconsumption: The Role of Mind-Set in Stressful and Chaotic Food Environments," *Environment and Behavior* 49, no. 2 (February 2017): 215–23, doi:10.1177 /0013916516628178.

Page 168. "When you sit at a desk all day": Anne Harding, "Why Gardening Is Good for Your Health," CNN.com, July 8, 2011, http://www.cnn.com/2011 /HEALTH/07/08/why.gardening.good/index.html.

Page 168. gardening helps people relax even more than leisure activities: Agnes E. Van Den Berg and Mariëtte H. G. Custers, "Gardening Promotes Neuroendocrine and Affective Restoration from Stress," *Journal of Health Psychology* 16, no. 1 (January 2011): 3–11, doi:10.1177/1359105310365577.

Page 168. older people who garden regularly are up to 36 percent less likely to develop dementia: Leon A. Simons et al., "Lifestyle Factors and Risk of Dementia: Dubbo Study of the Elderly," *Medical Journal of Australia* 184, no. 2 (January 2006): 68–70, doi:10.5694/j.1326 -5377.2006.tb00120.x.

Page 171. "Start-of-the-day mood can last longer than you might think": Nancy P. Rothbard, "How Your Morning Mood Affects Your Whole Workday," *Harvard Business Review,* July 21, 2016, https://hbr.org/2016/07 /how-your-morning-mood-affects-your-whole-workday.

Page 173. "When you sleep, your muscles lose tone": Luis Villazon, "Why Do We Stretch When We Wake Up?," *BBC Science Focus,* https://www.science focus.com/the-human-body/why-do-we-stretch-when -we-wake-up.

Page 179. "Losing yourself in a book is the ultimate relaxation": "Reading 'Can Help Reduce Stress,'" *The Telegraph,* March 30, 2009, https://www .telegraph.co.uk/news/health/news/5070874 /Reading-can-help-reduce-stress.html.

Page 185. according to a recent survey by YouGov: Gregory McCarriston, "58% of Americans Binge Watch TV Shows," YouGov, September 13, 2017, https://today.yougov.com/topics/lifestyle/articles -reports/2017/09/13/58-americans-binge-watch-tv -shows.

Page 185. The clinical psychologist Renée Carr explains: Danielle Page, "What Happens to Your Brain When You Binge-Watch a TV Series," NBCnews.com, November 4, 2017, https://www.nbcnews.com/better /health/what-happens-your-brain-when-you-binge -watch-tv-series-ncna816991.

Page 186. "We actually compete with sleep": Rina Raphael, "Netflix CEO Reed Hastings: Sleep Is Our Competition," *Fast Company,* November 6, 2017, https://www.fastcompany.com/40491939/netflix-ceo -reed-hastings-sleep-is-our-competition.

Page 186. a 2015 Boston University study found: Sarah Krongard and Mina Tsay-Vogel, "Online Original TV Series: Examining Portrayals of Violence in Popular Binge-Watched Programs and Social Reality Perceptions," *Psychology of Popular Media Culture* (2018), doi:10.1037/ppm0000224.

Page 189. In 1979, researchers George Lakoff and Mark Johnson published a study: George Lakoff and Mark Johnson, *Metaphors We Live By* (Chicago: University of Chicago Press, 1980).

Page 189. Northwestern University psychologists Hajo Adam and Adam Galinsky: Hajo Adam and Adam D. Galinsky, "Enclothed Cognition," *Journal of Experimental Social Psychology* 48, no. 4 (July 2012): 918–25, doi.org/10.1016/j.jesp.2012.02.008.

Page 190. According to the writer and ethnographer Leah Reich: Leah Reich, "A Bathrobe Can Make You Feel Like You're Home," *Racked,* September 1, 2017, https://www.racked.com/2017/9/1 /16183662/perfect-bathrobe-terrycloth-silk-chicago -athletic-association-hotel-robe.

Page 191. people who hold a hot drink in their hands: Lawrence E. Williams and John A. Bargh, "Experiencing Physical Warmth Promotes Interpersonal Warmth," *Science* 322, no. 5901 (October 2008): 606–07, doi:10.1126/science.1162548.

Page 197. Eight in ten Americans say they consider public libraries: David Beard, "Tale of Two Polls: What Do Librarians Have that Journalists Don't?," *Poynter,* January 19, 2018, https://www.poynter.org /ethics-trust/2018/tale-of-2-polls-what-do-librarians -have-that-journalists-don%C2%92t.

Page 199. "People may go to the library looking": Robert Putnam, *Better Together: Restoring the American Community* (New York: Simon & Schuster, 2003), 49.

Page 214. "The clutter competes for your attention": Erin Doland, "Scientists Find Physical Clutter Negatively Affects Your Ability to Focus, Process Information," *Unclutterer,* March 29, 2011, https:// unclutterer.com/2011/03/29/scientists-find-physical -clutter-negatively-affects-your-ability-to-focus-process -information.

Page 219. researchers at the University of London's Institute of Psychiatry: Will Knight, "'Info-mania' Dents IQ More than Marijuana," *New Scientist*, April 22, 2005, https://www.newscientist.com/article/dn7298-info-mania-dents-iq-more-than-marijuana.

Page 219. heavy multitaskers had less brain density: Kep Kee Loh and Ryota Kanai, "Higher Media Multi-Tasking Activity Is Associated with Smaller Gray-Matter Density in the Anterior Cingulate Cortex," *PLOS ONE* 9, no. 9 (September 2014): e106698, https://doi.org/10.1371/journal.pone.0106698.

Page 222. 2010 study found that Swedes are the least stressed workers: Anna Quito, "This Four-Letter Word Is the Swedish Key to Happiness at Work," *Quartz*, March 14, 2016, https://qz.com/636682/this-four-letter-word-is-the-swedish-key-to-happiness-at-work.

Page 222. "You can do it alone, you can do it with friends": Anna Brones, "What Is Fika? An Introduction to the Swedish Coffee Break," *Kitchn*, May 25, 2015, https://www.thekitchn.com/what-in-the-world-is-fika-an-intro-to-the-swedish-coffee-break-the-art-of-fika-219297.

Page 223. "The hierarchy breaks down during the *fika*": Gunilla Pravitz, "Time for *Fika*?," *LiU* magazine (Linköping University), no. 2 (2013), https://liu.se/liu-nytt/arkiv/reportage/dags-for-fika?l=en.

Page 225. Bright suggests choosing a particular action: Deborah Bright, "How to Let Go at the End of the Workday," *Harvard Business Review*, November 23, 2017, https://hbr.org/2017/11/how-to-let-go-at-the-end-of-the-workday.

Page 234. employees who report having close friends at work: Annamarie Mann, "Why We Need Best Friends at Work," Gallup, January 15, 2018, https://www.gallup.com/workplace/236213/why-need-best-friends-work.aspx.

Page 236. Researchers at the University of California, Irvine: Gloria Mark, Daniela Gudith, and Ulrich Klocke, "The Cost of Interrupted Work: More Speed and Stress," *Proceedings of the SIGCHI Conference on Human Factors in Computing Systems* (April 2008): 107–10, doi:10.1145/1357054.1357072.

Page 237. we tend to waste the time immediately *before* our meetings: Jeff Grabmeier, "Why an Upcoming Appointment Makes Us Less Productive," *Ohio State News*, May 23, 2018, https://news.osu.edu/why-an-upcoming-appointment-makes-us-less-productive.

Page 238. "Every Time Bandit has a Time Bandit": Brigid Schulte, "Work Interruptions Can Cost You 6 Hours a Day. An Efficiency Expert Explains How to Avoid Them," *The Washington Post*, June 1, 2015, https://www.washingtonpost.com/news/inspired-life/wp/2015/06/01/interruptions-at-work-can-cost-you-up-to-6-hours-a-day-heres-how-to-avoid-them.

Page 240. In 1910, President Taft announced: "President William Howard Taft Wanted All of the U.S. to Have 3 Months of Vacation," *All Things Considered*, NPR, August 1, 2019, https://www.npr.org/2019/08/01/747368652/president-william-howard-taft-wanted-all-of-the-u-s-to-have-3-months-of-vacation.

Page 240. According to a recent report by the Center for Economic and Policy Research: Adewale Maye, "No-Vacation Nation, Revised," *Center for Economic and Policy Research*, May 2019.

Page 240. Even when Americans *do* get vacation time: Hannah Sampson, "What Does America Have Against Vacation?," *The Washington Post*, August 28,

2019, https://www.washingtonpost.com/travel/2019
/08/28/what-does-america-have-against-vacation.

Page 241. 59 percent of millennials report feeling "shame": "Vacation Shaming in the Workplace: Millennials Most Likely to Feel Guilt for Taking Time Off Work," *PRNewswire,* March 4, 2016, https://www.prnewswire.com/news-releases/vacation-shaming-in-the-workplace-millennials-most-likely-to-feel-guilt-for-taking-time-off-work-300230829.html.

Page 241. A recent study by researchers from Columbia University: Silvia Bellezza, Neeru Paharia, and Anat Keinan, "Conspicuous Consumption of Time: When Busyness and Lack of Leisure Time Become a Status Symbol," *Journal of Consumer Research* 44, no. 1 (June 2017): 118–38.

Page 242. "Vacations tend to create memories": Alina Tugend, "Take a Vacation, for Your Health's Sake," *The New York Times,* June 8, 2008, https://www.nytimes.com/2008/06/08/business/worldbusiness/08iht-07shortcuts.13547623.html.

Page 245. most people have about three to six hours of truly productive time: Chris Weller, "Forget the 9 to 5—Research Suggests There's a Case for the 3-Hour Workday," *Business Insider,* September 26, 2017, https://www.businessinsider.com/8-hour-workday-may-be-5-hours-too-long-research-suggests-2017-9.

Page 248. "If you're waiting until the morning": Stephanie Vozza, "7 Popular Productivity Beliefs You Should Ignore," *Fast Company,* October 14, 2015, https://www.fastcompany.com/3052004/7-popular-productivity-beliefs-you-should-ignore.

Page 248. "On any given day, assume that you can only accomplish": Alex Cavoulacos, "Why You Never Finish Your To-Do Lists at Work (and How to Change That)," *The Muse,* https://www.themuse.com
/advice/why-you-never-finish-your-todo-lists-at-work-and-how-to-change-that.

Page 252. only one in five people: Barbara Plester, *The Complexity of Workplace Humour: Laughter, Jokers and the Dark Side of Humour:* (New York: Springer, 2016).

Page 252. "Do People Mix at Mixers?": Paul Ingram and Michael W. Morris, "Do People Mix at Mixers?," *Administrative Science Quarterly* 52 (2007): 558–85.

Page 256. subjects who were asked to perform creative tasks: Marily Oppezzo and Daniel L. Schwartz, "Give Your Ideas Some Legs: The Positive Effect of Walking on Creative Thinking," *Journal of Experimental Psychology* 40, no. 4 (April 2014): 1142–52, doi.org/10.1037/a0036577.

Page 257. workers who take walking meetings: Russell Clayton, Christopher Thomas, and Jack Smothers, "How to Do Walking Meetings Right," *Harvard Business Review,* August 5, 2015, https://hbr.org/2015/08/how-to-do-walking-meetings-right.

Page 265. "Brain games improve the specific function": Sandra Bond Chapman, "Do Brain Games Really Boost Brain Power?," *Psychology Today,* March 4, 2014, https://www.psychologytoday.com/us/blog/make-your-brain-smarter/201403/do-brain-games-really-boost-brainpower.

Page 266. "Although the crossword seems engineered for solo consumption": Adrienne Raphel, *Thinking Inside the Box* (New York: Penguin Press, 2020).

Page 274. "bridges the gap between us and the natural world": Qing Li, "'Forest Bathing' Is Great for Your Health. Here's How to Do It," *Time,* May 1, 2018, https://time.com/5259602/japanese-forest-bathing.

Page 274. When researchers tested whether a forest or a hospital: Insook Lee et al., "Effects of Forest Therapy on Depressive Symptoms Among Adults: A

Systematic Review," *International Journal of Environmental Research and Public Health* 14, no. 3 (March 2017): 321.

Page 274. trees and plants release chemicals called phytoncides: "Immerse Yourself in a Forest for Better Health," New York State Department of Environmental Conservation, https://www.dec.ny.gov/lands/90720.html.

Page 278. "There's no diploma in the world that declares you as an artist": "'There's No Diploma in the World That Declares You an Artist': Watch Kara Walker Lay Out Her Advice for Art Students," *Artnet News,* July 12, 2018, https://news.artnet.com/art-world/watch-kara-walker-art-21-1316030.

Page 293. "I'm not afraid to get lost": "American Traveller Who Became Famous for Getting Lost in Iceland Announces His Return," *Iceland Magazine,* February 6, 2017, https://icelandmag.is/article/american-traveller-who-became-famous-getting-lost-iceland-announces-his-return.

Page 294. as the music writer Sarah Eldred points out: Sarah Eldred, "Stop Skipping Tracks: Why I Listen to Entire Albums," *The Current,* November 25, 2016, https://www.thecurrent.org/feature/2016/11/23/listening-entire-albums.

Page 295. "Good art often takes time to make": Amanda Petrusich, "The Music Critic in the Age of the Insta-Release," *The New Yorker,* March 9, 2016, https://www.newyorker.com/culture/cultural-comment/the-music-critic-in-the-age-of-the-insta-release.

Page 298. In the anthology *Not Quite What I Was Planning*: Rachel Fershleiser and Larry Smith, eds., *Not Quite What I Was Planning: Six-Word Memoirs by Writers Famous & Obscure* (New York: Harper Perennial, 2008).

Page 301. "To walk, to see, and to see what you see": Megan Gambino, "Tales from the Appalachian Trail," *Smithsonian Magazine,* July 13, 2009, https://www.smithsonianmag.com/history/tales-from-the-appalachian-trail-34902244.

Page 301. 3 Biomechanics professor Daniel Ferris explains: Markham Heid, "Why Hiking Is the Perfect Mind-Body Workout," *Time,* July 5, 2017, https://time.com/4820394/hiking-walking-mind-body-workout.

Page 302. "Being out in nature, away from the business": Abigail Wise, "Proof That Hiking Makes You Happier and Healthier," *HuffPost,* July 18, 2014, https://www.huffpost.com/entry/how-taking-a-hike-can-mak_n_5584809.

Page 308. studies show that upbeat background music: Sara Bottiroli et al., "The Cognitive Effects of Listening to Background Music on Older Adults: Processing Speed Improves with Upbeat Music, While Memory Seems to Benefit from Both Upbeat and Downbeat Music," *Frontiers in Aging Neuroscience* 6 (October 2014), https://doi.org/10.3389/fnagi.2014.00284

Page 308. the music industry raked in a whopping $43 billion: John Lynch, "Musicians Only Got 12% of the $43 Billion the Music Industry Generated in 2017, and It Mostly Came from Touring," *Business Insider,* August 7, 2018, https://www.businessinsider.com/musicians-received-12-percent-43-billion-generated-by-music-industry-study-2018-8.

Page 311. why people take so much pleasure from "reconsuming": Cristel Antonia Russell and Sidney J. Levy, "The Temporal and Focal Dynamics of Volitional Reconsumption: A Phenomenological Investigation of Repeated Hedonic Experiences," *Journal* *of Consumer Research* 39, no. 2 (August 2012): 341–59, doi:10.1086/662996.

Page 315. "Our response to color is intensely emotional": Beth Harwell, "The Power of Flowers: Studies Link Flowers with Emotional Health," Lilium Florals (blog), September 2, 2016, https://liliumflorals.com/blog/flowers-contribute-to-emotional-health.

Page 325. "Above all, a haiku must be very simple": Jack Kerouac, *Book of Haikus,* ed. Regina Weinreich (New York: Penguin Books, 2003).

Page 325. "Writing haiku takes you right into the heart": Tricycle staff, "Haiku Mind: An Interview with Clark Strand," *Tricycle: The Buddhist Review* (Summer 1997), https://tricycle.org/magazine/haiku-mind.

Page 329. Researchers at Yeshiva University's Albert Einstein College of Medicine: Joe Verghese et al., "Leisure Activities and the Risk of Dementia in the Elderly," *New England Journal of Medicine* 348 (June 2003): 2508–16, doi:10.1056/NEJMoa022252.

Page 332. 99 percent of people in the United States and Europe: Michelle Z. Donahue, "80 Percent of Americans Can't See the Milky Way Anymore," *National Geographic,* June 10, 2016, https://www.national geographic.com/news/2016/06/milky-way-space -science/#close.

Page 333. In a series of experiments, the researchers found that participants: Paul K. Piff et al., "Awe, the Small Self, and Pro-Social Behavior," *Journal of Personality and Social Psychology* 108, no. 6 (June 2015): 883–99.

Page 337. According to the psychologist John Eastwood: Kirsten Weir, "Never a Dull Moment," *Monitor on Psychology* 44, no. 7 (July/August 2013): 54.

Page 338. "The difficulty of always feeling that you ought to be doing something": Eric Tamm, *Brian Eno: His Music and the Vertical Color of Sound* (Boston: Da Capo Press, 1995).

About the Author

JON STAFF is the founder and CEO of Getaway, a company that provides simple, unplugged escapes to tiny cabins outside of major cities across the United States. Getaway grew from Jon's lifelong appreciation for the great outdoors, having grown up in a cabin in rural northern Minnesota. He earned his AB and MBA from Harvard University and now lives in Brooklyn.

ADL

Also by Nigel May:
TRINITY

ADDICTED

Nigel May

bookouture

Published by Bookouture

An imprint of StoryFire Ltd.
23 Sussex Road, Ickenham, UB10 8PN
United Kingdom

www.bookouture.com

ISBN: 978-1-910751-03-9
EBOOK ISBN: 978-1-910751-02-2

ACKNOWLEDGEMENTS

Many people have my gratitude - I'm 'addicted' to you all. The hugely talented David & Kathy Rose (for giving me my first chance in TV), Wayne Brookes (for campery and critique), to Cazz Wright & Kim Welsh (for design and neverending support), Lottie Mayor, Vicky Letch & Nush Bellamy (for every joyful moment), Shelly Cooke (for a lifetime of friendship), 'sons' Steve, Nick & Joe (for extended 'family'), Sam Smith and Will Spilsbury (for the feelgood factor), Louise, Julie & Kath (for always being there, no matter what), the *more!* and *Sunlounger* girls. And of course to Alan for eternal love, guidance, glee and grounding. 'Scuddle baby!' To Vicky & Paul for the future. And to everyone who has read my words. I thank you all.

PROLOGUE

The heavenly strains of 'Ave Maria' ricocheted against the Gothic eighteenth-century walls of St Agatha's church, filling its interior with organ music. Accompanying it was a biting mixture of voices from the choir situated underneath the carved oak pulpit at the front of the church.

Busying himself with a mound of scribbled notes and pushing his metal-rimmed spectacles up his bulbous nose as he nervously scanned the congregation seated in front of him was the Reverend Michael Gregory. In his fifty-plus years of professional worship this had to be his most high profile funeral to date. Never before had he presided over a service that had attracted such media attention. He could already feel the rivulets of sweat running down his back under his cassock.

A mass of designer-clad mourners had spent the best part of an hour filing into the church. Celebrities from the world of television, some who'd been staring out from the newspaper gossip pages that very morning, caused whispers of excitement.

Alongside them was a scattering of film stars. Rugged, chiselled features and flawless, porcelain-doll skin that had only ever been seen locally on posters at the tiny village cinema or staring down from the sides of the buses that frequently trundled past the church's graveyard.

Representatives from London's West End and famed singing sensations were in attendance too, as was a peppering of politicians. Not old-school dinosaurs that any of the regular attendees of St Agatha's had ever voted for ... no, some of those supposedly trendy ones who were more interested in being seen on some Caribbean island with a rock star buddy than putting the country back on its feet. These were all celebrities for the twenty-first century. New, hip, happening.

Not that any of the mourners gathered had made it easy to be recognised, for once. Most wore large dark sunglasses covering their faces. Puzzling, seeing as it was hardly the height of summer. The sun had been hiding itself behind heavy pendulous clouds all day, so why the need for sunglasses? They were an odd crowd staring up at the reverend, many of them nervously twitching their heads left and right with alarming regularity, as if checking out just who was who and who was sitting where. The seating plan of this particular funeral had seemingly never been so important. There had been a frenzy of hurried footsteps rushing into St Agatha's the moment the solid church doors had opened.

That's what happens when segments of the service are being filmed for broadcast. Due to public interest, images would be shown on the news later that day. Being seen to mourn was obviously paramount in many of the gathered mass's minds.

There had been a bank of photographers and reporters outside the church. Every time a car with blacked-out windows had pulled up outside the ornate lychgate, the whole church had lit up with the popping flashlights from the cameras. The family of the deceased had been heard bemoaning that the funeral had become 'a bloody circus'.

For the locals, used to living in one of England's most green yet normally tranquil areas, the invasion of the media world was a pain in the backside but the various 'names' being escorted from their cars by a cap-peaked chauffeur were lapping it up, basking in the hollered screams of reporters clamouring for a decent headline-grabbing quote. From the tabloid hacks desperate for a tasty titbit concerning the mysterious circumstances that surrounded the deceased's demise to the fashionistas gagging for details of what the well-dressed celebrity was wearing to funerals these days, their constant high volume cries sounded like deranged seagulls. Not that any species other than humans would be able to come up with such vacuous answers.

'She was greatly loved, taken from us at such a crucial point in her life. I am beyond bereft, but shall try to cope.'

'Always a dear friend, she had so much more to give. Why is life sometimes so cruel and heartless?'

'The pain of losing such a bright light has dimmed my very existence. It will be so hard for me to shine again, but for my angel in heaven above, I know that's exactly what she'd want me to do.'

Every comment followed by a seemingly sincere face of misery and a beautifully manicured hand raised to the neckline as if clutching some imaginary string of pearls in a faux outpouring of angst and heartache. The falseness of it all was brutally obvious. Those who really seemed to care for the woman being buried today were few and far between. It was indeed a circus.

Gazing down from the pulpit as the final note of 'Ave Maria' petered out, the sunglasses-adorned faces of those peering up at Reverend Gregory spooked him slightly. Their big black compound eyes stared like mutant insects from a bad sci-fi movie. Adjusting his dog collar nervously, he began the service.

'Dearly beloved, we are gathered here today to celebrate the life of …'

———

The entire funeral service had lasted just under an hour. Despite the high profile nature of the day, as the mourners made their way from the church to the plot where the deceased was to be buried, it seemed that alongside the natural sorrow of the occasion, an extra feeling of disharmony stained the air.

The funeral had gone without a hitch, but something had been missing. Was it love? Warmth? At first it was difficult to decide just what it was, but as the congregation drifted out of the church and across the red carpet from the church path to the graveside, it became clear. There had been a sinister air of coldness from some of the congregation since the beginning. In fact, to anyone of a perceptive nature, an undeniable feeling that some were more than pleased to say goodbye to the deceased for the final time hung in the atmosphere.

As the coffin was lowered into its final resting place by the pall-bearers, a mass of piteous sobs filled the air. Some appeared too forced and too evident to be real. The genuine tear-laden laments came from the group of loved ones gathered at one end of the grave, a family hanging onto each other for support in their hour of woe.

The cries mixed with the heady scent of dozens of floral wreaths scattered around the graveside. But outweighing the floral odours and the flowing of grief was the rotting guilty stench of hatred, deceit and murder that coursed through the mind of one of the mourners. Unbeknown to those around her, she was the reason the lifeless body of a once 'dear friend' was now headed six feet under.

As the mourners moved away, one figure lingered by the open grave.

If anyone had been watching they would have seen a gentle curling of her lipstick-slicked mouth as she allowed herself a sardonic smile. In her hands she held a single red rose. It was as red as the blood on her hands ... the blood of a murderer.

Tossing the rose down onto the polished ebony casket, she watched it land on the gold engraved name plaque on top of the coffin. She felt satisfied at last. All of her scheming and hard work had finally paid off.

Reaching into her Miu Miu velvet bow clutch bag she pulled out a small mirror and her lipstick. As she finally allowed herself to smile broadly, she reapplied the make-up to her lips.

With a final glance at the coffin, she said, 'That will teach you to mess with me, you bitch'. She licked her lips, turned on her heels and strutted towards her waiting car, confident that she had got away with murder.

PART ONE

CHAPTER 1

Several months earlier ...

'What do you mean, the offers have dried up completely, Dale? Surely there must be some godforsaken reality show that wants me? I'd do anything – flounder around an ice rink, throw myself off a diving board, truss myself up in sequins and learn to master the bloody foxtrot ... even spend weeks in some rain-soaked jungle if need be. Isn't there anything?'

Nancy Arlow's voice had desperation knotted right through it. Sitting in her manager Dale Cousins' office in south-west London, she could feel tears pricking the corners of her eyes and her bottom lip begin to quiver as she pleaded with him. 'I can't be washed up at the age of twenty-five. It's just not fair. You should be banging people's doors down to get me decent film and TV work! I want to be the next Jennifer Lawrence.'

How had it come to this? After three years experiencing six top ten singles and a sell-out tour of Asia as a teenage pop sensation, then acting in *Eton Shore,* the biggest soap opera on British TV, Nancy's last job had seen her fighting an imaginary giant squid against a phoney backdrop in yet another straight-to-DVD turkey – *Squidosaurus: Monster From Below.* To add insult to injury she had spent most of her scenes naked, jutting her breasts towards the camera. Her career had nose-dived fifty fathoms deep.

As had become customary over the last few months, a bored Dale's eyes glazed over as he listened to Nancy. As far as he was concerned, her star had faded so greatly it was now at fizzle-out point. Virtually every casting director in the business had said no to her.

'Times are hard, babe, you know that. Give it a couple of months and hopefully there'll be another flick to work on. Maybe the squid one will be a cult success.' Dale knew that his words were floundering in an attempt to give false hope.

'You know full well that the stupid squid film is never going to give me any kind of credibility. And it certainly hasn't made me a lot of money, Dale. I need cash,' moaned Nancy.

It was true, times were harder than hard. Back in the good old days, Nancy had been raking in an absolute fortune for her wide-boy manager. Thank God he'd screwed her over for cash back when she was earning the big bucks. Hell, he'd screwed Nancy anyway he could, despite being twelve years older than her. She was a beauty worthy of the cover of Italian *Vogue*. Any man would find her hard to resist, which was why for many years their partnership had been both on paper and between the bedroom sheets.

As he watched her run her fingers through her long, pitch-black hair, the light streaming through his office window dancing across her exotic sienna skin as she pleaded with him, his mind began to wander. *Jesus, Nancy. You're still sexier than most women could ever hope to be but when did you get to be so fucking thick? Don't you get it – you're old news! Your career is dead.*

How things had changed. Their union had started when Nancy was sixteen after she'd seen an advertisement in a music industry magazine searching for the next big thing. *Wanted! Teenage singing sensation to set the world alight. Great looks essential, decent voice a bonus. Send a demo and full-length colour photo to...* The age-old rags-to-riches story but it had worked.

For a while they were unstoppable, but it had definitely been a case of make hay while the sun shone. After her time lighting up the music charts around the world and acting her heart out as part of Britain's hottest prime-time soap, Dale had been shocked at how quickly her media presence had diluted to almost nothing. The public had lost interest, her star had faded. He thanked his lucky stars that he'd bought his SW1 Roma Records office and his Notting Hill flat outright when he had the cash to do so. These days the main money-makers on his management books were cheesy groups from days gone by, reforming for nostalgia tours. Sadly, at twenty-five, Nancy wasn't even old enough to consider a retrospective singing career comeback. No, Dale had to admit that he needed to find a celebrity golden goose if he was going to carry on with his lavish lifestyle; Nancy's goose was definitely past its sell-by date.

'Dale, I have bills to pay that aren't going away. I need you to help me, for old time's sake.' As she spoke, Nancy stared directly into Dale's eyes, her own golden-brown eyes wide and begging. Dale felt she was looking into his soul, and at that moment all he could see before him was a pitiful version of the young starlet he had once loved. Maybe there was a little bubbling part of him that still did.

Leaning across his desk and taking Nancy by the hand, he said, 'How much do you need? Consider it a loan. I'll be taking it out of your fee from the next movie.' In the back of his mind Dale couldn't help but think the chances of Nancy actually making another movie were slimmer than Victoria Beckham's waistline.

Nancy smiled for the first time throughout their meeting. 'Ten thousand should be enough to see me through for a few weeks at least. I'll put it towards my tax bill and use some for my mortgage payments.'

Dale pursed his lips together and whistled in surprise. 'Ten grand? It's more than I intended but, seeing as it's you, I'll do it. How much is the tax bill, by the way?'

'Oh, not that much, really,' fudged Nancy. 'I've been saving for it, so this loan should sort it out.' Nancy could feel her skin heat up as colour flooded to her cheeks. She always blushed when she lied. Ten thousand was no more than the tiny tip of the iceberg that had become her financial woes. A six-figure tax bill and mortgage arrears were in danger of engulfing her life for good. She knew she could sell her flat and probably make a small profit, but the one thing that Nancy's pride would never let her do was downsize. Despite being rock bottom, in her dreams Nancy believed that one day she would climb back to the top of the celebrity tree.

'Could we make it cash, Dale? It makes things so much easier.' Nancy crossed her legs as she asked, her short denim skirt revealing a hint of lacy underwear as she did so. If she was going to be cheeky with her demands, then she knew that she would have to appeal to Dale's manly desires as well as his managerial duty. As his eyes travelled down to her lap, Nancy knew that he'd agree. If there was one talent that she still had in abundance it was her ability to wrap gullible men around her slender fingers – and she still knew how to pull Dale's strings.

'We can go and fetch the cash now.' Dale heard himself say it before he'd even thought about it. He'd been too busy picturing the heavenly hotspot between Nancy's legs. His cock twitched involuntarily as he did so. 'But use it wisely, Nancy, eh? As I said, work is hard to come by right now, so it might be a while before another payday.'

'I will, I promise.' Nancy was on her feet and linking arms with Dale, ushering him out of his office as quickly as possible. 'Now, which way's your bank?' As she spoke, she was sure that she could spot the telltale bulge in the front of his trousers. *I've still got it*, she thought. *And I always will ... God bless the power of a woman.*

As they walked onto the London street outside Dale's office, Nancy had to admit that the thought of £10,000 was proving to be quite an aphrodisiac for her too.

CHAPTER 2

Flicking through her black leather address book, Lauren Everett glumly stared at the multitude of names of one-time friends she no longer saw. Sports stars, actors, musicians, pop stars, models … her book read like a *Who's Who* of the celebrity magazine world. But you didn't have to be in *Who's Who* to know what's what … They were all people who only figured in Lauren's former life. Life before her husband: politician and potential future prime minister, Saul Everett.

'The sacrifices a one-time model and party girl has to make, eh, Barney?' bemoaned Lauren to the huge red and white Siberian husky sitting at her feet. A brown smudge of mud was evident against his wet black nose.

'Been digging the dirt again, have we? At least one of us is allowed to get dirty today, you lucky bugger. Your dad's out again for the night, so it's just you and me. I guess I should be used to it by now.'

Life with Saul could be lonely. *Could?* Hell, it *was*. Damn him, she was horny and had been looking forward to a night of pure seduction. But the message she'd just listened to on their house answering machine had killed that. It had been Saul – another night, another excuse. It was the usual tale.

> '*Hi, Lauren – Nathan has requested me for a meeting so I won't be back tonight, darling. Nathan wants to discuss something with me… silly old fart. I suspect it might be a messy one, so I'm booking into a hotel near the club we're*

drinking at. I'll be home tomorrow. Have a good night.
Give Barney a kiss from me. And Nathan says be good.'

'Nathan, Nathan, Nathan! That man is the bane of my life,' seethed Lauren to herself, pressing the delete button. Nathan Spilsbury – one time go-getting hot-shot political rattlesnake and influential ex-public schoolmate of the prime minister, but now a tubby, foul-mouthed, chauvinistic, old-school but very well-connected fifty-something spin doctor who seemed to control her husband in everything that he did or said. Lauren hated him. Saul, sadly for her, worshipped him. He was like a parasitic father figure, feasting on Saul's meteoric success up the political ladder.

It was Nathan who had told Saul to inform 'his buxom yet densely dim filly of a wife' – yes, those were his exact words – that if she was seen anywhere near one of those 'dreadfully freak-ish Z-listers the silly bitch used to ponce about with' – again his words – then it could spell curtains for Saul's career. And without his career, Lauren wouldn't have the annual holidays to hotspots like St Lucia and the Maldives, or the twelve-bedroom luxury residence with a swimming pool clad in iridescent tiles, an extensive drawing room lined with books she'd never read and two tennis courts out the back.

Being married to one of the country's most heralded politicians certainly had its benefits, but what was the point of having it all if there was no one to have fun with? Or at least no one on the same level as Lauren. Someone who shared her interests and would enjoy discussing designer frocks, killer heels and media tittle-tattle. Someone to skinny-dip and sip cocktails with at the pool. Someone who wanted to discuss man-eaters, not manifestoes.

Eyeing the list of names again, Lauren formed a mental list as to who she would have phoned first in her partying days. 'What's the point, Barney? They're all beneath me now ... or so

I'm instructed. They can go out and dance till dawn, laughing with beautiful strangers, and I will be tucked up here with only you and the latest Jackie Collins for company. Mid-twenties and I already feel like some sad old widow whose peak of excitement is deciding on which night to go to the bingo. How did this happen?'

Slamming the address book shut and bending down to wipe the smudge from Barney's nose, Lauren sighed and contemplated how she would fill another solitary day. 'A spa session in town and a touch of retail therapy. Sod you, Saul, I'm off to spend your money. Your body may be out of reach but at least I can get my hands on your bank account.'

———

Parking her Jaguar XK convertible outside one of her favourite West End clothes shops, Lauren stared through the window at the fantastic designer creations on display. All of them were easily within her price range, but what was the point? Not one of them fitted in with her husband's views of what she should be seen wearing in public. There was no point in buying a £3,000 flesh-flashing outfit if it was merely going to fester at the back of the wardrobe. Lauren had already traded her once-loved *prêt-à-porter* creations and moved onto much safer options such as wide-leg trousers, crêpe jackets and blazers to suit Saul. Heaven knows what her former friends would have said.

So, what to buy? she mused. *A new rug for the living room? New taps for the en-suite?* Lauren's thoughts bored her to the core. No, she needed to make herself feel as fabulous as possible, so there was only one thing for it. The common ground that she and Saul shared when it came to fashion — sexy, sultry, designer underwear. Pressing her Jaguar key fob to lock the car, she headed towards La Perla.

Once inside the shop, Lauren immersed herself in the goodies on display. Despite Saul's straight-laced conservative views of the world at large, Lauren knew that he had a decidedly kinky streak in the bedroom. Even though their love-making had become much less frequent due to his career, on the times they did become intimate, she had always been aware of Saul's liking of slightly deviant tastes. He'd been known to place her over his knee and slap her buttocks until they glowed salmon-red under the warmth of his palm. She had often handcuffed him to the bed as well, watching him squirm with desire as she tickled his underarms, nipples and manhood with a downy feather. Often he'd be so turned on by her actions that he would come before she had even guided him into her. He would always insist on returning the favour too.

Deciding that a spicy night in the boudoir was in order as soon as possible, Lauren thumbed through the racks, filling her arms with bustiers, bras and briefs made from the finest silk and tulle and decorated with glittery crystals. As an extra treat she picked up a black silk mask, decorated with a heart. She curled her lips with excitement as she handed her armful of super sexy garments over to the cashier, imagining the salacious look on Saul's face when she presented herself to him.

Glancing at her watch as she left the shop and headed up Sloane Street, Lauren saw that it was still early in the day. The last thing she wanted to do was return home to the empty, cavernous house.

It's almost lunch time, she ruminated. *A glass of white wine could be just what the doctor ordered.* Swinging her La Perla bags alongside her, Lauren crossed the road and headed into the first bar she came to. The interior was contemporary and stylish, the clientele the right side of cool. Seating herself, she ordered a glass of wine and stared around the bar.

Just as the wine was being placed on her table, Lauren's jaw fell open. Sitting on the other side of the bar was Nancy Arlow. Lauren had grown up loving Nancy, listening to her music and then watching her as a main player in her favourite soap opera, *Eton Shore*. Even though Lauren had met many famous people through her husband, they had always been stuffy politicians or dryer-than-dry councillors. Nancy Arlow was a true star. Or at least she used to be. As Lauren stared at Nancy, she couldn't help but notice the strikingly handsome man sitting opposite her.

Unable to stop herself, Lauren picked up her wine and walked over to their table. 'Excuse me, I'm so sorry to interrupt, but I just have to say that I adored you in *Eton Shore*. You were amazing!'

A grinning Nancy, still high from the fact that £10,000 in hard cash nestled in her handbag, looked up at Lauren. There was something familiar about her and she immediately liked her warmth and style. 'Thank you very much, that's nice of you to say. I sometimes wish I was still there.'

'You were the best thing on it, by a mile. I was gripped whenever you were on screen. And I used to love your songs too. I used to model and sing a bit myself back in the day but only amateur stuff, or pretending I was Madonna in the shower. I meet famous people all the time through my husband, but honestly, you have always been such an inspiration,' gushed Lauren. 'What are you doing these days? I haven't seen you on the TV for ages.'

'I'm contemplating my next move, shall we say … I don't want to rush into anything too quickly.' Nancy was keen to move the conversation on before it became obvious that she was, in fact, unemployed. 'Your husband? Who's that? Anyone we know? This is Dale Cousins, by the way. He's my manager. We've just come to celebrate a bit of business with a drink.'

Dale, who had not said a word so far, looked up at Lauren and shook her hand. 'Charmed,' he said, transfixed by the beautiful blonde apparition before him. Her rosy skin and fair hair made her the extreme opposite of Nancy – almost a photographic negative.

'My husband's Saul Everett, the politician,' continued Lauren. 'He's off working today, so I thought I'd have a touch of retail therapy.' She pointed over to where her La Perla bags littered the floor.

'Nice taste in underwear,' smiled Nancy. 'I love their stuff.'

A tad flustered at what to say next, Lauren started to ramble. 'Er … thank you. Well, I'll let you two get on. It was fabulous to meet you. Maybe we'll meet again, I do hope so. Bye for now. God, you really are amazing.'

As a fawning Lauren returned to her table, Nancy grinned at Dale. 'Well, I liked her. Anyone who thinks I'm amazing is OK with me. I knew I'd seen her somewhere before. Her husband's supposedly a real hotshot in Westminster. I've seen him on the news.'

'A stunner too. I mean her, not him, obviously,' commented Dale.

Draining his glass, he went to stand. 'Right, Nancy, I'll do what I can to secure you a job – and I know you want anything as long as it doesn't involve you fighting plastic monsters – so that you can pay that money back. Spend it wisely and I'll ring you if anything comes up. I'm off to a meeting.'

It was a pack of lies. Dale lied incredibly well – it was a crucial part of his job skills. Dale had no meeting planned and he had no intention of trying to secure Nancy more work. His focus had been redirected towards a different avenue of excitement. Lauren Everett. As he smiled across to her table and walked out of the bar he knew that their paths would cross again. He would make sure of it.

CHAPTER 3

'I want you dressed and ready to go by eight o'clock, Martha. Have you got that? So smarten yourself up and put something pretty on, for God's sake.' Wine empire owner and multi-millionaire Lewin Éclair's voice was gruff and laced with menace as he barked his orders at his only daughter. 'Four of us are eating at Le Quartier Français in Franschhoek.'

Martha had just walked back through the main doorway of the palatial South African Éclair estate house and into the entrance hall after an afternoon sexual liaison with Joseph, one of her father's loyal vineyard workers. She could tell that there was no point arguing with her father, though she'd already made plans to meet up with some of her friends that evening. Her happiness deflated immediately.

Her curiosity stirred however, Martha still wanted details. 'Just who are the *four* of us going to be then, Daddy? Is Mum joining us? And I suppose Adina will be coming too. It's not like her to miss a night of food at one of the best restaurants in South Africa, is it?'

Martha and her father's current squeeze, Adina King, had never really seen eye-to-eye. As far as Martha was concerned, former WAG Adina was a gold-digger in the true sense of the word. Despite the mere six-year age gap between them, they were at the opposite ends of the spectrum when it came to their views on life. The free-spirited lifestyle that Martha revelled in seemed abhorrent to Adina. For her, the only free spirits worth dealing with were the liberal amounts poured into her cocktail glass in VIP areas at South Africa's hottest clubs. If Adina was sidling up to an airhead celebrity and posing for the paps then she was in her element. Say 'Paris' to Martha and she would immediately talk of the artistic alleyways of Montmartre and the beauty of the Sacré Coeur. Say the same word to Adina and she would brag proudly about rubbing shoulders with the heiress Hilton and her socialite friends.

'Adina will be joining us, of course,' snapped Lewin. 'As for your mother – while she still insists on sharing the bed of that bastard Peter Bradford, then she and I will not set foot in the same room.'

It was true. Martha couldn't actually remember the last time she and her parents had sat down as a family and actually enjoyed some time together. 'So, who's diner number four? Not one of Adina's equally intellectual friends, I hope?' she smirked. She couldn't help but smile at her gentle dig.

Ignoring her, Lewin continued. 'A guy by the name of Roger Penhaligon. He's a bright young businessman. Bloody rich too. His computer company is one of the biggest in the country and they're interested in installing some new-fangled, up-to-date system here at the vineyards to govern our export, import and the suchlike. He's even talking about investing into the company as he wants to branch out. He's keen to win me over, so the meal's on him.'

Martha's brain numbed at the thought of the evening ahead. She would not exactly be hanging out with her ideal dinner companions, that was for sure. Her surly father, the vacuous Adina and a computer geek. 'Oh, kill me now …' she muttered sarcastically as she headed upstairs to her room. She was just reaching the top when Lewin bellowed a final order after her. 'And wear something revealing. One of those designer frocks. This Penhaligon chap is single, by all accounts.'

Why was it always about business? Was Martha surprised? No. Lewin had always insisted on putting his empire before his family. Ever since its launch some thirty years earlier, Lewin Éclair Wines had managed to establish itself as one of South Africa's most successful and highly respected family-owned boutique wineries. Perched high on the slopes of the majestic Helderberg Mountain in the Stellenbosch region of the Western Cape, it had become a multibillion rand company under the expert and ruthless eye of its owner.

Just like the grapes that were crushed each and every day to produce the Éclair estate's prize-winning Chardonnays and Merlots, Lewin had crushed many other local wine companies along the way to ensure that Lewin Éclair survived. It had brought him riches beyond his wildest dreams and a lifestyle of Donald Trump proportions, making his name a regular fixture on the annual Forbes Rich List. And one day he hoped the natural successor to his position at the helm of Lewin Éclair would be his daughter, Martha.

At twenty-four, she should have been ready to take the reins and move the company into the twenty-first century with a potent mix of glamour and business acumen. But, as far as Lewin could see, that was never going to happen. She'd tried to explain to him on many occasions. 'Daddy, I'm a free-spirit. You can't bludgeon me into showing an interest when I have none. I can't tell the difference between a palatable Pinot and a sassy Sauvignon. It's just not me. You and Mum know that.'

Her mother, Mariella, now separated from Lewin, was on her side. Martha was definitely her mother's daughter. 'You can't force the girl into a career, Lewin.' But her words, like Martha's, had always fallen on deaf ears. Blowing a thick cloud of cigar smoke into the air, an exasperated Lewin had merely coughed and muttered under his breath. 'The damn girl is a waste of space. She's no use to this company on her own. I need to find her a decent husband to run things for me.' Which was why Martha was yet again being displayed like a prize poodle for the latest candidate in her father's quest to find her a husband.

Martha didn't want a husband yet – far from it. There were plenty of men out there she wanted to savour, taste and try out. With a flirtatious appeal that was difficult to cork, it was very easy for her to indulge in her favourite hobby on a very regular basis. Sex.

Gazing into the full-length mirror in her bedroom and hold-ing up a stunning Roberto Cavalli dress with a plunging neck-line to her petite naked frame, Martha grimaced at the thought of the night ahead. 'Why can't I just be getting a repeat perfor-mance of this afternoon? Now that was my idea of a really good time ...'

Indeed, it had been skin-tinglingly divine. Enjoying the feel-ing of the strong South African sun beating down on her naked flesh and the sweet scent of the lush green grass underneath her long blond hair, Martha had been flat on her back, her clothes discarded, in one of the far-flung vineyards on the Lewin Éclair estate.

Alongside her lay Joseph, one of her father's many workers. He was also naked, his ebony skin still traced with sweat from their frenzied love-making. Martha had sampled the carnal de-lights of many of the vineyard's staff, but even for a woman of her voracious sexual appetite, she had to admit that Joseph was pretty special. She seemed to return time and time again to his thickly proportioned manhood and hard muscular body, loving the feeling of him thrusting inside her.

'Martha, I don't think I'll ever tire of making love to you,' grinned Joseph, flashing a row of magnificent paper-white teeth. 'Why won't you let me be with you on a more permanent basis?'

Propping herself up onto her elbow, Martha turned to face him, a cheeky grin spreading across her pretty and ironically angelic-looking features. 'You couldn't keep up with me, Joseph. And besides, I'm too young to commit to just one man, you know that. If I reach forty and need a fallback guy, then maybe. But for now, I'm just more than happy for a repeat performance if you fancy another quickie.' She gave his cock a playful flick.

'Whoa, lady. I need to get back to work. Your father would have my head on a stick at the estate gates if he knew what we got up to.' Joseph reached for his clothes as he spoke.

'I think mine would be alongside it, don't you? If he knew how hands-on I was with so many of his male employees, then I think I'd be sent into exile. It's not my fault if I find you all so attractive, is it?'

Joseph winced at Martha's words. Despite knowing about her other liaisons, his love for her still made her sexual admissions hard to bear. But he knew that he would always have to dance to Martha's tune. For now, he would have to content himself with their snatched moments, even though he considered them too few and far between.

Pulling his T-shirt over his head, Joseph kissed Martha on the lips and ran off across the vineyard. Martha watched his broad back disappear into the distance, dressed herself and headed back towards the house. Life was good, shining as brightly as the sun overhead.

As she wove her way in between the vines she picked a full, rounded grape from one of the many bunches and popped it into her mouth. It exploded as she bit into it, the taste mingling with the taste of Joseph's kisses still present against her lips. At that moment, Martha Éclair couldn't have been happier.

But happiness was not on the menu for Martha that evening. In fact, the entire evening turned out to be a complete bore, although not without incident.

Adina had posed peacock-like outside the restaurant with a huffy Lewin attached to her arm. The gathered press, tipped off by Adina herself as to her whereabouts, clicked away eagerly. If there was one thing even Martha had to admit Adina did well, it was pose expertly. The combination of her uber-short dresses, seemingly never-ending legs and a mass of rich, black curls framing her provocative features and toothpaste-advert smile, assured that she would always gain maximum exposure in the gossip columns. Martha chose to leave them to it and headed inside the restaurant to wait.

She was no sooner through the door when a tuxedo-clad man appeared at her side. He stood a touch too close for her liking and Martha was immediately taken aback at the invasion of her personal space. His suit was noticeably a size too big for his slender, boy-like frame, and when he extended his hand to Martha, she couldn't help but notice a ripple of over-eager excitement in his manner. His top lip was dotted with perspiration and his skin blotchy. He looked feeble and his manner unnerved her. There was nothing attractive about him.

'Hello there. I'm Roger Penhaligon. I believe we're dining together this evening. You're even sexier in the flesh than you are in photos. Dining with you will be an absolute pleasure.' As he spoke, any words featuring an 's' seemed to hiss from his lips. He reminded Martha of a serpent.

They were just seating themselves as Lewin and Adina appeared. 'Ah, Roger, I see you've met Martha. This is my girl-

friend, Adina King,' smiled Lewin. Adina reached out her hand
to Roger, who took hold of it and placed it to his lips. Martha
was sure that Adina grimaced as he did so, somewhat aghast
at the vision of patheticness before her. *Maybe Adina and I do
finally agree on something*, thought Martha.

The conversation throughout the meal had been strictly business. Martha tried to feign interest, smiling sweetly as much as
her bored features would let her. Adina was less subtle, openly
yawning at one point and excusing herself to make phone calls.

It had been halfway through the first course that Martha had
become aware that Roger seemed to be taking advantage of any
opportunity to inadvertently touch her. At first it had been the
light brushing of his leg up against hers underneath the table.
Then there would be the complimenting of her dress or her jewellery, where he would allow his fingers to linger on Martha's
flesh just a little longer than necessary. Then she felt Roger's
bony digits squeezing her leg under the table. Without saying a
word, she gently moved them away. A few minutes later, he tried
he same thing. Again she pushed him away.

If any man normally gave her unwanted attention, Martha
was ballsy enough to tell him where to get off, but she knew that
Lewin would be mad if she caused a scene. She knew better than
to come between her father and a potential investor. She would
just have to grin and bear Roger's touchy-feeliness until the end
of the meal.

As he said goodbye to her at the end of the night, Martha
forced herself to smile through gritted teeth. 'It was charming
to meet you, Martha. I suspect we'll be seeing a lot more of each
other.' He kissed her on the cheeks. Martha could still feel the
clamminess of his lips on her as she, Adina and Lewin climbed
into the back on one of her father's fleet of chauffeur-driven
limousines to take them back to the Éclair estate.

Lewin was pleased with how the evening had passed. Having downed copious glasses of wine, he slurred his words slightly as he spoke. 'I reckon he'll be investing millions. This could be the start of a whole new era for Lewin Éclair wines. Nice chap, as well.'

'If you like the sleazy kind,' said Adina, staring blankly out of the limo window. 'Anyway, why does your company need an injection of cash? It's not in financial trouble, is it?' There was a wobble of worry in Adina's voice.

'Far from it, but you have to look to the future. And Roger was not sleazy … he's just not been blessed with my good looks,' chortled Lewin,

Martha was quick to reply. 'Are you kidding, Dad? The man was slimier than a room full of slugs.'

'Well, he seemed to like you, judging from the way he was touching your leg every five minutes. I don't know what you're moaning about, Martha, he would make you a bloody good boyfriend. It's not like you've got them lining up, is it?'

Incensed by Lewin's words, Martha snapped back, 'When I do want a boyfriend, and right now I'm happy being young, free and single, thank you very much, then the last person I would consider is that sleazeball. And if he hadn't been a potential investor then I would have punched him the first time he tried to grab my leg, OK?'

'Way to go, girl!' deadpanned Adina, still staring vacuously out into the night sky.

Lewin continued to rant at Martha. 'It's about time you settled down and did something with your life, missy. A decent man would give you a good grounding, especially when it comes to the business. With a rich, sensible man like Penhaligon running things I'd be happy. And with my daughter by his side, at least I know that the company will still be in the family when

I snuff it. You're the only option I have. You could at least consider doing the right thing for me, for once in your life.'

Lewin punched the leather of the back seat to vent his annoyance. 'He told me he thought you were decent-looking. Why do you think I invited you out tonight, for Christ's sake? If it was just for schmoozing money out of the chap, Adina and I could have handled that. He likes you, and I want you to like him, for the good of this company.'

Feeling tears pooling at the corners of her eyes, Martha swallowed hard, searching for an explanation. 'So, you're telling me that tonight was about whoring me out to someone who you think might be interested in running Lewin Éclair wines in the future. What's the going rate for selling off your daughter to the highest bidder, Dad? He's not even my type. But then, how would you know what is? I am not some bargaining tool for you to play with.'

As the limo pulled up outside the estate, Martha reached for the door and yanked it open. She was determined not to cry in front of Lewin. Slamming the door in his face, she raced into the house.

Inside the car, adjusting her dress, Adina waited until the chauffeur came to open the door for her. Looking at Lewin, his face still red with rage, she sneered, 'I could run this business for you when you decide to retire. I do like a good glass of wine, after all.'

Lewin wasted no time in replying. 'You? You drink enough of the stuff, but you know bugger all about it. You'd be about as much use as Martha. In fact you'd probably be worse ...'

He had barely finished the sentence before the door had slammed in his face again.

—

Lying in bed that night, Martha couldn't sleep. Her mind was spinning with thoughts of what had happened that evening. The thought of creepy Roger's fingers on her flesh was bad enough, but the idea of her father looking on, hoping that it was to be the start of some joyous union disturbed Martha deeply. He had set her up on a blind date where the prize was his own ultimate professional satisfaction. Martha knew that she had to get away from him. Away from the estate, away from the pressure of the family business, away to somewhere where she could just be herself.

As the early morning light streamed over the beautiful hills of the Western Cape, Martha packed two suitcases, hastily wrote a note saying she'd be in touch and called for a taxi. By the time Lewin and Adina awoke, she was already at Cape Town airport deciding where to go.

CHAPTER 4

Opera diva Portia Safari was far from happy as she faced each and every one of the capacity crowd giving her a standing ovation after yet another night's awe-inspiring performance.

Not that her painted-on smile hinted at any of the inner angst flooding through her mind as the curtain lowered itself into place for the final time of the night on Budapest Opera House's enormous stage. The home of Hungarian opera, with its fine neo-Renaissance architecture, had been Portia's home for the last four weeks and finally her work on the epic production of Wagner's *Tristan und Isolde* was over. Playing the role of the tragic Isolde for five shows a week for the last month had been demanding, but for a woman of Portia's strength, stamina and professionalism, even the role that many critics deemed to be one of the most punishing in existence was well within her capability.

At the age of thirty-six, Portia had proved herself as the number one diva of the modern age. A woman spiced with a glamorous presence, passion and the power to allure. One who had smashed the notion that a diva was a portly middle-aged woman with a score of zero on the scale of sexual attraction. She had single-handedly made opera trendy.

Portia's stunning facial beauty had already verified that she was 'worth it' in the eyes of one of the biggest cosmetics firms on earth, having been one of their spokeswomen for nearly a decade. And the liquid curves of her body were in demand by the world's top fashion designers. She was the muse they all wanted to work with.

Her career had never been so lucrative ... so why the unhappiness? Her misery was tangible and when Portia Safari slipped into a bad mood, then woe betide anyone who found themselves in her impassioned way.

Even before the rapturous applause had died down on the other side of the curtain, Portia raised her eyebrows, pursed her lips and turned to the hulk of the man beside her. Her glare was Medusa-like. The muscular form of Piero Romeo quivered nervously, knowing that Portia's fury was about to be unleashed. Piero, an Italian by birth, was one of the world's leading heldentenors, and had been playing the role of Tristan opposite Portia.

'What the fuck were those random notes you spewed out halfway through that act, Piero?' Portia was puce with rage, tiny droplets of spit flying from her bottom lip as she shouted. 'Didn't you tell me that Piero meant *rock* in Italian? You, my dear, couldn't hit the right note with a boulder the size of the Coliseum. I will not have my performances ruined by amateurs like you. It's my character who is supposed to die onstage, not my eardrums listening to your inferior vocal offerings. Thank God this whole production is over.'

Before Piero had any chance to retaliate, Portia had spun away from him, her costume whirling around her like a tornado, and started to march offstage. As she reached the wings, she pirouetted back round to face Piero once more, a mass of flame-red hair gyrating around the striking feline features of her face as she did so. 'And your surname, Romeo ... I've never met a man more ineptly named. Your love-making skills are the worst I've ever come across.'

With that Portia was gone, striding back to her dressing room. She never saw an inflamed Piero being held back by three fellow cast members as he attempted to rush after the diva. Nobody would dent his macho Italian pride. Portia could slate his singing all she liked, the world's press and opera lovers knew that what she said was untrue, but nobody, not even a woman of Portia's magnitude and beauty, would attack his sexual prowess. As far as he was concerned, the Lothario in him had satisfied Portia's sexual needs more than adequately.

———

The two of them had become lovers in the first few days of being teamed in Budapest. They had both played there many times before, but never together. It had been after one of their final rehearsals that Piero had picked his moment.

'Would you permit me the honour of escorting you for a meal tonight? I have always found that delicious food and the finest wine taste so much better in the company of a beautiful woman.' His rich Italian accent flowed like velvet over Portia's senses and she had agreed immediately. If there was one thing that Portia appreciated as much as the adulation of a sell-out crowd, then it was the excitement of being romanced by a potential new lover. Flattery would get him everywhere.

Piero had hardly taken his dark hypnotic eyes off Portia as they dined. Portia was soon giddy with the shudder of emotion bouncing between them, and from the bottles of Elixir Cuvée wine they'd shared. The feeling of the alcohol oozing its way through her body pleased her. It was a feeling she enjoyed, even when she drank on her own in the comfort of her post-performance dressing rooms. But feeling its warmth rippling through her slender flame under the watchful gaze of Piero was even more pleasing.

They had made love in the huge four-poster bed at her Budapest apartment. A solid, muscled titan of a man, Piero's love-making had been just as athletic, flipping Portia into various positions to provide her with maximum enjoyment. His thrusts were hard and deep, the force of his body bearing down upon her. Portia loved it, her legs wrapping themselves around Piero's shaven body as she pulled her lover into her.

They had fallen asleep in each other's arms, Piero spooning Portia from behind. When she had woken up the next morning he had gone. There was no note on the bedside table. Portia had felt a wave of unease there and then. She had been right to experience it.

Despite feeling that she and Piero were hugely compatible both on and offstage, when the two singing stars came together again that evening for the first performance of *Tristan und Isolde* there was no mention of their sexual union just hours before. In fact, Piero had avoided her gaze all night. There was obviously to be no encore.

Portia had slept with enough men to know that she could add Piero to the long list of men who just wanted to take her to bed because of the star she was. Men had used her for years.

'Why is it?' she'd lament to her faithful manager and friend, Redmond Geller, one of the few males in her life who had never taken advantage of her, either sexually or financially. 'I have everything I crave in life except love. I have so much love to give the right man but always they cast me aside before they can actually experience the person I am on the inside. All they want are the heavenly curves of my flesh. I'm fed up with how men always find me so bloody two dimensional. I may have a hard exterior, Redmond, you don't survive in this industry if you don't, but I have a heart. There is romantic blood running through my veins and deep-felt emotion to share. But all I experience are young testosterone-fuelled chorus boys hoping that a leg-over with me will give their career the necessary leg-up, or swindling businessmen who have charmed their way into my bed only to run off into the distance with portions of my cash quicker than you could say *Carmen*. Where are the plans for the future? Where is the talk of growing old together? Where are the goddamn hearts, flowers and picking out baby names? All my heart bears is the scars of unrequited love.'

Fame-seekers lusting after a megabucks kiss 'n' tell; Portia had seen them all and emotionally suffered in their arms. Why should Piero have been any different? He was just another man who thought with his balls. She had made the mistake of giving herself too easily.

That became evident at the drinks party held after the first night's performance. It was held at the grandeur of the Orfeum Club, situated at Budapest's five star Corinthia Hotel.

Wearing a beautiful ivory Zac Posen full-length strapless gown, Portia had glided into the party fashionably late. She had rightly guessed that most of the cast and crew members would have been there for a couple of hours at least before she made her entrance. That way, she could be sure that all eyes would be present to behold her arrival. But just in case they weren't, she had been escorted to the hotel by Redmond. He had silenced the house band at the party and grabbed the onstage microphone to announce the arrival of 'everyone's favourite singing sensation'.

Indeed, nearly all of the heads in the room did turn when a stunning Portia, her long fiery locks pinned seductively high on her head, goddess-like, before falling into a cascading avalanche of rich curls, waved to those applauding her arrival. She smiled, revealing perfect Hollywood white teeth. But her teeth then clenched when she saw which two pairs of eyes were indeed not focused upon her. One belonged to Piero, the other to a ringlet-haired female member of the show's chorus. Her body was as curvy as her hair, a fact which didn't seem to be lost on Piero as he stood running his hands down her body.

They were oblivious to Portia, lost in their frenzied embrace in the far corner of the room. Portia winced as she watched Piero's fingers dancing across her flesh.

Portia stayed at the party for twenty minutes, politely saying her hellos and goodbyes to those who mattered. Grabbing Redmond by the hand, she ushered him away, spitting that she 'wished to go back to the apartment right now'. Used to Portia's mood-swings, Redmond simply obliged.

In the comfort of her own bed, the one in which Piero had made love to her, Portia had tossed and turned all night. All she could picture was Piero and the chorus girl locking lips. She asked herself over and over, insecurities running amok through her mind. 'What does she have that I don't? Why do men always do this to me? Chew me up and spit me out?'

Over the next four weeks, Piero had proved himself to be a womaniser of the highest degree, working his way through no fewer than a dozen of the female cast and crew members. It became a running joke on the set that there was obviously something wrong with you if you hadn't succumbed to the Italian's bewitching ways. Or maybe you were one of the lucky ones ... at least then there would be no potential for heartache.

———

Which is why Portia had made her mind up to try and belittle Piero with her comment about his sexual prowess. He may have been a totally skilled lover, but arrogance was not a sexy quality in any man, especially one who obviously had no respect for the women he bedded.

'That was below the belt, my angel,' deadpanned Redmond as Portia flounced past him on the way back to her dressing room.

'He deserves it. His notes have been rotten tonight. He near-ly croaked half of his words in the second act. And anyway, below the belt is where he keeps his brains, if the weasel has any! He picked on the wrong woman if he thinks he can just schmooze me into bed for the hell of it. I need a drink ...' Her voice peaked with rage. Portia pushed open her dressing room door and stepped inside, followed by Redmond. The room was a mass of brightly coloured bouquets.

'Calm yourself,' soothed Redmond. 'Think of your voice, my darling. Now, your champagne is chilled to perfection as ever. Krug, Clos De Mesnil 1995. Your favourite. As exclusive, expensive and as tasty as you are. If that doesn't put you in the mood for tonight's wrap party then I don't know what will.'

'I knew I employed you for a reason,' laughed Portia, pour-ing herself a glass and downing it in one. 'You say the nicest things. Now, this blessed party. I am determined to enjoy this one a lot more than the one after the first night's performance. Have you managed to collect the gifts I asked you for?'

'Yes, they're all wrapped up and ready to go. Well, all but yours, of course,' beamed Redmond devilishly.

Pouring another glass of Krug, Portia ran her finger across the pile of gifts, all wrapped up in white tissue paper and tied with big chocolate-wrapper-purple ribbon. She counted them ... 'Eleven, all present and correct. Now, Redmond darling, where's the twelfth?'

'Behind you!' he sang, as if in pantomime. 'On your ward-robe door.'

Fixing her gaze at the garment hanging there, Portia threw her head back and laughed. 'It's perfect!' she squealed. Taking it from the hanger, she held it up against her chest and admired her reflection in the mirror. 'Just make sure you snap a photo of Piero's face when he sees me wearing this tonight. And make sure you force the other eleven girls into wearing theirs as well. Even if you have to pay them. If that man is not prepared to see how nice I can actually be then he'll have to take me in fifth gear bitch mode.'

Downing another glass of Krug, Portia was still laughing as she stepped behind her dressing room screen, slipped out of her clothes and headed for a shower. Sometimes it was the simplest things that made the diva titter.

The white T-shirts were just as she'd envisaged. Tight enough to cling to all of the right curves, trimmed in faux rhinestones around the collar and sleeves, and all featuring the same phrase in bright neon letters: *I Went To Bed With The Italian Stallion And All I Got Was This Lousy T-Shirt.* Underneath the phrase was a picture of what, at first glance, looked like a stallion. Portia couldn't wait to tell everyone at the party, including Piero, that it was, in fact, a jackass.

CHAPTER 5

Nancy didn't make friends easily. She never really had. Even at school she had found it difficult to form a bond with any of the girls around her. She'd tried, but somehow something didn't gel – it was like trying to mix oil and water. Her first impressions about someone would always come with a big 'but'. *But* she's bound to not be interested in me. *But* she's already got friends. *But* she'll think I'm not good enough to hang out with. And post-school, being famous at such a young age had enveloped Nancy in a blanket of barbed-wire-coated vulnerability that was hard for any person around her to penetrate. Plus, Dale had always been her best friend as well as her lover. She'd not needed anyone else.

But as Nancy stared across at Lauren sitting on the far side of the bar she felt compelled to join her. She wanted to talk to her. The woman liked her, they had tastes in common and they were around the same age – Lauren Everett seemed normal and nice. Two things that had been missing from Nancy's life for the longest time.

'Mind if I join you?' asked Nancy. 'I fancy another drink and I hate drinking alone. My shout.'

Lauren didn't need asking twice. Nancy Arlow was standing before her! A woman she had virtually idolised on both CD and TV. A tad flustered but excited beyond belief, Lauren was quick to reply. 'Oh God … yes … let's get a bottle.' She'd phoned one of Saul's staff to come and pick her up and drive the Jaguar home. There was no way she was missing out on an afternoon with Nancy Arlow. This was the most exciting thing that had happened to her in ages.

The conversation was already flowing as quickly as the wine from the moment Nancy sat down. Without wanting to sound like a crazed fan, Lauren was desperate to hear Nancy's life story.

'So, how did your fabulous career begin? You've done so many great things for someone so young,' she gushed.

Nancy wallowed in the fact that Lauren obviously worshipped her. Going almost into chat show guest mode from the days when she used to be invited on them, Nancy couldn't wait to unravel the details of her formerly glittering career.

'Where shall I start?' she began, cherishing the beaming, satisfied smile that had already snaked its way across Lauren's face. 'Well, I was rubbish at school – totally. The only thing I could do was entertain. Despite all of my school reports slagging me off as someone with no real potential when it came to education, I was always the lead in the school productions with my singing, dancing and acting. I loved the rapturous applause and standing ovations. Who wouldn't? As I said when I appeared on *Oprah*, I was "a misfit for so much of my school life, it was only when I bathed in the warm glow of the stage spotlight that I felt completely at home".'

'Oh my God, I saw that episode on Sky! I remember you saying that. You looked amazing – so petite. Mind you, it was one of those periods when Oprah had stacked it on, so pretty much everyone did!' Lauren giggled at her own cheekiness, the wine and the company going to her head.

'Then I answered Dale's ad for a singer and it promised everything I had ever dreamed of. Something to take me away from my humdrum existence at home in inner-city London and transport me into the bright lights of fame around the world.' Nancy theatrically waved her hands either side of her head as she spoke, camping up the moment for Lauren's benefit.

'So, how did you do it?' probed Lauren. 'Did it happen over-night?'

'My career did explode pretty quickly if I think about it now,' giggled Nancy. 'I was very lucky, but true talent always shines through, darling,' she semi-mocked, loving the attention. 'I borrowed money from my mum to cut a CD featuring versions of my favourite songs and sent it off with a bikini-clad photograph of myself on holiday. Apparently the combination of my rich, soulful voice, my perfect skin and my cascading locks were just what Dale was looking for. He wanted me. Two months before I was due to finish at school, I dropped out, left home and moved in with him to pursue my career.'

'So, were you and Dale ... er ...?' Lauren stopped herself from completing the question, aware that maybe it was a little too personal for a first meeting. She needn't have worried.

'Were we lovers? Of course. He was my first. We were perfect together.' A little spike of jealousy stitched itself across Lauren's mind as Nancy continued. Nancy had the life that she had always dreamt of, and a drop-dead gorgeous man to boot. 'Well, we were perfect for a while. He was the silver-tongued wide boy no woman could resist. Totally secure and sure of himself, he was assertive and gave off an aura of power that I adored. He had *confidence* written right through him.'

And I bet his sexy dirty-blond hair, piercing blue eyes and evidently muscular body didn't exactly hinder the situation, thought Lauren, an image of Dale jigsawing together in her mind. The man was flirtatiously hot. 'So, what happened? You said you were perfect ... for a while?' She refilled their glasses as she asked.

'Dale has an eye for talent. He knew I had *it*. That undetermined *X-Factor* quality that turns someone into a star. He signed me to his record company, Roma Records, and within six months my first song had climbed to the top of airtime, sales and download charts across the UK. Weeks later I was a smash everywhere from London and Latvia through to Dublin and Dubrovnik. I had top ten hits around the world, a multimillion-selling album and became one of the most famous faces in the Far East promoting everything from chewing gum to credit cards. Plus I had a super-smooth lover who satisfied my sexual needs. That bag of goodies lasted three and a half years.'

'Wow. That is so completely incredible. You lucky lady!' enthused Lauren. 'Your album is still one of my all-time faves. And I was literally first in line waiting for your second album but it never happened. How come? You disappeared for a while. Where do you go?'

Nancy fell silent for a moment. She liked Lauren, but it was their first meeting and she wasn't sure exactly how truthful she could be. The honest answer would have been to say that it was when she disappeared into the studio for far too long to record her all-important second CD that things started to go wrong in pop-land. Dale, floating on the wave of constant flattery about his business acumen from those around him, had insisted that Nancy use only the best producers and the finest recording facilities for the CD. But working with the best meant waiting in line and negotiating the biggest fees, and by the time Nancy re-emerged into the spotlight of fame with another collection of hopeful hits, the cacophonous buzz that had originally surrounded her had subsided to a minimal whimper. Putting it simply, other starlets had taken her place.

When her next single failed to reach the top twenty, Dale listened to those surrounding him again, but this time he listened wisely. Nancy's bubble had burst and Dale refused to plough any more money into her singing career, shelving her second album. It also marked the temporary shelving of their relationship.

That was the honest answer. It was one that Nancy chose not to share. Not for now, at least. 'I fell out of love with the music so I took some time out for a while. I had a new flat in Bayswater, I wanted to chill there and enjoy my money, so I did. Dale went off travelling for a while – Thailand, South Africa, places like that. He wanted me to go, naturally,' she lied. 'But I was bored of five star hotels and seeing life through taxi windows so I thought I'd let people come to me for a change. My romance with Dale drifted for a while – he was away and I needed a man on tap, as it were. Dale was in South Africa when he received the call from *Eton Shore* asking me to sign up. The casting director had spent months trying to find a young woman to join the cast to play a cabaret singer. A colleague had suggested me, wondering if I would do it. Dale knew that it would be a money-making opportunity not to miss, so flew home and begged me to do it. I thought it would be fun so I signed up to play Alannah Kershaw. And it was fun, until Dale fucked things up … excuse my French.' The wine was obviously fairly strong.

Lauren felt herself sit upright in her chair, keen to know more. 'Why, what did he do?'

'He couldn't keep his dick in his pants. We became involved again when he came back from his travels and I stupidly thought we'd be monogamous. How naive. My long hours on the set of *Eton Shore* and my huge success meant that I was constantly tired or having to attend red carpet functions. Dale didn't like it and started screwing around.'

'Poor you. How did you find out? It must have been awful.' Lauren's voice was sympathetic. She imagined she would want to kill Saul if he ever strayed from their marital bed. 'God, if you ever write an autobiography it would be a corking read!'

'Watch this space, Lauren. You never know. Anyway, one of Dale's conquests was a fellow actress on *Eton Shore*. She had a minor role but when she spotted Dale on set when he'd come to visit me, she lured him to an empty dressing room with her slutty come-hithers and allowed him to ride her from behind in front of the mirror. She was a pure touch of class. She threatened to kiss and tell so Dale confessed to me and we stopped our relationship. He's still my manager and we have the odd moment of passion together but it's nothing serious.'

The table was silent for a moment as both women contemplated Nancy's story. Despite only knowing each other for less than an hour, the silence was far from awkward. It already seemed like a bond had formed between them and they were both enjoying it. It was Nancy who broke the silence.

'Enough about me. Let's talk about you. What's it like being married to a top politician? Downing Street here you come, eh?'

'I don't know about that. We'll see. Saul's a good man … a busy man … We have a dog, Barney. It's a happy life.' To Nancy her words sounded hollow and lacklustre and it was obvious that Lauren didn't really want to talk about it. Waters at home were seemingly not running smoothly. As another silence spread across the table, this time slightly awkward, Nancy suddenly remembered the £10,000 in her bag. She wanted to put it to good use and she knew exactly what that good use would be.

'Listen, Lauren, I have to go. I've really enjoyed meeting you. Would you care to meet up again? It's been fun and we can talk some more. I promise not to hog the conversation next time.'

How ridiculous, thought Lauren. *You can hog the conversation any time you like. Your life is so much more interesting than mine will ever be. I could never compare to you.*

'I'd love to. Shall we swap numbers? Maybe we can go shopping together or do lunch.' Something told her that Nancy would be a good friend to have, no matter what repugnant relic Nathan Spilsbury might have to say to Saul about it.

Having swapped numbers, the two women hugged and Nancy left Lauren at the table. As she exited the bar, Nancy patted her handbag, feeling the mound of the cash inside. Today was a good day.

———

It was less than five minutes later that Dale walked back into the bar. He had not been able to stop thinking about Lauren since he'd left. He found her sipping a mineral water – her attempt at calming her head after the wine – and looking through her La Perla shopping bags as he started to speak.

'Hello again. I'm Dale. Here's my business card. You heard Nancy say that I'm her manager. Well, I heard you say that you used to model and sing. Why don't you swing by my office and we can have a proper chat? We might be able to help each other.'

Slightly taken aback, Lauren felt a rippling of excitement run through her as he spoke. He had one of the most beautiful faces she had ever seen and his voice was like melted chocolate – deep and rich. Plus there was the fact that she knew a brief history about his past following her chat with Nancy. 'Er … certainly, that would be wonderful. Mind you, I've probably bigged up my singing a bit too much. I don't think Beyoncé or Leona Lewis need worry just yet.'

'I'll be the judge of that,' winked Dale. As far as he was concerned, he'd already decided. The woman in front of him could possibly be the new star he was looking for – the next big thing. If her singing was on par with her beauty then he'd have no worries.

Turning to walk away, Dale flashed his winning smile and said, 'And Nancy was right, you do have good taste in underwear. Very sexy. Your husband's a lucky man. Very lucky.'

'Thank you,' mumbled Lauren awkwardly. She waved to Dale as he departed. In her hand she was holding a silk bustier.

CHAPTER 6

'Two suitcases are never enough for the needs of a diva, my good man.' Portia was explaining her luggage woes to her personal butler at the presidential suite of the five star Atlantis Hotel in Dubai. He was busying himself with Portia's fourteen pieces of luggage that needed to be transported to the airport ready for her onward journey to the UK.

As he struggled to manoeuvre one of the trunks containing many of her stage outfits onto a trolley, Portia eyed him in the mirror as she lightly dusted her cheeks with a layer of foundation. 'Be careful with those cases, my darling, I can't afford to be seen with scratches on my Chanel luggage now, can I?' she purred. 'I do not want to be gliding my way through first class looking like an alley cat has been at them.'

Portia had spent five days at the Atlantis, the glistening focal point of Dubai's Palm Jumeirah, at the special request of its owners. She had performed to a celebrity-filled crowd to celebrate the hotel's anniversary and it had proved to be a magical evening, with glitterati from around the world flying in especially. As Portia had told reporters, 'Hollywood must be a ghost town tonight because the Fassbenders, Bullocks, Coopers and Johanssons of this world are all here to see me!'

Sport stars, chat show hosts, world leaders, even fellow operatic stars had jetted in especially. In fact, that was the one thing that her manager, Redmond, had been forced to complain about: a certain fellow operatic guest who'd appeared just before

Portia had taken to the stage. Piero Romeo had come to wish her well.

'Why was he invited, Redmond?' Portia asked for the hundredth time as they left the hotel. 'And why did he bother coming? After my humiliation of him at the wrap party in Budapest, he was the last person I was expecting to see. What was it he said to me? "You may have proven to be a bitch, Portia, but you're still a hugely talented one." He may be a cad but he's a smooth one, I'll give him that.'

'I just think he's a glutton for punishment. Or maybe a free Dubai trip is just too good to turn down,' scoffed Redmond. 'He's as smooth as you are privileged, my dear.'

Indeed she was. Portia was the only daughter of Lord and Lady Hartley, two of the wealthiest landowners in Britain. Irish-born Lord Nigel Hartley had been educated at Christ's College, Cambridge before forging a career in law. Shrewd with his money, he and his Egyptian-born wife, Omorose Safari, had invested in properties across the UK. Through buying and selling at exactly the right time, Nigel and his wife Rose, as she chose to call herself, became multimillionaires. As their only daughter, Portia had benefited from the cocktail of her father's auburn colouring and her mother's exotic, sultry features.

The diva's talent for singing came at an early age. In her first year at boarding school, she took to the stage of her school talent show and showcased her operatic skills. From then on, Portia was mesmerised by opera, forcing her parents to take her to London's Royal Opera House whenever possible. She soaked up the performances, learning as many female roles as she could by heart. When she left school, she enrolled in the Opera School of the Royal College Of Music, using her mother's maiden name as her stage name. Within four years she had encompassed the globe with her skills. She had found her true niche and a place where she could really shine.

It was a place that she still adored. The buzz she had experienced coming offstage in Dubai, a backdrop of fireworks lighting the sky behind her, had been one of the most euphoric she had known. But as she signed a few final autographs and sashayed out to her waiting car to head to the airport, Portia knew that she was ready to head home. To the sanctuary of Mara, the opulent Grade II listed building she owned back in the UK.

'Let's go, Redmond,' she declared, reaching for the minibar in the back of the car and pouring herself a straight vodka. 'One for the road, eh? It's going to be a long journey and we might as well start numbing those senses now.' She downed the drink in one.

'As long as you don't start numbing that voice of yours, Portia. Rehearsals for your next production start in a few weeks and I need your top notes top notch.'

'Darling, you know better than anyone how much I look after my voice. I drink plenty of water every day, avoid smoky areas, give spicy foods a miss, have humidifiers wherever I go, take my vitamins to keep my mucus membrane healthy ... need I go on?'

'And need I remind you that alcohol acts as a diuretic which may cause the body to lose water which can dry out the throat,' replied Redmond caustically. 'I love a drink as much as you, but I'm not the one with the million-dollar vocal chords, am I?'

'Oh, shut up, will you? It's like being managed by Dr Ross from *ER* with you sometimes. Except George Clooney is much better looking,' giggled Portia. 'We've just earned a cool million for one concert, for heaven's sake. I think we deserve a drink, don't you? Now, what will it be ... vodka, gin or brandy?' She smiled, surveying the minibar once again.

'Well, I'll have a gin then, seeing as we're celebrating.' Redmond smiled back. 'A splash of tonic, ice and a slice, if you please ... and for your information, in my opinion George Clooney is not aging well. I saw him in the lobby of the hotel.'

Pouring the gin into a glass and handing it to Redmond, Portia couldn't help but laugh out loud. 'Not aging well! Are you mad? As a red-blooded woman, I can tell you right now the man is totally divine. You are speaking as a man who is not exactly wrinkle-free and is therefore insanely jealous.'

'Hitting where it hurts as ever,' joked Redmond, stabbing his heart with a mock arrow. 'You utter bitch.'

'Touché, Redmond, touché. Now, cheers.'

———

It hadn't taken Martha long to decide just where she wanted to go. Peering up at the departures board at Cape Town airport, she had seen that an Emirates flight to the UK was leaving in just a few hours. A quick trip to the Emirates desk and she had bought her ticket and checked in her luggage. The flight would stop in Dubai for a few hours and then fly on to Heathrow. It was perfect. Martha wanted to get away from Lewin Éclair and any reminder of the family business as soon as possible. And if there was one place that Martha adored, it was the bright lights of London. She had spent a year living in the capital when she'd left school and her memories were of laughter-filled nights out in the West End, dancing all night and meeting the most eclectic pot-pourri of people she had ever come across.

She had rented a tiny flat in Soho, living above a rather dubious strip joint, loving the seediness of it all. Martha was sure that there was more to the club than mere stripping. Her favourite moment of the day would be wandering home at four or five in the morning to see the various strippers piling out onto the street, still dressed in their working clothes of rubber, leather and saucy uniforms, to try and weave their way to the nearest bus stop. It was a sight like nothing she had ever encountered before. She'd contemplated going there once, but had bottled it at the last moment. Maybe this time …

Martha slept for almost the entirety of the flight to Dubai, the tiredness of the night before finally catching up with her. She woke up just as the air attendants announced that the flight was about to land. It would be three hours before her connecting flight.

Once inside the airport, Martha busied herself browsing around the rows of luxury boutiques. She switched her mobile on for the first time since leaving Cape Town and saw a missed call from Lewin. He'd left no message. She had nothing to say to him anyway, and turned the phone back off.

Having bought a couple of magazines for the flight and some sushi, Martha headed to the VIP lounge within the airport. She had just seated herself and was contemplating a seaweed wrap and an article on the worth of celebrity paintings when she heard a commotion on the far side of the lounge.

Looking up she saw a portly man rapidly clicking his camera in the direction of a woman who clearly didn't wish to be photographed. From his accent when he spoke, she could tell he was American. 'Wait till my wife hears about this, she loves you. She saw you at Carnegie Hall once. You were awesome.' He carried on clicking as he spoke. The focus of his lens was a woman sitting on her own, her hands clamped to her face. A mass of deep red hair curled around her hands. She was screaming, 'Please, no pictures, I'll have to call security if carry on.'

Rising to her feet, Martha marched over to the man, grabbed his camera and pushed him away. 'Look, mister, the lady said no photos, so leave her alone, will you!'

The man looked visibly shocked. 'But this is Portia Safari. My wife's her biggest fan. All I wanted is a photo for her. And who the hell do you think you are, anyway? Give me the camera back.' The man's belly wobbled as he spoke.

'I'm the girl who will kick your fat sorry ass out of here if you're not a good boy. The lady doesn't want her photo taken, OK?' Martha was not going to back down. 'Here's your camera. Now I suggest you leave the lounge or at least go and sit in the furthest corner where neither I nor this lady can see you. Got it?' Defeated, the man lumbered off.

Running her hands through her hair, Portia looked at Martha and smiled. 'Thank you so much. There are times when I just don't want to be at everyone's beck and call. I signed an autograph for him and then he starts clicking away like crazy. I just want some peace before my flight.'

'Well, I'll leave you to it. If he gives you any more grief, then give me a shout. I'm sitting over there.' Martha pointed towards the half-eaten pile of sushi on the table. She made to leave.

'Wait a minute, please, why don't you come and join me?' pleaded Portia. 'Safety in numbers and all that. My manager will be back in a moment, he's gone to the little boys' room, but I'd like to thank you properly for saving me from that odious man. My name's Portia. You are …?'

'Martha Éclair from South Africa. On my way to London to escape my father who is driving me insane. Pleased to meet you. And you're that opera singer, aren't you? I recognise your name now.'

'I am indeed. And it seems we're both trying to escape men, doesn't it? Go and grab your belongings and come on over. If you're on the same flight as me to London, I know that I'd feel a lot safer if you're on one side of me and Redmond on the other. To keep that blessed barrel of a man away.'

'Did someone call my name?' It was Redmond returning from the bathroom. 'Have I missed something?

'Redmond, this is Martha, the rather brilliant and spunky young lady who just saved me from that loony of a fan over there.' She gestured at the man, who was still staring in Portia's direction. 'She will be travelling alongside us to London. And no matter where she's sitting, I want her seat changed to be alongside me. You don't mind first class, do you? I can't do anything less.'

Martha couldn't help but smile. There was something about Portia that she really liked. She was infectious with her bonhomie. She couldn't help but feel that her journey to London would be a lot more entertaining than she'd previously thought.

CHAPTER 7

Self-doubt had never been a phrase in Lauren's vocabulary, so she couldn't for the life of her work out what had stopped her from ringing Dale's number for the past few days.

She'd been bubble-headed with excitement ever since her chance meeting with Nancy and Dale. But what could she offer Dale Cousins? It wasn't like she had any real talent when it came to the world of entertainment, was it? What if Dale was expecting her to walk in and blow him away with her vocal performance? What if Dale was simply expecting her to blow him, full stop? She knew how these music types worked. He was deeply attractive, and if she'd met him in her partying days pre-Saul then maybe. But this was different – he seemed to be genuinely professionally interested in meeting up.

So, after another hour or two of singing along to some of her favourite tunes – she'd attempted every style of vocal warbling from the unnatural highs of Mariah Carey through to the velvety dark riches of Grace Jones in a hope of finding what suited her voice best – she finally plucked up the courage to dial Dale's number.

Her heart pounding with trepidation, Lauren waited nervously for him to pick up. 'Hi there, Dale Cousins, can I help you?'

'Hi, Dale, this is Lauren Everett. We met the other day when you were with Nancy Arlow. You told me to ring you.' Lauren's throat dried as she spoke. She coughed nervously, worried that maybe he wouldn't remember her.

If Lauren had been able to see Dale she would have seen a broad, somewhat smug, smile spread across his face. 'Hey, Lauren. I'm so glad you phoned. I've been thinking about you ...' He paused for a second before continuing. 'A lot.'

'Really? That's good, I guess. Sorry I haven't rung before. I've just been really busy. Parties with Saul, that kind of thing,' she lied. In honesty, her schedule over the past few days had amounted to just one rather kinky night of passion with Saul, thanks to the La Perla underwear, and endless days of dog-walking and back-to-back episodes of *Diagnosis Murder*. Saul was away on a conference yet again. Lauren had offered to go, but according to Saul Nathan Spilsbury had said that she'd be 'uninterested'. The phrases Nathan had actually used were 'totally out of her mind-numbingly stupid depth as people would be using words of more than one buggering syllable' and 'bored because nobody would be discussing some trashy and talentless big-boobed scrubber's hen party with a bunch of bleeding tarts and faggots'. Saul had not argued with him, even though he wasn't sure that Nathan always judged his wife particularly fairly. In Nathan's eyes, Lauren would never be good enough.

'You like a good party, then? My kind of girl,' replied Dale. 'Well, in that case, you couldn't have phoned at a better time. I have an invitation on my desk for a music awards show tonight. Usual boring stuff ... watching a few scraggy-haired groups collecting trophies they don't deserve, but it's free food and drink and there are always a good number of industry types up for a laugh. And poor old me ... well, I'm lacking a plus-one. Why don't you join me? We could talk about your singing possibilities and get some studio dates booked for try-outs.'

Lauren was agog. 'Wow, that sounds fabulous. I'm not sure though. I won't know anybody and it's not the usual crowd I'm used to. I've been hanging out with cabinet ministers all week.'

Despite her words though, she already knew that she loved the idea.

'You'll know me. That's all that matters. And besides, you wouldn't want to leave a poor, defenceless fool like me all on my own like Billy No Mates, would you?' mocked Dale.

'I should imagine you're about as defenceless as a school full of piranha fish!' retorted Lauren. 'But, when you put it like that, I suppose it's my duty to keep you company for the night. Where and when?'

Dale furnished her with the details and said that he would arrange for a car to pick her up and take her home afterwards. Lauren adored his efficiency. 'It's no wonder Nancy loves you as a manager if you're always this attentive to a person's needs,' she joked. 'Will she be there tonight? It'll be nice to see her. I would have thought she might have been your plus-one or invited in her own right.'

'No, she's busy tonight ... turned it down, I seem to remember. Something about looking at a new script for her next project,' fudged Dale. 'So, I'll see you tonight. I look forward to it.'

'Me too. What's Nancy working on next—' But it was a fruitless question; Dale had already rung off. He needed to ring Nancy to tell her that she wouldn't be coming to the awards ceremony after all. If he'd known that Lauren was going to ring, then he'd have never asked Nancy to accompany him in the first place. Now, he just needed to think of a way of letting Nancy down gently.

———

Nancy was not going to let the fact that yet again Dale had let her down spoil her day. As if he really expected her to believe the old 'family problems' excuse as a way of getting out of the awards ceremony. As far as she could remember, Dale was the black sheep of the Cousins family and hadn't spoken to most of them for over a decade. *Doubtless he'll be taking his latest stupid little slapper with him, desperate to impress her in the hope of a leg-over*, she thought to herself as she lay back naked on the crisp cotton sheets of her bed.

No, nothing was going to spoil her day: spread out on the bed around her were hundreds of bank notes. She'd counted them earlier and there was at least £25,000. Not bad going, considering that just a few days ago it was merely £10,000. Despite the lack of work opportunities coming her way, the last few days had been some of the luckiest that Nancy had ever encountered.

When she'd left Lauren in the bar, the money had been burning a hole in her bag. She was itching to put it to good use, but she knew that using it to pay off some of the money she owed was only going to give her a momentary thrill. In fact, if she was honest, no thrill at all. The money was useful, but she needed more. She needed to speculate to accumulate. That's when it had come to her. She'd read about a woman in the newspapers earlier that week who was a professional gambler. She hadn't started out that way. As far as Nancy could remember she'd been a cleaner or a staff nurse or something low-paid. But one day she'd stumbled across a website where you could bet on everything from which celeb couple would divorce next through to whether the Royal family would be in the papers that day. Little by little her earnings had increased. She'd also studied the form of racehorses and begun to place bets at her local bookmakers. She'd bought scratch cards and lottery tickets by the score and, somehow, she'd managed to win big. Within a year, she had quit her job and turned 'pro'. The sun had obviously been shining on her. If she could do it, then why couldn't Nancy? It would be the end of all of her financial worries.

Nancy's knowledge of horse racing amounted to no more than having once made a personal appearance on a huge stage at a racecourse, but there was no time to worry about that. She was sure she'd passed a bookies on the way to the bar. Locating it, she pushed open the door and walked inside. Posters on the wall offered up 'endless chances to win'. Happy, smiley faces peered down at her. The dazzling allure of people who were obviously flushed with cash from their love of gambling.

Nancy hadn't realised there were so many choices about what to gamble on. Roulette, blackjack, poker, greyhounds, sports events from around the world … the choices seemed endless. But the woman in the newspaper had hit the jackpot with horse racing so that was where Nancy wanted to begin.

She scanned the list of upcoming races listed on the wall. Doncaster, Aintree, Sheffield, Newmarket … where to try? Newmarket, that's where she'd made her personal appearance. It was a sign. The next race began in just a few minutes. Moving to the counter at the front of the shop she asked the assistant how to place a bet on the race.

'You need to pick a horse and hope it's going to win, love,' replied the dour, scrawny-bearded teenager behind the counter. 'It's not hard. If you want to choose a horse for that race, you'll have to be quick. It's starting in a few minutes. Here's the list of racers.'

He passed her a sheet with a list of names written on it and their odds of winning alongside them. Nancy let her eyes scroll down the page. The odds were just a mass of incomprehensible numbers. She would use her instinct and pick a name she liked. Gingham Gal, Dolly May, Hurricane Alley, Pussycat Diva, Waffles Woo … Nancy laughed at the strange names. Then she spotted it: Becoming Nancy. It was another sign. It was way down the list, but it sounded like a winner if ever there was one. Looking up at the sullen assistant she said, 'That one', pointing at the name.

'First time you've taken a flutter, eh? With odds like that, I've got more chance of winning the race than that horse. How much you want to bet?' he smirked.

Reaching down into her handbag, Nancy pulled out two fifty pound notes. 'A hundred pounds to win, please.'

'Don't say I didn't warn you,' laughed the teen as he took Nancy's money and gave her a betting slip. There was no sign of any mirth from him a few minutes later when he handed Nancy her winnings. Becoming Nancy had romped home in a surprise victory at odds of 20/1. Nancy had just pocketed £2,100.

The blissful rapture of her first win spread through Nancy, heating her senses like volcanic lava. What a rush. It was something she had to repeat. So she did. At least twenty times over the next three days. There was no system to her gambling. She went to different bookmakers, chose races at random and names that appealed to her. There were losses, of course. But for some unknown reason, Nancy was touched by the lucky hand of fate. Out of the twenty races she betted on, she won thirteen of them. Unlucky for some, but not for Nancy. Within seventy-two hours, her £10,000 cash handout from Dale had ballooned to £25,000. It was the easiest money she had ever earned.

Gazing at the crystal chandelier that hung above her bed, Nancy spread her arms out either side of her, feeling the joyous coolness of the notes against her naked flesh. 'No, Dale. Take your slapper to the awards bash, honey. I shall be out making some money that, for once, you can't take a cut of.'

And Nancy knew she'd be lucky. She could feel it. It had said so in her horoscope that morning. 'Scorpios will profit if they're willing to take the risk'. Well, Nancy was more than willing to take risks, and she knew just the place, and just the person she wanted to come with her. Picking up the telephone on her bed-side table, she dialled Lauren's number to see if she was free for the night.

CHAPTER 8

'Darling, you must come visit me at my home; you have my number and address. I have thoroughly enjoyed meeting you. You've made the journey back from Dubai an absolute pleasure and thanks once again for saving my bacon with that piggy little man.'

With that, Portia was gone, installed in the back of her Rolls Royce, with Redmond at her side, heading for home. Martha smiled and waved at the car as the personalised number plate, SAFARI 1, disappeared across the airport car park.

'I think I will. You are one crazy lady.' Martha still felt vaguely light-headed from the journey. That's what comes from eight hours of virtually constant drinking. The champagne had flowed from the moment that Portia, Redmond and herself had taken their seats. Portia had drunkenly entertained her with stories of the men who had seduced her over the years, including the latest episode with Piero. 'Despite what I told him, Martha, he was a bloody good shag. Fabulously big cock. You know when a man just knows what to do with it. It reaches the places other dicks can't reach. Sometimes, with a smaller man, you feel like they're just waggling their cock around in a warm room. I remember one chap whose dick was so long and thin I didn't know whether to go down on it or floss my teeth with it.' Martha had been more than happy to soak up Portia's bawdy stories, revelling in her favourite subject yet again. She told Portia all about her x-rated interludes with the workers at Lewin Éclair and about her father virtually offering her up to Roger Penhaligon.

The two women had loved sharing their stories, despite a red-faced Redmond listening on throughout. In the end, he'd drunk more than either Portia or Martha, keen to blot out their gratuitous descriptions of the male members they'd sampled in a blur of champagne-coloured fizz.

Picking up her luggage, Martha walked to one of the deluxe taxi information desks within the terminal. She would hire a car and a chauffeur to take her into the heart of London and then book herself into a hotel. A few days of pampering and five star service would soon take her mind off her father. Within moments, she was being told that a chauffeur-driven Jaguar would soon be at her disposal.

When it arrived, a peak-capped man placed her luggage in the boot and opened the back door for her. He was strikingly handsome and his ebony skin and winning smile immediately reminded her of Joseph. An undulation of lust rippled through Martha as she stared, wide-eyed into his face. As he belted himself into the driving seat and asked Martha 'where to?' in the rear-view mirror, she was sure that he had an all-too knowing twinkle in his eye too.

'A fancy hotel in the centre of London. That's all I need. I don't know their names, so I guess I'm in your hands.' She smiled, keen to tread the thin line between minx and floozy. Staring directly into his eyes in the mirror, she raised her eyebrows and ran her tongue along her top teeth.

'I know just the place. You leave it to me, madam. I'll be sure to take you all the way.' He winked, put the Jaguar into first gear and pulled away from the kerb.

Martha pushed herself deep into the back seat, spread her legs a little wider than necessary to get comfortable and made sure that the chauffeur had seen her actions. He had. 'Sounds good to me,' she purred. This was going to be yet another enjoyable journey.

———

The journey back home had been a solitary one for Portia. Redmond, who lived in one of the many wings at Mara, had spent the entire journey with his head flopped back, snoring into the air, the combination of the flight and the alcohol having exhausted him. Portia's mind drifted to her conversation with Martha.

The Winelands of South Africa, such a marvellous place, she thought as she watched the lush green fields of England pass outside the Rolls Royce window. *I must try and book myself in for a visit, when I next get the chance.* If she kept in touch with Martha, which she had every intention of doing, then maybe she could go and stay at the Lewin Éclair estate. It sounded divine. And, of course, the thought of all of those tastebud-tantalising wines to sample would suit Portia greatly. She hadn't been to South Africa in years, quite possibly because her first great love still lived there, as far as she was aware. The man who'd truly shattered her unguarded heart. The man who murdered any love she had at the time. The one man in her life she would have readily stayed with and the one man she hardly ever talked about.

She'd met him while on one of her first ever tours abroad, a six-week run of *Madame Butterfly* in Cape Town. He had been there on the opening night, a vision in a white linen suit at a VIP party for the cast and crew. He'd made a beeline for Portia, seeking her out across the crowd. He was fifteen years her senior, but that didn't matter to Portia. From the moment she laid eyes on him, she fell in love. For the next six weeks they were inseparable. At every performance, Portia would look down from the stage and see her beau seated there. They would talk for hours afterwards about their common love of opera and make love until the break of dawn. It was he who took Portia's virginity. Until then, she had never wanted to give herself wholly to a man. When she did, she knew that she had chosen wisely. His love-making seemed both vibrant and gentle, taking Portia on a ride of sensuous, sexual peaks. It was with him that Portia felt that she had truly become a woman.

She would have stayed with him in South Africa. She would have given up all of her operatic success at the time to become a wife and mother. He was a successful businessman and she would have gladly accompanied him wherever he chose to take her. But then it had all gone wrong. On her last day in Cape Town, on the day that she had decided that she wouldn't be taking the flight back to the UK with the rest of her opera troupe, she had made her way to his hotel suite before the performance. She wanted to tell him the news that she thought he longed to hear.

Knocking on the hotel bedroom door, she could hear voices coming from inside. 'Must be room service, darling. I'll get it.' The voice was female. The door opened to reveal a young woman in a revealing babydoll nightie. Her full breasts nearly spilled out over the top. 'Oh, I thought you were room service. Can I help you?' she chirped. Portia could still hear her voice in her head all these years later.

'I think I must have the wrong room … I thought this belonged to …' stumbled Portia.

'Are the oysters and champagne here, ready for some bedtime fun, then?' The voice came from a man who appeared in the doorway behind the woman. He was naked apart from a pair of pyjama bottoms. He slapped her backside playfully before looking up.

'Portia … what are you doing here?' The colour drained from his face. But Portia left without saying a word, running down the hotel corridor with tears streaming down her cheeks. She never saw him again. In her mind, he was the man who had made her distrustful of the male species ever since.

As the Rolls came to a halt under the cedar trees either side of Mara's opulent entrance, Portia looked out through nostalgic tears. If she'd stayed in South Africa, things would have turned out so differently. She would never know what would have been, but she did know that Peter Bradford had a lot to answer for. She just hoped that whatever he was doing these days, his betrayal of her had been worth it.

———

'I'm going to come, baby. Come with me, let me feel you inside me. Give it to me, screw me nice and hard.' For a sweet-faced girl, Martha could talk as filthily as any conquest her chauffeur had ever had the pleasure of banging on the back seat of his work Jaguar.

'Take it all. I'm about to explode. Get ready, honey.' She could feel the shaft of his ebony rod rubbing against her clitoris. With a final, urgent thrust, he unleashed his seed. Beads of sweat dripped down onto her from his forehead and carved chest as she felt his come flood into her. She clenched the walls of her pussy, draining every last drop from his cock and then pulled him out of her.

'You are one horny lady. Are they all like you in South Africa?' he sighed, relishing the moment. 'Most of the customers I've shagged at work have at least waited until we reach their hotel.'

'What can I say, I was feeling horny. Where exactly are we anyway?' Martha picked her jeans and panties up off the car floor and attempted to put them on before rubbing the condensation off the window to look out. As far as she could see, they were in a car park. There were no other cars in view.

'It's a quiet spot my brother knows. He comes here at night when he wants to get his rocks off. It's hidden enough to be fairly safe but can still get busy when the weather's warm.'

'People come here for sex?' beamed Martha feverishly. 'Cool. So, do they all get to watch each other? And don't give me that bullshit about it being *your brother*. After the performance you've just put on, I bet it's you who's down here on a regular basis,' she teased. 'You were really going for it.'

In spite of his colouring, Martha was sure that she could see his cheeks redden a little. 'No, I'm more of an indoors kind of lover. He says people watch each other and get off on the pleasure of it all because it's kind of forbidden.'

'It's a shame there's no one here now. Maybe I'll have to join him down here sometime.' Martha could feel a thrill she'd never experienced before coursing through her as she said the words. The thought of other sex-hungry people watching her as she lost herself in pleasures of the flesh brought goose pimples to her skin. Hell, why should they just watch, she'd be quite happy for them to join in.

As she watched the chauffeur getting dressed back into his uniform, Martha couldn't help contemplating that maybe Portia Safari wasn't the only natural born performer around. She couldn't wait to put on a show of her own.

CHAPTER 9

Nancy was a London girl born and bred. If it hadn't been for Dale, she would probably have been stealing hubcaps, smoking dope and being a battered single mother on one of the inner-city estates she'd grown up on. But he had changed her life and now, thanks to his latest handout and her streak of gambling good luck, Nancy had money to play with. And playing was definitely on her mind as she stepped out of a black cab outside a West End casino. Wearing a black figure-hugging Preen layer dress that she'd bought earlier in the day, Nancy looked like a true star as she threw a fifty pound note at the driver and marched up the stairs outside the casino entrance. As she stood at the top, her body silhouetted against the London night sky, Nancy took a moment to contemplate what she would spend tonight's winnings on. More designer attire, a holiday in the tropical sunshine, a pampered spa visit. Maybe she'd ask Lauren to join her. She couldn't make it tonight but their phone chat had still been friendly and flowing. She was easy to talk to.

Nancy had chosen the W1 casino specifically. As a celebrity she wanted somewhere she would definitely blend in. The extravagant interior of the casino had entertained millionaires, royalty, politicians and playboys since its opening many decades before. Nancy knew that with her stunning looks she would be able to play the men there as well as the slots and roulette. She would be more than happy if they wanted to flash the cash in her direction. It was a win-win situation as far as Nancy was concerned.

She'd originally decided to set herself a budget for the night. It was to be a rather sizable £10,000, the amount of the initial loan from Dale. But blinded by good fortune, Nancy had placed the entire £25,000 inside her Prada clutch.

Strutting her way to the casino bar, she ordered herself a cocktail. It was an aptly named High Roller. She was aware of at least three pairs of male eyes banqueting on her good looks as she consumed the cocktail. She smiled at each of the men in turn, seductively taking the cherry that adorned her drink and running it across her lips. Making direct eye-contact with the most striking of the three, she popped the fruit into her mouth with a smile. He nodded back and as Nancy walked from the bar into the main casino gaming area, the man followed.

Removing a wad of banknotes from her bag, Nancy exchanged them for roulette chips and made her way to the table. She was aware of the man following her but, as yet, he still kept his distance and avoided conversation. *Like a lamb to the slaughter*, thought Nancy. Sure enough, as she took her seat at the roulette table, he sat down alongside her. The time was not yet right for Nancy to make the first move.

Placing a pile of chips randomly across a variety of numbers, Nancy tried to look as if she knew what she was doing. She had no idea how much she'd placed on the table, although she knew that she'd exchanged about £10,000 to play with. She'd watched enough of those late-night casino shows on the TV to know that if she placed her chips across a variety of red and black numbers, hopefully something would pay dividends.

'Table closed, no more bets, please,' the croupier announced and spun the roulette wheel. As the ball clicked its way around the numbers, Nancy felt the exhilaration of the unknown surge through her. After what seemed like an epic amount of time, the ball rested on red number 21. Nancy looked down at the table, where a pile of her chips rested on that very number. Unable to contain herself, she let out a squeal. Despite a few minor losses on other numbers, the result had definitely meant she was winning after her first spin.

'Well done. Doubtless it's a lucky number for you. Your age, I assume?' The voice came from the suave stranger alongside her. About thirty, immaculately dressed in a black tuxedo, there was a slight air of pre-*Dallas Buyers Club* Matthew McConaughey beach dude about him. Nancy was even more impressed with his ruggedly handsome features close up than she had been from across the casino bar. There was a trace of accent in his voice but Nancy couldn't place it.

'I'm a little older, but who am I to argue if a good-looking man says otherwise?' Martha swivelled her chair towards him as she spoke, crossing her long slender legs in the process, advertising them to perfection. She noticed the man's eyes gravitate towards them as she did so. 'You must be my lucky charm,' she jested.

'I consider it an honour. Are you ready for your next choice? Roulette is all about conditional probability. But I'm guessing an expert like you knows that already. Any suggestions for a struggling novice?'

He thinks I'm an expert, I'm obviously more convincing than I realised, thought Nancy. 'Well, from my time in Monte Carlo, I seem to remember that if red comes up on your first spin, then the odds say that it will be black next,' she fudged. Nancy had never set foot inside Monte Carlo, let alone one of its famed casinos. The excitement of the night was already flowing through her veins, causing her to spout lies. If she could convince the stranger that she was an expert, then maybe he'd play right into her hands and flash his cash in her direction.

'Well, in that case, black it is. Seeing as you're such a beauty, I shall place every chip I have on black. If it doesn't come up, you can buy me a drink ... deal?' He smiled, a brilliant flash of white radiating across his face.

'Deal,' winked Nancy. They both pushed a large pile of chips onto the table, placing them across various black numbers on the baize. Just as the croupier was calling no more bets, both Nancy and the handsome stranger pushed a column of chips each towards black number eight. Their chips collided, spilling across the table.

'Care to share?' he laughed. As he did so, he placed his hand against Nancy's back and stroked it seductively. Nancy knew that he was hers for the taking.

'It's another lucky number for me, I can feel it. And it looks like you're feeling the same way. I'd be happy to share,' she said. She regrouped the spilt chips back into two piles and slid them onto number eight.

Once again, the croupier spun the ball around the wheel. It bounced back and forth, weaving its way up and down the numbers. When it started slowing, Nancy could feel the hairs on the nape of her neck rising to attention. She prayed that the white ball would come to rest on a black number. It did: number eight. Nancy couldn't believe her luck. In just two spins, she had virtually doubled the amount of chips she had on the table. She punched the air with glee as the croupier pushed another huge mountain of chips towards her. He did the same to the man alongside her.

'I guess it's *you* who are my lucky charm,' he beamed. He leant over and kissed her on the cheek to show his appreciation. His lips were soft and warm. 'I definitely owe you a drink. Shall we cash these in and head to the bar?'

Nancy was eager to join him, but didn't want to seem too eager. *He's keen, I'll give him that, but I don't want to play straight into his hands.* As the thought went through her head, another met it straight on. She was on a winning streak and nothing would stop her. If she seemed like an expert, then maybe she was. Perhaps there was a sure-fire winning system to the way she was playing. If her luck carried on as it had done, then she wouldn't have to worry about Dale getting her another crappy film to star in. She'd have enough money to sort out her debts. Maybe tonight was to be the first of many nights where she could win big.

Considering the stranger's offer, she ran her fingers through her long dark hair, draping it flirtatiously over her shoulder. 'You go and cash your chips in. Years of playing the table have told me when good fortune is on my side. I've still got another few spins in me. I'll see you in there in five?' She pointed towards the bar. 'I think we can both afford the finest wine on offer, don't you?'

'I know just the one. Rich and full-bodied … just like you. I'll see you in a moment.' As he spoke, he gathered his chips from the table and juggled to keep them in his hands. Standing, a couple of the chips dropped to the floor. 'Guess I'm not used to having this many to deal with,' he laughed and bent down to pick them up, before heading off to cash them.

'As sweet as honey,' sighed Nancy under her breath. 'But he'll have to wait a while. I have some winning to do.' Turning back to the table, she could feel a rush of inexplicable bravado run through her. She felt invincible. The night was going much better than she had ever planned. In fact, her life seemed more fruitful than it had in ages. Nothing could topple her from the crest of a wave she was currently surfing. Impatient to feel the sensation of victory once again, she placed all of her chips on black number six. It was a split decision, the number of top-ten singles she'd had as a pop star. It felt lucky. It felt right. She knew that it would come up trumps and literally win her tens of thousands of pounds in the spin of a wheel. As she placed the chips, a sharp inhalation of breath sounded from the other disbelieving players around the table. Their rational minds told them that the chances of Nancy winning were stacked against her.

'No more bets.' It was too late, Nancy had made her choice. The wheel spun, the ball snaking its way around the numbers. Nancy wanted to close her eyes, unable to watch, but something kept them wide open. The cocktail of fear and exhilaration of what she had done. As the ball came to rest, it was the fear that won through.

'Red number fourteen.' The croupier's words seemed to truncheon their way into Nancy's brain. It was not black number six. All eyes around the table seemed to be resting on her. As she watched the mountainous pile of her chips being dragged away from her, Nancy tried not to calculate just how much money she had just lost. She wanted to cry but wouldn't let herself be seen as weak and frail. She needed to retain her composure. Fighting back the advancing tears, she rose to her feet and gave a forced, cheery 'easy come, easy go' to the people gathered. It sounded as empty to them as it did to Nancy.

At least I still have the rest of the money in my bag, she contemplated. At least I wasn't completely stupid. She reached down to pick up her Prada clutch from where it had been nestled at her feet. A battering ram of panic slammed into her. The bag was gone. It was there just now. She'd been sure of it. But now it was nowhere to be seen. Getting down on her hands and knees, Nancy scrambled around under the table to try and find the bag. It was definitely missing.

Trying to stop her hysteria from erupting, Nancy took a deep breath, stood up and stumbled away from the table, confused about what had happened. She couldn't have lost all of her money, she couldn't. The mere thought of it jolted through her body like an electric shock.

Maybe the handsome stranger had seen it. Maybe when he bent down to get his chips he had seen the bag there. Maybe he'd moved it. She ran to the bar to see if he was there. He wasn't.

Placing her palms to her cheeks with worry, Nancy revolved a full 360 degrees, scanning her eyes around the entire bar. Just like her bag, the stranger was gone. There were no maybes left. He had evidently stolen the bag when he bent down to retrieve his chips. He had made off with all of the money in Nancy's bag. She had been duped. Those were definites.

As the tears started to stream down her face, Nancy ran through the casino and out into the London night air.

CHAPTER 10

There are moments in life when a person feels like they have gate-crashed into someone else's idyllic world. Lauren was having one of them as she rocked her body around the dance floor at the awards ceremony. Dancing opposite her, obviously feasting on the enjoyable vision of her perfectly rhythmic moves, was Dale. Around them, in various states of hedonistic inebriation were some of the biggest names in the music business today. Lauren had spotted at least a dozen bands she had on download, and various acts on a night off from selling out stadiums around the world. She hadn't felt this good on a dance floor in ages. In fact, she couldn't even remember the last time she'd been given the chance to strut her sexual stuff with such freedom. For ages she'd not been out and in one day she'd had offers from both Dale and Nancy separately. She still felt guilty about turning Nancy down, using Saul as an excuse, but staring across at Dale she knew she had made the right choice.

'Have I told you how amazing you look?' yelled Dale above the music, leaning in to place his mouth alongside Lauren's ear so that she could hear.

'Just once or twice,' giggled Lauren. In truth, it must have been at least a dozen times in the last half an hour, but Lauren wasn't tired of hearing it yet. For once, she'd picked out something that she'd really wanted to wear for the evening, not something that merely fitted in with Saul's views on how the accessory wife should look. She'd teamed her imported Max Azria silk georgette V-neck gown with a pair of Jimmy Choos and trendsetting jewellery from her favourite designers, Dyrberg/Kern. Even she thought that she looked the belle of the ball. Dale had looked slicker than black ice in an Ozwald Boateng suit and tie, but both the tie and his jacket had been jettisoned during the evening as the party heated up.

'So where did you learn to dance like that?' questioned Dale.

'It's a long story,' smiled Lauren. 'I used to be a real club girl.'

Motioning her need for a drink, she and Dale quit the dance floor and walked over to the one of the bar areas. The dim lights surrounding it gave it an air of seductive romance. Taking their drinks to a table, they sat down in one of the secluded booths nestled against the walls.

'Well, we've got all night, I hope,' said Dale, 'so tell me more.' Lauren began to fill him in about her past ....

———

Mayhem was the nightclub to hang out at in London when a teenage Lauren Wilde, as she was known then, was keen to be seen in her modelling days. *Hanging out* quite literally, more often than not, given that her outfits tended to amount to little more than two strips of chiffon ribbon strategically swirling around her voluptuous breasts, and a pair of tiny golden hot pants clinging to her pert buttocks.

She lived for Mayhem, and would find herself gyrating around its neon-lit dance floor most nights, brushing shoulders with people she'd read about in the tabloids. One day she longed to be as famous as they were, seen with a different esteemed man on her arm every night, flicking her hair to perfection as the paparazzi flashlights exploded around her. Gossipmongers hungry for her latest news, like which million-dollar campaign she was modelling for next. But things didn't always go to plan.

Lauren's modelling career was far from million dollar. Despite a beauty that most women would scratch eyes out for, with her rosy-pink skin and soft, tumbling sunshine-blond locks, Lauren had never really made it out of the minor league. She'd appeared at a few catwalk shows, but it was always Maida Vale not Milan, Putney not Paris. Low key. Low rent. Low paid.

She'd shot a few photo sessions for magazines. Nothing hardcore, despite her nightly clubbing attire, but the lads' mags lapped her up as a good-looking blonde with a body curvier than an ampersand, who could get her kit off yet remain within the realms of decency. She'd never made the covers though.

She'd been offered a job on one of those late-night porn channels once, jiggling her ass to the camera whilst rubbing a telephone between her breasts, enticing viewers to ring in. She'd been tempted to do it at first but when she watched one of the channels with her then-housemate and fellow model, Kelly, she realised just what a bad career move it would be.

Thank God she hadn't accepted, because gigs like appearing full frontal on TV had a bad habit of coming back and biting you on your perfectly formed behind.

Lauren had worked her way through a string of boyfriends, but none of them had lasted beyond a few weeks. She was an *equus ferus*, a wild horse incapable of being tamed by a mere man. They may have had beauty, brains or bank accounts in abundance, but not even they could win Lauren's heart. She didn't love love, she loved life, and as long as she and Kelly were dancing themselves dizzy and turning heads, then that was all that mattered.

Which is why the arrival of Saul Everett had been a complete shock. Lauren had just finished dirty dancing alongside Kelly to another funk-fuelled slab of delicious R 'n' B in the middle of the Mayhem dance floor at the end of another dazzling night.

As usual, all eyes were upon the two models, and Lauren loved the feel of her body as she ran her hands seductively over her contours. A sea of men flocked around her and Kelly as they danced, hoping to catch their attention. They had no chance, most of them staggering into each other under the influence of drink or drugs. Lauren may have been a party girl but she hardly ever drank back in those days, and drugs were a total no-no. Her vice came in the bedroom. She loved the feel of a man making love to her, throwing her recklessly onto the bed and skilfully bringing her to orgasm. Another reason she avoided the sea of pissheads at Mayhem. If they couldn't keep themselves upright, then how would their cocks manage?

As the predatory circle of men dispersed, Lauren had spotted Saul Everett at the edge of the dance floor, his face highlighted by a thunderstorm of laser lights bouncing across the club. He wore an immaculate suit and tie, which in itself was a novelty given the sweaty nature of the club. Lauren had read enough glossy magazines to know that the tailored outfit was a designer one, Savile Row, no doubt. Saul's face was striking, his cheekbones raised and proud, the lower half of his face dark with shaving line. His jet black hair was slicked across his forehead in a perfect wave. He sipped at a bottle of water, normally favoured by those pilled into oblivion, but his cool, calm demeanour suggested that maybe eau minerale was naturally his beverage of choice.

Lauren liked what she saw. Saul was the epitome of composed, sophisticated elegance. The antithesis of all around her. Staring at him, Lauren felt her nipples harden and a burst of excitement flow between her legs. There was no way a man dressed like Saul would ever cast as much as a second glance in her seminaked direction.

But he did. He didn't just look, he smiled. The widest, brightest, most inviting smile Lauren had ever seen. Before she could stop herself, Lauren had smiled back and gravitated towards him. When he spoke, his voice was deep and clear, peppered with the accent of an upper-class education. 'Your dancing was amazing. Would you care to join me for a coffee? I'm a member of a private club around the corner. It'll be quiet there and we can talk.' Trusting him completely, they were there within five minutes.

Lauren had never met a man like Saul before. He was intelligent and charming, the most captivating man that she had ever encountered. And he seemed equally bewitched with her. Saul talked to her about all sorts of different things and his masterful, masculine voice could make even the most bewildering subject sound joyous. Most of all, Lauren enjoyed his pillow talk.

It wasn't until their third date that Saul took Lauren to bed. Used to men who couldn't wait to pull her panties to one side and climb on board, Lauren was a beautiful ball of pent-up excitement laced with frustration by date three. She'd watched Saul from across the table on their dates and seen how his shirt stretched tightly across his chest and biceps when he gesticulated. She'd never seen him without a tie, let alone in any state of undress. So when he escorted her back to his Westminster apartment for 'a nightcap', Lauren could feel her heart beating in anticipation.

They had barely set foot inside his palatial apartment before Lauren started to loosen his tie and drag his suit down over his shoulders. Saul returned the favour, unzipping Lauren's figure-hugging minidress and letting it fall to the floor, revealing her matching bra and thong. Soon they were both naked.

Lauren had been right about Saul's body. It was hard and sinewy, not an ounce of excess fat to be seen. His stomach was flat and striped with muscular abs. His erection stood proud, possessing both thickness and length, rising from a dark thicket of hair. Lauren inhaled with delight. She knew that their sexual partnership would be mind-blowing.

Saul was a master of foreplay, and when he had finally entered her, it was at his choosing. As he increased the speed of his strokes, he tenderly touched Lauren's hair and cheek, telling her to enjoy the experience and remember how gorgeous she was. They came together, Saul's smile beaming down at her from above. He had certainly secured her vote. Lauren was smitten, as was Saul. Six months later they were married, Lauren's modelling days, clubbing nights and her friends, such as Kelly, jettisoned.

———

As Lauren sat opposite Dale at the ceremony, that first night of love-making with Saul seemed like a million years ago. She missed regular sex with Saul. But now was not the time to brood about that.

'So, do you like the idea of being part of the music business?' enquired Dale. 'It's a fun scene, isn't it? I want to get your voice recorded in the next few days to see what we can do with it. I'm assuming you're interested, otherwise you wouldn't have phoned. You're not here for me, are you? This is a great party, things are just getting going now. We'll be here till dawn.'

Lauren could feel herself blushing. Of course she loved the idea of singing and becoming part of the world she was experiencing this evening, but she had no idea what Saul would say about it all. Politicians like him did not have wives who partied till daybreak. Plus, she really was enjoying spending her time with Dale. There was something she found deeply exhilarating about him. 'There's no way I'm going to last until morning, Dale. I'm shattered as it is. I don't know how you do it.'

'Let me share the secret.' Reaching into his back pocket, Dale pulled out a sizable bag of white powder. Lauren knew it was cocaine. Placing it on the table, he turned to her. 'Try some. It'll perk you up a treat. You'll be looking even more delicious on that dance floor.'

Pushing the bag away from her, Lauren protested, 'Look, Dale, drugs are so not my thing. I'm a politician's wife. I don't do things like that. It's ridiculous.' Starting to panic, she went to stand. 'Maybe I don't fit in with all of this. This singing nonsense is nothing more than a pipedream. Thank you for a lovely evening but I'd really rather go home.' She tried to leave the table but before she could Dale placed a hand on top of hers. He squeezed it gently yet tightly enough for Lauren to stop in her tracks.

'C'mon, Lauren. I thought you wanted all of this. You've got the look, I'm sure you've got the voice. I could make you a star. And don't worry about the odd line of charlie. Everyone does it. The secret is just not getting caught. And if you're worried about photographers, then don't be. The organisers ban them after the first few awards to spare the blushes of a hundred music stars off their heads. They were kicked out hours ago. What have you got to lose?' Dale's voice seemed strangely hypnotic to Lauren. Her head told her to leave, but something inside her gnawed away at her, urging her to stay. She found Dale mesmerising and she was eager to please him. What was the worst that could happen? She wouldn't like how the cocaine made her feel, might be sick and obviously never do it again. At least if she was sick, then Saul was away at his conference for the rest of the week. She'd have time to get over it. And she didn't want to make Dale think she wasn't serious about his offer of help.

Five minutes later she found herself snorting a line of coke off the booth table. It was her first line of the night, the first line ever. When she was still happily gyrating her body around the dance floor at five o'clock the next morning, she'd lost count of how many lines she'd had. She didn't care. She loved the feeling of being part of the in-crowd around her. Dale was pleased with her and Saul would never find out. That was all that mattered.

CHAPTER 11

Still flushed from her back-seat encounter, Martha's head was whirling with the thrill of what the chauffeur had told her. Groups of people meeting for sex in public – just the thought of it brought goose pimples of excitement to her flesh. She had been questioning him about it ever since they'd resumed their journey and her mind was still racing as they pulled up outside her hotel in Kensington Gardens. He'd handpicked the hotel especially for Martha. He'd heard the views from the uppermost floors were said to be some of the most spectacular in London.

'This place looks amazing,' cooed Martha, looking up at the striking building before her. 'You've picked well. It's the second impressive erection you've shown me today.' She laughed at the crassness of her joke. Turning off the engine, the chauffeur turned to face Martha. 'It's one of the best in town. My twin brother stays here a lot with some of his clients. It has the air of decadence I feel you deserve.'

'Your *twin* brother? You never said he was a twin!' Martha's mind started to race with sexual possibilities – a ménage à trois brewing in her mind. 'You mean to say they didn't break the mould when they made you?' She stopped her mind from wandering further. He could be gay or hit with the ugly stick for all she knew.

'His name's Tom. We're identical twins, although I always tease him that I'm the one with the good looks. He comes into

the city for work sometimes.' He paused before adding, 'When
the need takes him.'

Martha could feel her sexual fantasy reigniting. At least the
ugly stick option had been dismissed. 'What does he do, then?
You said he comes here with his clients?'

'He's a life coach. He works for The Abbey rehabilitation
centre. You might have heard of it, it's pretty much world famous. He has a lot of female clients who like to show him their
… er … appreciation for turning their lives around.'

Bingo, thought Martha. That's the gay option erased too. Despite her lack of interest in the celebrity world, even Martha
had heard of The Abbey. 'God, that place is like the Mecca for
addicts. Virtually every celebrity in Hollywood has booked in
there at some point. I bet he's got some stories to tell.'

'You can ask him yourself if you like. Give him a ring – it
sounds like you two should go *out* together. I think you'd like
him … and I know he'd like you.'

———

Not too far from Martha's hotel, Lauren clicked off her mobile
phone and walked into the reception of the recording studios
where she was to meet Dale. She had been having a conversation with Saul and was still feeling incredibly guilty about her
depraved night out with Dale. Not that she'd mentioned it to
him. As ever, he'd been too busy filling her in about his conference on economic self-sufficiency or whatever it was. She'd not
been able to listen. Firstly because of her horror that she'd enjoyed the feeling she'd achieved from taking the cocaine and had
been beating herself up about it ever since; and secondly because
he was boring her senseless. She couldn't help feeling that she
was drifting away from her husband and his stuffy, bureaucratic
ways. Nathan Spilsbury was keen to drive a wedge in between

them and Lauren couldn't stop the nagging doubt that since meeting Dale, she herself was planting a gap between her and her husband's ambition. Besides, she had discovered that she had ambitions of her own – but Saul would never understand that. Now was hardly the time to drop into conversation that she'd love to be the next Miley Cyrus. No, for now, this part of her life would have to try and remain a secret. Away from her husband, and away from the paps. A guilty pleasure that she needed to explore.

She pushed all thoughts of her angst about Saul out of her mind as she approached the over-styled Jessica Biel-wannabe seated behind the reception desk. 'Hi, I'm here to see Dale Cousins. He's expecting me.' She gave her name and the receptionist directed her to the elevators to take her to the studios on the top floor. Lauren could feel her nerves escalating as the lift doors shut behind her.

At the top floor the doors opened. Standing directly in front of her was Dale. In his hand he held two flutes of champagne. 'I saw you coming across the street so this is still nicely chilled,' he said, indicating the glasses. 'Welcome to the day that will hopefully change your life – and mine.'

'I bet you say that to all of the girls,' she joked. 'So this is what the inside of a recording studio looks like.' She stared around at the sound booths on the far side of the room and at the framed photos of star names hung on the walls. She spotted one of Nancy. The thought of having her own photo up there one day thrilled her. *If only*, she mused to herself.

'So, how's your head after the other night? You seemed to be having a good time. You dance like a dream. I can see your first video already. You dancing against a backdrop of neon lights, beams of colour bouncing off the sequins on your dress. Maybe somewhere like Vegas. The backdrop of Mandalay Bay, The Venetian or The Luxor always looks magnificent. It's worked for Britney and Katy Perry. It could work for you, Lauren.' Dale handed her the glass as he spoke and she took a sip. The champagne and the talk of making her very own video were an enticing cocktail and acted as the perfect elixir to any jitters she'd been experiencing. Lauren felt her nerves melt away.

'It's a place I've always wanted to go. Saul tends to think it's a bit trashy. But, before you saddle up and have me heading off to the deserts of Nevada, are we not running before we can even walk here? You haven't even heard me sing.' She blushed as she spoke.

Smirking with satisfaction, Dale replied, 'Actually, I have. The coke seemed to obliterate any worries you had the other night. You were putting Barbra Streisand to shame when you climbed into the cab. I seem to remember you attempted to give me her entire back catalogue. You may not be on her level – nobody is – but you sure can hold a tune.'

Lauren put her hands to her face and groaned with embarrassment. She could feel the heat in her cheeks increasing. 'Please tell me I didn't. I must have been messier than I remember. Just shoot me now!'

'You were far from messy. In fact, you were quite beautiful. I loved the way you sounded … and looked. Which is why …' His voice trailed off as he produced another bag of cocaine from his packet. 'I was thinking that if your voice sounds that good on coke, then maybe it might be wise to get a little wired for the demo today.' Putting down his champagne, Dale licked his finger, dipped into the coke and rubbed it onto his gums. He didn't take his eyes off Lauren throughout the entire process.

In just a matter of seconds, a rush of different thoughts ricocheted through Lauren's mind. She knew that taking the coke again would be a massive mistake. Saul would be livid, not to mention politically ruined if word got out. But Lauren looked at Dale and saw his handsome features merge with the gold discs and famous faces on the studio walls. An explosion of twinkling Vegas lights framed her thoughts. It was no good. Despite any worries, she walked over to Dale and repeated his actions, dipping her manicured finger into the bag and rubbing the white powder onto her gums. The hit was almost instant.

For the next hour they talked about everything, their speech becoming more frenzied after every narcotic line. They listened to everything from Gwen Stefani and Missy Elliott through to bygone classics from Blondie and Donna Summer on the studio's huge sound system. Lauren swayed to the music, singing along with the notes. All of her inhibitions seemed to vanish. She sounded good in her own head and from the captivated smile running across Dale's face, it seemed that he thought so too. Pointing her towards one of the sound booths, he mouthed 'Let's do it'. For a split second, she was not sure what he meant. As he guided her into the booth and shut her inside it became obvious that he was talking about the vocals. Why did she feel a touch disappointed? Had she wanted Dale to mean something else? Would she have succumbed to his desires if they had been just that? Lauren wasn't sure. Now wasn't the time to analyse.

Placing the headphones to her ears, Lauren started to hear the backing tracks of some of her favourite songs filling her head. Dale gave her the thumbs up and she started to sing along. Shutting her eyes, she became lost in the music. The taste of the coke and the thumping beat of the song fused together and as she reached the last lengthy note of the song, she felt as if she had given it her all. She couldn't wait to do it again and sang her way through the next two songs. Every time she opened her eyes she could see Dale on the other side of the glass. He pounded his fist in the air to the beat of the music. It looked almost tribal.

Lauren loved watching him, his T-shirt stretched tightly across his chest and biceps. As he lifted his hands, his shirt rode up over his stomach. Lauren noticed the deep blond line of hair that aimed its way up to his navel and onwards to his defined abs. She found the sight deeply thrilling.

All too soon the songs had come to an end. Lauren felt as if she had experienced a mental orgasm. Her body seemed alive, her senses finally tuned in to what she'd always aspired to. Dale beckoned her out of the booth. She pushed open the door and he rushed towards her, taking her in his arms. He bear-hugged her tightly. His body felt good against hers.

'That was amazing, Lauren. I knew you'd not let me down. I'll spruce it up a bit and get the big boys in to make it sound as slick as possible, but you'll fucking rock this industry. You're better than anyone I've ever worked with … and I mean anyone.'

As he spoke, Lauren couldn't help but notice that he seemed to be staring directly at the photo of Nancy on the wall. 'Even Nancy? She has an amazing voice. One of the best – she's a great girl, Dale, I Iike her a lot. She asked me out with her the night of the awards ceremony. I would have gone. She needs a friend. I want to be there for her.'

'Nancy doesn't need friends, she never has. She's trouble, no … she's worse than that … she's history. Forget about being her mate, she's never been a best-buddy kind of girl. And anyway, you're going to be so busy with me from now on getting your music career started that you won't have time for anything, let alone girly nights out with a has-been. Now, let's celebrate – another line?'

Lauren couldn't help feeling that Dale was wrong about Nancy. They could be friends, but her potential new career would have to come first. As for the coke – there was no way she was going to decline.

CHAPTER 12

'What do you mean, she's run off? She didn't bother to let you know she was going? Martha is *your* daughter, darling. You would think she'd be considerate enough to tell you she's as good as emigrating.'

Turning away from the dressing table mirror where she had been applying a slick of night cream to her already age-defying face, Mariella Éclair turned to look at the muscular, naked body of her lover, Peter Bradford, as he stretched out on their bed. For a man of his advancing years, Peter was still a fiercely attractive man, and decades of building up his wine empire had given him a body that women half his age still lusted after. But Mariella knew that he was hers. One look at his sculptured chest and arms, his deep-set autumn brown eyes and his thick head of silver hair and she was forever certain that she had made the right decision in leaving Lewin.

'She's hardly emigrating, Peter,' corrected Mariella. 'From what I can gather from Lewin and that dreadfully skanky Adina woman, Martha has gone to the UK for a while. She left a message to say that she's staying at some hotel in Kensington. It seems that Lewin has managed to annoy her yet again by trying to marry her off behind her back. You would think he would have learnt by now that his daughter marches to her own drum. She gets that from me, thank the Lord.'

'I can see where she gets her dislike of Adina King from as well,' said Peter. 'I thought you'd be happy that Adina is keeping the cranky old bastard happy. At least it keeps him out of our hair. I don't think he'll ever forgive me for stealing you from him. Silly sod. Doesn't he know the best man won?'

'That's as may be, but he'll always be Martha's dad and he'll always be worried that she's not good enough to take over the reins of Lewin Éclair wines when he croaks it. And, to be fair to Adina, she was actually defending Martha's decision when I saw them both earlier. She said Lewin was completely vile. Not that I find that at all surprising. His temper was one of the reasons I fell out of love.' Mariella smoothed more cream down her neck as she spoke. Peter watched her, transfixed.

'How could he let a beauty like you slip through his fingers? You're a goddess.' He returned to the matter of Martha's leaving. 'So, what's he been up to this time then?'

Mariella recounted the story of Lewin's attempts to pair Martha up with Roger Penhaligon and how Lewin had accused her of being a waste of space. Peter placed his hands behind his head and listened intently as she spoke. He only commented when she finished.

'Does that man not have a fatherly bone in his body? She should be allowed to marry who she bloody well pleases. It's not up to him,' he scoffed.

'But, darling, the whole point with Lewin is that he wants Martha married off to someone who can take over the family business. I was cut out of the equation the moment I climbed into bed with you. You know better than anyone what a billion-rand empire he's perched on.'

'Indeed I do. Now, talking of bed, how about you come and perch yourself on this.' Peter placed his hand on his cock, which had grown erect as he'd watched Mariella.

Forty minutes later, as Mariella lay in her lover's arms, basking in the glow of their post-coital union, she could feel herself drifting into sleep. Just before she did, she heard Peter's voice. 'Where did you say Martha was staying in the UK. Which hotel was it?'

'Somewhere in Kensington. I have the name of it in my diary. I can tell you tomorrow. Why?' she murmured.

'No reason, just wondered,' said Peter. But Mariella never heard him, she was already asleep. It was a good job, because if she had have been awake she may have correctly suspected that Peter Bradford, the man she'd left her husband for, was up to no good.

CHAPTER 13

When Martha woke up and checked the time on her phone, it was two fifteen a.m. – she had slept solidly for the best part of eight hours. *Looks like the journey finally caught up on me*, she thought groggily as she rose from the bed and went to look out of her hotel room window. It was a clear night and she could see off into the distance, the magic and the mystery of the London skyline sucking any tiredness away from her. Within two minutes she was in the shower – within ten she had dressed and was heading out of the door.

The air was chilly against her skin as she strolled along Kensington High Street; it was certainly a lot cooler than it had been back home in South Africa. But there was something about the freshness of the air, combined with the urban middle-of-the-night smells of fast-food joints and bars throwing drunken customers out onto the streets, that Martha loved. She knew she would choose to stay in London for a good while. It surprised her just how much she'd missed being there. But, vibrant though the bright lights of Kensington may have been, Martha longed to be in one particular part of the capital. Climbing aboard a red double-decker night bus, another of the things she loved about London, Martha headed to Soho.

Jumping off the bus near Leicester Square it was just a few minutes' stroll to the clip joints, sex shops and media hang-outs of Soho. Martha found it with the instinct of a homing pigeon. Even though it had been years since she had graced its litter-laden pavements, she immediately felt at one with her surroundings. The night was still crackling with the electricity of the people immersing themselves in its shabby chic. Merry revellers poured from the late-night drinking holes, many staggering from street to street under the influence of God knows what. Gay couples walked freely, hand-in-hand, sharing their love with kisses and blatant fondlings, happy in the rightful acceptance of those around them. Prostitutes of all ages positioned themselves, hoping for another financial bite before the night was through. The whole Soho vibe made Martha smile, a genuine warmth surging through her body.

Checking her phone again, she could see that it was just after three. She wanted a drink, to experience some of the London life she thrived on. She decided to head to one of the area's strip joints. She had money, she had no inhibitions and she had no qualms about probably being the only non-working girl in there. She ventured into the first one she could find.

Martha was expecting the interior to be a dark, damp, seedy place with blackened walls, sticky floors and full of salivating men in raincoats furtively playing with themselves. The truth was pretty much the complete opposite – a mass of neon-lit areas and chrome surfaces greeted her. The clientele was far from men-only. There were lone guys of all ages dotted around the bar, but mixed in between them were couples, dressed in everything from high fashion through to tight, curve-clinging fetish wear, refilling their champagne flutes from a bottle chilled in an ice bucket alongside their table. Martha could almost smell the sexual haze that seemed to filter through the club. She drank it in, enjoying the idea of being part of it.

On one side of the bar, three girls writhed their bodies up and down poles on a raised stage, coiling themselves into sexually provocative positions for the titillation of the customers. A sign

on the wall instructed *Do Not Touch* but all three girls seemed
happy to let a mass of hands of both sexes rub against their skin.
Turned on by the spectacle, Martha ordered a drink and placed
herself in front of the stage. The girl in front of her was naked
apart from a skimpy thong and a pair of killer heels. A mass of
platinum-blond curls tumbled around her face. Her breasts, full
and naturally pert, wobbled deliciously as she wrapped her legs
around the pole. Gripping it with her thighs, she arched her
body backwards and formed a crescent with her body. Her face
upside down, she stared straight into Martha's eyes, smiled and
winked. Martha had experimented with girls before but there
was something about the female flaunting herself in front of
her that excited her like no other woman had. It was all she
could do not to jump onto the stage and join her. The crowd applauded wildly, and just as the woman who had excited Martha
was about to disappear into the wings, she turned and winked
directly at her again. It was a wink that spoke volumes. The attraction had been mutual. Martha knew what she had to do.
Draining her drink, she paid her bill and headed outside.

Finding the stage door for the strip bar was easy. It was situated in a dim side alley and had the name of the club written boldly upon it. Martha decided to wait there. She was wide
awake, despite the early morning hour thanks to her body clock
still being totally off-kilter. She had been there twenty minutes
when the blond-haired stripper appeared.

'Well, there's a pretty new face in town to greet a working
girl after a night of spinning around a pole. I'm glad to see you
understood my wink, honey. I was hoping you'd hang around.'
The stripper immediately linked arms with Martha and pulled
her close. It was an overly friendly gesture, almost intimate, but
to Martha it seemed natural. Even though she didn't know the
woman's name, there was an instant bond between them.

Martha knew that they would be friends and introduced herself to the woman. 'I'm Martha and I'm completely in awe of what you manage to do on that stage. You are amazing.'

'At the end of the evening half of the punters in there are too pissed to notice. I could have been doing the Macarena and most of them would have still been jerking themselves sore. I'm Kelly, by the way, or at least I am when I'm not pole dancing. My stage name is the highly fabulous Twinkle Stimulation. Catchy, eh?'

Martha couldn't help but laugh. 'Pleased to meet you, *Twinkle*. Do you fancy a coffee?'

In a matter of minutes the two women were seating themselves inside a coffee shop, the aroma of freshly ground beans and the multi-cultural chatter of the customers filling the air. As Martha sipped at her espresso, she studied the woman opposite her. Her dyed-blond hair hung in wide curls around her face, the make-up was deep and dramatic, splashes of colour across her eyes and shaded across her cheekbones. She wore a faux fur bolero jacket, tight T-shirt, and second-skin jeans. It was designer trash at its coolest and Kelly wore it well.

'So, how long have you been strutting your sexy stuff onstage?' enquired Martha.

'Long enough to know that I'm good at it and that it pays my bills,' Kelly replied. 'I actually really enjoy it. I've tried all sorts of modelling in the past and despite what the Tyras and Cara Delevingnes of this world have you believe, it's not always a bed of sweet-smelling roses. I've done everything from photo love stories through to getting my snatch out at stag parties and this is the first time in my life I've had regular money coming in. I'll stay at that club as long as the punters will have me … not that I get any complaints in that department.' Kelly jiggled her breasts and chuckled. 'These puppies see me right. Plus I only live round the corner.'

Her curiosity rising inside her, Martha continued with her questioning. 'You must find all sorts in there. Do you have regulars who come back to see you time and time again? I've seen you once and I can't wait for a repeat performance.'

'The works! Pop stars, soap stars, film stars, politicians. Of both sexes too. And some of them pay incredibly well, especially if you give them a little something extra after hours. My flatmate, Lottie, has just left me high and dry to run off with some horny internet tycoon she's been shagging. He came to the club, took a liking to her, and now she's shacked up with him in Mustique. Lucky bitch. Now I'll have to find her share of the rent this month.'

'I'll move in … if you like!' Martha had said it as quick as a flash, the notion springing into her head and spilling out of her mouth before she'd even had time to consider. 'I love Soho, and you seem like my ideal kind of flatmate. And I can pay a deposit in advance, no worries …' Her voice trailed off, wondering if she'd already overstepped the mark.

'Fabulous, when can you move in? The only house rules I have are that I never get up before midday, I have a pet goldfish called Marilyn who needs feeding when I'm not there and if you touch my Clinique night cream you're dead. Apart from that I'm the perfect housemate. Another espresso to celebrate? I assume that's what you're drinking again. Something dark and strong.'

'Just how I like my men,' joked Martha.

'Another thing we have in common then, babe,' said Kelly. 'I met a black politician once who was gifted like a pit pony in the trouser department and possessed a heavenly body sculpted like a Michelangelo. I love the politicians in general as they're great tippers. We get a lot of the Westminster crowd spilling into the club after a day putting the world to rights on their soapboxes.'

It was true. In fact, one of the visitors to the club that very evening had arrived there after a string of back-to-back political meetings. He'd perched himself in a dark corner watching the vampy movements of Twinkle Stimulation and her colleagues with an erect penis stabbing at the inside of his tweed trousers. On leaving the club, he'd headed to a shabby doorway in the next Soho street. It was a door he'd visited many times before. A faded postcard pinned there advertised the BUXOM STU-DENT BEAUTY two floors up. There was still life in the old dog yet – and a misogynistic Nathan Spilsbury was determined to prove it.

Finding a spaced-out prostitute lying on the bed, he'd thrown a wad of banknotes at her. She gathered them together as Nathan tore off his clothes. Climbing onto the bed, he slammed his sweaty groin across the girl's face and shouted harshly, 'Suck me like a fucking Dyson, you dirty whore, and earn every last pathetic penny I'm giving you. I want to leave here with my balls sucked drier than an old woman's tits.' Nathan was never one to mince his words.

CHAPTER 14

Hurriedly stashing away a virtually empty bottle of vodka in one of her cupboards, a flustered Portia looked over at Redmond who was seating himself at Mara's huge oak kitchen table.

It was the start of another working day and Redmond placed his thick A4 pad in front of him – his lifeline when it came to the day-to-day running of the professional life of one of the world's biggest opera stars. In a world of smartphones and palm computers, Redmond was still happiest with old-school pen and paper.

Sure she'd manage to conceal her trickery, Portia began placing slices of fruit into her blender, ready for her daily smoothie. As usual the *fruit du jour* was pomegranate. Portia was a great believer in its antioxidant properties supposedly helping with all manner of ills. She'd often been heard at parties across the globe telling those gathered that a martini was 'so much healthier with added pomegranate'. A martini at this hour of the day would have been scorned upon, but, as far as Portia was concerned, what Redmond's business head didn't know, his business mouth couldn't moan about. Which was why she'd already added a hefty dose of the vodka to the deep red liquid sloshing around in the blender. She'd spent her life being good for her art, and if a woman with millions of fans worldwide couldn't treat herself to a little kick-start in the morning then what was the point? Besides, it made her lonely yet lucrative life more bearable.

'So, who is desperately in need of my talent today?' she asked, seating herself opposite Redmond. 'I warn you now though, I don't want to stray too far from Mara until the new production starts, so anything I consider doing will have to be UK-based for the moment. Unless, of course, there's a million pound price tag attached. For that, you can send me to Uranus if need be.'

'Well,' Redmond scanned his notes, 'there's the usual round of TV requests. Some BBC show wants you to retrace your family tree and see if they can uncover anything riveting. I suppose they're hoping that you might be related to some Elizabethan harlot from the mists of time.'

'No,' Portia was quick to bark. 'My genes are dipped in diamonds and glamour, darling, not tainted by some tawdry backstreet grandmother who got her kicks on her back with her knickers round her ankles. Apologise sweetly to the BBC and say I have no time. Next.'

Redmond was used to Portia's routine dismissals of most ideas that he was required to put to her. 'Gossip girl Nush Silvers wants to interview you for her latest in-depth music article. She normally sticks to dynamic young things but apparently you've got a cult status among her readers and students are lapping up your back catalogue.'

'No, the last thing I need is to be interviewed by someone who normally grills people half my age, Redmond. I may look fabulous but I look more fabulous if I stick to people who look nowhere near as good. Simple logic. It's another reason I employed craggy old you!' Portia threw back her head in laughter, her russet curls bouncing wildly. She found the idea ridiculously amusing. Maybe she'd put a touch more vodka in her smoothie than normal.

'Every wrinkle I have is thanks to you and your wicked-witch treatment of me,' replied Redmond, poker-faced. 'Now, there's one more request, and even you and your hard-nosed ways would be pushed to turn this one down. London's theatre land is having a special charity weekend in a fortnight's time and all of the productions are donating money from ticket sales to charities. It's a bit last-minute but ticket sales have been down and it's a way of drumming up bums on seats and raising awareness of some worthy charities. All of the big names from the world of stage and theatre are confirming their attendance. The culmination of the weekend is a glitzy show at the Royal Albert Hall. The organisers want you—'

'They shall have me,' interrupted Portia. 'Top billing, I trust. I shall sing an aria from *La Bohème*. "*Si, Mi Chiamano Mimi*" – always one of my favourites.' Portia burst into song at the breakfast table, causing Redmond to wince.

'I'll chop your head off and call you Anne Boleyn if you don't let me finish,' he snapped. 'There's no choice about what you sing.'

Portia's vocals stopped in mid bel canto. 'What do you mean, no choice? Portia always has a choice.'

'The organisers want you to record the official theme song for the weekend. It's a duet especially written by Lloyd Webber. You'd be required in the recording studio for most of this week. There's no pay, but it's great kudos and doubtless if you turn it down then divas like Sarah Brightman or Malena Ernman will be in there like a shot. The diary is free this week. I could get you down there tomorrow for meetings and book you in at the Savoy.'

'Do I have a choice? It would appear that you've made your mind up already, Redmond,' sneered Portia, draining her glass and heading to the blender for a refill. 'Do what you need to do.' She paused for a moment before adding, 'And did you say a duet? Any idea who they're teaming me with?'

A stain of colour spread across Redmond's face. 'I was just coming to that. Piero Romeo has already confirmed. He was their first choice,' he mumbled, hoping that saying it quieter would soften the blow somehow.

'That jackass again? Goddamn it. I work with the man once and now he's following me around like a bad smell. Why him?' shouted Portia, banging her glass down on the granite work surface. A pool of rich red pomegranate juice splashed over the side of the glass and puddled itself across the counter.

But, despite her annoyance, there was a part of Portia that couldn't help thinking about the night they'd spent together in Budapest. Despite his wandering eye, she had to admit she'd be more than happy for it to wander in her direction again.

'I'll take that as a yes, then, and book the Savoy,' piped Redmond, before scuttling out of the kitchen.

CHAPTER 15

'I'm sorry, sir, I can't help you. Miss Éclair checked out of the hotel yesterday. She left no forwarding address, so if you are a friend of hers then I suggest you ring her to find out where she now is. That's the only answer I can give you.'

The perfectly groomed receptionist behind the desk had been trying for the last twenty minutes to explain the same thing to the, in his opinion, downright rude man standing in front of him. A queue of disgruntled guests were now beginning to huff impatiently behind the man. He seemed oblivious, continuing with his rant. 'But I've told you already, I've lost her number. I'm an old friend of hers, she phoned me to say she was here at the hotel and that we should hook up.'

'Well, I would have thought that her number would be stored in your mobile from the call, then, would it not, sir?' The receptionist was pointed with his answer.

'For God's sake, man. She must have rung me from a hotel phone. It was a withheld number. I don't know. All I want is to find out where my friend, Martha Éclair, is now?' His voice was becoming more and more enraged, the decibels increasing with every word. 'She's my friend, we want to catch up. If you could just tell me where she is, then I'll get out of your face and then you can serve this bunch of losers.' He spun round to face the sixty-something suited guest behind him, who cowered visibly at his stare.

The receptionist was adamant. 'I'm afraid I'm going to have to ask you to leave, sir. Your behaviour is becoming fairly threatening and if you don't go now, then I shall be forced to call security.'

'Screw you, you jobsworth little prick!' The man angrily pushed a mound of tourist pamphlets that were piled on the desk and watched as they scattered across the floor either side of the receptionist. As the hotel worker bent down to pick them up, the man stormed across the reception and headed out through the revolving door. A sea of eyes followed him as he did so.

The man was just about to climb into a taxi at the front of the hotel when a voice from behind him made him stop in his tracks. 'I'll take you to where Martha Éclair went.' As the man turned to face the voice, he was greeted by the sight of a stout, bald-headed man. 'I know exactly where she went. It was my cab she went in. She told me her name, not exactly a hard one to remember. Good-looking lass. I heard you shouting about her in reception. I can have you there in half an hour. It'll cost you though. I'm not exactly supposed to tell people about other fares.'

'How much?' He delved into his pocket and pulled out a roll of banknotes. 'Fifty pounds do you?'

'Make it a hundred and I'm yours,' replied the taxi driver. 'Plus the fare on top, all right?'

'Let's go.' If it meant he was able to find Martha, then the man considered it money well spent.

CHAPTER 16

'You have underwater speakers. That is just too cool for words!' yelled Nancy as her head broke the surface of Lauren's grandiose swimming pool. 'You can actually listen to music as you swim. That is totally wicked – it must have cost a fortune.'

'I have no idea. Saul had it installed as one of his friends was raving about how cool it is for pool parties. Not that we ever have any. Saul is hardly ever here lately.' Lauren was becoming increasingly bitter about her husband's increasing absence.

'Screw him, girlfriend ... get some hunks in trunks round and have a pool party. That would make Saul stay at home more, I bet he'd be worried about you then,' giggled Nancy. 'And if you do decide to get the pumped-up-pec brigade over then I'm inviting myself, OK! You'll need to share those boys around.'

Reaching for a cocktail the women had made before hitting the pool, Nancy smiled. It was the first time she'd done so since the night at the casino. She'd been elated when Lauren had phoned her inviting her over. It had forced her to get out of bed, dry her tears and actually leave the house. A girly afternoon with her new friend had been the perfect remedy for her anguish.

Not that it had gone quite as Nancy had hoped. There was something odd about Lauren. She seemed so much more jittery than she had done when they first met. Her mind seemed to be wandering and she'd lose her train of thought halfway through a conversation. When Nancy had questioned her about it, she'd been fudging and vague.

'I'm just tired. Barney's been keeping me up at night whining because his dad's not been here. And then on the one night Saul has been, he kept me up for completely different reasons.' Lauren smiled, Nancy thought a little stiffly – as if she was trying to divert the conversation onto a much juicier subject. Nancy took the bait nevertheless.

'He's a bit of a dish, your shiny politician man. Is he as good in the sack as he is on screen? You can tell me now we're friends.'

'Let's just say he makes his mark,' giggled Lauren. 'The other night in particular—' She was just about to continue when the front door bell rang. Stepping from the pool, she grabbed a towel and patted her hair dry as she went to answer it.

'Hurry back, I need to know more,' screamed Nancy. 'And please tell me it's the Chippendales or the male cast members of *True Blood* at the door … in skimpy swimwear!'

It wasn't – it was Dale's drug dealer making a delivery. He'd been coming round more and more often at Lauren's request.

———

There had always been certain things that Lauren would never be without in her handbag. Credit cards, bank notes, chewing gum and the essentials of lipstick, powder and mascara. The one thing that had never been hidden there, until now, was a bag of cocaine.

At first she was only taking it with Dale, but the packet of nose candy had started seeping into her home life as well. In between taking Barney for a walk and practising singing she would feel herself becoming despondent and her mind wandering. *Would Saul allow her to sing? How would he react if she told him? Was Dale just leading her on?* Every time her answer had been the same – to reach inside her handbag and dip into the coke.

Saul had only been home one night in the last six. But, as she'd hinted to Nancy, it was a memorable evening and Saul, pleased to see his wife, had been eager to show her how much he'd missed her and *make his mark*.

Saul had no sooner arrived than he was pulling his tie and shirt off. Scooping a sniffing Lauren – she blamed catching a chill whilst walking Barney for her runny nose – into his arms, he'd whisked her upstairs and into their bedroom.

'Have you missed me?' he yelled with authority. Thrilled by his masterful voice, Lauren whimpered that she had. She knew where the scenario was taking her. Within seconds he had reached down and pulled out their 'play box' – full of nipple clamps, butt plugs, vibrators, dildos and bondage rope. It was the rope that Saul had reached for to tie her to the bed.

'You've been a bad girl, haven't you? I know you have.' For a second, Lauren's mind had begun to panic. *Did Saul know that she'd been seeing Dale and doing coke? Had word got back to one of his cronies that she'd been seen at the awards ceremony?* Her mind raced. If he did know, then she was in serious trouble. She needn't have worried though – Saul was merely playing a role. He took a riding crop from the box and snapped it down across her butt. Her cheeks began to sting. They had been stinging ever since.

———

As Lauren sat herself down at Dale's office desk a few days later, her backside still smarted with the sexual pain that Saul had inflicted. She fidgeted awkwardly in her seat, trying to achieve the most comfortable position. Her butt cheeks were still a criss-cross of bloody hairline scratches and rosy red skin. The line of coke she'd just taken with Dale was yet to have the desired effect of numbing her pain. As she stared across at Dale, she'd never seen him look more stylish. His Ben Sherman T-shirt and skinny-leg jeans suited him immensely.

'So, Lauren, I've been touting your CD around to record companies and everyone is highly excited. The one thing I haven't told anyone as yet is who exactly you are. They know you're gorgeous, they know you can sing ... what they don't know is that you're married to a politician. If it was someone else – an actor or a plastic surgeon, or best of all a footballer – then we'd have no worries. You playing pop star would be par for the course. Personally I reckon a dose of your sexy ways is just what the opposition needs to get us all voting them into power. You could be the sexiest leader's wife since Carla Bruni married Nicolas Sarkozy. Have you told Saul yet?' he enquired, raising an eyebrow. He knew what the answer would be.

'No, I figured that until something definite was going to happen, we could keep it between us. If my singing is as good as you say it is, then even as a woman of mystery I should be able to secure a deal. You do your job, and I'll deal with mine when the time comes.'

'Fair enough. Sounds like you've made your mind up. But there is the little matter of you signing to me. We've not actually made this working partnership official as yet, and business is business. I'd like you to look over the contract I've had written. You've got everything I need, and I think I'm just the man for you.' Dale pushed a stapled pile of papers across the desk towards Lauren. As she reached over to pull it across to her, her hand accidently came to rest on top of Dale's. A spark of electricity ran through her at his touch.

Staring into his eyes, Lauren left her hand there for a silent second or two and then pulled the papers towards her. 'I'll read it, Dale, and I will sign it, you know I will. I just need to work out what's best with Saul. Leave it with me.'

'I want you to sign as soon as possible. There's an event going on in London next weekend. A big charity bash for the movers and shakers of the music biz at the Royal Albert Hall. There will be loads of influential bods milling around and I want you there on my arm. If you charm them like you've charmed me, then bright lights here we come, baby. It'll be a good press opportunity too. No pressure, but I think it could definitely play to your advantage in the long run. You would do anything to make this work, wouldn't you?' Dale's words were almost blinding to Lauren, drawing her in like a moth to a flame.

Slipping the contract into her handbag, Lauren stood to go. 'You know how much this means to me, Dale. I never expected this, but it is what I want. And I'm not the only one who's managed to turn on the charm.' She was aware that she was flirting and suddenly felt awkward at doing so. 'I'll be in touch,' she proceeded nervously.

'It will be a great weekend and I want you there, Lauren.' Dale's rich tones were still sinking into Lauren's brain when he leant over to kiss her. She let his lips brush against hers, clueless as to how they had arrived there. Despite every bone in her body telling her not to, the tingle of Dale's lips, on top of the coke, made her leave her lips locked with his for longer than necessary. It was all Dale needed.

Pushing his lips urgently against hers, he wrapped his arms around her and pulled her towards him. Lauren responded, opening her lips and allowing his tongue to loop with hers inside her mouth. He tasted delicious; a surge of forbidden excitement galloping through her. Dale's hands moved up the side of her body and he let one of them brush against the fullness of her breasts. When he met no resistance, he cupped her breast in his hand, bringing her nipples to attention.

It was then that the office door flew open with no warning. A teary Nancy fell through the door, mascara running down her cheeks. It was the first time Lauren had seen her since the afternoon she'd spent at her pool. She looked like she hadn't slept since. 'Dale, I need to speak to you, something's happened …' Her words petered away to nothing as she took in the scene before her. Lauren wrapped in Dale's arms, his hand still cupped around her breast. As Nancy stared into Lauren's eyes, her horrified expression showed clearly that she did not appreciate what she saw.

At that moment, it wasn't just Lauren's buttocks that were flushed red, the cheeks on her face were too. Nancy had just managed to catch her red-handed.

CHAPTER 17

Exiting her chauffeur-driven car as it pulled up outside London's Royal Albert Hall for a press launch, Portia appeared to slink out of the back seat and manoeuvre her body expertly for the journalists and paparazzi gathered there. Her winter white faux fur cape and a classic Alexander McQueen leopard-print dress were a winning combination. It was a couture safari that she felt suited her wildly beautiful features to perfection.

A hassled Redmond hovered behind her, a bundle of pads and papers clutched in his arms. It had taken a lot of persuasion to get Portia to the launch for the charity weekend event, but even he had to admit that, as ever, she was working the assembled press magnificently.

'Darlings, I'm here working with the crème de la crème of musical theatre. It couldn't get any better. We all need to dig deep into our pockets and drag people back to the West End. Musical theatre and opera should be adored by everyone, and if I can help, in my own unique way, then how could I ever say no? God gave me this talent for a reason.' She brought her speech to a rousing denouement with a glass-shattering pitch-perfect operatic note, raising her arms Evita-style before those gathered. The force of it caused even Redmond to flinch slightly. Happy with her performance, Portia headed inside, an obedient Redmond following two steps behind her.

'Well, darling, that should guarantee you coverage on the evening news,' he grinned. 'Very *je suis arrivé*, if you please.'

'You should know by now, my dear, that when I agree to do something then I will put my heart and soul into it and make my presence felt … unlike someone else I could mention,' barked Portia.

Less than thirty seconds inside the building, reflected Redmond. He'd been counting the seconds ever since Portia had vacated the car, seeing how long it would be until she made reference to a certain somebody.

As was becoming more common, the object of her annoyance was Piero Romeo, her singing partner for the charity single. The same single that she was to perform in front of the press that very morning alongside Piero, even though she hadn't actually laid eyes on the athletic singer since her performance in Dubai.

'Just who the hell does he think he is? Demanding that he record his vocals completely separately from me. If I can rework my hugely busy schedule to fit in this blessed song then so can he. What was the limp-wristed excuse he gave again? Useless creature.' Portia huffed her annoyance, flaring her nostrils as she did so.

'Just hold your horses, Cruella.' Redmond was in no mood for one of Portia's tantrums, especially one that he'd already explained to her countless times during the four days of recording she had completed for the song. 'Your vocal chords may be working perfectly but your ears seem to have forgotten their purpose in life! I have already told you that Piero has had to record his vocals abroad because he's been working on a new opera production. He sent his apologies, alongside more bouquets of flowers than your hotel suite actually has room for, and says that he can't wait to perform with you again today. Surely even you, the archdiva of melodrama, must have got that into your head by now!'

Portia knew when she was pushing her prima donna ways a little too far with Redmond. 'So he says,' she whimpered. 'It's just not the kind of professionalism a star like me is used to, that's all. And sending me over a dozen bouquets of flowers doesn't excuse him, in my books. Now, come on, Redmond, let's get in there and give everyone a touch of that musical magic that only I'm capable of.'

It had been over a dozen bouquets – fourteen, to be exact. Portia had counted each and every one of them and compiled all of the message cards that accompanied them. Why send so many? To Portia it was obvious. Piero was evidently realising what a fool he'd made of himself in Budapest romancing other inferior women when he could have been with her. To her it was like dining on stale nibbles and soda water when he could have been feasting on Beluga and Krug. And what pleased her more was that the more indifference she treated him with, the more he seemed to be trying to get back in her good books. She would actually look forward to seeing him today, not that she would give him any indication, of course. No, he'd have to woo her like a platinum Casanova if he wanted their love-making to develop into a second act.

CHAPTER 18

Since living together in Soho, both Martha and Kelly had discovered that they were like peas in a pod. They shared so many interests.

The first was their taste in music. Kelly had covered most of the walls in the main living area with posters of her favourite bands – Bon Jovi, Paramore, Foo Fighters, U2. All groups that Martha had in her CD collection back home in South Africa. Sandwiched in between them were posters for classic musical productions that had lit up London's West End – *Hairspray*, *Chicago*, *Love Never Dies*, *Les Misérables*. Martha would never have pegged Kelly as a lover of musicals but adored the fact that she seemed somewhat of an aficionado. Her eyes had widened with passion the moment Martha questioned her. 'My best pole-dancing routine is to *Big, Blonde and Beautiful* from *Hairspray* and going to see *Les Mis* a few years ago when Portia Safari was in it was one of the highlights of my life. That woman has a voice that's been dusted with diamonds,' she gushed. Martha made a mental note to introduce Portia to Kelly at the soonest opportunity.

Their second common interest seemed to be of a more exotic nature – a broad-minded sexuality. Posters for the Fetish Saloon, Club RUB, the F Club, Torture Garden and Spankers Club decorated the walls too. Martha loved the images of people wrapped in skin-tight rubber and sexy flesh-exposing outfits and the mention of masked balls, erotic masquerades and burlesque nights. She found herself aroused as she took in adverts for grope rooms, atmospheric dungeon playpens and gothic harems. It was a world she longed to experience. She couldn't wait to pump Kelly for information as they sat listening to music as daylight dawned after one of Kelly's late-night shifts at the club.

Drawing on one of her nightly relaxing spliffs and passing it to Kelly, Martha felt her head swim with the cocooned feeling of the drug circulating her senses and began to ask about the clubs. 'Are they places you've been, then? They sound …' she paused, contemplating the correct word, before adding, 'hot.'

Kelly raised her eyebrows and smiled. 'That's one way to put it. It's a little guilty pleasure I have now and again. The fetish scene in London is the best place to liberate your desires. I can get dressed up and become whoever I want to be. Schoolgirl, mistress, uniformed … the dressing up is completely empowering. I remember the first time I went, I didn't have a clue what to wear, so I threw on some tight jeans and a crop top. The woman on the door took one look at me, smiled and gave me a roll of bondage tape to fashion my own outfit. You'd be surprised how sexy you can look just dressed in strategically positioned tape.'

Martha could feel her senses crackling with excitement. 'Did you have lots of sex?'

Stubbing out the spliff Kelly grinned. 'Now you're talking about a completely different scene, honey. Fetish is about playing, sticking to dress codes and being respectful of those around you and having a consensually kinky time. Sex clubs, on the other hand, don't tend to have a dress code and there's a somewhat looser grip on what's acceptable. You should try fetish – I guarantee that you'll be pleasantly surprised and totally addicted.'

'And what about the sex clubs?' Martha's mind was a fusion of obscenely appetising images.

'I think they'd fit you like a silk glove. You're a girl who loves sex, Martha, I knew that from the moment you eyed me up onstage at the club. Now, I think it's time for bed, don't you?'

As she spoke, Kelly pushed the tiny denim skirt she was wearing further up her legs. It was a deliberate move and Martha's eyes darted automatically to it, causing her to experience a slight intake of breath. Kelly wasn't wearing any knickers, her pussy exposed for Martha's veneration. Taking Kelly by the hand, the two women walked to Martha's bedroom. In was only a matter of seconds before all of their clothes lay discarded on the floor as Martha and Kelly became intimate for the first time. They both knew it wouldn't be the last.

—

Ever since she'd kissed Dale Cousins, Lauren had been in no doubt that it wouldn't be the last time either. She hadn't planned it, yet she knew deep down that she'd wanted it. He was giving her everything that Saul seemed to be lacking right now.

For one, he was spending some time with her. Saul's nights away from home were becoming more and more frequent with every week, just as his phone conversations to her were becoming more infrequent. He seemed to be busier than ever at a time when her life with him had never appeared so empty. If it wasn't for her endless spirit-lifting phone chats with Dale about how he considered her to be on the verge of 'something big' then Lauren was capable of spending all day without speaking to another soul. She couldn't even phone Nancy any more. Not since she'd caught her and Dale together.

With Dale, at least Lauren felt part of something. Thanks to Saul, and more so Nathan, Lauren couldn't help feeling that she was surplus to requirements when it came to the world of politics. The only place that she really seemed to have become the wife that Saul craved was in the bedroom. When he wanted to reach for the play box, then Lauren became the perfect slave to the rhythm of his domineering ways. She enjoyed it, but there was something so incredibly tender about the kiss she'd shared with Dale that seemed to highlight the sexual spark that maybe she was missing. Dale's kiss had seemed less military, less demanding and altogether more affectionate and caring. It was a kiss she had been thinking about constantly.

That was the constant nagging irritation that buzzed mosquito-like at the back of Lauren's mind. She and Dale had been caught kissing by Nancy and it was clear that Nancy had been far from pleased. In fact, the look of venomous horror on her face at the time suggested that the idea of Lauren and Dale locking lips was too much for Nancy to bear.

What if Nancy decided to say something about what she'd seen? What if she decided to go to the papers? Saul would never forgive Lauren – she'd stand to lose everything. But then so might he. Lauren knew that she was out of her depth, letting the thoughts of what-might-be cyclone around her brain.

Dale had tried to placate her during their first meeting at his office since their kiss. 'I've spoken to Nancy, she was just surprised to see us kissing. She's assured me that she wouldn't say a word to anyone. She knows better than to cross me. I am still her manager, after all.'

'But she looked so upset,' cried Lauren, her voice dripping with insecurity. 'She could ruin everything, just because of one stupid kiss.' Her eyes began to fill with tears as she spoke. 'How can you be so sure, Dale? She didn't exactly look stable that day, she was a mess.'

Reaching out for her hand, Dale tried to calm her fears. 'You have to trust me on this one, Lauren. I've looked after Nancy for a long time, she knows I will always be there for her, but only providing she plays by my rules. I was the one who turned her into a star, the one who put her exactly where she wanted to be.

Now, talking of turning people into stars, have you signed that contract yet? You know how important it is.'

Placated somewhat by Dale's words, Lauren reached down into her bag and pulled out the contract. She'd signed it days ago, whilst happy on the highs of coke. She'd contemplated tearing it up when the downer of finishing another bag hit her, but a phone call to Dale and another bag had been couriered her way. It seemed the best way to alleviate any insecurity.

She handed the contract to him and he unfolded it, letting his eyes rest on her signature at the bottom of the page. Squeezing her hand again, Dale stared deep into Lauren's eyes and said, 'You've done the right thing, Lauren. I promise you that this will work for you. But you have to tell Saul about the music, if you really want him to be part of all this. Unless, of course, you don't want to say anything until you've really decided just what you want … and who?'

Leaning towards her, Dale ran his hands through the tresses of Lauren's blond hair and pulled her face towards his. Their lips met and Lauren found herself responding, running her own hands through Dale's mop of dirty blond hair. She'd known that they would kiss again. Just like the cocaine, being with Dale was starting to become an addiction.

'Are you sure about Nancy? I don't want this ruined, Dale, please. She could so easily tell Saul what she saw.'

Holding her close, Dale answered, 'Don't worry. She knows that I'm all she has right now. She needs me. Let me handle Nancy the way I know best, OK? You have to trust me.'

'I do,' whispered Lauren.

Lauren wouldn't have been anywhere near as trusting if she'd known what Dale considered handling Nancy in the best way to be.

CHAPTER 19

'How dare they? How fucking dare they? They must think I'm stupid.' Nancy had been saying the same thing over and over for days. That's how she'd felt when she'd run into Dale's office to find his lips locked with her so-called friend. She was married to a famous politician and he was Nancy's first true love.

That had been the moment that the pilot light of opportunity had switched on inside Nancy's head. Lauren had let her down and she was evidently just about to do the dirty on her lucrative, newspaper-worthy husband. Money sign at reel one. Lauren probably didn't want her husband to know about it and would pay for someone's silence. Money sign at reel two. Nancy needed as much as she could get. Money sign at reel three. Kerching – jackpot for Ms Arlow.

But then Dale had completely taken the wind out of her sails. As Lauren ran apologetically from the office, before Nancy had time to get an explanation from Dale, he had run towards her and held her tightly in his arms. He had pulled her close into his heaving chest and whispered 'I'm sorry' in her ear. His breath felt hot and sweet, his lips brushing against her earlobe. It was an action that had completely disarmed her. Any bullets she had been about to fire Dale's way had suddenly become blanks. She was enjoying the closeness between them, suddenly aware of the years of history they had shared.

It all became too much to bear and Nancy let her misery rise to the surface. Huge rivers of tears ran down her cheeks and she sobbed into Dale's T-shirt. 'Dale, I've done something incredibly stupid.'

She unravelled the story of her night at the casino to Dale, telling him about the money she'd lost. She stated the total as £5,000, making no mention of her winning streak on the horses or the fact that she had blown the entire amount Dale had given her. She knew how incredibly naive she'd been already, without having Dale rub his managerial salt into her wounds.

As she finished her story, Dale cupped Nancy's face in his hands and kissed her softly on the lips. 'It doesn't matter, angel, it doesn't matter.' The action again threw her off her guard. This was the last thing she'd been expecting, but then maybe it wasn't. She knew that Dale would always have a soft spot for her. Their love light had burned too brightly to be extinguished for good. She kissed him back, her lips urgent and feverish. It felt good to know that he still found her irresistible, despite all they'd been through. For the first time in a long while they made love. Nancy had forgotten just how good Dale was able to make her feel. As they climaxed together, Nancy heard herself say, 'You know I'm the best woman you'll ever have, no matter who you try it on with.' It was the first veiled mention of what she'd seen when she'd first entered the office.

Their love-making complete, Dale walked to the far side of the office. He pulled open a drawer and took out a cheque book. Writing Nancy's name onto it, he wrote the amount and signed it.

'Don't worry about money. There'll be more work around the corner to help out, but this one's on me. Call it a gift for all the things we've worked on together in the past. You know I still care for you, Nancy.'

Reading the cheque, one from Dale's personal account and not his business one, Nancy saw that it was made out for £5,000, the amount of money she'd said she'd lost.

Bollocks, why didn't I tell him the whole truth, she cursed under her breath as she lay sated across his desk. 'So, is this what you think I should be charging for the sex we've just had then, Dale?' She winked cheekily before adding a little more seriously, 'Or is it the cost of my silence as far as Lauren is concerned? I bet her bigwig husband would love to know that she's been sleeping around behind his back. I just hope she was worth it.'

'You're a sly one, Nancy. For your information, we haven't slept together and I have no intention of doing so. She just tried it on because she wants me to sign her up. She reckons she can sing, tracked me down here and thought that I wouldn't say no if she threw herself at me. I was chuffed when you turned up, to be honest. It stopped me having to get heavy handed with her and blowing her off.'

'So, I'm still you're number one client, then?' beamed Nancy, pulling her panties and jeans back up.

'And you always will be,' retaliated Dale. 'But I would appreciate it if you could keep what you saw under your hat. The last thing I need is some Westminster wanker on my back accusing me of political treason just because his wife wants a bit of extra-curricular to try and become another Cheryl Cole. She couldn't even sing, anyway.'

'As long as she doesn't see herself as the next Nancy Arlow, then I'll leave her be. And thanks for this, I owe you,' she said, tucking the cheque into her jeans pocket. 'It was worth every penny.'

Five minutes later, Nancy was gone. Dale stood bare-chested at his office window and watched as she climbed into a black cab on the street below. 'Silly bitch,' he muttered. 'Not even I thought she'd be dumb enough to believe that load of old bullshit. Still, it's five grand well invested if she keeps her gob shut about Lauren.' With that, Dale returned to his desk, reached for his laptop and turned it on. He needed to transfer £5,000 from his business account over to his personal one. There was no way he intended to pay for Nancy's silence from his own pocket. He'd just have to get his weasel of an accountant to expertly lose it in the business somewhere. Once he'd done that, he treated himself to another line of coke.

As Dale's office disappeared out of sight from Nancy's cab, she looked at the London buildings whizzing past the window. She could still smell the scent of his aftershave on her skin. She too muttered to herself. 'Stupid bastard. If he thinks for one minute I won't try for Lauren's money then his brain is thicker than his cock. I saw the contract she's signed – it was there on the desk, Dale. Nancy Arlow is back in action. Nobody makes a fool out of me, especially you and your new trollop on the block. But I won't be doing anything until I've cashed this baby first.' She raised the cheque in her hands to her lips and kissed it lightly.

CHAPTER 20

Watch your thoughts; they become words. Watch your words; they become actions. Watch your actions; they become character. Watch your character; it becomes your destiny.

Such was the essence of addiction. It could envelop a person like a mist rolling in over a sleepy seaside town. At first it would seem innocent, almost mystical, a magical place to be. But then, just as the mist can get thicker and conceal hidden dangers, so can addiction. It surrounds a person, leaving them blind and unable to see a way out. As a result, the only thing to do is to go deeper and deeper into the mist – deeper into your addiction.

———

Portia was finding it harder and harder to get through the day without focusing on how she could shoehorn her next drink into her busy schedule without those around her noticing it.

She would start the day as ever with freshly blended fruit juice, served by the staff at her London hotel. She would in-sist on always eating alone, telling Redmond that it allowed her thinking time to 'map out how to make the most of the day'. In truth, it allowed her to add miniature bottles of vodka from the hotel minibar into her juice. She found it the best way to kick-start the day. After breakfast she would then stash some more bottles around the suite, for those moments when she could take a few minutes' relaxation there before heading off to her next appointment. There would be one inserted down the back of the sofa, one placed out of view on top of the ornate teak dresser in the corner of the suite. One would be hidden behind the thick, leather volumes of books that stood on the shelves. But Portia had recently discovered some excellent new ways of trying to conceal her habit. She'd tested it out back home at Mara and Redmond hadn't cottoned on, and as far as Portia was concerned, if a wily old buzzard like him was none the wiser, then general Joe Public would never clock a thing.

First of all, Portia had taken a bottle of mouthwash from her bathroom cabinet, emptied the contents down the sink, rinsed the bottle and then refilled it with vodka. It was the perfect hiding place. Nobody, not even Redmond or one of her Mara staff, would interrupt Portia while she was in the bathroom. They wouldn't dare. A much-needed swig, a brushing of her teeth and then back to business. It was divinely simple.

It was as Portia placed the bottle back inside her bathroom cabinet at Mara one day that another idea came to her. What about a bottle for her bedroom? She was always paranoid that one of her staff would discover the mini bottles she hid in the drawer of her bedside table. There was enough alcohol in the cellars of Mara to cater for the most drunken of party seasons. The odd drink was fine, that was expected. But one of her maids finding bottles stashed by her bedside would arouse suspicion and Portia couldn't risk that. The last thing she needed would be some blabbermouth menial striving for a quick buck with a telltale scandal in the national press. No, she needed to remove those and find a much more subtle place to stash her bedroom supply. Scanning around her room she had found the answer – where were there bottles in her bedroom? Of course: her dressing table contained an array of exotic and colourful perfume bottles, housing a wide variety of eclectic scents that Portia adored.

Not your usual celebrity nonsense from the likes of Sarah Jessica Parker, Jennifer Lopez or Montana Phoenix. Heaven forbid. Portia had picked up her love of handmade, bespoke perfumes and beautiful bottles from her mother, who had travelled around the world in order to buy exactly what she wanted. A teenage Portia used to spend hours studying the voluptuously shaped bottles decorated with gold script or squirting one of the designer atomisers, watching as a fine cloud of sense-awakening fragrances filled the air. It was the start of a love affair she'd never left behind.

Portia had collected dozens of bottles over the years, spending thousands of pounds on them, and many of the bottles remained empty. The idea was hatched. Within minutes, she'd poured the vodka into one of the empty bottles. Picking it up, she squirted the atomiser directly into her mouth. The sheer Hollywood glamour of it all and the taste of alcohol as it hit the back of her throat made her laugh. From that day on, her bottle of 'favourite perfume' had gone everywhere with her. And not just the one. Another of the smaller atomisers immediately found its way into her handbag for those 'emergency' moments when she was out.

Yes, Portia was savvy enough to know that if she fancied a drink, no matter what the hour, there was always a way to do it without the concern and interruption of those around her. It was none of their business if her perfume was a hundred-proof.

Not that Portia's alcoholic intake wasn't causing her a modicum of concern; it was. For a woman who tried to watch her calorie intake, the addition of a few clandestine tipples throughout the day and the abundance of mints she seemed to be eating were starting to form telltale signs across her body. Even Redmond had commented on the mints. 'Have you bought shares in Trebor, darling? You're smelling mintier than a salver full of

After Eights lately.' Portia, thinking on her feet, had thrown her answer right back at him. 'The joy of decaf mint tea, Redmond.'

No, Portia had noticed that the extra calories from the alcohol and the minty sweets were beginning to distort the flowing curves of her body. Not much, but enough for a diva of her hypercritical ways to worry. As she looked at herself naked in the full length mirror of her hotel bedroom before heading off to her charity press launch, she was not happy with what she saw. *My belly doesn't seem as perfectly flat as it used to be. Is that the hint of a saddlebag I'm seeing on my waistline? God forbid, is that flabby underarm flesh?* Her mind raced with dissatisfaction. *Maybe it's time for some kind of treatment*, she mused. Yes, maybe she'd book herself in somewhere. She'd worry about that later; first off she had to go and see Piero for the press launch.

Bloody men, ruination of my life, she thought to herself. *Despite having it all, I still can't bag a decent one.* It was the one part of her life that had never really worked out as she'd hoped. Trying to lift herself from a moment's melancholy, Portia stared at her reflection and said, 'C'mon, Portia, men aren't everything …' After a brief pause, she couldn't stop herself from adding, her voice much more downbeat, 'They're the only thing.' With another oral squirt of the atomiser, she went to get dressed. If she was to see Piero again, she might need a little Dutch courage.

———

The final flawless notes of Piero's and Portia's duet together came to an end, bringing the gathered press at the Royal Albert Hall launch to their feet with a thunderclap of ovation. Despite it being their first performance of the song together, Portia and Piero had worked the stage beautifully, bringing their bodies close as they stared into each other's eyes and harmonised Lloyd Webbers' latest masterpiece. Taking their bows, the two stars walked offstage hand in hand. As soon as they made the wings, Portia pulled her hand away from Piero's. There was anger brewing in her eyes.

'Just what did you think you were playing at? Don't think for one minute that I couldn't feel your erection pressing against me when we were singing. You were like some rampant Jack Russell rubbing yourself against me. This is neither the time nor the place and if you think I have any interest in you then you're sorely misguided—'

Portia's words were cut short as Piero lifted his finger and placed it against her lips, with a teacherly 'Sshhh'.

'It's what you do to me, Portia. I'm a red-blooded Italian – what can I say? I'd like to take you to bed again, to make love to you. You feel the same, I know it. Those unkind words of yours in Budapest hurt me to the core, but I know they're not true. You enjoyed the sex we had together. I have a lot of love to give—'

'Yes, and you couldn't wait to give it to half the cast as soon as you'd climbed out of my bed,' snapped Portia, cutting him dead. 'That didn't exactly make me feel wanted, you know.'

'I didn't think you'd want me again. A woman like you can have anybody she wants. You are so beautiful, so talented, so … *squisito* … exquisite. I assumed I would just be a one-night stand for you. Did I assume wrong?' For such a colossus of a man, Piero's question seemed childlike and pitiful. It was not what Portia had been expecting.

'Er … maybe you did. How dare you assume that I'd be shagging my way through half of Hungary. I don't like being made to look a fool, Piero. I've had enough heartache to last a lifetime, so, despite what you might have felt, I do not jump into bed with any passing co-star who happens to come my way.'

'Then maybe I have been the fool, Portia. Let me try and make it up to you. We have to work together on this single. I'm here in London for the next week, as are you, so let me take you out. Let's start afresh. No assumptions, just two people enjoying each other's company. If nothing else, we can guarantee our faces in the newspapers and magazines to promote this event. Agreed?'

Portia could feel her icy demeanour defrosting. 'I suppose it can't do any harm. You have my number. And you're paying, so make sure it's somewhere ridiculously expensive. You're lucky I'm giving you a second chance.'

'*Bella donna, vi saluto* … I salute you,' beamed Piero. 'I can't wait. Let's say tomorrow night at six.' Before she could react, Piero bent forward and kissed Portia on her lips. She felt a frisson of sexual anticipation run through her, ignited by his touch. A little flustered, she headed to her dressing room. She needed a squirt of her favourite perfume.

CHAPTER 21

'Hi, I'm Tom.' The voice was deep, rich and as delicious as melted chocolate. The full, rounded lips it came from were some of the most tantalising Martha had ever seen. They were succulent in a Lewis Hamilton kind of way without being too big and Jagger-esque. The sight of Tom's ebony face caught Martha's breath as she slid into the passenger seat of his SLK 230 alongside him. He was puppy-dog beautiful with a Tyson Beckford masculinity to his face.

'Nice to meet you at long last,' cooed Martha. 'Nice wheels. The Abbey pays well then, I assume.'

'I do all right, but we're not here to talk about work. Tonight is all about playing. Are you sure you're up for this?' Tom placed his hand on Martha's knee as he asked. A spark ran through her body.

'I have thought of nothing else. It's not every day that a girl gets to go dogging with a beauty like you.' Martha was loving the flirtation. Tom was beautiful and she had no need to win him over – he was already a guaranteed result.

'Believe you me, when the people there see you, I will be forced to the back of the queue,' said Tom. 'I hope you've got some stamina.'

'Well, let me see …' she said, patting the pockets of the cotton blazer she was wearing. 'Condoms – check, lip gloss – check, mobile phone in case I lose you – check … Oh yes, stamina …' She patted her lap minxily before saying, 'Check.' Tom licked his lips appreciatively. 'Now, Tom, how about some Pink to get the party started.'

'God, you are keen, but keep it under wraps for now as we've got a two-hour journey to get to tonight's entertainment. I want that pussy of yours in perfect working order,' enthused Tom, raising his eyebrows and placing the key into the ignition.

'Believe it or not, I wasn't talking about that pink, I was talking about the singer. "Get The Party Started", "Just Give Me A Reason", "Blow Me (One Last Kiss)" … you know, Pink?' Martha held up a CD to prove her point. 'I was thinking this might keep us both buoyant on the long journey. We're not going to get there until midnight, after all.'

'Ladies choice it is,' said Tom, taking the CD and inserting it into the in-car system. 'Right, sexual heaven here we come. Let's just hope it doesn't rain.'

They needn't have worried. It was the perfect summer's night, the sky still bright and the night air pleasantly warm as they pulled away from Martha's Soho apartment and headed towards their destination. In fact, it was clear enough for Martha to have spotted the car that pulled out directly behind them should she have cared to have looked. The man behind the wheel had been watching her ever since she'd vacated her flat. In fact, he'd been watching her for days.

———

Earlier that night, on the other side of London, Portia was also settling back into the luxurious comfort of an expensive car. Unlike Martha though, she had no idea where the end destination was and where the chauffeur was taking her. In fact she'd been letting her designer-clad body sink into the leather for well over the last hour, Piero Romeo alongside her. 'Just where exactly is this restaurant, Piero? I should have known that it would be miles away when you said you'd pick me up at six. Ridiculously early. If this J'Aton gown is creased to hell by the time we get there then I'll not be best pleased. It cost me an absolute fortune on a trip to Australia and it's one of my favourites.'

'You look sensational,' said Piero, his voice smouldering with more than a hint of desire. 'You said you wanted tonight to be special and it will be. Now, here's where we get out.'

As far as Portia could see through the side window, the car had turned into what was little more than a field. Scanning through the glass all she could see were patches of sun-scorched grass and what looked like some kind of brick outhouse in the distance. À *la mode* glamour with the finest à la carte menu it was not. Perturbed by the vista before her, Portia was quick to erupt. 'Piero, if you think I'm walking around a field in my dainty little Calvin Klein heels, then you are more misguided than even I thought. Turn the car around and take me back to the Savoy ... now!'

Piero frowned in frustration, before allowing himself to smile. '*Mamma mia*! So quick, so tempestuous. I suggest you look out my side of the car.' He opened the door, allowing Portia to stare out. What she saw caused her to raise her eyebrows and one side of her mouth to curl into a wry smile. Parked about five hundred yards away from the car was a light executive jet. Having flown in them many times, Portia knew that the one in front of her was top of the range.

'So, the journey is far from over, then?' she enquired.

Taking her by the hand Piero led her from the car and walked her towards the steps descending from the jet. Immaculate in his tuxedo and crisp white shirt, Portia had to admit he made a striking escort. As they reached the steps, Piero brought Portia's hand up to his lips and kissed the back of it. '*Bella signora*, the night has only just begun.' They walked up the steps and into the jet. Portia had no idea where they were flying to, but at that precise moment, she didn't care. Destination unknown was fine with her. She was already beginning to float on the wings of exhilaration at the thought of the night ahead.

—

Martha had enjoyed the journey to wherever it was she and Tom had just arrived. The two of them had talked non-stop for the entire journey, much of the conversation laced with shameless, saucy flirtations at the night that lay ahead.

Martha had been keen to grill Tom about his job as well. It wasn't every day you secured a captive audience with a life coach from the top rehabilitation centre in the country.

'So what does a life coach do? How long have you been at The Abbey? Who have you treated?' The questions were fired in quick succession, tumbling from Martha's lips without a pause. Tom grinned, thrilled by her natural enthusiasm. His teeth were perfectly even and bright white, an extreme contrast to the deep, dark tones of his skin. Martha let a judder of anticipation spiral through her body, thinking of how those teeth would hopefully be nibbling against her willing flesh before the night was through.

'I help people with issues to try and achieve goals and develop skills and to generally make them feel good about themselves. I've been at The Abbey for three years and I love it and I'm not giving you any names as yet but let's just say I've got a client list that could fill the tabloids cover to cover.' Tom's answers had been volleyed back at Martha just as quickly as she'd asked them. 'My client list has allowed me to experience some of the best restaurants and hotel rooms in the country.' He winked, before adding, 'A life coach seems to make a good plus-one for a lot of troubled ladies out there.'

There was a confidently cool air to Tom's words. He was cocksure but bordering on the right side of smug. It was undoubtedly a job that suited him and the cheeky look on his face told the story of how he obviously profited from it in many different ways. Martha liked his style and she could feel herself becoming turned on just by being in his presence. It was no wonder the ladies at The Abbey fell for his charms. He'd already cast his spell over her and she's only been in his company for a few minutes.

'Well, here we are,' he said as they pulled into a stretch of picnic area. 'It doesn't look like we're the first. According to the directions I was given on the website, there should be lots of action going down here tonight. It should be a good introduction for first-timers,' he added, looking at Martha. 'Not that anybody will be able to guess that you're getting your dogging wings tonight. When they see you on all fours they'll be thinking you've been at it for years. And take that as a compliment, because it's meant as one.'

'Oh I do,' grinned Martha, staring out of the car window into the night. Even in the near-darkness she could see a variety of cars and vans parked around the area. A few people were milling from vehicle to vehicle, furtively peering into them to see what, if anything, was happening inside. It thrilled Martha, her eyes widening as a bubble of giddy apprehension popped inside her stomach. She felt like a hungry child staring into a sweet shop window at the candy delights on display.

'What are the rules and what are … the risks?' The word 'risk' hurdled through Martha's mind. There had to be risks. That was part of the thrill of it all for her: the thought that she was about to do something that not many people could attempt, could achieve. Martha loved her body, loved the sex … now she wanted others to love it with her.

'If the interior light of a car is on then that generally means the people inside are up for being watched from a suitable distance. If the light flashes then that is often an invitation for people to come closer. If you get up close and the window or the door is open, then you can climb on in and get dirty. I always like to ask first though.' Tom winked. 'My mother raised me to have good manners, you know. Ready for action?'

'Ready, willing and able. Lead the way.' Martha licked her lips to show her eagerness and the two of them walked from their car and headed towards the mass of vehicles parked nearby.

———

Even for a woman of Portia's globe-trotting gastronomic expertise, she had to admit that the meal she was just finishing was one of the most gratifying she had ever experienced. She'd known that she wouldn't be settling for pizza and chips with Piero, but the rapturous variety of blue lobster, scallops and black figs she'd treated her tastebuds to had surpassed any preconceived expectations she'd had of the opera star. And the setting for their evening was, in Portia's eyes, *magnifique*.

They had been in the air for no more than an hour when the pilot had announced that they were about to land. Portia had no idea where they were going but as they descended, her heart raced as she spotted the telltale signs below them. The proud structure of the Eiffel Tower was easy to spot thanks to the cloudless summer night, and the Arc de Triomphe, positioned like a historic bull's-eye at the centre of the Place de l'Étoile, starfished out below them. Paris – one of Portia's favourite cities in the world. The art, the fashion, the style – it had it all. It was her first time in the city since a sell-out run at the Paris Opera House and the thought of being back there, however brief, melted any frosty doubts she had previously considered about the evening.

Lifting her freshly filled flute of champagne from the table in front of her, she reached out and squeezed Piero's hand across the table. 'Wasn't it Cole Porter who said "I love Paris in the summer when it sizzles"? Well, if ever there was a city I get a kick out of, then it's Paris. What a lovely surprise. Here's to a sizzling night.'

Upon landing, a car had whisked the two stars off to Le Bristol, a hotel that housed a restaurant which had become synonymous with the best in fine cuisine. Its Michelin-star chefs and poll-topping menu had made it one of the must-visit hotspots in the world for dining. The attentive staff had greeted Portia and Piero with open arms, showing them to their table in the summer restaurant. The finest wine had flowed, the perfect accompaniment to their dining. Portia was loving it. And it wasn't just the constant flow of alcohol and the fit-for-a-king food that was pleasing her. She had to admit that Piero was incredibly good company, something that neither of them had allowed themselves to experience before, other than their one night in Budapest. They talked about their lives in the operatic world, their favourite singers and how they came to be two of the biggest names in their field. It was an enlightening evening and as they slid into the back seat of their car, ready to take them to the private air field where their jet had landed, Portia knew already that she didn't want the night to end. It had been *une nuit parfaite*.

'The night air has become a little chilly, has it not?' Portia deliberately eased herself closer to Piero as she spoke, longing for him to share the warmth of his body with her. He took the hint, removing his dinner jacket, placing it around her shoulders before looping his arm around her and drawing her towards him. 'Let me keep you warm,' he whispered. They remained silent for the rest of the journey, Portia's head nestled in the crook of Piero's shoulder. It was a comforting silence, both of them content to be sharing each other's company. She could feel his chest rising with every breath beneath her face and the virile aroma of his body. Mixed with the medley of alcohol that she had enjoyed, Portia shut her eyes and savoured the moment.

When she opened them again, their car was pulling up alongside the private jet. It wasn't until they were both inside and seated ready for take-off that Portia spoke once more. 'I'm sorry for how I treated you in Budapest, Piero. You know my reasons but I shouldn't have tried to make you look so foolish.'

Just as he had done backstage at the charity press launch, Piero hushed Portia by placing his finger to her lips. There was something more sensual about the action this time round though. 'And I beg your forgiveness for my stupid assumptions. I would never have cheapened myself with those other women if I had known that maybe there was a chance again with you. I guess I can't believe my luck.' The intensity of his chocolate eyes penetrated straight to Portia's soul. It was at that moment that she made her mind up – she was definitely falling for Piero Romeo.

As the jet evened itself out after the climb of take-off, Portia rose from her seat. She was a little unsteady on her feet, not sure whether it was the alcohol or the movement of the flight. 'A new beginning, then? For us both. Now we've taken off, I guess we have an hour to kill before landing in London. How about we do a little *taking off* of our own?'

Unhooking her gown, she let it fall to the floor and stood over Piero in her lingerie and heels. He was already undoing the buttons on his shirt. 'Time for some in-flight entertainment of the mile-high kind,' teased Portia.

'*Mamma mia ...*' cooed Piero.

—

Martha was fastening up the buttons of her blouse in the back seat of their car. She had just enjoyed the delights of having Tom take her from behind as she leant into the back seat from outside. He had simply pulled her knickers down, lifted her skirt and inserted his cock into her. She'd squealed with delight at its impressive size and in the knowledge that a group of about eight people had gathered around the car to watch them in action.

Tom and Martha had both enjoyed their evening. They had spent at least two hours at the picnic area and had been pretty much constant with their sexual activity. All of the males there had swarmed around Martha like bees as soon as they had seen her. Martha was more than happy to be their honeypot, at first teasing them with glimpses of her round, inviting backside. After twenty minutes of teasing, she had leant back onto the bonnet of one of the cars there and let Tom fuck her. A crowd had quickly amassed, many of them in states of undress, men and women of all ages pleasuring themselves at what they saw. It was the first of many equally erotic encounters throughout the night.

Driving away from the picnic area, Martha's face beamed with the newness of the thrill she'd experienced. 'I take it you've enjoyed yourself, then?' said Tom.

'I loved every sensual minute. I can't wait for the next time. I'm addicted already.'

As Martha's mind flashed back to all of the sinful symphonies she'd enjoyed that night, their car lost sight of the other sexual thrill-seekers behind them. Also now out of view was a car that had been parked there all evening. It was the one that, unbeknown to Martha and her latest lover, had followed them all the way from Soho. Sitting inside, totally amazed yet hugely turned on by what he'd witnessed, was the driver. On his lap he held a camera. Its night vision and long lens had allowed him to take as many photos as he could from his somewhat distant vantage point. He scrolled back through his photographic efforts to see what he'd captured. Many of the shots were just a mass of indistinguishable bodies in the gloomy darkness. But a few were pictorial gold. At least three of them showed Martha's face quite clearly as she immersed herself in the carnal joys of the night, a crowd of people around her.

Checking his watch, he grabbed his mobile phone and rang a number. There was no reply so he left a message. 'Hi, it's me. Sorry for the late hour. I've got some photos for you that I think you'd like to see. I'll email them through in the morning.'

Hanging up, he started to turn his key in the ignition, but the throbbing in his trousers stopped him. He'd been constantly erect for the past few hours, the voyeuristic nature of the night pleasing him greatly. He needed to do something about it, and from what he'd seen there were a vast range of women who would be quite happy to come to his aid. Stashing his camera under his seat and stepping out of the car, he made his way over to the picnic area. Martha wasn't to be the only person sampling the art of dogging for the first time that night.

CHAPTER 22

When Adina King had first started going out with Lewin Éclair it had all seemed to make sense. She needed a constant supply of readily available cash which meant she didn't have to dip into her own somewhat substantial fortune at all, and for Lewin it meant the macho status symbol and power trip of having one of South Africa's most glamorous ladies on his arm. But she had recently been aware that their relationship was becoming harder to palate than a corked bottle of the most acidic, vinegary wine. Their conversation had dried up like picked grapes left to desiccate in the South African sunshine, and their love-making had become little more than a few urgent stabs in the dark while Adina went through the motions of faux-climaxing. The dark, unpleasant odour of cigar smoke on his breath as he clumsily shifted his sweaty bulk of a body on top of her in bed was still bearable in Adina's mind for two reasons.

First of all, she was indulging in amazing, nerve-tingling sex with one of South Africa's sexiest up-and-coming male models. They'd met in the VIP area of one of Cape Town's hottest nightspots and the attraction between them had been mutual and instant. Adina had barely had time to finish her cocktail before she found herself with her minuscule G-string pulled to one side and the model's mammoth member slipped inside her in one of the club's toilet cubicles. The pair had been meeting regularly ever since.

But the second, and main reason that Adina could cope with Lewin's clammy attempts at copulation was by thinking about the money behind the man. If she could make it work with Lewin then she would be financially set for life. One day, potentially, the vineyards could be hers. It would be the alcoholic gift that kept on giving. People would never tire of the produce that Lewin Éclair exported around the globe and even though she had no intention of running the estate herself – mental brain work was *so* not her thing – Adina had visions of one day staring out at the land around the estate and knowing that it was hers, all hers.

Thirty-year-old Adina King was one of South Africa's most notorious celebrities, and also one of its most controversial. A former WAG to a footballer, the beauty had relegated her one-time boyfriend and shown him the red card as his own career hit the skids due to a bad car accident. Puncturing his lungs had not just deflated his chances of international play, it had popped Adina's bubble of love towards him. Call it cut-throat ambition, but she no longer had a use for him. The oh-so-caring Adina had hitched up with Lewin before the footballer had barely come out of the operating theatre. Lewin, with his ever-expanding bank balance that seemed to outshine any worries Adina may have had about the age difference between them, was flattered into bed and schmoozed into showering her with the designer luxuries only few could afford.

Sitting on the veranda at the estate house with Lewin alongside her, they both had large glasses of the latest in-house red wine in their hands and Lewin, as usual, was puffing on one of his beloved Cohiba Esplendidos Cuban cigars. They had been silent for the last ten minutes, the only sound coming from the clink of their glasses as they placed them on the table in front of them and the lip-smacking as Lewin dragged heartily on his cigar.

Regarding Lewin out of the corners of her kohl-pencilled eyes, Adina knew that if one day she was to be queen of all she surveyed then she had to try and steer Lewin in the right direction. At the age of fifty-five Lewin wished to take a step back from the Herculean task of running one of South Africa's most successful industries so he could enjoy life a little more. He wasn't getting any younger, as his full head of thick grey hair testified. And now that Martha had gone AWOL and Mariella was definitely *persona non grata*, Adina hoped that she may be moving up the wine list. Her impatience fuelled by the satisfying richness of the drink, Adina sidled gently towards Lewin. She manoeuvred the fabric of her Valentino side-drape dress sexily up her thighs as she did so, exposing even more of her perfect upper legs. Shaking her mass of panther-black hair she placed her hand on Lewin's shoulder. He turned towards her, blowing a billow of smoke as he did so. It pricked at Adina's eyes but she chose to ignore it.

'It's a beautiful night, darling, isn't it? Just you and me gazing out at the world. And what a world it is, you must be so proud of what you've achieved. It's all yours.' She ran her manicured fingers down one of his cheeks as she spoke. Lewin seemed somewhat oblivious.

'Not that any of my bloody family realise it,' he huffed. 'I've sweated blood and tears for this place and how do they repay me? A woman who runs off with my biggest rival and a daughter who vanishes quicker than a magician's assistant. No bloody respect from either of them.'

'Which is why you need a real woman in your life. Someone you can be proud of, someone who is just as competitive as you.

Someone who is perfectly … compatible.' Adina leant over to kiss Lewin's lips before adding, 'In every way.'

'I'm fully aware your attraction in me is all about my wallet, Adina. You wouldn't look twice at me if I was some poor little deadbeat from the townships, so don't pretend otherwise.' Lewin aggressively stubbed out his cigar as he bad-mouthed his lover.

She was determined not to let him spoil the moment though. 'You know me too well. We're so alike. I know you've walked over people to get what you want in the past, you're always bragging about what a ruthless operator you've been. That's why we're perfect for each other.' Standing up as she spoke, Adina began to undo the buttons holding her dress in place. 'I'll be the first to admit that my initial attraction to you was maybe a little money-heavy, but that's changed, Lewin. The more we're together the more I realise just how harmonious we are. You excite me – the money, the power, the sex.' At the mention of the last word, Adina let the dress fall to the floor. She was naked apart from the cage Louboutins she wore on her feet. The overall effect was one of statuesque dominatrix. It was obviously a look that, despite his general vexation of womankind, worked for Lewin. He could feel his cock twitch to attention.

Stepping out from the dress, Adina placed herself in front of a seated Lewin and dropped to her knees. She could detect his arousal as it tented his trousers. She was pleased to be having her desired effect. She spoke as she unzipped his flies. 'You are all the man I need, Lewin. I know I could have anybody, but it's you I want. You I've fallen for. Only you can give me what I want.'

Adina wrapped her lips around his member, took him deep within her mouth and worked her way up and down Lewin's shaft. He let out a satisfactory sigh of exultation at the pleasing warmth of her mouth. 'You do that better than any woman I've ever known, I'll give you that, you dirty bitch.'

Ignoring the smell of stale sweat on his cock as she expertly worked her way along its length, Adina grabbed it with one of her hands and removed it from her mouth. She smiled lasciviously as she stared up at Lewin. Rising to her feet again, she straddled him and lowered herself onto him. Using the strength of her thighs to lift herself up and down his rod, she used her hands to unbutton his shirt. Lewin groaned with pleasure and watched as Adina's full breasts bounced up and down in front of his eyes.

'This is all for you, Lewin. You could have this for a lifetime, you know,' she panted, placing her hands either side of his face, pulling it towards her breasts, encouraging him to take her nipples in his mouth. 'I want to be with you, Lewin, I want us to commit.' She could feel herself nearing orgasm, her clitoris tingling as a teaser of things to follow. Lewin's body juddered with her, his head, silent and buried within her breasts. 'Marry me, Lewin, let's be together. I need to be with you, just you, no one else. Marry me!' Adina quivered to a rapturous orgasm, and waited for Lewin's response and the feeling of his liquid explosion inside her. Neither came. *Shit, I've pushed it too far.* Her mind flashed with the thought.

Pushing his head away from her breasts, Adina suddenly realised why Lewin had been silent. His face was contorted into a collage of pain, his eyes wide and all colour drained from his features. His mouth hung open, tiny weak pants of air coming from within.

Pulling herself off him, Adina started to panic and lightly slapped Lewin's cheeks. Any force behind her slaps was a mix of half alarm, half fury – anger that she'd gone to all the effort of the seduction for nothing.

'Lewin, speak to me. What is it? Tell me what's wrong.' With that, Lewin's head flopped to one side, his mouth still open. The fragile breaths seemed to have stopped, replaced by a fatalistic silence. Grabbing her dress, Adina ran naked into the house looking for help. Her mind ran riot with a firework explosion of thoughts, none of them pleasant, not all of them caring. *Jesus Christ, I've fucked him to death. The stupid bugger has gone and died on me. He can't be dead … he can't. I need to get his money first. I have to marry him before I bury him …*

CHAPTER 23

Lauren was ranting at the wolf-like facial features of her Siberian husky, Barney. 'How am I supposed to even talk to your father if he doesn't bother coming home? You'll be forgetting what walkies with him looks like at this rate. How can I tell him about what I'd like to be going on in my life, how I'd like to stand on my own two feet, how I'm bored out of my sodding skull, if all I get from him are snatched conversations saying that he's fucking busy planning political world domination with that prick Nathan?' Lauren pulled at her mass of blond hair in frustration and let out a shrill scream. A scream of frustration, confusion and coke-induced paranoia.

Dipping into her latest bag of gutter glitter had been the first thing she'd done after coming off the phone from Saul. She had desperately needed to speak to him. She wanted to tell him about the recording contract with Dale, she wanted to tell him that she was fed up living in his shadow and that she wanted to try and do something for herself. But she needed to do that face to face. What she certainly couldn't tell him was about the kiss she'd shared with Dale or indeed about her newfound love of grade A cocaine. That would hopefully stay a secret for ever.

But her latest phone call with Saul had been a snatched one-way conversation that had amounted to little more than her politician husband saying he was likely to be away for the next few days on business and that she wasn't to worry. 'Nathan says the prime minister has been talking about me again, Lauren, so we're making sure I'm getting seen at the right places. I'll make it up to you when I get back home.'

Lauren was about to ask whether that meant manacling her to the bed and beating her buttocks as red as Satan again. She was beginning to tire of his hands-on ways in the bedroom. But, as normal, just as she was about to let rip, she could hear the odious Nathan squawking in the background. He reminded her of the Penguin from *Batman*. His droning was incessant and rambling. He obviously thought Lauren couldn't hear what he was saying but she could, and she was pig sick of him. 'C'mon, man, tell that tacky footballers' wife of yours that politics is no ruddy place for her. Saul, I'll take you so high up the political ladder it'll induce a fucking nosebleed but you need to stop that airhead limpet of yours dressing like a bloody slut. Tits spilling out and showing too much leg – there's a time and a place for that and it's not in public when the PM's around. You need to nip it in the bud. Now come on, man, we need to leave here quicker than a shit vacating my arsehole after a night on the curry…' Saul signed off with an abrupt yet agitated, 'Got to go, darling, Nathan's got a car waiting for me.' With that, he was gone, leaving her more frustrated than ever, hence the scream. Why didn't Saul ever defend her? Why was that ogre of a man allowed to be so horrid about her?

The cauldron of rage inside her boiling over, Lauren picked up a large bubble vase from the table in front of her and threw it violently against the wall. She and Saul had bought it together on a romantic weekend to Florence for their first wedding anniversary. As she watched the vase shatter into dozens of pieces and fall to the floor, she couldn't help feeling how it was symbolic of her marriage. Something so deluxe and delightful, her once joyous union with Saul now seemed ready to break down into a myriad of sharp, pain-inducing shards. Was she ready to be the one to throw everything she had with him against the wall and ruin it? Lauren wasn't sure she was. But why should she give up on her dreams?

Barney ran from the room, scared of the loud explosion the vase had made as it shattered. Lauren sank to the floor and began to sob. Why did she feel so wretched? She had a gorgeous husband who was successful in his own field, the potential chance of a great singing career ahead of her if Dale was to be believed, and an opulent home that she would never have dreamt of achieving back in the days when she was kicking up her heels on the dance floor at Mayhem. And, of course, there were the kisses she'd shared with Dale. But why did the mix feel so awkward?

In the words of one of her favourite songs, she knew that there was little chance that she could 'get the balance right'. She'd discovered the Depeche Mode classic on one of her father's old twelve-inch singles and loved the genuine eighties electro-feel of it. Even though it had first hit the charts when Lauren was little more than a twinkle in her father's eye, the tune had become an instant winner with her. She'd rushed out to buy the band's Greatest Hits CD and savoured nearly every track. It had been one of the pre-club tracks she'd adored playing at home when she was getting ready for her girls' nights out.

As Lauren sobbed, mascara running down her face, words from the song ran through her mind. *You think you've got a hold of it all. You haven't got a hold at all. When you reach the top, get ready to drop. Prepare yourself for the fall, you're gonna fall. It's almost predictable.* A flow of tears dripped from her chin onto the floor as Lauren rocked back and forth. There was a predictability about the situation brewing in her mind. A storm was coming and however she attempted to try and achieve some kind of balance, she was certain there was no way she was going to be able to tip it in everyone's favour.

Her thoughts were interrupted by the sound of the doorbell ringing. At first she decided she'd leave it, but thinking it might be more coke from Dale she headed to the door. Wiping her tears away with her sleeve, she checked her reflection in the mirror hanging by the front door. She looked a state. The mascara had formed smudged stains across her cheeks and her normally sunshine-blond hair was definitely having a dull, cloudy day. Her nose ran from both her misery and her ever-increasing coke habit. She needed to do something. She'd grab the coke and then pour herself a bath. A good long soak and a face mask pampering session would do the trick.

Opening the door, the last person she expected to see was standing there. 'Hi, mind if I come in? I'd like to talk. I think we've got a few things to discuss, don't you? And I didn't bring my swimming costume this time.' The overly sneery voice of a grinning Nancy grated against Lauren's brain, but she knew she had no choice. Opening the door, she ushered Nancy in.

——

Lauren had left Nancy in her living room, fussing over Barney, while she made her excuses to head upstairs and make herself look presentable. An inquisitive Nancy couldn't help but snoop around a little. There were photos of Lauren and Saul together everywhere. On their wedding day, Lauren resplendent in a fig-ure-flattering gown. Nancy spotted it as being from one of her favourite designers, Ana Cristache. On the mantelpiece stood photos of a suave-looking Saul shaking hands with various po-litical figures that even Nancy, who would normally be hard-pushed to know a Tory from a loony lefty, recognised. Well, one was the man running the country after all. In nearly all of them Lauren stood, sentinel-like, alongside him, the smiling innocu-ous wife. Others showed them at various vacation destinations around the world. In front of the Taj Mahal, with Hawaiian leis around their neck on some paradise beach and reclining on the deck of what looked like a private yacht. Their faces were seemingly a vision of joy and happiness. 'Looks like someone has a pretty cushty life. I think it's time to rock a boat of our own,' Nancy muttered to herself, before returning to fuss Barney once more. As she did so she eyed the broken vase on the floor. Patting Barney's head, she pulled him close to her. 'You stick with me, boy, you don't want to be walking anywhere near that mess.'

A fresh layer of make-up applied, a much more presentable Lauren walked back into the living room. 'Sorry about that. It's been quite a day.'

'I can see that,' sneered Nancy drily. 'Have you had a bit of an accident?' She motioned towards the broken vase.

'Yes ... er, yes ... it fell off the shelf,' lied Lauren, fully aware that there wasn't actually a shelf in the room for it to have fallen from.

'I would imagine it was quite pricy. Still, you and Saul are obviously not short of a pound or two, are you? This place is rammed with designer items.' Lauren could tell where Nancy's conversation was going. She could feel her heart starting to beat faster.

'Can I fetch you a tea, Nancy, or something stronger? A cocktail like the other day?' Lauren's lip wobbled nervously as she spoke and she sniffed loudly.

Nancy narrowed her eyes as she stared directly at Lauren. She could sense that Lauren appeared to be marginally out of control again; her eyes flickered nervously as she spoke and she wrung her hands together constantly. Nancy was obviously spooking her more than she'd planned. The thought pleased her. 'No, I'm not staying long. I've just come to find out why you were kissing Dale. I thought we were mates, Lauren. You're married and you know I still like Dale. And don't try to tell me that it was just a gentle peck because it wasn't. He had his hand wrapped around your boob and he was obviously up for a lot more. Sorry I was Ms Coitus Interruptus. Still, your loss, my gain.'

Lauren could feel a wealth of colour overheating her cheeks as she listened to Nancy. She could have guessed it was coming, but hadn't Dale promised that he'd deal with Nancy? Why did she have to find herself in the firing line? Taking a deep breath, she attempted to answer. 'It wasn't what you think.' She could hear how limp her excuse sounded. 'It was a one-off, we were just caught up in the moment ... it won't happen again.' She paused, a wave of irascibility running through her. 'But what the hell has it got to do with you, anyway?'

'Does your husband know? I would have thought a seedy affair behind his political back would be a great way to fill some column inches and bring his glittering career tumbling down. I wonder what the prime minister would say?' mocked Nancy, indicating the photo on the mantelpiece. 'Dear Ten Downing Street, guess what Saul Everett's wife has been up to ... signing a contract to try and sing and getting her end away at the same time.'

'No one would believe you. It would just be your word against mine. And anyway, you wouldn't do that to Dale. He's still your manager, even if he does now represent me as well. That's what this is all about, isn't it? You're washed up, Dale's told me, and you're worried that he's going to lose interest in you now he has classier fish to fry. You're a good actress, Nancy. You know I'm a fan, or at least I was, but anyone can see that your career has not exactly been at its peak recently. You're jealous, aren't you?' Despite her defiance, Lauren's bottom lip still trembled as she spoke and she sniffed throughout.

'Why would I be jealous of a dirty piece of work like you? I'm not the one doing the dirty on my husband, I'm not the one thinking Dale's going to get me a singing career. I've been there, done that, got the T-shirt. Dale and me have a lot of history, lady, and I know darned well that he's only good for one thing right now, and it's not turning you into the next wannabe Minogue.' Nancy continued to smooth the fur on Barney's face as she spoke, an eerie calm oozing from her. She was enjoying herself.

'What do you mean, he's only good for one thing? Dale's an expert, one of the best in the business.'

'Maybe back in the day, but look at the facts: besides a few tribute acts and me, who as you so bluntly put it is "washed up" in your eyes, Dale's not exactly surrounded by major talent, is he? So, unless you want me to go running to your husband to tell him what you've been getting up to with a second-rate Simon Cowell then I suggest you pay for my silence.'

Lauren knew that it wouldn't be long before the ugly mention of money raised its head. Her head told her to pick Nancy up off the sofa and throw her out in the street on her sorry, money-grabbing ass, but something else told her that maybe a quick financial fix was the way to stop the problem from snowballing. She made her mind up.

'How much? A one-off payment and that's it. Nothing happened with Dale and me, and nothing will. But you wouldn't understand that. Money talks with you and that's that.'

'A hundred grand – it buys my silence and keeps you and your husband together. And the transaction is just between you and me. You don't mention this to Dale. If he gets wind of it, then I might just forget what I'm supposed to be staying silent about. Deal?'

Lauren could see no way out other than to accept Nancy's terms. 'Fine, I'll get the money. I can have it by tomorrow. Where will you be?'

'I'll write down the address for you. Have you got a pen and paper?' Nancy couldn't help but smile as she spoke, unable to hide her happiness. Lauren had been putty in her blackmailing hands.

'I'll get one from the kitchen.' Lauren walked out of the room, Barney following behind her, leaving Nancy alone. She returned with a pad and pen a couple of minutes later.

Nancy wrote down the address of a bar near her Bayswater flat. 'Be there, with the money, at twelve noon.' She rose to her feet, handed the pad to Lauren and headed towards the door. 'Right, I'll be off. Nice doing business with you. Do give my regards to Saul. It would be such a pity for him to get involved in all this. And obviously, if you do ever have that pool party we talked about, you can strike me off the invitation list from now on.'

Lauren snapped again. 'Just fuck off and leave us alone. I'll be there tomorrow with your money.' She held open the door and allowed Nancy to pass through before slamming the door behind her and punching her fist against the wall as she did so.

Standing outside, Nancy breathed in the summer air and reached down into her bag to pull out her car keys. But before climbing in, she wanted to check something. She was sure she'd spotted something in the kitchen as she'd been leaving the house. She'd just had a quick glimpse as she'd walked past the door, but something had aroused her suspicion. Moving her way deftly to the kitchen window she gingerly peered inside to try and confirm what she'd seen. She was right, there on the table lay a bag of cocaine. Racked out alongside it was a line, currently being snorted through a bank note by Lauren. Moving away from the window and dashing back to her car, Nancy climbed back inside and drove down the long driveway, away from Lauren and Saul's house.

'Well, who'd have thought?' cooed Nancy. 'Lauren Everett is obviously a lot more fucked up than even I realised. At least that explains the sniffing.'

Flicking on her car stereo, the voice of the DJ burst forth. 'Let's head back to the eighties now with one of the classics from Depeche Mode. This is "Get the Balance Right".' Nancy pressed another button and the radio switched over to her own CD. The soulful sounds of Kelly Rowland's voice filled the car.

'That's better,' said Nancy. 'Nobody in their right mind likes that old shit any more.'

CHAPTER 24

'This is a hedonist's delight! I don't know how much this is costing you, Martha, but it's worth every bubbly, rejuvenating penny. I swear I could stay here all day.'

'My pleasure,' said Martha who, just like Kelly, was enjoying the ticklish sensation of the hot tub bubbles bursting against her skin as the two women lounged in the frothing waters. 'If there's one thing that is sure to raise my spirits to the heavens then it's a day of pampering.'

The flatmates had been enjoying the delights of one of London's premier women-only spas all day. After her daredevil night out with Tom, Martha had been keen to spend the next day doing nothing more strenuous than wrapping a fluffy white towel around her and lying back in complete luxury. When a bleary-eyed Kelly had raised herself from her bed after yet another energetic night of pole dancing, Martha had decided to treat her new friend to a day out as well. So far, their day had consisted of a facial, an all-over deep-tissue massage and a skin-softening body booster. After a soak in the hot tub they were both lined up for manicures, pedicures and a bikini wax.

'It sounds like you needed it after last night, as well,' winked Kelly, playfully flicking some of the hot tub water at Martha. 'Sounds like you were on fire. I can't believe you went dogging. I thought I was liberal, but blimey, girl, you must have loins that burn stronger than Vesuvius. I've never met a girl who's so highly sexed.'

Martha's cheeks flushed with colour, not sure what to say. 'Not that I can blame you,' continued Kelly. 'That guy you were with was major cute – if his twin is just as hot then they're the sexiest twins I've seen since Kyle and Lane Carlson. And you've managed to try them both out. Talk about brotherly love.'

'Who? Are they famous?' quizzed Martha. 'I'm not exactly up to scratch on my celebs.'

'Jesus, girl,' frowned Kelly with a smile. 'The Carlson twins? Armani, Abercrombie & Fitch, Calvin Klein … They've done them all. Do you never read the gossip mags? You're wasted in here. I've spotted at least half a dozen big names in here today while we've been treating our pores.'

'I'll search for them on the net when we get back to the apartment,' promised Martha. 'No, last night was a real eye-opener, and I can't wait to do it again. You should come.'

'I think I'll stick to swivelling around my pole or hanging out in the fetish clubs for now, thank you. Talking of which, I have my first night off in ages tonight and there's a sexy little club not too far from home having a rather tantalising Privates on Parade theme evening. We should go.'

'Privates on Parade? Does that mean we have to walk around with our bits hanging out?' Martha seemed genuinely shocked.

Kelly rolled her eyes in dismay and lifted herself from the hot tub, wrapping a towel around her naked flesh as she did so. 'Coming from a girl who literally had it all on show in a lay-by last night, how you can even feign mock-horror is beyond me. But it's a uniform theme as it happens – the chauffeur and the groom, general and the maid, the nurse and the soldier, that kind of thing. Think kink. I'm sure we can find something appropriate.' She held up Martha's towel, spreading it wide. 'Come on, let's get that bikini wax. It may come in handy later.'

'You're on. It sounds divine.' Martha let Kelly wrap the towel around her, dabbing gently at her wet skin as she did so. 'My mother would be so proud.' A wide smile flashed across her face, 'She always wanted me to be a nurse.'

———

Martha's mum, Mariella, had been reclining up to her neck in bubbles as well when her phone had rung. Annoyed to be interrupted during her daily lengthy soak in the round-top bath that stood pride-of-place in the middle of the Bradford estate bathroom, she cursed herself for bringing her mobile into the room with her. Relaxed by the scent of intoxicating ginger lily that filled the air, Mariella picked up the phone from the edge of the bath and looked at the display. It was the Lewin Éclair estate number, one which for years had been her own.

'What the hell does he want now?' she cursed, annoyed that her ex was still able to instil an air of incensed nausea into her. All feelings of relaxation left her body. She contemplated not answering, but thought that maybe it might be news of Martha. Vexed, she pressed the button to answer. 'This had better be good, Lewin, my bath time is sacrosanct, as you should well know.'

She was startled to hear a female voice at the other end of the line. Especially when she recognised it as Adina, who was not exactly her first choice for a girly chinwag. In fact, she would go as far as to say she loathed the woman.

Adina's voice was hassled. 'I'm afraid I've got bad news – it's about Lewin. He's had a heart attack and been rushed to hospital.'

Mariella leapt from the bath as soon as she had hung up and ran into the study where Peter was sitting at his desk and staring at his laptop. A look of fright spread across his face as Mariella entered.

'What the hell is it, my love? You look like you've seen a ghost.' He was out of his chair and rushed over to her, holding her naked frame, covered with soapsuds, in a split second. 'What's the matter?'

'I need to get to the hospital now. Lewin's had a coronary. It's not looking good. I need to be there. I must get hold of Martha too. She'll need to know.' Mariella stood wide-eyed as she spoke. Her voice was robotic, spitting out her thoughts as they entered her head.

'Of course.' Peter's rugged arms felt comforting around her. 'Go and get dressed. I'll try and phone Martha.'

As soon as Mariella had left the room, Peter walked back over to his desk. He picked up the phone, ready to dial Martha's mobile. Before he did he shut down the windows on the desktop of his computer and logged off. He wanted to make sure that no one saw what he was looking at. It had shocked even him. Three photos of Martha being sexually pleasured on the bonnet of a car. In each one a group of people were gathered around her watching. He'd have to deal with that later.

He dialled Martha's number and waited …

———

Enveloped in their towels, Martha and Kelly walked away from the hot tub and made their way towards the room where they were to have their bikini waxes. They were about halfway there when a voice boomed from behind Martha.

'Darling girl. What a small world. But then I might have guessed that a girl of your good taste would be pampering herself at London's finest spa.'

Spinning around, it was Kelly who spoke first, her mouth falling open in surprise. 'Oh ... my ... God!' She left it open, as if catching flies at the sight of the woman standing before them.

'Portia, how wonderful!' gushed Martha. 'Portia, this is my flatmate, Kelly. She's a fan of yours, but not a deranged one like the man at the airport. Kelly, this is Portia.'

Kelly held out her hand. 'Pleased to meet you ... ma'am.' She curtsied a little, unsure how to react, before nudging Martha in the ribs. 'You never told me you knew Portia Safari.'

Facing Kelly, Martha giggled at her friend's awkwardness. 'Up until a few days ago, I didn't. We met on the journey over here.' Turning her attention back to the diva, Martha moved forward to hug her. She too was wrapped in one of the spa towels. 'How are you?' Are you in London for a while?'

'I'm performing in a concert at the weekend at the Royal Albert Hall, and I insist that you come along too. I was going to telephone you about it actually. There will be loads of fabulous people there, but all industry, darling, and I could do with a friendly face in the ranks. And you must come visit me at Mara too. You both must.'

'We'd love to – to both invites,' fired Kelly, still unable to comprehend just who was in front of her.

'Yes, we would. That would be great,' thanked Martha. A flash of worry suddenly spread across her face. 'Oh my God, my phone! I've left it by the side of the hot tub. I'll just run and fetch it before somebody swipes it. Will you two be all right chatting for a minute?'

Leaving Portia to one of her favourite subjects, namely finding out why somebody adored her so much, Martha ran back to the hot tub. Luckily her phone was still perched on the side. She bent to pick it up, but as she did so, the oily nature of whatever potions had been placed into the tub had made her hands slippery. As she went to grab it, it fell from her hand and slid, as if in slow motion, into the bubbling waters. She watched it sink to the bottom.

'Damn it!' Sitting on the edge of the hot tub she reached down to the bottom and attempted to grab the phone. After several attempts and countless lost minutes, she succeeded. It was too late for the phone though. When she pulled it back out of the water, it was no longer working.

CHAPTER 25

The exchange between Lauren and Nancy had been quick and to the point. 'You've got the money?' 'Yes.' 'Hand it over, I trust it's all there.' 'Yes.' 'Nice doing business with you.'

Lauren's meeting with Nancy to hand over the £100,000 had brought her to one of the lowest points of her life. The Bayswater bar had been mercifully empty when she had wandered in, the weight of the cash housed within her handbag pulling at her shoulder. She'd spotted Nancy in the corner straight away, sipping on a glass of wine, her head smugly leant back against an etched glass partition awaiting her arrival.

Lauren had left her house early in the morning. She had a meeting at the bank to arrange withdrawing the money from her own account. If she'd taken it from her joint account with Saul then the evidence would have been there in black and white next time he cared to look at one of their bank statements. At least if she took it from her own savings, not that there was hardly anything left after the six-figure withdrawal and her recent habit of siphoning off cash for her own growing narcotic habit, Saul was less likely to find out.

It was only as Lauren turned to leave the bar that she knew that she'd have to confront Nancy one last time. Returning to the table where Nancy was finishing off the glass of wine, Lauren spoke, her voice as clear as her nerves allowed. 'So, we're settled, aren't we? You have what you want and neither Saul nor Dale will ever know. I get to work with Dale and you can carry on doing whatever it is you do these days. I never want to see or hear from you again.'

'It's fine with me, love. I'm the one with a cool hundred grand at my disposal now. You shouldn't worry about anything. God, anyone would think you're getting a touch *paranoid* about something. Paranoia is such a *bad* thing. Not to be *sniffed* at.'

Lauren froze at Nancy's choice of words. Did she know more than she'd already chosen to mention? Lauren couldn't let her get the better of her again.

Choosing to ignore any implication, Lauren carried on. Something had been playing on her mind all night and she knew that now would be her only opportunity to assuage any further worries she had. 'There's just one more thing before I go. You said yesterday that Dale is only good for one thing. What did you mean by that? You obviously don't rate him highly as a manager, so what is he good at?'

Nancy stood up from the table and leant over to Lauren's ear. She whispered what she had to say. 'Sex, darling, sex. The one thing that man can manage to do is bring me to orgasm every time. It was the first thing he did once you'd run your raggedy little ass out of his office.'

Watching as Nancy left the bar, Lauren blinked back her tears. No matter how much she tried, she couldn't wash the filthy image of Dale and Nancy having sex from her mind. And she couldn't help wishing it was her.

CHAPTER 26

With Saul away on business and nothing arranged with Dale until the charity event at the weekend, a despondent Lauren found herself at the loosest of loose ends. It was an empty feeling that ran through her body like a virus.

After her rendezvous with Nancy, Lauren had walked the streets of west London trying to make sense of what Nancy had told her. It shouldn't have mattered to her, it shouldn't have engraved itself wound-like into her thoughts, but it had. Lauren had to admit that her feelings for Dale were becoming more than just professional and the realisation just added another layer of confusion and suffering to her already stratified life. She felt pained and needed something to take away the sadness.

Wandering into a bistro, she found herself a small corner table at the back. Having ordered a large glass of white wine, she took a healthy swig and placed her bag on the table. Unclasping it, she looked inside to seek what she wanted. Nestling there was the bag of cocaine. Checking round to see that no one was looking in her direction, she licked her finger, dipped it swiftly in the bag and then placed her powder-coated finger in her mouth. She rubbed the drug over her gums, enjoying the faint scratchy sensation as she did so. It was only a few moments before her mouth started to become numb and the normally stress-lightening ways of the coke began to cascade into her emotions. But this time, the coke didn't give her the instant gratification she'd joyfully experienced in the past. The morning's actions and the niggling imagery of Dale and Nancy in her head still left her crestfallen and wretched.

Reaching down into her bag again she contemplated a second dose. But something stopped her. Resting in one of the many inner folds of her bag was her address book, the one link to her former life that she could still lay her hands on. The one avenue back to her modelling days, back to the days when her most important quandary for the day ahead would be the decision about which hot pants to wear for a euphoric night out. Just the mere thought of those halcyon days lifted her spirits. Grabbing the book, she flicked through the pages, perfectly aware of the number she was looking for. Without hesitating, she found the number and punched it into her mobile, praying that it still belonged to the same person. After a few rings, the chirpy voice at the other end of the phone proved that it was.

'Hi, Kelly, I know it's been forever and a day, but I could really do with meeting up – it's Lauren Wilde ... er, Everett these days, of course. '

After a somewhat stupefied silence at the other end of the phone for what seemed like the longest time to Lauren, Kelly's voice replied. 'Well, bugger me, talk about a blast from the past. My old dancing partner. I thought I'd lost you to the stuffy ways of Westminster. I'd love to meet up. When?'

'Are you still in London?' enquired Lauren, buoyed by her old friend's cheeriness.

'Sure am. I'm just getting changed as I've been pampering myself at a spa not far from home, but I live in Soho and still earn my living in the big smoke. Nothing can drag me away from the pollution,' she laughed. 'So, when do you want to meet?'

'How about now?' Lauren was aware that her voice sounded almost pleading, but she didn't care. She needed to take her mind off everything and the sooner the better. 'It would be great to see you.'

Intrigued by Lauren's eagerness but genuinely pleased by her reappearance in her life, Kelly gave Lauren her home address. 'Give me an hour to get there at least but I'm sure there's something chilled and bubbly in the fridge. We'll make an evening of it if you fancy?'

'Wonderful. I'll see you there,' said Lauren, before hanging up.

As Kelly slipped back into her clothes at the spa changing room, she let out a smile at the thought of seeing Lauren again. It was proving to be quite a day – the pampering, meeting Portia and now Lauren's phone call. She told Martha about the conversation as they walked from the spa. Something in her mind niggled Kelly though. She knew Lauren of old, and there was something about her phone call that wasn't right. Lauren had always been one of the most effervescent people she'd known and there was an air about her voice that had seemed flat and a little unanimated. Why choose now to ring after years apart? Kelly guessed that they'd need the chilled bubbly to get to the bottom of things.

——

Martha had recognised Lauren the moment she'd spotted her skulking outside the apartment. She looked older than she'd remembered her and her dress sense wasn't anywhere near as wild as it had been when she'd last seen her propping up a nightclub bar, but there was no mistaking her deep blond locks and model-esque features. She was the same girl that had shared many neon-lit dance floors with Martha when she had first come to London.

'What a small world. I can't believe you two know each other as well,' enthused Kelly, popping the cork from a bottle of champagne inside the apartment. 'Who'd have thought? So how come I never ran into you back in the day, Martha? Lauren and I went everywhere together.' Kelly handed the two women their drinks and sat herself down on the sofa. She placed a comforting hand on Lauren's bare knee as she did so. It was good to see Lauren again, but there was definitely a sorrow in her eyes that needed investigating. But that would come as the evening progressed.

It was Lauren who spoke. 'It's not that we really knew each other to talk to. We just used to hang out in the same clubs. We chatted a few times in the toilets. You must have been working on a modelling job or something, Kelly. Or spinning yourself corkscrew-like into the dance floor. I could dance all night, but you always managed to have that little extra something to keep going with some seductive moves.' Lauren laughed. It felt like the first time she'd been able to laugh freely in days, all thoughts of Dale, Nancy and Saul momentarily draining from her mind. She was enjoying catching up with her old friend, and seeing Martha too was an added bonus. 'Then you disappeared. I never really thought about it. We were club-mates who passed like trendy young ships in the night.'

'I went back to South Africa. So, that's us explained but how come you two lost touch with each other?' enquired Martha. 'It sounds like you were a force to be reckoned with back in your dancing days.'

'I fell in love,' responded Lauren. 'Hook, line and sinker for the most amazing guy, but let's just say that my married life and my life with Kelly didn't mix.' Lauren explained about her marriage to Saul and his political work.

'She became the good little wife,' mocked Kelly. 'I don't blame you though. Saul was a great catch and a real dish to boot. I watch with avid interest whenever he comes on the news.

You've bagged yourself a good one there, Lauren, so make sure you hang onto him. Despite his dislike of me.'

'Don't take it personally, Kelly. Saul tends to not really like anything associated with *life PS* – Pre Saul! You're the first person I've been in touch with from those days for years. And I mean … years!' Lauren's voice was coloured with a stain of deep unhappiness. It was something that both Kelly and Martha noticed.

'Well, let's just say that you're the one with the great big house and a swimming pool and I'm the one playing Twinkle Stimulation round a dance pole.' Kelly winked at Lauren as she spoke.

Upon hearing the name, Lauren sprayed her mouthful of champagne everywhere. Wiping her lips with the back of her hand, she placed her glass on the table. 'Who the hell is Twinkle Stimulation?'

'It's my stage name. I work in a pole-dancing joint round the corner. Twinkle pays the bills, honey, and will continue to do so until my mega-rich knight in shining armour comes galloping into the bar and slips a fifty pound note down my G-string with his telephone number and the promise of a new life in Acapulco.'

'Life isn't always rosier, believe you me. There are moments when I'd love to stand on stage, twirl myself into blissful oblivion and not have to give a thought about what to wear for a meeting with the deeply dull chancellor of the exchequer at some chi-chi restaurant. You know me of old, Kelly – and you, Martha – I'm not exactly the best wife for a politician to have, am I? Not that I see him a lot lately though. He's always away working.'

Martha and Kelly let Lauren carry on talking. As they drained the bottle of champagne, she told them about how bored she had become with her stay-at-home life and how the chance meeting with Nancy and Dale had led to the hopeful possibility of a singing career. Martha listened to her tales, unaware of just who Nancy was and what a successful star she'd been, but Kelly, a sucker for a name-drop, sat open-mouthed as Lauren unravelled her tale.

'You're telling me that Nancy Arlow's manager has signed you up for potential stardom? This is amazing. We need to celebrate – I'll get some more fizz. We want to hear every detail, and then I'm feeling a girly night out might be in order.'

As she watched Kelly heading towards the fridge for another bottle of bubbly, Lauren had to admit that the thought of a night out with her and Martha sounded like just what she needed. As for them hearing every detail, well she'd leave out Nancy's pay-off, Dale's kiss and her own coke habit for now. Talking of which … Lauren grabbed her bag and asked Martha where the bathroom was. 'I just need to powder my nose.'

CHAPTER 27

You only had to take one look at the ashen face of Lewin Éclair as he lay, eyes shut, in his hospital bed to know that he was a very sick man. According to the doctors looking after him he was lucky to be alive. About a third of all heart attacks proved to be fatal and for a man like Lewin, the chances of him surviving one were not good, as the Éclair family doctor at the end of Lewin's bed was currently telling both Mariella and Adina.

'He's extremely fortunate that his heart didn't just give up completely. I've known Lewin for years and his love of wine, cigars and a far from healthy diet have been pointing this way for a long time. Plus he's been very anxious of late. God knows how, but his heart must be as tough as rhino horn because he's survived a good few hours now since the attack itself, but I need to warn you both that there could be complications. There's a strong risk of cardiogenic shock – we could be looking at heart conduction blocks, life-threatening rhythms to his heartbeat and tears and ruptures within the heart. I'd be lying if I didn't tell you to prepare yourself for the worst case scenario. I can say that as a family friend, Mariella. Lewin's age goes against him. He may be tough, but he's not that tough. What exactly was he doing when he suffered the heart attack? Was it you who found him … er, Ms King?'

He checked his notes to make sure he had got Adina's name right. The doctor had spent most of his time with the two women directing his conversation at Mariella. As far as he was concerned, she would always be the only woman in Lewin's life. He'd been their family doctor for decades and he thought highly of both of them. To him, Adina was no more than Lewin's latest squeeze. He found her quite vulgar to look at, if he was honest.

Adina seized the moment, aware that for once since Lewin had been admitted, she herself was the focal point of conversation. 'We were enjoying a romantic interlude out on the veranda. An intimate moment as we did most evenings.' She turned her head between the doctor and a cringing Mariella as she spoke, keen for them both to soak up her information. 'Lewin had been telling me how much he loved me and about our plans together for the future. How he was more in love than he'd ever been,' she lied, keen to make herself top dog. 'We were in the throes of love-making when he suffered the attack. His last words to me were along the lines of how he'd never felt so connected with a person, both spiritually and physically. I believe he was on the edge of asking me something of the utmost importance – making the commitment for us to always be together.' It was clear what Adina was hinting at.

Mariella, totally aghast at Adina's schmaltzy performance, was quick to knock her off her pedestal. 'Are you mad, woman?' There was venom in her voice. 'If you think for one minute that Lewin would consider marrying you, then you're crazier than a springbok caught in a bush fire. He's a top businessman – that will always be his number one priority and there's no way he'd consider marrying a gold-digging slut like you. And if he did, it would only be because you can obviously suck an orange through a straw and drop your knickers quicker than the speed of light. It was probably the thought of spending his life with you that brought on the heart attack in the first place. It's enough to scare the life out of anybody.'

Unsure of what to say and surprised by the ferocity of Mariella's verbal attack, Adina ran from the room. Left alone with the doctor, Mariella could feel herself shaking with rage. The savagery of her feelings against Adina had surprised her too. Struggling to compose herself, she turned to the doctor. 'I'm, er, I'm sorry, doctor. But really, that woman is nothing more than a parasitic whore. Who the hell does she think she's trying to kid with all of that mumbo-jumbo about a spiritual connection? The only connection I'd like to give her is the toe of my Jimmy Choos firmly rooted up her repugnant rear end.'

Leaning forward to hug her, the doctor lowered his voice to speak in her ear. 'I know it's highly unprofessional to say so, Mariella, but I couldn't agree more. Not your class, dear. And I thought your little speech there was marvellous. I just hope Lewin heard it in his sleep.'

As the doctor departed through the ward door, Mariella was left alone with Lewin. She looked at him, bare-chested and his eyes closed, wired up to the machines around his bedside. He'd never looked more vulnerable, more pitiful. Despite all of the bad things that had passed between them, as she looked at his frail figure lying there, she couldn't help but think about all of the good moments they had spent together: cruising down the Nile, holidays on the snow-capped mountains of Kenya or the peaceful splendour of Provence. There had been many souvenirs of a lifetime together to choose from, the most precious of all being their daughter, Martha.

Yes, despite recent times, there was still a dim candle of devotion that burnt within Mariella's heart when she looked at Lewin. She knew that was why she'd been so poisonous with Adina. *What was he thinking of, being with her? It couldn't be anything more than physical, surely, no matter what Adina said.* Walking to his bedside, Mariella held one of Lewin's hands and squeezed it gently. As a tidal wave of sadness splashed through her, she found herself talking out loud to the man recumbent in front of her. 'You stupid old bugger, Lewin. You'd better pull through this. Your last action on earth simply can't be having sex with that dreadful woman. I won't allow it. It's just not right. How on earth would I explain that to Martha?'

CHAPTER 28

Portia was far from happy with the reflection staring back at her from her hotel bathroom mirror. Redmond had told her countless times already that morning how beautiful she was. But that was part of his job, was it not? Piero had certainly thought she was beyond beautiful as he explored her body and made love to her on the private jet coming back from Paris, but still it was not enough to satisfy the most demanding of divas.

'I'm beginning to look like Sharon Osbourne before she discovered the marvels of a Hollywood surgeon. Maybe I should ask her for his number next time I'm in LA,' she muttered to herself, pulling back the skin either side of her chin to try and accentuate what was already a jawline that most women of thirty-six would drown puppies for. She then lifted her eyebrows with the middle finger of each hand. She liked what she saw. 'A soupcon of Botox might make me a little less hatchet face and a touch more Teri Hatcher, I suppose.'

Picking up her bottle of supposed mouthwash Portia unscrewed the cap and took a swig. 'God, I need this today,' she said, and took another gulp. Popping an extra-strong mint into her mouth, she looked at her reflection for the final time, happier at what she saw, and made for the bathroom door. 'Time to face the firing squad,' she murmured.

The firing squad in question was one woman – fashion and beauty journalist Madeline Strong. Having worked for virtually every UK tabloid newspaper in existence, Madeline was the sin-

gularly supreme voice to listen to when it came to the ways of
looking good and feeling great. Never had a woman been more
aptly named. She was more forceful than an FBI investigator
with her questioning and had an industry reputation as a real
ball breaker. Having slept with most of the publishing industry
bigwigs on her meteoric rise to the top, it was rumoured that she
had more secrets about their extra-marital bedroom habits than
other woman in the industry. Due to her constant threats of kiss
'n' tell, she had them all by the balls and could name her price
when it came to securing jobs. She was curt, crisp, abrupt, biting and penetrating with her manner. She made Kelly Cutrone
look like Marcia Brady and was one of the few women on earth
who actually scared Portia.

But Redmond had said that being interviewed by her about
her beauty regime in order to publicise the charity event was
necessary. A double-page spread in Britain's highest circulation tabloid with the UK's most respected fashion and beauty
hack was bound to garner major interest for the forthcoming
weekend. Portia had spent the day at the spa desperately hoping
to give her skin the much needed boost she felt it required. If
she was to face Madeline then it was absolutely imperative that
she looked her best. Especially as she was flying solo. Normally
Redmond would sit in on interviews with Portia just to make
sure that the line of questioning stayed on the straight and narrow, but Madeline was insistent that the early-evening interview
would be strictly a one-on-one. As she'd said to him on her arrival at the hotel, 'I did not get where I am today, Mr Geller, by
bowing down to pesky managers and their interfering ways. The
feature will be up to my normal standard of excellence – that is
all you need to know.'

Redmond had known that he was beaten and that there was
no way he could make the journalist change her mind. Embar-

rassed by her overly tart manner, he had blushed, his face man-
tling a poppy red. As he showed Madeline into Portia's suite, she
had taken his chin in one of her hands and moved his face from
side to side. 'You can leave me now. We'll call when I'm finished,
and remind me to suggest something for those broken veins
and open pores around your nose. A man of your age shouldn't
have so many.' With that Madeline closed the suite door in Redmond's ever-reddening face, leaving him to run off and find the
nearest mirror.

Sweeping into the main area of her suite from her bathroom,
Portia extended both hands out to Madeline who was sitting on
a leather armchair flicking through the thickest fashion magazine Portia had ever seen. Putting it down, Madeline rose to
her feet and extended her hands in reply. The two women air-
kissed, a good three inches remaining between their lips and
any chance of them skimming the other's cheeks. 'You're looking good, darling,' oozed Portia, eyeing Madeline's killer sweater
dress. It clung to the curves of her dainty body with perfection and its brightly coloured dot design seemed to illuminate
both the room and Madeline's expertly decorated face. 'Is that a
must-have designer gown I'm spotting? It's exquisite.'

'It's a Diane von Furstenburg. Divine to wear. I'm interviewing Angelina after you this evening so I thought I'd better pull
out the big guns. What are you in today, darling? What's the dis-
cerning diva wearing in her suite these days?' There was almost
a sneer in Madeline's voice.

'I've had a day at the spa, my sweet, so I like to chill a little
when I come back here. I'm head to toe Gucci – a classic black
cotton shirt and a pair of capri pants.' Why did it sound so
weedy and pathetic in comparison to Madeline? Portia felt like
she'd just admitted to shopping in TK Maxx or Ross Dress For
Less.

Madeline eyed Portia's ensemble from top to bottom, as if critiquing it, ready to give marks out of ten. Portia couldn't help feeling that she wasn't scoring very highly. 'Capri pants don't suit everyone, darling, especially if you're prone to calves like Henry VIII. They're not exactly forgiving.' Portia had no idea whether she was actually aiming the dig at her or at capri pant wearers in general. She chose to remain tight-lipped and attempt a faux smile. 'The black is a good choice though. Contrasts your hair beautifully and it's always wise to pick a colour that will slim you down and elongate the body. Not everyone in the public eye dresses so astutely, I can assure you. I had to interview the so-called fashionistas of US soap *Peregrine Palace* the other day at the Mondrian in LA. Montana Phoenix and her bunch of cronies. Some of them have no idea about fashion. Sleeveless dresses when you have an arm like a ham hock is never a good move, and as for a nasty shoe – one word to say for most of them – trotters! How they expect to squeeze a piggy foot into a kitten heel is beyond me.' Madeline had a trait of singularising everything to give it more emphasis.

Half enjoying Madeline's slating of one of the world's biggest soap operas and its stars and half dreading that she might be next in line for character assassination, Portia took her seat and ran her fingers through her mass of flame-red hair. 'Shall we begin, Madeline?'

'Yes, I do believe we should. I won't want to keep Angelina waiting, will I? Now, Portia, you're loved by the masses but like so many women out there, you're at an age now where maybe things aren't as firm as they once were. Sculptured contours and curvaceous breasts can become saggy old knockers overnight.' Madeline smiled as she spoke, a painted-on professional façade that attempted to disguise the toxic nature of her questioning underneath. 'Do you have to watch what you eat as you get older for fear of piling on the pounds?'

Portia knew that she would have to consider every word of her answer very carefully. Madeline's sickly sweet smile was fooling no one. She was like a swan – graceful and beautiful to look at, a vision of cool, calculated calm. But Portia was under no doubt that she would raise her ravishing wings in attack and bite you into submission without a moment's thought.

Portia sat upright in her chair and sucked her stomach in as she began to answer, conscious that she needed to make sure that she looked good from every conceivable angle.

———

'There is no way I can wear this out in public, girls. What will people think?' Lauren turned herself around a full 360 degrees, determined to see herself at every conceivable angle too in Kelly's bedroom mirror. She liked what she saw – it was just the fact that she'd never seen herself like it before.

She was wearing a skin-tight olive rubber latex dress. It was so tight that Lauren had been forced to remove all of her underwear and talcum powder her body to actually get it on. She loved the feel of it against her flesh. A large aperture at the front forced up her braless breasts, squeezing them together like two perfect flesh-coloured melons, leaving them exposed from just above the nipples. It was zipped all the way from the base of the dress to just under the breasts, allowing Lauren to reveal as much cleavage as she desired. The olive rubber fastened around her neck with two shiny poppers. 'Where the hell did you get this, Kelly? I need to wear it for Saul. He'd love it.' She looked amazing and could tell it wasn't just her own opinion – both Kelly and Martha looked on with admiration.

'I have a few of them that I've collected over the years. They always come in handy on my fetish nights out. You totally rock that outfit. It's the boot-camp look and will be perfect for tonight,' said Kelly. 'And you're not telling me that Saul loves a bit of kink, are you? I always had him down as mister straight-laced.'

Worried that she'd said too much, Lauren was quick to correct herself. 'Oh … only in the bedroom,' she mumbled. 'He has a healthy sexual appetite when he's at home.'

'And are you sure that he's not coming home tonight? You wouldn't want him turning up and then finding out that you're all rubbered-up in a fetish club, would you?' mocked Martha.

The talk of Saul brought Lauren down to earth with a bump. 'No, he's not coming home. I've arranged for Barney to be looked after and I'd love to go out with you girls. But who am I trying to kid? I can't go out like this. I'm a politician's wife – it would ruin everything. You two go out to your Privates On Parade or whatever it's called and I'll go home. We can meet up another time and go for a drink.' She started to unzip the dress, a glaze of sadness spreading across her eyes.

'Just you wait one minute, Lauren Everett.' It was Kelly's voice, vehement and slightly stern. 'The Lauren Wilde I knew of old would be wearing that outfit out the front door in a flash. I do appreciate that maybe hubbie dearest wouldn't be too keen on his wife having a good time though, which is why I think I have the perfect solution. Say hello to the cat mask.' Kelly held up a mask made of black latex. It was large enough to cover the top half of the wearer's face, with oval cut-outs for the eyes. On its peak were two pointed cat's ears. Lauren's eyes lit up as she saw it.

'Let's give it a try, shall we?' proposed Kelly. 'Martha, can you scrape back Lauren's hair and pile it on her head? Then we can get it all under the mask.'

Martha did as she was instructed, grouping Lauren's mass of blond curls together with her fingers. Holding it tight and placing an elastic band around it from Kelly's dressing table, she pooled it fountain-like on the peak of Lauren's head. Kelly stretched the latex mask and slid it down gently over Lauren's hair and onto her face. The result was perfect. Lauren was unrecognisable in her outfit.

'You see,' affirmed Kelly, turning Lauren back towards the mirror. 'You shall go to the ball! Not even your own mother would recognise you now. I believe we've found your absolute disguise. Some sexy red lips and you're good to go. Now all we need to do is find an outfit for Martha and myself.'

Admiring the complete stranger she saw peering back at herself in the mirror, Lauren squealed with delight. It was a sexy delight that tingled every nerve ending. 'You're right, I don't even think Barney would recognise his own mother now, not dressed like this. And he loves chasing cats …'

CHAPTER 29

*'All the women who are independent, throw your hands up at me.
All the honeys who makin' money, throw your hands up at me.
All the mommas who profit dollars, throw your hands up at me.'*
Nancy had been in fine voice all day. But then having £100,000
of delicious cash at your disposal was enough to turn even the
most depressive of people into a warbling songbird. And as she
sashayed around her flat, harmonising to Beyoncé and co she
was looking forward to the night ahead.

Nancy wanted to prove her own independence yet again, and
show Dale just how capable she was of standing on her own
two feet without succumbing to the murky TV depths of eating
witchetty grubs or kangaroo testicles in some far-flung jungle.
She was determined to maximise her potential yet again with
the cash that had fortuitously come her way: the hundred grand
from Lauren, and a little bit extra. In fact, quite a lot extra.

She had spent part of that afternoon at a pawnbroker near
her London apartment. Her objective was to try and earn some
extra cash by selling off two diamond rings. She wanted as much
as possible, but didn't really care if she was short-changed that
much. After all, they weren't her rings. They were Lauren's. Nancy had taken them from a small onyx trinket box positioned
amongst the photos on Lauren's mantelpiece. She'd flipped the
lip open on the box and found the two rings inside when Lauren
had been fetching a pen and paper for her from the kitchen.
Nancy wasn't even sure what had possessed her to steal them and

place them in her bag, but she had done so before giving it a second thought. Lauren deserved it for betraying their friendship. It was a new risky addiction to add to her love of gambling. The two rings had both been antique and thanks to the quality of the yellow gold and the sizable rocks, they both fetched four figure prices. It was that money that Nancy intended to use that very evening as she headed off into the balmy night air. Undeterred by her last experience, Nancy had chosen another high-end casino to wager her luck at and this time she would leave nothing to chance.

—

'We look like a kinky Charlie's Angels,' joked Lauren as she, Martha and Kelly walked down the stairs into the dark and inviting world that was hidden in the east London basement bar. It was true, the three women, who had spent the best part of four hours getting ready back at Kelly and Martha's flat, were already turning heads before they even set a black patent vertigo-inducing heel inside the venue. They may have taken their time, but the end result had been worth every sybaritic minute.

Alongside Lauren's boot-camp dress and cat mask, which she'd teamed with black patent sandals and the deepest blood-red lipstick, Martha was wearing a latex nurse's outfit, complete with face mask and a nurse's cap, also made from rubber, which rested sexily atop her long, poker-straight hair. Around her neck hung a highly polished metal stethoscope. Kelly's outfit of a rubber body wrapped wetsuit-like around a figure made for sin and a pair of extreme platform zip thigh boots completed the uber-sexy trio.

Kelly knew what to expect, having visited the club many times, and nodded welcomes and gave out kisses to a few regulars she'd seen there before. To both Lauren and Martha it was a brand new experience, one which left both of them wide eyed and open mouthed. For Lauren it was a world she'd never dreamt of and one that she wasn't sure as yet she was going to enjoy. The club was packed and wherever she gazed a mass of people in various states of attire looked back at her. As yet she wasn't sure if they were staring at her because they recognised her or just because she looked so stunning. Men of all ages wandered past, wearing everything from full military regalia through to the skimpiest shorts, a rubber waistcoat and a Stetson. Everywhere was a sea of bare chests, peaked caps and coal-black jodhpurs. The women wore some of the most flesh-exposing outfits that Lauren had ever seen, breasts straining within the flimsiest of gauzy fabrics ready to be unleashed if so desired. It took some getting used to, but the smiles on the faces of everyone inside the club proved two things to her: it was both a friendly and a sexually charged atmosphere. She felt herself smile and began to feel enjoyment from underneath her mask.

For Martha, the tantalising thrill of the club had danced across her senses like a cat-o'-nine tails as soon as she'd walked in and seen the people around her. The fusion of the exhibition-ism of the mass of bodies on display coupled with the mystery of hidden identities housed behind rubber masks and mul-ticoloured wigs lit the touchpaper of Martha's deepest desires. Standing between Kelly and Lauren, she felt for their hands and took them in hers. 'Have you ever seen anything so provocative, girls? It's like *Lady Chatterley's Lover* meets Lady Gaga. I am go-ing to absolutely adore every minute of this. Let's explore,' she gasped, the excitement tangible in her voice.

As they moved into the main body of the club, Kelly hitched down the zip of her outfit to expose a juicy portion of cleavage. 'It's packed in here and I suspect it's going to be a hot one, la-dies. Let's get a drink. I think we're all going to need one.'

—

Nancy's night had panned out just as she'd hoped. In fact, better than even she'd desired. With near to five grand's worth of cash inside her bag, Nancy had entered into the casino in the right frame of mind. If she lost, then all she was losing was the money from Lauren's jewellery, but if she won, then it was Lady Luck not just shining down on her but picking her up by the plunging neckline of her Versace and baptising her fully in the font of good fortune.

She'd played the roulette table all evening, her knowledge of where to place her chips no wiser or shrewder than it had ever been, but her lack of any logic or system seeming to hit pay dirt. By the time she decided to call it a night, the cash totalled an impressive £7,500, more or less.

Nancy went to cash in her chips. 'You look happy,' ventured a woman alongside her, also waiting to cash in her winnings. She was easily past retirement age, eloquently dressed and had an air of unbridled glamour about her that reminded Nancy of the cinematic sirens of days gone by – the likes of Rita Hayworth or Greta Garbo. Her hair was immaculately set and she personified the word 'wealth'.

'That's because I am. I figure if I'm leaving with much more than I came with then someone is loving me tonight and that, my friend, is reason to celebrate,' enthused Nancy.

There was something about the exuberance in Nancy's voice that sent a rush of satisfaction through the woman. 'People like you, my dear, are the reason I love coming here and the reason I love gambling. I don't know what I'd do without it. It's the easiest money I've ever made – and the most enjoyable. Not that I ever needed to do it, of course – marrying an oil tycoon sorted my finances out. He had more money than he knew what to do with when he was alive, and now it's mine. It's just the thrill of it all is just so ... so ... *addictive*, I suppose. But it is lovely to see someone walking out of here with such a pretty smile on their face. I've seen both men and women leaving here crying like bawling babies.'

'Lady Luck is my new best friend,' replied Nancy.

Again the old lady's face lit up with glee. 'Oh ... the Lady Luck. Now there was a quaint little hotel if ever there was one. Downtown Vegas. It's gone now, demolished as far as I'm aware. It's all of those grandiose hotels now with chandeliers the size of private islands and nightly shows from two-bit singing stars and circus acts. Mind you, Vegas is still the gambler's dream and some of the newer hotels are out of this world. Have you been?'

It was now time for Nancy's face to light up. Las Vegas. Of course – it would be the perfect place to try and maximise her gambling potential. And it was one of the few places in the world that neither her singing nor her acting had taken her. Now would be the ideal opportunity. She had time on her hands, money to play with and the feeling that nothing could stop her now that she was back on a winning streak. 'No, I've not been, but if you reckon I should then maybe it's about time. Do you have any tips?'

'Let me cash these and then I'll buy you a drink. It'll be a lovely way to end the night. I'll tell you what I know. My name's Betsy Hartley.'

Five minutes later the two women positioned themselves at a table in the casino bar and started talking. They were still there an hour later. Nancy was enjoying Betsy's company and her tales of bygone days spent gambling in Vegas. 'It's an amazing place. Back in the day I had the pleasure of seeing all the greats there – Sinatra, Sammy Davis Jr, Dean Martin ... even Elvis, although he was always a touch too graphic in the hip department for me, my dear.' Nancy found herself enthralled.

Betsy continued to weave her tapestry of words, her upper-class English accent adding an air of noble grandeur to her stories of the place that many dubbed Sin City. 'Back when William was alive – he was my husband – we found ourselves in Las Vegas at least three or four times a year. He used to attend conferences and seminars and I was quite happy to find myself a wall of one-armed bandits, a blackjack table or a roulette wheel to have some fun with. I suppose, looking back, it's where my love of gambling must have begun. If one's going to play the game then one might as well play it in style.' She raised her glass and chinked it against Nancy's.

Style indeed, pondered Nancy, staring at the sizable diamond cross hung around Betsy's neck as the lights of the casino bar danced across its facets. 'Do you still go there?' she enquired.

'Not since William's death, no. Plus these old bones of mine are far too delicate for the hustle and bustle of modern-day Vegas. This casino is the closest I manage these days. I do read up on it though, a sort of hobby by proxy, if you like. I was reading a wonderful article in one of my magazines about the *loose* machines in Vegas – they're the ones which are said to pay out more often than the others. They have a high hit frequency but tend to give you lots of little payouts. But the real money to be won is from those with a high payback percentage and a lower hit frequency. It's fascinating stuff – all of the gambling strategies are quite an art really. Vegas is the only true place to go if you're a real gambler, in my opinion. Even if one of your more influential friends invites you to Monte Carlo for a long weekend on their yacht – it may be closer to home but it doesn't have that spicy edge that Vegas always manages to conjure up.'

Nancy could feel herself becoming wrapped up, cocoon-like, in Betsy's words. She could feel dollar signs of success sinking into the tissue of her brain as she listened. Tonight had been a good night, a financially rewarding night, but if she was to really try for the big bucks and not just content herself with minor wins, then maybe she needed to move further afield. To the glittering heat of the Nevada desert.

'Now, my dear, these old bones of mine have stayed up far too late,' said Betsy rising from the table. 'My driver will be wondering where I am. Can I give you a lift or have you already arranged your transportation?'

'I'm going to stay for another drink,' replied Nancy. Her mind was racing with the thrill of the unknown. 'But it's been lovely speaking to you. I hope I see you again and you can guarantee that I'll be booking a trip to Las Vegas as soon as possible.'

Pulling an address card from her gold sequinned evening bag – Nancy was guessing it was antique from the retro look of it – Betsy handed it to her new friend. 'This is my address and telephone number. If you want to come and read that article or need more hints on what to do in Las Vegas, then give me a ring. It's been a pleasure for me too. I could talk about that splendid city all night. "I like to think of Las Vegas in terms of a well-dressed man in a dinner jacket and a beautifully jewelled and furred female getting out of an expensive car." God bless Howard Hughes ...'

As Betsy walked from the bar, Nancy slipped the card inside her own bag and watched the elderly lady glide out of sight. As she ordered another drink she muttered to herself, 'Howard who?' She'd have to Google him when she got home.

CHAPTER 30

To say that Lauren's eyes had been well and truly opened by the fetish club would be an understatement. In fact, underneath her cat mask she couldn't help but feel that her eyes were as wide as a manga character as she feasted on the sights surrounding her.

Charged by the regular trips she'd been making to the Ladies to snort yet another line of cocaine, Lauren had become separated from the other two women and had ventured blindly into all areas of the club. It was surprisingly cavernous with many dimly lit areas and hidden rooms around every corner. The air was electric with flesh-pricking expectation and the combination of the drug in her system and the erotic enigma of the disguised people around her was proving to be a heady and potent blend.

At the far end of the club, a doorway housing a curtain of vertical strips of rubber came into view. It was an area that Lauren hadn't encountered before and safe in the knowledge that her real identity seemed to be securely clandestine underneath her costume, she pushed back the rubber strips and walked inside. A selection of furniture and equipment filled the room. It was obviously what Kelly had been describing to the women earlier as the dungeon. Lauren could see a huge X-shaped cross positioned in one corner and a spanking bench alongside it. The only reason she knew it to be a spanking bench was because of the bare-buttocked woman leaning over it.

Along from it, Lauren could see a cage, its polished bars catching the small rays of light seeping from the doorway as more people entered the room. Inside the cage a man was hanging by his wrists from the top of the structure. Around the cage various women reached in to touch and grope his body.

Making her way to the end of the room, Lauren found what she could only describe as another play area. Canes, crops, whips, blindfolds and chains hung from the walls. Yet the entire kinky spectacle laid out before her was friendly and uncritical. Welcoming, almost.

A woman stood in the middle of the area, a riding crop flexing between her hands. She was dressed as a nurse. It was only after a few moments that Lauren realised it was Martha. Standing in front of her was a man. He wore tight combat trousers, an open camouflage shirt and a full army mask over his face. His chest was toned and firm – he was masculine and masterful. But it was clear from what was happening that it was Martha who had the upper hand in their play.

Flexing the crop into a semicircle before letting it spring back to attention, Martha brought it down on the man's stomach. The firecracker-quick noise cut through the air. The man tensed his muscles, their definition highlighted even more. He nodded his masked face, showing both his submission and his gratitude. His enjoyment swelled beneath his combats. Lauren spotted Kelly standing there too, smiling as she fondled the jock-strapped groin of the man stood next to her. 'These are two kinky girls,' she smiled, enjoying the bizarreness of the situation.

Having finished with the man, Martha headed for the bar – as she did so she walked straight into Lauren.

'I was wondering where you were,' she teased. 'Did you enjoy the show? I know I did. I was that close to ripping both our clothes off. I'll have to get his number.'

Kelly joined the women. 'I'm glad to see we're all enjoying the dungeon. Nice display, Martha. I'm thinking I might need to put one on of my own. There's a pole over there with my name on it. I have a fan here who needs to worship me a little. He's one of my regulars at the strip joint. Good tipper, but he can get a bit too touchy-feely. At least here he's under my control. I make the rules, don't I, sweetie?' She turned to face the man alongside her.

The man she was talking to was the same one she'd been fondling throughout Martha's performance – despite his advancing years, he wore leather chaps and a jock-strap.

Kelly turned back to the girls, but found only Martha there. Lauren was already pushing her way across the dungeon area and frenziedly running to the front of the club. Despite the heat in the place, she had started to shiver, an icy chill running to her core. It had happened the moment she had laid eyes on the man with Kelly. The man she had come to hate – the pompous Nathan Spilsbury.

———

Martha and Kelly found Lauren hidden in one of the cubicles of the women's toilet. It had taken them the best part of half an hour and a continual banging on every door to locate her. Even when they'd found her it took them both a few minutes of gentle coaxing to get her to open the door and let them in. The look of horror on her face and the double stream of mascara-stained tears down her cheeks told both of them that she was deeply upset.

Locking the door behind them, the three women huddled together as comfortably as the confines of the cubicle would let them. 'What the hell has happened to you? I've never seen a woman run so fast in heels that high,' said Kelly, trying to lighten the atmosphere.

'That ... that man,' stammered Lauren, sniffing as she tried to explain. 'Is he still here? The one you had on a lead. Nathan bloody Spilsbury. He knows me. I was scared he'd recognise me. He's Saul's spin doctor and a nasty piece of work to boot. If he knew I was here he'd skin me alive and tell Saul about it. I shouldn't have come. I just shouldn't ... Why did you make me?' Her voice was pathetic and sobbing.

'That silly tosser knows your husband? I knew he had some kind of political connection, but I know him from the pole dancing. He comes in to the club and leers at me a few times every month. Daft little prick, to be honest,' accounted Kelly. 'I've seen him down here a few times too. He always plays my slave and tries to shock me with subservient dirty talk. I'm sure he didn't recognise you, so I wouldn't worry.'

'And even if he did,' said Martha, 'surely he would be in just as much trouble as well? I thought there was something familiar about him, I must have seen his photo in the press.'

'He's virtually at the end of his career – he could just retire comfortably if he wanted to. A bit of scandal wouldn't do him any harm. But he could screw things up for me. He hates me, thinks I'm not worthy to be married to Saul. Are you sure he never said anything, Kelly?' Lauren's sobs became more urgent.

'He'd have said something to me if he did. He worships me. I think you're being a bit paranoid, don't you?' Kelly reached behind Lauren and picked up the bag of cocaine she'd spied lying on top of the cistern. 'And is it any wonder? Since when have you been into this? You used to scream at me for doing weed.'

Snatching the packet back, Lauren snapped, 'I'm not being paranoid. You don't know him like I do. He's evil ...' She wiped her face with the back of her hand and shoved the cocaine into her bag before adding, 'And what I choose to do is up to me, all right? Can we just leave please?'

Pushing her way between the two women, Lauren unlocked the door and checked her reflection in the toilet mirror. She looked a mess, but at least she was still unrecognisable under the cat mask.

'I'm ready for the off, I've had my fun for the night,' said Martha, somewhat confused by the way the evening was ending.

The three women walked from the club and waited in line for a taxi in silence. Just as they reached the front of the queue, a black car pulled up on the other side of the street. The back seat door facing them opened and Nathan Spilsbury got out. Lauren said nothing and hung her head down, praying that he wouldn't recognise her. She eyed him surreptitiously from under her mask. He walked to the doorway of the club and raised his hand, beckoning someone. The man in the combat mask who had been playing with Martha ran out of the club and over to the car. He dived into the back seat, followed by Nathan. As Nathan entered the car he accidentally pressed one of the buttons on the door. It worked one of the blackened electric windows which started to slide down. 'Fuck and bugger, stupid bastard car!' he shouted. Panicking, he stabbed at the button to reverse the process.

Neither Martha nor Kelly were paying any attention, but for Lauren the action came too late. Unable to stop herself, she continued to gaze into the car where Nathan's fellow passenger had removed his mask and was running his hands through his crop of thick black hair. The face was instantly recognisable as her husband, Saul.

Lauren wanted to run over to the car and ask him what the hell he thought he was doing. Wasn't he supposed to be away on business? She wanted to drag Nathan from the car and confront him about every snide little belittling remark he'd ever made about her. But she knew that she couldn't. She was a mess, her mind was too slow and she knew that she had no more right to be there than he did. Without saying a word to the other women, she climbed into her own cab behind Martha and Kelly and watched as Saul's car drove off in the opposite direction.

CHAPTER 31

According to the charity event brochure that Portia was flicking through backstage as she ran through her vocal warm-ups, over 350 events were held every year within the splendour of London's Royal Albert Hall. And tonight, she and Piero would be the main attraction – the maestro masterpieces at what the press had already billed as *the greatest collection of singing stars ever housed under one roof.* They'd all given up their time and their usual appearance fees to show their support for the evening's event. If you hadn't been asked to appear or your name wasn't on the invitation list then, quite frankly, the shine on your star was evidently somewhat tarnished. And to know that she had been specially requested to top the bill alongside Piero, the man who was now sharing her bed again, thrilled Portia to the very depths of her soul.

Pushing open her dressing room door, Redmond piled into the room. In one hand he carried one of the hugest bouquets of blood-red long-stem roses that Portia had ever seen. In the other he balanced waiter-like a pile of newspapers.

'Jesus wept, I feel like I should be doing silver service trying to balance this lot,' he complained throwing the newspapers down onto the nearest sofa. They fanned out across the fabric. 'It's today's press, sweetie. I thought I'd see what they're saying about tonight's bash. And these' – he indicated the flowers – 'are from Piero to wish you well for tonight. Not that you'll need it, darling, you and he seem to be quite a dynamic duo right now.

He's put a smile on your face, that's for sure. You've been posi-tively pleasant over the past few days. Up until then you could have curdled milk with some of your sour faces.'

It was true. Since they'd flown back from Paris together, Por-tia had seen as much of Piero as possible, and that included let-ting him into her bed. His love-making had been just as memo-rable and orgasmic as she had recollected, and the fact that he seemed ultra-keen to satisfy her desires night after night had her heart singing.

'Let's just say things are going well and I'd like it to stay that way,' cooed Portia, checking her make-up in the mirror before turning to peruse the flowers. 'How lovely. The man is so thoughtful. Now, put these in water, Redmond. We don't want them wilting. Although if they're anything like Piero they'll be standing proud all evening.' She winked playfully at Redmond and continued with her vocal exercises.

Busying himself with the roses, Redmond looked at his own reflection. He was sporting a brand new jet black Hugo Boss suit. Its narrow fit gave him an eye-pleasing sleek silhouette. 'I am so glad I dressed up. Have you seen it out there? More stars than the blessed Planetarium. I think there's more money in this building tonight than there is in the Royal Mint. I almost couldn't get to you, darling – not without some agile weaving in and out of the glitterati. Mind you, I'm sure I nearly stuck these flowers up Catherine Zeta Jones's nose as I tried to get through. I heard some choice swearing and the accent was defi-nitely Welsh, but I didn't stay around to find out.'

'Is she looking good?' enquired Portia, breaking off from her exercises.

'She looked better than you sound, Portia. Touch raspy, aren't we? You're sounding like Marlene Dietrich,' Redmond noted. The expression on his face was one of genuine concern.

He was right, Portia's vocal gymnastics did not seem to be as multifaceted as normal.

'Oh, don't worry about me, Redmond. I do have a little tickle but it'll pass. It's probably one of Piero's hairs caught in my throat. He may shave his chest hair but those short and curlies down below just seem to get everywhere!' She rubbed her fingers up and down her throat and coughed comically.

Redmond's expression changed from concern to one of mock horror. 'Too much information, thank you very much. But seriously, you watch your vocals. Just because you're suddenly having a sex life worthy of Linda Lovelace doesn't mean you should not look after your chords. If I'm to carry on making money from you then I need your voice to be as sharp as your tongue.'

'Oh Redmond, I'm happy for once, and not even you and your whinge-bag ways are not going to bring me down.' Portia moved directly in front of Redmond and placed her hands on his cheeks, before pinching each one buoyantly. 'My voice will be fine. Have you ever known me to be anything other than total perfection?' He had to admit he hadn't and that he couldn't remember the last time he'd seen her in such a good and carefree mood. Horizontal dancing with Piero was certainly softening her personality.

Redmond moved to the sofa, seated himself and started flicking through the newspapers. Nearly all of them featured articles about the evening's events. Portia's flawless face stared out from every one. Leafing through the final newspaper, he came to the double-page spread written by Madeline Strong. A look of panic gripped him and he took a sharp intake of breath as he scanned across the feature. Without saying a word, he shut the newspaper as quickly as possible. It was too late – Portia had already been alerted by his sharp inhalation and was standing over him. Her voice was no longer a happy one. 'Open it back up, Redmond. I assume you were looking at that dreadful woman's interview with me. What's she got to say for herself? I thought the interview went quite well considering she's more acidic than a bathful of vinegar.'

Knowing that there was no way he could refuse, Redmond reluctantly turned back to the article. 'She's a silly bitch, Portia. She said I have open pores and I've not had them since puberty. Honestly, she doesn't know what she's talking about.'

Portia wasn't listening though. Her eyes were fixed on the article. A rather unflattering photograph of her arrival at the press launch a few days earlier was the main image. It featured a rear-view of Portia, her head turned to one side, her mouth open as if taken mid conversation. It was a photo that any picture desk across the land would never have chosen to use – unless, of course, it suited the tone of the article. The angle at which it had been taken seemed to accentuate every curve of her body and not in a pleasing way. The leopard-print design of the dress clung to her backside, horizontal creases stretching taut across her buttocks creating the illusion of it being too small for her. A printed arrow ran down from the title at the top of the article, pointing at Portia's backside. It read COSSI FAN BOOTI. Underneath it, the strapline read AS DIVA PORTIA SAFARI ROLLS INTO THE CAPITAL FOR A CHARITY PERFORMANCE, STYLISTS ASK WHETHER SHE'LL BE SINGING THE MARRIAGE OF PIG-ARO!

Feeling her face flush with fury, Portia continued to read, Redmond tutting disgustedly in the background. The first paragraph, underneath a heavily air-brushed photo of Madeline Strong, was brutal.

Meeting Portia Safari as she guzzles sweets in the hidden comfort of her London hotel, one can't help but notice that

maybe the diva is not as careful about how her once mil-
lion-dollar body looks these days. The rolls of fat that I spot-
ted squidging out from underneath her Gucci cotton shirt
and perched on the oh-so-stretched waistband of her capri
pants would have the fashion house choking on a plate of
overly oiled pasta – something that Portia's obviously been
no stranger to lately. It makes me wonder whether these
days she's not so much about Rigoletto but Pig-a-lotto!

The rest of the copy was beyond harsh and equally damning. There was hardly any mention of the actual charity event,
the interview having been turned into one of Madeline's famed
character annihilations. It was Redmond who broke the silence
as they stumbled across the minefield of words. 'We'll sue her,
Portia. They've doctored the photo and I'll demand a retraction.
There's not an ounce of spare skin on you.' He slammed the
newspaper shut, screwed it into a ball and threw it to the floor.
'Gutter press at its worst.'

But Redmond's rant was like white noise to her. She was
aware that he was speaking but unable to take in any of his
words. In her mind, the cutting text in the article had confirmed
what she had been thinking for a while. Her body was not as
good as she herself demanded it to be. She'd stopped being so
strict about her regime lately, unhappy about the loneliness in
her life. But now she needed to make it perfect for Piero. If they
were to have any chance together then she needed to be the
drop-dead gorgeous diva people, especially lovers, expected of
her. Portia made a snap decision. She would book herself into
The Abbey. She'd been there before. They knew how to be dis-
creet and deliver results. She'd phone the owner, her old friend
Duncan Porte, after the weekend. Cancel everything else and
book herself in for a bit of bodywork.

Snapping back to reality, Portia answered. Her tone was staccato and devoid of any emotion. 'Quite. May the wicked witch rot in hell. Now, I do believe I've got a song to perform. If you'll excuse me, Redmond, I need to continue getting ready. Will you go and thank Piero for me and tell him that I hope he's planning something rather decadent and glamorous to toast our success after the concert.' Picking up the screwed-up newspaper, she handed it to Redmond. 'And get rid of this, would you? Dump it in the bins outside. I don't even want it in the same building.'

Amazed at the composure in her voice, Redmond took the paper and left the room. He'd been expecting her to explode like an over-pumped balloon.

Alone in the room, a mortified Portia walked to the mirror and allowed herself finally to scream. The force of it scratched at her throat. She winced, horrified at the feeling. She needed to numb it and knew just the thing. Picking up her perfume atomiser, she went to squirt it into her mouth. Just before she did, she changed her mind. Not because she was worried about the effects of the alcohol, but because she knew that just one squirt would not be enough. Unscrewing the bottle top, she removed the lid, placed the bottle to her lips and poured the contents into her mouth, draining it dry.

CHAPTER 32

Lewin Éclair had always taken his health for granted. And he was used to being number one. At high school he had been captain of both the swimming and the rugby teams. He'd always known he would be. Just as he'd known that when he ventured into the wine business he would be the man to make his name, his company, the most famous one in South Africa. He'd always thrived on the cut and thrust of it all. Adored the speculation of where the business could expand to next, watching its vines of success grow around the globe, strangling other businesses nowhere near as robust. It was what he expected to happen – for others to fall by the wayside as Lewin Éclair marched on to victory.

The riches had come, the success had come, the superstar lifestyle around the world had come, and so had the enemies. People who were just as keen to see Lewin Éclair wines wiped off the map as Lewin was set on destroying others. But where he had succeeded, others had only managed to fail. Lewin was always shrewder, sharper, more cut-throat. He was indestructible.

But waking up in his hospital bed, his entire body sore from his recent heart attack, Lewin realised for the first time ever that he wasn't invincible. In fact, if the tight pain in his chest was anything to go by, he surmised that he was lucky to be alive.

Blinking to let his eyes come into focus, Lewin realised that two figures stood at the end of the bed. It was the first time he'd seen them since his attack. Mariella was one of them and next to her was the powerful form of Peter Bradford. Lewin took one look at him and asked, 'What's that sneery-faced bastard doing here? Are you trying to kill me off, Bradford? Not content with just grabbing my wife, you've come to stick a pillow over my face and smother me? You and whose fucking army?'

Peter raised his eyebrows and stared at his rival. 'You're awake again then? And just as vile as ever I see.'

Mariella turned to her lover. 'Look, leave this to me. You get home and keep trying to get hold of Martha. At least now we can tell her that her dad's awake and back to his normal noxious ways. I'll see you later.' She kissed Peter on the cheek and watched as he left the ward before turning to Lewin.

'I think I preferred you when you were asleep. You need to take things easy from now on. According to the docs your heart has taken quite a bashing and your body isn't exactly as sporty and chiselled as it was in the days when you and I got together. In fact, the doc said you're bloody lucky to have come through. There may be complications though.' She repeated everything to Lewin that the doctor had said to her and Adina and also about how Peter had been trying to get hold of Martha, to no avail. As she finished she walked round to the side of the bed to get closer to Lewin. 'Despite everything, you old goat, I'm glad you're awake and that all this,' she pointed towards his chest, 'didn't kill you off. Despite what you think Martha loves you dearly – she just finds your interfering a little hard to bear. Maybe this attack will teach you to lighten up a bit. And, on a personal note, I'm not ready to see the love of my life pushing up the daisies just yet, OK.' She took his hand and squeezed it. 'So, you take it easy, and no more nightly escapades with Adina out on the veranda. She's been telling everybody that that's what you were up to when you had the attack.' She lowered her voice before adding, 'Sordid little slut.'

Lewin was somewhat touched by Mariella's actions and for a few seconds he was transported back to their happy days together. *Love of my life, eh?* It was only at the mention of Adina that his mind snapped back to the present. 'Where is she? Is she off getting her nails done or her hair weaved or whatever she bloody well does?'

'She was here earlier, but she went off ...' Mariella's voice was drowned out as a scream of excitement came from the ward door.

'Darling, you're awake again. The doctors said you'd woken up before but I was at Pilates at the time. Thank God my little baby is back from the brink.' It was Adina, dressed in what Mariella could only describe as one of the shortest skirts she had ever seen – and she had virtually lived in Mary Quant when she was younger so she knew how short they could go. A figure-hugging black crop-top which reached down to a few inches above Adina's navel completed the ensemble. Hospital-visiting-wear it was not and if ever an outfit had been put together to induce a coronary in a red-blooded male then this was it. Scanning Adina in disgust, Mariella became self-conscious of the fact she was still holding Lewin's hand and let go of it before Adina noticed.

It was the first time Adina had seen Mariella since her recent outburst; something which she still hadn't forgotten. Looking directly at her, she flashed a forced smile, showing a perfect set of polar white teeth. 'You can go now. I would like to see my boyfriend alone, if you don't mind. It's all been very traumatic for me and Lewin and I need to talk.' She raised her right hand and waggled her fingers at Mariella to say goodbye.

Resisting the urge to bite her head off, Mariella bent down to kiss Lewin on the cheek again, said, 'I'll be back when we get hold of *our* daughter. You take it easy and don't let anything ... or *anyone* ... upset you, OK?' She stressed her chosen words to perfection. She didn't even look at Adina as she walked from the ward.

Adina tottered over to the edge of the bed, her heels clipping against the tiled floor. She hugged Lewin as closely and as tightly as his tubes and the machines around him would allow. 'You're all better, my soldier. That's so good to see.'

'You're not exactly Florence Nightingale, are you? I'd hardly say I'm better, Adina. I've had a heart attack and I've got to be careful about what I get up to in the future to try and make sure I don't have another.' Lewin wasn't too sure that he was that pleased to see his girlfriend. Even her mere presence seemed to annoy him.

'That's why you need a good woman in your life. Someone to look after you and take the reins while you just relax and recuperate. Do you remember what we were talking about when you suffered the attack, Lewin?' asked Adina.

Lewin tried to think back. He could remember their lovemaking but the conversation was far from lucid in his mind. His puzzlement obviously showed on his face, a fact not unnoticed by Adina.

'We were making love, Lewin, as only you and I can. Supreme, harmonious sex. And we were both saying how we fit together like the perfect jigsaw puzzle and how we should be together and well, then you asked me …'

Afraid both of where the conversation was apparently leading and at his lack of memory concerning his last conversation with Adina, Lewin tried to keep his calm. 'Asked you what?' he questioned tentatively.

There was no stopping Adina. 'To marry you. You said it was what you wanted and that we should do it. You do remember, don't you? You've made me the happiest woman alive.'

Lewin could see his heartbeat quicken on the monitor along-side his bed. He took deep breaths to try and keep it as settled as possible. 'No, I don't remember, but I have no intention of marrying you, Adina. I know that I don't want to get married. You're nothing more than a rather beautiful accessory to me. Like a sleek and slender Porsche or a beautifully painted Monet. And I am nothing more to you than a rather heavily stocked cash machine. If I did say we should get married then obviously it was the strain of the heart attack talking and nothing else.'

Gritting her teeth, Adina was determined not to take no for an answer. 'You really don't remember what we talked about, do you? You are *so* much more to me than, as you rather bluntly put it, "a heavily stocked cash machine". So much more ...' She let her words sink in before adding with a smile, 'Lewin, you're the father of my baby: I'm pregnant.'

Lewin's heartbeat on the monitor by the bed suddenly shot up. This time it would take more than a few deep breaths to bring it back down to normal. Pressing the panic button to call for the doctor, he knew that he would never take his health for granted again.

CHAPTER 33

Betsy Hartley's house was situated along a tree-lined street within the Royal Borough of Kensington. As Nancy climbed the stone steps leading up to the heavy wooden front door she guessed that there wouldn't be much change from five million pounds, should she ever find herself in a position to purchase such a property. It was grand without being showy, decorated with old-school money that had taste running naturally through it.

Just staring briefly inside it at the first of its four floors through the bay window, Nancy could see that it was beautifully decorated – huge velvet drapes cascaded down the windows and the walls were punctuated with classic black and white photos from days gone by. It was elegant simplicity and simply elegant.

As was Betsy when she opened the front door, dressed in a pleated silk blouse and dark trousers. Her face was immaculate, her make-up symmetrical and precise. She'd been expecting Nancy ever since their phone conversation earlier that day.

'How lovely to see you, my dear, do come through. I'll get Bloodworth to bring us some tea and scones and we can talk about your forthcoming trip to Las Vegas. I'm thrilled you're going. I'd be tempted to come with you myself if flying still agreed with me.'

Nancy, suddenly feeling hideously underdressed in jeans and T-shirt despite the heat of the summer day outside, entered the hallway. It was like stepping onto the set of a Merchant Ivory film. A solid mahogany byzantine telephone table stood against

the wall, an original classic handset-and-cradle telephone resting on a crocheted doily at its centre. On the other wall a stag's
head was mounted on a shield-shaped wall-hanging and a row
of brass hooks stood out proudly, a selection of fur coats hanging from them. Nancy guessed they were real.

'Let me take your bag and hang it up, my dear,' said Betsy,
motioning to take Nancy's Gina bag. 'Bloodworth is preparing
the food and tea so I'll have to do it myself.'

'Bloodworth?' questioned Nancy. 'Is he ...?' She didn't know
what to say.

'He's invaluable. He's my butler and has been with William
and me for years. When William died I couldn't see any just
reason to dispense with his services. He lives here with me. I'd
get pretty lonely otherwise.' Betsy hung the shoulder bag on one
of the hooks and walked into the reception room. Nancy stared
in wonder at her surroundings as she followed the old lady in.
The double reception room was at least fifty feet long, dark
floorboards and Persian rugs giving it the distinct feel of having
been crafted by people of opulent, regal breeding. Separating
the room into halves were two floor-to-ceiling stone columns,
and equidistant on either side of them were some of the largest
chandeliers Nancy had ever laid eyes on.

The room led onto a pretty patio area that overlooked a garden which seemed to stretch as far as Nancy's eye could see. It
was beautifully tended, with two leylandii hedges flanking both
sides and a row of topiaried bushes at one end. As Betsy escorted
Nancy out onto the patio to seat herself at the garden furniture
there, Nancy felt as if she was walking into Narnia. The whole
feel of the house and garden was truly magical.

'Now, shall I be mother?' A charming teapot, with brightly
coloured flowers and etchings of gold on it sat on the table,
a hot plume of steam rising from its spout. 'I see Bloodworth

has delivered the tea. How do you like it?' Nancy answered and Betsy began to pour. As she did so, a portly gentleman of comparable age to Betsy, with barely a hair left on his head, shuffled out onto the patio. In one hand he carried a cake stand piled high with scones, while in the other he balanced a tray housing jam and whipped cream. 'Ah, Nancy, now this is Bloodworth. Bloodworth, this is Nancy,' said Betsy. 'These scones look divine, just what we need on a day like today. Now, I do hope you're not one of these silly young women who won't touch dairy and can't eat scones because you're worried that the few calories in them will go straight to your hips. I always think good food should be relished, don't you? I don't think you can beat a decent scone.'

Nancy couldn't help but smile at Betsy's exuberance and helped herself to one of the scones, layering on both the jam and the cream. Betsy looked pleased. 'Oh marvellous. A girl who loves gambling and a decent spot of tea. You and I are going to get on a treat. Now, when are you off to Las Vegas?'

Nancy filled Betsy on what she had been up to since meeting her at the casino. She'd gone online the next morning and booked a direct flight to Las Vegas after the weekend. At the same time she'd made a reservation for a suite at the Bellagio. Now that Nancy had some money at her disposal she was determined to relax in style – there was no way she was going to book herself into a two-bit fleapit of a motel with just a sleazy owner and a family of cockroaches for company. If she was to try and hit it big in Vegas then she needed to look the part, and that meant staying in the right places. It was money that she should have been using to pay her mortgage and decrease her tax bill, but as far as Nancy was concerned, if she could hit the jackpot in the glitzy city of neon lights then she could end her money troubles for good. Mundane mortgage worries and troubling tax bills would have to wait.

Betsy was thrilled to hear that Nancy was heading stateside and couldn't hide her merriment when Nancy mentioned the Bellagio. 'Oh, sweet girl, the Bellagio is thirty storeys of grandeur and luxury. The lobby has over two thousand hand-blown glass flowers in it. It was one of the last places William and I stayed together. The dancing fountains shooting skywards to the sounds of Gene Kelly or Andrea Bocelli are a sight to behold,' she gushed. Nancy didn't have the heart to tell her that she'd only booked it because she'd read it had been featured in *Ocean's Eleven* with Brad Pitt.

The two women were still talking about Vegas as the sun started to set and a vague chill started to tiptoe across their bodies. Nancy could see goose pimples forming on Betsy's skin. 'I think I'd better be going. It's been wonderful to see you again. I'll let you know when I'm back from Las Vegas and hopefully we can go out and spend my winnings. Thanks for sharing your tips with me, Betsy.' If she were honest, Betsy's tips weren't exactly rocket science. They'd amounted to little more than handing her the magazine article she'd been telling her about, paying a visit to the loose slots of the MGM and advising her not to stick to one particular colour when it came to roulette. Nancy couldn't help but feel that Betsy's love of gambling was one that stemmed from not having the necessity to win. Unlike herself, Betsy was obviously sitting on a fortune and gambled merely for the indulgent thrill. Winning was a bonus, but it had not become a compulsive necessary addiction.

'May I just use your toilet before I leave?' said Nancy, standing from the table. 'I think it's this sudden chill and all the cups of tea. I'll never make the journey home otherwise!'

'Of course, my dear. I suggest you use the bathroom on the fourth floor. I suspect it will appeal to you. I may be an old lady but that bathroom is my little haven of fun and frivolity. It's all the way to the top of the stairs. I'll clear these plates and take them to Bloodworth ... where has that man got to? He's probably nodded off – he normally does when the summer comes.'

Leaving Betsy to collect the plates, Nancy headed back through the reception and into the hall, before starting to climb the four flights of stairs. As she went, she surveyed the host of photographs on the wall. Most of them were black and white photos of well-to-do families stood in front of impressive, dynamic homes. Wartime images of men in military uniform stared out from a few of them. In others, a lady that Nancy guessed was a younger Betsy stood alongside a moustached man in front of a country cottage, a child on the grass in front of them. One of the photos featured Betsy and her husband standing in front of the Flamingo Hotel in Vegas. From the way her hair was stacked beehive-high on her head and the fashions that both she and her husband were wearing, she guessed it must have dated from the nineteen sixties or seventies. It was a fashion that had come back into vogue several times since and one that Nancy loved. 'Way to go, Betsy – you are a cool old dame.'

Nancy liked Betsy, which as she arrived on the fourth floor struck her as something of a pain. She didn't want to like her. She'd only come to her house for one main reason and now was the time to try and put her plan into operation. She needed money and it was clear that Betsy had more than she knew what to do with.

Nancy had no more urge to go to the toilet than she did to swim with sharks. Bypassing the bathroom, she headed to the first bedroom she could find. It was immaculate and definitely not the one that Betsy slept in. Scanning around the room Nancy dismissed what she saw and moved on. The next one was smaller but equally immaculate. It reminded Nancy of a room in a show house or in a hotel that had not housed any guests for a long time. Again she ran from it as quickly as she could. It was only when she went into the third bedroom on that level that she found what she wanted. It was the largest of the three she'd visited so far – heaven knows how many the house actually contained – and from the dresses hung on the wardrobe doors and from the boxes, bottles, lotions and potions fanned out across the huge dressing table cradled in the window, it was obviously a room that saw daily use.

Checking that there was no one in sight, Nancy ran over to the dressing table and flipped the lid on what she assumed was a large jewellery box. It was. There was a mass of jewellery inside – more in one box than she had ever owned in her life. Nancy had been thinking about Betsy's jewellery ever since she'd spied the necklace she'd been wearing the night they'd met at the casino. She couldn't imagine for one minute that Betsy would have anything except jewellery of the highest – and most expensive – quality. She was definitely more De Beers and less QVC.

She knew she'd have to be quick. Reaching inside the box she grabbed a handful of rings and a necklace. She placed them quickly inside her shoulder bag that she'd grabbed off the hook on the way up the stairs. The jewellery box still looked full. Hopefully Betsy wouldn't even notice that some of it was missing. She shut the lid back down on the box and took a handkerchief from her pocket. She wiped it across the box's lid, hoping to eradicate any fingerprints. With lightning-quick speed she placed the handkerchief back in her pocket and ran from the room.

Nancy was just about to head downstairs when she passed the bathroom again. Maybe she should make this look and sound as realistic as possible. She went in and flushed the toilet chain. Her eyes scanned the room. It was completely different to the other rooms and the style of the rest of the house. It was no wonder Betsy had directed her there. It was like a tacky, yet incredibly well presented homage to the home of gambling. A large neon Las Vegas sign hung on the wall, a row of snow globes were lined up along the window sill, each depicting a Vegas scene, and a pair of furry LV dice hung over the bathroom mirror. The bathroom mat spread across the tiled floor was a copy of a roulette table. Everything from the soap dish through to the toothbrush holder and indeed the brushes inside were emblazoned with dollar signs, cowboy hats and the words 'Las Vegas'. If it hadn't been in such stark contrast to the rest of the immaculately decorated house, the whole room would have been deemed a chavvy eyesore, but having heard Betsy talk with such fondness about the place, Nancy couldn't help but find the room somewhat charming. It reminded her again why she liked the woman, the thought making her feel cold and worthless about what she had just done.

Heading downstairs as fast as her feet would carry her, Nancy hung the bag back up on the hook and headed out to see Betsy. She and Bloodworth were in the kitchen. 'That bathroom is awesome, Betsy. I love it,' she raved, somewhat out of breath.

'I knew you would,' beamed Betsy. 'Now you get yourself home and all ready for Las Vegas. Good luck and I want to hear all about it when you get back. I suspect we'll have something to celebrate, because you, my dear, are a true winner. I can feel it.' She leant over and kissed Nancy on both cheeks.

As Nancy walked down the tree-lined street back to her car with her jewellery-laden bag tucked safely under her arm, she felt far from a winner. When she'd stolen from Lauren, she could justify her actions – the woman had ruined their friendship, she deserved to be punished. But Betsy – she was nothing more than a harmless old lady with a fun love of gambling who had taken Nancy to her heart. And Nancy had repaid her by robbing her blind. It was the first moment where Nancy felt that maybe her money woes and her insatiable need to fund her gambling were getting out of hand. What had happened to her? It wasn't supposed to be like this. Perhaps she needed help. She knew where to find it. But Vegas had to come first – and that, to use a gambling term, was a dead cert.

But as Nancy climbed into her car and drove off she'd never felt more of a complete and utter loser.

CHAPTER 34

'Will you try and hold it together, for God's sake, Lauren? This is a hugely important night and you're staggering around like Oliver Reed in a frock.' Dale's voice was far from pleased. 'Just how I'm supposed to sell your singing talents to record bosses when you can hardly string two words together is beyond me. What the hell's got into you?'

At that precise point of questioning, it had been the best part of a bottle of the finest champagne and several lines of coke that had got into Lauren. As a result of which she was staring around one of the many reception rooms at the Royal Albert Hall with eyes blurrier than an untuned TV. She had not been able to hold herself together since seeing Nathan and Saul at the fetish club a few days earlier. She had not spoken to her husband since, avoiding his phone calls whenever he'd rung. As far as she was concerned, his being at the club and obviously having a good time with Martha, and undoubtedly countless other women, was something she couldn't comprehend. He was playing with fire but, if anything, his actions, accompanied and seemingly cheered on by the monstrous Nathan, spurred her into a situation of 'what's good for the goose is good for the gander'. Why should she beat herself up about wanting a career? Why should she feel guilty about having feelings for Dale? And why should she not try and find some answers hidden in the powdery depths of her coke bag? As far as Lauren was concerned, if they were both keen to sample new recipe ideas that weren't on the menu at home then that gave her carte blanche to do whatever she liked. Whatever the consequences …

It had only been the clever actions of Dale, Martha and Kelly that had kept her away from the cataclysmic consequences of her attracting the unwanted attention of the press so far that night. Sadly for Lauren, one person she hadn't been able to avoid was Nancy.

'Well, don't you look wobblier than a newborn Bambi,' scoffed Nancy as she spied Lauren clinging desperately to Dale's arm. 'And I've seen you look prettier, I'll be honest. Must be the wacky dust she's been shoving up her nose, eh, Dale? Her face looks like she's had a stroke. What are you thinking? You could do so much better – but then you have in the past.'

Dale was in no mood for small talk. 'Get out of my face, Nancy. What the hell are you doing here? The door policy is supposed to be pretty picky tonight, so I'm surprised that a has-been like you has been let in. And leave Lauren out of it.'

'Out of it? Such an apt phrase – look at her gurning mug. What would her husband say? If only I had my camera. And as for my invitation, well … I have you to thank for that. I spot-ted yours on your desk at your office when you fucked me the other day. It's funny how your mind and eyes can wander during so-so sex. I made a few phone calls and here I am. It's amazing what doors open if you offer up a sizable donation. Thanks for the tip-off.'

Dale could feel his blood starting to boil. So Nancy was out to humiliate him – terrific. The last thing he needed was a slang-ing match with her, especially in front of potential investors into Lauren's new career. And there was the small matter of Lauren beginning to slump dangerously down his arm in her severely smashed state. Determined to get rid of Nancy as soon as he could, all he could say was 'Fuck off.'

'My pleasure – there's enough influential people at this gathering to mingle with all night. Who knows, I may even be able to bag myself a new manager; a decent one who can satisfy me both professionally and personally. See you around.' Nancy took one step away from the group before turning back, her dress swirling around her as she did so. 'Oh, and best of luck selling Little Miss Nostrils to the masses. You're going to need it.' With that Nancy was gone, leaving Dale, Martha, Kelly and a floppy-headed Lauren.

'Was that who I think it was? Christ, she's a class act, isn't she? Last time I gyrate around a pole to one of her tunes,' remarked Kelly.

'Nice dress – just a shame about the person wearing it,' stated Martha.

Martha and Kelly were there at the invitation of Portia, not that they had seen her as yet. Her performance with Piero was to be the finale of the evening. Kelly didn't mind waiting – she had already found herself in conversation and swapping numbers with an afro-headed rock star that she'd lusted after from afar when she'd seen him in *We Will Rock You*. She'd also been sharing tips on how to find the perfect-fitting bra with the 36-DD lead singer of one of her favourite groups.

Martha was enjoying feasting her eyes on the varied visions of beauty that mingled around her. Having spent the night before out dogging again with Tom, Martha's sexuality had never been more heightened. Every person she looked at was rapidly becoming little more than a number on her scoreboard of shaggability. Already within the media crowd of the evening, she'd earmarked at least half a dozen ten-out-of-tens that she was determined to speak to, and maybe more before the night was out. She had to admit that Dale had easily scored a nine when she'd first spied him with Lauren.

Not that Dale seemed to be thinking about anything other than keeping Lauren in control since the four of them had met up before the event at a bar around the corner. Lauren was already well on her way to woozy when she'd tumbled from the cab Dale had sent to her house to pick her up. He ushered her into the bar where she'd told him she'd arranged to meet Martha and Kelly, and then subsequently into the Royal Albert Hall through a back door, avoiding the gathered press and TV crews at the front of the building. The last thing he wanted was to see a plastered Lauren plastered all over the papers before he'd even managed to bag her a megabucks deal.

Martha and Kelly still assumed that Lauren was just upset about the close call with Nathan at the fetish club and whisked her off to the Ladies' toilet as soon as they arrived inside. They splashed water onto her face in an attempt to sober her up. It hadn't really worked and Dale was becoming more and more annoyed.

'There's no point me trying to engage in conversations with the people behind everyone from Lorde through to Rihanna if you're going to stand there all glassy-eyed. Tonight was supposed to be your night to shine,' he snapped as Lauren clung to his arm to try and steady herself. It wouldn't have been a good look at any time but landing face-first on the carpet wearing a four-figure Marchesa dress would have been the equivalent of walking into The Ivy and ordering a kebab for dinner. It just wasn't done.

'She's had a rough week, that's all,' ventured Martha, trying to make excuses for her friend. 'She just needs to sleep it off.'

Dale wasn't in the mood for excuses. 'Thank Christ I booked a box for us to sit in. I'm going to take her there now and she can sleep it off all she likes. We're not leaving here until we've worked this place and the party ain't over until the fat lady sings.'

Martha and Kelly couldn't help but laugh at his words. 'I assume you're talking about Portia, then? You've seen that dreadful piece in the newspaper today about her. Complete load of rubbish, but then what isn't in this celebrity world?' Martha was talking to Dale, but he'd already hurried off in search of his box, attempting to surreptitiously drag Lauren along with him.

'Poor cow,' said Kelly, watching Lauren as she stumbled off. 'She needs help. She should book herself in somewhere to try and sort out her head. She's obviously pretty screwed up right now.'

A bell sounded, signalling that the show was about to start in five minutes. Kelly clapped her hands together with excitement. 'C'mon, let's go and take our seats. I don't want to miss a moment of this.'

Martha's face was etched with thought, caused by two reasons. The first was what Kelly had just said about Lauren. Maybe she did need to find herself somewhere to go to get her head together. And from Martha's conversations with Tom she knew exactly the place – The Abbey. Maybe a little life coaching and TLC was just what Lauren needed. She made a mental note to slyly question her about it when she was back in the land of the sober.

The second reason for Martha's pensive air was a strikingly handsome man staring directly at her from the other side of the room. His eyes seemed to burn deeply into hers, wrapped in their own intensity. He scored an eleven for looks and immediately sent a thirst of sexual longing through her body. His dark blond hair was slicked back onto his head, two days' worth of designer stubble peppering his cheeks. There was an air of undaunted maleness about him – heroic and irresistible. Martha could tell that they were both thinking the same thing. She didn't know how and didn't care to question.

'You go ahead,' she said to Kelly without taking her eyes off the man. 'I'll be there in a minute. I just need to go to the little girl's room.'

As Kelly headed off, Martha made her way directly over to the man. Without saying a word, she stood on tiptoe in front of him and reached up, placing her lips against his. He was a good few inches taller than her and he tasted good. As their lips parted he smiled and took her hand. 'Follow me,' he whispered. Unable to stop herself and not wanting to for a second, Martha did as instructed. It felt reckless and irresistibly raunchy.

The corridors of the venue were clearing as people headed for their seats. They were virtually empty by the time the man stopped outside a door and inserted a key into it. He pulled it open and took Martha inside. It was a private box, seemingly not in use for the evening's event. Chairs were stacked up in the corner and the lights remained off, with just a dim light feeding into the area from the main arena of the Hall. The man had no sooner shut and locked the door behind him than he made his move. Martha was more than ready.

Their lips came together, the stubble on his cheeks grinding seductively against her face. She felt his tongue explore deeply within her mouth as he pushed her dominantly up against the wall of the box. Martha reached down and started to undo the belt looped around his trousers. As she did so, she could hear the sound of the orchestra in the arena below filling her ears. She recognised 'All That Jazz', 'Cabaret', 'Any Dream Will Do' … all songs from theatrical productions being celebrated at the event. The crowd cheered and began to clap along, showing their appreciation. Unleashing the man's cock from the confines of his trousers, Martha dropped to her knees and showed some appreciation of her own, taking his solid member in her mouth. She worked his shaft for a good five minutes.

Below them a troupe of dancers burst onto the stage, high-kicking and spinning their way across it. Pulling Martha to her feet, the man put his hand underneath the skirt of her ruffled D&G dress and yanked at her knickers. They came away easily, leaving her wetness exposed. He ploughed his fingers inside her, causing Martha to flinch with pleasure. He found her clitoris and rubbed his fingers against it. The pounding volume of the orchestra seemed to increase and the dancers onstage expertly beat out their rhythm in time to the music. His movements became faster and faster as the pace of the music increased.

Pulling his fingers from within her, the man placed them around his cock and guided it into her. Its girth filled Martha and she gritted her teeth to stop herself from crying out with desire. At first his motions were deliberate and slow, allowing her to savour every inch of his manhood. But then his pace grew faster. The drums of the orchestra below became more tribal, the banging of the cymbals more urgent. The music was reaching its peak. It wasn't alone. As the man's strokes became more forceful Martha could feel her own climax rising. She let out a moan of pleasure as the first waves of orgasm released themselves between her legs. Wave after wave of pleasure followed until finally the man unleashed his own seed, emptying what seemed like rivers of hot liquid inside her. As he did so the music below became louder and louder before finishing with an almighty crash. A line of pyrotechnics exploded behind the dancers, sending jets of flashing lights pirouetting into the air. Martha and the man watched the fireworks subside and the dancers leave the stage to rapturous applause before separating themselves.

'That was quite something. Care to do it again sometime?' said Martha.

'I'd love to. I knew you were thinking the same as me. I could tell. You're very easy to read,' he said mysteriously before adding, 'Sorry I made you miss the start of the show.'

'I'll watch it if they release a DVD of the event,' giggled Martha. 'I'm Martha, by the way.'

'I'm Kieran. Nice to meet you.' Martha spotted a slight accent in his voice. It reminded her of back home. 'Are you from South Africa? You're a long way from home too, aren't you?'

'I was born there but I've been here for the longest time now. Guess the accent will always be there though to portray my roots.' Buckling up his belt, he looked at Martha. 'Look, I've got to go. We should go and take our seats, but if you'd like to get in touch with me again and work on an encore performance then take my number.' He took a pen from the inside pocket of his jacket and dropped to his knees. At first Martha thought she was in for a second delirious dose of love-making. She was wrong. Lifting her skirt once again he wrote his mobile number on the bare flesh of her thigh with his felt-tip pen. It tickled as he wrote, a sensation Martha found deeply pleasant.

'This way there's no way you can misplace my details during the concert,' he said, before kissing her thigh next to where he'd written. Martha thought it was one of the horniest and most intimate actions she'd ever experienced.

'Now, let's go,' he said before opening the box door. Adjusting her dress Martha walked out into the full light of the corridor. Kieran locked the door behind him and kissed Martha fully on the lips again before saying goodbye and running off.

Martha watched him go, still tingling from their love-making. 'Wow, hot man!' she said to herself. 'He must work here. How else would he have the keys to a box that's not in use?' Without giving it another moment's thought, she made her way to her seat.

She pushed past the people on her row to take her place alongside Kelly. Portia had secured them excellent seats near the front of the auditorium. As Lauren sat herself down, Kelly turned to her. 'Where the hell have you been? You've missed the start. The orchestra played this cool medley of musicals. It was a wicked number.'

'Not to worry, replied Martha, stroking her thigh through her skirt. 'I've been getting a wicked number all of my own ...'

—

Still smarting with rage about the newspaper article, Portia took Piero's hand and wafted onto the stage ready to deliver yet another commanding and majestic performance. Her duet with her new lover was to be the dynamic denouement to the charity evening's events. Staring into Piero's eyes as the audience rose to their feet in adulation, Portia knew that the swarthy Italian had already started to melt her heart. Even in the short few days they had been in each other's company, Portia had the feeling that she had met her equal, her true match. Someone as strong and independent as she was, yet someone who was looking for a partner to look to the future with – whatever it may hold.

As the sound of the orchestra filled the venue, Portia watched as Piero started to sing, his deep, rich tones calming any rage that still bubbled within her. His voice was as delicious as the purest caviar. It was the best Portia had ever heard it, suiting the dramatic romantic-love-affair nature of the song to perfection. When she had sung with him in Budapest she had searched to find fault with every performance – not that there was really any to be found – but then she had been looking at him through the eyes of rejection.

As she wrapped herself in the rugged sanctuary of his arms heading towards the heart-stirring climax of the song, she was beginning to think that she was looking at him as someone she could fall in love with. And that was an emotional pool that Portia hadn't let herself swim in for the longest time.

Then, for Portia, came the moment she would look back on for the rest of her life with a sense of horror and defeat. A total sense of failure. To her trained ear, her own voice had felt slightly forced throughout the entire song. The notes weren't as diamond-cut as she was used to. Her throat, normally so fluid and dripping with refined nuances for each and every word seemed to be edged with roughness. It was as if the glitter in her voice had been replaced with the coarsest granules of sand. People in the audience marvelled at her vocal gymnastics, unaware that Portia herself knew that something was wrong. For a woman who had carried numerous note-perfect operas around the world and showcased her unparalleled talents to millions of fans, Portia sensed that her voice was not at a hundred per cent.

Suddenly, with no control from within her own body, her voice started to crumble. The high note she attempted petered out to nothing – the silence louder than any note of her career. As she attempted the next line, mercifully the last, her normally reliable delivery cracked under the strain and all that emitted from her voice box was a raspy, breathy, unpleasant sound. She raised her hand automatically to her throat as if to grab the unwanted sound and jettison it. An audible gasp of horror rose from the crowd. Petrified at what was happening, Portia stared into Piero's eyes and could see a surge of alarm deep within. Her own eyes began to fill with tears. As the music came to an end, Piero pulled her close to him, as if to protect her, the warmth of his body still wrapped around her. She buried her head in his chest and allowed her tears to come.

As the audience applauded, unsure about what to do after what they had heard, Piero guided Portia offstage, leaving his arm protectively around her. He kept it there until they reached her dressing room.

Portia was too scared to talk. She was still reeling from what had happened. She had not given the performance that people expected of her. Her voice, the tool of her trade that she always took for granted, hadn't let her. She had failed and in her mind she wondered if she'd ever be able to succeed again.

———

Handing the key back to one of the security guards at a back entrance to the Hall, Kieran slid a wad of bank notes into his hand at the same time. There must have been at least two hundred pounds, adding to an already substantial sum he'd bribed the man with earlier. 'I appreciate the loan of the key, mate. Everything's locked up so no one will know anybody's been in that box, OK?'

'Good job, too. My boss would string me up by the knackers if he knew I was dishing out keys,' said the guard. 'Although why you'd want to only watch a fraction of a show from a disused box is beyond me. With the money you've given me you'd have been better off buying a proper ticket instead.'

'I achieved exactly what I wanted,' grinned Kieran. 'Exactly what I wanted.' And it had all worked out just as he'd hoped it might. He'd wanted to make love to Martha ever since he'd followed her the first night she'd gone dogging with Tom. In fact, he couldn't wait until he did it again. Just as he'd suspected from watching her in action from afar, Martha was one of the most satisfying shags that Kieran Bradford had ever experienced. Not that he'd tell his dad that when he phoned him later, of course. He'd just tell Peter that he'd made contact with Martha as instructed and that his mission was well under way.

PART TWO

CHAPTER 35

The Abbey Rehabilitation Centre had been the number one refuge for any famous figure with a problem for nearly a decade. For any name with an issue that needed to be treated and who was prepared to pay through the nose to achieve a solution, it had become the only place in Britain worth considering. Everyone from royalty to reality stars had booked into one of the many rooms housed behind its neo-Grecian façade at some point and strutted out a while later with their seemingly clean head held high and a 'how I got my act together' story for the tabloids.

Built at the epicentre of nearly two hundred acres of some of the UK's lushest natural beauty, The Abbey had secured itself an untouched reputation as being the promised land for problems, the utopia for the under-pressure and an Arcadia for the addicted. As the Latin engraving, carved into the stone lintel supported by two gargantuan pillars at the entrance said, *Hic Pro Panton, Hic Pro Sulum – Here For Everything, Here For Everyone.* A welcoming statement indeed, but not strictly true.

Only those with bank balances that most people can merely daydream about could pay the entrance fee into this particular Xanadu.

Which is why a crestfallen Portia had headed there as soon as she possibly could after her disaster at the charity event. Madeline Strong's feature about her mammoth media-land weight gain – in the real world it was merely a few pounds – and an emergency meeting with a Harley Street doctor confirming that she had damaged her vocal chords – more than likely due to a severe scream (she had Madeline to thank for that again) – had resulted in her demanding Redmond to clear her diary and book nothing for the foreseeable future.

Over the years, The Abbey had become like a sanctuary for Portia at much-needed times of rest and recreation. But her latest visit was one with a mission she was keen to discuss with her old friend – the dashing and debonair owner of The Abbey, Duncan Porte.

'If you've read that dreadful woman's tabloid feature on me – not that I suspect you have, darling, you've always been more of a culture section kind of man – then you'll know that she crucified me about my weight. I admit I've gained a few pounds here and there but I trust it's nothing that your fabulous team can't put right, Duncan. When I see the outside world again I want to possess a body more heavenly than Aphrodite. Plus, thanks to that tabloid tart and me screaming like a banshee, my lovely man in Harley Street has told me there'll be no singing for me for a while. It appears I have strained my vocal cords a little, hence my slight huskiness. I shall be on antibiotics for a few weeks and be drinking lots of water to prevent drying of the throat. But I trust we can talk strictly between ourselves, Duncan? I need to ask you something rather delicate.'

Duncan, a powerhouse and an athletic figure of a man from years of physical exercise and treating his body as a temple, leaned forward in his chair and took Portia's hands in his own across the table. They were virtually twice the size of hers and immediately filled her with an inner security. They had never been lovers but there were times when she let her brain indulge in giddy moments of consideration about just how expert a sexual partner the eligible bachelor might be. As he spoke, his voice was Barry White deep. 'Portia, we've known each other long enough to know that anything we speak about within these walls is confidential.'

'I think one of the reasons my voice has suffered slightly is because I've been drinking rather a lot. As you know I've always been partial to the odd glass of Krug, but over the last few months I've noticed that I've been drinking more and more. I know I shouldn't, but somehow I can't resist. Every singer knows that alcohol dehydrates. I think it may be why my voice gave way so easily. I enjoy drinking, Duncan. But it's become somewhat out of hand...'

Duncan continued to hold onto Portia's hands as she explained about her breakfast routine of adding alcohol to her juice, about the perfume atomisers full of spirit and the secrets of her bathroom mouthwash. His eyes showed nothing but concern as she admitted out loud for the first time that she considered herself to have a problem. 'I want to stop, I do. I drink because I'm unhappy, because I'm lonely, because I'm nervous about what the future may hold for me. Nerves tighten the voice, Duncan. Have I been so immersed in my career that it may be too late to find happiness in other areas? I'm heading towards my late thirties, and my body clock is ticking. My life can be so solitary. The four blank walls of a dressing room look soulless wherever they are. And every man that's come my way has either ripped me off or ripped open my heart. The warmth of a crowd is joyous, but it's no substitute for the warmth of a man.'

Portia pulled a silk handkerchief from her bag and dabbed at her eyes as the tears started to fall. 'You're the only person I've told, Duncan. Redmond doesn't know I drink. He'd go crazy. I need you to help me stop, especially now I might have found something ... someone ... to try and stop for.' She told Duncan about Piero and how she felt she may be falling for him. 'I'm just scared that if things go wrong with Piero I might not be able to cope.'

Duncan rose from his seat and walked around to Portia. He placed his hands on her shoulders and leant down to kiss her on the top of her head. 'You're in the right place, for all of your issues. As far as the few pounds you seem to think you've gained are concerned, we have a dietician here who will put you on the straight and narrow. As for your other concern – I'd like to put you under the care of Dr Bruno Fielding here at the centre. He's a leading light in the field of clinical psychology. I believe he'll be able to get to the root of why you feel the need to drink – to understand it and hopefully relieve it. In the meantime, we'll make sure that there is no alcohol available to you here at The Abbey, and we'll search any visitors you have. Plus I'll need to search any luggage you have. I trust that's OK, Portia.'

Raising her hand to her shoulder and placing it on one of Duncan's, Portia stroked the back of his hand and spoke softly. 'You really are a marvel, Duncan, and so is this place. I knew you'd be able to help. Now, are you sure you want to search my luggage? You may need to bring the entire staff with you. I may be here to relax and recuperate but there's no excuse for not having the right outfits, darling. I've five cases in the Rolls that my driver can bring in. I've no idea how long I'm going to be here but when have you ever known me to travel light?'

CHAPTER 36

Peter Bradford had started to bully his son in his teenage years. He had been a bully ever since.

Kieran Bradford had loved his childhood. Growing up as the only offspring of one of South Africa's richest couples, Peter and Roberta Bradford, the young Kieran had experienced the perfect idyllic existence. Holidays around the globe, endless summers at their beach house collecting shells with his mum and being taught how to surf by his dad, even safari expeditions to learn about wildlife.

Roberta had been a devoted animal conservationist and Kieran had followed her on many of her endeavours to save endangered species or ban illegal trade. But when Roberta had been killed in a light aircraft crash over the Winterhoek Mountains everything in Kieran's life seemed to change. He was only eleven years old. With only his dad to look after him, Kieran's once carefree life and nature-loving demeanour was slowly stamped out of him.

Roberta's death had hit Peter hard too but he was a man's man, a man who would never allow himself to portray weakness to those around him. He was a man who believed that if Kieran was to survive in life, then it was his job, as his father and remaining parent, to make sure that his son's skin was as tough as an elephant's and that his instincts for survival were as speedy and ruthless as a cheetah's. The once placid lad, who under his mother's eyes would never have hurt so much as a fly, became a malevolent predator under the boot-camp-like tuition of his father. It was with his father's brutal teaching that Kieran went from a boy to a man. He had the utmost respect for him, almost a fear, but one thing was for sure – Kieran would always do as his father requested.

Knowing that one day he would take over his father's wine empire, Kieran had left Cape Town full of wanderlust at the age of eighteen to travel the world. He'd traversed America on Route 66, island-hopped his way through Thailand, bungee-jumped in New Zealand and tried rafting and ice climbing in Chamonix before eventually settling in the UK. He was a daredevil and a playboy – someone who had devoted his life to the pursuit of pleasurable activities.

His powerful, firm torso had allowed him to sample more women than he could possibly remember. A womaniser, a rake, a man-about-town, a philanderer, a socialite, a pleasure-seeker, a lady-killer – they were all terms that he wore with pride. Women were for humping then dumping. For using then abusing.

Which is why his first sexual liaison with Martha had taken him by surprise. Despite the frenzied nature of their sex and the relatively little conversation between them, Kieran had not been able to shake her from his mind. Like him, she was a person who loved to play life to the full, to live it with a heaped serving of danger. That had become obvious ever since he'd started to follow her at his father's orders. He'd obtained her address from the taxi driver at the hotel, sat outside her Soho apartment and watched her laughing on the arm of her flatmate; shadowed her on her night out to the fetish club, sitting hidden in his car outside until the wee small hours of the morning when she'd reappeared with her two friends. He'd even stalked her on her dogging trip. That had turned out to be a real horny eye-opener, even for a man of Kieran's considerable carnal experience.

And then, of course, there was the evening out at the Royal Albert Hall. He'd known by then that he wanted to fuck her. By that point he'd become dissatisfied with just being on the periphery of Martha's life – he'd seen enough of it over the last few days to know that there was something about Martha Éclair that was drawing him in to her bright, inviting yet definitely dangerous flame. And that was something that his father would surely be pleased about. It was what he'd demanded him to do, after all. Kieran could remember the words exactly. He always could with his father. Each and every one of them:

According to Mariella, Martha's tosser of a father's trying to marry her off. That's why she's done a runner. Track her down and win her over, Kieran. Do whatever it takes. You've been around the block enough to know the way into a woman's heart. If she falls for you, then when Lewin croaks it, Lewin Éclair wines will go to Martha. With you as her other half, that means we have a stake in it. Divorce her in the future and half goes to you, giving Bradford Wines the power to be number one. We're talking billions here, so don't fuck this up. If that girl is going to get married then make sure it's to you. And whatever you do, don't tell her you're a Bradford.

For a physically strong man, Kieran was incredibly weak when it came to saying no to his father. He was sure he could get Martha to fall for him. But the fact that he'd already sent x-rated photos of Martha to his father – his dad wanted any material that could be used to blackmail her in the future – and the fact that he would have to lie about his identity perturbed Kieran. For the first time in a long while he wanted to be honest.

But if he did and things went wrong with Martha, then his father would blame him for messing up. And that was something he couldn't risk. His fear of Peter and his increasingly genuine attraction to Martha were both strong but they were both filling Kieran with a huge amount of weakness.

CHAPTER 37

Nathan Spilsbury was spewing vitriol yet again about Lauren. 'Bloody stupid bitch – she's obviously not here. You should get her tagged like a spotty-faced teenager with an ASBO. How do you explain to the bloody PM that your wife couldn't be bothered to attend a Downing Street bash? No point in having a woman if you can't rely on them to do what you want. You need to knock some sense into her.'

He and Saul had just arrived at Saul's house, hoping to find Lauren, but instead they'd found complete darkness. It was the first time Saul had been home in days.

Flicking on the hallway lights and wandering into the kitchen, an aggravated Saul was quick to snap back. 'That would explain why your own wife left you sad and lonely, Nathan. And coming from someone who likes women to lead him around on a lead like some kind of circus animal, you'll forgive me if I don't take your advice when it comes to the ways of matrimonial domesticity.' Saul was beginning to ever-so-slightly tire of Nathan's pig-headed ways.

'It was a bloody good night, though, Saul. You have to admit that. Mistress Kelly was looking wickedly wonderful and you seemed to be enjoying yourself.'

There was no denying it. The club night had been one of the best Saul had been to. Since Nathan had first invited him into his underground world a few months back, Saul had wallowed in the attention and feelings he experienced there. It was a place to take him away from the bureaucratic rifle range and the gravitas of government issues that he had to face day in, day out.

He'd been to half a dozen of the fetish events, both in London and across the country, always disguising himself in a full facial mask. It was like his secret superhero identity – the Batman to his Bruce Wayne or the Spiderman to his Peter Parker. He'd contemplated asking Lauren, but wasn't sure she'd understand his desire for 'play' with others. And anyway, Nathan has dismissed the idea of telling her as ridiculous. 'Any husband needs his secrets, Saul, and the loose-lipped bloodsucker would only kiss and tell if you ever ditched her.'

Saul needed obedience from his wife – at home, in the bedroom and on the occasions when his job demanded it. Like now … but she was nowhere to be seen.

Saul had been trying to ring Lauren all afternoon. Her phone had remained unanswered, switching to the messaging system every time. An important last-minute party had been called at 10 Downing Street for an impromptu visit from a European head of state and both Saul and 'his wife' had been invited. Unable to reach her by telephone, Saul, accompanied as ever by Nathan, had driven straight home to try and locate Lauren.

Turning on the kitchen lights, Saul's attention was immediately drawn to a folded sheet of paper on the table. It had his name written across it. He recognised it as Lauren's handwriting. Snatching it up, he unfolded it and read the contents as a snooping Nathan peered over his shoulder.

Dear Saul,

I've had to go away for a few days. I need to get my head together. I've been going a little bit crazy and something's come up that I need to do. Don't try and contact me because I won't respond. I love you but we need to speak,

*need to communicate a little more. I'm sorry. I've wanted
to speak to you for a while but you're always busy with
work and doing whatever Nathan wants you to do. It's
like there's three people in this marriage right now. Such
a cliché but it's true. I love you, I do, but I need to get a
few things sorted.*

Sorry again. I'll be in touch.

Lauren x

*PS: Don't worry about Barney – he's at the kennels. He
loves it there.*

Nathan couldn't help but comment, his voice becoming all told-
you-so. 'What the hell is all that bollocking claptrap supposed
to mean? You've married beneath you, sunshine. She's from bad
stock – a rotten maggot-infested apple. It was bound to happen.
And three people in the marriage? Doesn't she realise it's me
who's steered you in the right direction? Three people indeed –
how bloody Princess Diana!'

Smoking with rage, Saul screwed up the piece of paper and
threw it across the table. He turned to Nathan and grabbed him
by the neckline of his shirt, forcing him onto tiptoe. 'Just shut
it, will you, you ignorant fool!'

He was tempted to punch him but held back knowing that it
would be unwise. Attempting to calm his fire he pushed a flustered Nathan away and headed for the front door. 'Screw her.
Let her have her time away and we'll see what she's like when
she comes running back to me. Now, you and I have a party to
go to. Let's move it.'

Slamming the door behind them, Saul was steaming. Nobody dictated to Saul Everett, no one. What the fuck did Lauren
think she was playing at?

At that moment Lauren was strapping her seatbelt into place across her lap as she settled into her first class seat on a transatlantic flight. Dale was sitting alongside her. Despite still feeling incredibly rough and itching to take 'a trip to the bathroom', she was determined to remain as quiet and reserved as possible. She wanted Dale to know that she was grateful to be getting a second chance ...

Lauren could hardly remember any of her time at the Royal Albert Hall. She could remember her head spinning out of control in the cab on the way there and she vaguely remembered talking to Martha and Kelly and seeing Nancy. She had a tiny notion in the back of her mind that she'd seen Catherine Zeta Jones onstage and heard Portia Safari singing, but other than that the whole fiasco of an evening was still a blackout. She was glad, if the glowering face of Dale was anything to go by when they'd met the next day.

He'd dropped Lauren off at her house after the event and had put straight to bed. She'd woken up still in her Marchesa dress with a note alongside her telling her to ring him when she 'could string two words together and walk as opposed to wobble'. The tone of the note and the relentless pounding in her head told her that the previous evening had evidently been a messy one. She still blamed Saul. How could he be so dishonest with her? Trying to deal with the mounting pain in her cranium, Lauren had undressed, thrown herself under the power shower and phoned Dale. He was there within half an hour. She'd sheepishly opened the door to him, trying to gauge his mood.

'Dale, I am so sorry if I ballsed things up last night. I just needed to try and deal with a few things in my head ...' She tried to apologise.

Dale was quick to cut her off, obviously in no mood for chit-chat. 'And you decided to do it with enough alcohol to float HMS *Victory* and enough coke to empty Bolivia. Yeah, whatever, Lauren, it's forgotten. Now, you need to pack a couple of suitcases and grab your passport. You and I are taking a trip. I want you looking a million dollars and ready to go in an hour at the most. I need your outfits to be sparkly, metallic, loads of sequins – that kind of thing. Nice and young too. Nothing too fuddy-duddy. Pack what you can but if it's not right then we'll buy stuff when we get there. I'll be in the car – I need to sort out arrangements and make some phone calls.'

He'd turned his back on her and walked towards his car before Lauren could reply. She hadn't known what to expect but Dale's travel update was the last thing she'd forecast. Charging upstairs, a rush of excitement flowing over her, she momentarily forgot about the throbbing inside her skull and her heartache over Saul. Something intoxicating was about to happen and she wasn't going to let anything or anyone spoil it – whatever it was.

Forty minutes later she'd packed every outfit she'd deemed suitable into two suitcases and descended the stairs. She made a phone call to the kennels where Barney had spent the night and asked them if they could house him until further notice. There was no point relying on Saul coming home to look after the dog. He'd be somewhere with Nathan getting low down and dirty or trying to worm his way up the political ladder.

Lauren knew that wherever she was going, whatever Dale had planned, it was her time to shine. She went to the kitchen and wrote Saul a note. Grabbing her passport she headed out to Dale's car, dragging her cases behind her.

It wasn't until they were under way that Lauren had the courage to bring up the night before. 'It won't happen again,' she bleated. 'I won't touch another drop.'

Dale turned to her and smiled warmly. Whatever he was hiding was certainly good news. He placed his hand on her leg and squeezed her knee, causing her to flinch a little. 'Honey, if this all comes off, then I'll buy you enough champagne to keep a colony of Playboy bunnies up to their nipples in the stuff.'

Smirking at his good humour, Lauren replied, 'So, I guess I'm forgiven, but do you mind explaining to me what all of this is about? I've just left my husband a note saying I'm going away and that he shouldn't bother contacting me, and I'd like to know why.'

'Well, despite you nearly ruining everything last night something amazing has come out of it. When you were catching up on your sleep in that ludicrously expensive private box, I went back out to the bar to get myself a drink. I bumped into a guy that I used to know from the days when I first managed Nancy. He's a bit of an entrepreneur – likes to plough his cash into something if he feels it's going to be worth it. He's a bit of a wide boy but I like him. Imagine *Dragon's Den* meets second-hand-car-salesman and you get the idea. Well, he invested a bit of money into Nancy back in the day and it served him well. He asked what I was up to these days and I told him about you. I would have brought him to the box to see you but I figured an open-mouthed snoring vision wasn't exactly billboard material so I showed him a photo of you and played him your CD. When I told him the only thing we needed to make the package complete was a stylish video he offered to stump up the cash for a percentage of the profits from any record sales.'

Lauren could hardly comprehend what she was hearing.

'You're telling me this man is intending to give you money to help make a video for me?'

'There's no intending to about it, Lauren. The job is already done. He transferred the money over to Roma Records this morning. More than enough for accommodation, foreign film crew, location fees and two first class flights. The video for your first song for Roma Records will be in the can within days. It's the easiest deal I've done in ages,' enthused Dale.

'And I was snoring instead of schmoozing? Classy.' Lauren's head was ready to explode with information overload. She was amazed at how fast things were happening. Her mind blurred with the excitement of it all. See, what the hell did Nancy Arlow know? Dale had proved himself to be off the Richter scale when it came to management skills. She erased the image of Nancy in her mind. The other person she'd managed to involuntarily expunge from her thoughts was Saul. For the first time in days he wasn't at the forefront of her mind.

'So, where are we going?' she ventured.

Slipping on a pair of Giorgio Armani sunglasses, in Lauren's mind Dale had never looked more handsome as he replied, 'Well, my potential little pop star, we're off to the airport for a first class flight to Las Vegas.'

CHAPTER 38

The drive from London to The Abbey through the crisp summer vibrancy of the English countryside was one which Martha enjoyed immensely. The fields full of sunshine-yellow rape and the sweet-smelling stretches of greenery that whizzed past appealed to her inner love of nature. She feasted on the sight of kestrels hovering, seemingly motionless, above the fields, and the hundreds of rabbits that hopped gaily along the side of the road.

It was a part of the UK that she hadn't seen before and it reminded her of the beauty of her life back home in South Africa. It felt peaceful and provided her with a calmness and tranquillity – something that was at complete contrast to her life over the last few days.

Since meeting Kieran at the charity event, Martha had hardly stopped. From the moment she had woken up the following morning to the time that she finally tumbled into bed at the end of yet another sin-drenched night, her mind had been constantly fit to burst with lustful images of how incredibly spicy and sexual her life had become. Her need for sex was becoming an obsession and it was Tom, the life coach at The Abbey, who had made her realise that perhaps her habits were getting a little out of hand. Martha had not stopped having sex with a string of suitors for what seemed like days.

———

'Martha, there's no way I can go again. You've drained me dry. Besides, I need to get back to work. Enough's enough.' Tom's voice was riddled with more than a hint of annoyance as he pushed Martha's hand away from her attempts to stroke his wilted cock back into life. They were lying on her bed at her Soho flat. 'We've been at it for hours. You're amazing but I can't take any more today.'

It was true, they had. When Tom had rung her at the apartment – she'd still not bothered to replace her mobile – to announce that he wasn't due at work until that evening, Martha had leapt at the chance of enjoying a bit of one-on-one with the well-hung life coach. He had walked into the flat to be greeted by an already-naked Martha, who had stripped him bare and guided his manhood into her within seconds. Their love-making was forceful and animalistic but having achieved two orgasms already, the muscular Tom was ready to call time.

As he rose off the bed and started to pull his jeans back on, Martha snapped, angry at his refusal to satisfy her yet another time. 'Surely you can manage to screw me again. I thought you were supposed to have the stamina of a lion. They can mate up to a hundred times a day if the mood takes them.'

Pulling his T-shirt over his head and down across his washboard stomach, Tom was not about to be slated. 'My stamina is as good as the next man, Martha, but I do have a job to do. I have clients at The Abbey tonight and I can't let them down, despite your needs.'

Disappointed by his resistance, Martha knew that she couldn't tempt his back into her bed. But if Tom was going to turn her down, then she wanted him to know that there were indeed plenty of other willing partners that she could choose from to satisfy her desires. 'I'll have to get one of the other men in my life to satisfy me then, won't I? Maybe some of those guys we met dogging might like a rerun, or there's always the man I met when I was out with Kelly ... he had real stamina. He came round this morning and was one of my most relentless lovers ever. He just kept going and going, ready to appease my every need. I knew he would be when I met him. He was a *real* man.' She emphasised the word to again try and prick at Tom's masculinity.

For all of her bravado and bragging, Martha wasn't lying. She had spent the morning in the arms of, and pinned to a hotel bed by, Kieran Bradford. When she'd woken up early in a ball of sexual frustration that morning, her first thoughts had been about the stranger who had skilfully made love to her at the Royal Albert Hall and left his number on her thigh. She'd written it down in her little black book before washing it off. A phone call to an apparently delighted Kieran had resulted in them meeting at his hotel room by mid-morning. They had made love on the bed, up against the wardrobe and underneath the jets of the power shower, choosing to indulge in the language of the flesh rather than dwell on any kind of conversation.

It was something Kieran was grateful for. Martha's phoning him proved that some kind of connection had been made between them, but the last thing he wished to do was have to fend off any awkward questions about his background. That was why he chose to book a hotel room for their rendezvous instead of meeting at his riverside flat. There were too many family snapshots of life-back-home lying around that would give the game away.

The one thing that Kieran hadn't planned for in his pursuit of Martha was the fact that he seemed to be harbouring what felt like genuine attraction and desires towards her. But how could he mix that with the fact that he was chasing after her on his own dad's instructions? It was not yet the time to fess up.

Martha had just had time to take a taxi back to her apartment after her rendezvous with Kieran to get changed and then head across London. She asked the driver of her cab to wait outside her flat as she raced inside to change. It was an outfit she had asked Kelly if she could borrow especially for the occasion: a latex maid's costume teamed with a sexy pair of black suspenders from her own collection and a pair of four-inch patent ankle boots overlaid in satin and lace. The overall effect was of some fervid menial from a backstreet bordello who was obviously keen to supply her master with a lot more than just a flick of light dusting.

Having slicked on a thick layer of devil-red lipstick, Martha checked her appearance in the mirror and wrapped herself in a lightweight knee-length coat she'd bought. It was not coat weather, thanks to the balminess of the summer day outside, but the last thing Martha wanted was some lecherous cab driver questioning her on why she was dressed so provocatively.

The object of Martha's lustings for the next ninety minutes – and that was all it would be, she'd been informed of that when he'd phoned – was to be another man that had been on her mind ever since their first meeting. There was something about him that had ignited her senses. They had flirted, they had played, and they had swapped numbers with a covert and almost cryptic manner. This man was an enigma. She had never seen his face, but she knew that his body was one of the finest she had ever seen. She knew that he was a man who knew exactly what he wanted.

His words to her as he'd asked for her telephone number had made that clear. 'I'd like to ring you to play again. We could get together.' It was not a question, but more of an order. Martha had willingly given him her name and telephone number. When he'd phoned and left a message late the night before it was clear and concise. 'Message for Martha. It's the man from the club.

I'll be at this address tomorrow at one p.m. for ninety minutes, no more. I'd like you there if you want me to serve you. I'd like that. Dress accordingly.' He left the address and rang off.

When Martha had listened to the message, the sound of the man's voice and his authoritative ways had tweaked at every nerve ending in her pussy. She knew she'd be there to meet him again. There was a mysterious sexuality about the stranger that set him apart from men she'd met before.

When she arrived at the address, she was surprised to see that it was a rather fairytale-style wooden cottage situated in a secluded private garden on the outskirts of London. She paid the cab driver and knocked on the cottage door. To her surprise it was opened by Nathan Spilsbury. She decided not to mention about Lauren's reaction to him and merely uttered a timid 'hello'.

'He's expecting you and is most glad you've come. He is keen to please. Will you come in?' replied Nathan. He pulled open the door and beckoned Martha inside. It was only once she was inside that Nathan made to leave. 'I'll be back in ninety minutes,' he said and pulled the door shut leaving Martha alone in the dimly lit cottage.

Her eyes started to adapt to the candlelight that flickered around the cottage and she realised that she wasn't alone. The masked figure of Saul, naked from the waist up, was kneeling on the floor in the middle of the room, his hands behind his back and head tipped forward. It reminded Martha of photos she'd seen in films where criminals are about to face Madame la Guillotine. Lifting his head, Saul looked directly at Martha through the peepholes of the leather mask and spoke. It was just one line, but it said volumes. 'I am ready, mistress'.

Slipping her coat off and letting it fall to the ground, the penny suddenly dropped in Martha's mind. It was clear that

Saul wanted her to dominate him and looking around the room it became clear that there was an abundance of ways she could achieve his desires. Attached to the ceiling was a vast array of hooks and clips, many of them attached by ropes or heavy chains and a criss-cross pulley system. It didn't take an expert to work out that they would be strong enough to hold the weight of a person and suspend them as required. There were shelves and racks packed with equipment ready to be used. It was like a Santa's Grotto for an open-minded adult's deepest erotic fantasies. Whips, masks, hoods, paddles, floggers, gags – they were all proudly on display, ready for use. A huge throne dominated one corner of the room.

This was a new world for Martha, one in which she was happy to walk. As she picked up a small multi-tailed whip from the shelves and marched towards the ever-obedient Saul, a strong surge of sexual rapture undulated through her body. She wasn't just happy to walk into this world, from now on she was going to march into it in the sexiest and kinkiest pair of heels she could find.

'Right then, it's time to play …' she purred. 'Let's begin …' She only stopped ninety minutes later when Nathan came back and knocked on the door to tell her he'd arranged a cab to take her wherever she liked. It was as she sank into the back seat and gave her home address to the driver that she realised just how horny she still felt. That's why she'd been so pleased when Tom had called.

———

Tom had listened to Martha's detailed account of her sexual activities over the last twenty-four hours with his mind swinging between admiration and incredulity. He was not a man egotistical enough to become concerned over the number of sexual partners any of his conquests experienced while he was servicing them, but even he had never met a girl like Martha before.

'You need help. You're a sex-addict, or at least a severe nymphomaniac. Can't you ever give it a rest? If a man like me can't keep up with you then you're in trouble!' He was only half joking. 'What are your plans for tonight?' he asked enquiringly.

'Who knows … there are so many men out there. Maybe I'll visit Kelly's club.'

'See … it's not exactly a night curled up on the sofa watching some chick-flick with a box of chocolates and a bottle of wine, is it? It's all about sex with you – does your brain ever switch off? Or, more to the point, does that?' He pointed to her pussy. 'I bet you if you came to The Abbey and saw the doc, he'd say you can't survive without sex.'

Martha had to admit that sex had always formed a huge part of her adult life, but even for her the amount of sex she'd had since arriving in the UK had been both colossal and colourful. But she wasn't an addict – was she? Tom's words to her had laid down a gauntlet that she couldn't resist. She was just about to accept his challenge when he spoke again.

'Dr Fielding's a brilliant doctor, he's treated everyone. He's working with that opera woman at the moment – the one whose voice went crazy at that charity event. Apparently she's in there to try and stop drinking. I'm not supposed to talk about it but it's not like you know the old lush.'

As Tom blew her a kiss, checked his watch and darted from the room, Martha lay back on the sheets of her bed. They still smelt of sex. She let her mind wander. *So, Portia's at The Abbey? Maybe I should go and see Dr Fielding. It might be nice to see the place if nothing else, and I can catch up with Portia at the same time.*

CHAPTER 39

Retail therapy was item number one on Nancy's agenda as she finished unpacking her cases in her Bellagio suite. Her head had been lit up like the Las Vegas strip on the flight over and she needed to take her mind off some of the deeply worrying thoughts that kept entering her brain.

She still felt incredibly bad about having stolen the jewellery from Betsy, so much so that she hadn't actually been able to bring herself to sell them. And what if Betsy realised and involved the police? For all Nancy knew every London jeweller from Tooting to Tottenham may already have photos of the stolen items waiting for the hapless thief to come strolling in.

The truth was that Betsy hadn't even noticed that some of her prized diamonds were missing, but Nancy, full of fear and shame, had buried her stolen stash at the bottom of her underwear drawer and headed for the airport. It wasn't like she needed the money just yet – she still had Lauren's six-figure sum to play with. That was the other notion that kept pinballing around her mind as she traversed the Atlantic. What would happen if Vegas didn't pay out as expected? Even with her glass-half-full mentality, Nancy knew that the odds were not necessarily in her favour.

But as she flounced into the illustrious shopping heaven of Via Bellagio any ideas of self-loathing or self-doubt drifted away like tumbleweed across the Nevada desert. With money in her handbag and some of the biggest fashion names on the planet at her disposal, Nancy was ready to shop to an excess that would put the flashiest of WAGs to shame. 'Let's face it, it's been ages since I had money to burn,' she cooed as she headed through the mall.

It was true. Growing up in the dingy, grimy world of inner-city London, Nancy's shopping trips had revolved around cheap clothes stores and charity shops, customising second-hand items to try and make the most of the little money she could scrape together. Even when she'd found success as a singer and actress and had enough money to allow her to relocate her family to the leafy countryside of middle-England and finally kit herself out in the designer names she'd always read about, more often than not she would never get the time to really appreciate the opportunities given to her. And since her fall from *Eton Shore* and her descent into straight-to-DVD hell, her shopping trips had become more and more penny-pinching again.

As she gazed around the luxurious setting of the Via Bellagio and almost drooled at the lavish list of world-famous names, she intended to make the most of each and every one. Hermès, YSL, Gucci, Chanel, Dior, Prada, Tiffany & Co – these weren't names that every Vegas traveller could afford to shop in with ease. But while Nancy could, she intended to do just that.

Walking into Prada, one of the shop assistants eyed her politely and sidled alongside her. 'Can I help you, madam?'

As someone born to shop, Nancy's heart raced. 'You bet you can. I want outfits so sexy and jewellery so blinging they make Jennifer Lopez look like Susan Boyle. And money is no object ...'

———

Just as Nancy was considering the first in a long line of designer dresses the complaisant Prada assistant was parading in front of her, Lauren was pulling her own designer creations from her suitcases in her hotel room under the watchful eye of Dale. As she placed each of them on the kingsize bed in front of her Dale would give either a 'yes' or a 'no'.

They had been in Vegas less than three hours and already he had been a typhoon of activity. He had checked them into two over-the-top rooms at the MGM Grand. He'd also made contact and met with the producer of the film crew he'd picked to use in Vegas to shoot Lauren's video. According to him, the camera ops, director, location manager, hair, make-up and a rough storyboard of how the video would look were all ready to go. Now all that was needed was the right outfit for Lauren to wear and that was something that Dale himself had chosen to decide as part of his managerial duty. And he wanted to do it as soon as possible. There was no stopping him.

Lauren herself was beginning to flag. She was desperate for a line of coke to pick herself up but Dale had made her leave any that she had in his car at the airport instructing her that 'getting done at customs is not the way to start a potential singing career'. She'd obediently, if begrudgingly, left it in his glove compartment.

As the case lay empty and two piles of dresses – one 'yes', one 'no' – lay on the bed, Dale, remarkably awake considering the potential of jet lag, started to sift through the 'yes' pile.

'We start shooting the day after tomorrow. We'll be shooting along the strip and also out in the desert. I want at least three outfits. One needs to be long and flowing for some dramatic, sweeping shots in the desert. A wind machine blowing onto you with a trail of material billowing out behind you. I want you to look more scorching than the fucking landscape, baby. Then for the scenes filmed on the strip we'll be shooting at night when everything is lit up like bonfire night and I want you in two different metallic outfits. Something shiny to reflect the Vegas lights around you. When people see this video I want you to look like you're wrapped in a fucking diamond.'

As he spoke, he paced up and down the room, holding his hands together as if in prayer and tapping them on his bottom lip. Lauren couldn't help but feel that he was in his true element; organising something that could potentially make him – and her – a hefty wedge of money. There was a power and insider knowledge to the way he spoke. 'We're in good hands with this crew. They've just finished working with Taylor Swift so they know what I want with you. Innocence, yet a sexiness that makes you appeal to all. If we make you slutty then girls will hate you but we need to make sure that the guys are beating off to your video as well so we need to ramp up the sex appeal a bit too. It's a thin line, but we can do it with you.'

All of a sudden, Lauren found herself rocked by Dale's words. Yet again she found herself in a position that she wasn't ever expecting. What if she couldn't deliver? And, moreover, what the hell was she thinking? She'd run out on her husband to go and make a music video and he still didn't have the first clue about it. A jolt of nausea streaked through her brain and she sat herself down on the side of the bed.

'I can't do this, Dale. It's all wrong. Not until I tell Saul what I'm doing. Now that someone has invested in me word is bound to get out and it could ruin our relationship. He is still my husband, after all. I owe him that.' Lauren's mind raced into top gear with the issues that she still needed to address: *he owes me an explanation for what he was doing at that club, what he was doing with Martha, why he was playing with fire and why he was risking his own career. How could he criticise me if he's already hiding something from me?* 'At least if I tell him what's going on then I can hold my head high and say I've been honest to him.

That way he knows how I feel, what I want from my life. Why I want to do this.'

Dale stopped pacing and positioned himself alongside Lauren on the bed. He took her hand and smiled. 'I understand what you're saying – you're bound to be nervous, but wouldn't it be better telling Saul when you've got something concrete to show him? This video completes the package. You can show him what I'll be presenting to the world when it's all ready to go. The only people who really know about this so far are us two and a couple of industry players. You were too blitzed at the Albert Hall to meet anyone which, in hindsight, could actually be a blessing. The very few people who know can be silenced easily enough. We can get this video shot and edited. The end result will be a sure-fire hit to knock the pompous socks off even *your* priggish husband. By the time I start selling you to the press and the music channels I swear he'll have been in the loop for a long time. He'll be using you to sing his party political broadcasts.'

Priggish? If you only knew, thought Lauren. But she knew Dale was correct. If she told Saul now he would erupt with fury, demand she fly home and all the investment money would be wasted. Plus she wouldn't be able to stop herself from telling him about her discovery of his sordid little secret and that would lead to more upset. No, she was in Las Vegas, she was here to make the all-important video for what would hopefully be her first single. It was more than she ever dreamt of and she would be stupid to look a gift horse in the mouth and ruin everything because of her feelings for Saul – whatever they were any more.

'You're right, Dale. You believe in me. That's all I need. And like you say, not that many people have a clue what we're up to as yet. Although you did forget one – Nancy. She knows that you're working with me, doesn't she?'

'You do not need to worry about Nancy Arlow,' laughed Dale. 'She'll be sat at home in her flat with the blinds drawn watching *Devious Maids* or *Honey*-fucking-*Boo Boo*. It's got fuck all to do with her – what does she know?'

A mesh of worry flashed through Lauren's head. *But she does know you've signed me. She saw the contract and knows there's something between us. She's had £100,000 of my money and told me not to tell you. What if she wants more for her silence? Nancy is as sharp and as poisonous as a dart from a blowpipe.*

She chose not to tell Dale what she was thinking but consternation was obviously written all over her face as her head hung down.

Lifting Lauren's chin and stroking her hair away from her face, Dale gazed longingly at her. 'You look tired, Lauren. The jet lag must be kicking in. Care for a pick-me-up? You're not filming for another thirty-six hours so I reckon we can let our hair down a bit, don't you?'

'I feel in dire need of sleep. It's been a mad few days,' sighed Lauren.

'Not yet you don't. I have plans for you. How about some of this?' Dale reached into his pocket and pulled out one of the fattest bags of coke that Lauren had ever seen. 'One line or two?'

Lauren's jaw fell open. 'How the hell did you get that through customs? You made me leave my bag in your car and it was nowhere near the size of that. It couldn't have been in your case – you wouldn't have been that daft. Unless you hid it on your body.' Lauren began to laugh, a giggle at first and then a raucous belly laugh as an image gripped her thoughts. 'Oh my God, you didn't it smuggle it in up your ... up your ...' She pointed her finger downwards to Dale's backside.

'No I didn't!' exclaimed Dale, wincing at the thought. 'I got it off the guy in charge of the film crew. He said he'd sort me out and I kind of figured that you would want a top-up when we got here. So, shall I rack out a line, then?'

Lauren didn't need to reply, her smile said it all. 'I guess I'll wait until later for some beauty sleep then.' She began to roll up the fifty dollar note that Dale had given her, ready to snort the coke.

'Good, because we need to sort out your clothes.' Dale finished separating two fat lines of coke on the bedside table and waggled the credit card he'd used to do it in Lauren's face. 'And I know the best place to shop in Vegas, so get snorting and let's go spend some of our backer's money.'

CHAPTER 40

'At this precise moment I'd contemplate impaling Snow White on a sharp stick for a bottle of vodka, Dr Fielding, and happily watch her squirm to death as I get merrily tanked. Does that tell you how much I'd like a drink right now?'

Portia was in one of her moods. A mood that takes no prisoners as her raised voice testified. Since checking herself in to The Abbey the day before she had been alcohol-free and the burning need for a drink was beginning to weigh heavier than a juggernaut. And even though he was considered to be one of the best in his field, the structured and pseudo-understanding questioning of Bruno Fielding was definitely rubbing her up the wrong way.

'I suggest you don't speak louder than is necessary, Ms Safari. Your voice is damaged enough as it is and will need time to rectify itself. I understand from speaking to your consultant in Harley Street that the damage is not too extensive, but becoming upset about a lack of alcohol when that has more than likely contributed to the problem is not exactly wise, you understand.'

Dr Fielding's tone reminded Portia of her days at the Royal College of Music when a tutor would reprimand you for hitting a bum note. Portia had never been a lover of an authoritative intonation unless, of course, it was her own.

Her irritation mounting, Portia was quick to bite back. 'What I understand, Dr Fielding, is that if most people asked themselves why they drank, they probably wouldn't have an answer, but I am not most people. I know why I drink. It makes me forget how lonely my life has become. If I have a drink it helps me convince myself that I'm having the time of my life. The odd tipple takes me out of my own head and makes me forget. I search for my necessary dose of love out of a bottle because it's much more reliable than having to depend on men. You should know what spineless, parsimonious pricks they can be – you are one, after all!'

'A prick, a man or both of the above?' Dr Fielding couldn't resist volleying Portia's comment right back at her. 'But from what Duncan has told me about you, and what I've read in the newspapers, I understand that you may have a new suitor who you think could be more than capable of making you happy – Piero Romeo.'

Just the mention of his name brought a smile to her face. Piero had been phoning Portia constantly since her admission into The Abbey. As far as he was concerned, Portia was in there for a little body work, something which he deemed completely unnecessary. They had talked for hours. Well, Piero had talked. He had insisted that Portia merely whisper to relax her voice. At the end of his last conversation with her he had promised that he would visit her as soon as he could. Portia prayed that it wouldn't be too long, as she was aching for his touch. If he could bring a bottle of 150 proof with him as well then he would be the picture of total perfection. But she knew that wouldn't happen.

'I can only share knowledge with you, Ms Safari,' continued the doctor. 'Everyone has their own path in life and I can't choose yours for you, but I can give you guidance. I'm not a preacher, I'm a clinical psychologist and I will share any experience and advice with you that I can. But I must say one thing to you now: you can have enough fake-enthusiasm to fill the largest opera house on earth but you will never get clean away from the alcohol unless you genuinely want to. I say the same to all of my clients who succumb to an addiction. *You're* the only person who can really help *you*. Only *you*, Ms Safari, will be able to really make a difference. Do I make myself clear?'

'Perfectly, Dr Fielding. You're right, there is someone I've met who I do believe could be pivotal in my life. I am buoyant, and hopeful, shall we say, that we may be able to … make a go of things.'

'So, do it for him as well as yourself, Ms Safari. How do you think he'd feel knowing that you have to sneak off for a crafty squirt of alcohol in the bedroom or that your bathroom cabinet doubles up as a minibar?'

Portia didn't think that Piero would exactly be thrilled, especially given that a top class diva was expected to treat her voice like gold dust. 'I see your point, so how do I stop myself? And for God's sake will you stop calling me Ms Safari, it makes me feel like some wrinkled old aunt. I'm thirty-six, not eighty-six. My name is Portia. If I'm to listen to you then please call me by my first name!'

'OK, I'll tell you how I see things right now, Ms— er, Portia. But if we're making things informal then please call me Bruno. It's only fair.'

For the next forty-five minutes Portia listened as intently as she could to what Bruno was saying. By the end of her first session with him, she walked away feeling that maybe, just maybe, he could hold the key to stopping her secret drinking, and if he could do that, then maybe he could hold the key to her future happiness with Piero. She didn't want anything to spoil that, especially her own actions. And if that meant going without a drink, despite her longing for one, then she would try and do everything the doctor had said.

She left his office having taken quite a liking to Bruno Fielding. She'd rarely met a more challenging yet deeply charismatic
man. Or one that was as strikingly handsome. *Not a patch on my
Piero*, she thought as she headed back to her private room, *but
deeply attractive nevertheless*. It was obviously a trait of the men
at The Abbey.

———

Or so she thought. As she entered the room where she was to
meet her dietician for the first time an hour later, any notions of
the men at The Abbey all being cut from the same classic cloth
popped quicker than a balloon speared by the largest of knitting
needles.

The man, in his late twenties or early thirties – it was hard to
tell – was wearing a running vest stained with patches of sweat
across the front and a pair of the most ill-fitting tracksuit trousers
that Portia had ever seen. His body was obviously in good shape
– she was hardly expecting to be taught the whys and wherefores
of food intake from someone who resembled Homer Simpson
– but his face was at best quirky, at worst downright weasely.
As someone who liked her men to be broad and masculine and
rugged, the man standing before Portia was the complete antithesis. His shiny face was pockmarked, a hangover from adolescent
acne, no doubt, and his cheeks seemed to sink into his face as if
unsupported. His lips were thin and a patchy attempt at a goatee
beard circumnavigated his mouth. His dark hair was thinning
greatly, the top of his head virtually bald. The hair that still survived was grown longer at the sides to compensate and tied in a
ponytail which sprouted pathetically from the back of his head.

God, he must be good, despite appearances, thought Portia
wickedly as she stood before him. *Duncan did employ him, after
all, and he only takes the best.*

The man stretched out a hand to Portia, but not before wiping it down his trouser leg first. 'Hi, sorry I'm a bit sweaty. I've been out for a run in the grounds. Getting your body tip-top is all about exercise as well as the food you put into it. I'm Ed, by the way. Nice to meet you, please sit down.'

Portia took his hand and shook it. She may as well have been asked to handle a poisonous tarantula for all of the enthusiasm she showed. Wiping her palm as covertly as she could on the back of the chair, she sat down. As she did so a pungent aroma of sweat filled her nostrils. She wrinkled her nose automatically, unable to hide her dislike.

'Oh, sorry, do I stink a bit. It was quite a run. Let me slip into another T-shirt and hopefully it won't be so bad.' Before Portia could say anything, Ed slipped his vest off over his head and grabbed a towel from the corner of the office to wipe himself down. Portia had to admit that his body looked amazing. There wasn't an ounce of surplus fat anywhere to be seen and his physique was toned without being bulky. More jockey, less stocky. His chest was well-rounded and the definition from his abs was the kind that most gym-going males could only dream of. It looked like his bespoke body had been custom-made to be the perfect size to advertise his muscles to perfection. *At least he's model material from the neck down*, mused Portia, still drinking in the sinewy supremacy of his body as he pulled a clean T-shirt over his head.

'That's better,' he grinned, before seating himself opposite Portia. 'So, I'm told you're unhappy with your body shape and want to trim down a little. I can't exactly see what the issue is from the outfit you're wearing but we'll get you what you want, don't you worry.' Maybe the voluminous silk blouse and baggy linen trousers she'd chosen weren't exactly the most appropriate given the nature of the appointment. 'So, let's get you undressed and see what's going on. If you'd like to go behind that screen and strip down to your bra and knickers and I'll come and take a look.'

The next ten minutes were among the most excruciating Portia had ever experienced. Standing in front of the dietician in nothing but the skimpiest of lacy bra and panties was one of the most awkward things that she had ever done. For such a sexual ensemble it was a highly un-sexual situation, especially when Ed studied his way around Portia's curves as if he were examining the instruction manual on a faulty tumble dryer. He gave her his honest opinion. 'Your body is in phenomenal shape. Everything is in proportion and there's no way I would recommend any kind of bodywork at all. Your curves are beautifully feminine. I think I'd be wasting your time.'

That was the last thing that Portia wanted to hear. She could feel her anger rising inside her. If she wasn't happy with her body then she wanted results and she wanted them fast. 'Well, I don't pay *you* a huge amount of money to hear *your* recommendations, do I? I pay you to do what *I* want. I want my body to look sleek and slender. I will not head towards forty with the onslaught of bingo wings, saddlebags, double chins and a jelly belly. I want you to sort them all out by whatever means possible to stop me from wobbling around onstage like Mama Cass. You're supposedly one of the best in the business so I suggest you prove it. And whatever I have done, I want it to look natural. So, you do whatever it takes to make this body at least ten years younger. Portia Safari does not do womanly curves. Womanly curves are called "fat" in the media, and I will not go through that again. I will do anything to avoid that ... anything!'

Ed had heard it all before. There was hardly a week that went by at The Abbey without some celebrity moaning about how their body was 'out of control' or 'simply ballooning' when it fact they were in near-perfect shape. He'd dealt with them all and their diva tantrums. The paying customer was always right and always willing to pay for something a little extra. As he watched Portia dress herself again he knew that he would be able to appease her.

'OK, so maybe there is the odd issue that we could address,' he lied. 'I can draw up an eating plan and some light exercise work. If you follow my expert guidance and do exactly as I say then I think we could be seeing a dramatic change in your body shape in a short space of time. Some of my measures may seem a little ... unorthodox ... and I may be straying from the path of what my bosses always want, but you did say you'd do anything to regain the perfect figure. There are always options, it just depends how far you're prepared to go.'

There was a layer of mystery and cunning in Ed's voice that made Portia think, for the first time, that maybe they would be able to work well together. 'My public and my lover want to see me at my best. I trust you will find the most effective way to ensure that. I want results and I want them quickly. I will do whatever it takes and whatever you recommend at whatever the cost. And don't worry about your bosses. I trust that whatever method you decide will be strictly between us.'

A light switched on inside Ed's brain. 'Leave it with me. I'll look at the options ... all of them ... before our next meeting. You have my word that you'll be leaving The Abbey in perfect condition.'

As Portia left his office, Ed formed a gun shape with his fingers, aimed it at her back and softly mouthed the sound of fire. *Like a lamb to the financial slaughter. Another talent vacuum of a celebrity willing to cough up for a quick fix.* Working at The Abbey was proving to be the easiest money that Edward Collie had ever earned and he was sure that Portia Safari could be his next easy-to-milk cash cow.

CHAPTER 41

Men have always been slaves to their emotions. Whether good or bad, a man and his affectations will always try to deal with whatever situation life throws at him in the best way possible. Sometimes the strongest of men will become weak with love, or the frailest of men will somehow rise to the strength-testing challenge placed before him.

As Vincent Van Gogh said about the male species: 'Let's not forget that the little emotions are the great captains of our lives and we obey them without realising it.' Captains that steer the ship of an individual's life into all sorts of raging and tempestuous seas.

———

Lewin Éclair felt weaker than he had ever done in his life, but if his heart attack had done anything it had made him strong about one thing. He no longer wanted Adina King in his life. From the moment that his ex-wife Mariella had stood by his bed and called him the *love of her life* he had known what a fool he'd been letting her go in the first place. She was the mother of his child and despite her seeming devotion to his rival, he knew her well enough to know that there was a hint of sadness in her eyes at the way things had worked out between them. As Lewin lay in his hospital bed he didn't know what his future held as far as Mariella was concerned, but he knew that his relationship with

Adina was now scraping the bottom of the trash can. He needed to bin it once and for all.

But then Adina had announced that she was pregnant with his baby. For a split second it had turned his world and his heart upside down. A baby at his time of life was not on the menu. But as he looked into Adina's animated face as she broke her news Lewin had seen right through to her soul. It was cold, calculating and deceitful. Her eyes flickered with self-doubt and there was more than a hint of desperation sketched there. Lewin was convinced that she was lying, but he needed to be sure.

When his doctor arrived in response to Lewin pressing his panic button, his patient had two jobs for him. One was to calm Lewin's heart from the current heightened outburst it was experiencing, but the other was much more important in putting both his heart and his mind at rest. If Adina was trying to deceive him then he needed to prove it as soon as possible. He'd informed the doctor, an Éclair family friend for many years, about her news. As he did so, Adina chewed nervously on her bottom lip and attempted a smile.

'I'd like a full examination of Ms King right now, here in the hospital. I want to check that my child is in good health,' Lewin instructed.

A flustered Adina suddenly went into overdrive, gushing with excuses. 'No, it's fine, there's no need. My own doctor has checked everything perfectly. The baby is in the best of health. It comes from perfect genes, after all.' She tried to hold Lewin's hand as she protested, but he shoved it away.

Lewin's voice was stern. 'Adina, my doctor checks you here and now or else we're through. Finished for good. You don't want that, do you? A baby needs a father, a rich one who can give him everything he or she needs. What are you worried about?' There was an eerie calm on Lewin's face as he turned to the doctor again. 'If you could take Ms King to another room for a thorough examination, that would be much appreciated, doctor.'

Lewin was sure he could see tears falling down Adina's cheeks as she was escorted out of his ward by the doctor. He returned to Lewin alone five minutes later. 'She's gone, there is no baby,' he said, a knowing smile forming across his face.

'Did you examine her? Are you quite sure?'

'There was no need – we were just about to take her to be prepared when she blurted out that she was making it all up. Why do you get yourself involved with these women, Lewin? You were so much better off with Mariella. Mind you, Ms King seemed quite tearful, sad that she'd made up the baby story, to be honest. She ran out of the hospital as fast as her daft heels would allow.'

Vindicated and pleased with his swift actions, Lewin was sure that he'd seen the back of Adina for good. 'She'll be running off into the arms of some other rich bastard so I wouldn't feel too sorry for her, doc.'

He was right. Less than three days later there were stories in the South African press about her shacking up with a top male model and telling the world that she'd 'never been happier'.

———

Draining the last slug of brandy from his glass and placing it on the table in front of him, Saul was far from happy. The overly loud clash of the glass as it landed on the table caused those sitting around him to raise their inflated, red faces from behind their broadsheets and tut in his direction.

'Just fuck off, the lot of you,' Saul muttered under his breath. He was in no mood to be berated by the fellow members of the men-only London drinking club he was seated in. He'd come to try and arrange his thoughts into some semblance of order and so far it wasn't working. Ordering another brandy, he leant back in his leather armchair and tried to fathom the root of his problem.

Saul was a man who liked things done his way and in an order that suited him best. He'd always been the same. As a teenager he'd insisted on alphabetising his vinyl collection so that he knew exactly where to find a particular selection of songs; and at the end of every weekend he would spend hours in his boarding school dorm meticulously ironing and folding his garments for the entire week ahead. A crease out of place would mean starting again. Second best was never good enough for Saul and if things weren't organised into neat, orderly structures in his life then he found it unacceptable. And that included his emotions for those around him.

Lauren had always been someone he knew he could depend upon – the obedient wife looking after his castle, stunningly fabulous to look at, a willing partner to his sexual escapades in the bedroom and a model other-half in the pretentious world of politics. Although Saul had to admit that the last of those had required some severe remoulding at times.

But where was she now, when he needed her? She should have been with him at the prime minister's party. If he was to get anywhere in his advancement up the political ladder then he needed Lauren by his side. He expected it – and would demand it when he finally saw her again.

He'd tried ringing her but her mobile had remained unanswered. The tone of the ring suggested she was abroad. The thought of it made him madder. *How could she leave without even telling him where she was going?* He didn't even know which continent she was on, let alone what she was thinking. That was what irked Saul the most. Lauren was not fitting in with what he needed her to be and that was … well, almost unforgivable. She'd certainly have some explaining to do on her trek back to the UK. Especially now that she had competition.

That was the other thing that was chiselling its way across Saul's brain. Of all the women he'd 'played with' during his nights out with Nathan on the fetish scene, none of them had stirred any post-party lustings in him like Martha. Normally he would be able to forget their expertly corseted figures or latex-wrapped breasts as soon as he'd served them.

But from the moment he'd laid eyes on Martha's blonde beauty at the club he'd known that he'd wanted a repeat performance with her.

That's why he'd arranged to meet her again at the private cottage. Cleared space in his diary especially to be with her. There was something bewitching and mesmerising about a girl who looked so clean yet played so dirty. His body still ached from their time together. Maybe it was good that Lauren was away for a while. She wouldn't have to question the telltale bruises and veiny lacerations that streaked his body. He'd allowed Martha to take things further with him than he'd ever done with any other woman outside his marriage. They hadn't made love, but he suspected that they soon would. He wanted it, and Saul always allowed himself to have what he wanted.

Emptying his glass again and banging it loudly on the table once more, Saul ignored the repeated tuts and shushes from those around him. As he left the club he knew that his strictly organised life was changing. And maybe deep down Lauren wasn't the only one who wanted it to. Perhaps he did too.

CHAPTER 42

'Portia, darling, are you there?' Tapping softly on the wooden door to Portia's private room at The Abbey, Piero waited for the call of his lover to beckon him in. There was no reply.

The woman on reception had stated quite categorically that Portia was in her room after her meetings and that she was allowed visitors, so where was she? Placing his ear against the door, he was sure that he could hear something. He couldn't tell what but a gentle repetitious noise reached his ears. Unsure what to do, he turned the doorknob.

The door opened, allowing Piero to peer into the room. Portia lay fully-clothed in a foetal position on the bed. As she raised her face to look at him, Piero could see that huge rivers of tears flowed down her face. Her make-up was smudged and clumped into uneven patches across her skin. Recognising Piero through her waterlogged eyes, Portia let out a huge, desperate sob and buried her head into her pillow once more. Touched by how pitiful and vulnerable she looked, stripped of her strong imperious façade, Piero rushed to her side and sat on the bed alongside her.

Cupping her face in his hands, he lifted it off the pillow and stared deep into her eyes. Despite her obvious misery, she was still strikingly beautiful. In fact, he'd never seen a more exposed beauty in his life. It was as if he could read through to her very core.

Whatever the cause of her anguish, he knew that he wanted to be there for her. To make things better, not just for now, but for a lifetime. Before they'd even exchanged a word, it was at that moment that Piero knew he'd fallen in love with Portia. And falling in love was not something that a womaniser like Piero had ever planned.

Throughout his entire life Piero Romeo had never had any trouble tempting women into his bed. He'd seduced his private singing teacher at school, most of his mother's best friends, a list of co-stars that read like an operatic all-stars, and even a flurry of journalists from some of the world's top publications who had been sent to interview him. One lucky reporter had once knocked at his hotel suite for an interview and subsequently not filed her copy for the next forty-eight hours. Piero played women like puppets. He pulled the strings and females did exactly what he wanted. His behemoth-like masculinity lured women to him like insects into a Venus flytrap. At the age of thirty-five, he had more notches on his bedpost than he did bedpost. And he'd never fallen in love, it wasn't in his nature – until now.

'Il mio bell'angelo,' he growled softly. 'My angel, what is the matter? Why are you crying like this?' He leant down and kissed her on the lips, the taste of her tears splashed across them. He wrapped his arms around her and pulled her towards him. Portia remained silent, but from the way that she held onto him, her fingers drawing him urgently against her, Piero knew that the diva was happy to see him.

The two of them remained mute for a few minutes, both glad to share the warmth of the other's body. It was Portia who eventually spoke first. Her voice was faint. 'I feel so lonely and wretched, Piero. My voice might never be the same again and my body is not as it should be. I'm supposed to be a role-model and an inspiration to millions and I'm a wreck. Plain and simple. I have million-pound advertising contracts that will toss me aside quicker than day-old headlines. I'm yesterday's news.'

'How can you say that?' Piero stroked his fingers across her flame-red waves as he answered. 'You are the most beautiful woman I have ever met. Clever and witty, talented and strong.'

'But I've ruined it all. My talent will go. Without my voice I am nothing,' said Portia somewhat melodramatically. Despite her gushing sentimentality, she clearly believed what she was saying. 'My body needs work. I'm not as toned as I once was. That woman called me fat.' It was an obvious reference to Madeline Strong. 'She's right, I am.'

'You are perfect, my sweet. I know you are. But if you don't feel right about yourself then this place is going to put that right. That's why you came here. To get what you want.' Piero was keen to put a doubting Portia at ease. In his eyes she was indeed perfect, but he was wise enough to know never to argue with a woman about their appearance. The lady was always right.

'But I've realised it's all my fault, Piero. I've been so stupid. I'm the one who's destroying both my figure and my voice. It's all down to me ... you don't understand.'

It was true. He didn't, but as he listened to Portia spill out her explanations as to why she was in such a state he held her close, letting her know that she could share whatever she needed with him. He listened intently as she explained about her drinking, about the hidden stashes of alcohol and her daily cravings. He could feel her tears soaking through the material of his shirt as she spoke, her face pressed into him.

'But why do you do it, Portia?' he implored.

'Because I'm lonely. I have everything I want in my life but no one to share it with. Do you know how that feels?' Portia gazed upwards into Piero's eyes as she spoke. 'I hate being alone. Men hurt me and I'm fed up.' Her voice trailed off pitifully, her eyes resting directly on his. They were pooled with tears and once again as he stared into them Piero made a split decision.

'I'll make sure you'll never be alone again, Portia. This may not be the perfect location, but I don't care. You're perfect and that's all that matters.' He went down on bended knee alongside the bed. A thrilling wash of expectancy burst through Portia's tears as he did so. 'Will you, Portia Safari, make me the happiest man alive and marry me?' It was a question he had never imagined himself asking in a million years.

There was a tap on door. Portia opened it to see who was there. She could hardly believe her eyes when she realised it was Martha. The South African could see that she'd been crying. 'Oh my God, are you OK? I haven't come at a bad time, have I?' she questioned.

A radiant beam of joy spread across Portia's face. 'Just the opposite, Martha. Your timing couldn't be better. Piero's here. I'm getting married and you're the first to know. Would you do me the honour of being my bridesmaid?'

CHAPTER 43

Nancy's first night in Vegas has been, in a word, disastrous. Despite the wealth of advice from Betsy days before and feeling hotter than an enchilada in her brand new Prada dress, her attempt at trying to win big in the entertainment capital of the world had been as stony and as dry as the nearby Grand Canyon.

She'd spent the last few hours chancing her arm at the blackjack table of the Bellagio's Club Privé hoping that the elite exhilaration of the high-limit lounge would bring a permanent end to her financial woes. But despite looking the part, Nancy soon realised that she was out of her league trying to play against the professional gamblers and casino-savvy experts sharing the table with her. After two hours of attempting to score the elusive twenty-one with her given deck, she had heard herself say the word 'bust' more times than the editorial in a randy teenager's porn mag. Nancy's attempts to make Vegas win for her were the equivalent of expecting a lame donkey to win the Grand National. It just wasn't happening.

Realising that she'd already used up virtually three-quarters of the hundred grand she'd come to Las Vegas with in just one sitting, a dejected Nancy decided to head back to her suite. Tomorrow would be another day and hopefully the age-old expression of 'another day, another dollar' would prove itself correct. As long as the dollars had at least six figures.

Pressing the elevator button and watching the lift doors open in front of her, Nancy was just about to step in and retire for the night when a thought crossed her mind. Betsy's tales of the loose slot machines and their bigger chances of paying out echoed through her thoughts. They were supposed to dish out money – more than any other slot machines in Vegas. Hadn't she recommended some at the MGM? Nancy was sure that was the hotel she had mentioned. An urban myth from a dotty old woman? Perhaps … but perhaps not.

Maybe she could claw a little bit of her losses back after her catastrophe at the blackjack table. Unable to curb her desire to win, within two minutes she'd left the Bellagio, hailed a cab and headed to the MGM.

When it had first opened the MGM Grand Hotel had been declared the biggest in the world and nothing had quite prepared Nancy for the sheer enormity of it. As she surrounded herself by the constant sound of falling money and the dazzling flash of a million casino lights, Nancy felt as if she'd shrunk down to the size of a tiny Alice entering Wonderland.

Intoxicated by the excitement of her surroundings and the fact that she was drawing admiring glances from a group of four tuxedo-clad men nearby, Nancy sashayed over to them and flashed her best seductive smile. 'Hi, boys, care to help a lady?'

The men's voices tumbled over each other like rugby players in a scrum in an attempt to be the one to win her attention. She could tell from the drawl in their accents that they were probably from the deep south of America. 'Sure thing, pretty lady – always happy to help a damsel in distress.'

Nancy asked them where she could find some of the famed loose slots that she'd been hearing about. As one, they all pointed in the same direction across the casino. 'Straight through there, missy, all along that wall. Shall we join you to help slip your coins into the right slots? See if we can bring you some good old-fashioned southern style luck.' There was something remarkably seedy about the way he spoke, but at least Nancy knew that the group were telling the truth.

'That won't be necessary, fellas, but thanks all the same. I'm meeting my fiancé over there. He's a boxer. We're in town to hold talks about a fight with Manny Pacquiáo. He's the jealous type, if you know what I mean.' The four men had hurried off as soon as she'd said the word 'boxer'. Nancy laughed at their predictability as she watched them disappear. *God, it's like being chatted up by the Beverly Hillbillies*, she mused to herself. *Right, time for me to try and strike it rich.*

Making her way across the immense casino through a sea of hopeful tourists, Nancy headed to where the men had indicated. She was a few metres from her destination when something made her stop. Through the continual rhythmic beat of money and the sound of amusement that filled the air, two voices seemed to emerge through the din. They were laughing and joking wildly, seemingly louder than anyone else. At first Nancy thought that she was imagining it, but she tuned her ears into the voices and tried to work out which direction they were coming from.

Her mouth dropped as she spotted an excited Dale and Lauren playing one of the machines. A stream of coins clattered from it as Lauren scooped them into her plastic casino bucket. Immediately the vibrant air of the casino seemed to become stale and yellow around her.

Itching for a fight, Nancy was ready to march up to the couple, when she stopped herself. Dale was running one of his hands down the centre of Lauren's back, bringing it to rest on her pert derrière as she continued to rake out her winnings. There was no sign of the tumble of coins slowing down. Afraid that Dale and Lauren would spot her, Nancy ducked behind a machine and watched them in secret. It was obvious that they were both having a fabulous time, as if in celebration.

I wonder how much they've won, contemplated Nancy, a prickle of jealousy nipping at her skin. It was blatantly enough to cause jubilation. As Lauren finished ladling the money into the bucket she turned to hug Dale. It became more than just a hug as the two of them locked lips. For a few seconds, but for what seemed like an eternity to Nancy, she watched as her manager and the latest signing on the Roma books embraced each other. Their kiss was deep and full of passion. They had no sooner let their lips part from each other than they joined them together once more, as if unable to control their feelings.

'That bitch!' muttered Nancy. Seizing the moment she reached into her bag and grabbed her phone. Switching it to camera she pointed it in their direction and snapped as quickly as her fingers would allow. Checking the image, Nancy saw that it was a clear and damning picture of Lauren being more than just professional with Dale. It was a photo that she knew would come in useful.

It was to be the first of two that night. As Dale and Lauren linked arms and drifted across the casino to a row of elevators, Nancy followed them from a distance. Maybe losing at the Bellagio hadn't been such a bad thing after all. There were other avenues of fortune to follow.

CHAPTER 44

The desire for making a fast buck regardless of how dishonest it seemed was obviously something that flowed like a virus in many people.

Ed Collie had just finished printing out and photocopying a four-page document about a new wonder drug to help *people lose weight in the quickest and simplest way possible.* According to the bullet-points at the top of the first page there was *no need for a change of diet, no need for a severe exercise regime* and *no worry of your friends thinking that you've had invasive medical procedures as the results will be 100% natural.*

Scanning through the pages that he'd handed to her, Portia's eyes lit up as she looked at the claims and the before and after photos of stunning young women with firm, tight, model-material bodies.

'But there must be a catch, Ed. If it really is as good as it says here then surely it would be putting dieticians like you out of business. Everybody would be taking it.' Despite her reservations though, she loved what she saw on the pages.

'You told me you wanted fast results and these are the fastest on record. A hundred per cent success. And you'll want a super-quick impact now that you've got a special date in the diary. Nobody looks good waddling down the aisle like a globular meringue ball, do they?'

Ed winked at Portia as he spoke. She'd been ecstatic about Piero's proposal ever since he'd popped the question and if there was one day that she didn't want to look anything other than physical perfection it was on the day that she gave her heart to Piero.

She'd already ordered Redmond to leak a story to the press that the happy couple would soon be naming the day and venue. In true media style, the tabloids were already naming them *Portiero – Opera's hottest couple*.

'There is a *but* coming though, I presume,' probed the opera star. 'It's too easy. A couple of tablets twice a day and the weight drops off. There wouldn't be a woman on earth above a size zero if that was the case.'

'Which is why most of today's hot young stars are back-to-skinny two weeks after ballooning to their heaviest ever, Portia. How do you think Hollywood stars drop the baby weight so fast? They're not exactly fit enough to go back into the gym as soon as they cut the umbilical cord, are they? Everyone needs a little help and that's where the wonder drug comes in.'

'At a cost, no doubt,' speculated Portia.

Unseen by her, a bead of sweat formed on Ed's top lip as he began to explain. It was the moment that required him to go in for the kill. Do or die for his career. 'Well, that's the only thing about it. These drugs are not readily available. They're being kept secret for the privileged few – those who can afford the luxury of guaranteeing the results they require. I wouldn't recommend them to everyone and if you do decide to try them then it has to be just between you and I. If my boss finds out then I will deny everything. I mean it, Portia. This is not something that I would offer everybody. The supplier in this country only deals with a handful of people. I'm lucky that my kudos here at The Abbey makes me one of them.'

As a look of satisfactory devilment started to ooze across Portia's face, the dietician could see that his speech was having the desired effect. He had been sure that if Portia wanted to lose weight, then she would do whatever it took and whatever it cost to do so. Even if she didn't really need to in the first place.

Portia's response was clear and precise. 'I'm in. But if I don't see my figure changing into a slimline shape that would make an LA It-Girl green with envy then your ass will be disappearing from here quicker than a vampire in a field of garlic! So, how much will this cost me?'

Feisty, foolish and ready to flash the cash, reflected Ed. *This one is going to be easier than most to fleece.* Despite his mind racing with the thrill of a prospective cash avalanche, his face remained poker-straight as he answered. 'I can supply you with a month's course of tablets. It will take a few days to sort things out and I will need you to stick to the diet I prepare for you. But if you take the drug as instructed then you'll see the results. Let's just say you can order your wedding dress two sizes smaller than you are right now ... how does that sound?'

Portia raised her eyebrows in delight. 'Exquisite, young man. Now, let's talk money.'

Ed could feel his throat drying as he licked his lips and swallowed hard. *What could he get away with?* As his head whirled with a cycle of numbers, he looked directly into Portia's eyes. He could sense a band of deep yearning within them. The number in his head doubled. Something told him he could afford to run the risk. 'Fifty thousand.'

Without even flinching, Portia folded the printouts, placed them in her bag and stood up. 'Very well, you shall have the money in a few days. I shall stay at The Abbey until you secure me the ... *medication* ... and then I shall be on my way.'

'One other thing, Portia. Try to cut down on the alcohol. These drugs will work, but too much alcohol could affect them and I know from your case notes that Dr Fielding is seeing you for a minor addiction. It wouldn't be wise to scupper your chances of the perfect figure with an excess of liquor.'

Portia stopped in the doorway as she made to leave Ed's office. 'I intend to make my wedding the most fairytale affair since Grace Kelly married Prince Rainier, and despite my liking for a drink, young man, the thought of gliding down the aisle with a figure like a winner from *The Face* is possibly the best incentive to try and keep me sober. My weakness for a glass of decent fizz will be outweighed greatly by my strong desire to give my fiancé the most physically perfect body I can on my wedding night. So I suggest you make some phone calls and procure these drugs as soon as possible. Now, if you'll excuse me, I have a wedding to plan.'

Shutting the door behind her, Ed was left alone. There was something he liked about Portia. Which was why he'd told her to stay off the alcohol. It was all complete lies. It wouldn't affect the drugs at all, in his opinion. But surely he could do one good thing for her. If his words could help her ditch that particular demon then he wouldn't feel so bad about ripping her off to the tune of £50,000. It was his best result yet.

Fifty grand would be the price that would give Portia peace of mind that her already proportionally perfect body would be sinfully perfect for her husband-to-be. It was also the price that would contribute very nicely thank you to whatever status symbol Ed Collie chose to buy – maybe a new car or an exotic holiday. Why should other members of his family always have all the glamour? He was just as worthy of it as any of them.

Slipping his tracksuit on, Ed thought about his lucrative day's work. Poor Portia. *She'll be expecting me to make that all-important phone call now to my supplier. She hasn't got a clue. She's no idea that she's about to pay all that money for nothing more out of the ordinary than several packets of aspirin decanted into a new jar with a fancy label on.*

He'd print one up on his PC. The same PC where he'd created the pages of wonder-drug documents that had convinced Portia and a few others before her to part with their cash. It was amazing what a few photos pulled from the internet and a document design programme could do. The drugs would do no more than maybe halt the odd headache, but if Portia believed that they were the wonder drug then more fool her.

Ed picked up his copy of the document off his desk and fed it into his office shredder. He didn't want Duncan Porte to see it.

Zipping up his tracksuit, Ed checked his pocket for some money. He found a ten-pound note. That would do nicely. He'd head to a few of the nearest pharmacies and buy a stash of pills. That should keep Portia going for a month. As he stepped from his office he saw Portia standing at The Abbey entrance desk talking to the receptionist. He squeezed her on the arm as he walked past.

'I'm off for a run. Happy planning,' he said. He had some planning of his own to do. What to do with all the money coming his way. The sooner he had the pills, the better.

CHAPTER 45

The sun-drenched hills of her South African home looked almost cinematic in their drama and beauty as Martha's taxi pulled up outside the Lewin Éclair estate. But despite the artistry and glow of her surroundings it was not a place that Martha had planned to see again until she had been good and ready. But a phone call to Mariella had forced her to fly back as soon as possible.

Martha hadn't been in contact with her parents for days. Ever since her phone had short-circuited in the bubbly depths of the London spa, she had been incommunicado.

But after her catch-up with Portia at The Abbey and the jaw-dropping news of her forthcoming marriage to Piero and Martha's intended role on the big day, she knew that she had to phone home.

Martha knew that Mariella would be thrilled with the news. Certainly more than she would have been had Martha chosen to tell her about the rest of her day-long stay at The Abbey. After a meeting with Dr Fielding in which she had informed him about her recent carnal activities and he'd informed her that she was indeed borderline addictive when it came to sex, Martha had immediately tracked down Tom, and instructed him to 'bang her to within an inch of her life' across his bed.

He'd dutifully accepted, riding Martha with the skill of a virtuoso porn star. Sharing every horny detail of her sex life with Dr Fielding had lit up Martha's sexual senses with more depravity than a Roman orgy. Doubtless her antics with Tom were not what the good doctor would have prescribed but Martha didn't care. If she was borderline addicted to sex then it felt good – darned good. It was only when she'd satisfied her need for yet another nerve-tingling orgasm that Martha had left a drained Tom and gone to visit Portia.

Martha had spent the evening with Portia and Piero talking about their union. They seemed good together, she had to admit. When she'd first met Portia at Dubai airport she would never have earmarked her as the marrying kind but there was something about the way Piero finished her sentences and let his fingers entwine with his fiancée's as they chatted that kindled the flames of Martha's romantic core.

In spite of not wanting to admit it to herself, she had been unable to shake the image of Kieran Bradford from her mind ever since she'd met him. She'd even fixed his face in her mind as she played mistress for Saul. There was more to Kieran than just sex.

It had been past midnight before Martha realised, the evening a blur of cooed admirations and musings about potential wedding venues. She was contemplating asking Tom if she could stay the night at The Abbey when Portia had insisted on phoning Redmond to come and collect her young friend. 'You will stay at my home for the night, darling. It's not far from here and you could be there in half an hour. You too, Piero. After all, it may well be where we live together when we're married – you may as well get used to it.'

Both he and Martha were obviously keen to see the diva's home and readily accepted the offer. After they'd left, Portia found herself in solitude. Undressing herself, she climbed into bed and drifted off to sleep, her mind full of promising wedding destinations – the historic beauty of London's St Paul's Cathedral, the bougainvillea gardens of a Red Sea hotel in Egypt, a mountain-top villa overlooking the turquoise Caribbean ocean? Portia's mind bounced between them all as she fell asleep. It was the first time in an absolute age that she had not craved a drink before retiring. Maybe being in love would be just the non-alcoholic tonic she needed.

———

Martha had loved Portia's home from the moment a runway of lights illuminated the cedar-lined drive leading to it. Redmond, still somewhat stunned by Portia's news about the wedding, had shown both Martha and Piero to their rooms for the night. He instructed them that breakfast would be served at eight the next morning and left them in peace.

Martha slipped out of her clothes down to her underwear. Climbing between the crisp cotton sheets of the four-poster bed in her room, she listened to the sound of the night. It was silent. More silent than any other place she'd known, the room pitch-black when she switched off the bedside lamp. She lay in the dark, waiting for sleep to take her. Eventually it did.

It was six o'clock when she woke the next day, the early morning sunshine streaming through the huge floor-to-ceiling window at one end of her room. For a moment she tried to figure out her surroundings, and then as the penny dropped she smiled and pushed the sheets back from her body. She was at the house of one of the most famous operatic divas on earth. Mariella would love this too and Martha longed to speak to her. She cursed herself for not having replaced her mobile phone yet.

She showered and dressed herself and walked into the main hall at Mara. Redmond was already there, a laptop computer perched on his legs. 'Morning, you're up early,' he smiled. 'Did you sleep well? I'm just checking my emails to see what requests are coming Portia's way, although I suspect everything will go on hold now we have a wedding to think about. Who'd have thought? Those two were at each other's throats when they first met and now look at them …'

'Well, they definitely love each other,' Martha replied. 'They were all over each other at The Abbey like a couple of lovesick teenagers. I didn't know where to look! I think they'll be happy together. It's nice to see two people who seem to be so well suited – most marriages break up these days. My mum and dad's did.' There was a hint of sadness in her voice as she thought about her parents. 'My mum back home would love this place and the fact that it's Portia's – it's amazing. I'd phone her but I managed to drown my mobile. Don't ask how …'

'Feel free,' signalled Redmond, indicating a telephone in the corner of the room. 'I'll fix us some coffee. You phone whoever you like.'

Martha called Mariella. As soon her mother answered she could tell that something was wrong. She listened, tears pricking her eyes as her mother told her about Lewin's recent brush with death and his break-up with Adina. At the end of the conversation, Martha simply said, 'I'll be home as soon as I can. Love you,' and hung up. Within twenty minutes Redmond had organised a car to take her back to London to pack a suitcase and then on to the airport, and had let her use his laptop to book a flight to Cape Town.

She'd cried all the way to her Soho apartment, and continued to do so as she checked in at Heathrow a few hours later. She may not have always seen eye to eye with her father, but he was still the only one she had and the thought of him not being around any more filled her with a black streak of sorrow.

———

Mariella ran out to greet her daughter just as Martha was paying for the taxi. They hugged each other tightly, joined by the love for the man they had nearly lost.

'Darling, you're here – thank God. Your father's inside resting, not that he's particularly good at that. They let him out of the hospital yesterday. He'll be so pleased to see you again. Leave your case there, I'll get one of the staff to come out and fetch it.'

Martha placed her suitcase on the gravel. Her mother seemed completely at home, despite not having lived at the estate since her separation from Lewin. *The staff?* Obviously she was revelling in her second-time-around position as mistress of the house. The thought pleased Martha.

'Is Dad giving you the run-around, then? Not listening to the doctors? I should have guessed. He hates being dictated to, after all.'

'Your father is a stupid old bugger, Martha. He's no one to blame for this heart attack but himself. Cavorting around with that strumpet of a woman. What was he thinking? She tried to convince him that he'd proposed to her because of this imaginary pregnancy of hers. I think your darned father has ridden the *marry-go-round* enough, don't you, after everything that he and I went through. At least I was never the gold-digging bitch Adina was. I respected your father, loved him. I still do, despite all the water under the bridge. He may be a silly old bugger … but he's *our* silly old bugger, and we have to make sure that he recovers as speedily and as efficiently as possible.'

Martha could see that Mariella was indeed relishing her role as nursemaid. They rushed to Lewin's side and she took his hand in hers. Martha was genuinely pleased to see her dad once again. He looked pale and tired, but his eyes still possessed a twinkle that suggested happiness behind them. As Mariella stood on the other side of the bed and tenderly held Lewin's other hand,

Martha felt a wave of happy confusion. Mariella seemed filled with an inner glow too. Martha couldn't help but feel that you didn't need the intellect of Albert Einstein to work out the reason for it. Maybe Lewin's heart wasn't the only one that needed looking after …

CHAPTER 46

There are telltale signs that can hint at or expose the innermost secrets of even the most complex of people. As Martha and her mother left Lewin sleeping and headed off to join Peter Bradford for dinner back at his estate, Martha had no expectations of the night ahead except for knowing that she would be dining on some of the world's finest food and that it would be intriguing to see how Mariella and Peter were in each other's company. She was right on both accounts.

The three of them had feasted on South African lobster tails, prepared to perfection by the estate staff. Conversation had been stilted between her mother and her rugged beau, the businessman obviously vexed somewhat by Mariella's insistence on talking constantly about Martha's father. Peter had tried to divert the conversation, forcing it down other avenues, but each time Mariella would steer it back to Lewin. Martha couldn't tell whether this was intentional or not, but she could see the stormy cloud of flushed anger spreading across Peter's face every time the *L-word* was mentioned. Mariella seemed oblivious, but to Martha it was strikingly obvious. The air between Peter and Mariella seemed frostier than a Matterhorn glacier. Something had changed between them and it would take more than a heated portion of the finest seafood to get them warmed up again.

Peter tried once more to alter their topic of conversation. 'So, how are things over in the UK then, Martha? Any news to share? Have you found yourself a nice British guy as yet? I imagine a pretty girl like you can't be without offers.' Naturally the question was baited. The photos on Peter's PC proved exactly what kind of offers Martha had been accepting. But now was not the time to broadcast his possession of them.

Kieran's face etched itself across Martha's thoughts, making her smile. 'It's early days, but we'll see ... I'll keep you informed.' The tone of her voice indicated that her few words were all she was prepared to say on the matter. 'I do have some rather amazing news, though. I met a truly fabulous woman on the way to the UK and we've struck up quite a friendship. I didn't really have a clue who she was at first but it turns out she's pretty famous. Anyway, she's getting married and she's asked me to be her bridesmaid. I've no idea where the wedding is but I know it will be mind-blowing. She's contemplating pretty much anywhere in the world. Money is no option. And what's more she's told me I can invite my family and friends if I wish. I guess she figures the more people there the better. Doubtless it will be in some celebrity magazine. So, it might be time to dust off your fascinator, Mother.'

Mariella raised her eyebrows and nodded her head at the news. 'There's no guarantee your father will be well enough to travel, but we'll see.' Her words ploughed into Peter like a corkscrew.

'So, who is this woman who has tempted my beautiful princess into being her lady-in-waiting? Maybe we could supply the wine for the wedding – sounds like it could be a big order,' enquired Mariella as Peter pushed his plate angrily across the table. He wasn't sure if she was talking about Bradford Wines or touting for business for her ex.

Martha paused a little longer than necessary, building an air of tension with her silence, before replying, 'Only the biggest opera star in the world today, Portia Safari. Aren't you a fan? Don't you have some of her CDs in your collection?'

But before Mariella could answer, a huge crash sounded from the other side of the table. Peter, the colour now seemingly drained from his face, had dropped his glass of wine onto his china plate. Both of them had broken, spilling a pool of deep red Pinotage across the table. Without thinking, a flustered Peter attempted to remove some of the broken glass fragments from his plate. In his attempt to do so he accidentally ran one of his fingers along a sharp edge. It formed a long, nasty gash that began to ooze thick splashes of blood. 'Shit! Fucking stupid glass. That fucking hurts!' he cried in pain as droplets of blood mingled with the wine.

Martha remained silent but Mariella leapt to her feet. 'There's no need for language like that, Peter. For God's sake, what the hell happened?'

But Peter didn't answer. Grabbing a napkin and wrapping it around his bloody finger, he shot up from the table, causing his chair to fall backwards as he did so. He'd left the room within a couple of seconds. Something had obviously spooked him and Martha was pretty sure it had been her news about Portia. Maybe he was a fan too?

———

At his London apartment, Kieran Bradford stepped out from underneath his shower and wrapped a towel around his waist. He would normally be getting ready to go out on the hunt, ready to seduce yet another victim into his bed. But for once, the hunter felt listless and could see no point in sharpening his claws for a night of action. His head was concentrating on one thing – the delicious features of Martha. He'd tried phoning her at her apartment but Kelly had informed him that she had flown back to South Africa due to an emergency. The news had filled him with dread. Firstly that he wasn't able to see and make love to the woman who had somehow managed to change the way he'd always seen the female species. *Was he falling in love with her?* But secondly, if she was back in South Africa at the Éclair family home then there was a good chance she would be seeing his father – and he held the photos Kieran had taken of Martha dogging. *What did his father intend to do with them? Whatever it was it couldn't be pleasant, could it?* If it wasn't for those photos Kieran could be honest with Martha and say who he really was. She wouldn't mind him being the Bradford heir, would she? But now it was too late. He'd e-mailed the photos from his personal account. His father had the evidence. Whatever Peter intended to do with them remained to be seen.

Yanking off his towel, a naked Kieran lay on his bed and stared at the ceiling. His father held all four aces but at least he himself could try and do whatever was within his grasp to stop any damage. Rolling over and reaching underneath his bed for his camera, he scrolled through to the photos that he'd taken of Martha having sex in the car park. Diligently he deleted them one by one. Having done that, he turned on his laptop and logged onto his e-mail account. Moving to the 'sent' folder, he found the e-mail he'd sent to his father containing the photos. Again he permanently deleted it. Why was he doing this? To Kieran it was obvious. He wanted to minimise any possible harm coming to Martha – a telltale sign that he was definitely falling for her. But how would he explain that to his father?

CHAPTER 47

Nancy had booked herself on a flight home from Las Vegas the morning after she'd spotted Dale and Lauren together. Having failed miserably in her quest to make a profit at the blackjack table, she had decided to quit while she still had some, if not that much, of the money she'd taken from Lauren. Besides, if the night before had taught her anything, it was that maybe gambling wasn't always the best way to gain the money she craved. Maybe the guaranteed winning hand could only be played when it came to blackmail and not blackjack.

As she waited for her luggage to satellite around the carousel at Heathrow Airport, Nancy stared at her phone and flicked between the two photos. She wasn't sure which would have the higher price-tag – the one of Dale and Lauren embracing would doubtless be of major interest to Saul. He'd want to keep that out of the papers to save his career, but the other one … well, that was pure gold dust. It had been well worth the risk following Dale and Lauren from the MGM Grand casino.

She'd watched them stumble in each other's arms into one of the hotel elevators. They were the only people inside when the doors shut so it was easy to watch the number display ascending until it came to a lengthy halt. Like lightning, Nancy ran into another elevator and pressed the button for the corresponding floor. As it whirred to a halt at the desired number, Nancy gingerly stuck her head around the lift door as it opened to catch sight of the backs of Lauren and Dale weaving their wobbly way down the hotel corridor. They had no idea she was right behind them.

Nancy watched as the couple stopped outside one of the numerous hotel doors and Lauren reached down into her handbag for her hotel swipe card. Pulling it out, she waggled it in Dale's face and giggled as she asked, 'Are you coming in for a little nightcap?' As she did so, a bag of white powder fell to the floor. 'Ooops!' she tittered. Dale bent to pick it up and hand the packet back to her. He leant forward to kiss her before saying, 'I'd love to. Why don't you get started without me? I just need five minutes to freshen up. You finish off the coke and I'll bring some more from my room.'

Lauren inserted the card into the door and pushed it open. Dale disappeared off to his room at the other end of the corridor. In her drugged-up state, Lauren didn't push hard enough on the bedroom door as she went to close it behind her, and left it ajar. Without a moment's hesitation, Nancy grabbed her opportunity and ran towards the room. As quietly as she could she pushed it open just enough to gaze inside. Lauren was sitting cross-legged on the floor tipping out a line of cocaine onto a glass table. The soulful sounds of Alicia Keys poured from the room's music system. It was sufficiently loud and Lauren was sufficiently wasted for her to have no clue what was going on behind her.

Aware that she could be discovered any minute, Nancy grabbed her phone again and pointed it at Lauren just as she leant over to snort up the line. She clicked at the perfect moment, securing the photograph. She was just about to leave the room when a noise at the door alerted her that someone else was about to push it open again. It was Dale. As quickly as she could, Nancy ducked into the bathroom before he could see her. She just had to pray that Dale wouldn't want to use the bathroom before joining Lauren.

For the next few minutes, Nancy remained behind the door, unable to move for fear of being seen. She could hear the sound of laughter and the telltale snorts of drug-taking coming from the room. It was only after a while that the voices died out. Either Dale and Lauren had both crashed out or something of a more intimate nature was happening. The moans of desire that followed proved that it was the latter.

For a moment, Nancy considered using her phone again to take a photo of the couple in action. But she knew she couldn't. She had no desire to. Dale was her first love and she didn't want to witness him ploughing his length into someone else, whatever the price tag. Tiptoeing from the bathroom, she crept towards the door and opened it, praying that she wouldn't be spotted. She needn't have worried. Lauren had her eyes shut in ecstasy and Dale had his face buried eyebrow-deep in a place where he was unable to see anything.

Pulling the door closed as quietly as possible, Nancy ran to the elevators and made her way back to her own hotel. En route, she decided to quit Vegas. She couldn't bear to see Lauren and Dale together – something about it hurt too much. At least if she quit Vegas now she wouldn't be a total loser, she had at least two visual aces on her telephone. Hopefully they would come up trumps.

A few hours later, back at her own Bayswater apartment, Nancy downloaded the images from her phone onto her computer. They looked even better full-screen. Nancy was proud of her handiwork and was imagining Saul Everett's reaction to them when her phone rang. She picked it up to hear a familiar voice.

'Hi, Nancy, it's me. You are not going to believe the latest stupid celebrity to fall for my schemes. Only that idiotic opera woman, Portia whatnot,' he bragged.

Nancy liked speaking to Ed Collie. They didn't chat very often but when they did he never ceased to make her smile with his tales of deception. As she listened to him explain about the weight-loss scam a sudden thought came into Nancy's head. With her recent bout of stealing and gambling becoming something of an addictive obsession, maybe a visit to see him at The Abbey would be the perfect way to formulate how to deal with it. And at the same time, she could ask Ed's advice on the going rate for trying to blackmail a straight-laced political hotshot with rather incriminating photographs of his not so straight-laced wife.

'What are you doing tomorrow? I need to come and see you. It's not just you who's been busy on the deception front. I need some advice.' Nancy put the phone down and smiled.

CHAPTER 48

In his fifteen years of working at private clinics and rehabilitation centres around the world, Dr Bruno Fielding had received more than his fair share of sexual advances and blatantly obvious suggestions from female patients hoping that he would be prescribing them more than just a course of treatment.

Hardly surprising, given his brooding good looks and charismatic matinee-idol masculinity. If ever there was a man who could envelop women with a treacle-thick layer of confidence-building charm then it was Bruno Fielding. But at the age of thirty-eight, he was still to find the right woman to spend his life with. He'd fallen a handful of times, always ready to give his heart, but falls had often led to hurt and injury. A hurt pride as yet another woman wanted him for nothing more than a pumped body to satisfy her in bed, and injury as he heard his romantic heart shatter into a shower of misery-making shards when he was subsequently tossed to one side. Despite possessing a brain that had been filled to the brim with medical expertise, making him one of the best in his profession, Dr Bruno Fielding's heart still wallowed in a squidgy starry-eyed sentimentality that had not secured him the partner he craved. He was sure that one day it would happen, but when remained to be seen.

Those around him said that he was 'married to his career' but Bruno would have gladly given it all up to sail off into the sunset with the woman of his dreams by his side. But his search for that elusive companion had remained fruitless because when it came to choosing a partner from the menu of life, Bruno had definitely become what you would call a fussy eater. If a woman didn't strike his heart with Cupid's arrow from the moment he laid eyes on her then it was a sure-fire bet that no amount of wooing or chivalrous cooing was ever going to turn her into 'the one'.

Which was why over the years he'd turned down some of the most beautiful women on earth – both inside and outside his consultation room.

So Bruno was more surprised than anyone when his cock stiffened to attention the moment Nancy appeared in the open doorway of his Abbey office. She was the most beautiful woman he had ever seen. As he took in the deep, roasted rich colour of her skin and the figure-skimming contours of her T-shirt and jeans combo, it was a few seconds before he was able to speak to the smiling stranger before him.

'Hello there, can I help you?' Bruno shifted awkwardly in his seat as his erection throbbed lustfully and his heart appeared to skip a beat.

'I sincerely hope so, doctor. Ed Collie, the dietician here, recommended that I come to see you. I have a few issues that he reckons you can help me with,' said Nancy. She curled her lips on one side and turned her head coquettishly towards Bruno. There was a definite air of flirtation about the way she spoke. 'I sincerely hope he's right. He tells me you're the best and I think I can tell that …' she paused before adding, 'just by looking at you.' She stepped into Bruno's office and shut the door behind her. There was something almost predatory about Nancy's actions, as if she was cornering the doctor with no chance of escape.

But at that precise moment Bruno Fielding was more than happy to be the prey she had her desirous eyes fixed on. Like a dazed buck caught in the headlights of an oncoming car, Bruno was momentarily paralysed by the vision in front of him. A voice inside his head told him to stay professionally focused, but it seemed to be drowned out by the beating of his heart and the throbbing between his legs. Was Cupid playing a trick on him – even for an avid believer in love at first sight this was something extraordinary. There was an instant attraction that if he wasn't mistaken, was not merely one-way. But within the walls of his office was not where this was supposed to happen.

'Come in. Please, sit down. My secretary normally deals with appointments but seeing as you're here, I'm sure we can sort something out. I'll just need to make some notes.' Bruno could feel his mouth run dry as he spoke. He'd never felt so flustered before in front of a patient ... or so turned on.

Rising to his feet, he moved to a filing cabinet situated behind his desk. He opened the top drawer and pulled out a large pad of paper. As he turned back to face Nancy, he found her standing directly in front of him, no more than six inches from his face. Without saying a word, she dropped to her knees and began to unbuckle the belt holding up the doctor's trousers with one hand while unzipping his flies with the other. She was determined to free the thrilling bulge she had spied straining against the fabric of his trousers as he had risen from the desk.

Bruno, his head telling him to stop but his arousal saying otherwise, remained silent as the woman in front of him unleashed his manhood and placed her lips around it. He allowed himself to rock back and forth as she worked her lips up and down his thick shaft, letting out a moan of desire as she did so. She teased it with light, feathery strokes before taking his full length deep inside her mouth. She could feel his body shudder with joy as she placed her lips as far down his shaft as her throat would allow her. He was completely at her mercy, a feeling she adored.

Bruno placed his hands either side of Nancy's head, allowing his fingers to entwine in her long dark hair. He knew that at any moment his office door could open and one of his colleagues could walk in. But the warmth of Nancy's mouth wrapped around his hard rod defied him to care. It was a delicious contrast to the coldness of the metal filing cabinet drawer pressed up against his bare buttocks as he worked his member in Nancy's mouth. Unable to stop himself he could feel his seed rising within his cock. She wrapped her hands around his butt cheeks, allowing her nails to dig into his soft flesh and pulling him towards her as she savoured every drop. It was only when she could feel the doctor's cock beginning to languish that she got to her feet. She wiped her lips erotically with the back of her hand.

'I'll tell you what, doc, why don't I speak to your secretary after all? But how about we scrap the appointment? Maybe we should arrange for you to take me out instead – a dinner date. I reckon that will be the answer to any issues I have festering away. Suddenly they don't seem so pressing. My name's Nancy Arlow, by the way. I look forward to eating out. You can probably guess I'm a girl with a healthy appetite.' Nancy winked and slipped out of the office door, leaving Bruno standing there, his trousers still around his ankles.

As he hitched them back up and tucked his cock back inside his underpants, Bruno Fielding couldn't believe that he'd finally had sex with a patient in his office. But then he thought about what Nancy had just said. She wanted to arrange a dinner date, not an appointment. She didn't want to be his patient. So if he wanted to have sex with her again, then he could ... wherever he darned well pleased. Nancy seemed unlike any other woman he had ever met. Cupid had scored a bullseye. The warm glow inside his heart told him that. And for the first time in a while,

Bruno was going to allow his heart to govern his highly academic head.

Bruno couldn't wait to see her again. But first he needed to bring his mind back to work – he had an appointment with Portia Safari to contend with.

———

Nancy herself had been amazed at how attractive she had found Dr Fielding. Why hadn't Ed told her what a good-looking man he was when they'd met up earlier?

Possibly because they'd been too busy discussing Ed's plans to scam Portia out of £50,000 and the fact that they'd been pouring over the Las Vegas photos that Nancy had taken of Lauren and Dale. She'd told Ed about everything that had happened to her over the last few weeks and how the gambling and stealing had become something of an addiction.

Ed had laughed it off flippantly at first, finding it amusing that his celebrity sister was coming to him with her woes. 'Go and see Dr Fielding if you're worried about it. He'll prescribe something to sort you out but, if you ask me, the best way to stop nicking stuff and gambling is to cash in your winning hand right now. These photographs could be worth a fortune. Go and see this Saul bloke and if he doesn't cough up the dosh then hit the papers with them. You could easily be looking at a good six-figure sum for the coke one. The tabloids will eat it up. Cold hard cash wins over a doctor's advice any day of the week.'

But nothing had prepared Nancy for her first encounter with Bruno. He was the epitome of the classic older man that she'd loved so much when she'd first met Dale. And as soon as she laid eyes on him, she was determined that she would be just what the doctor ordered – with a man as handsome as Bruno Fielding obviously interested in her, she'd forego the advice and concentrate purely on just the vice instead.

Leaving his office, Nancy made her way to The Abbey reception to speak to Bruno's secretary. She left her name and number and said that Dr Fielding needed to speak to her urgently. In Nancy's mind the sooner they met up, the sooner they could experience a repeat performance of what had just happened.

Having given her details, Nancy turned away from the desk, ready to leave. As she did so, she bumped straight into Portia who was making her way to her appointment with Bruno. The force of their collision made Nancy drop the Gucci bag she was carrying, spilling the contents across the floor. Both women bent down to try and retrieve the cosmetics, keys and phone as they tumbled from the bag.

'Oh, I'm so sorry, my dear,' gushed Portia, fully aware that she hadn't really been looking where she was going. 'Do forgive me.' She snatched at a lipstick as it started to roll across the floor and picked up some car keys as Nancy grabbed her phone and a compact and started shoving the items back into her bag.

Portia's attention was drawn to the ring that Nancy was wearing on her left hand. It was one of the ones that Nancy had stolen from Betsy and had become one of her favourites. She knew that she shouldn't really wear it in public but its unique design and flawless diamond had become irresistible.

Taking Nancy by the hand, Portia spoke, an evident flood of appreciation soaking her voice. 'What an exquisite ring, my dear. It's divine. Where on earth did you get it?'

Unsure of what to say, Nancy tried to fudge her way out of the situation. 'Oh … this old thing. It's been in the family for years. An heirloom passed down from my gran to my mum and then to me,' she lied.

Portia lifted Nancy's hand nearer her face so that she could take a real close-up look. She was a touch forceful. Nancy was unable to pull her hand away as Portia twisted the ring round to one side to look at the finer design details on the shoulder. A tiny ornate crest was marked onto the yellow gold. Portia took a sharp intake of breath as she studied it.

Nancy could feel herself beginning to worry. There was something about the woman's inspection that she felt uneasy about. She yanked her hand back from Portia as quickly as she could. 'Excuse me, you're hurting my hand,' she said defensively. 'Now, if you'll excuse me, I need to leave. I don't know what your business is with my ring, lady, but I really can't stay here to find out, OK? So stop manhandling me.' Her tone was becoming aggressive.

Portia was quick to reply. 'My business is none of yours, young lady. There is no need to be rude. I was just looking at the rather beautiful handiwork …'

But Nancy was up and out of The Abbey entrance before Portia could finish the sentence. As Portia placed her finger to her lips in contemplation she could hear the sound of Nancy's car speeding away across the gravel. She turned to the secretary behind the counter, who was busy typing details into her computer.

'Who was that vile little creature?' she barked.

Looking up from her PC, the secretary stared smugly at Portia. 'Now, Ms Safari, you know full well that I can't divulge any information about other visitors to The Abbey. We run a strictly confidential service here.' She returned her gaze to the computer screen, complacent in her own officious power.

Portia was not to be beaten. There was no way she was taking no for an answer and she let rip accordingly. 'And you know full well that I have just announced my forthcoming wedding to Piero Romeo which will be at one of the most deluxe five-star resorts in the Caribbean. It's the kind of place that the likes of you could only ever read about in some Danielle Steel novel, so how about we make a deal? You get a fully paid-for invitation to the wedding for you and a plus one and I get the name and details of that skanky little bitch who just walked out the door. Do we have a deal or does the idea of sipping champagne in an infinity pool under the pure-blue Caribbean skies not appeal to your holier-than-thou ways?'

Portia had Nancy's name and telephone number within thirty seconds. In less than a minute she was back in her room and dialling her mobile. 'Hello, is that Betsy? It's Portia here. I need to talk to you. Do you know a woman called Nancy Arlow …?'

Portia had always liked Betsy, ever since she had regularly stayed with her and her husband, William, when she was younger. Any time Portia's own father, Lord Nigel Hartley, and his wife were out of the country on business, Portia had been more than happy to stay with her favourite aunty and uncle – they had always shown her nothing but the purest love. She was a wonderful lady, and one that she certainly didn't want taken advantage of.

CHAPTER 49

When two people enter into the union of marriage and make their vows to each other, no one knows where the saying of 'till death do us part' and 'for richer, for poorer' will lead. Not one couple who have ever walked down the aisle to become man and wife have known for certain what their supposedly joyous merger will bring.

For Lewin and Mariella their two-million-rand wedding nearly three decades ago had brought them, at first, many years of happiness, one of the world's most successful wine empires and the ultimate prize of a beautiful, healthy girl in the form of Martha.

For a long time their existence was as celebratory as the sound of a thousand champagne corks popping but all of that had changed when Lewin had started to relegate the wants of his wife to below his cut-throat business desires. Lewin's trips away from home for weeks on end and a slow-but-sure demise of what had once been a full and active sex life meant that Mariella had become lonely, unloved and unfulfilled. Before she could stop herself, Martha's mother had found solace in the arms and between the sheets of other men's beds. But none of the men meant anything until she met Peter Bradford. He was the man who made her feel like a woman again, who managed to fill the empty gap in her life. After a year of feeling her heartstrings pulling in two polar-opposite directions – one weakly towards the sanctity of her marriage and the other forcibly towards the newfound freedom she found with Peter, she made her choice.

With her husband out of the country on business yet again she packed her bags and moved in with Lewin's arch rival.

But ever since the heart attack and the contemplation of losing Lewin for good, Mariella's heartstrings had been tying themselves in knots once more. Her love for him was one that she would never be free of, and every day since the attack she couldn't help but feel that it was one she didn't actually want to be free of any more. She still loved Lewin, and in spite of everything that had passed between them she knew that Lewin felt the same.

Martha had noticed it too and was desperate to quiz Mariella as her mother drove her to Cape Town airport to catch her flight to the UK. Now that Lewin was well on his way to recovery, Martha knew that the time was right to return to London. Besides which, she was missing her life there.

'You're still in love with Dad, aren't you?' Martha's questioning was straight to the point. The journey to the airport wasn't going to take too long and she wanted to gain as much information from her mother as possible while they weren't in earshot of either Lewin or Peter.

Mariella knew there was no point pussyfooting around her daughter. She'd spotted the look on Martha's face every time she saw her parents together and she wasn't going to hide her true emotions from her own flesh and blood. 'I never stopped loving him, Martha. We've climbed through life together. It's just that we seemed to lose our footing somewhere along the way. He was my first true love and I guess he always will be.'

'Do you want to get back with him now that Adina's out of the picture? I love the thought of you guys back together so we can all be one big happy family. Maybe his attack will mellow him. He's certainly been nicer to me since I've been back. At least he's not trying to marry me off to any wealthy stranger.'

Mariella cracked a wry smile. 'Your dad loves to interfere but he's learnt his lesson on that front, I'm sure. Despite what you think, he hates it when you're away from home. The trouble with your dad and I is that we became strangers. I never saw him and I needed to feel ...' She paused, searching for the right words. 'To feel loved.' Martha was sure that she could see the glisten of tears welling up in her mother's eyes as she continued, 'When your father loves me then he's the most perfect man on earth, it's just that I have to remember how he made me feel before and why I ended up with Peter. Peter's a good man too.'

Martha wasn't so sure. She'd always been wary of the macho ways of Peter Bradford. There was something about him that she'd never liked and his reaction to the news of Portia's wedding was still sitting heavy on her mind. His response had been completely out of character. 'He may be a good man, Mother, but is he the *right* man? That's what you need to ask yourself.'

A single tear rolled down Mariella's cheek as she turned the car into the parking area at Cape Town airport. She was quick to wipe it away, hoping that Martha hadn't seen it. 'Since when did you turn into Oprah Winfrey, Martha – dishing out advice on all things romantic? I didn't have you down as the love guru. Maybe this new man of yours is mellowing you too.'

'Maybe ...' Martha let her voice trail off, deep in thought as she watched a plane coming into land through the side window of the car, wondering where it had flown in from.

It was the beeping of her new mobile phone that interrupted her daydreams. She had finally replaced her old one the day before and it felt good to be contactable again at last, no matter where she was. She'd received a text. She was thrilled to read it was from Saul, or 'Mr Kinky' as he was listed on her contacts. It read: *I want us to play again, mistress. I need you ... only you ... ring me when you can. Humbly yours.* A deckle-edged sexual quiver ran across Martha's thighs as she read it, imagining Saul's receptive flesh. She would text him before boarding the plane. No, she loved the idea of being with Kieran, but the thought of dark, dangerous, delicious sex with Saul was definitely a major turn-on. She was far from mellowing.

Once inside the airport terminal, Martha checked in her bags and headed to one of the first class lounges with her mother for a final farewell. As they sat themselves down and ordered two glasses of wine, Martha picked up a newspaper that had been left on the table. The headline on the front page read DIVA NAMES DAY – PORTIA AND PIERO'S £5M CARIBBEAN WEDDING. The copy underneath a photo of the two stars onstage at the Royal Albert Hall revealed that the couple had chosen to get married in just a matter of weeks at an exclusive resort on the private Peter Island, situated amongst the British Virgin Islands in the Caribbean. The celebrity names hinted to appear on the guest list read like a who's who of the entertainment world and was said to include famous faces from every single continent. Bridesmaids and best men were *yet to be confirmed but it was believed that Martha Éclair, the daughter of South African wine baron, Lewin Éclair, has already agreed to perform the honours.*

Martha squealed with joy. 'Oh my God! The next time I see you will be in the Caribbean. It's only a few weeks too. I hope you and Dad have got your passports and suntan cream in order. Or should I say you and Peter? Who will you take, Mum? You're all invited …'

Mariella didn't respond. Not because she didn't want to, but because she had absolutely no idea what the answer would be.

———

When Betsy had married William Hartley it had been a sophisticated and stylish gathering in the mosaic and stained—glass-bedecked beauty of Soane Hall at London's One Marylebone. Surrounded by friends and loved ones it was a synthesis of beautiful food, the finest champagne and polished music from a 1940s big band. Betsy and William were made for each other and were a classic case of the perfect match. She was as beautiful as he was handsome, as charming as he was charismatic.

Their years together were outstandingly happy. Although never blessed with children, they surrounded themselves with the family they did have, especially enjoying the time they got to spend playing 'adoptive parents' to Portia Hartley, the daughter of William's brother Nigel and his exotic wife, Omorose. Portia was a joy as a child, singing to Betsy and William at every opportunity. Even at an early age, Betsy had earmarked Portia as having 'star quality'. It was no surprise to her that Portia had become one of the world's leading operatic divas. Both she and William had collected every newspaper cutting they could about their famous niece and couldn't have been prouder about her talent. When William had been diagnosed with a brain tumour in his mid sixties, he had been given two years to live. He died in hospital with Betsy, Nigel, Omorose and Portia by his side. Even on his deathbed he managed to communicate that he wished his family to always care for each other. It was something they would always do.

William would have been thrilled to know that Portia was finally finding love. When Betsy learnt of the news from Portia about her forthcoming Caribbean wedding to Piero, she knew that William would be 'smiling down from above'. Despite her advancing years, Betsy promised that she would make the effort to attend, as long as Bloodworth could be there to look after her every need. Portia was ecstatic.

The conversation had been marred somewhat, though, by the mention of Nancy Arlow and the story of the ring. The ring was a diamond one which had been in the Hartley family for years and bore the family crest on it. It had been one of Betsy's most treasured possessions, a gift to her from her husband on their honeymoon. A young Portia had often gazed at it, wide-eyed with envy at its beauty. In her eyes it was as beautiful as Betsy herself. As the years went by, Betsy's fingers had become thinner with old age, and she had chosen not to wear the ring any more, storing it at her dressing table instead. Occasionally she would get it out to clean, buffing it until both the yellow gold and the diamond sparkled before placing it lovingly back into her collection.

When Portia told her that she had seen what she thought was the ring on Nancy's finger, Betsy couldn't believe it. 'It must be a mistake, dear. I do know the girl, but she was perfectly charming and lovely company. I am sure she wouldn't take something that didn't belong to her. There must be a perfectly reasonable explanation.'

But there wasn't. Placing Portia on hold, Betsy had gone to search through her jewellery collection. The ring was indeed missing, as were other treasured items. She returned to the phone with a heavy heart, knowing that she had been duped. Between sobs down the telephone, she wept, 'Oh Portia. What shall we do? I must phone the police, I suppose.'

The pitiful cries of her favourite aunt felt like razor-sharp knives stabbing at Portia's heart. She knew she had to do something for her elderly relative. Betsy had always shown her unconditional love. 'No, Aunt Betsy, don't phone the police just yet. You leave things to me. I know exactly what to do. We'll get your jewellery back, I promise. That woman will pay for this, believe you me. I'll stop at nothing to make sure she does. Nothing at all …'

—

When Lauren Wilde had married Saul Everett in the fairytale beauty of her enchanting summer wedding, it had been everything that she had ever dreamt of. The elegance of her Ana Cristache dress, the sophisticated class of the Rolls Royce Phantom that had chauffeured Lauren to the entrance of her village church, the four-tiered butter-cream-iced wedding cake draped with vibrant sugar flowers – everything had been picture perfect.

As she gazed deeply into Saul's eyes that night as they made love as a married couple for the first time, Lauren had honestly believed that they would be together as one forever.

But things had changed – the love they shared, the flames which had once burned bright, were rapidly extinguishing themselves. The gap between them had never been so wide, both geographically and emotionally.

As Lauren gazed into the lens of the camera focused on her as she lip-synched the words to her potential first single, she was pleased that she was approaching the end of the video shoot. The heat of the sweltering Vegas desert sun beating down on her sizzled against her skin and it was becoming too much to bear. She had been filming for the best part of eight hours with only the tiniest of breaks for food and water, and despite her head telling her that the mere idea of shooting a video was beyond glamorous, her head pounded and her feet ached from the ridiculously elevated designer heels she was wearing.

Only the encouragement that Dale had been giving her about her performance and the lines of coke she'd been sneaking off the video director throughout the day seemed to be keeping her body buoyant. Dale – the man who had made love to her again last night, the man who she had allowed to slip between her sheets and turn her into an adulteress, the man who had made her not think of her own husband for the best part of seventy-two hours – the man who was destroying her one-time dream marriage.

—

As Lauren mimed her heart out, nearly five and a half thousand miles away on the other side of the Atlantic, Saul sipped at a brandy from the minibar in the back of his Mercedes parked outside one of the terminals at Heathrow Airport. He stared out at the aeroplanes coming into land from around the globe and wondered if this had been the airport from which his wife had flown out of the country. He'd tried ringing Lauren again to find out what the hell she was playing at but again the foreign tone sounded before clicking through to the phone's message service. Saul had given up leaving messages. Let the bitch rot for all he cared. Besides, Saul's mind was now elsewhere, concentrating on the appealing delights of Martha and her body built for sin. To him she was like a firecracker housed inside a velvet glove – soft and serenely beautiful on the outside but underneath beat an explosive heart soaking in its own lustful juices. It was an explosion that had ignited the rapacity of Saul's carnal longings for her. He had to have her – as a mistress, as a lover, as a sexual dominatrix. This was why he was waiting at the airport.

Martha had texted him the details of her flight and arrival time from Cape Town. Saul had answered immediately, telling her that someone would be there to meet her as she arrived. He couldn't wait to be with her again – to banquet on her flesh. Saul had sent Nathan to the arrivals hall bearing a huge bunch of flowers and a board with her name on it. Martha had seen him as soon as she arrived, despite his squat, portly frame being virtually swamped by the size of the bouquet. He had escorted her straight to the Mercedes and into the arms of Saul. It was the first time Martha had seen him without any kind of mask on. His face was as handsome as his body was firm and strong. There was something familiar about him but Martha couldn't place it. As she climbed into the back seat alongside Saul, she didn't even have time to utter a word before he took her face in his hands and placed his lips against hers. Immediately she could feel her nipples rising to attention. His kisses were urgent and strong, his breath ripe with the odour of the brandy.

Saul moved his hands down her face and let them dance across her neckline before starting to unbutton her blouse. Martha could feel the hardness of his erection pressed against her leg as he freed her breasts and swooped down, lapping his tongue around her buds. He placed one of her nipples between his teeth and nibbled gently. Martha pulled his head towards her, burying his face in her willing flesh and let out a moan of absolute joy. She could see Nathan staring at her in the rear-view mirror as he salivated over the image of her breasts spilling from her blouse. Martha didn't care – she was used to being watched, the thought thrilled her, and Nathan was obviously used to seeing his friend in action. Nathan had hardly slipped his key into the Mercedes' ignition and begun to drive out of the airport car park before Martha had freed Saul's determined cock, stripped them both of as many of their clothes as possible, repositioned themselves as best they could and guided his rigid shaft into her.

Martha could feel her eyes glaze over with euphoria as Saul thrust his cock inside her. She could tell that he was a master when it came to matters of the flesh, despite the confines of their location. As their bodies rocked together, she gave herself up to the pleasure of the moment and let her juices flow into orgasm as Saul released his own seed into her. For a few moments they lay there in silence, their bodies still linked, relishing the after-glow of their impassioned fireworks. It was only as she caught sight once again of a lecherous Nathan's eyes darting across her naked flesh in the rear-view mirror that she manoeuvred herself away from Saul and rearranged her clothes to cover herself.

'Well, that was an amazing welcome, I must say. I'll have to leave the country more often,' she grinned at Saul. 'I thought you only liked the kinky stuff.'

'I'll do whatever you like, Martha. I want you.' It was more of a demand than a request.

'Even if we have the beady eyes of Peeping Tom watching us?' she whispered, indicating Nathan, who seemed to be fidgeting awkwardly in the driver's seat, no doubt trying to move himself into a more comfortable position for the stumpy hard-on which pressed against his boxers.

'Nathan's used to it. You saw him at the club. I do what I like when I like, regardless of who's around. But I am normally a little more incognito when things are more public. I have to be with my job, hence why you've seen me in the mask and all that before now. I hope I haven't disappointed … out of costume, as it were.'

'Not at all, far from it. Your face is as sexy as the rest of you. Mind you, I'll be wanting a repeat experience of the kinky stuff soon enough. Dominating you makes me horny.' Martha cast her mind back to the night that she had first met Saul. The firmness of his body, the mystery of the man behind the mask, the subservience of his manner – it had been a great introduction to the world of fetish. If only it hadn't all ballooned out of control thanks to the hysterical Lauren. She'd freaked when she'd seen Nathan.

The thought of Lauren and her reactions that night seemed to spark a domino effect inside Martha's brain. Lauren had been spooked about seeing Nathan because he worked closely with her husband, Saul. Yet Nathan was always with the man who had just made love to Martha. Was this more than mere coincidence? Martha had absolutely no idea who the sexy, mysterious stranger sitting alongside her really was. She only knew him as

'Mr Kinky' – he'd never told her his name. Surely he couldn't be …?

Before she could stop herself, she turned to ask him. 'What's your name? Mistress Martha would like to know,' she said jokily, hoping that if she played the dominator, at least she may receive an honest answer.

It worked. 'Saul, mistress. At your service.' He leant over to kiss her full on the lips again. Everything fell into place. Martha had just had sex with Lauren's husband. She was his mistress in more ways than one. As Martha started to see Saul's cock rising to attention again, all she could think about was how Lauren would react to the news that she was intimately involved with her husband. As she wrapped her hand around his cock and felt it twitch deliciously again, she knew that she had no intention of ever telling her. Saul was too good to give up and Martha was determined that he should be hers from now on. Wife or no wife. He was definitely something to savour. She lowered her head and took his member in her mouth …

———

As Martha enjoyed the taste of Saul's manhood in the back seat of the Mercedes, his wife was lying face up on the back seat of Dale's hire car, rushing from the set of the video shoot back to their Las Vegas hotel. Dale had placed Lauren there immediately after she'd collapsed on set at the end of the shoot, determined to get her away from the curious eyes of the crew around her. Her body shook and her mind raced, her skin switching from hot to cold. A lack of food and water and the searing heat of the sun had been contributory factors to her collapse, but Dale could tell exactly what had been going on. The rings of white powder lodged inside her nose told the story. As did a deep-red flow of blood that ran in a solitary line from one of her nostrils. Lauren had taken too much cocaine. Snorting it back in their room at the hotel or on a night out was one thing, but taking it to excess in front of people working for you – people being paid for by a generous investor to try and launch your career, was another. Dale knew that if Lauren's singing aspirations stood any chance of success, then she would have to be in total control of her love of coke. Nobody likes a fuck-up, not even a hedonistic livewire like Dale. He had made a decision. As soon as they arrived back in the UK, he would be booking Lauren into The Abbey. Their Vegas trip had brought them closer together and he was becoming increasingly fond of her, but business was business and he had too much to lose now. He wouldn't let her screw things up.

CHAPTER 50

As Duncan Porte picked up his office diary and scanned the list of patients currently being treated at The Abbey, he smiled to himself. In his decade as owner, the place had never been busier. The continuing flow of famous faces desperate for a quick fix or a professional shoulder to cry on showed no signs of drying up. And long may it continue ... as long as there were celebrities with issues that needed addressing then the trousers of his Savile Row suit would always be lined with cash. Cash that had allowed him to jet around the world to his many homes and to furnish his life with the best decadence and decor he could. As far as Duncan was concerned, God bless the delicate minds of the deranged within The Abbey walls because their worries were his welfare, their issues his income, their addiction his ambrosia.

His office phone rang as he shut the diary. Reaching across his desk, he picked up the receiver and placed it to his ear. Recognising the voice at the other end of the line, a joyous loving smile unfolded across his face. 'Hello, darling, I was just about to ring you. You're going to love me more than you already do. Portia's invited me to her wedding and naturally you shall be by my side. Caribbean here we come.' Had there been anyone in the office with Duncan right then, they would have been able to hear the loud squeal of delight that came from the other end of the phone line.

—

As one of Duncan's many affluent and vanity-riddled flock currently utilising The Abbey, Portia was enjoying how things seemed to be looking up for her since she'd entered the hallowed healing walls. Under the guidance of Bruno Fielding she had managed to tackle her drink problem head-on and was already beginning to understand just what had made her search for solace in the bottom of a vodka bottle. It was her lack of emotional fulfilment. And if fulfilment was something that could be bottled, then currently her heart was overflowing with enough happiness to fill a jeroboam. Her wedding plans were in motion and in a matter of weeks she would be walking down the aisle to become Mrs Portia Romeo – not that she'd use that name, of course, to her public she would remain Portia Safari. If there was one thing that Portia had never had any understanding of it was the trashy way some celebrities decided to change their names after a wedding as if trying to stamp some self-indulgent seal of approval on their union. All that double-barrelled Knowles-Carter and Pinkett-Smith business was downright unnecessary and often foolish. She would not be changing her professional name for anyone – not even the delicious Piero.

For Portia, the one thing that was still lying *heavy*, no pun intended, on her mind, was her weight. But as she slid £50,000 in cash across the desk at Ed, she knew that the bundle of crisp notes was about to give her the wedding-dress body she wished for. She still found the man opposite her repulsive, but if he was the magic genie who could grant her wishes then the cash was a small price to pay.

'You needn't bother counting it. It's all there,' she barked. 'Now, if I can have the wonder drug, please. The sooner I start, the sooner I can shift my unwanted kilos.'

Ed pulled open one of the desk drawers and took out a small clear bottle of about fifty white tablets. He handed them to Portia. 'Wave the weight goodbye, Portia. Come that Caribbean wedding you'll be gliding down that aisle skinnier than Kiera Knightley. Now, I trust that concludes our business, and not a word of this to anyone, especially not the boss.'

Portia placed the bag in her pocket and went to leave the room. 'You have my word. I look forward to never seeing you again.' As she exited the office, her mind was drawn to Kiera Knightley. She'd met her once at a Hollywood party. She'd instruct Redmond to send a wedding invitation to her via her agent. Another A-lister would always look good in the wedding photos.

———

One person who had already been invited to the wedding was Bruno Fielding. Portia had been keen to show her gratitude for his advice about her addiction and he'd gratefully accepted. And he knew exactly who his 'plus-one' would be. He'd known without doubt the moment Portia invited him during her appointment in his office just after he'd met Nancy for the first time.

They'd met several times since, both at The Abbey and outside. Each time they had ended up making love, both of them unable to control their urges and longing for each other. Nancy was the most electrifying woman that Bruno had ever met and he was determined to do everything he could to satisfy her – both for her troubled mind and her yearning body. And Nancy was far from complaining.

As far as her yearning body was concerned, Nancy was basking in the heated glow of a jaw-droppingly stirring orgasm delivered from the expert tongue of Dr Fielding as it lapped around her clitoris while she spreadeagled her naked body across his office desk. Even before they had begun to talk, their clothes had been shed quicker than a rampant teenager on a prom night promise.

Smoothing her shift dress back into place as Bruno buttoned up his own crisp white shirt, Nancy listened as her lover told her about the wedding invitation. Her eyes widened with elation as the full glory of what he was saying sank in. 'You are freaking kidding me? You've been invited to that woman's wedding and you want me to go with you? To the Caribbean? Let me think about that, will you?' Without a millisecond's thought, she added, 'Yes, yes, yes!'

'Great,' beamed Bruno. 'I'd like us to be there together ... you know ... really together, as an item. You're so special to me, Nancy. I know I've only known you for a short while but I'm falling for you ... you know that, don't you?' He could feel himself blush as he spoke.

Before Nancy could answer, the telephone on Bruno's desk sounded, signalling an internal call. He picked it up and listened. Nancy watched as his forehead furrowed with concern at what he heard. 'Take them to one of the private suites and I'll be there immediately.'

Clicking off the phone, Bruno leaned over to kiss Nancy. 'There's an emergency, a new arrival that I need to see straight away. I need to split. Call me later and you can tell me what the fashionable twenty-first-century man is supposedly wearing in paradise these days. With you on my arm at this wedding I'm going to need clothes that are sharper than Joan Rivers' tongue.'

Bruno rushed from the office, leaving Nancy alone. Normally he would never leave a patient on their own in his office, but Nancy was hardly a patient, was she? As far as he was concerned, she was now his girlfriend. One that he intended to not let slip through his fingers.

Pulling her compact from her bag, Nancy checked her reflection in the mirror and lightly dusted some powder across her cheeks. Her face was flushed with the afterglow of sexual excitement. As she stood to leave, she eyed Bruno's suit jacket hooked over the back of his chair. He'd placed it there as he undressed before their love-making. The deep violet silk that lined the inside stared up her at, beckoning her. Unable to stop herself, she walked over and started to rifle through the pockets, cautiously looking towards the office door as she did so. She found Bruno's wallet and opened it up. Tiers of credit cards were housed within. A Coutts Gold one caught her eye, as did a cluster of banknotes all lined up neatly at the back. She pulled the cash out and counted it – £350. Without thinking about it, she rolled up the money and tucked it in her own bag.

She placed Bruno's wallet back into his pocket and scuttled from the room. As she shut the door behind her, she turned quickly and bumped straight into Tom, The Abbey life-coach. She almost bounced off his hard, muscular ebony body as they collided. She recognised his face from the employees' photos board situated in the reception. She remembered thinking how good looking he was in the photo. In the flesh he was even better.

'Sorry, my fault,' smirked Tom. 'I'm just rushing to a meeting. Forgive me.'

'Forgiven,' smiled Nancy, 'I should watch where I'm going.'

As she left, Nancy knew exactly where she was going. Central London – there was clothes shopping to be done. She had £350 of disposable cash and that would buy one or two items for her forthcoming trip to the Caribbean.

Speeding away from The Abbey in her car, Nancy's body may have been satisfied, but her troubled mind was obviously far from cured. Yet another dose of deceit and stealing behind someone's back proved that. Not that she was letting it worry her, far from it. Her mind was focused on deciding where to shop for the best body-boosting bikinis.

———

'Fit-looking woman,' thought Tom as he watched Nancy disappear out of sight after their collision. 'I wouldn't mind a piece of that.' He'd have to find out who she was and why Dr Fielding was treating her. Maybe she could become another notch on Tom's bedpost. She looked his type, but then pretty much anything with a pulse and spreadable legs was these days.

Not that he was going short when it came to the pleasures of the flesh. He had a rather enjoyable horny interlude planned with Martha.

She'd arrived at The Abbey that morning for a meeting with Dr Fielding and had texted him after her appointment saying that she'd be 'waiting for him' at his room. He loved her devil-may-care attitude. She may have been a patient at his place of work, but as far as a hormonally fuelled Tom was concerned, she was a highly sexy one and that was all that mattered.

She was lying on her front, her chin resting on one of her hands, her blond locks falling across her face. She grinned knowingly as Tom moved towards the bed, eyeing the perfect soft rosy cheeks of her backside as he did so.

'So, how's my favourite sex addict?' he winked, pulling his T-shirt over his head.

Martha rolled over onto her back. 'According to Dr Fielding I'm borderline addictive when it comes to sex,' she purred.

'*Borderline* addictive … well brace yourself, soldier, because I'm crossing those borders and preparing for an invasion of the horniest kind. Let me reacquaint you with my weapon of mass seduction!' he joked. A joyous Martha gave a gratifying groan of ecstasy as he did so.

—

As Martha was letting out groans of appreciation, on the other side of The Abbey, Lauren Everett was emitting a groan of displeasure as Bruno Fielding injected a dose of sedative into her arm. He had decided to administer it as soon as he'd laid eyes on his new patient. Her limbs shook and she chewed at her bottom lip as she nervously stared around the private room she'd been brought to.

It seemed like a mere two minutes ago that she'd been savouring the high life of Las Vegas with her new lover, Dale – the whole experience a vibrant neon whirl of the clichéd sex, drugs and ... well, the funky flowing rhythms of her hopeful first single, if not rock 'n' roll. So how had she gone from that to the quivering, jelly-like, mascara-stained mess that lay on the couch at The Abbey, forcibly held down by Dale and Dr Fielding?

The journey back from the States had been horrendous – at least it had for Dale. Lauren had not known a huge amount about it. He'd cleaned her up back at their hotel and given her two sleeping tablets, which knocked her out within a short space of time. While she slept he packed both of their suitcases and rearranged their flights home, securing them an earlier plane than scheduled. Within six hours, both he and a zonked-out Lauren, her puffy bloodshot eyes hidden behind a huge pair of sunglasses, had headed to the airport, checked in and boarded their flight. A shattered Lauren returned straight to sleep, not waking again until virtually touchdown at Heathrow. From there, Dale had driven her straight to The Abbey. There was no time to waste.

As a woozy Lauren watched the room blur around her and drift into darkness under the effects of the sedative, Dale explained to Bruno about the excess of drugs she had taken in Las

Vegas and why they had both been there in the first place. There seemed to be genuine care in his voice, and if Bruno was right, it sounded more than just professional concern.

'I need her clean, Dr Fielding,' stressed Dale. 'This mustn't happen again. I don't have to explain to you that drugs are everywhere in the celebrity world, but until this woman's first single is being played on every radio station out there and knocking the likes of Adele and One Direction off the top of the Billboard chart then I need her to deal with any temptations that come her way. I want results as soon as possible, which is why I brought her here. You guys are the best, so prove it. My own neck's on the line here. I already manage one fuck-up, I don't need another.'

'She'll be in good hands, Mr Cousins, you have my word on that,' assured Bruno. 'I need to run some tests but I'd suggest we should prescribe some beta blockers to begin with as Lauren's addiction and overdose could definitely put a strain on her heart and leave her open to cardiac risks.' There was a moment's silence before he added, his curiosity obviously piqued, 'So, you manage a lot of celebrities, do you? You're used to people, as you put it, *fucking up*?'

'Most of them are loopier than a fairground ride, Dr Fielding. But when talent like this little lady comes along ...' he pointed at an unconscious Lauren as he spoke, 'then you need to grab it with both hands. She is going to make me a shed-load of money as long as she can hold herself together. Even an educated man like you must have read about stars like Amy, Britney, Nancy ... you name them, they've all car-crashed their way through their careers at some point. I do not want to add Lauren to that list.'

Bruno furrowed his brow at the list of names. 'Amy ... I presume you mean the much-missed Winehouse, Britney speaks for itself ... as for Nancy ... you lose me, I'm afraid. Sinatra is the only one who comes to mind, and I'm sure you don't mean her.'

Dale laughed at the doctor's refreshing lack of celebrity savvy. 'Two out of three, doc. I was talking about Arlow. She's the other fuck-up I manage right now. Sang for a while, acted for a bit, last seen working with a plastic squid in a hellishly bad straight-to-DVD turkey. Once Lauren makes it big, I'll be dumping her. It's no wonder you didn't know her, doc – that's the fickle nature of showbiz for you. She's very much yesterday's news.'

Dale stopped talking as he watched the colour appear to drain from the doctor's face, leaving his once flushed complexion sallow and ashen. 'Er … are you OK, doc? You look a little peaky.'

'I'm fine,' bumbled Bruno, trying to compose himself. 'I've worked long hours lately and the shifts are catching up on me a bit,' he fudged. 'I'll run along and fill out the paperwork for Ms Everett. You have my word that we'll try and get her problem sorted as soon as possible. She'll be out there singing her heart out before you know it.'

Bruno left the room, his thoughts racing. *How dare that man say that Nancy was washed up? How could he even contemplate ditching Nancy and trashing her into the celebrity dustbin? Not Nancy … not my Nancy. That was who he was talking about, surely?* Bruno knew that there was no way on earth he should breach his sacred medical code of patient confidentiality and inform Nancy, but now that they were together, then surely telling her would be the right thing to do, wouldn't it? They shouldn't keep secrets from each other, should they? Heart over mind yet again.

He reached into his pocket to pull out his phone. It was empty. He must have left it in his jacket. He marched back to his office, his mind made up. He knew what he had to do.

Back in the patient room, Dale had made a decision too. After what he'd heard and seen with Lauren in Las Vegas, he knew that he potentially had a lucrative money-making geyser of talent on his hands.

In his eyes, Lauren had both the look and the sound to explode worldwide. He needed to make sure that nothing and no one could ruin it. Taking Lauren's phone from her clutch bag, he scrolled through the contacts list until he came to the number he required. Highlighting it, he pressed the dial button. It rang twice before answering. 'Hello, is that Saul Everett? My name's Dale Cousins. I need to speak to you about your wife – there are a few things I think you need to know …'

CHAPTER 51

It's called the snowball effect. The figurative term for the process that will begin from an initial state of seemingly small yet necessary significance and will then balloon and amplify into something much larger and much, much graver. From the most minuscule of seeds can grow a rampaging plant of destruction that is capable, triffid-like, of destroying any who find themselves lured into its poisonous path.

The initial seed was the split-second decision made by Dale Cousins to pick up the phone and dial Saul. It was something that, really, Lauren should have been doing. She was his wife, it was her duty. If she was intent on forging a career for herself in complete contrast to that of her husband's then it was her rightful place to inform him. Maybe by sitting down over a serene dinner in a private room at Kensington Roof Gardens, or a make-or-break weekend away in the splendour of Capri or the chi-chi glamour of Biarritz. Certainly not from the mouth of your cocksure manager and lover as you lay unconscious from the sense-stunning aftershock of a narcotics' haze.

But life was never predictable and once the ignition button of panic had been pressed then it was inevitable that an explosion was surely bound to follow.

Both stupefied and incensed by what he was hearing as he stood in his own front room, Saul had listened to the words that had spewed from Dale's mouth, informing him about his wife's actions. He had felt his blood pressure reach critical as he learnt about her trip to Las Vegas and tried to calm his rage as he heard Dale, a mysterious stranger he had never met and a man he never cared to meet, inform him that he was 'guiding Lauren to greater things'.

Greater than what? Than being married to a groundbreaker in the world of politics? *Who did this man think he was? Who gave him the right to play God Almighty and sit on his managerial cloud dispensing commandments to someone of Saul's calibre?*

In the few short minutes that Saul and Dale spent on the phone together, the politician had an important insight. The first was that he hated Dale Cousins. He hated the new man in Lauren's life. Not because he was guiding his wife to new things, possibly to new heights. Not even because he was serving information to Saul in a fait-accompli take-it-or-leave it media bullshit way. No, he hated him because he was taking away the stranglehold of security Saul thought he'd always had over Lauren. A trophy wife was no use to Saul if the metal was tarnished. In Saul's mind a man could only be top dog if his bitch wasn't let off her leash and allowed to sniff around elsewhere.

In a flash of the utmost clarity, in a life-changing moment that Saul would remember for the rest of his days, he made a decision. He didn't need Lauren. He didn't care. In fact, he wasn't even sure if he wanted her any more. He had tasted a better, more exquisite fruit. One that he knew he could really be himself with – his equal. The woman who had flooded his mind ever since he'd first *served* her.

For the first time for as long as he could remember, the staunch, rocky rigid exterior of cool, calm, collectiveness that was Saul Everett began to crumble. His focus on his career, on his life with Lauren, on his aspirations for the future seemed to blend into one image. It was the crystal-clear image of the woman he knew that he had to try to be with. Martha. She was the key to unlock any future happiness. The door on his life to Lauren needed to be shut and bolted forever.

Words tumbled from his mouth with a venom that contrasted sharply with the neat, calculated uniformity of his appearance. For a man so structured in his everyday life, Saul let the words flow freely. 'Next time you see my sneaky bitch of a wife, Mr Cousins, you can tell her that we're through. I'll instruct my press team to furnish the newspapers with the news that we've *drifted apart*. If she wishes to speak to me then I suggest she does it through her lawyers. I assume she's there with you. You're on her mobile, after all. I've wasted enough time trying to contact her over the past few days. She can play her little games and try to be some jumped-up pop star if she wishes, but as far as I'm concerned we're over. Better to do it now than have her embarrassing me writhing around on some godforsaken singing show. Nobody calls the shots with me, you tell her that. If she wants to play around then so be it, but I don't need her … I don't want her …' there was a slight pause, a momentary faltering of his voice before he concluded the sentence, '…not any more. Our time is done.'

Saul slammed down the phone, leaving Dale open-mouthed at the other end.

Within half an hour a phone call had been made to Saul's press team and an announcement drafted. It was short and to the point, telling of their separation and how Saul, making sure the tone of the statement was still politically correct, 'wished Lauren all the best for the future, whatever it may hold'. As soon as Nathan Spilsbury saw a copy of it, he was elated, his portly frame waddling around like an overexcited pheasant – overjoyed that his friend had 'finally seen the light and canned that silly bint of a wife'.

Mentally making it his own personal mission to find Saul a future wife who would do as required – one who would just sit, stay, never let herself off her leash and give Saul some snotty-nosed little rugrats to fill Downing Street – he immediately tried to phone him. It was engaged. The politician was already on the phone leaving a message for Martha, telling her that he urgently needed to see her again.

———

It wasn't until a few hours later that Lauren finally awoke from her unconsciousness. She'd been moved to a solitary suite at The Abbey and was lying underneath the crisp cotton sheets of her bed. Her throat was dry and her head hurt.

At first she was unaware of where she was, but as her eyes adjusted as she looked around the room, her memory became clear. She saw Dale sitting alongside the bed, his head hung back and his eyes closed. He was a welcome sight.

'Dale …? I need some water.' Her voice was weak and raspy, but still loud enough to rouse Dale from his slumber.

'Hey you,' he murmured, stretching his arms in a Y above his head as he did so. 'Sure thing … how are you feeling?'

'As rough as rats, to be honest. I want to get out of here, Dale. Can we go, please?'

Passing Lauren a glass of water from the jug by her bed, Dale took Lauren's other hand in his and squeezed it tenderly. 'Not until we sort out the issues you've been having. I need you fit and well if we're going to make the most of you as a budding Madonna. And that means no more overdoses, so we need to do what the experts here say, OK? They're putting you on tablets and you'll be receiving the best treatment money can buy.'

Pushing her hair from her face and sipping on the water, Lauren looked directly into Dale's dazzling blue eyes. 'I'm sorry, Dale … for everything. You're giving me an amazing chance and I keep messing it up. I'll do what I need to do, I promise.

And that includes talking to Saul. There's no way I'm risking him ruining what we have here. Not now, it's gone too far.' It was clear that Lauren wasn't just talking about her star potential. She'd enjoyed her intimate moments with Dale in Vegas just as much as he had.

A wave of seriousness washed over Dale's face. 'I need to apologise too, Lauren. There's something I need to tell you. I've spoken to Saul ...'

Lauren lay there wide-eyed, her eyebrows raised in shock as she listened to Dale's account of his conversation with Saul. As she did so, streams of tears twisted down her cheeks. They were a mixture of emotions – a tinge of sadness and an outpouring of relief.

———

'Those were the most heavenly chocolate truffles I have ever tasted,' cooed Nancy as she dabbed the corners of her mouth with her napkin. 'Rich and deliciously decadent – just how I like my men,' she added. 'Mind you, I have to admit, Bruno, the chocolate was a lot more free-flowing than the conversation has been this evening. Is there something wrong?'

It was true. Despite the grandeur of their restaurant surroundings, Bruno had not exactly been talkative during their three courses. Nancy was worried that maybe she'd been caught out and that Bruno had evidence to prove that she had taken the money from his wallet but, as yet, no mention had been made about the missing cash.

'I'm sorry, Nancy. It's just been a hellish day, that's all, and I'm just glad you agreed to come out this evening. I know it's only been hours but I have been desperate to see you, honestly. I think I could have finally found what I've been looking for and I don't want anything to spoil it.'

'And what could that be, exactly? A gorgeous restaurant, excellent food and wine and a devastatingly sexy man opposite me. And to think I was contemplating an evening watching reruns of *Game Of Thrones* and *Breaking Bad* on the telly. I think I made the right decision, don't you?' There was more than a lashing of sarcasm layered through Nancy's words. 'What on earth could spoil this? You wait until you see the bikinis I've bought for the Caribbean, Bruno.'

'I look forward to it – not that they'll stay on for long, I can assure you of that,' winked Bruno, a glint twinkling across his face. 'I need to talk to you seriously, though, and you have to swear to me that what I tell you will go no further. I'm telling you because I like you, Nancy. I like you a lot and if it didn't affect you then I wouldn't even consider it. I've been beating myself up about it all day, which is why I've been a bit quiet tonight.'

'Bruno, you're rambling and gushing and making no sense. If you have something to say then tell me. While I still have the taste of those truffles in my mouth there is nothing on earth that could upset me,' she joked, although inwardly her stomach flipped with dreaded anticipation. She had an inkling this was not going to be good news.

Taking her hands in his, Bruno leant across the table towards Nancy. 'When I left you today, I had to go and see a new patient.'

'Yes, I know. You're always the busy little psychologist. Now cut to the chase and tell me what's on your mind. You don't have to be a medical expert to know that you're freaking me out a little at the moment.' Nancy shifted nervously in her chair as she waited.

'Well, the patient is a client of Dale Cousins, the same guy who manages you. She's come in for a drug overdose problem and I've put her on beta blockers, but that's neither here or there. It's what he said that I need to tell you …'

Like an excited puppy who had just been promised *walkies* or a child who had just found out they were going to Disneyland, Nancy's ears sprang to attention. All thoughts of truffles and stolen cash evaporated form her mind as she listened to what Bruno had to say. She could feel her skin darken with a purple stain of anger as he described what Dale had said about dumping Nancy professionally once 'his client hit the big time'. She didn't need to be psychic to work out just exactly who the client was. It wasn't until she was sure that Bruno had finished his story that she formulated her response.

'Darling, that man has been threatening to dump me for years, despite me bringing in more money for him in my time than any other client. It's bullshit. And anyway, who's to say this *client* of his will make it big? I had top ten hits all around the world and you don't see me snorting coke and going crazy, do you? She's obviously a crazy bitch. Drug overdoses are so trashy. Very late Whitney!'

'So, you're not worried? If he dumps you then you're not screwed? He did say your career has taken a bit of a nosedive.'

'Rather nosedive than nose candy, eh? Dale needs me more than I need him. I think it's time I changed management after all,' bluffed Nancy, fully aware that her name was about as welcome on most management books as the Wicked Witch of the West.

'How did you know it's cocaine?' asked Bruno, his eyes narrowing with a slight suspicion. 'I never said—'

Nancy shifted nervously again. 'Because it's the only thing white about the black murky world of the music industry and I've never known Dale not to have a bag or three concealed about his person. He's got nostrils that look like they've been iced there's so much coke up there. Now, is that everything you were worried about, because I'd rather talk about something much more important like when you're going to check me out in those bikinis. I need to make sure my man is more than happy, don't I?'

A broad, wanton grin spread across Bruno's face. 'Why don't you come back to mine tonight? I'll show them my appreciation.'

'Because they're at *my* house. Why don't we head back there and I'll try them on for you. You're going to love them. One Betsey Johnson and one Victoria's Secret.'

'You say that like I'm supposed to know what that means, Nancy. As long as they're easy to get off that's all I ask. Right, I'll go and pay the bill. Yours it is.'

It wasn't until Bruno had left the table to go and settle the bill that Nancy allowed her anger at Dale to bubble over. She clenched her hand into a fist and banged it firmly on the table, causing her wine glass to wobble. *How dare he tell people she was washed up? It was Lauren who had to worry – the drug-crazed slut. She'll be wishing she went the whole hog with the overdose when I've finished with her*, she thought, pursing her lips in fury.

Oh yes, Nancy didn't need to worry about Dale cutting all financial ties with her. She had a mega-rich suitor on her arm in the shape of Bruno and she'd soon have her own payday rolling in thanks to a certain politician.

In fact, just as Nancy was choosing the truffles from the menu on her night out with Bruno, at the home of a still livid Saul Everett an A4 brown envelope with his name typed on it turned up on his doorstep in the leather-gloved hands of a motorcycle courier. Assuming it was something from Nathan or a necessary document for his work, Saul had ripped it open.

Inside he found two eight by ten inch colour photos. One showed his soon-to-be ex-wife snorting cocaine off a table, and in the other she was wrapped around a mystery man in a casino. He surmised rightly that they were both taken in Las Vegas and that the man in question was the man he'd spoken to on Lauren's phone. A white sheet of paper accompanied the photographs. On it were typed the words MR EVERETT, THESE PHOTOS OF YOUR WIFE BEING FAR FROM RIGHT AND HONOURABLE HIT THE PRESS UNLESS I GET EXACTLY WHAT I WANT. AND THAT MEANS CASH. DON'T MESS WITH ME BECAUSE I MEAN BUSINESS. Following it was a mobile phone number and Nancy's name.

'What the fuck …?' hissed Saul. If they had arrived a day before he'd have been devastated, certain that his career would be ruined, but after his conversation with Dale and his decision about Martha he was now looking at the photos in a completely different way. It had been a pivotal day for Saul.

Placing Nancy's handiwork back in the envelope he poured himself a Scotch and logged onto the internet. He typed the words 'Dale Cousins' into a search engine and found the Roma Records website. Clicking onto it he looked at the clients listed there underneath a smiling photo of Dale, which confirmed he was the man in the Vegas photo with Lauren. Running his eyes across the photos there was no mention of Lauren, but one name stood out above all the others: Nancy Arlow – the woman trying to blackmail him. *Interesting*, mused Saul, downing the rest of his Scotch.

Nancy was just downing the remaining splashes of her red wine when Bruno returned to the table, his wallet in his hand. A deep line of worry was etched across his forehead. 'That's really weird,' he said, 'I withdrew some money this morning as I hoped we'd be eating out tonight and I know for sure it was in my wallet. I just went to pay and it's not there any more. I had to use a card instead, not that it matters. But I know that money was there. I left my wallet in my jacket when I left you in the office. Somebody must have come in and taken it. But that's not likely at The Abbey. I'd trust them all. You didn't see anything strange, did you?'

Worried that she was suspected, Nancy was quick to try and detour his thoughts. 'Well, I hope you don't think I had anything to do with it?' she stated, somewhat over-dramatically. 'Maybe it dropped out somewhere. Have you tried your pockets? Mind you, I did see something, now I come to think of it.' She was feverishly trying to angle the spotlight of suspicion off her.

'When I left your office that life-coach guy was outside your door. He was looking incredibly shifty and said he needed you for something. He was quite flustered,' she lied. Unable to stop herself, Nancy continued, 'I'm not a hundred per cent sure but I am fairly certain he went into your office as I was leaving. He looked very devious when I saw him. Maybe he took it. I daresay the coaches are not paid as much as you psychologists, are they? Perhaps he was trying to top up his salary.'

'Tom would never do that ... he's a good man. Or at least I think he is.' Nancy could almost see the seed of doubt germinating inside Bruno's brain. 'Are you sure?' he asked.

Nancy nodded without saying a word. On the way back to hers, Bruno made a phone call to Duncan Porte. Duncan said he would deal with the situation. By morning, Tom had been relieved of his duties at The Abbey, pending enquiries. Once more, Nancy's handiwork had done its damage.

CHAPTER 52

As a desolate Tom was being marched off The Abbey premises the next morning by a burly security guard and an almost tearful Duncan Porte, Kieran Bradford was speeding his sleek Aston Martin V8 Vantage across the gravel at the front of the rehabilitation centre. He'd been requested there by text from Martha in the middle of the night. Her message had been vague, short and not overly sweet, striking a chord of concern through Kieran's mind: *K – we need to talk. Can you meet me at The Abbey tomorrow, I'm here sorting out some stuff but I need to see you. M.*

For Martha it had not been the most restful of nights. Her lengthy love-making session with Tom had been as filthily glorious and as explosive for her clitoral nerve endings as ever. But just as she'd been drifting off to sleep in Tom's arms, the warm post-coital sanctuary of his muscular arms around her, both she and Tom had been woken up by a loud rapping at the door. Slipping on his boxer shorts, a confused Tom had rushed to the door to confront the cause of the disturbance. His confusion escalated further when he was greeted by a solemn-faced Duncan Porte, usually one of Tom's biggest fans, sandwiched by a pair of thickset men whom Tom recognised as part of The Abbey security team. A bleary-eyed Martha pulled the bedsheets high across her body to cover her naked form as Tom, feeling somewhat obligated, invited the trio of men into his room. She could feel the eyes of the two security men scanning her opportunistically, like a couple of starving dogs with a bone. Wrapping the sheets around her she grabbed her clothes and moved to the bathroom to get dressed.

When she returned, Tom too was fully dressed, sitting on the edge of his bed, his head in his hands. Duncan and the two security men still stood over him. Martha could see that distress was branded across Tom's face, tears threatening to fall.

'I've been accused of stealing,' he said, his voice riddled with disbelief. 'My boss has asked me to leave straight away. I can't work here again until all of this has been sorted out. This is shit, man, I didn't steal anything.'

'I want to believe you, Tom, I do,' said Duncan. 'You know I think you're a huge asset to this place but we've a witness who saw you going into Dr Fielding's office for no apparent reason. Until we can prove that she's in the wrong I'm afraid we need to suspend your work here. When all of this blows over, as I'm sure it will, we can take a look at your job again. But for now I need to think about the business. I can't have important clients here who think that there might be a thief on the premises. I have always prided myself on the fact that The Abbey has a flawless reputation. I will not have anything tarnish that ... no matter how unfounded the accusations might turn out to be. You can stay here tonight, but you'll have to leave in the morning.'

Duncan turned to leave, flanked by the guards. As he reached the door he turned to Martha. 'And Ms Éclair, given the nature of your addictive issue with us here at the moment, may I suggest that sleeping with the staff members is possibly not the best route to finding a solution, no matter how attractive you may find our life coach. I trust you'll not be staying the night in here? If you do wish to rest overnight at The Abbey then I suggest you check into one of our client rooms.' Despite the pointed nature of his conversation, there was a hint of a wry smile forming on Duncan's lips as he left the room.

As soon as Duncan shut the door behind him, Tom became angry. He walked to the bedside table and lashed out at the lamp and glass of water placed there with a turbulent swipe. He let out a snarl as the glass shattered against the wall, spilling its contents.

'I never went into Dr Fielding's office, Martha. I would never steal money from him – I would never steal full stop. I don't need to. I earn a good living here and I have other sources of income as you well know. I haven't even been near Fielding's office all day. I've been busy, man. The only time I was anywhere near there was on the way here.'

Tom cast his mind back to his collision with Nancy outside Bruno's office. A fit-looking woman like that was not easy to forget. She'd been coming from his office, hadn't she? She must have been a patient of his. There had been something a little bit shifty about her though, almost hurried and agitated. Looking back, and given the accusations that had just been levelled at him, Tom wasn't sure that the woman wasn't the root of his troubles. 'I think I may have been stitched up,' he declared, staring at Martha.

She listened intently as he told her about his encounter with Nancy, not that he was able to name her, but his description of her hair, face and skin tone was incredibly detailed. By the time he had finished the story, Martha had already formulated a plan. She had a clear picture of the woman and knew exactly who might be able to reveal her identity. Kissing Tom fully on the lips, Martha gathered her things and headed towards the door. She was determined to try and help. She may not have known Tom for long, but even she didn't have him pegged as a petty thief.

'Leave it with me,' she urged, 'I think I might know who that woman was. If she is your boss's mystery witness, then we'll find out exactly what she thinks she's seen. I'll let you know how I get on. Don't worry – we'll sort this mess, trust me. Speak tomorrow. And besides, after what your boss has just said, I had better not stay the night, had I? Won't do my "borderline sex addiction" any good at all, will it?' she winked.

Right, let's see if we can work out who this woman is, she pondered. *I hope Portia's got her Miss Marple head on …*

———

Portia was finally thoroughly enjoying her time at The Abbey. Her sessions with Dr Fielding and following his valid expertise had made her think less and less about alcohol. She could still down an ice-cold flute of her favourite Krug with relish given the chance, but the knotted ball of desperation and craving that she'd once felt for regular doses of alcohol was definitely unravelling.

There was a new addiction in her life and it was causing much less of a hangover than her previous one – her forthcoming wedding to Piero. In between visits from Redmond, informing her of future professional requests for appearances around the world and confirming the ever-expanding guest list for the wedding, Portia had spent her day on the phone to Piero, whispering sweet nothings into his operatic ear and declaring her ever-growing love for him.

For the moment they could not be together as he had been called to Ukraine to discuss a forthcoming engagement at the National Opera House in Kiev, but there wasn't an instant when Portia wasn't literally counting the seconds until she could have him in her bed again.

The other thing that had kept Portia's mind well and truly out of harm's way from the dangers of the drink was the seemingly never-ending list of things that needed to be arranged for her forthcoming ceremony. Redmond was, as ever, the pinnacle of giddy organisation, revelling in the details such as magazine deals and press opportunities, but Portia was determined that the finer, more intimate ideas for how her special day was to flow would be tailor-made from her own mind. There were first class guest flights from around the world to organise, guest transfers to the secluded splendour of Peter Island, limos, helicopters, villas, wedding dresses, bridesmaids, flowers, decorations, hair and make-up, entertainment, party planners to arrange ... the list and the price-tag seemed to increase by the hour. Five million and counting, but to Portia the price was beyond questioning.

Since she had secured the slimming wonder-drug from Ed, she had felt that finally everything was coming together. Losing those final few pounds that had been so apparent to her as she stared into the mirror, if not anyone else, would be the succulent cherry on the icing on the wedding cake of her dreams. There was no way that the chosen designer for her wedding dress – she was yet to decide which of the many designs on offer was most flattering – would make her look anything less than red-carpet fabulous.

Portia was just about to slip her silk Elle Macpherson dressing gown from her shoulders and take her first dose of the wonder drug before retiring when there was a knock on her door. It was late, but maybe Redmond had yet more news for her about the wedding. *Why doesn't the blessed man just ring,* she thought as she glided to the door. She was pleasantly surprised to find Martha standing there.

'Dear girl, how marvellous to see you again,' she cried excitedly, ushering her friend in. 'I trust you're looking forward to the big day? How's your father? Redmond told me that you had to fly back home to South Africa? Will he be well enough to come to the wedding? I do hope so. It's all coming along rather marvellously. I've been booking all kinds of entertainment today. Everything from steel bands to torch singers. I was thinking about your housemate, the stripper girl … is it Kelly? Would she consider performing at Piero's stag night in Tortola before the wedding? I am sure his red-blooded friends would adore it. Might as well give him one last tantalising look at another female body before he gets to feast his eyes on mine and mine alone for the rest of his days.'

Portia's succession of bullet-quick questioning came to an end as she suddenly realised what an odd hour it was for a visitor. Sliding her dressing gown back on she motioned to a coffee maker on the far side of her room. 'Can I make you a drink? I'd offer you something stronger, but given my current situation, no can do I'm afraid, Martha. Now, what on earth are you doing here in the middle of the night?'

'Well, I'm hoping you can help a friend of mine. I think he's been accused of something he didn't do.'

Portia listened fixedly as Martha described the woman who had bumped into Tom earlier that day. There was no doubt in her mind as to who she was and she was quick to inform Martha about Nancy. 'If it is her, and it certainly sounds like it is, then she's a devious little bitch and I'd bet my future happiness that she's the one who shafted your life-coach friend. Stealing is obviously second-nature to her. It seems that she's been pretty light-fingered at the house of my aunt Betsy. Lovely woman, Betsy, you'll meet her at the wedding. She treats me like her daughter.' Portia went on to tell Martha about her own chance meeting with Nancy when she'd first spotted her aunt's stolen ring. 'I'm plotting my revenge though; I have her name and number and she'll rue the day that she messed with my family. Nobody messes with me. I'll make her pay – at whatever cost I decide.'

It was well into the early hours of the morning before Martha left Portia's room. Portia had offered her accommodation at Mara again for the night, but Martha turned it down, preferring to find herself a room at The Abbey. She wanted to see Tom again in the morning to let him know once more that she would do everything she could to prove his innocence. Rubbing her tired eyes as she walked to the reception, she enquired with the woman behind the desk about the possibility of a room for the night. She was just taking a room key from her when her phone rang. It was Saul. He'd left a message for her earlier and in the drama of the evening she had forgotten to return his call. But as his mistress, she could make him wait. The mere thought of him though filled her with an inner melting pot of passionate desires, more so than any of her other lovers. Saul had definitely become the front-runner in the race for her heart.

She answered it, expecting to hear his deep, clear masculine tones – instead his words were slurred and frenzied. He had obviously been drinking heavily, something that was completely out of character. She tried to interrupt the rambling words that spewed from his lips but to no avail. She could only listen to try and decipher his words. Even in his drunken state it was still clear what he was saying. *He'd left that bitch Lauren, she'd been taking him for a ride and he now knew there was only one woman for him. He wanted to be with Martha.* As Saul rang off, seemingly unaware that Martha had even answered the phone and that he wasn't talking to a machine, his last few words drilled into Martha's mind. 'I need you, Martha … mistress … Martha … we belong together. I want to be with you. I love you … I need you so much … please, please be with me. I love you.' His pleading words were drenched with genuine emotion, revealing a soft, vulnerable side of him that she'd never seen before.

Despite his drunkenness there was no doubt in Martha's mind that he meant every word. She trusted him, which was more than she could say for her feelings towards Lauren. At the back of her mind Martha wasn't convinced that Lauren wouldn't fight to get her man back, despite her recent protestations of marital misery. She and Saul had major history and the thought of Lauren trying to reignite a seemingly extinguished flame with Saul if things didn't run smooth in the future incensed her more than she cared to admit.

She had no idea why he'd left Lauren and at that moment she didn't really care. After weeks of swaying her affections between two of the many men in her life – the two men who actually meant more to her than just another round of sex – the normally free-spirited Martha made a conclusive decision.

She wanted to be with Saul. There was something about him that she'd never experienced from another man, and it wasn't just his love of kinky sex. There was a light that came from deep inside him and reflected and refracted on each any every surface of his multi-faceted personality. She'd become more and more fascinated and captivated by him at each and every one of their rendezvous.

Maybe Martha had found her Mr Right. Lauren's marital loss could be her emotional gain. It was just as she climbed into bed, the first rays of early morning light breaking over the horizon, that Martha had texted Kieran. If she was to be with Saul, then she owed it to Kieran to be honest and tell him how she felt. They needed to meet and she needed to end it – if she didn't then how could she ever give herself fully to Saul?

CHAPTER 53

Kieran had known exactly what Martha was going to say. He'd sensed it in her text. Even though he'd never really stated his growing feelings for her face to face, he had known from the first time that he had started to follow her on Peter's command that there was something bewitching, alluring and ultimately heart-enveloping about the heiress to the Éclair empire.

And he'd thought that maybe she was beginning to feel the same. He thought he'd seen it in her eyes, that maybe there was a common glimmer of both sexual and sensual admiration between them. She had gone from being the target of his stalking to the object of his affections. That was why he'd destroyed the photos he'd taken of her dogging. He loved her free spirit, he loved her *joie de vivre* and he hated the thought that the photos could be used against her.

But all of that didn't matter any more. All of that had been taken away from him when Martha had said that she didn't want to see him again. She'd been honest. There was someone else and she wanted to make a go of it with him. She didn't offer names and Kieran didn't ask for any. There wasn't any trace of deceit in her eyes or threads of dishonesty in her voice. Martha had just been straight with him and for that, he respected her. If he didn't respect her he could have told her how he'd been ordered to follow her by her mother's lover, how he was supposed to seduce her into a loveless marriage – at least it would supposedly be – just so a dutiful son could please his bully of a father.

But Peter Bradford hadn't counted on Kieran genuinely falling for Martha. In a parallel universe, without the meddling Peter demanding and orchestrating their initial meeting, maybe they could have met on their own terms and honestly fallen for each other. But their union was built on the foundations of deception and that would never build a true house of love. No, Kieran would walk away from Martha and leave her be. Let her carry on with her life.

He'd kissed her tenderly on the cheek as he said goodbye and wished her well. Maybe the international bed-hopping, cruel-hearted philanderer had learnt something from Martha. Perhaps the hard exterior that had been crafted from his boot-camp years under his father's watchful and critical stare had finally begun to crumble a little. Maybe there was more to life than just the accumulation of wealth and power at the pitiful expense of others. Had Kieran the playboy played his last?

As he walked out of The Abbey reception and back out into the warming morning air towards his car, he didn't know. He was just glad that Martha was not aware that she had been originally intended as another one of his victims. Or so he thought … one phone call from Martha ruined that …

———

Over the course of the next hour, a weeping Martha phoned her mother, Mariella, to tell her what had been going on in her life. She never talked of Kieran or Saul by name, but she told her mother that she'd been caught between two men, one of them born in South Africa, and that she'd finally made the choice. She informed her that her chosen man was married, but that didn't matter for now. She knew that Mariella couldn't judge her – wasn't she, after all, currently torn between two men? Surely she'd understand the situation her daughter found herself in better than most?

'So, who's coming to the wedding with you then, Mother?' enquired Martha again, just as she had done in South Africa. The geography was different but the answer was still the same. Silence. How could she say anything when her current partner, Peter, was standing right behind her trying to earwig her conversation?

As Mariella ended her call with her daughter, Peter leapt to interrogate her. She shared the confessions that Martha had divulged on the phone, not realising just what she was saying or indeed starting. Peter's brain zigzagged with a web of thoughts. 'Born in South Africa' – Kieran, dumped – Kieran, betraying his father – Kieran, failing his father – Kieran. The boy had not done as instructed. There would be consequences. So strong, yet so weak – had he not learnt anything from his father? Had he not learnt how to succeed?

Peter walked to his study and logged onto his e-mails and found the photos of Martha dogging. Clicking his icon on the 'print' button, he watched as the photos started to appear through the printer in glorious, immaculate, scandal-revealing colour. The time had come to put the photos to good use.

———

As Kieran went to climb back into his car at The Abbey, a hand grabbed his shoulder and twisted him round roughly. He barely had time to focus on the woman in front of him before he felt a hard, harsh slap across his face. The first was followed by an equally strong second, a backhander that stung against his cheek. The ring the woman was wearing cut into his flesh, drawing a small line of blood. It was Nancy.

'You bastard! Enjoy stealing from people, do you? You're the fucker who took my money at the casino. You took my bag and everything – thousands of pounds. I recognise you.' She was thumping her hands on his shirt as she shouted, unable to control her rage. 'I'm going to call the police. They'll have you, you thieving wanker.'

Kieran recognised her. She was right – he had taken her money. It had been like taking candy from a baby. The stupid woman had been all gooey-eyed over him from the moment he'd sat down beside her at the roulette table. He'd enjoyed spending her twenty-five grand but he couldn't risk her phoning the police. If they searched his place they'd still find her Prada clutch bag there. He hadn't ditched it yet – he'd been too busy chasing after Martha. He grabbed her arms and wrapped his hands around her wrists to stop her continual thumping. Painting the biggest and most sincere smile he could across his face he tried to calm Nancy down.

'Look, I can understand you're a bit upset about something, but you should accuse the right guy before you start whacking the living daylights out of somebody. I don't know what you're talking about. I hope you find the guy who's ripped you off, but it's not me, Ok? So, unless you want me to tell the police that you've just assaulted me for no reason whatsoever then I suggest you don't bother calling the boys in blue just yet.'

Kieran knew that Nancy wouldn't believe him. She was right not to. But for a few seconds he could see a formation of self-doubt cloud across her mind. It was all the time he needed.

He climbed into his Aston Martin, turned the key in the ignition and reversed the car away from Nancy. He could see her looking at him, wondering whether she should let him drive away from her. She was still left wondering as Kieran's car sped out of sight, the wheels spinning across the gravel.

As The Abbey disappeared from sight Kieran decided that perhaps it was time that he fled the country for a while. With no

Martha to chase and a potential brush with the law courtesy of Nancy, it seemed the right time to fade into the great unknown.

Back at his London apartment, he packed a suitcase, grabbed his passport and headed to the airport. He dumped Nancy's Prada clutch bag in a skip en route.

CHAPTER 54

Blackmail has never been a fast track to a happy ending – in fact, quite the opposite. Nobody with blackmail in mind enters into their trickery without a stain of hatred for those around them branded onto their souls.

Nancy's soul was becoming darker every day and as she waved Bruno off at her front door, she felt an excited anticipatory charge of electricity run through her at the thought of what the day ahead might bring. Bruno was heading back to The Abbey and would no doubt be attempting to treat Lauren and her tragic addiction.

Nancy was still smarting from what Bruno had told her the night before at the restaurant. The news about Lauren's condition had pleased her dark side immensely but the brutal fact that Dale wanted to dump Nancy as a client had frozen her to the core. *How dare he? Despite all of their highs and lows, they worked well together, didn't they? Theirs was a special bond that could never be severed completely.* Plus he was all she had right now when it came to her career. He'd soon forget about Lauren when Saul intervened – especially now that he was in possession of the photos she'd sent. Payday for Nancy and a petrified Saul dragging a wayward and drug-fucked Lauren back into the bosom of her marital home were surely just moments away.

It was a little after midday that Nancy's mobile rang. It was a withheld number. Nancy's heart raced as she answered. 'Hello ...'

'Is that Nancy Arlow?' The voice on the phone was deep and rich. She recognised it as Saul Everett's.

'I knew you'd ring. I trust you've seen the photos of your wannabe pop-star wife. Has she told you yet?' Saul gave no answer so Nancy continued. 'Such a shame that she's so keen to spread her wings and fly away from home – poor little sparrow – she's flying in the wrong airspace though by straying into mine. She needs shooting down. I want cash to stop the photos hitting the press and I need you to nip her career in the bud. Do you understand?' Nancy was relishing the surge of power tearing through her. It came to an abrupt halt as Saul spoke, his words hitting her like a baseball bat.

'You listen to me, woman. I have your photographs, and I know all there is to know but there will be no cash, you stupid bitch. I daresay a woman of your suspect intellect hasn't read the newspapers today, but if you had you'd see that my wife and I have announced our separation. Our marriage is over and I couldn't give a shit if she wants to go off and sing with a bunch of thick-necked rappers or snort enough cocaine to kill a herd of caribou. We're over. If you want to take your photos to the press you do it. She'll suffer and so will Dale Cousins. Good – they deserve each other. If you want to piss off your own manager, then you do it, but if I know anything about the music business, then a star that sticks drugs up her nose is pretty commonplace. The press might not do me any good at first, but it'll be forgotten before you know it. You show me a politician who hasn't had a hefty dose of mud and controversy thrown at them at some point. We all bounce back, which is more than you'll do if Mr Cousins dumps you as a client. I didn't have to spend too long on the internet to find out just how washed up your career is. Put your name into any search engine and the words "loser" and "has-been" are featured in every result. You can whistle for your

cash because it won't be coming from me, OK? If I hear from
you again, you'll regret it … I mean that. You picked the wrong
man to blackmail …'

A shaking Nancy could only scream as she heard the sound
of Saul hanging up. It was not how the conversation between
them was supposed to unfurl. She was supposed to be seriously richer at the end of it, with Saul's short and curlies firmly
gripped between her avaricious fingers. Instead, he had shafted
her – played an ace for which she had no winning move.

She switched on the TV in her bedroom. It was true, she
hadn't seen the papers today. She'd spent the morning lazing in
the bath and applying a face mask. She'd arranged to meet Bruno
again that evening and she was determined to look her best. She
pressed the interactive button on her remote and a series of news
headlines appeared on the screen. *Oscar-winner's baby scandal,
internet usage linked to depression, glamour model marries cage-
fighter boyfriend in surprise ceremony, society girl found murdered*
… Then she saw it – the headline that confirmed what Saul had
said. POLITICIAN EVERETT SEPARATES FROM WIFE. It
was near the bottom of the page. It didn't even have top billing.

Nancy slumped onto her bed and felt her eyes begin to burn
as tears tumbled from them. This wasn't supposed to happen.
She was relying on that money. Her debts were spiralling and
those photos were meant to be her passport to solvency. Why
was it all going wrong?

Thank God she had Bruno in her life. The doctor could be
just the diagnosis she needed to ease the pressure. Wiping her
tears away with the back of her hand she reached across to the
bedside table and picked up a packet of cigarettes that lay there.
Despite having given up smoking years ago, Nancy had started
again over the last few weeks, her lack of willpower getting the
better of her.

It wasn't a cigarette that she took from the packet though. Slipping her fingers between the packet's gold lining paper and the box itself, Nancy pulled out Bruno's Coutts Gold credit card. She'd taken it from his wallet as he slept alongside her in the middle of the night. She needed cash and having seen his PIN and memorised it when they'd stopped at a petrol station for fuel on the way to hers, she knew that the card was now her only option. She planned to replace the card in Bruno's wallet again that evening. Hopefully he wouldn't even notice that it had gone. She hadn't been sure that she'd actually use it, but after her conversation with Saul, her mind was made up.

Twenty minutes later Nancy found herself slotting Bruno's credit card into a cashpoint not far from her apartment. It was a major risk, but Bruno must have more money than most people could dream of. He was at the top of his field and would be paid a fortune for what he did. *He wouldn't notice if some extra cash disappeared from his account ... would he?* Unable to stop herself, Nancy entered the PIN and withdrew as much cash as the machine would allow. It was a four-figure sum. An anxious ripple of unease spread across her mind. She shouldn't be doing this to Bruno – he was one of the good guys. But now they were together and relationships were about give and take. For now, she would be the one doing the taking.

——

Martha was just about to experience the squalid nightmares of blackmail too. Not that she knew it as she left The Abbey to visit Saul. They had spoken on the phone as soon as she had finished her confrontation with Kieran – something which, despite its somewhat harsh nature, had left her with a feeling that she had done the right thing. She knew that her mind was focused on Saul and even though she still enjoyed her adrenalin-inducing liaisons with Tom she knew that there was something different about Saul. He seemed her perfect match – a deviously delicious soul wrapped in a magnificent outside shell laced throughout with a lusty libido. Many partners would find Saul daunting but Martha adored him.

Saul had informed her that Lauren was staying at The Abbey and was being treated for an addiction to cocaine with a course of beta blockers. Martha had been tempted to visit Lauren to wish her well, but a thunderclap of guilt and hypocrisy sounded within her as she mulled over the thought. *Hi, Lauren, how are you? By the way, you know you and Saul have split – well, I'm tickled pink because I think I love him. No hard feelings? And by the way, if you are under any sneaky illusions about trying to patch things up with him then I'll be round to put a pillow over your face to make sure that never happens.* It was hardly the best bedside conversation to have with her so-called friend, was it? It would come out sooner or later but hearing about Martha's feelings towards her husband was hardly the kind of medicine even the most sadistic of doctors would prescribe right now.

Saul had also informed Martha about the blackmail package of photos of Lauren that had been delivered to him and about Nancy Arlow's unsuccessful attempt to extort money out of him. It was Nancy that Martha was uber-keen to discuss upon arrival at Saul's.

'I've heard that woman's name twice now in less than twenty-four hours and it's been connected with three totally separate but equally low-down and dirty things. First off, your photos of Lauren. Secondly, I'm sure she's the one who has managed to have my friend, Tom, suspended from The Abbey, and finally, she stole some jewellery from my friend Portia's aunt. The woman is evil, it would seem. If she is behind Tom's suspension I swear to God I'll kill her. She needs to be halted.' For a soft-natured free spirit like Martha, her words of hate to those around her were becoming surprisingly harsh.

Saul raised his eyebrows as he looked at Martha. 'I have her number if you want to take things further.'

'Portia has it and wants to get her own back so I wouldn't want to deny her the pleasure,' smiled Martha. 'She was the reason I was at The Abbey.' She paused before adding somewhat mysteriously, 'Amongst other things.' It was almost like an invitation for Saul to question her. 'I'm bridesmaid at her wedding and naturally I'm allowed to take someone with me. Seeing as you're top of my wish list, would you care to come?'

'I don't see why not. It's in the Caribbean, isn't it? I read about it in the newspapers. I saw your name mentioned as bridesmaid. It'll be worth it just to see you all dressed up like a meringue. It'll be a huge turn-on to see you dressed in pretty white frills.' Saul smirked and wrapped his arms around her waist, drawing her to him.

'Easy, mister. My dress is neither white nor frilly ... but you can guarantee I'll have a pair of latex panties on underneath it just for you – with a peephole for easy access.' The thought obviously excited Saul as Martha could feel his swollen erection, harboured inside his trousers, pressing against her body.

'Now we're talking. In that case, it's a definite.'

'Are you sure you'll be able to come with your job? The wedding is about six weeks away.'

'I'm my own boss. And besides, the job isn't the only thing that concerns me. Especially now that you're around. Let's just say that I want to concentrate on my policies for having a bit of fun for a while.' Saul twitched his cock, emphasising his desires. 'Now, who's this Tom? Should I be worried?' He leant in to kiss her, allowing his tongue to dance across her lips as he did so. As their lips parted, Saul sank to his knees in front of Martha and started to unbutton her satin trousers. 'I need to show you that I am the man who can serve you best, mistress. I want to satisfy you,' he moaned, his voice drenched with sexual adventure.

Martha, a warmth spreading between her legs, knew just how to react. 'Oh, Tom's a big beautiful man who pleases my body greatly, but I need you to show me your own skilful ways. Serve me, Saul … serve me. You know how to please me, don't you'

There was no way that Saul could answer. Having pulled Martha's thong to one side, he had his mouth buried deep within her pussy, lapping at it with his tongue. He was still on his knees, his face enshrined between her legs, when she reached orgasm.

Having rearranged her clothes, pleased with *the service* Saul had provided for her, they both sat alongside each other on the couch in his front room. Martha looked up at the oh-so-happy wedding photos of Lauren and Saul together that stared down at her from the mantelpiece and felt a sharp stab of plaited worry and guilt run through her. It was something she wasn't used to. She turned to look at Saul, her eyes quizzical.

'Is it definitely over between you and Lauren? It seems a bit quick. You both seem so together in the photos and I know that Lauren was crazy about you. I am supposed to be Lauren's friend, Saul. I daren't think what she will say when she finds out about us. She told me and Kelly all about you. What went wrong?' Martha gently let her fingers run down one of Saul's cheeks, enjoying the feel of the five o'clock shadow that was beginning to grow there.

Saul looked Martha directly in the eyes as he spoke. There was a softness to his voice that she was not used to hearing from him. 'We've been drifting apart for a while. What with my job taking me away and my … er, *other interests*, shall we say, I've been making excuses to stay away from home. I still care for

Lauren but I don't love her. I honestly wonder if I ever did. She ticked all the boxes for what I needed at the time. She's beautiful, sexy and easy.'

'Why easy? If she was that easy you'd still be with her, surely?' asked Martha, confused.

'She was easy to mould. I turned her into what I needed for my job. I was in control. She would always do what I wanted, and ultimately that wasn't enough. I was always her master, her tutor, her dictator ... call it what you will, and I needed to be challenged. I needed to have someone tell me what to do once in a while ...'

'Hence the trips to the fetish clubs?' Martha could see where the conversation was leading.

'Yes, Nathan introduced me to it. He told me about it and I loved the idea. He's been getting his kicks there for years but obviously he's too old to bother about getting caught and his real career is pretty much behind him. I tried it incognito with the mask and had one of the best nights I'd ever experienced. The danger and the thrill and the heady atmosphere of people who were ready to push the boundaries of their experiences, to extend their capacity for pleasure, were intoxicating. It was the complete opposite to my work, my upbringing, my existence. I could worship someone who needed me. I'm not sure that Lauren and I needed each other any more, which is why she's gone off the rails a bit, I suppose.'

'So, do you need me? Do I challenge you?' Martha enquired somewhat nervously.

'Like no woman I've ever known. You've made me question everything. I know it's only yesterday that I decided it was over with Lauren. I haven't even spoken to her, but I knew ages ago, back when I first met you, that it was dead between us. I didn't want to lose my trophy wife, scared what it might do to my career, but now none of that seems important. I want to be with you, Martha ... if you'll have me.'

Martha laughed happily, any doubts briefly erased. 'Have you? Of course I'll have you. I'd be mad not to. Great-looking guy, body to die for and a sexual appetite that needs constant feeding. You're my perfect man – Romeo to my Juliet. You had me back when you first worshipped me at the club ...'

Saul couldn't help but laugh too as he took in Martha's words. 'How very Shakespeare! Do you really think those star-crossed lovers were as kinky as we are?'

'Not for a moment, but I'd love to imagine them with a box of sex toys under their Verona beds, wouldn't you? Maybe it wouldn't have all ended so tragically. Now, talking of lovers, let me show you where Portia and Piero are getting married. It's too fabulous for words! Can I log onto your internet?'

'Make yourself at *home* ...' Martha was sure that Saul emphasised the word in such a way to convey his true feelings for her. 'My iPad is in the kitchen. I'll pour us a glass of wine. I don't normally drink but seeing as it's a day for celebration in some ways then I'll make an exception. Will red do you?'

'As long as it's South African ... I find it has the best body – just like the women,' teased Martha as she found a website showing the delights of Peter Island where Portia had chosen to marry Piero. As Saul handed her a glass of wine and stared at the screen he was blown away by the idyllic scenes of sugary sand beaches and cerulean blue seas laid out before him. 'Wow, amazing place ... perfect for a wedding. Your friend's picked well.'

'Portia has impeccable taste, especially for a celebrity. Normally it's all Cinderella pumpkin coaches and releasing a flock of doves into the air. I'm assuming this will be much classier,' replied Martha. 'Is it OK if I check my e-mails while I'm here? I haven't done it for a few days.'

'Sure. I'm just going to ring Nathan. The old fool talked me into an appearance on *Newsnight* this week, but I'm going to tell him to cancel it. My heart's not in it right now. I have other things on my mind – namely you!' Saul ran his fingers through Martha's sunshine gold hair and leant to kiss her on the lips before turning to leave the kitchen. 'Plus I need to phone the kennels to arrange about the dog, Barney. With Lauren gone I think he should stay at a friend's house for a while. Poor thing. Casualties of love, eh?'

Left alone, Martha typed in the address for her e-mail account and entered her password. It listed that she had four new e-mails. 'Aren't I the height of popularity,' she deadpanned. 'Two asking me if I want to extend my penis – no thanks, I don't have one – one offering me house insurance – delete – and one from back home.' The one from back home was from the account of Peter Bradford. It was titled NOT FOR YOUR MOTHER'S EYES.

I assume this will be something about Mum's birthday, mused Martha to herself. It was only three weeks away and maybe Peter was after girlie hints about what to give her. Her assumption could not have been more wrong. When she clicked onto the e-mail, one of the lurid, pornographic photos of herself and Tom on their dogging night out revealed itself. Martha nearly dropped her wine glass with horror. *Why was Peter sending her this? And how on earth did he have it?* The message underneath the photo explained all.

WHO'S BEEN A NAUGHTY GIRL, THEN? I GUESS YOU WON'T BE WANTING YOUR MOTHER TO SEE THIS (I HAVE PLENTY MORE). KIERAN TOOK THEM (MY SON, IN CASE YOU DIDN'T KNOW). HE'S BEEN FOLLOWING

YOU FOR WEEKS ON MY INSTRUCTION. BUT YOU DUMPED THE STUPID IDIOT JUST AS HE WAS WINNING YOU OVER. GET BACK WITH HIM BEFORE IT'S TOO LATE – I WANT YOU TOGETHER AND COMMITED OR ELSE THESE PHOTOS GO STRAIGHT TO YOUR MOTHER. BREATHE A WORD ABOUT THIS AND I'LL SPREAD THEM FURTHER THAN JUST THE FAMILY – I'M SURE THE PRESS HERE WOULD LOVE THEM. I'LL EXPECT TO SEE YOU AND KIERAN AT THE WEDDING – AS AN ITEM. IT WOULD MAKE MARIELLA SO HAPPY. BE A GOOD DAUGHTER AND DON'T DISAPPOINT HER.

Martha felt a blanket of incredulity wrap around her. She was being blackmailed. Blackmailed by her mother's boyfriend. She'd never been a huge fan of Peter's but this was an all-time low. She'd quit South Africa because her own father had been trying to marry her off to any passing stranger, and now it was happening all over again – and she wasn't even in the same continent. She couldn't let Mariella see those photos – they were as close to each other as any mother and daughter could be – but there were definitely some things you never wanted to share with your nearest and dearest. And Martha's al fresco adventures were definitely among them.

And after all she'd been through with Kieran, he'd been stringing her along all the time. He only wanted to be with her because his father had demanded it. What a weak bastard. Thank God she'd decided to end it. But if she didn't attempt to be with him and stay with him, then Martha was running the risk of Mariella seeing the photos and also potentially having them leaked to the press. It would destroy her parents and could destroy the run-up to Portia's wedding. She couldn't risk that. But what the hell was she going to do?

Making sure that Saul was still ensconced in his own telephone conversations, Martha took her mobile phone from her bag and scrolled through to Kieran's number. It clicked straight through to answerphone. She didn't leave a message.

Martha was just pressing the off-button on her phone as Saul sauntered back into the kitchen. As quickly as she could, she logged off from her e-mails afraid that he might spot the photo. He didn't, but he was aware that Martha looked far from happy. In fact her face was creased with anxiety and her cheeks were marked with a deep red blush.

'Are you OK?' posed Saul, taking her in his arms. 'You look all hot and bothered.'

'Er … yeah … yes … I'm fine,' lied Martha. 'I think it must be the wine – it's gone straight to my head. I'm not used to drinking in the day.' She pressed her face deep into Saul's chest to stop herself from crying. She was a million miles away from fine, as she had no idea what she was going to do about Peter's vile e-mail.

Plus there was Saul. The last thing she needed right now was any trauma that could possibly see him running back in Lauren's direction. Saul was hers, she was almost a hundred per cent sure, but while there was still a vein of doubt in her brain about Lauren, Martha couldn't help but let her thoughts bubble with worry.

CHAPTER 55

As Peter sat at his desk planning a huge export order of Bradford Wines to the Far East, his mind kept wandering off the job in hand to the e-mail he had written to Martha. It had been hours since he had pressed the send button and he'd still received no response. Not that he was overly worried. He had visions that Martha would no doubt be phoning Kieran and arranging to be with him. Maybe they would even be talking of a quickie wedding. That is what Peter wanted, after all. How else would he be able to get his hands on Lewin Éclair Wines?

It would have been better if Lewin had dropped dead from the heart attack, but he hadn't so, *c'est la vie* ... and sadly not *c'est la mort*. At least then, the estate would have gone to Martha and it was pretty certain that Mariella would have then had a hand in the day-to-day running of it. A hand that a work-savvy Peter could guide himself. A hand that could suggest a merger of two individual wine giants, forming an unstoppable beast of business.

But now that Lewin was on the mend and quite possibly ready to try and marry off Martha again, Peter was determined that if her heart was up for sale then it should be his son who turned out to be the successful top bidder, no matter how devious his offers may be. Otherwise, Peter's dreams of owning Lewin Éclair Wines could be going, going, gone for good ...

—

While Peter was planning his stranglehold domination of the wine market, Mariella and Lewin were sitting on the veranda at the Éclair estate staring out at the lush landscape that displayed itself before them. It was a beautiful day and the sun shone proudly in the blue sky overhead making the scene more colourfully vibrant than ever. It was their own little slice of heaven on earth. Or at least it had been theirs once, theirs together as a team.

It was a thought that was foremost in Lewin's mind as he stared across at his ex-wife, her face bathed in the golden glow of the sun's rays. He'd invited her to the estate to be with him. He'd craved her company since the heart attack and felt safer, stronger and even healthier when she was by his side. She had readily come, making sure that Peter was immersed in his work before sneaking off without his knowledge. Not that she had any reason to lie to Peter, yet it just seemed more sensible to not tell him the truth by saying nothing at all.

'On a clear day you can still see as far as Robben Island,' Lewin said softly. 'Where Nelson Mandela spent twenty-seven years as a prisoner, God rest his beautiful soul. Imagine being held captive for such a long time, it's incomprehensible. And in such a beautiful place too. It's barbaric that he had to live in a cell no bigger than an outside toilet when just beyond the four walls of the prison lay an incredible world of ostriches, springboks, cormorants and penguins. Pure, natural beauty and I don't suppose he got to experience much of it at all. He was trapped.'

'Why so wistful, Lewin? It's not like you. You only normally mention the likes of springbok and ostrich if you're ordering them off a menu,' replied Mariella, a smile curling from her lips.

'It's how I feel … trapped. There's all of this beauty around me. Wondrous scenery, amazing mountains, crystal clear waters, dazzling feats of nature and yet the most beautiful thing of all is constantly just out of my reach. If I can't have that then there's no point being here. The heart attack has taught me that.'

Mariella listened in silence as he continued to talk. 'I've spent years concentrating on just one thing – making sure my business was as lucrative as it could be. It's given me so much but it took away the one thing I should really have been looking after – the most beautiful thing of all – you.'

Mariella could feel her cheeks colouring as she listened to Lewin's words – words that immediately transported her back to the happy, carefree days when they were first together. She soaked in every syllable. 'Oh, Lewin ...' She went to continue but Lewin raised his hand gently, silencing her before she could continue.

'Let me finish. I have something I want ... that I *need* to say. I might be a fool for saying this but I don't want to live my life half-lived. Not now. I nearly lost it all when I had that heart attack and it's made me realise that I am not invincible. I almost died. When I do die I want it to be with the woman I love by my side. And I want it to be somewhere that's as far away as possible from the stresses and strains that this place puts me through.'

'Lewin, what are you saying? You're leaving? Giving up the estate?' interrupted Mariella. Her voice was enveloped with confusion and a hint of expectant excitement.

'I feel trapped by it all. It's one of the most beautiful places on earth, but just like the late Nelson Mandela, I feel unable to enjoy it. It's holding me back. But I'm not actually imprisoned. I can escape. I'm free to do what I want, with who I want ... if they'll have me. I've been busy making calls and trawling the internet. I'm employing a manager to look after the estate. It's made me enough money to live like royalty for the rest of my days and it will still earn me thousands every day even if I'm not here.'

Mariella's voice croaked with nerves as she spoke. 'But where will you go? I don't want you to go ...'

'That's what I was doing on the internet. I've bought a house. It's near that Portia Safari woman's in the UK. Martha was telling me about her property when she was here and showed me the land around that part of the UK. It's stunning, and without the stresses of work, I'd be able to enjoy it. Martha has no intention of coming back here anytime soon and I have plenty of family of old in the UK, so why not?' He took a sheet of paper out of his pocket, unfolded it and handed it to Mariella. There were three photos on it – one of the outside of a wisteria-covered Cotswold-style manor house and two interior shots of immense rooms, their ceilings held up with beams of dark, dependable timber. It reminded Mariella of the houses she'd seen on programmes on the History Channel about royalty in days gone by. She thought it was one of the most singularly pleasing and charming sights she had ever laid eyes on.

'Come with me,' said Lewin. 'I love you so much. I've never stopped loving you, even when I was with Adina. I've bought it for us. Let's leave and go to England.'

There was a moment's silence and to Mariella it felt like an eternity. She could hear her brain ticking inside her head as if on countdown to her eventual answer. In years to come she would look back at that moment and wonder why it took her so long to answer. She had known what she wanted to do even before the question had been asked. In fact, she had gone to spend time with Lewin with the express wish of telling him her own desires. But something stopped her giving Lewin a definitive answer. She needed to be sure.

'Live in England? But we couldn't, it's a pipe dream, a myth ... our home ... our homes are here,' she stuttered.

'A myth? Well, every myth needs a hero and I want to be yours again. Leave Peter …' he pleaded. His words were direct yet heartfelt.

'I'd already planned to.' Mariella's words had jumped from her lips before she'd even had time to contemplate them. They stopped Lewin in mid-flow.

'You'd what?' The two words fused together as one as a confused Lewin tried to take in what he'd just heard.

'I want to leave Peter. I've been thinking about it for days, weeks even. I don't love him any more. I need you in my life, Lewin. I always have done – but without the hardships of work keeping us apart. Are you serious about leaving the business in someone else's hands? Could you do that? If you promise you can, then I'm yours. When I thought that you might die, a piece of me died too. It hurt too much. I knew I had to have you again, but I didn't think you still wanted me. I thought I was part of your history. I thought I was too old …'

Lewin threw his head back and let out an almighty belly laugh. It was the first time Mariella had seen him laugh since his health scare. 'Too old? Are you mad, you daft woman? You're more beautiful now than you've ever been and you've always been the best-looking woman in my eyes. You're like a fine wine … you just get better with age. Now, tell me about this plan to leave Peter. The old bastard won't know what's hit him. Serves him right for stealing you from me in the first place. So you'll come to the UK?'

Mariella nodded. Lewin's face beamed with delight as she informed him of her plan to leave Peter. She knew it was the right thing to do but a corner of her soul still felt exceedingly callous about the thought of dumping him. *Surely he'd be so upset.*

She wouldn't have had any such charitable thoughts if she'd have known about his e-mail to Martha.

CHAPTER 56

It had taken until the age of thirty-six for Portia to be complete-ly happy with her life. Her wedding to the only man she felt she'd really loved in over a decade was mere weeks away. Thanks to the loved-up blossoming of her heart she hadn't so much as thought about reaching for a bottle of alcohol in days, and with Ed's wonder drug in her hand she would soon have the svelte, supermodel-figure she'd been dreaming of. Everyone around her from Redmond and Piero through to Martha and Duncan had been telling her that her figure was already a symphony of curves hitting all the right notes, but the diva was having none of it. She could see a few excess wobbles and areas that needed tightening in her opinion, and it was her opinion that counted.

But, as she prepared to take the first of the little white pills Ed had given her, she knew that before too long, her life would be perfect. And now that she'd instructed Redmond to cancel all of her professional commitments for the foreseeable future, her diary was clearer than it had been in years. A multimillion-pound wedding to the divine Piero in the Caribbean, then she would concentrate on their life together at Mara – she and Piero had decided they would live at Portia's home until they found a new place together, maybe one where their first child could be born.

Being a mother was definitely something that Portia would love to experience in the future – she'd love to show the uncon-ditional kind of love that she had received from her own parents and also from Betsy and William. Yes, if the powers above decreed that it wasn't too late for Portia's body to bear children, then she would love to be a mother one day.

The only pesky wasp currently hovering around the sweet, heavenly honey pot of Portia's life was Nancy. And boy, did she need swatting. Especially now that she knew just how low the woman would appear to stoop, having just heard from Martha about the saga with Tom. Portia was adamant that she would pay for that and for stealing Betsy's jewellery. How dare she flaunt herself in public wearing the Hartley family crest on her finger? Portia would cruelly rip the ring off her when she tracked her down and replace it with one made from apatite. She'd already pictured it in her mind. Apatite – a gemstone with a hidden meaning, its origin from the Greek word *Apate*, the Greek goddess of lies and deception – it fitted perfectly. Portia would ram the cheapest apatite ring she could find onto Nancy's finger and let burn with her fiery temper as she destroyed Nancy for deceiving Aunt Betsy. The little trollop would know that she had messed with the wrong family. When Portia had finished with her she would make sure that she could never deceive anyone again.

But Portia had no idea when that would be. Let her sweat. She was small fry compared with the forthcoming wedding, and seeing as Redmond was arriving to pick her up first thing in the morning to escort her back to Mara, she had other, more important things on her mind. She was going to have a ring of her own on her finger soon – one that was sparklier and more joyous than the bubbles from even the finest of champagnes could ever be. No, Portia was happy and as she popped the white pill into her mouth and headed for bed, she knew that in a few days' time, just as Ed's documentation on the wonder drug had stated, she would be body sculpted to perfection.

—

Portia was awoken by the sound of her own name being shouted, but the voice shouting sounded as if it was coming from another room. It was almost muffled, as if wrapped in cotton wool. As she opened her eyes she could see that it was daylight but a cloud of dizzy confusion seemed to be clinging onto her and it took her a few moments to actually remember where she was and what action was required to reach the voice calling her name.

She felt groggy and even the mere thought of trying to move seemed a monumental effort. But she recognised the rather urgent cries as belonging to Redmond and knew that she would have to let him in. *God, that wonder drug has knocked me for six*, she thought to herself as she blearily pulled back the cotton sheets and slid out from under them. *Still, it'll be worth it.*

'Portia, darling, are you there? It's Redmond … I've come to get you. I think people out here are a little fed up at me shouting for you. I've been doing it for ten minutes now …' His voice was jokey yet still laced with panic. He could sense that something wasn't right. The woman on reception had told him that Portia was still in her room.

'Calm down, you fool. Can't a girl get her beauty sleep any more?' Portia winced as she attempted to say the words as she moved to the door, her chest feeling tight and her mouth finding it hard to form the words properly. They sounded slurred to her. *Great*, she mused, *I give up alcohol and end up taking a drug that makes me sound bladdered anyway. How bloody ridiculous.* 'I'm coming.'

She turned the key in the door and pulled it open to reveal the trusty Redmond on the other side. His head was turned down, concentrating on his mobile phone. He had been in the process of trying to ring Portia's number again. With an air of relief he stopped as he heard the key turn in the door. 'Thank God for—' His words came to an abrupt halt as his mouth dropped open and his eyes widened.

'What the hell …? Get in, Portia, get in.' He ushered Portia hurriedly into the room and shut the door behind them, unable to comprehend what he was looking at and worried that other Abbey-goers might have had the chance to see. 'What the hell has happened to you?' Every inch of Redmond's face was scarred with panic. 'I thought you were here to make yourself feel better, what have you done?' He reached out to touch Portia's face but she flinched before he could gain contact.

'What the hell are you on about, you crazy man?' Again Portia's voice sounded affected, the words running into each other with no definition. As she spoke, she turned to look at herself in the mirror. Her heart pounded, repulsed at what she saw. In operatic terms, the horrific scream she let out was comparable to a glass-shattering soprano note of the highest pitch. What stared back at her was not the same beautiful face that had bid herself goodnight just hours before with the happiest of hearts. Her cheeks, lips and the entire area around her mouth had swollen up to grotesque proportions. Her lips appeared chubby and slug-like and her cheeks had risen to bloated, gluttonous Augustus Gloop-like domes of flesh, stretching her face out of recognition. Portia raised her hands to her face, half in an attempt to cover her hideous new features from herself and also in a faux attempt to try and wipe them away with her fingers.

Not sure what to do, Redmond pulled Portia towards him and hugged her tightly. 'Don't worry about this. It's a bee sting or something … don't worry, it'll be gone by the end of the day, I'm sure …' But he wasn't. He had no idea what could have caused Portia's face to balloon in such a fashion. He needed to fetch help. 'You stay here, I'm going to get Duncan. He'll sort this out. Here, in private, no one will see you like this, no one, I promise.'

Leaving a completely distraught Portia in front of the mirror, staring at her deformity through the tears that had puddled in her eyes, Redmond left the room in search of Duncan. She was still there, transfixed by the horror of her own face, when both Redmond and Duncan returned just a few minutes later. Portia unleashed her venom as soon as the pair of men came into her vision.

'What kind of godforsaken freak factory is this, Duncan? Look at me, I'm like Frankenstein's fucking monster. How could you let this happen to me? I'm supposed to be front page on every celebrity magazine in just a matter of weeks looking the epitome of beauty as I walk down the aisle and instead I'm going to look like bloody Bridezilla released from the depths of hell! I'll have this place condemned! Redmond, call my lawyer, now ... I'll sue this place for every penny!'

Determined to placate his client, Duncan tried to conceal his alarm at the monstrosity before him as he attempted to unravel the facts of the situation. 'There's no need for that, dear Portia. You have obviously suffered a reaction to something. Now, may I suggest one of our doctors looks at you immediately to try and uncover what has caused this? Have you eaten anything strange in the last twenty-four hours – shellfish or something you're allergic to?'

Like a hysterical wolverine fighting for its life, the ferocious torrent of anger continued to pour from Portia's mouth. 'Shellfish! For heaven's sake, Duncan, you know me well enough to know that I've tasted the finest oysters, lobsters, cockles and sodding mussels that planet earth can dish up. If I've lived through them I hardly think any of the prawn baguettes this place offers up are going to turn me into the Bride of Wildenstein over-night! This is not a reaction to something I've eaten.'

Redmond could see that Portia was becoming more and more tempestuous, her acidity spewing from her swollen lips like the frothing of a rapid dog as her voice became louder. 'Please, Por-tia. Try to calm down, think of your voice. It's taken such a battering and we don't want you to do any further damage—'

'My voice is the least of my worries, Redmond. Nobody will ever come to see me again when they find out I look like an extra from *Night of the Living Dead*. Thank God Piero's still in Ukraine, I would simply die if he saw me like this. Please tell me this isn't going to stay like this, Duncan, please ...' It was the first time Portia's words had been vaguely pleading since Duncan had entered her room. 'There must be something we can do ...'

Duncan placed his hand on his chin and stroked it contem-platively, looking around the room as he did so. As with all of The Abbey patients, Portia's room was devoid of windows to stop any potential for the prying lenses of the paparazzi from gaining lucrative photos to sell to the press. He stared around at the piles of papers and scribbled notes laid out across the coun-ters, details concerning Portia's forthcoming nuptials, no doubt. 'Redmond thought it might be a bee sting, but that's highly unlikely. Quite how one would fly in without any windows is beyond me and besides, you would have felt it in the night or at least heard it. You're a light sleeper, if I remember your medical notes, are you not?'

'This is not a bloody bee sting. I may not be David Attenbor-ough but even I know that!' barked Portia. 'Martha Éclair was here with me until the early hours and she'll tell you there was no blessed bug swooping around the place.'

'Martha? Oh yes, Ms Éclair ... I had to move her out of one of our employee's rooms as sadly I've had to escort him off the premises this morning. We've had a bit of trouble with things going missing.'

'Well, you can add my exotic looks to the list, Duncan, unless you count a deformed puffer fish as exotic,' she said, referencing her face. 'And anyway, I know all about that and I'm sure that will all get sorted in time,' she added dismissively.

'Well, if you were fine until just a few hours ago and you've not eaten or taken anything in the interim then I'm at a total loss as to what could be causing it. We may have to get you transported to the nearest hospital. If I knew how to help more, Portia – you know me, as a dear friend, I would.'

A niggle of doubt weaved its way through Portia's thoughts. *Taken anything ...?* There was only one thing that had passed her now-swollen lips since Martha's departure and Redmond's arrival. The wonder drug. But it couldn't possibly be that ... there was no mention of any face-altering side effects in the literature from Ed. In fact, all of the smiley happy people staring out at Portia from that were blessed with model-perfect faces that would not look out of place on a Times Square billboard campaign.

But, even in her hysterical state, Portia knew that every avenue needed to be explored. 'There is one thing ...' she mumbled. She hesitated before adding, 'Now, Duncan, please don't be annoyed at me, but I have treated myself to a little boost to try and shift this vexatious extra weight I've been sporting ...' Both Duncan and Redmond listened intently as Portia explained fully about buying the wonder drug from Ed, their mouths simultaneously falling open in disbelief as they took in her words. As the colour drained from Redmond's face, leaving his normally rosy complexion ashen, the opposite appeared to be happening to Duncan. His chiselled features seemed to be flooding with a spread of red anger as he listened to his client and friend, and his teeth gritted together.

Portia could see that the cauldron of rage bubbling inside Duncan was ready to erupt. She walked to her bedside table drawer, took the literature about the drug from it and handed it to Duncan. 'Please don't be angry with me, Duncan. This wonder drug has worked miracles for so many people around the world. Ed assures me that many celebrities have seen their figures improve in a matter of days. Look at them all. Beautiful, sculpted people. What is the point of one having money to burn if we can't use it to burn off the calories after all?'

Duncan snapped, his patience having reached breaking point. 'Bullshit, Portia!' The force of his words shocked Portia into silence. 'You are one of the most intelligent people I know, but you're also, forgive me for saying, one of the vainest, and we all know that vanity kills, darling. Surely if this drug was such a miracle in Hollywood and among the rich and famous, do you not think for one darned second that I would know about it? That I would actually have it readily available for my clients at The Abbey? Isn't our motto *Hic Pro Panton, Hic Pro Sulum* – Here For Everything, Here For Everyone? Well, you and I both know that that's true as long as you can afford whatever we deem necessary, but the one thing I pride myself on here, Portia, is that whatever is recommended to you, it's all been tried and tested and regulated by professionals to make sure it's the best thing for you—'

'But Ed is a professional, Duncan, he works for you,' protested Portia, her words both pathetic and pitiful.

'And you know me well enough to know that I would never employ someone who would charge you a shitload of extra cash for something off the record. Your body is a sacred temple, Portia, and I will never suggest you putting something into it that hasn't been cleared by me beforehand. Talking of cash, I assume you were charged heartily for this ... so-called wonder drug?'

Portia hung her head down like a scolded schoolgirl standing in front of a headmaster she'd obviously let down badly with her behaviour. A tear ran down her nose and fell onto the floor as she mumbled her answer. 'Fifty thousand pounds,' before adding as way of an excuse, 'Well, I can afford it, Duncan.'

Duncan let his rage explode. 'Well, I can't afford to have it going on underneath the roof of The Abbey, Portia. I won't stand for it. I have a reputation to keep up. Where are the pills Ed gave you? Give them to me now, I'll have them checked out and get back to you. In the meantime, I suggest you and Redmond stay here and keep yourself hidden away from prying eyes. We'll get this sorted, Portia, you have my word, but we do it my way. There will be no lawyers involved, that's the last thing I need, and if we do find that these pills have caused this reaction, then we'll compensate you all we can and make sure that everything is done to turn you back into the beautiful woman I know.'

Taking the pills from Portia, Duncan headed towards the door. 'I'm going to see Ed to see what he has to say about this. I need to know where he got these bloody pills from.'

As Duncan made to leave Portia shouted after him, 'Go easy on him, Duncan. The boy was only trying to help me out.' Despite his underhand ways and the fact that Portia's face was beyond distorted, there was a little part of her that actually felt sorry for Ed.

—

Any sympathy that Portia may have had for Ed disappeared faster than a bullet from a gun when Duncan swept back into her room a few hours later. She had spent the time sitting down, staring at her face in the mirror, still unable to comprehend the warped vision that gazed back at her. Redmond had fruitlessly tried placating her at every opportunity, insisting that any deformation would be gone as quickly as it had evolved. His words had fallen on deaf, and still somewhat muffled, ears. Portia leapt from her seat as soon as Duncan arrived.

'What news? Tell me I'm not going to stay like this, please. I'd rather die,' she said, her words smothered in more than a theatrical dose of melodrama.

Duncan sat her down and held her hands. Then a hint of a slight smile painted across his face. It was enough to calm any major worries that Portia could still feel crashing around her body. He began to speak. 'I've had the pills tested and they're nothing more than aspirin. Plain and simple. Normally they would do no more than dull a few aches and pains and they certainly wouldn't help shift any weight – not that you need to anyway – but I've been checking your medical records. You're allergic to aspirin, naproxen and ibuprofen. That's why you've suffered this reaction. It's severe but we can get it treated – both promptly and privately, Portia. No one need ever know. The doctors here can make sure that you get everything you need for a full recovery. The swelling should go down within a few days and naturally we'll compensate you – providing we can keep this between us. This is not the kind of publicity that The Abbey needs and, believe you me, I am distraught that a dear friend like you has been deceived by a member of my staff. Edward Arlow has been dealt with accordingly. I've fired him. He admitted to getting the pills at a local chemist after I threatened him with a court case. He'll pay you back the fifty thousand, I'll make sure of that. He's the second member of my team I've had to escort off the premises today – it has not been a good day for The Abbey. Thank God we've all got your Caribbean wedding to look forward to. And Portia, you will look amazing for your wedding, you have my word on that. I've never known you look anything less than pure perfection.'

But Portia wasn't listening. She'd taken in the information about the aspirin but her mind had become distracted at the mention of Ed's surname. Edward Arlow. She thought his name was Collie? Arlow? Surely he couldn't be linked to Nancy?

'Duncan,' she barked. 'Isn't his name Edward Collie? That's what it says on his door. Why are you calling him Edward Arlow?'

'Collie's his working name, but he was born Edward Arlow. I needed to confirm his identity for The Abbey records when he started working here and he handed over his birth certificate as verification. He told me he'd changed his surname a few years back. Some family reason, if I remember rightly. The name Arlow stuck in my brain because I had a tutor at university of the same name and I remember thinking it's not that common,' stated Duncan.

'Common? I'll tell you about common ... He's not related to that common, low-rent, thieving little tramp called Nancy Arlow, is he? She's been seen in here. I bumped into her in the reception and Martha knows of her too. Used to be a big music and TV star but she's staler than a six-month-old cheese these days. If you ask me, she's the despicable little reason behind your robbery woes.'

A wave of confused recognition streaked across Duncan's handsome features. One eyebrow raised quizzically. 'Now you mention it, I do recall Ed mentioning he has a famous sister, or something along those lines. That's why he changed his name. He was always getting people asking whether they were related and I seem to recall it started to piss him off, being the "poor relation". I guess he wanted his own identity. I'm sure Ms Arlow has been to see us here about potential treatment recently. I don't think she ever booked herself in though. Small world, eh?'

'Yes, but this place is big enough for her to swoop in like a thieving magpie and steal anything she can get her hands on. The clients here are prize pickings. She stole a precious ring from my aunt Betsy and I'd put money on the fact that she's behind the money that's gone missing from Dr Fielding's office. Martha told me about it. The woman is scum and it obviously runs in the family. Birds of a very nasty feather resting in their own evil nest. Splintered chips from the same block!' she spat, unable to contain her hostility. 'Let me guess … what was the treatment she enquired about? How to conquer gambling and severe kleptomania? The trashy little scrubber.'

'You know I can't comment on that, Portia,' said Duncan, but the look on his face told her that she was right. It suddenly made sense and Duncan knew that somehow, he would have to deal with the subject of Nancy Arlow. He couldn't prove that she was involved in the theft but it certainly looked like she was currently suspect *numero uno*.

As for Portia, her soul was feeling even darker and more twisted than her facial features. Ed Collie, born Arlow, brother of Nancy, had made her look like this. He'd duped her, fleeced her of fifty k and given her something potentially life-threatening. He'd been fired, he'd lost his livelihood. He'd never work again – she'd see to that. As for Nancy, well, Ed's family ties and deception had just given Portia reason to hate her even more. She needed to be stopped, permanently if necessary – and Portia's venom was potent enough to know that she would do whatever was needed. Hell hath no fury like a diva crossed.

CHAPTER 57

The countdown was on. Virtually every news station around the globe from the pearly-white upbeat smiles of New York's NBC through to the sombre heavy-browed delivery of London's ITN was talking about, analysing and discussing what was being billed as the musical wedding of the decade. The forthcoming Caribbean nuptials of 'Portiero' was vital airspace-filling news – speculation of bridal outfits, guest lists, entertainment and possible honeymoon destinations gushed forth from the screens of millions of televisions worldwide, a thousand different languages giving their expert take on the latest rumours. In the age-old media tradition of the starlit celebrity world, every one of them delivered their very own insider-gossip exclusive – none of them even dusted, in fact, with a speck of truth.

As the bride-to-be reclined on the leather sofa at Mara, her hand outstretched as a viscous slick of crimson nail varnish was applied by one of the many beauticians Portia employed almost on a daily basis, she listened intently to the latest apocryphal puff of industry gossip frothing from the mouth of a rather portly male fashion expert gracing her sitting room TV screen. Ever since leaving The Abbey – the damage to her face from the aspirin allergy now mercifully behind her thanks to Duncan's team of quick-thinking medical experts – early mornings at Mara had become a ritual of watching just what the media world was going to invent next about her wedding. Over the few short weeks she'd locked herself away at her palatial home, making sure that no one would see the thankfully short-lived distortions to her face, she had heard it all. Everyone from Michelle Pfeiffer to Michelle Obama was said to be coming to Peter Island. Piero had employed a personal hair stylist to cater solely for his expanse of chest hair and Portia had been learning how to give her fiancé a flamboyantly sexual burlesque wedding night dance to remember courtesy of Dita Von Teese. All nonsense.

According to the so-called fashionista on today's programme, he'd had a bona fide one-to-one conversation with the Italian designer who had been commissioned by Portia to create the dazzling outfit she would exchange vows in. The dress would be, in his words, 'furnished with hundreds of flawless crystals that had been handpicked by Portia herself from around the world' and would be 'one of the most expensive dresses on record'.

'What a crock of shit,' sighed Portia, waving her now decorated nails at her beautician to end the session. She surveyed her talons to check that they were up to the standard she required for the day ahead. Luckily for the beautician they were. Portia shooed her from the room.

'What is? Yet another tragic excuse for TV journalism, I assume,' enquired Redmond, beavering into the sitting room with his usual ultra-efficient mix of bonhomie and causticity.

'Of course, darling. Today they are speculating about my wedding dress. That sweaty Shrek of an expert, and I use that term as loosely as possible, thinks that I've been swanning around the globe handpicking jewels to please some jumped-up Italian fashion designer. As if ... Could you imagine me, decked out from head to toe like the front counter at Tiffany's? Wear that much bling underneath the rays of the Caribbean sunshine and I'd be bouncing light around like some hellhole nightclub laser display. What do these people take me for, darling? As you well know, my dress will be the finest haute couture. Simple, stylish, flattering to my diminishing curves' – Duncan had supplied Portia with a personal trainer to help shed the excess pounds she believed she was carrying – 'and above everything else it will be tasteful. I will not be festooned in enough gemstones to make me look like some cheap redneck tourist on a dream holiday to Dollywood. Do these experts never fathom out the real truth?'

Sitting himself alongside the diva on the sofa, Redmond raised an eyebrow, curled his lips into a slightly mocking smile and picked up the TV remote control to flick the screen to black. 'It's good for you that they don't fathom the truth, my sweet, isn't it? What do you think the tabloid likes of Madeline Strong would have been saying if they'd known you'd just spent the last two weeks with your face wonkier and more misshapen than a Salvador Dali? I can tell you now you're back to your usual sickeningly beautiful self, but there were moments when I thought the only job I could book you for in the future was going to be understudy for the warty witch in *Wicked*.' Redmond attempted to placate Portia with a swift wink before she could unleash any possible anger. It worked.

'And you, Redmond dear, would be the first thing I'd make disappear with my magic wand. For good. Now, I assume you've come to discuss the wedding guests as instructed? Who's confirmed? All A-list, I hope,' enquired Portia, tapping her crimson nails expectantly on the arm of the sofa.

'Let's just say that every concert venue and movie set around the world is looking like it might be void of big names on your wedding day, eh?' smiled Redmond.

Portia smiled back – a genuine beam of happiness. As the sun streamed in through the sitting room window it illuminated her face. Redmond found himself taken aback by just how stunning she was. He'd never seen her more radiant. Portia was a women who thrived on looking the best possible. Thank goodness the monstrosity of her malformed features just a few days earlier had remained a secret.

———

Except it hadn't – not to everybody. Nancy had relished in every juicy detail. She'd made the loved-up Bruno tell her time and time again, coaxing him into describing just how swollen Portia's lips were, just how puffy and alien-like her eyes appeared and whether there were any photographs that Nancy could look at. Thankfully for Portia, the only ones there were had been stored on The Abbey's computer system out of harm's way. Duncan had been as professional as he could, making sure that only those really needing to know were informed of Portia's predicament. One of those people was naturally Dr Bruno Fielding. What Duncan hadn't bargained on was a loose-lipped Bruno spilling the entire story to his girlfriend, Nancy, during an energetic bout of bedroom gymnastics.

Bruno's intellect may have been definitely one that most medical practitioners would gouge out their own eyes for, but he certainly lacked in sense and reason when it came to pleasures of the flesh and giving Nancy exactly what she always wanted, both physically and verbally. You could have the intellect of Stephen Hawking and still be as short-sighted as a pipistrelle when it came to pillow talk.

Not that Duncan even knew that Nancy and Bruno were together. Although he suspected that Nancy was involved in the missing money from Bruno's office after Portia's hinting, he'd refrained from pursuing her at Portia's request. As the opera star had informed him quite categorically, 'I shall deal with that tramp, Duncan, when I'm ready. She will get what she deserves.' Seeing as it was a member of Duncan's team who had caused Portia's misery at The Abbey, he felt it was the least he could do to allow her to exact her revenge her way. And besides, Nancy hadn't been seen at The Abbey since the time that Tom had been suspended and her brother had lost his job. She'd decided that a low-profile was in order, especially with her detestable rival, Lauren, now in residence at the rehabilitation centre.

In the weeks leading up to Portia's wedding, Nancy had no need to go to The Abbey. She had all she needed in Bruno. He was strong, handsome and a constant source of cash. And as long as she told him what he wanted to hear, he seemed more than willing to supply her with any information she required. Some would say lapdog, but to Nancy he was the perfect partner.

She'd heard about Portia through her brother, Ed. He'd run straight to Nancy's door, terrified after being dismissed from The Abbey, his bank account fifty thousand lighter. Despite their blood ties, Nancy was far from sympathetic. She'd sent him packing after supplying him with a handful of £50 notes she'd yet again extracted from Bruno's bank account. Despite his expert medical mind, Bruno was pitifully hapless when it came to minding over his finances, something which Nancy had abused to the max, stealing his bank card whenever possible and taking what she required. As long as she supplied Bruno with regular sessions of orgasmic sex he was putty in her hands.

It was as she straddled across Bruno's naked body at her apartment one evening, the walls of her pussy pulsating to drain the last drops of his desire from his cock, that she'd first raised the subject of Portia's allergic reaction. Aware that Bruno knew that Ed was her brother, she was keen to show him where her allegiance lay. And for now it wasn't with her family ties. 'I can't believe Ed would do such a thing,' she'd feigned as she dismounted from Bruno's now wilting hard-on. 'He came here looking for sympathy and told me what had happened. He said Portia's face was really bad ... is it true?' She leant down to kiss Bruno fully on the lips and his cock twitched. As it started to swell with desire again, Bruno's mouth flooded with the information that Nancy longed to hear.

As Bruno drifted off to sleep later that evening in the after-glow of yet more torrid sexual fun and games, Nancy's head was overflowing with what she had learnt. She couldn't wait to see Portia's face at the wedding of the year. She couldn't help but wonder if it would even be fully recovered. *Maybe a heavy veil might be in order*, she mused as she herself drifted into slumber. Her last thoughts before sleep finally engulfed her were of Portia. If that woman even so much as caused her a tiny ripple of trouble – whether it be her sibling connection to Ed or the fact that she'd obviously had more than a passing interest in the ring that Nancy had stolen from Betsy, then Nancy would know exactly what to do.

She could throw the secrets of Portia's recent bout of Quasimodo beauty right into her face. One word out of line from the opera star and Nancy would head straight to the papers. Info like that would have to be worth a fortune – even if it did mean sacrificing her brother's career in the process.

———

Lauren's singing career was definitely on hold for the moment. With her first video in the can and a huge flutter of interest surrounding her following the newspaper revelations of her split from Saul, the timing had never been better, in Dale's managerial opinion, for her pop career to be launched.

Word had been leaked at Dale's orchestration that Lauren would be attempting to launch herself as the latest rival to the legion of air-brushed beauties filling the Billboard charts with their smooth, sultry tones, but until she had managed to curb the coke intake, there was no point in Dale pushing her into the musical spotlight of fame.

As Lauren's days and nights of treatment and observation at The Abbey under the watchful guidance of Bruno Fielding progressed, each hour seemed to give Dale more indication that Lauren's addiction could hopefully soon be controlled and, in time, forgotten. She responded well to the treatment and with every day gained more control and knowledge about the perilous situation she had allowed herself to slip into.

Life had changed so much for Lauren over the last few months – the politician's bored housewife had branched out, spread her wings, let herself fly towards the sunshine of the life she'd always dreamt of. But the squalid bags of nose candy she'd been dipping into had become the metaphorical wax that had melted from her Icarus-wings and caused her current demise. The realisation of waking up within the confines of The Abbey day after day, her body aching and her head craving for yet another hit, had made her comprehend exactly what she was risking. There was no point striving for a life that could potentially reward her with so much satisfaction if she was prepared to throw it away on so very little.

Lauren had thought about Saul less and less each day. She'd read no newspapers, seen no TV. Dale had successfully managed to shield her from any prying journalist, anxious to find out exactly what she thought about her recent separation from her husband. Her marriage may have failed but she began to acknowledge that it had, in fact, died a long time ago. She was determined that she would not die with it.

For days the only people Lauren saw were the medical staff at The Abbey and the ever-present Dale. He'd become her rock, the one person who truly seemed to be on her side. He acted as her protector, her inspiration to get better and her hope for the future. He'd sit at her bedside hour after hour, his laptop perched on his knees, mindful that despite her current predicament, the foundations of what could happen for her career when she left The Abbey needed to be put into place. He fired off e-mails, took business calls and liaised with those people he needed to turn Lauren into the next big thing. She knew that his interest in her was more than just professional. In her eyes, even in a groggy state, she could see that between Dale's feelings for her and Bruno's guidance, she could beat her demons.

What she didn't know was that both of them were, in fact, letting her down in their own way. Blinded by love, Bruno was sharing yet more professional secrets with Nancy every night as he lay in her arms, informing her of Lauren's condition and therapy, unaware of Nancy's deep loathing of his patient. And Dale – for someone who was so intent on setting his would-be starlet on the straight and narrow – showed no real signs of letting up. The long hours of work and worry at Lauren's bedside were taking their toll – as soon as Lauren shut her eyes or was taken elsewhere for another session of healing, he would find himself leaving her room, heading to the restrooms and chopping out fat lines of cocaine, which he'd snort greedily from the top of the cistern. It's what he'd always done – he saw no reason for change. He just wouldn't flaunt it in front of Lauren, he couldn't risk putting temptation her way.

It was after yet another buzz-inducing line that Dale rushed into Lauren's private room full of excitement. The smile on his face literally spread from ear to ear.

'Someone looks happy,' noted Lauren, feeling brighter than she had done in days. 'Care to share?'

'I'm just imagining you with a golden tan. I bet it looks fabulous with your blond hair,' smirked Dale.

Lauren appeared confused. 'Now I may be full of beta blockers and God knows what else but even I know that I'm getting no sun on my skin flat on my back in here.'

'But you will be … sooner than you imagine. I think I've just been handed the perfect tonic to give you the ideal reason for getting yourself fit and well. How do you fancy a few days in the Caribbean? I've just come off the phone from a music contact of mine. An opera star called Piero Romeo. I worked with him years ago on a London production. I bumped into him again at the Royal Albert Hall a few weeks back – not that I expect you to remember that. He's getting married to Portia Safari in the Caribbean – it's been all over the news – and I've just been invited. Result!' Dale's words became faster and more animated with every syllable. 'And you, Lauren, are coming with me. It'll be full of music industry people, no doubt, which will be crucial for contacts and it'll be fabulous press, and I think it could be just the thing you need to put all of this behind you.' He circled his finger around the room to signify what he meant. 'It'll be a great chance to get away from everything, to relax and recuperate.'

Perhaps Dale wouldn't have been so keen for either himself or a radiant Lauren if he'd known just who else was already confirmed and on the guest list.

—

Despite her imminent bridesmaid duties, Martha's mind was as far removed from contemplating just how she'd attempt to shine at Portia's wedding as it could be. If a wedding is traditionally thought of as being 'white' then Martha's thoughts were at the opposite end of the spectrum – she was channelling 'black', as in blackmail.

The e-mail she'd received from Peter Bradford stared up at her from her inbox as it had done since its arrival. She had memorised every nasty, threatening word and the photos were seared onto her brain, even as she slept in Saul's arms at night. She couldn't shake it from her thoughts, hanging over her like a sword of Damocles.

Not that she'd been able to see a great deal of Saul recently. He'd been busy finalising work commitments with Nathan and had been trying unsuccessfully to avoid the press as they hounded him about his recent break-up with Lauren. He had expertly fended off most of their questions, used to having the upper hand when it came to a duel of words, but even an expert speaker like Saul had become flummoxed when a hardcore hack from one of the trashiest of national rags had asked if 'anybody else was involved in the break-up'. At first, a defiant Saul had stated 'no, absolutely not' but something inside him had snapped as he said it. Why lie? He knew he wanted to be with Martha. They fitted together perfectly. What did he have to hide? Was he trying to protect Lauren? She'd not been concerned about his feelings when she was wrapped around Dale in Las Vegas, had she? In an instant, he had followed up his initial denial with a counter statement. 'Well, actually, I am seeing someone else but that has nothing to do with my break-up from my wife. Our relationship had been sadly drifting apart for a long time. The announcement may be new to you, but it's old news for us, I'm afraid. We'd both just like to be left alone to sort out our private lives.' It was a risky move and one that Saul would never have made a few months back. He would have let Nathan advise him on every word, but something about Martha had made him more carefree and made him care less about his political career than ever before.

Needless to say, the next day, Saul had been quoted word for word in every national newspaper, speculation raging about who the new woman in his life may be. His image was tarnished, no doubt, Nathan seething at him down the phone for letting a 'stupid tart blind him into stupidity by flashing a bit of flesh' but Saul didn't care. He remained silent, spoke no further on the subject and within days his headline-grabbing story was replaced with something else equally banal and trivial. The media world had moved on, and it meant that Saul and Martha could too.

Saul had told Martha about what he'd said before the story hit the press. They'd met that evening at a private members' bar around the corner from Martha's Soho flat. She loved the fact that he had been man enough to say that he was with somebody else – it made her realise that she had made the right choice in following her heart to be with him. But there was one nagging doubt at the back of her mind. She needed to be straight with Saul – she needed to tell him about the photo and Peter's attempt at blackmail. His mouth fell open as she relayed the whole story – including the story of how Peter had employed his own son to chase after Martha.

Saul was quick to respond. 'The man's sick, why is your mother with him? And what is it with me and sodding blackmail photos lately? They're everywhere I look!' He smiled – lifting a weight off Martha's shoulders. She knew he wouldn't, but the fact that he never judged her about the dogging photos proved that he was the man for her. Equally sexual, equally loving.

They had sneaked back to Martha's flat – separately, just in case any paparazzi were lurking – to look at the e-mail. Saul stared down over Martha's shoulder as she opened her inbox and squeezed her shoulders tenderly as he felt her entire body tense as the images downloaded and he read the words from Peter.

'This was sent over a week ago and you've neither replied nor had any follow-up from him?' He spoke as if he was addressing the House Of Commons, his words both clear and direct. Martha could feel that he was taking stock and taking control of the situation. 'You've tried to telephone Kieran but he's seemingly abroad and doesn't want to be contacted. You don't care about the photos – I think we're both broad-minded enough to know that it's actually pretty hot, but the last thing you want is for your mother to see it. I may have to keep one, though, as it's incredibly horny,' he joked. 'So, it's you versus your mother's lover – you can hardly tell her about it if she's in love with him.'

'I'm not sure she is, but that's hardly the point,' said Martha. I just need to stop him from doing anything else. Imagine if he goes to the press. He wants control of Lewin Éclair Wines and to gain that, he needs me married off to Kieran.' Martha contemplated the dead-end nature of the situation.

'Well, that will happen over my dead body, let me tell you,' said Saul sternly. 'Now I have you in my life I'm sure as hell not going to let another person come between us. As far as I can see, we only have one possible option.'

'Which is?' Martha tried to sound as hopeful as she could manage, but it was obvious that her spirit was already defeated.

'We buy him off. We pay to make sure that he destroys the photos. How much do you think he'll want? I should know the going rate for blackmail these days but I figure the exchange rate might be different in South Africa – I've only sampled it in the UK recently. Half a million?' deadpanned Saul.

'That's chicken feed to Peter Bradford. He's one of the richest men back home. This isn't about money, it's about control. He wants control of my dad's business and the only way he can do it is to infiltrate my dad's ranks. Even if Peter offered dad three times the value of Lewin Éclair he still wouldn't sell it to the man who stole his wife. He'd rather see it go bankrupt. But if I'm married off to Kieran then there's a chance that one day Peter can have the control within his family. He could arrange mergers and allsorts and turn his own company into the biggest wine company on earth. I think I have to face the fact that I'm fucked, Saul, and as a supposed sex addict I don't mean in the good way. Whatever I do, someone is going to get hurt.'

There was a minute's silence between the two of them as neither one knew what to say. The air of silence was only interrupted by the sound of the apartment telephone ringing. 'I assume that'll be Kelly – she's out perfecting her Twinkle Stimulation stripper routine tonight for Piero's stag party – she's talked of nothing else ever since she found out. I've not told her about you and me as yet,' said Martha.

'Well, I wouldn't tell her over the phone. There will be plenty of time for that at the wedding. That's when I guess the whole world will realise we're together.'

'Well, at least we'll get it all over and done with in one fell swoop,' offered Martha. 'I'll get the phone, it might be important.'

Picking up the phone, Martha expected to hear the giddy tones of Kelly squealing from the receiver. It wasn't her flatmate. Instead she was faced with the rather upset-sounding and somewhat nervy voice of her own mother. She could tell that Mariella had been crying. Two thoughts rocketed into her brain at the same time – either Peter had shown her the photos or, worse still, something had happened to her father.

'Oh my God, Mum, what is it? Are you OK? It's the middle of the night for you guys there … has something happened to Dad? Please tell me he's OK.' Martha's voice became more urgent with every word.

'He's fine, Martha. He's fine. I just need to speak to you. I'm sorry it's so late, but I needed to talk to you once Peter was sound asleep. He's in bed and I needed to get away from him.' Mariella's voice was hushed slightly, as if she was afraid to speak too loudly, for fear of being overheard.

'Mum, you're scaring me ... has Peter done something to you? If he's hurt you, I swear I'll never forgive him—'

Mariella silenced Martha by launching into the reason she'd phoned. 'No, I'm just worked up about a decision I've made. Peter and I are going to finish, Martha. I don't love him any more. I wanted you to be one of the first people to know ...'

Martha sat agog as Mariella whispered her plans down the phone – of leaving Peter, not that he knew it yet, of being with Lewin once more and the pair of them moving to the UK to get away from the smothering lifestyle of the wine business. Martha was elated, momentarily forgetting about the nightmare she was facing with Peter. Her parents were to be reunited again.

She was only reminded of Peter's malodorous presence when he heard his voice cry out in the background of the phone conversation, obviously roused from his bed.

'Martha, I've got to go, Peter's woken up and is wondering where I am. Keep this a secret – we'll both see you at the wedding. Love you.' Before Martha could reply, her mother had rushed to end her confession and hung up.

'Trouble at home?' enquired Saul.

'Kind of, but it might just be one of the best pieces of news I've had in a while.' She explained to Saul about the conversation. She was just coming to an end when the phone rang again.

'This will either be Mum again or this time it will be Kelly.' She picked up the receiver, which was still warm from the previous call. It was neither Kelly nor Mariella. In fact it was the last person she was expecting to speak to. 'Oh my God, it's you ...'

she exclaimed, her sentence heavy with dismay. 'What the hell do you want?'

———

No, the countdown to the wedding was certainly under way for everyone, and the speculation about what the joyous union would bring would continue right up until the moment when the operatic stars would finally exchange vows. But not a single TV broadcast or newspaper column could correctly predict what would happen at the marriage. For all of their insider scoops and exclusive headlines, not one of them came even close to the intrigue, deception and horror that the wedding would unfold. Because as much as they cared to guess the designer labels and accessories that would be on show, as much as they tried to compile a list of definitive guests and as much as they tried to find out just what the exact cost of the multimillion-pound wedding would be, not one of the media outlets would have guessed in their wildest crowd-pleasing dreams that the wedding would end in a death. Not so much 'I do' for somebody, but more a case of somebody who would 'never again'.

CHAPTER 58

Piero Romeo had played many different roles throughout his operatic career but tonight he was to play one of the most important roles of his life – the role of stag at his own pre-wedding party.

The venue was a huge yacht, owned by one of Piero's guests, which was anchored a mile from shore at Soper's Hole Marina on Tortola Island, the largest of the British Virgin Islands. The yacht towered majestically over many of the visiting boats that had sailed into the marina, a centrepiece of excellence among the smaller vessels – most of them containing paparazzi with camera lenses that appeared to stretch on for forever in the hope of obtaining a photo of the party in action. Something which was unlikely to happen, given the walls of security men marching up and down. Piero and his all-male party were all at sea and all ready to party.

The stag event was billed as 'Piero's Pirate Party' and all of the guests had been instructed to dress accordingly. Soper's Hole had been home to one of the most famous pirates of all, the Brit buccaneer Blackbeard during the eighteenth century, and both Piero and Portia had thought it would be fabulous for the groom-to-be and his guests to celebrate in fancy dress. All invitees had been told to gather in private at one of the Soper's Marina brightly coloured bars in full pirate regalia, where they would be treated to local rum cocktails, before a team of speedboats would ferry them to the yacht itself.

Piero was already on the boat but was not allowed to join his guests until everyone was in place. His team of best men, three handsome and virile fellow opera stars had organised the evening – with a soupcon of suggestion from Portia – with strict precision.

As Piero waited in his private room on the yacht, he could hear the hustle, bustle and bawdy laughter of his guests as they tucked into the specially prepared seafood dishes spiced with the authentic West Indian flavour of the Caribbean. Piero knew it would be a spicy night all round if his compatriots had anything to do with it. He'd already downed a bottle of mystery liquid that had been left in his room with an *Alice In Wonderland*-style label reading DRINK ME attached around the neck. The potion, he was guessing a heady mix of some of the strongest rum he'd ever tasted and a fusion of fruit juices, had warmed his body to perfection, spreading through his veins like lava. As three of his friends burst through the door with a chorus of pirate-style cries and waving faux cutlasses, Piero could feel his head beginning to spin. As the men hoisted him onto their shoulders and carried him from the room to greet his guests, Piero was already grateful that he would have another two days to sober up before exchanging vows with Portia.

———

Portia herself had decided to shy away from a hen party. After her recent dalliances with alcohol she had decided that there would be enough temptation at the wedding itself without putting herself at risk with a champagne-drenched party beforehand. She had already left Tortola by private yacht to be taken directly to Peter Island, where the wedding would take place. As she told waiting reporters at the marina before sailing, 'The moment I become joined to Piero, the most wonderful man

I have ever met, I will finally have received the standing ovation I have always been longing for.' Asked why she wasn't going to party with her friends and fellow guests at Tortola, she told them that she 'wished to be alone before the big day, to prepare for the most wonderful occasion of my life'. The word 'alone' hardly seemed apt when she was actually on board the yacht with an ever-expanding team of hair and make-up artists, party planners, beauticians, stylists, Aunt Betsy and her trusted Bloodworth, and her bridesmaid, Martha. She'd have been more alone at the opening ceremony of the Olympics.

———

A huge cheer erupted as Piero was carried before his guests. Dressed in a muscle-hugging white shirt, slashed to the waist revealing his solid, hirsute chest and frilled to perfection on the cuffs, Piero looked every inch the rippling, matinee idol pirate. His hair was tied into place with a bright red bandanna, and a patch of black leather hung over one eye. Added to the mix he'd accessorised with a large gold hoop earring and a skull and crossbones pendant made from diamonds – a gift from Portia for the occasion. The overall effect was a powerful mutineer medley combining the machismo of Marlon Brando, the womanising charm of Errol Flynn and the seedy sexiness of Johnny Depp.

Within seconds a drink had been pushed into his hands and a blaring sound system started to pump out a pulsating beat of tropical tunes. The combination of the drink and the rhythmic sounds was intoxicating and the whole room seemed to come alive.

Scanning round the room, Piero could see many of his fellow musical peers as well as actors he recognised from both stage and screen, all of them kitted out to perfection in leather waistcoats, wigs, long coats, many with beads threaded into their hair, some of them sporting the ultimate pirate accessory of a toy parrot on their shoulders. There were people he recognised from his visits to Portia at The Abbey, and even that politician he'd read about in the papers who'd recently split from his wife. As he stared across the room, he could see him talking to Dale Cousins, who Piero had worked with in the past. Neither looked overly happy. Well, he'd speak to them in a while, a few more drinks and he defied anyone not to be happy – this was set to be a night to remember. But as he drained his glass and felt his hips start to sway to the ex-hilarating beats of the calypso music he wasn't sure just how much he'd be able to remember come the morning. The night had only just begun and nearly everyone seemed in the mood to party ...

——

Well, nearly everyone. Neither Saul nor Dale had ever really contemplated that there might be a time when they would be in the same room together. If they had, then they certainly wouldn't have imagined it being on a yacht in the Caribbean dressed as a pair of pirates. It had been Saul who had spotted Dale first. For a split second he had considered ignoring him completely; he had nothing to say to the man. But then, he realised that they were likely to find themselves in each other's company a great deal over the next three days. He was obviously part of the wedding party. Questions started to swim around Saul's mind. *Was Dale here alone? Did he bring Lauren with him? How had Lauren reacted to their separation? Would Lauren be bumping into Martha?* The thirst for knowledge was too great. Saul strode over to Dale, who would have been less shocked if he'd bumped into the Pope, and immediately barked in his face.

'What the hell are you doing here, Cousins?' he snapped through gritted teeth.

It took Dale a few moments to reply, his brain still wondering if the local cocktails and the coke he'd been regularly snorting since arriving on the yacht were in fact a cross-pollination capable of hallucinogenic properties. Saul as a salty seadog was a mightily trippy vision.

'I know Piero of old. Personal invite from the groom-to-be. You?' Dale volleyed the question back at Saul with super quick speed. It was the multimillion-dollar question. Saul could lie or just come out with the truth. Going against what most people would imagine a politician would do, he spoke the truth.

'I'm here with their bridesmaid, Martha Éclair. She invited me and after all the shit I've been through recently with my own home life I figured this might be just the tonic. I've got to say it was ... until I met you.'

'The feeling's mutual, buddy, so let's just deal with it.' He paused, then added, his curiosity obviously tweaked. 'Here with the bridesmaid? Together? You don't waste any time, do you? You've only just served Lauren divorce papers. She won't be chuffed,' snorted Dale, an air of sarcastic derision hanging in the air.

'I don't think my soon-to-be-ex-wife has any reason to feel, as you put it, "chuffed" or otherwise. Any seedy accusations about my love life would definitely be somewhat ironic, given the photos I received of you two in Las Vegas. They proved that you and her are more than just work colleagues.'

The news floored Dale. 'What photos? Our trip to Vegas was purely business – your ex is set to be a big star. You'll see her tomorrow, she looks amazing.'

'Providing she doesn't overdose, thanks to hanging out with the likes of you. A dead star is no use to anyone,' countered Saul. 'And it strikes me that your client list doesn't exactly have the best track record, does it? Full of losers – Lauren makes a great addition,' he smirked.

'Now, hang on a—' Dale tried to stop Saul in his tracks, but the politician was not going to be bulldozed into silence.

'I suggest you ask another of your clients about the photos, seeing as it was her who sent them to me – seeing as it was her who wanted to blackmail Lauren and me with them. She wanted me to take Lauren back and get her off your hands. I told her where to go but she's still got the photos. I would imagine she'll send them to the press someday soon as she's obviously got the morals of a sewer rat – you must have taught her well.'

'Who the fuck—' Again, Dale's interjection was pointless.

'Doubtless she's off her face most of the time too. She certainly doesn't seem to be doing much work lately from the CV I read on your website. I suggest next time you see her you ask Nancy Arlow just what she's after in a manager – because it seems to me that right now she's after any ill-gotten gains she can lay her grubby little hands on. Lauren's welcome to your seedy little existence. She obviously fits in a treat. Now, if you'll excuse me …'

Saul turned to walk away, leaving a somewhat shell-shocked Dale both livid and stunned by his news about Nancy. He was still stupefied when Dale turned back to him. 'And may I suggest you watch your coke intake here, Mr Cousins, your nose is running like a leaky tap. You might think it's a good look in your world, but I doubt it is in the groom's.'

———

Over on the far side of the room, one of the other party guests would have been just as interested to hear the name of Nancy being mentioned. Bruno Fielding was happily tucking into a bowl of broiled fish and talking to his boss and friend, Duncan

Porte. In a similar vein to Saul and Dale's impromptu encounter, the two colleagues had both not known that the other had been invited.

'I should have guessed,' commented Duncan, scanning the room as he spoke. 'Portia is a very giving person and will always help those who help her. She and Piero are obviously incredibly well connected. I've never seen so many names in one room. I've spotted the opera baritone Simon Keenlyside already – he is simply one of the best singers I've ever witnessed and I'm sure that's the Hollywood actor Jeremy Pinewood over there. I'm tempted to say half this room has been to The Abbey at some point, you know.'

Wiping the traces of fish from around his mouth, Bruno readily agreed. 'I know, Dale Cousins is here and he's brought Lauren with him. She's responded so well to treatment – she just needs to keep up the medication and I truly believe she'll be fine. And obviously Martha Éclair is the bridesmaid. This wedding is like *addicts on vacation*!'

'Recovering addicts, Bruno. It's what The Abbey prides itself on. If anyone can turn people around then it's you. I just wish all of our clients were as professional as you. That business with Ed Collie could have exploded out of control. We're lucky Portia didn't sue the ass off us.'

Mention of Ed pricked at Bruno's heart. He hadn't yet told his boss that he was seeing Ed's sister and that she had accompanied him to the Caribbean. He hadn't really considered it before, but then he hadn't figured he'd be running into Duncan. He went to say something, feeling that maybe now was the moment to broadcast it, but before he could confess the pair of them were interrupted.

'Here you go, boys, two Painkiller cocktails ... guaranteed to numb even the butchest of men into submission. And look who I've been talking to at the bar – Portia's right-hand man. He's a regular visitor to The Abbey so doubtless you two both know him, but just in case you don't, let me do the introductions. Redmond, this is Dr Bruno Fielding, the best medic in the business, so I hear, and this is my husband, and owner of The Abbey, Duncan Porte.'

Redmond couldn't help but squeal. 'Your husband? How fabulous. Does Portia know – she's been questioning herself for years as to why Duncan and she never quite managed to get it together. She's always had a soft spot. Now the truth is out. She'll love it.'

'I do hope so, I've been dying to meet the woman myself. Been a fan for years,' said the strikingly handsome stranger who had escorted Redmond from the bar. His head was devoid of hair, shaved virtually to the skin, and his eyes were a deep penetrating shade of blue. His body was thickset and obviously chiselled from hours in the gym. Redmond could see why anyone would find him alluring. 'Her sense of style is beyond compare. I can't wait to see her wedding dress – it is bound to be sublime.'

'Here we go again. Fashion this and fashion that,' scoffed Duncan. 'I'm afraid my husband is rather obsessed with all things designer. If it's been seen on Mila Kunis or, who's that American soap star you're obsessed with, Montana Phoenix, then Adam is happier than a cat with a bowl of cream.'

Adam held his palms up as if to confess his dependency. 'Your clients have their addictions, Duncan, and I have mine. It takes me away from my day job.'

'Which is?' enquired a jubilant Redmond.

'I'm a policeman. DCI Adam Hall at your service, Redmond.'

Portia's manager nearly choked on the fruit in his cocktail. He couldn't wait to tell his boss. Not only was Duncan gay but he was married to a high-ranking police officer. Portia would love it. 'Well, there's a revelation,' he gushed.

'And talking of revelations, I think from what I heard at the bar, someone is about to reveal all tonight as Piero's stag night treat,' stated Adam.

Right on cue, the lights in the room dimmed, the calypso sounds muted themselves and a deep, expectant cheer filled the air. A stage had been set up at one side of the room with a pole positioned in the middle and as a spotlight flooded onto it, a pirate stood motionless centre stage, swamped from head to toe in a long coat and wearing a three-cornered sea bandit hat. It was impossible to tell who was underneath. All was revealed as the focus of everyone's attention flung the coat to the floor and twirled the hat into the air. Standing there, deafened by the roar of the crowd in front of her, wearing nothing but a tiny black sequinned bikini decorated with white skull and crossbones, was Kelly. As the cheers subsided, she spoke. 'Well, evening, boys, I'm Twinkle Stimulation, the most buxom buccaneer on the high seas. Just call me your *yo-ho-ho*. Who's ready to splice their mainbrace and set sail for a jolly roger? I think I need to show you my hidden treasure chest.'

The room erupted again as music burst from the speakers and Kelly started to gyrate her body sensuously in front of the crowd, pirouetting around the pole as she did so. She was determined that it would be her finest performance. For the next twenty minutes she worked the stage to perfection, thrusting her hips, her pert buttocks and her ample cleavage towards the crowd. She even pulled Piero onstage at one point, to give him a lap dance to remember as she pulled away her bikini and daringly danced her breasts in his face. Piero, awash with the copious cocktails he'd downed throughout the evening, loved every minute of it, any inhibitions he may have had having walked a metaphorical gang plank into a sea of drunkenness.

As the final bars of Kelly's performance climaxed through the speakers, she shed the bottom of her outfit too, giving the assembled males a tantalising glimpse of her naked body before the lights dimmed once more. When they illuminated again, she was wrapped back up in the coat. Thrilled with the applause and wolf-whistles, Kelly bowed and left the stage.

'Well, what do you know, boys, a brief snatch of snatch to keep the party rocking!' laughed Adam. 'Piero looked like he was loving that – well, at least he was when he could keep his eyes open! The man is wasted.'

Neither Redmond nor Bruno answered at first. They were still staring at the stage, transfixed to where Kelly had performed. Bruno was trying to picture the delicious curves and beauteous body that Kelly had momentarily revealed to them. Redmond was slightly horrified. 'Did she have the hottest body on earth or what?' cooed Bruno.

To no one's surprise, Redmond, Duncan and Adam didn't echo their agreement. They were much keener on the body on view at the end of the night when a drunken, naked and heavily well-endowed Piero was tied by his best men to the main mast of the yacht as the party guests were ferried back to shore. As Adam said as they climbed into their speedboat, still eyeing the pendulous girth between Piero's legs from afar, 'No wonder Portia's marrying him. If anything's capable of making her hit those high notes than it's having *that* inside her! Lucky girl.'

CHAPTER 59

The ultra-exclusive, six-bedroom Falcon's Nest Villa on Peter Island had been the setting for some of the most star-studded weddings celebrity magazines have ever chased after – everyone from footballers and their doting WAGs through to media moguls and their exquisitely coiffed, diamond-dipped girlfriends have been seen living the highest of high lives at the mountain-top villa. For those with cash to burn like Portia, it was definitely money well spent. A round-the-clock butler, chef and housekeeper made sure that everything was in order and kept tidy, leaving the lucky houseguests to simply sit back and enjoy the spacious master bedrooms, each boasting an ocean view, the exotic en-suite bathroom with a colourful laser-lit rain shower and the scented gardens containing a two-tiered infinity pool.

Portia had chosen the venue specifically and had booked not just the villa for her and Piero to share with Betsy and Bloodworth, but also the entire five-star Caribbean resort nearby, where the beach-front suites and sea-view rooms would house her hallowed guests. The guests who were now arriving either by private yacht or by helicopter from their overnight stay in Tortola. It was the day before the wedding and at least half of the wedding party, namely the men, were bleary-eyed, hung-over and sporting dark glasses as they booked into their deluxe rooms.

Piero's stag party had been a success, as a fuzzy-head count proved. The cocktails had flowed and the whole island's supply of headache pills had been snapped up by the revellers the next morning, hoping to ease their pounding brains. Piero was worst of all and was grateful for the smoothness of the private jet carrying him and his best men to the island. As soon as he reached Falcon's Nest, he retired to his bedroom. He would have adored to have made love to Portia, who greeted him at the door wearing the sexiest of bikinis, but he was barely capable of raising his hand let alone anything else. Portia didn't mind – there would be plenty of time for that on their wedding night and besides, she was far too comfortable discussing her plans with Martha and Betsy around the infinity pool. Piero flopped into bed on his own and immersed himself in much needed sleep for most of the day.

Dale and Lauren had taken one of the first helicopters to leave Tortola in the morning. Dale was still spitting about Nancy and what he'd heard from Saul. *How could she?* Her hatred for Lauren he could fathom but deep down he never thought Nancy would attempt to try and destroy him too. He'd always been able to twist her around his little finger.

He had told Lauren about it over breakfast at their Tortola hotel and had feared at first that it might have hindered her recovery, but if anything Lauren had left The Abbey stronger and seemingly more resolute and level-headed than he had ever seen her. She was ready to attack the music world with her first single and was determined that nothing or no one would get in her way.

'Let her do what she wants. She's washed up and knows it. Thank God Saul had the decency to send her packing. Not that I'm thrilled to learn that he's here, let me tell you. Why is he here exactly? Who's he with?'

This was the only part of the stag night's revelations that Dale hadn't yet shared with Lauren. *Wasn't Martha supposed to be her friend?* 'I can't remember,' he fudged. 'I just know that he said that we were hardly in a position to criticise his being with somebody else after Nancy's photos.'

'Fair enough. If I'm moving on, then so can he. Neither he nor that skank Nancy will stop me from enjoying all of this Caribbean air. I'm taking my beta blockers, I'm feeling on the road to recovery and I'm determined not to touch the charlie again. Weddings are a time to celebrate and I need to rejoice in the fact that I'm still alive and kicking.' She allowed a smile to unfurl across her rosy-pink face before adding somewhat ominously, 'Besides, Nancy Arlow will get exactly what she deserves and I shall personally deliver it with relish. I saw her last night in the hotel bar, actually. We didn't speak but she looked a lot more upset to see me than I was her.'

Lauren got to her feet, pushing away the plate of half-eaten breakfast fruit in front of her as she did so. 'Now, I just need to take a trip to the little ladies' room, Dale, so if you'll excuse me.'

She was just about to walk away when Nancy and Bruno sauntered into the breakfast area. The snarl that released itself from Nancy's mouth as she locked eyes with Lauren was almost audible. Enjoying the tension between them, Lauren walked round to the table to where Dale was seated and leant towards him, kissing him fully and a little over-passionately for such an early hour on the lips. Speaking much louder than she had been, she chirped, 'I'll see you in a minute, lover' and skipped somewhat gaily from the room, leaving Dale flushed with embarrassment.

When she returned to the table thirty minutes later – she'd been talking to one of her favourite actresses, a fellow guest at the wedding, who she'd bumped into in the restroom and had lost track of time – Dale was nowhere to be seen. Assuming he must have needed to answer a call of nature himself and that he'd wondered why she'd been so long, Lauren sat herself down at the table, reached down into her bag and pulled out her bottle of beta blockers. Pouring herself a glass of water, she popped the pill into her mouth and swallowed. She spied Nancy watching her as she did so. Unable to resist, she raised her glass in Nancy's direction and cried 'cheers'. Nancy didn't react.

She waited another five minutes for Dale to return but there was no sign. Assuming his call of nature was maybe a little bit more troublesome than she first thought, Lauren picked up her bag and walked back to their room to wait for him there.

Lauren had been right about Dale's whereabouts. He was indeed in the toilet, but it wasn't due to any kind of weak bladder or morning-after-the-night-before stomach. He needed a line of coke. Locking the cubicle door behind him, he pulled his wallet from his back pocket and opened it up. Lauren was also right about him being troubled. As he frantically worked his fingers around the wallet he couldn't find his cocaine anywhere. He'd placed his entire stash there when they'd arrived at Tortola. It had been there last night on the yacht because he'd enjoyed a series of fat, lip-numbing lines. He was certain he'd had it when he was ferried back to port. Or was he? He was pretty wrecked. Maybe he'd dropped it on the yacht, or worse still maybe it had fallen into the ocean. Either way, one thing was sure – wherever it was, it certainly wasn't with him any more. Banging his fist against the wall in frustration he opened the door and headed back to his room.

———

There had been banging on the wall of Duncan and Adam's room as well during the night. The couple had been fuelled into a rather noisy and passionate bout of sex back at the hotel after the stag party, both of them doubtless still visualising the sight of Piero's mammoth appendage in their horny minds. Unable to control their animalistic tendencies, they had both been pretty vocal, causing their neighbours, an elderly pair of Piero's Italian relations, to bang on the wall in protest and phone the hotel reception in order to complain. Duncan and Adam had only ceased when a rather timid-looking female staff member knocked on the door to ask them politely to 'stop making any loud noises'.

The gay men walked rather sheepishly towards breakfast the next morning. While Duncan spoke to the hotel concierge to organise a time for their helicopter flight to Peter Island, Adam milled around in reception, people-watching the exclusive parade of high-end fashion that seemed to be draped around every hotel guest. *This is definitely one uber-swank gathering*, he mused, noting Marchesa, Dolce & Gabbana, the late Alexander McQueen and a simply huge Neil Lane diamond sparkler within the space of a few minutes. It was haute couture heaven.

'Nice outfit,' he smiled as yet another vision of red-carpet glamour sashayed past him. 'YSL, if I'm not mistaken, and that bag is a prime example of first class Salvatore Ferragamo. You're one stylish lady, if you don't mind me saying.'

'A girl always likes to hear she's in vogue,' she answered back, 'especially if it's from such a good-looking guy.' She couldn't help but let her eyes drift the full length of Adam's robust, athletic frame. 'Pleased to meet you, I'm Nancy Arlow. I assume you're here for the wedding to end all others.'

'Got it in one. I'm Adam Hall. My other half is just sorting out our chopper to Peter Island.' Adam pointed towards the reception, turning as he did so and virtually coming face to face with Duncan who had evidently done what he needed to do. 'Oh, talk of the devil, here he is now. Duncan, this is Nancy Arlow. I was just admiring her fashion savvy.'

Duncan faltered for a second before holding out his hand. 'Oh … er, hi. You're here for the wedding?' he enquired.

'Yes, my doctor boyfriend was invited by the bride. He treated her for something recently. Doubtless you'll meet him at some point.'

'Dr Bruno Fielding, perchance?' The question raced from Duncan's lips before he really considered whether he actually wanted to ask it. It took Nancy by surprise.

'Yes, spot on. Do you know each other?'

'I should do, he works for me at The Abbey. He's a good man. How's his head this morning? We were all a little the worse for wear on the yacht last night.'

'Nothing that a hearty breakfast won't sort out. I must go and find him, actually, as he'll be missing me, no doubt. I only popped out for a smoke. I'll see you guys later.'

'Indeed you will,' muttered Duncan under his breath. 'Indeed you will …'

As Nancy walked off, she couldn't help but look around at Adam once again. She loved a compliment, no matter where it came from. *Such a shame he's gay*, she thought to herself. *Mind you, I should have guessed – straight guys never know that much about fashion, do they?*

CHAPTER 60

The weeks before Mariella's exit from South Africa in order to watch her daughter act as bridesmaid at Portia's Caribbean wedding had been organised with a military precision and a top secret efficiency that would have pleased even the highest officers of the SAS. They had also been some of the most emotional times she had ever experienced – her feelings of excitement about her new life with Lewin and her terror at Peter's eventual reaction to her choice flip-flopping through her head like an oxygen-starved fish out of water.

She knew that she had made the right decision. When Lewin spoke to her about how he had found a business manager to look after his company, about how he had already organised shipping of their most treasured items to their awaiting UK home and about how he longed to spend the rest of his days with the one woman who had truly meant more to him than any placing on the Forbes Rich List, she knew that they were destined to be together again. For a lifetime. She would have been with him already had it not been for the matter of the wedding.

The last thing Mariella wanted to do was take the spotlight away from Martha as she performed her duties at Portia's wedding. Mariella and Lewin had discussed it. While Mariella and Peter flew to the Caribbean, Lewin would take the time to organise for the rest of Mariella's belongings to be shipped to the UK and then he himself would take one of the Éclair private jets and leave the Rainbow Nation behind for good to begin a second

chance with his perfect partner in the UK. Mariella would tell
Peter that their life together was over once the 'Portiero' wedding had taken place and she would fly to the UK while Peter
would hopefully fly back to South Africa.

That was the plan and on paper it seemed an easy thing to
do, but as Peter and Mariella stared out of their ocean view
window at their grandiose Peter Island Resort room, the atmosphere between them seemed heavier than the smell of the
fresh-grilled fish they had just pushed awkwardly around their
plates at one of the resort restaurants. She could hardly look at
him. The man before her had become a stranger to her. They
were both on edge, and although Mariella knew exactly what
was causing her own distress she was bewildered as to why Peter
seemed so riddled with angst. They had hardly spoken on the
flights from South Africa, Mariella blaming a feigned headache
and pretending to sleep for most of the journey and Peter burying his head in a Sidney Sheldon novel to try and escape his
own inner thoughts.

If Mariella had been able to see inside Peter's mind, she would
have witnessed a storm of dark secrets more forceful than the
worst of tropical cyclones. Peter knew that the Caribbean wedding was his opportunity to confront Martha about the dogging
photos and make sure that she and Kieran were together – not
that he'd been able to contact his wayward offspring. Somehow,
Kieran's mobile phone clicked constantly to the messaging service. But Peter knew that when he did track down his obedient
scion he would do just as Peter required.

The other issue that rocketed around Peter's mind was the
matter of seeing Portia again. He had hardly been able to stop
thinking about her since Martha had first mentioned the wedding. His darling Portia. It had been virtually the best part of
two decades since he had last seen her in the flesh, running away

from his betrayal of her and into the distance at the hotel in Cape Town. Why *had he been so stupid? Why hadn't he run after her? How could he? Just seconds before he had been making love to another woman.* He'd let his libido get the better of him. He'd tasted forbidden fruit behind the back of the sweetest woman he'd ever known. The memory may have become distant but the stupidity he'd felt about losing her had lingered on for forever. He'd loved Portia – both as a person and as a performer. Upon seeing her again, he was determined to show her that he had spent years regretting his actions.

———

The chance came that evening, the night before Portia and Piero's ceremony, at an exclusive pre-wedding party at the Falcon's Nest Villa. Portia had billed it as 'an intimate gathering of friends who would privately wish her and Piero all the love in the world for their forthcoming union'. It was to take place in the sumptuous setting of the scented gardens at the villa's outdoor entertainment area. It was beautiful and dignified. But there was nothing dignified about the intimate gathering as the night unfurled. In fact, instead of wishing love, it seemed that most people would have gladly wished each other motionless and face-down in the serene waters of the villa's infinity pool.

Even before Portia and Piero's planned grand entrance, as the diva busied herself sliding her never-ending curves into the most flattering of Chanel gowns in her upstairs suite, the guests gathered below were eyeing each other with pointed looks sharper than the sticks skewering the pineapple pieces in their cocktails.

Not that Lauren was sipping anything stronger than a glass of iced water. She had avoided alcohol like the plague since her release from The Abbey and was determined that nothing would coax her into temptation as far as drugs were concerned. And for once, she was pretty sure that Dale was clean too. Despite a certain twitchiness and the fact that he was downing the cocktails as if the party bar had announced it was soon to run dry, she was sure that he'd not sneaked off to snort a line of coke all evening. She was right, but a restless Dale was not off the coke out of choice – he'd still not been able to track any down after losing his own stash at Piero's stag party.

Lauren was pleased that she felt in control – she needed to be, her palpitating heart had a lot to be coping with – as standing no more than ten yards away from her was her soon-to-be-ex-husband, Saul. And as if seeing him hadn't been enough of a shock to her already fragile system, observing her so-called friend, Martha, wrapped around him and running her fingers through his jet black thatch of hair in such an intimate way had made her see a red deeper than the blood which seemed to be beating more frenziedly though her core with every second.

Reaching into her purse, she pulled out a beta blocker and swallowed it. The thought of her dependency on them scared her slightly but as soon as she'd taken it, an air of sanctuary spread across her. As long as she took the tablets as Bruno ordered and avoided the lure of cocaine then Lauren could survive anything, even Martha's betrayal with Saul. Leaving a jumpy Dale to head for the bar to order another drink, Lauren strolled over to where the giggling couple were standing. Their laughter stopped as soon as they saw her.

'Well, this is a turn up for the books. I never had you down as the raving party animal, Saul. You were always too busy with piggish Nathan to bother with nights out with me, but it seems a lot of things have changed.' She scanned Martha from head to toe before adding somewhat cattily, 'And not all of them for the better. I assume you two came here together and didn't just fall into each other's arms under the heat of a Caribbean sky?'

A thousand thoughts streaked through Martha's head. She'd been watching Lauren since her arrival at the party. *Was Lauren looking at Saul through regretful, nostalgic eyes? Had Saul been returning her looks? Was there still a frisson between them? Why did Lauren have to look so bloody good? Why did Martha doubt herself and why was she still plagued with a ripple of doubt about Saul? He'd stated his feelings for her time and time again in glorious heartfelt clarity.*

Martha could feel her skin turn the same colour as the raspberry dress she had chosen for the evening. It was a mix of embarrassment and rage. She had known this moment would come, but there was no way she was going to let Lauren get the better of her in front of Saul. She was quick to reply.

'We've both moved on, Lauren. Saul and I want to be together. I didn't know who Saul was when we first met, but now I do – and it changes nothing. You can despise me all you like if you wish, but you haven't really got a leg to stand on, have you?' She smiled, an out-of-character fusion of spite and malice crossing her features. 'I've seen the photos of you and your manager. Very cosy, Lauren. Very *devoted wife*. I'm the least of your worries, lady. If Nancy Arlow sells those babies to the papers, then your singing career could be crushed before it even begins. I'm glad you're out of The Abbey, I'm glad that the overdose didn't put you in an early grave, although God knows there are times when I actually think I could put you there myself for what you've put Saul through, but more so I'm overjoyed that your husband, sorry … ex-husband in a matter of weeks, has chosen to be with me. After seeing those photos, I think it's a definitely a step-up for him, don't you?'

Her words hit Lauren like a truck. 'What photos?' She turned to Saul, somewhat bewildered. He replied, his voice calm and uncaring. 'Sex, drugs and rock 'n' roll – the classic trinity, Lauren. Except you can forget the music – it was just the first two. But then, I suppose you can forget the music altogether if that piece of work has her way and pushes those pics to the papers. Career over. She tried to blackmail me with them, Lauren. She wanted cash. I refused, but not out of any loyalty to you. Far from it. You and Dale deserve each other. He evidently breeds monsters – ones hungry for fame. You and Nancy obviously have a lot in common, more than just the same manager. I suggest you go and discuss it with her and leave Martha and me alone.' Saul pointed across the pool to where Nancy was talking with Bruno. 'Maybe she'll show you the photos first-hand – that way you'll know what to expect in the gossip columns.'

Her heart racing with hatred, it was now Lauren's turn to turn the colour of Martha's dress ...

———

Nancy's heart was racing too. She had been watching Lauren ever since she'd arrived at the party. She despised everything about her and to see her with Dale pierced her heart with a stabbing annoyance that would not go away. Thank God she was alongside Bruno. His evident devotion for her was the only thing that was making the sun-drenched evening fiesta at all bearable – that and the constant supply of drinks. As she flicked her cigarette ash into the infinity pool and instructed Bruno to fetch another cocktail, she gazed around at the other guests. Virtually half of them seemed to be staring in her direction, and not one of them, except maybe Adam, seemed to be admiring the Gustavo Cadile dress she'd chosen for the evening's festivities.

Duncan Porte had certainly been staring at her with a heavy-browed intensity that unnerved her. She knew that he and Bruno had talked about her because Bruno had told her – although, somewhat mysteriously, lapdog Bruno had been incredibly vague about what exactly had been said. Martha and Saul had been showering her with disdainful and derisive glances too. She could understand Saul's revulsion to her after her attempt to blackmail him, but what was Martha's problem? The Éclair girl didn't even know her so why was she so intent on dishing out looks that could pierce the hide of even the hardest of people and send them six feet under? Obviously Saul had filled her in.

They could all go to hell as far as Nancy was concerned. And besides, their abhorrence seemed minute in comparison to the anger registered on the face of Lauren who was currently stomping towards Nancy as fast as her Louboutin heels would allow. She'd already seen her talking to Saul and Martha.

Spying Lauren's shoes, Nancy raised her eyebrows in appreciation. 'Killer heels, killer looks ... bring it on. Seconds out, round one,' she slurred quietly, her head spinning slightly. She lit another cigarette as Lauren drew nearer and raised her voice enough for those gathered nearby to turn in her direction. 'Well, if it isn't Dale's latest wannabe on the block. Watch you don't totter into the infinity on those heels, darling. It takes class to walk in those and you're far from that, aren't you? Mind you, you'd hardly drown would you ... you could empty the pool of water in one snort, given your recent nasal capacity, from what I hear. Actually, from what I've *seen*, as you no doubt know. I assume your ex has been telling you about the photos—'

A loud crack echoed around the pool as Lauren allowed the full force of her palm to connect with Nancy's face. Nancy reeled slightly at the impact. Raising her hand to her face and rubbing her cheek, she smirked superciliously at the blonde woman in front of her. 'I'll take that as a yes. Now, just what are you prepared to pay me to keep these photos away from the tabloids?'

———

Neither Bruno nor Dale had seen or heard the fracas that their women had been causing around the pool, as they were both at the bar. Dale was talking to the doctor about how well Lauren had been doing since leaving The Abbey and deliberately avoiding the subject of Nancy. Dale liked the medic despite his current choice in partner. They had just finished their conversation when Dale's attention was drawn to the other side of the bar. A good-looking mature lady stood there, alongside a somewhat serious-looking man. Dale was sure he knew her from somewhere. Carrying his two drinks, he weaved his way to where they were standing. Up close the woman was even more striking than he first imagined. 'Hi there, I don't think we've met, my name's Dale Cousins. Are you enjoying the party?'

'Peter Bradford from South Africa. Owner of Bradford Wines. This is my partner, Mariella, mother of the bridesmaid, Martha,' snapped the man, keen to stay away from engaging in small talk. 'Now, if you'll excuse us.'

The couple moved off from Dale before he could say anything else, but as they did so, Mariella stared him directly in the eyes and a look of nostalgic yet fearful excitement flashed across her face. As she smiled at him and moved off, the penny dropped. He did know her. In fact, he'd once known her incredibly well, at least intimately. She'd been pleasured by him at her beach house in Cape Town when he'd been travelling all those years ago – in fact he'd been with her when he'd received the call about Nancy's casting for *Eton Shore*. The phone call had acted as their coitus interruptus. 'Small world,' mused Dale, laughing to himself as a vision of their love-making filled his mind. His cock pulsed in his trousers. God, he could murder some coke ... surely he'd be able to get some from somewhere.

Cape Town was on Peter's mind too as he walked away from Dale. The last place he'd seen Portia, and in a matter of minutes she'd be standing before him again. *What would she say? Would she recognise him and still hate him? How would he feel?* All of that was to come but first he needed to speak to Martha. She'd been strangely silent about the photos he'd sent to her and he wanted to make sure that she was still intent on being with Kieran, despite her current appearance of being wrapped around some uptight politician. Mariella had told him who he was. She seemed happy for Martha to be with him. *Didn't the stupid woman realise that Martha being with Saul was wrong?* It had no future. Not for them, and certainly not for Peter. She had to be with Kieran. There was no choice.

Martha was still shaking with rage and getting over her confrontation with Lauren when she spied Peter and her mother strutting towards her. With a sharp intake of breath she took Saul by the hand and squeezed it tightly. She knew she had to be strong. This was the moment she'd been waiting for. And now was the time. She'd known ever since she'd spoken to Mariella and discovered that she longed to be with Lewin again and that they desired to start a new life together in the UK. The moment had to be perfect.

'Long time no speak. You're looking lovely, Martha,' said Peter, his voice unconvincing. He leant in to kiss Martha on the cheek and as he did so, he whispered in her ear, 'Although naturally I am surprised you've not been in touch before, and even more so by your choice of partner for this wedding. Didn't I make myself clear?'

The menace in his voice drilled into Martha's brain. She hated him, more than she'd ever hated anyone, which was saying something given the animosity ricocheting around the party and her continuing dark thoughts about Lauren.

Composing herself, she began to talk. 'Hello, Peter. Welcome to paradise. I couldn't think of a better place to be – especially when I'm surrounded by the people I love. And that includes Saul. I don't believe you two have met. But forgive him if he doesn't shake your hand, he knows what a wanker you are already. It's just a pity my father isn't here to complete the picture of family bliss. I'm sure he'd love to see what's about to happen.'

A king of the business world, a normally unflappable Peter suddenly felt pushed from his own throne. This had not been what he'd expected to hear, but if Martha was choosing to ignore his threats then so be it. He would just have to put her in her place and remind her who was harbouring the trump card – namely the explicit photos. He turned to Mariella to see her reaction to her daughter's words. She remained silent but tears were forming in her eyes, leaving her with an appearance of abject sadness. None of it made sense to Peter.

'Are you going to let your daughter speak to me like that, Mariella? I thought you'd taught her respect.' There was a false bravado in his voice. Despite his physical strength, he could feel himself weakening before the two women and Saul.

'You need to earn respect, Peter, and you don't do that by trying to blackmail my daughter into a phoney marriage.' A solitary tear fell from Mariella's eye.

'I don't ... I don't know what ... what you mean?' stuttered Peter, as all the ruddiness of his complexion seemed to ebb away from his cheeks.

'My mother knows, Peter. She knows.' Martha's words were clear. 'I've told her about the photos, I've told her about your son, Kieran, and I've told her about your blackmail attempts to get control of Lewin Éclair Wines. She's known for weeks. You can't hurt her ... or me. And you'll never have any inroads into my father's company.'

'You're mad. Of course I can hurt you. I'll send those photos to the press. Your family will be ruined by the scandal. How can a successful business family like yours survive when photos of you getting fucked over the bonnet of a car are plastered all over the press? It's hardly the right image for a wholesome family wine empire, is it? You wouldn't want your mother to see you like that, would you?' Peter could hear his voice starting to crack under the pressure of what he was saying. Like a clockwork toy that needed winding up, he could feel all of his energy flowing from his body, his fight grinding to a halt. He could almost taste his own defeat.

'I've seen the photos, Peter. You can't hurt me any more than you already have.' Mariella's bottom lip trembled as she spoke. 'I found copies of them in your suitcase. What Martha chooses to do is her own business, whether I like it or not, but nobody will ever try to use my daughter against me. I thought you loved me, Peter. Maybe you did, but it would seem not as much as you love the thought of improving your business power. Lewin's more of a man than you'll ever be, and he may be ruthless in business and he may have made mistakes but he'd never stoop this low. I was going to do this after the wedding tomorrow, Peter, but Martha was insistent we sort this as soon as possible. We're through. We came here together but we leave separately. I've already had my belongings moved out of your house. I can't be with a man who would do this to my own flesh and blood.' Mariella took hold of Martha's hand as she spoke, sandwiching her between herself and Saul. 'And to be honest, even if I knew nothing about it, I don't think I want to be with you any more anyway. I don't love you, Peter, and this proves to me I'm right.'

The waves of shock crashing over Peter were evident as he listened to what Mariella was saying. They were through? If that was the case, then he would never have any power of Lewin Éclair Wines. This was not over – he wouldn't allow it.

'Those photos in my case were just printouts!' he barked, narrowing his eyes in anger. 'I've got enough intelligence to back everything up on my computer. Those photos will be with every press association around the world before you catch the bride's bouquet tomorrow. You'll ruin this wedding, destroy any integrity this family ever had and kill off your boyfriend's political career. Do you want that on your conscience? Of course, if you did decide to be with Kieran, then maybe I could forget all about the photos – at least for as long as you're married – and make sure that the Bradford Wine empire can have a stranglehold on your poxy business.'

'That's never going to happen …' It wasn't Mariella, Martha or Saul who spoke. There was a silence as Peter turned round to stare in the direction of the additional voice. He knew the owner, but only had his worst suspicions confirmed as he heard the final word, '… Dad.' Staring back at him was Kieran.

'What the hell are you doing here? And you'll do exactly what I want you to do. That's how I raised you, you stupid bastard. You do as I say … or else.'

'No, Dad, I don't do as you say. I'm through with all of that. The lies, the deceit, the running scared of my own father. I fell in love with Martha, but she chose not to be with me. I don't blame her. Our meeting was hardly built on an honest foundation, but I can at least rectify some of the damage that's been done here. She's with Saul now. I respect that. What I don't respect is you trying to blackmail her into being with me. I'm man enough to choose my own relationships. I'd rather just be Martha's friend than be her enemy.'

'Stupid little prick. I'm ashamed to call you my son if that's the attitude you're going to take. And the photos will go to the press. I can make sure of that.' Peter pushed roughly against Kieran's shoulder with his hand in an attempt to assert his authority over his son. Kieran had expected it and remained upright, defiant against his domineering father.

'There are no photos, Dad. They're gone – destroyed. I phoned Martha at her flat in London a few weeks back – bit of a surprise for her, to be honest, but I wanted to do the right thing and explain what you'd made me try and do. She told me about the wedding and Mariella bringing you here. I knew you'd try and bring your laptop with you to keep the photos safe so I had Martha instruct Mariella to unpack it before you left and leave it at the house in South Africa. That's where I've just flown from. It's always easy to get one of the family jets to ferry me around the world if I choose. I've wiped your laptop and desktop clean. Every photo I could find, including any of Martha. I opened the safe for copies too. There were none, I'm guessing the only ones you printed out are the ones you packed to come here. While I was in the safe though, I did borrow £25,000 – I owe someone some cash I stole from them and I figured it was the least you could do as way of payment for the dirty work I've done for you.'

Peter looked shell-shocked as his son continued. 'You've achieved more in life and reaped more financial success than most people can dream of, and I'm proud of you for that, Dad, but you can't buy other people's love with blackmail. Mum would have never taught me that if she were still alive. You've taught me to be dishonest and bad and steal and cheat. They're all the things that she hated – that she tried to fight against. She was a free spirit … just like Martha. Two boundless hearts with nothing but love to give. I can't see that destroyed. You're my dad and you always will be and I'll always love you, but right now I just don't like you very much. You can't hurt me any more, you can't … and you can't hurt Martha.'

Peter knew that he'd lost. All of the pawns he had intended to manipulate in his game had turned against him. It was checkmate. He'd not made copies of the photos and Kieran was right, if they'd been wiped from his computers then they were gone forever. He'd lost the game, he'd lost his son and he'd lost Mariella. Unable to stand the situation any longer, Peter stormed across the gardens and headed away from the gathering. He needed time to think.

Just as he was passing the main doors of the villa, a voice boomed out from a microphone in the corner. It was Redmond. 'Ladies and gentleman, will you please welcome at their last social occasion before they become man and wife tomorrow, Portia Safari and Piero Romeo.' As the bride-and-groom-to-be entered into the gardens, Peter couldn't help but stop and stare at Portia. She was just as beautiful as he remembered, in fact, even more so.

CHAPTER 61

Portia's entrance into her own pre-wedding party was a bitter-sweet one for the diva. On the one hand, she had never looked more radiant, she had had the Chanel gown made to measure for showing off her traffic-stopping billboard body to perfection. She had spent weeks working on her outfit – tiptoeing her way delicately through every designer style from billowing sleeves and plunging necklines, through to beaded accessories and embroidered flapper panels, but in the end she had chosen pure, simple, unadulterated class with fabrics that simply kissed the skin and flaunted her ageless femininity. To her guests she looked a paragon of perfection, but they couldn't see the jet black streak of horror that zoomed lightning-quick into her head as she walked into the sunshine. Portia was like a beautiful Faberge egg with an unwanted rotten yolk festering inside.

The cause of her sudden dramatic downturn in humour was the first person she laid eyes on. Nancy Arlow. Nancy stood there, a cigarette in her hand, blowing smoke rings into the air, staring directly at the diva. Never had somebody looked more contemptuous. A consummate professional, Portia didn't let a flicker of her inner horror show on her face as she glided past Nancy, hand in hand with Piero, taking in the applause from those gathered. In fact, she forced a smile as she drew alongside her and allowed herself to take in the full length of Nancy's appearance. Before she could halt her own thoughts, she wished her dead. Her sienna skin suited the Caribbean heat and her dress was stunning, but all of that blurred into the background as Portia noticed the ring on Nancy's finger as she lifted her hand to her mouth to drag on her cigarette. It was the one that she had stolen from Betsy.

Not that Nancy knew that at that precise moment, she was having too much fun blowing smoke directly into Portia's face as the opera star walked by. She curled her lips in delight, only to have all expression fall from her face a mere second later as she spied Betsy and her butler, Bloodworth, walking directly behind Portia.

Nancy's cigarette dropped from her hand in horror and rolled across the floor and into the infinity pool where it extinguished with a short fizzle. Before Betsy caught sight of her, Nancy turned on her heels and went in search of Bruno. Now was definitely the time to try and get lost in the assembled throng.

Portia and Piero made their way to the corner of the garden where Redmond had placed the microphone and a raised stage. It was from there that they addressed their guests. Piero, his face covered in the largest sunglasses he could find to dull his still raging hangover, was grateful that Portia had taken it upon herself to deliver their thanks. 'Thank you, everyone, you are too kind,' she gushed as the applause started to die away. 'I would like to thank *all* of you for coming. It means such a lot to me that each and *every one* of you is here to celebrate the joyous step that I shall take with Piero tomorrow. It's wonderful to see so many familiar and, dare I say it, famous faces. Family members, friends and fans all gathered to honour both Piero and me as we become one. Tomorrow promises to be an amazing day and I have it on good authority that the weather will be incredibly hot – although naturally it won't be as hot as my outfit or my plans for the wedding night.' Portia laughed at her own joke and a murmur of mirth emanated from the guests. 'But before tomorrow, we have tonight, and I hope you all have an amazing time. So eat, drink and be merry – but not too merry as I don't want to see any panda-eyes staring out from the wedding photos when they pop up on the newsstands ... and that includes you, darling!' She poked Piero in the ribs to make her point. 'I think the hangover you've had today was large enough to last a lifetime.' Piero knew that she was only half joking.

For the next hour or so, Portia and Piero mingled amongst their guests, exchanging pleasantries and making sure that everyone was catered for. Under the watchful eyes of both Redmond and Piero, Portia managed to stay away from any kind of alcohol. Not that she had any intention of drinking – she wanted to be completely in control of all that was going on around her. She floated her way from a hopelessly fawning Adam and his mildly embarrassed husband, Duncan – 'what a surprise, Duncan darling, I never even contemplated you batting for the other team, although it does explain why you and I have never got together, you gorgeous man! I'm surprised Redmond never guessed!' – to a far from deep conversation about the state of British politics with Saul and Martha – 'I would run for prime minister myself, Saul,' she cooed in jest, 'but I think I'd find Ten Downing Street a touch cramped for my tastes.' But no matter who she was talking to, Portia kept a watchful eye to make sure that two of her guests didn't leave the party before she'd had a chance to talk to them. They'd been lurking in the background all night and it was just as the sun was setting over the horizon signalling the end of her last day as a single woman that she noticed that Nancy and Bruno – not that Portia had realised they were together when she'd invited him to the wedding – were making moves as if to leave.

'Will you excuse me, my precious,' she announced to Piero. 'I just need to go and powder my nose. I trust I can relinquish the duties of entertaining our guests to you.' Leaving him talking to Dale and Lauren, who Portia had been quite horrified by – *How could she leave that heroic hunk of a politician for a common record company owner? Where was the class in that?* – Portia headed towards the pool, taking the arm of her aunt Betsy as she did so. 'I have someone I'd like you to meet, Aunt Betsy. I think she has something to give back to you.'

Nancy and a complaining Bruno – he'd not even said hello to Portia yet and Nancy seemed intent that he shouldn't – were just in the process of leaving the garden when Portia and Betsy stepped right in front of them alongside the pool.

Bruno's face lit up as his ex-patient appeared. 'Portia, I've been trying to talk to you all night. You always seem to be busy with someone. May I introduce my girlfriend, Nancy Arlow.'

'And may I prescribe that you trade her in for a new one, Dr Fielding!' snapped back Portia. 'How can someone of your intelligence be so foolish when it comes to picking a partner? I've met Nancy before at The Abbey. And I believe she knows my aunt Betsy incredibly well. They have a love of gambling in common … as well as a love of jewellery, it appears.'

Nancy had never wanted the ground to open up and swallow her as much as she did at that moment. Portia she could deal with – she still had a trump card to play if needed – but seeing the sweet face of Betsy standing in front of her stabbed her to the very centre of her heart. Betsy had been nothing but kind to her and she had repaid her by stealing. The look of disappointment on Betsy's face told Nancy that the old lady already knew.

'Hello, Nancy, as we gamblers would say, I guess me being Portia's aunty is where your luck runs out. Now, I believe *that* belongs to me.' Betsy signalled towards the ring. 'We can either call the police and discuss it with them, or you can give it back to me, say you're sorry and then get the hell off this island. You can forward the other jewellery onto me. I am assuming you won't be wanting her at your wedding, Portia.'

Nancy knew that she had no option. Slipping the ring from her finger, she handed it back over to Betsy and muttered an apology. 'I didn't mean to hurt you, honestly. I have been feeling bad about it. I just got so into debt with the gambling and my lack of work and well, I intended to sell it but I couldn't. It's so beautiful ...' Her words trickled out to a pathetic whisper.

Bruno listened on, amazed that the woman he was in love with was capable of stealing from an elderly lady. 'You're telling me that what Portia says is true, Nancy? You stole it?'

Nancy was unable to answer before Portia responded. 'Yes, this tramp is nothing but a common thief, Bruno ... and you should know it. Haven't you had money disappear from your wallet recently? One of your work colleagues gets the blame despite a previously spotless CV and suffers a suspension that could have ruined his career. I'd be checking your bank balance if I was you and seeing if your gold and silver has started disappearing mysteriously. Quite the light-fingered criminal is Ms Arlow, and her brother, Ed Collie, is just as dishonest, as we well know. Treachery and inner ugliness obviously runs in the family.'

Unable to control herself at the mention of her brother, Nancy snapped. 'For God's sake, you stuck up two-bit Maria Callas. Just listen to yourself – slagging off *my* family. At least Ed and I have worked hard to get everything we have. Not all of us had fancy backgrounds and rich little aunts in their posh London homes to help us out. You've never wanted for anything – silver spoon in your mouth and a pompous rod up your ass – you couldn't fail, could you? Well, lady, I may be a thief and have had that coach guy at The Abbey suspended for my handiwork but if you think I'm going down on bended knee to ask for your forgiveness then you can shove your holier-than-thou attitude where the sun don't shine. You think I'm ugly on the inside – well, let's see how you like it when the whole world sees how ugly you are. I think some photos of your face swollen up like a fucking axolotl leaked to the press should put you in your place. You deserved everything Ed gave you.'

Grabbing Nancy roughly by the arm and swinging her towards him, Bruno was next to explode. 'You stole my money, Nancy? And how can you possibly have any photos of Portia? I was the only person who took photos of her face after Ed tried to butcher her. There's no way you can have those.'

Feeling that everyone was now ganging up on her, Nancy turned on Bruno, unable to stop herself. 'Just how thick are you, Bruno? I was told you would have taken photographs for potential evidence, so I rooted through your bag when I was staying at yours. I guessed you might have downloaded some from The Abbey computers – you were always bringing work home and telling me what was going on – so I tried every CD I could find and eventually found them. Even I couldn't believe what a mess she was. And as for your money – well, I'm hardly with you for any other reason, am I? The sex is good, but I've had better. Having a girlfriend like me on your arm costs, all right?'

Nancy could see how much Bruno was hurting. He'd not wanted to believe that Nancy could be so bad but her words sliced him into pieces. Staring into his eyes, Nancy felt rotten. Bruno had just become an unnecessary casualty in the war taking place around him. She was making a habit of hurting people that she actually liked – first Betsy and now Bruno. Her destructive desire for money was beyond control, as was her mouthing off. But it was too late for regrets now. She needed to make her exit before she made matters worse.

Portia's voice was calm and collected, keen not to make a scene at her own party. 'Just get out of here. Leave the resort and get off the island. Sell your photographs to the papers if need be and see how many lives you ruin in the process, including his,' she spat, indicating Bruno. 'The poor lovefool will never work again due to a lack of patient confidentiality. Destroy the photographs and you have my word that I won't take you and your brother to the cleaners. I could have you both banged up for this. Am I understood?'

'I'll be gone, don't you worry. You lot are all welcome to each other. But aren't you keen to find out how I knew about your freaky face in the first place though? You're all wrongly assuming it was brother Ed who told me. It wasn't,' she lied. Nancy knew she was down and out but if she was making her exit then she would have to do it with the flourish of a true actress and try to hurt someone she really despised.

'It was Lauren Everett. Drugged off her face on coke with her manager and as loose-lipped as they come. She told me at The Abbey. God, you have some classy guests at this farce of a ceremony. I'm glad I won't be there. I wouldn't be seen dead at your wedding.'

Nancy turned to leave, but a raging Portia, perturbed by Nancy's revelation, was determined to have the last word. 'If I do see you tomorrow then I swear that's exactly what you will be. Dead …' She paused for a split-second before adding, 'And so will Lauren Everett if what you say is true …' Portia knew there was a reason she hadn't liked the woman – nobody who left a prize specimen like Saul and did drugs could be trusted. She'd have to be dealt with another time and the sooner the better. But Portia had had quite enough confrontation for one night. Or so she thought …

—

It was about an hour after Nancy had stormed from the party that the body of guests started to disappear back to their rooms. Thankfully the altercation with Nancy had been mostly unseen. Piero and Redmond had spotted the exchange but didn't question Portia when she returned to them smiling, Aunt Betsy on her arm and the ring back on Betsy's finger. By the early hours of the morning the last guest had been transported back to their accommodation and only Piero and Portia were left staring out across the ocean. It was a beautifully clear night and the reflections of thousands of stars shone brightly on the surface of the water. Taking Portia in his arms, Piero kissed her deeply, allowing his tongue to delve into her mouth. She pulled away in mock disgust.

'Somebody has been having a cigar. I can taste it on your breath. That will not be good for your voice, Piero.'

'Tonight I can do whatever I want, my angel. I'm the happiest man alive and it's thanks to you, Mrs Romeo.' He held her tightly against his chest, his arms forming a cocoon of safe haven around her.

'I can't use that title until tomorrow, my darling. But I do love the sound of it. Now, you go and brush your teeth. I want a moment on my own to savour my last night as a single woman. I shall be up in a moment, although naturally we shall not be sharing beds tonight – tradition is tradition no matter how sexually irresistible the groom may be.' She kissed him again and sat herself on one of the chairs looking out to sea as Piero disappeared inside. The silence of the Caribbean night filled her ears. It was peaceful and she'd never felt happier. Tomorrow she would marry the man of her dreams. The night had been eventful and even though it appeared there were still a few *personal* issues to sort out, everything was going to plan. The silence was broken by a voice behind her.

'Hello, Portia. You look as utterly enchanting now as you did all those years ago when I first saw you onstage. The moonlight highlights your heavenly face like a spotlight shining down on you.'

Portia heard herself gasp as she stared into the face of Peter Bradford. 'You …? What are you doing here? You shouldn't be here.' She couldn't help but think that Peter looked equally striking and handsome now as he had done when she'd last seen him.

'Yes I should. Because otherwise it would be too late. You'd be married to Piero and I wouldn't be able to say what I feel. To tell you how stupid I was to let someone like you slip through my fingers. To admit that I was young and impetuous and have spent the last few years regretting what happened between us when you caught me at that hotel.'

'But you cheated on me, Peter. I loved you and you betrayed me.' Memories of their time together came flooding back into Portia's brain, but somehow the good times they shared seemed to outweigh the brutal finality of that last time they saw each other.

'And you'd be betraying Piero if you married him tomorrow. Because I think you still love me. I know you do, Portia. Even now, after all this time. I was your first love and that never goes away. Those feelings we shared can burn bright again, Portia. Marry me instead …'

His words made no sense, the idea was ridiculous. *Why would she marry a man who betrayed her and broke her heart so brutishly?* But Portia found his words hypnotic, mesmerising and dangerously alluring – just as he had been all those years ago in South Africa. In the heat of the torrid Caribbean night, she found herself in a bittersweet blur and unable to give him an answer.

CHAPTER 62

Portia had not slept well the night before her wedding. Her gruelling dreams had been full of painful images of her body being stretched beyond recognition in two different directions. As if her own frame had become the makeshift rope in an emotional tug of war, the men pulling at her on either end tearing her heart to breaking point. It was clear why.

But after a night of sweat-inducing tossing and turning, when one of her villa maids woke her up the next morning, pulling back the curtains to allow the bright Caribbean light to stream in upon her face, a shattered Portia knew that the day ahead would be her greatest performance yet. A day on which she would finally fulfil her dreams of marrying the man who really deserved her as his bride. She just hoped she was making the right choice and that the hours ahead would not be ones she would regret for the rest of her life.

Blinking her tired eyes as they adjusted to the harsh luminosity, she turned to her maid. 'Can you instruct the hairdressers and make-up artists that I shall require them here at least two hours earlier than planned? I suspect even I will need all the help I can today ...' As she caught sight of her weary reflection in the bedroom mirror she knew that she was right.

———

Just as Portia was seating herself for a pre-nuptial coiffeur later that morning, Nancy was buckling herself into the airline seat as the jet transporting her away from Peter Island prepared for take-off. Things had not gone to plan with her trip to the Caribbean – in just a few short days her life had spiralled out of her own control. She had flown into one of the most luxurious places on earth with a high-earning and gullible boyfriend, a distinct feeling that her money woes were soon to be at an end for good and completely unaware that she would ever have to face Betsy Hartley again. But in true Nancy style, yet again she had let the walls come crashing down around her. She'd lost Bruno, been slapped by Lauren and had to endure her newly found cloud of smug relationship bliss with Dale, had to face Betsy and watch as her kind, fine-lined face had become etched with the deepest of disappointment. She also had to face the wrath of the bride-to-be. Even the goddamned bridesmaid and the owner of The Abbey had laid into her about placing Tom in the firing line and blaming him for her own treachery. The only highlight of the day had been a chance meeting with Kieran Bradford and a surprise cheque for £25,000. Seemingly, she wasn't the only one with regrets about a previous dose of purloining and deception. No, Portia's pre-wedding party had not been the happy house of revelry Nancy had originally planned. But as she felt the surge of the engines as her plane jetted skywards and watched the shape of Peter Island become a pinprick below her, a warm glimmer of malodorous cunning still bubbled inside her. Things were not over yet.

———

Lauren wrapped up her long blond hair in a post-shower towel and walked back into her resort bedroom where a naked Dale was still dozing on the bed, his cock proud and erect and pointing appetisingly in her direction. But now was no time for another bout of sexual contortions, no matter how nectarous his body seemed. They were already late.

'Eh, mister ... this is no time for morning glory. It's already early afternoon and we have a wedding to go to in just a few short hours. I suggest you and your hard-on head for a shower to cool off.'

'I feel as rough as an old dog's tits ...' slurred Dale, his eyes still closed. 'Just another hour in bed will do the trick.'

'No, Dale, I'm not going to be late for this wedding. There's people there you think I need to impress and I'm not going to be doing that by rolling in late with an old soak on my arms. So, get up ... now!' Ripping it away from around her body, she threw her sodden towel at him to prove her point. She was annoyed at him and despite her forced joviality she was unable to hide it.

Raising his body up and running his hands through his dirty-blond hair, Dale yawned as he stared at an obviously aggrieved Lauren standing before him, naked apart from the towel on her head. 'Now, there's a pretty sight to greet a man with the horn first thing,' he said, letting his gaze run down the curves of her rosy-pink skin. 'But someone is not exactly smiling like Coco the Clown today. What's up?'

It was true. Despite the cleanliness of Lauren's freshly scrubbed body, her mind was a dark and dirty place swimming with angry confusion. Dale only needed to ask once. 'For a start, what the hell are we going to do about those photos of me and you in Vegas, Dale? Nancy made it clear she wants paying off. She could ruin everything for me and now I'm finally back on the straight and narrow she's the last thing I need to hinder my potential career. The silly bitch was adamant that I'd have to pay. And then there's Martha fucking Éclair swanning around with Saul, who's suddenly gone from being Mr Uptight Politician with only his career to think of to being Mr Perfect Boyfriend who seems happy to act all loved-up and laidback. Let that bitch try and play the politician's wife and see how she likes it. And there's something wrong with Portia – she obviously doesn't like me much and there was a definite flotilla of daggers sailing my way from her at the party last night. After Nancy left, our hot-headed hostess could barely look me in the eye without seething. Something's not right ... when did all of these women turn into devils? I feel like they're all out to get me.' Pulling the towel from her hair, Lauren marched towards the bedside table and reached for her beta blockers

'You *are* in a foul mood, aren't you? You know Dr Fielding said you had to try and stay calm until any possible heart palpitations passed. Today is a day for celebration, so let's enjoy it ... together.' Dale reached out to try and touch her hand as Lauren picked up a glass of water and swallowed one of the pills. She didn't respond. Instead she reached for Dale's wallet, which was also lying on the table, and threw it at him. A thick wrap of cocaine fell out from within, as she knew it would.

'And this doesn't help, Dale. I'm trying to stay clear of this stuff and you're wandering around with enough of it in your wallet to supply Woodstock. It was clear you were buzzing off your tits at the end of the party. Happy to put me at risk, are you?'

Any semblance of jocularity disappeared from Dale's unshaven face. 'Oh, you're the last person I wanted to see that. I picked some up at the party last night from one of the guests, but obviously I didn't plan on you catching me out. I was a bit tired and thought it might help. It was strong stuff – my head's pounding this morning.'

'Seeing it? I'm not stupid, Dale. The signs are pretty obvious ... I just thought ... you'd be more careful around me, that's all.'

A bolt of panic suddenly crossed Dale's mind. 'You didn't take any, did you? Bruno said you mustn't.' He stared directly into Lauren's eyes, searching for any telltale clues.

'Like I said, Dale, I'm not stupid. I don't want it. I've got too much to lose.'

As he grabbed the wallet and took it with him to the bathroom, Dale wasn't convinced that she was telling the truth. He blew his nose over the sink, clearing his nostrils of the night before's excess. He shouldn't have let himself be so stupid. If Lauren had taken the coke then his nose wasn't the only thing being blown. Their chances of a successful money-making music career could be too.

———

Martha had been doing some *blowing* of her own before the wedding too. But hers was of a purely sexual nature. It had been her parting gift to Saul as she rushed out of the door of their resort accommodation and made her way back up to the Falcon's Nest Villa to prepare alongside Portia for the main event. She would not see Saul again until she emerged resplendent in her bridesmaid outfit into the two-storey glass Great Room at the villa where the wedding vows would be exchanged.

She was sure that the day ahead would be an occasion to remember. Hopefully a happy one for her. The night before had laid a lot of demons to rest. Her parents were to be reunited, Peter Bradford and his threat of blackmail was no more and Kieran had been true to his word and made sure that all evidence of her dogging activities had been destroyed *and* been man enough to face his father. On top of that, Saul had managed to secure Tom his job back at The Abbey. And more importantly, at long last, Martha had managed to face Lauren with the truth about her happiness and cement her feelings that Lauren would not be a threat to her and Saul in the future. It had been no wonder she was so sexually charged when she'd woken up in Saul's arms that morning.

The previous evening had been an eventful one with altercations at every turn. As Martha followed Portia into the Great Room for the wedding itself, a celebratory display of Casablanca lilies cascading from her hands as she walked between the symmetrical rows of guests gathered, she assumed that the day ahead would unfold without any hitches, doubts or indeed further altercations.

She obviously wasn't able to hear the ever-swirling discordant mass of bridal emotions whirlpooling around the head of the star attraction walking a few steps ahead of her. Portia's mind was still a lava-pit of scalding, dangerous thoughts that showed no signs of subsiding as she listened to the operatic sounds of her wedding march and stared at the back of the man standing at the front of the room. The man who would soon be her husband. Had she made the right choice?

CHAPTER 63

As Portia reached the front of the Great Room, she turned to the man alongside her. As quickly as her doubts and worries had arisen the night before, one look into his beautiful love-laden eyes made them dissolve into nothingness – eclipsed by the safe, unadulterated love that she could feel pouring from her partner's soul and enveloping her. How could she have ever doubted? He was the man for her.

Without saying a word, she turned around and looked towards Martha. She smiled, her grin reaching from ear to ear. It was a smile of pure gratitude. She had Martha to thank. She had helped with one of the toughest decisions she had ever had to make …

———

The night before, as Portia had seen Peter Bradford again for the first time in years, the force of sudden emotion that shot like a bullet through her had winded her more than she had ever imagined. She had thought many times throughout her life about the man who had taken her tender virginity, trying to understand how something she had deemed to be so pure and blissfully joyous had become so catastrophic and soul-destroyingly bad. *Why had he strayed? Was it something she herself had done? Had she failed him as a partner? Had she caused the love they had, a love that she had carried with her virtually ever since, to extinguish itself? What if she had been able to give him a second chance back then? Should she allow him a second chance right now?*

In the stunned silence that followed his proposal to her after her party, Portia, normally the quintessence of certainty, was for once lost for words.

It had been a voice from the other side of the infinity pool that had brought her back to her senses – the voice of Martha Éclair.

'Who the hell do you think you are? What are you still doing here – there's nothing for you here.' Her words were aimed at Peter, who seemed more than a touch injured to see his nemesis's daughter again so soon.

'I've come to see Portia. The reason why is none of your—'

Peter attempted to continue but Martha was quick to cut him off. 'I know why you're here. It is my business. I just heard it all. I had no idea you two knew each other. Small world. But if you think for one minute you can crawl back into Portia's life, then you're sorely mistaken. The only place you should be crawling is under the nearest stone or heading back to South Africa with your sorry tail between your legs.'

Martha machine-gunned more words at him before either he or Portia could speak. 'It's my business to look after those I love. And I include Portia in that. If she had the misfortune to know you once then so be it, but you've tried to ruin enough lives tonight without adding hers to the mix.' She turned to Portia, whose head had turned to blancmange with all that was going on around her. 'Let me tell you about the man you think you know, Portia. You'll realise that Piero is more of a man than he'll ever be and you are more of a woman than Peter Bradford will ever deserve.'

Portia listened dumbstruck as Martha told her about what had happened between herself, Saul, Peter and Mariella that night. About the blackmail, although she was spared the exact details of the photographs, about how he had bullied his son into wooing Martha and about his plans to try and take over the Lewin Éclair Empire.

It was only when Martha had finished that Portia was finally able to speak. She gave Peter her response. 'Is this all true, Peter?' She could see from his face that it was. 'Just go. What we had is long gone. For years I thought about you and how you betrayed me. For years I thought about what might have been. I wanted you – so many times I thought about you and wondered about maybe pursuing you for a chance at what we once had. But you were bad then, and from what Martha has said, you're just as bad now. Cheating, bullying and deceiving your own family and those close to you. Do you think I want a man like that? If you do, then you don't know me at all. You haven't known me for years. I had no idea you'd be part of this wedding, no idea I'd even ever see you again, but I thank you for coming. I do. Because now I can finally lay you to rest, like I tried to all of those years ago. You came, I listened, but now it's time for you to go. I won't marry you, Peter, not a hope in hell. I deserve better and that's what I've found with Piero. I'd rather you didn't come to the wedding tomorrow. I think it's best under the circumstances, don't you? Goodnight, Peter …' Her words trailed off slightly as she stared at the man she had once loved so strongly. She could see a ribbon of tears flowing down his face, the brightness of the Caribbean moonlight reflecting in their moisture. Without saying a word, a defeated Peter turned from Portia and allowed his face to sneer with derision in Martha's direction before marching away from the villa.

It was only then that Portia allowed her resolve to crumble. Unable to contain her emotions any more, a barrage of sadness fountained down her face and she crumpled her body in her arms. Martha ran over to her and wrapped her own arms around her friend, pulling her close and allowing her to sob freely into her shoulder. They both remained silent for what seemed like minutes, the only sound filling the air being Portia's weeping. Eventually it was the diva who spoke.

'Why did you come back? Did you know he was here? I might have said yes to him, you know. He's always had a hold over me.'

'Not any more. He's gone. And I came back because I have stupidly lost a stone from one of my rings. It's only a tiger's eye stone but I really like it and I thought it might have dropped off during all the commotion tonight. I'll find it tomorrow after the wedding, no doubt.'

Portia smiled to herself. 'We'll find it now. That gemstone fell out for a reason, let me tell you. I know something about the meaning of gemstones – Betsy and I used to study all about them when I was younger – and tiger's eye symbolises the solving of difficulties. You coming back here tonight has solved a difficulty for me that I might not have been able to do on my own. God bless you, Martha, and you have my word that if we don't find that stone tonight I will buy you every single tiger's eye on earth to make up for it!'

—

They had found it. It had been nestling by the edge of the pool. Martha had reattached it to her ring and was wearing it as she stood behind Portia and Piero as they exchanged vows and diamond-encrusted rings the next day. She had never seen Portia look more beautiful and Piero more handsome. As the reverend announced the happy couple 'man and wife', Martha allowed herself to look round into the assembly of guests applauding behind her. She spotted Saul straight away, his eyes salaciously feasting on the tight fit of her dress. She winked at him. She could see Mariella beaming at her, her proud expression at complete contrast to the glaring swords of hatred Martha seemed to be receiving from Lauren. Staring across the crowd, Martha made sure that the one guest she didn't want to see there was nowhere to be seen. Much to her relief, he wasn't.

As she'd hoped, at the exact moment the newly-weds were posing for their exclusive wedding photos, Peter Bradford, still smarting with rejection, was on his way back to South Africa.

CHAPTER 64

The only person who didn't really enjoy Portia and Piero's lavish wedding reception was Lauren. Despite tantalising her palate with some of the best caviar, crab, salmon and seabass the culinary world could ever dream of serving, no amount of fabulous cuisine or eclectic entertainment could persuade her that she was enjoying herself. Even with Dale's best efforts to drag her onto the dance floor and let her body move freely to the ripe tropical music filling the night air, she could barely bring herself to move awkwardly from one foot to the other.

The only two times she had smiled all night was when she was requested for the official photos – all press, no matter what magazine they ended up in, was good press with her career to think about – and when Dale introduced her to some music industry shakers who might be able to help her with a beneficial leg-up the career ladder in the future. But despite being drunkenly promised everything from potential collaborations with *American Idol* winners through to a touring support slot with Celine Dion, Lauren sported a false smile so expertly painted on that the likes of Picasso would have been proud. Even though she was within touching distance of the life that she had always wanted, as she stared across the reception at Piero and Portia lovingly draped across each other, at a well-inebriated Dale gyrating his hips in the direction of an embarrassed Mariella and an absolutely smashed Bruno Fielding being supported by Duncan Porte and Adam Hall as they slumped him across one of the reception tables, Lauren would have willingly swapped her place to be anywhere else in the world. Curled up on the sofa, stroking Barney's head would have been perfect. Saul had already told her off like a naughty schoolgirl about having to house the dog elsewhere. For the first time in ages, she was almost missing her old life and the solitary day-to-day existence of dog-walking and shopping.

Who was she trying to kid? Saul was the reason she was so annoyed, knotted and hurting as if a string of rose thorns was wrapped around her heart. *How could he be so happy with Martha so soon?* It wasn't right. He'd suddenly become the man Lauren had wanted him to be for ages. Suddenly he seemed carefree, not afraid to let himself go. As she watched Martha and Saul twirling warmly around the dance floor, she could feel her skin prickle as Martha ran her hands down his neck and undid his tie, sliding it from him and then draping it casually over his shoulders. He'd have never done that with Lauren. He'd have been too scared of letting his guard down, especially if Nathan was busy snooping with his pathetic spin-doctor ways. And there was no way Saul would have been seen at a social gathering with his tongue down Lauren's throat, as he was now with Martha. *Heaven forbid – what would the dear old PM have had to say about that?*

Feeling alone and angry, Lauren spied the bottle of Krug champagne on the table in front of her. She'd avoided alcohol ever since her treatment at The Abbey. Bruno had recommended she do so, not that he was exactly the best advert for resistance right now. In fact, he'd never know if she had a glass, would he? He would barely know his own name tomorrow, let alone be able to read her the riot act on the way home. As the annoyance of seeing all around her enjoying themselves engulfed her, Lauren picked up the bottle and placed it to her lips. She tipped it backwards and enjoyed the chilled feeling as it flowed into her mouth and down her throat. It immediately made her more tolerant of her situation.

Aware that her heart was beginning to palpitate within her ribcage, Lauren opened her purse and popped another beta blocker. Thank God she had those – they made her feel more in control even if she was downing this latest one with the finest bubbly.

Deciding it was high time to join Dale on the dance floor, Lauren got to her feet. It was bad enough Martha being with Saul but she was determined that Dale would not be swivelling his intoxicated hips any nearer to the aging body of Martha's mother than he was already attempting. She was a good-looking woman, but she was still an Éclair and at that moment the family tie seemed like the ugliest thing in the world to Lauren.

Weaving between the tables, Lauren could feel her mind becoming fuzzy. She reached out to steady herself on the back of a chair and could feel a coating of heat creeping across her body. Beads of sweat began to form on her face and back and her eyes became heavy as she tried to concentrate on the scene around her. Unable to stop herself from falling, the last thing she could try and focus on as she felt her legs give away beneath her was the sight of a worried Dale running towards her. Sensing that her heart was ticking like a time bomb inside her she slumped to the floor, the reception fading away to be replaced by intense blackness.

———

The next thing Lauren knew was a hazy feeling of opening her eyes and trying to focus on the rotating fan on the ceiling of her resort room. The natural brightness of the daylight around her suggested it was the next day. She had obviously been sleeping or unconscious for a long time. Her mouth dry and uncomfortable, she licked her lips and attempted to cough. A dry rasp erupted. The noise attracted Dale who had been packing on the other side of the room. He rushed towards the bed and sat down beside her, taking her hand in his as he did so and handing her a glass of water.

'Hey, you're awake. You had us all worried, you know. You've been asleep for hours. But at least you were the centre of attention at the reception. Anything to take the media spotlight off the bride and groom, eh? How are you feeling?' He leant down to kiss her on the cheek as he spoke and Lauren enjoyed the softness of his lips against her skin as he did so.

'What happened?' she stammered. 'I remember watching you dance and then ... nothing. Until now.'

'You collapsed. The local doctor gave you the once-over and says you must have been a touch overheated. Looks like you overdid it. He's recommended you rest for a few days when we get back. You did swig the champagne back though. I saw you at the table. I think the combo of that and the heat and your recent troubles sent you over the edge. I would have made Bruno look over you but he was not exactly much use. I think discovering Nancy wasn't the girl he thought she was hit him hard. He'll have a sorer head than you this morning.'

The mention of Nancy's name made Lauren recoil inwardly. 'At least she wasn't there to see me collapse – she'd have loved that. I thought I was having a heart attack. I shouldn't have had the champagne but everything was getting a bit much. Thank you for looking after me.'

'You can thank Duncan and Adam as well. They helped bring you back here and arranged for the doctor. And as for things getting a bit too much, well, you can put Saul and Martha, and Portia's evil eyes out of your mind now as we're leaving this afternoon. The helicopter will collect us at four to take us from the island. Then we take the private jet from the airport. We'll be back in the UK before you know it and after a few days' rest we can concentrate on turning you into a superstar.'

'You really believe that? Can we really do this, Dale?' Lauren questioned, her words sprinkled with more than just a speck of self-doubt.

'I know we can. I've not let you down yet and I have no intention of starting now. Give me six months and it will be Perry-who and Gaga-whatever. But, first things first, even superstars have to pack their cases, you know ... so if you're feeling up to it, there is a pile of designer dresses over there that I may know how to undo and slip from your body but I have no idea how to fold.' Lauren couldn't help but laugh at his male uselessness. It felt good to laugh and to not be angry. The wedding was over, all confrontation momentarily behind them. They could fly home and concentrate on the future – maybe both professionally and personally.

———

Redmond had been busying himself all day making sure that every one of Portia and Piero's guests was assigned to a relevant helicopter, yacht or private jet to transport them away from the 'Portiero' wedding. It was a mammoth task but as he seated himself on the last of the jets to leave the island he allowed himself to sink back into the comfort of the oversized chair and be proud that the entirety of the wedding festivities had gone pretty much without a hitch. Sure, there had been the woman collapsing at the reception and the odd fracas over whose suite was the biggest and most palatial, but apart from that, both Piero and, more importantly, Portia, were elated with how things had turned out.

Redmond knew all about Portia and Betsy's run-in with Nancy and had arranged for her to leave the day before. Mercifully for his boss, she was now out of the picture. What he didn't know about was the animosity that had occurred between some of the guests. If he had, then his chosen passenger list for the private jet transporting himself, Piero and Portia back to the UK might have been slightly different. Just by looking around him he could see that the jet didn't exactly contain the happiest bunch of people, but he put that down to post-party fatigue.

Dale and Lauren were seated on one side of the jet. Lauren still looked shattered after her collapse the night before and despite her happiness when she had been packing with Dale earlier that day, a cloud of darkness had spread across her face again as soon as she had settled herself at the airport. The reason was seated directly opposite her – Martha and Saul, hand in hand, smiling and joking maybe a little more than was actually necessary. Their actions, especially Martha's, seemed a little forced, more so when Lauren's eyes were upon them. Both of them had full champagne glasses in their hands even before take-off and were keen to keep toasting the newly named Mr and Mrs Romeo, who were seated at the front of the plane.

Not that Portia had any intention of using her married name. Still deliriously happy on the wings of love and wisely having no need or desire to toast her future happiness with alcohol, Portia had flitted around the cabin telling all of her guests that she couldn't possibly. 'Portia Romeo – darling, I sound like some kind of chauffeur-driven car for an empty-headed Hollywood heiress. I think Portia Safari has so much more sexiness to it and thankfully my dear husband agrees.' The only passenger she wouldn't converse with was Lauren, determined that she wouldn't spoil the journey by unloading her forked tongue of venom onto her just yet in return for her apparent spilling of the beans about Portia's disfigured face to Nancy. *Best to avoid Lauren for now*, mused Portia, certain that revenge would be hers sooner or later.

Seated behind Saul and Martha were Mariella and Bruno. Seeing as both of them had gone to the wedding with partners and subsequently traded them in as damaged goods, they made an unusually strong pairing, both of them putting the world to rights and demanding, only half-jokingly, that all potential partners should have to sit a suitability exam before even being considered as relationship fodder. 'If they don't pass with flying colours, then sod them, I say ...' said Bruno, still nursing the mother of all hangovers and downing a Bloody Mary.

'Too right, Dr Fielding,' stated Mariella. 'If I wasn't retreading an old path with dear Lewin then I would never trust another man again.'

Duncan and Adam were placed behind Dale and Lauren respectively. Adam had his head immersed in a folder detailing some police cases he had to work on after his arrival back in the UK, while Duncan was happy to browse through a pile of business magazines he'd bought at the airport. The only other passengers on the jet were Kelly, Betsy and her trusty Bloodworth.

It was a few hours into the flight that the authoritative voice of the captain came through to tell the passengers that they would be landing in approximately ninety minutes' time. The long journey had passed relatively quickly with Portia and Piero keeping most people's spirits high with their harmonised banter and bonhomie. Betsy and Bloodworth had slept most of the way, while Kelly, Bruno and Mariella had joined Martha and Saul in their drinking. Duncan and Adam had spent their time leaning forward chatting to Dale and Lauren.

Lauren found the two gay men charming and while Dale and Duncan were deep in conversation, she was keen to learn more about Adam's police work. 'So, a DCI sounds very high up and grand. I'm guessing you'll be inundated with things to investigate when you get home?'

'Yes, I dare say I will,' sighed Adam, his voice tinged with a layer of resignation. 'It's been wonderful to get away as Duncan and I hardly have any time together. A few days in the sun have been incredibly liberating, especially as everybody there was so fabulously fashionable. If I start talking about Prada or Pucci at work then everyone thinks I'm stark raving mad. Some of the outfits were beyond catwalk magic – yours included.'

Lauren was enjoying the flattery. 'Thank you, I do my best – not that *everyone* always appreciated it!' she deadpanned, nodding towards Saul. 'At least with Dale he knows what really looks good on me. I know I'm in safe hands now when it comes to my singing career as Dale has an eye for knowing what suits me best.'

'I should say. His heart is obviously in it too, which is wonderful. You make a good team. I shall look forward to loading your first chart topper onto my iPod,' gleamed Adam.

'I'll send you a copy as and when it happens,' smiled back Lauren. 'Now, talking of hearts, I must take my tablet. I suppose your other half has told you all about my recent visit to The Abbey. I got a little bit *rock 'n' roll* a little bit too soon and did myself some damage.' As she spoke, Lauren pulled her bag out from underneath her seat and reached into it to find her beta blockers.

'Duncan never discusses work with me. We keep all of that off-limits. He doesn't bore me with medical jargon and I don't send him to sleep with talk of stake-outs and shoot-outs! I think that's why we've been together for so long. Now, enough shop talk,' uttered Adam, his eyes opening wide with relish as he stared at Lauren's bag on her lap. 'Let's talk fashion. That bag is to die for. Designer heaven or what? That must have cost you a small fortune.'

Lauren began to reply. 'A one-off, sweetie, nothing but the best—' Her words stopped sharply in mid-flow as she clutched her hand to her chest. Her breathing became short and jagged and all colour seemed to leak from her face as panic branded itself across her features. Trying to stand up, her bag fell from her lap and landed on the floor. The noise of its contents spilling out caused those around to look up from what they were doing. They all panicked at what they witnessed.

Adam, Duncan and Dale were the first out of their seats and it was Dale who spoke first. 'Oh my God, Lauren, what the hell's the matter? Doctor!' he screamed, shouting across at Bruno who was already up from his seat. 'What's the matter with her? Her eyes are bulging out of her head. Do something.' As he finished the sentence, Lauren fell to the floor, her body becoming motionless. Her eyes still open, she slumped onto the carpet of the private jet, her hair falling across her face. It looked like there was nothing the doctor could do.

Falling to his knees, Bruno Fielding checked Lauren's pulse and tried to listen for any sign of activity inside her body. As he did so, a circle of people stood over him, each of them looking down at the scene in front of them in horror. Not so much a circle of life, but a *circle of death*.

'There's nothing I can do. I would guess she's suffered sudden cardiac death. He looked up at Dale and then at Saul, and then back to Dale again, uncertain as to where he should really be looking. 'I'm so sorry. She's gone … dead.'

Every one of the people surrounding Lauren's lifeless body audibly gasped as Bruno said the words. Disbelief in surround sound.

Kelly screamed, sad for the loss of an old pal.

Saul's body went numb from head to toe as he stared down at the body of the woman he had shared most of his life with. A flicker of the love they'd once shared sparked momentarily across his heart. He reached out and squeezed Martha's hand.

Martha looked on at a love rival and a former friend, but now a woman she'd been capable of detesting because of her former love for Saul. She and Lauren would never make amends but at least it was now certain that Lauren would never try to win Saul back. Martha had won her man once and for all.

———

Duncan, deeply sorry and shocked but still unable to stop himself, immediately thought of the bad press that Lauren's death may generate for The Abbey.

Betsy felt a tear run down her face, respectful and chilled at the loss of such a young life.

Dale shook with disbelieving rage at the abrupt death of the woman he believed he was growing to love and nurturing for success.

Portia, surveying the scene before her, couldn't help but feel that Lauren had got what she deserved for blowing the lid on the diva's disfigurement at The Abbey.

Redmond couldn't help but hope that Lauren's death wouldn't overshadow Portia and Piero's wedding and keep it off the front pages.

And Adam … well, as he looked down at Lauren's corpse, at her bag and its contents scattered across the floor, something uneasy tiptoed across his brain, nagging at his reasoning. Call it a policeman's sixth sense or intuition but there was something about Lauren's sudden death that didn't make sense. He couldn't put his finger on it, but something wasn't ringing true. As he and Duncan lifted Lauren's body and moved it to the back of the plane, where they covered it with a white sheet for the remainder of the journey, DCI Adam Hall said nothing, but couldn't help but feel compelled to take control of the situation. Something was telling him he needed to.

CHAPTER 65

A few days later, as Adam stared out of the rain-streaked window of his London office, he knew that his anxious feelings on the private jet had been justified. Like a bad equation, something hadn't added up and as he fixed his gaze on Lauren Everett's autopsy report for the umpteenth time, the unease that he'd chillingly felt course through his body was spelt out in black and white yet again. Lauren had died of sudden cardiac death caused by 'cocaine usage'. A quantity of cocaine had been found in her system which had led to severe heart palpitations and then to a fatal cardiac arrest. Lauren's body apparently didn't stand a chance.

Cocaine usage? She'd sworn to those around that she hadn't touched it in weeks. *Would she have been so lacking in willpower?* The wedding would have been the easiest place in the world to obtain the drug, surmised Adam, seeing as it was full of high-flying, nostril-abusing media types, but he genuinely didn't believe that Lauren would have let herself slide once more into the narcotic abyss she'd formerly occupied.

Plus, the autopsy revealed another fact that Adam couldn't comprehend. Lauren's system was completely devoid of beta blockers. Despite having seen her take the medication at regular intervals himself throughout the stay on Peter Island, according to the experts there was no trace of the drug within her system. Adam had spoken directly to both Bruno and to Duncan at The Abbey to confirm that Lauren had been prescribed the beta blockers and that she had definitely been taking them.

Both men were unable to explain why the drug was not showing in the dead woman's system. But the more Adam looked at
the report, the more he had to arrive at the same conclusion.
There was no reason for the young starlet, who the tabloids were
already mourning and heralding as 'a great loss to the music
world', to risk her own life.

   She'd seemed happy in the Caribbean when he'd spoken to
her. When she and Adam had talked together it had been about
the future, about how her life was moving onto a new Chapter –
her days with Saul behind her. She was still his wife but she was
sure that she was moving onwards and upwards in a new, much
more gratifying direction by being with Dale.

   Saul had been hounded by the press ever since his arrival
back in the UK, and had escaped with Martha to go and stay
at Mara with Piero and Portia. The newly-weds were putting
any kind of honeymoon on hold until after Lauren's funeral,
although this couldn't be arranged until her body had been released by the police.

   No, the more Adam Hall's intuitive professional brain
whirred around like the accurate cogs of a precision timepiece,
the more he realised that there was only one answer to his worries – Lauren Everett's death was beyond suspicious. He had no
reason to believe it was just accidental causes that had snuffed
out the life of one so young, in fact he believed that somebody
had to be behind it. He believed it could be murder. Now he
just had to try and prove it. There were questions that needed
to be asked …

———

Dale had not been able to concentrate on anything since Lauren's death. His office at Roma Records had been inundated
with floral bouquets and seemingly heartfelt media messages

from well-wishers but each and every one of the blooms seemed to drill into his brain, reminding him of the beautiful flower he had lost in Lauren. Even Nancy had phoned to ask if there was anything she could do to help Dale through his 'deeply troubled time'. But despite their sorrow at his loss, none of their banal, meaningless words or par-for-the-course platitudes were able to solder his heart back together. Dale simply couldn't believe that Lauren was gone.

Never again would he see her smiling face beaming across at him with glee about the possibilities of meeting one of her idols, or watch the sunshine-filled sparkle of her eyes as she made love to the cameras on her one and only video shoot. It was ruthlessly savage to think that the curtain had already come down on her career before it had even been given the chance to rise. It would have been so lucrative, but now it was lost.

Dale had spent hours watching the video that Lauren had made in Las Vegas, regret pricking his eyes and sadness eventually tumbling down his cheeks as he watched her rhythmically working the screen. It was such a waste. Another great talent taken before their time. *Why had life been so cruel to take her away from him just when he needed her most? Why now?* Sitting at his office desk, Dale paused the video clip, leaned back into the comfort of his leather chair and closed his eyes. The butter-soft leather cradled his back and tiredness washed over him. He'd not been sleeping since his return from the Caribbean and his whole body ached with misery. Allowing his body to finally obtain the sleep he craved, he drifted off …

He was awoken by a loud knock at his office door. A glance at the clock on the wall told him he had been asleep for the best part of an hour. He still felt wretched and rubbed his bloodshot eyes as he moved to the door. Opening it, he found Adam standing there. Without saying a word, he ushered him into the room.

Seating himself, Adam scanned the office, taking in all of the flowers on display. 'She was a popular lady, it seems. How are you feeling?'

'Like crap. She *was* popular and she was going to be huge. I just know she was. Look at her ... a vision, a goddess ... she could have had it all.' Dale pointed his fingers towards the TV screen where the image of Lauren in Vegas was still paused. 'I'm intending to release the song posthumously. It's what she would have wanted. The backers will demand it anyway ... So, what can I do for you, Adam?'

'I'm here in an official capacity. I need to ask you a few questions. I think you're right, Dale, Lauren would have been a sucess, which gives me great reason to believe that there is no way she would have jeopardised her own health and risked her own life. Why would she compromise her own potentially bright future? I've just come from talking to the pathologist who performed the autopsy. They have reason to believe that it was cocaine that killed her. I need to know if you saw her taking any?'

Dale's face turned as white as a spray of proud lilies that stood behind his desk and his mouth fell open in disbelief. 'Coke? She loved it before her treatment at The Abbey but she'd not touched it ever since, I swear. She had a right go at me for doing it just before the wedding ...' Dale's words dried up, suddenly realising what he'd said. Adam was quick to react.

'So, it's fair to say that she could have got hold of some quite easily in the Caribbean. It was readily available to her if she wanted to take it?' There was an air of condemnation in Adam's voice, but he'd been around long enough to know that the usage of coke for industry players like Dale Cousins was hardly shocking front-page news. 'Did you supply her in the Caribbean, Dale?'

Running his hands through his mop of hair, Dale could feel his head spiralling out of control as he contemplated what could have happened. 'No, I swear, Adam, I didn't. I had some on me the night of Piero's stag party but I lost that at some point during the evening. I was so pissed I probably dropped it overboard or lost in watching that stripper. I'm sure I never gave it to Lauren. I was trashed, out of it. I honestly don't remember what happened. But I didn't have it the next morning. I craved some the next day at the pre-wedding bash so I bought a few grams from one of the guests. Lauren found it in my wallet the morning of the wedding but I'd stake my life on saying that she hadn't taken any. Look, Adam, I'm no saint but I beg you to believe me, I didn't give any coke to Lauren, not since she was admitted to The Abbey. I'd have too much to lose ...' Dale jumped up from his seat in agitation, desperate to prove his innocence, before adding woefully, 'Mind you, I've lost it now anyway. She's gone ... forever.' He sat straight back down.

'Do you still have the coke you bought? We could see if it matches the coke in her system,' enquired Adam.

'No, I may be a fool, but even I know not to transport drugs between countries. I binned it before we left the island. The last thing I would risk is any sniffer dogs at customs.' Dale's brain was a hive of buzzing worry. 'So, are you saying that if Lauren did take some of that coke – which I don't think she did, but if she did – then it might have been that which killed her? *I* might have played a part in her death?'

'It's a possibility, Dale, and one which I will have to explore, but there is something else I need to talk to you about. You were with Lauren ever since Dr Fielding first prescribed the beta blockers to her. Was she taking them diligently? Did you see her taking her medication?'

Dale's confusion was evident. 'Sure, she took them every day. I saw her take them at The Abbey, I saw her take them in the Caribbean. She was pretty reliant on them. I don't think she felt safe without them. She was certain she wanted to try and stay off the booze and take the medication as regularly as she could. Why wouldn't she take them?'

'So if I told you that there was no trace of beta blockers in her system then you would find that hard to believe?'

Slumping back into his chair, Dale rubbed his forehead and stared straight across the desk into Adam's eyes. 'I am telling you now that I saw Lauren taking those beta blockers every day since she was prescribed them. They were in her system, that's for sure. You have to believe me.'

DCI Adam Hall didn't comment but there was something deep within the eyes of Dale Cousins that told him that he was telling the truth. But the truth was that Lauren had no evidence of beta blockers in her system. The autopsy had proven that. But Dale had seen her taking them, so had he … he'd watched her taking one just before her death on the plane. Somewhere in the story of Lauren's demise, there were huge black streaks of deceit and lies that needed to be found and uprooted. Adam needed the evidence to locate them.

Pulling open Dale's office door, Adam turned to speak before leaving. 'Just to let you know that Lauren's body has been re-leased. Her family can arrange the funeral now. I daresay it will be quite a star-packed affair. Lauren's life may have been short but it was certainly a full one. It makes it all the more tragic if you ask me …'

'Thank you for letting me know. I swear I didn't do it, Adam. The coke never came from me. I wouldn't risk it … I didn't, I swear …' Dale's voice was weak and pleading.

'Off the record, Dale, I don't think you did. We just need to prove it. I'll see you at the funeral.'

CHAPTER 66

The funeral had been tough for Dale, almost like an out-of-body experience. His very being felt like a shell vacated by a hermit crab – empty and lifeless. He knew that he was in the worst trouble he'd ever faced and he wasn't sure how to try and make things right. Or indeed if he could ... too much had already happened.

Deep within, his soul was elsewhere, unable to comprehend that Lauren was finally gone. He had watched as her coffin had been held aloft and brought into the church, stared down at the Order of Service and lost himself in the stunning photo of her looking back at him, and he had listened as the reverend and Lauren's own family had talked about what a sad loss her death was to the world. But as he stood at the gates of St Agatha's watching the mourners departing – back to their lives, back to their dreams – his body seemed little more than a husk. He was loath to leave, not until he had finished what he came to do. If he was to move onto a new chapter, then he needed to make sure that all around him was in order.

Ever since he'd spoken to Adam a few days before at his office, he'd been unable to shake the feeling that he was responsible for Lauren's death. That his gung-ho nature and playboy lifestyle had contributed to her untimely demise.

Why had he introduced her to coke in the first place? Why had he pushed her to extremes? Why had he insisted on immersing her so deeply into the media world? Why had he trusted a certain someone?

Why? It was the word that would plague him for forever, until the day when he too was placed six feet under.

Looking around the graveyard he smiled softly as he saw that only a few mourners remained, including the person he needed to speak to. He had no idea how long he'd been standing there. Long enough for the mass of reporters and camera crews to have dispersed with their armada of pointless quotes ready to be showcased in their various rags and TV shows.

Lauren's funeral had been a feast for the hungry hacks eager to secure quotes from politicians, stars of stage and screen and theatreland who had all turned out in force to celebrate Lauren's life. Some of them had never even met her, but were keen to jump on the bandwagon of publicity her recent life-story had caused and show their bereaved faces. Column inches and publicity were everything.

St Agatha's had never seen such a funeral. Its quiet slice of rural England was not noted for celebrities. It wasn't every day that worldwide stars like Portia and Piero could be spotted in the locality. At least the service had been dignified.

Portia had been silent throughout the entire service, her hands linked across the front of the black Isabell Kristensen dress she'd chosen for the occasion as she sat next to Piero at the front of the church. She was keen to be seen but remained silent throughout the day, only talking to those around her. She'd not even given quotes to the masses of reporters waiting, choosing to let a team of burly bodyguards usher her and her new husband into the Gothic church in peace. Redmond and Betsy had joined them – Betsy keen to pay her respects to the young woman who had died in front of her own eyes. Both Portia and Betsy's eyes had kept drifting during the service to the other side of the church where Nancy Arlow sat, dabbing at her own immaculately made-up eyes with a silken handkerchief. They both surmised that the faux outpouring of misery was only for the purposes of the camera recording the service.

Lewin and Mariella were holding hands, united in their new life together in the UK. As planned, while Mariella had been serving her revenge to Peter at Portia's wedding, Lewin had upped sticks and moved to the UK, leaving his business behind in the capable hands of a relief manager. Their new home near Portia's very own Mara was ready for Mariella by the time she touched down. Martha had never seen them look happier and more determined to be together, memories of Adina and Peter already far behind them.

Martha had originally said that she thought it best that she sit away from Saul at the funeral, but the politician wouldn't hear of it. They were together now. The world knew that he and Lauren were separating and press from the 'Portiero' wedding had linked him to 'the beautiful heiress to the South African wine empire'. They had nothing to hide, and Martha was alongside Saul throughout, her hand firmly linked in his as he faced the press and answered their questions. She'd won her man. He only remained silent when pressed as to his political plans for the future, much to pompous Nathan Spilsbury's bewilderment. Not that Nathan gave it too much thought for once, even though he couldn't help but feel his hold on Saul wasn't as tight as it had once been. For today, Nathan was too busy secretly enjoying the fact that his escort was 'mistress' Kelly. Although even he and his seedy mind knew that her normal procedure of walking him around by a leather dog collar wouldn't have been overly apt given the sombre nature of the occasion.

As Dale stood alone at the gates of the church, he had never felt more cheerless or charged with an electricty of fear that ran through his body. Sad about what had happened in the past and frightened about what may happen in the future.

'Why so sad? Oops ... maybe not the most tactful of questions.' The voice brought Dale back from his dark thoughts. It was Nancy who stood before him. 'You look half scared to death. It's nice to know I can still generate a powerful effect on you after all these years.' There was an arrogance about her voice that Dale had expected. *How could she be so transparently upbeat on today of all days? How could he have doubted that she would have been anything but?* They hadn't been on-off partners for years without getting to know each other's personality traits inside out.

'You will always have an effect on me, Nancy, you know that. And it will always be a good one, I hope. There's too much water under the bridge to ever let anyone, dead or alive, come between us.' Dale reached out and brushed his fingers tenderly across Nancy's cheek as he spoke. 'We'll always be together somehow. I shouldn't ever have doubted that.'

His words seemed to disarm Nancy's thoughts and all traces of arrogance faded from her voice as she stared into Dale's eyes and spoke. 'We do work well together, Dale, I never doubted that either and something deep in my heart always told me that, even when you were with her ...' Nancy motioned her gloved hand towards Lauren's grave and allowed herself to smile. 'Not that she's a problem any more, and not that I was the one with the dodgy ticker, if we're talking about hearts.'

Cupping Nancy's face in his hands, Dale could feel his fingertips tremble as he felt the coolness of Nancy's skin. 'Time to start again, I think, don't you? Lauren could have been big, but no one will ever be bigger, brighter, or more beautiful than you, Nancy Arlow. My Nancy. We belong together. We're meant to be, now and forever. Let me love you ... let me make the world love you again. Nothing ... or no one ... can stop you and I when we're together. I just wish I'd realised sooner.'

Dale's words danced inside Nancy's brain, causing her senses to pirouette. They were the words she'd been longing to hear. Finally he'd seen sense and realised just what he had in her. The wait and everything she'd been through had been worth it. Her mouth shaped itself into a quizzical smile.

'Why now, Dale, why didn't you tell me before? You know deep down I've never stopped loving you, despite your ... *minor distractions* with other people.' Once more she looked towards Lauren's grave.

'Now is the perfect time to tell you how I feel, Nancy. It's only now that we're alone that I realise just how far you were prepared to go to make sure that we could be as one again. That you would stop at nothing. You've been a very clever and a very calculating girl. I should never have underestimated you. There was no doubt really that you would stop at nothing to make things right.'

He pulled Nancy towards him and wrapped his arms around her, allowing his lips to brush against the soft flesh of her ear as he did so. 'I know what you've done for me ... for us,' he whispered.

Thrilled by his words, Nancy hugged Dale tightly towards herself and emitted a huge sigh of relief. 'Thank you, Dale, thank you. You know me better than anyone ever has ... or ever will.' Suddenly aware of their location, Nancy pulled away from Dale, keen that their sudden closeness shouldn't cause suspicion.

'Well, there's a huge gap in your clientele that needs filling again and believe you me, I'm ready to step back into the spotlight.' She reached into her bag as she spoke, her words soft and seductive. 'Do you have a light? I could *murder* a cigarette,' she purred. The intonation on the word was somewhat marked. She was choosing her words carefully, lacing them with a smug pride.

Reaching into his pocket, Dale pulled out a silver lighter and gave it to Nancy. Pulling off a black glove, she placed the lighter to the tip of her cigarette and ignited the flame. She handed it back to him with a deep, satisfactory intake of breath. 'I've been *dying* for that.' Again the intonation was calculated and stressed. 'Thanks. So, when did you work it all out?'

'I don't know how you did it, Nancy, and I don't care. I just know that you did. You're the only one clever enough to have gone through with it. The perfect murder. That's what it was, wasn't it? The police think Lauren was murdered. They've been to see me. They think that she was taking coke and it caused her heart attack but they can't prove anything. They think I might be involved but I know I wasn't. Well, no more so than the fact that the woman I've always loved did it for me. You killed her and you weren't ever there. Now we can plan for the future. I'm no saint, but neither are you ... that's why we're perfect together. Nobody has ever done what you've done for me. That's why I love you, more than ever.' Dale could feel his heart beating as he spoke. 'How *did* you manage it?'

Flicking her cigarette away, Nancy couldn't wait to confess, elated by Dale's passionate words. There had been times when she had doubted his love, but finally he was standing before her, echoing her own emotions. 'We're better off without her. I knew we would be. That's why I did it. She was trash ... low-rent, talentless trash. She had to be got rid of. She had to go. I did it for us.'

Remaining as calm as he could, Dale spoke, his voice rich and coaxing. 'What do you mean, Nancy, you did it for *us*?'

'Killed her off so we could be together again, just as it should be. You never stopped loving me, Dale, and I feel exactly the same about you. We're made for each other. We fit together. The police won't prove anything. Your coke killed her but they'll

never know that. You and I can work our way back to the top
and make people realise that we're the best there is. The dream
team. No one else comes close, especially dead-end Everett. She
was no more than a passing dalliance to you, you know that.'

Dale felt his bottom lip quiver as he asked, 'How did *my* coke
kill her?'

There was an icy joy to Nancy's answer. A cold-hearted, destroying frost that had penetrated to her very core. 'I stole it
from you. Like candy from a baby. When you came back to
the hotel after Piero's stag night you were trashed. I'd waited for
you in the bar. You could hardly walk but it was clear you were
still in the mood to drink. I offered you another cocktail and
you readily accepted. I asked you for your wallet to pay for it,
nabbed the coke, finished the drink and headed off to bed leaving you a considerable amount of coke lighter. Easy.'

'But that still doesn't explain how you gave it to Lauren. She
would never knowingly take it after everything she'd been told
at The Abbey.'

'Stage two – wait for my opportunity, which luckily enough
you gave me at breakfast the next day. Bruno had told me Lauren was on the beta blockers for her decrepit little heart way
before the wedding. I could get whatever info I wanted out of
him with our pillow talk. Go down on him and he'd gush the
info. I asked him about the pills – what they looked like, how
they worked and he told me they were plastic capsules with a
powder inside. Bingo. All I had to do was swap the powder for
coke. My brother, Ed, gave me the idea when he duped Portia
Safari with the dodgy pills for her *woe-is-me* weight gain. She's
another silly bitch. People will take anything if they think it'll be
doing them some good.

'I figured the beta blockers would be in Lauren's bag so when
she left the breakfast table, leaving you in charge of her bag,

and then you disappeared to God knows where, I grabbed the chance to take it. By the time I'd emptied your stash into her pills and got back to the table with them, she wasn't even back from powdering her nose. Lady Luck was on my side. Mind you, she sort of powdered her nose when she took her next beta blocker. She was taking pure coke. The silly tramp was killing herself and all I had to do was sit back and watch until her heart gave in.' The confession seemed to amuse Nancy, giddy at her own treachery and pleased that she could finally tell it to the man she loved. The man who she now knew still loved her.

Dale could feel his own heart pounding within his chest at a force he'd never experienced before. 'You made her poison herself? You devious bitch – and you used me to do it.' He forced a smile as he stared into Nancy's eyes. 'You killed her – don't you have any regrets?'

'Sure I do, Dale – that I wasn't on that plane in person to see her keel over and take her last breath on the way back from "the wedding of the decade". I had no idea how much longer it would take for the pills to kill her off – a day, a week, a month … who knew? I was kind of hoping it would be before she managed to hit the airwaves with her screechy tones though. And it was. Which leaves you and I free to concentrate on us. It was the foolproof murder. She killed herself, at least that's what the police are going to have to believe. Who's going to tell them otherwise? Not you, Dale. You're on my side, plus you're the man who supplied the killer coke.' There was a soulless matter-of-factness about Nancy's confession which scared Dale, but maybe she was right. How would he ever be able to prove his own innocence to the police?

'Right, shall we go?' said Nancy, slipping her black glove over her hand once more. 'I don't know about you but I'm finding this getting away with murder thirsty work. I could *kill* for a rum and coke … of the fizzy kind, of course. Let's toast our future happiness again, shall we, the past is literally dead and buried.'

She held out her hand to Dale for him to take. He simply placed his hand in hers and the pair of them walked, their hands linked, to Nancy's waiting car.

CHAPTER 67

It was less than twenty-four hours later that DCI Adam Hall turned up at the Bayswater flat of Nancy Arlow to arrest her for the murder of Lauren Everett. She hadn't expected it, she was convinced she had managed to get away with committing the perfect crime, but then she hadn't expected the man she loved, Dale, to betray her.

They'd driven back to London together, him listening to Nancy's fairy tales of how their life would now be united and perfect. But instead of going for the drink as promised, Dale had made Nancy drop him off at his office, saying that they should meet the next morning to discuss 'exciting and new' and naturally non-existent 'work offers' for Nancy.

As soon as he'd watched her car disappear around the corner he paid a visit to DCI Hall and informed him of Nancy's confession. Dale's suspicions about Nancy's involvement in Lauren's death had whirled around his brain from the moment Adam had visited him at his office days before. It had killed him emotionally to trick his former love into confessing, but he knew that it was something he had to do. Being devious came naturally to Dale, especially where Nancy was concerned, and he wanted justice for Lauren. She deserved that. The callous nature of Nancy's actions had hit Dale like a sledgehammer, extinguishing any last droplets of sympathy he had once harboured for her. He knew he had done the right thing.

At first Nancy had professed her innocence to the policeman, putting on a performance worthy of an Oscar-winner and not one of her usual straight-to-DVD turkeys. It was the performance of her career, and also destined to be her last. The evidence was stacked up against her.

Adam himself was a pivotal player in the evidence used for Nancy's downfall. After Dale had informed him of Nancy's post-funeral confession, the pieces of the deadly jigsaw suddenly slotted together. It had been Adam who had seen Nancy with Lauren's bag as she'd headed off to fill the beta blockers with coke. With his flair for all things fashion he'd recognised it as a designer accessory and had thought then that it might be a one-off. When he'd seen Lauren with the same bag on the plane then momentarily he'd doubted his own fashion knowledge, but Lauren had said herself that it was a one-off. They were her last words. How prophetic that they should be the words that would orchestrate the damnation of her own killer. He'd checked with the designer and indeed they had confirmed that Lauren Everett was the only person who could have possibly owned the bag at that time.

Adam had kept the bag after the flight. He'd known all along he'd been right to. All of Lauren's belongings surrounding her death had been kept and sealed at the police headquarters. An analysis of the beta blockers proved that they were all indeed filled with cocaine. The fingerprints on the bottle and also on each of the tablets matched the fingerprints on the silver lighter that Dale had supplied to Adam after taking it back from Nancy at the graveyard.

When faced with all of the evidence against her, Nancy had crumbled, devastated by Dale's betrayal but seemingly proud of her handiwork. As Adam and his team handcuffed her and marched her away, a defiant Nancy couldn't stop herself from arrogantly screaming, 'She deserved it. She stole my life, so I stole hers.' She meant it.

There was still a relentless arrogance in Nancy when she was jailed for life later that year.

EPILOGUE

The baptism of Amadora Omorose Betsy Romeo was another star-studded affair and featured the proud parents, Portia and Piero, on the cover of nearly every celebrity magazine around the globe. Virtually eight months to the day after Lauren Everett had been laid to rest, a smiling bundle of joy had been born unto the world. Portia had known she was pregnant when she had been at the funeral, protecting her stomach with her hands throughout. The baby, conceived just before the Caribbean wedding, was a true 'gift of love' in her parents' eyes which was why they had given their first-born the Italian name meaning just that. Amadora was to be the first of two children, another coming just a year later, who would share a blissful life with Piero and Portia at Mara, where the couple had decided to stay.

Martha and Saul were named as Amadora's godparents, and the pair of them had flown in from South Africa especially to fulfil their duties. They had moved to the Stellenbosch region of the Western Cape about a month after the funeral. Saul, a new man with Martha by his side, even though he felt racked with guilt at how things had turned out for Lauren, had decided to turn his back on politics and longed for a new challenge. Lewin and Mariella, now blissful in their tranquil UK home, had suggested that maybe the running of Lewin Éclair Wines was just the role Saul was searching for. It worked for everyone – Lewin was keen to keep the business in the family and even Martha could finally see the delights of living her days with Saul in the picturesque joy of the Helderberg Mountains. They even shipped Barney to join them with their new life in South Africa. Six months after returning to South Africa Saul and Martha were married, with Kelly – now a success in her own right with a string of *Twinkle's Strip-Yourself-Fit* DVDs reaping huge sales all over the world – acting as a rather risqué bridesmaid. Martha and Saul had celebrated their wedding night by making love alfresco in one of their many vineyards. Their sex life was as active and creative as ever and both of them became regulars on the South African fetish scene, enjoying their 'play' together. One of their regular scenemates was Adina King, often accompanied by one of a never-ending line of successful and hideously rich boyfriends.

Not that everybody had relished Martha and Saul's move to the winelands. Nathan Spilsbury was as peeved as a snowman who had just been booked on a package tour to Hell. When his protégé announced that he was through with politics and his spin doctor's bombastic ways, Nathan's first reaction was to blame Martha. It was always easier to blame a woman. According to Nathan they were always at the root of any major problem. 'Another bit of wiggling skirt comes along and turns your bloody world upside down. You're thinking with your dick, man, not your head. Keep her for sex and sprog-making, matey, but your career comes first, for God's sake – you're so close to the top now you can virtually smell the current PM shitting himself – he knows you're the next great contender. Why throw it away on some bang-worthy bimbo? Have I been wasting my fucking time? Be a man, Saul, not a pussy-whipped asshole in love.' The only thing Saul had whipped was his fist across Nathan's face in disgust. It had been a long time coming and he had savoured the moment. The sound as Saul's fist connected with the flabby skin of Nathan's face would repeat itself rapturously in his mind for years. Nathan's constant criticism of Saul's choices in life had finally turned Saul against him. Architect of his own downfall, it had been three months before Nathan had worked up the balls to speak to Saul again. When he did, Saul had never returned his call.

As for Dale, the initial months after Lauren's death were emotionally hard. He had been let off with a caution about his possession of drugs as he had been so helpful and instrumental in bringing Nancy to justice, but there was part of him that would always blame himself for Lauren's death. If it had taught him one thing, it was that maybe he could survive without having his head buried constantly in a bag of nose candy.

As emotionally difficult as the months were, the period that followed Lauren's death was one of Dale's most financially rewarding. The posthumous release of Lauren's one and only ever single was welcomed around the world with the song becoming a multimillion bestseller in over thirty countries. With the cash it afforded Dale, he was able to reward those who had believed in Lauren from the start.

Nancy too enjoyed a resurgence in success, although she was far from able to enjoy it from her squalid isolation behind bars. Her last movie, *Squidosaurus: Monster From Below* became a cult classic with underground fans lapping up the fact that the star of such a low-rent piece of mediocre movie-making had turned into a Machiavellian killing machine. A clever deal by Dale when it came to royalties meant that he again reaped the rewards of his banged-up ex.

Dale put the money to good use, moving out of his Roma Records office and setting up at bigger premises in the heart of London's Soho. His own star was burning brighter than ever before. All he needed now was another surefire winner to make sure that his spotlight of success retained its intensity. His chance came one evening after another busy day at the office, as he wandered into a trendy bar just around the corner from Roma, desperate for a beer.

Two girls were sitting at the bar, virtually identical to look at, their petite delicate faces enveloped by long straight blond hair flowing down almost to their waists. As if fated, they both turned round and looked in his direction as he walked through the revolving doors of the bar. Simultaneously they both flashed him a perfect pearlescent smile that in Dale's mind appeared to magically illuminate the room.

Taking his chance, he walked up to the bar and stood between the two girls – he guessed they were twins – and asked, 'Can I buy you two ladies a drink?' Less than five minutes later, as he watched them wrapping their glossy lips around the straws leading down into their cocktails, he fired off the question he'd been desperate to ask: 'So, have you two ever considered singing or acting before …'

LETTER FROM NIGEL

Hello glam-fans! Well that was a real adventure. Did you guess what was going to happen? I really hope that you loved reading Addicted as much as I enjoyed writing it. Spinning a tasty whodunit involving four fabulous ladies – Lauren, Martha, Portia and Nancy – was a real pleasure and one that thrilled me with every chapter.

The women of Addicted all have the things that most of us can only crave – fame, money, an ability to head off around the world whenever they like on exotic journeys but obviously, as you've just witnessed, things are not always as happy as they seem. I loved plotting their adventures as it gave me a chance to do a bit of travelling too – all in the name of research of course. It would have been rude of me not to take a trip to Dubai or head to South Africa to experience first-hand the lives of my four leading ladies. I know….any excuse to pack a suitcase and head to the airport!

If you enjoyed the book I would LOVE you to leave me a review on Amazon. Hearing what readers think is a true joy and makes all of the hours of writing truly worthwhile. Who was your favourite character? Are you Team Portia, the total diva (I love her!), Team Martha with her free-spirited ways, Team Nancy with her cheeky chart-topping aspirations or Team Lauren who never stops dreaming of what may be around the corner?

And, if you liked this book, then perhaps you'd like to read more of my stories! I'd love to talk all things spicy on Twitter, Facebook and Goodreads. Let's make the world as diamond-dipped and glamorous as possible.

To keep right up-to-date with the latest news on my new releases just sign up at the following page:

www.bookouture.com/nigel-may

Here's to more sin-sational reads with a whole host of incredible characters – we can all immerse ourselves between the pages of another action-packed blockbuster.

Keep it gritty and glam, Nigel x

🐦 @Nigel_May

www.nigelmay.net

TRINITY

'Move over Jackie Collins, there's a new blockbuster star in town.'
New! Magazine

When friends become enemies there are no rules…

Ambitious gossip queen **Anoushka Silvers** is the daughter her abusive
father never wanted. Determined to prove herself to her family, she'll
stop at nothing to get what she wants. But when her bitchy tongue
gains her death threats and the unwanted attention of a stalker, it
could be Anoushka who is making the headlines.

For actress **Evie Merchant,** her childhood dreams of becoming the
world's hottest movie star are just about to come true. But a string
of hurtful liaisons with lovers out to use her fame, has made Evie
uncertain about her future. And with Oscar day looming, Evie's biggest
prize of all could be cruelly snatched from her.

A loveless upbringing has made wild child **Regan Phoenix** search for
quick-fix highs from drink, drugs and meaningless sex. But when the
opportunity of starring in her own reality show comes along, Regan
grabs it with both hands, hoping to put her trashy past behind her.
From fashionable London to stunning Venice and glitzy LA,
Trinity **takes you into a glamorous and thrilling**
world you won't want to leave.

'**An addictive plot that is packed with twists and turns.** Prepare for
larger than life characters, fabulous locations
and plenty of humour.' *The Sun*

'Sex and scandal abound in this full-throttle thrill-ride through the
hidden lives of the mega-rich. **Trinity sizzles with bitchery, bling and**
betrayal, and is the perfect accompaniment to your sunlounger this
summer' Victoria Fox

Read on for an exclusive extract from Nigel May's new novel, *Scandalous Lies,* **coming soon…**

Hell's Canyon, California

Daytime

The heat was intense. The sun, still burning lava-bright in a one-colour tapestry of the purest idyllic blue despite the late hour of the afternoon. Clouds non-existent as a monotonous heat continued to blur the lines where horizon introduced itself to sky. The ground, shouting a natural desire to be quenched by the waters of the heavily depleted river nearby had its request left unanswered as its skin began to crack, an aging process no imminent meteorological surgery was likely to repair. Shriveled plants, those who had survived the brutal heat of one of the fiercest summers on record so far, were only moments from oblivion, a death that would be a welcome one to their moisture-searching veins. Any furry inhabitant that had once scurried across the canyon floor was either long gone in a hunt for food, or showed the idiocy of their tardiness by now remaining as now more than a skeleton. Mother Nature was a bitch and despite the beauty of the canyon and the surrounding area for most of the year, at that precise moment the globe of raging white embellished above the canyon was a dangerous one. A lethal one. Nothing could survive.

Unless, of course, you were currently opening the heavy, curved door of a floor to ceiling fridge freezer combo within the confines of your air-conditioned RV and reaching for a chilled bottle of Moet & Chandon Bi Cuvee Dry Imperial, one of six housed within the confines of the chiller. At a cost of nearly a grand each these were diamond-dipped bubbles. And fizz that could extinguish even the most barbarous of sunshine. In that case, then survival was easy.

'A sneaky peak to put you in the mood?' asked Foster Hampton, pushing his blond surfer-dude curls, pure Bondi Beach even though it was pure Brit blood that ran through his veins, away from his eye line as he reached for the bottle. The whirl of chilled air from within the fridge enveloped his naked skin as he stood, bottle in hand and faced his lover, lying on the double bed on the other side of the road vehicle.

'You should turn back around and show me that peachy backside of yours again. I was enjoying the view from over here,' answered Mitzi Bidgood. 'It's something I will never tire off. It should be added to every British female tourist's itinerary for a road trip across America. Mount Rushmore, Dollywood, Golden Gate Bridge and Foster Hampton's bubble butt. A pink, glowing spectacle of an ass. A wicked wonder of the world. The tourist board could make a fortune in ticket sales. Not that I'm keen to share it with any passing Yank though to be honest. That rump is mine all mine. The view from this angle is totally appetising,' remarked Mitzi, pointing towards the sizable pendulum of meat currently rising to attention between Foster's legs. 'And what, to answer your question, makes you think for one orgasmic moment that I am not already in the mood?'

Foster smiled as Mitzi spread-eagled her naked legs and dipped the finger she'd been pointing at his cock with into the fleshy, wet folds of her pussy. The weapon between Foster's legs rose to its full length, blood flooding through it with anticipatory desire.

'Now, pop that cork, pour me something beautiful and bring that body of yours onto this bed right away. Mitzi needs some loving after that long drive today. I assume we have all night?'

'We are going nowhere until dawn,' Foster replied as he poured the champagne, a flow of frothy bubbles rising to the rim and cascading down the body and stem of the glass and onto the tiles below his feet. 'I did not drive the entire length of this canyon in this monstrosity to just turn around and head back out again. There aren't many cars that can make it this far, so we might as well make the most of our surroundings and the fact that we're the only ones around for miles. Not that I'm going out in this heat. The dashboard thermometer says it's about 113 degrees Fahrenheit. That's way too hot, even for a beach-loving boy like me.'

It was true, the road they had driven on to reach the secluded spot at the far end of the canyon was impassible by most vehicles. It was only top of the range RVs like the one Foster and his girlfriend of three years, Mitzi, had hired for their month-long USA vacation that were able to cope. The camper was outwardly perfectly equipped to deal with even the rockiest of terrains and its lavish interior was equally custom built for sheer luxury while travelling with its satellite system, surround sound, DVD player, huge TV and wireless internet. On the few occasions they had used the internet during the previous three weeks of their journey it had only been to check emails from their lives back home in the UK. As a professional dancer on one of her home country's top TV shows, Mitzi needed to find out what the next season of the hot show held for her when she returned in just over a week's time. The rumour mill was circling with the notion that Mitzi's celebrity partner for the next six months would be a fellow reality TV star from Surf N Turf, the same show which had

seen Foster rise to fame four years ago. The show, about a group
of Cornish surfers who also ran their own landscape gardening
business at the same time, had been a huge hit and Foster had
been the breakout star, securing a spot as Mitzi's dancing partner after only one season on *Surf*. Viewers loved his relationship
with Mitzi, which quickly spilled from the ballroom and into
the bedroom. Their Barbie and Ken blond perfection meant
that when the two of them lifted the glitter ball trophy aloft at
the end of the series, the offers came flooding in for them both.
Sponsorship deals, lucrative cruise tours to showcase their dancing prowess and a massive pay increase for Mitzi to stay on the
show, saw both their kudos and their bank balances snowball.
Foster's latest project, a documentary in which he would put
his gardening skills to the test to turn a downtrodden Cornish
council estate into a thriving oasis of green shrubbery and happiness, was due to commence on his return to Britain.

But for now, all that was on the cards for the next few hours
was a nerve-tingling, gymnastic, symphony of love-making,
something their sporty, supple dancer's bodies allowed them to
indulge in as often as possible and in positions most sexual partners could only dream of.

'I'll show you what's hot,' moaned Mitzi deliriously as she
moved her finger faster inside her, the body arching with pleasure as crests of desire snapped through her inner core, spreading from the heat between her legs. Shift that six-pack of yours
over here now and ride me like a Texas rodeo athlete.'

Foster didn't need asking twice. Moving to the bed, he emptied his own glass of champagne and handed the other to Mitzi.
As she placed the glass to her lips, Foster pushed his face deep
into the open layers of joy between her legs. The feel of her wetness thrilled him, encouraging him to force his face deeper. It
was only once his mouth was completely enveloped by the flower

of her pussy that he allowed his lips to open and the pouring of champagne to icily flow from his mouth into the sexual cavity of her vagina, swirling around his tongue and Mitzi's finger as it did so. She let out a squeal of joy and dropped her now virtually empty glass onto the sheets alongside her. The remaining droplets of champagne dribbled onto the material underneath her body.

Foster looped his tongue around Mitzi's finger and felt an increase in the ferocity of her excitement as she moved her finger faster and more pressingly inside her. The fusion of the sweet champagne and her own natural womanly flavour washed across Foster's tongue as her finger rubbed against his taste buds. Mitzi's breathing became more urgent. Beads of sweat formed on her forehead and she felt them run down her face and weave down between her round, cherry-peaked breasts. Only Foster could turn her on so quickly, his love-making as pleasing now as it had been when they had first given in to temptation years before. If there was another skill that Foster could add to the many that he already possessed it was his cunnilingual technique. She wriggled with pleasure as his tongue seemed to reach places that her finger could not.

She felt the three-day old stubble on his chin graze over her tender flesh and a hunger gnawed within her. It was a hunger that only one action could assuage. She let out a whimper, a gasp as the roughness of his feasting centred on her clitoris and reached her hands down to move his head away.

A smiling Foster looked up at her from between her legs, his face shiny with sweat and Mitzi's juices.

'Why don't you fuck me' she stated. It wasn't a suggestion.

Foster flicked his tongue along the thin line of hair decorating her pussy, circled it around her belly button and feather-kissed his way up to her breasts, taking her to the edge of bliss. He maneuvered himself into position and, as he bit down onto one of Mitzi's erect nipples, allowed his erection to plough into her. Firm, long and proud, his dexterous crescent of flesh caused her to bite down of her bottom lip as he thrust faultlessly into her. She could feel her euphoria rising. No lover had ever made her feel like Foster. There had been many, but he was unique.

A scream escaped her lips but volume control was unnecessary. Who would hear her? Only the man causing her to ride the waves of joy in the same skilled way Foster himself could ride those on the ocean. She was ecstatic for him to hear her appreciation. But no more words came as she pressed her mouth onto his and kissed him deeply. A knowing look from deep within his eyes, one of trust and shared love, told her what was to follow. Mitzi's eyes blurred, her vision smudging as she felt him unleash his liquid into her and her own orgasm climb to its perfect peak. She wrapped her arms tightly around him, attempting to coax him even deeper. He kept his cock, still semi-stiff in his post denouement delirium, inside her. Foster and Mitzi were still in the same position, united in their love, half an hour later.

—

Nighttime

'This has been the best holiday ever, Foster. Both sexually and otherwise,' giggled Mitzi, somewhat tipsy from the third glass of champagne she'd drunk, accompanying the Caesar salad Foster had prepared her for dinner. 'I mean it. The places we've seen have been amazing and it's wonderful to just spend so much time together without cameras and press interviews and people screaming for autographs. Just to be you and me, us, together. Doing whatever we want, whenever we want. I have loved it so much, and I love you so much.'

'I'll have to make you drink champagne more often,' said Foster, 'if it makes you this mushy. You weren't such a softie when you were barking dance moves at me when we first met, were you? Are you becoming softer with age?' He winked playfully.

'You were my professional partner then and I was doing my job. Now my job is to let you know how much I love you. Do we have to go back home?'

'Not for another week or so, there are plenty of adventures to come yet. It's not over til the gorgeous lady starts dancing, and that's not until we reach UK shores again.'

'Actually, I was thinking of putting on a bit of a show for you now? I love this song!' said Mitzi rising to her feet from their table outside their RV. It was late evening and the air was finally cool enough to be outside, where they had eaten. The sky had moved from blue to almost black, only a moon and a dotting of stars illuminating the air. She ran inside the camper van, and moved to the sound system which had been playing some of their favourite tunes all evening. It was Beyoncé's *Drunk in Love* that had just started. Turning up the volume, Mitzi sashayed back to the doorway of the camper van and let her body sway seductively to the beat. Silhouetted by the light coming from behind her in the RV, her actions were a perfect mix of flirty and dirty. The beat of the song throbbed as she moved, her timing perfect.

Just as Foster could feel his cock rising to attention again in his sweatpants, a sudden flash of light further across the canyon startled him away from Mitzi's gyrating. Staring out into the darkness he could see a flicker of bright orange. What was it?

'Stop the music will you, Mitz. What is that over there?'

Mitzi paused the music and silence fell around them. Joining Foster again, Mitzi too gazed out into the night.

'It's a fire?' There was questioning in her tone, but there was no doubt.

'But I didn't know there was anybody else out here,' said Foster. 'Maybe the sun started it earlier. We should take a look. It could be blocking the road out of here. And you never know it may have been some dirty old men watching us through the RV windows earlier. We put on quite a show.' The thought didn't displease Mitzi, she was a showgirl after all. And their afternoon sex session had certainly been a spectacle to behold.

Foster was sure that he could hear something in the air. The sound of music. Was the champagne playing tricks on him? He didn't think so.

'Shall we go take a look?' he asked.

'Why not?' giggled Mitzi, 'maybe it's another hot young couple out here just like us. And maybe they're just as adventurous as us…and just as horny.' She gave Foster's ass a playful squeeze as they ventured off towards the bright orange glow.

The sky was pitch black yet the air seemed clear as they stumbled, a little giddy on bubbles, in the direction of the light. Mitzi kept losing her balance slightly on the pebbles and loose rocks beneath her feet. Foster took her hand to steady her. 'We can't have you twisting an ankle before dance season, can we?'

Mitzi found the whole situation borderline erotic. Her and the man she loved, miles from anywhere, in the pitch blackness of the Californian wilderness. Alone and wild.

Except they weren't alone.

Narrowing their eyes to try and scan the glow, the couple blinked until the crackle of orange came into focus. What they saw made Foster gasp. If Mitzi's gasp earlier during their love-making had been one of total rapture, Foster's was the complete antithesis.

'What the fuck…?' His words petered out.

'What is it, Foster, what's going on?' It didn't look like they were going to run into an amorous couple interested in a bit of fireside alfresco shagging. As she focused, a chill ran through Mitzi's body and she let out a slight shiver.

'Holy shit.

Dancing around the fire, which they had obviously built themselves, to a heavy tribal musical beat, were a series of figures. They were all dressed in head to toe outfits obscuring their faces. They looked like robes, heavy, maybe made of hessian, almost monk like in appearance, all topped with wide hoods. There must have been about six of them. As the flames flickered higher, one of the figures stripped off the hood and untied the robe allowing it to fall to the floor. It revealed a naked woman, Mitzi guessed about the same age as her, mid-20s. She possessed full, round breasts and a small dark triangle of hair between her legs.

'What the fuck is going on?' Mitzi whispered, reconsidering the alfresco sex theory. Maybe they were just about to witness some kind of outdoor dogging scene with a difference. Mitzi always thought dogging was a load of dirty old men whacking off in a lorry park with some rough old housewife. Maybe the Yanks did it with glamour and lit by a naked flame.

The sound of the beat became louder and more frantic in the air. Foster and Mitzi could see that the other figures surrounding the young woman had stopped, but all bar one of them remained with their hoods in place. The one who revealed his face was a man of about 50 with what looked like a head of salt n pepper hair. It was hard to work out his features exactly as the flickering of the firelight distorted the air.

From one of the sleeves of his robe he pulled out a long, wide-bladed knife. The blade caught the firelight and reflected shards of colour shot into the air.

All of the other figures around the fire held their hands aloft. The music stopped almost instantly. Silence filled the air. 'What's happening, Foster? This is beginning to freak me out' stammered Mitzi. The atmosphere had turned from daring to deadly.

Foster was unsure what to say.

Then it happened.

The man holding the knife, drew it aloft and brought it swiftly across the woman's throat. Even from their somewhat distant position, as the female clutched her hands to her throat, the spurt of deep crimson blood that flowed from her neck before she fell to the floor could be seen by Foster and Mitzi. Disbelief and fear stuck in their throats, threatening to choke them.

For a moment, time stood still, nothing daring to move. Then the full horror of what the couple had just seen hit them. Before she could stop herself, Mitzi screamed. A loud, terrified, blood-curdling scream. 'They've killed her.' It was all she could shout. Her voice pierced the air. Sensible it wasn't, but the noise had escaped from her lips before any semblance of rationality could form.

Once again for a second it seemed like all movement halted, nobody sure what their next action should be. Then as Mitzi and Foster watched on in horror, the figures turned to face the direction of the scream. A sense of anger and panic wrapped itself around the group.

Moving away from the fireside and the body on the floor, the figures began to run in their direction.

'Fuck, they've heard us, they're coming this way. Foster, we need to get out of here now.'

Foster and Mitzi raced towards the camper van, the sound of footsteps and shouts coming from a mass of directions behind them. They needed to get back to the van and drive away from the canyon. Neither was in any fit state to drive, both over the limit, but fear and abject terror spurred them into sobriety. This was a race to survive.

Mitzi could feel her heart burning within her chest as she fumbled her way towards the van. The flip flops she was wearing slid beneath her feet on the loose canyon floor. As one fell off, she jettisoned the other leaving her barefoot.

Foster ran beside her, his panting just about audible alongside her own. A cacophony of voices sounded behind them. They seemed to be getting closer.

The light of their camper van, guiding them to hopeful safety, didn't seem to be getting any nearer. They hadn't walked for more than a few minutes towards the fire, had they? Maybe it was further than they realised.

Mitzi was suddenly aware that the sound of Foster's breathing behind her had disappeared. Where was he? She called his name, her voice dry with fear. There was no answer. She didn't dare stop and look back. She kept running towards the light. She'd soon be there, soon. Maybe Foster was there already, he was stronger than her.

A voice sounded behind her. Was it Foster? She couldn't tell above the sound of her own heartbeat. Turning to glance, her ankle twisted beneath her as another loose rock slid beneath her toes. She fell to the ground. As she did so, she bit down into her tongue as the force of the canyon bottom slammed into her face. The coppery taste of blood filled her mouth.

She had to keep going. The light was brighter, she was nearly there.

Dizzy from her fall, she tried to stand up and keep running. She felt wobbly, a stabbing of pain from her leg. Had she broken something? For a second all she should think about was her dancing career. The bright lights of the dance floor filled her head. Would she ever see it again? Would she ever escape the darkness?

Still on her hands and knees as she tried to stand back up, Mitzi felt the brushing of hessian against her skin before feeling hands either side of her neck. She didn't even have time to scream before a different kind of darkness took her.

———

The next morning as the sun rose over Hell's Canyon and remorselessly beat down onto the arid land, there was no sign of life again. No animals scurrying, no lush green vegetation thriving, and no sign of the RV or the two famous Brits who had been there the night before.

Printed in Great Britain
by Amazon